Microsoft Intune Cookbook

Second Edition

Practical recipes for configuring, managing, securing, and automating identities, apps, and endpoints

Andrew Taylor

<packt>

Microsoft Intune Cookbook

Second Edition

Portfolio Director: Kartikey Pandey
Relationship Lead: Prachi Rana
Project Manager: Sonam Pandey
Content Engineer: Sayali Pingale
Technical Editor: Simran Ali
Copy Editor: Safis Editing
Indexer: Manju Arasan
Production Designer: Alishon Falcon
Growth Lead: Shreyans Singh

First published: January 2024
Second edition: February 2026

Production reference: 1260226

Published by Packt Publishing Ltd.
Grosvenor House
11 St Paul's Square
Birmingham
B3 1RB, UK.

ISBN 978-1-80580-723-0
www.packtpub.com

This book is dedicated with all of my love to my amazing daughters, Lili and Poppy. Keep on making me proud!

– Andrew Taylor

Foreword

Language is one of the most powerful forces we have—it shapes understanding, bridges complexity, and transforms raw information into meaningful action. As the landscape of endpoint management and AI-driven security continues to evolve at extraordinary speed, the need for clarity, accessibility, and grounded expertise has never been greater. Andrew Taylor delivers exactly that.

What stands out in this book is not just the technical depth—though Andrew brings that in abundance; it's the rare ability to make the intricate feel intuitive. He takes the expanding universe of Intune, Security Copilot, automation, and agent-based intelligence and presents it in a way that feels both approachable and empowering. His writing reflects a deep respect for the practitioner: the admin troubleshooting late at night, the architect designing for scale, and the learner seeking confidence amid constant change.

Andrew doesn't simply describe technology; he interprets it. He translates evolving capabilities—many of which can seem overwhelming at first glance—into workflows and insights that feel natural, almost obvious, once he has shown the way. That is the hallmark of a true teacher.

This book arrives at a pivotal moment. AI is shifting from being an optional accelerator to an operational necessity. Organizations are navigating new models of automation, proactive intelligence, and policy-driven security at scale. And with that shift comes the need for guidance that is both technically rigorous and deeply practical.

Andrew delivers that balance masterfully. His chapters illuminate not just the "how" but the "why," the "when," and the "what's possible next." He invites readers into a future where admins are augmented by intelligent systems, where workflows are elevated by automation, and where clarity—in strategy, configuration, and execution—becomes a competitive advantage.

As someone who has spent years at the intersection of product, security, and AI innovation, I am inspired by the way Andrew approaches this work: with empathy for the practitioner, with precision in detail, and with a genuine desire to help others succeed.

It is a privilege to introduce this book. I hope you find in these pages what I did—guidance, insight, and a renewed excitement for the future of endpoint management.

Lavanya Lakshman

Principal PM Manager, Microsoft Intune

We are standing at the threshold of a new era in technology. The conversation has shifted rapidly from digital transformation to the adoption of **artificial intelligence** (**AI**), and the promise of what AI can achieve for organizations is staggering. But as we look toward a future driven by intelligent automation and generative insights, we must confront a critical reality: AI is only as secure and effective as the data it consumes and the environment in which it operates.

There is a misconception that the "AI era" is strictly about algorithms and models. In practice, for the enterprise, it is about architecture. It is about knowing exactly where your data lives, who has access to it, and the health of the endpoints that interact with it. This is where Microsoft Intune transcends its traditional role. It is no longer just a tool for device management; it is the entrance portal to the AI era.

To be ready for a secure, AI-focused future, organizations need robust data governance, granular controls, centralized management, and comprehensive reporting. You cannot effectively deploy tools such as Microsoft Security Copilot or secure your estate against AI-driven threats without a unified control plane. Intune provides that foundation. It allows us to standardize security baselines and ensure that the "inputs" feeding our AI systems are trusted and verified.

This is why Andrew Taylor's work is so vital right now. Andrew, a distinguished Microsoft MVP, does not just teach you which buttons to click; he teaches you how to think architecturally about modern management. He understands that centralized management is the prerequisite for the agility that AI requires. Through these pages, he demonstrates how to leverage Intune not merely to manage devices but to establish the governance guardrails necessary for innovation.

Andrew's technical approach is grounded in the reality of today's threats but aimed squarely at tomorrow's opportunities. He breaks down complex concepts—from compliance policies to advanced reporting—showing how they act as the building blocks for a resilient, AI-ready organization.

As you read this book, I encourage you to see Intune through Andrew's lens: not just as an admin console but as the command center for your organization's future. The AI era is here, and with the guidance provided in these chapters, you will be ready to navigate it securely.

Lior Bela

Microsoft Intune Business Director

Contributors

About the author

Andrew Taylor has been working in the IT industry for over 20 years across a variety of roles and industries, but always with a passion for end user computing and automation. He now works as CTO at Software Central, building tools to make working with Intune even better! He is also a keen blogger and shares many popular scripts with the community, as well as attending community events worldwide.

Andrew is a four-time Microsoft MVP in both Microsoft Intune and Microsoft Security Copilot and holds many Microsoft certifications (10 at the time of writing). Outside of work and family time, he is a film fan and can often be found at the local cinema or practicing his archery skills.

A very special thanks to Julia, Lili, and Poppy for giving me the time to write this book and also making sure I actually sat down to complete it; I could not have done it without the three of you.

Thanks also to everyone in the Intune community and everyone who has assisted at Microsoft, especially Lavanya and Lior, for always being available and making time for me.

And, of course, thanks to you for buying this book. I really hope you find it useful!

About the reviewers

Joost Gelijsteen is a specialist in the modern workplace and security landscape. At Secure at Work, he guides organizations in taking clear control over a safe and forward-looking digital environment. His background spans more than 25 years of hands-on experience with large-scale workplace deployments and deep technical work in Windows management, Intune, and identity-driven security. As a Microsoft MVP, he follows new developments from close by, studies how features behave inside the platform, and turns that knowledge into practical steps that teams can apply without noise or guesswork. He also writes an in-depth technical blog at `joostgelijsteen.com`, where he publishes research, analysis, and practical insights for engineers.

Joost values clarity. A modern workplace should be automated, secure, productive, and pleasant to use. Achieving that balance requires technical depth combined with persistence and curiosity. He brings that mix to every project and aims to help organizations build workplaces that remain strong, simple, and ready for what comes next.

Jon Jarvis is a Microsoft MVP for Security and Windows & Devices/Windows 365, and serves as a security solutions architect at Advania UK. With over a decade of experience in the Microsoft cloud ecosystem, he began by helping organizations migrate to Exchange Online and now leads secure modern workplace strategies, focusing on Microsoft Intune, Microsoft **Defender for Endpoint** (**XDR**), and Windows 365 Cloud PC deployments.

Recognized as the first Windows 365 Microsoft MVP in the UK, his dual-award status underscores his community leadership in endpoint security and device management. He regularly presents at international conferences and publishes technical articles that translate Microsoft's best practice guidance into real-world implementations.

Table of Contents

Chapter 5: Android Device Management 169

Chapter 6: iOS Device Management 211

Chapter 7: macOS Device Management 253

Chapter 9: Monitoring Your New Environment 367

Chapter 10: Looking at Reporting 425

Chapter 15: Using AI with Security Copilot 627

Preface

Microsoft Intune is the modern way to manage your end-user devices across all platforms (Windows, Android, iOS, macOS, ChromeOS, and Linux). With a huge shift to hybrid working and cloud management, traditional domain-joined devices often struggled with maintaining contact with management platforms. With Intune, everything is managed from the cloud; as long as your devices have internet access, they will receive all applications, policies, and more.

Not only that, but you can also send devices directly to users by utilizing Autopilot to provision them, saving IT admins many hours of provisioning and shipping devices.

Configuring and managing a new or existing environment can be a daunting task with thousands of settings, hundreds of reports, and many little settings that could quickly catch you out. *Microsoft Intune Cookbook* runs you through the entire process, from purchasing your licenses through to configuring, deploying, monitoring, and administering the tenant.

Based on many years of experience and many hundreds of tenant builds, you can learn from my experience on both what to do and what not to do.

As you progress with your Intune career and tenant management, you definitely want to look at automation. If a task is repeatable, it can be automated to both free up your time for more proactive and exciting tasks and also reduce the risk of user error.

While running through every step in the UI, this book also shows how to use PowerShell and Microsoft Graph to complete the same tasks at the API level, which you can then build on in your environment.

Included at the following URL are links to some excellent community resources, which are worth reading and following as you embark on your Intune journey: `https://github.com/PacktPublishing/Microsoft-Intune-Cookbook-Second-Edition/blob/main/blogs-links-communities.md`.

In this second edition, the chapters and scripts have been completely refreshed with changes within Graph, as well as many changes, updates, and new functionality within Intune itself. On top of that, there is a new chapter looking at Security Copilot and how to leverage AI in your daily tasks.

Who this book is for

If you currently manage an Intune environment, are building a new environment, want to pivot yourself into end-user computing, or take a bold step in your career, this book is for you. For those more experienced, learning Microsoft Graph will propel you to the next level.

As this is a hands-on cookbook, while it touches on architectural considerations, the primary demographic is technical staff who are implementing a solution.

While the book does not cover the basics of PowerShell scripting, you should be able to follow the scripts with a limited knowledge of PowerShell commands.

What this book covers

Chapter 1, Getting Started with Microsoft Intune, runs through what Intune is and how to purchase your licenses and configure your first tenant. It then looks at some key Microsoft Entra settings and group creation to build a solid foundation for your Intune build.

Chapter 2, Configuring Your New Tenant for Windows Devices, looks at the policies available for Windows devices once your tenant is configured, and how to configure them to manage your fleet.

Chapter 3, Securing Your Windows Devices with Security Policies, looks at the more critical security policies available for your Windows devices and how to best implement them for secure, but usable endpoints.

Chapter 4, Setting Up Enrollment and Updates for Windows, continues covering your Windows device management, looking at Windows Update, Autopatch for update management, and Windows Hello for Business for secure authentication. It then covers enrolling devices using Autopilot and the Enrollment Status page.

Chapter 5, Android Device Management, covers the end-to-end management of your Android devices. Starting with configuring your Google Play account, connecting that to Intune, and using the Play Store for application deployment. The chapter then looks at configuring enrollment profiles and the different policies available, including those for original equipment manufacturers. For those managing personal devices, it also covers app protection policies.

Chapter 6, iOS Device Management, looks at how to use Intune to manage your iOS and iPadOS devices, covering enrollment into Apple Business Manager and using the Apple Volume Purchase Program for application deployment. It then covers connecting Apple Business Manager to Intune, setting up enrollment profiles, and configuring policies to manage devices. As with Android, it also covers application protection policies.

Chapter 7, macOS Device Management, covers the very popular and increasingly powerful management of macOS devices. Starting with configuring policies and deploying Shell scripts, it then moves on to deploying applications and ensuring your devices are always updated.

Chapter 8, Setting Up Your Compliance Policies, explores the critical area of compliance to ensure that only healthy, supported endpoints can access any data within the tenant (when paired with a Conditional Access policy). This chapter covers compliance for all supported Intune platforms and for Windows devices, and also looks at the more complex, but infinitely more powerful, custom compliance policies.

Chapter 9, Monitoring Your New Environment, looks at the monitoring options available within Intune to ensure that your new environment always offers the best experience to your end users. It covers monitoring applications, application protection policies, and the devices themselves. At the device level, it looks at reviewing your policy deployments, device enrollments, and compliance, before looking at device update status. It finishes by looking at administrative tasks and audit logs within the Intune portal.

Chapter 10, Looking at Reporting, covers the numerous reports available throughout the many areas of Intune, including the very useful Endpoint Analytics. It then expands into Power BI with Intune Data Warehouse, and also Windows Update reports within Azure Log Analytics. To take things one step further, it also covers exporting events into Azure for alerting and management.

Chapter 11, Packaging Your Windows Applications, dives into application packaging and deployment, often seen as an art in itself. This chapter covers all of the available application formats for Windows using the official tools before delving into the world of dependencies and supersedence.

Chapter 12, PowerShell Scripting across Intune, looks at all of the areas of Intune where you can develop and use PowerShell scripts. It starts with device platform scripts, then moves on to proactive remediations, and finally, using them in applications, during deployment, and in detection and requirement rules.

Chapter 13, Tenant Administration, runs through all of the options within the Tenant Administration menu in Intune, looking at the daily monitoring and administration tasks. It then moves onto the set-once style configuration options, such as roles and customization, before finally looking at filters, custom notifications, and multi-admin approval.

Chapter 14, Looking at Intune Suite, covers all of the additional functionality available as part of Intune Suite, including Endpoint Analytics, Remote Help, Endpoint Privilege Management, Enterprise Application Management, and more.

Chapter 15, Using AI with Security Copilot, runs through all of the advantages Security Copilot and AI bring to your daily management tasks, starting with the native functionality, then looking at Explorer, using the Microsoft-supplied agents, and finally, building your own in Security Copilot.

To get the most out of this book

For the sections on automation, you will need a machine capable of running PowerShell; version 5 or version 7 will work fine. While you can simply download and run the scripts, using an editor will aid in following the steps.

Software/hardware covered in the book	Operating system requirements
PowerShell 5 or 7	Windows, Linux, or macOS
A web browser	Any operating system

If you are using the digital version of this book, we advise you to type the code yourself or access the code via the GitHub repository (link available in the next section). Doing so will help you avoid any potential errors related to the copying and pasting of code.

> **Note**
>
> The Microsoft Intune UI is constantly being updated, so while we have kept the number of images down, there is still a chance you may notice minor differences between what is seen/described here and what is available in the portal.

Download the example code files

The code bundle for the book is hosted on GitHub at `https://github.com/PacktPublishing/Microsoft-Intune-Cookbook-Second-Edition`. We also have other code bundles from our rich catalog of books and videos available at `https://github.com/PacktPublishing`. Check them out!

Download the color images

We also provide a PDF file that has color images of the screenshots/diagrams used in this book. You can download it here: `https://packt.link/gbp/9781805807230`.

Conventions used

There are a number of text conventions used throughout this book.

`Code in text`: Indicates code words in text, database table names, folder names, filenames, file extensions, pathnames, dummy URLs, user input, and Twitter handles. Here is an example: "For these devices, remove them using `Remove-MgDevice`."

A block of code is set as follows:

```
$Headers = @{
    "Authorization" = "Bearer " + $resourceToken
    "Content-type"  = "application/json"
    "X-Requested-With" = "XMLHttpRequest"
    "x-ms-client-request-id" = [guid]::NewGuid()
    "x-ms-correlation-id" = [guid]::NewGuid()
}
```

Any command-line input or output is written as follows:

```
((Invoke-MgGraphRequest -Method GET -Uri "https://graph.microsoft.com/beta/
deviceManagement/configurationSettings?&`$filter=categoryId eq'4a5e4714-00ac-4793-
b0cc-5049041b0ed7'" -OutputType PSObject).value| select-object name, description,
'@odata.type', rootDefinitionId,options,@{Name="Platform";
Expression={ $_.applicability | Select-Object
platform}},@{Name="technologies";Expression={ $_.applicability| Select-Object
technologies}},valuedefinition, id) | out-gridview
```

Bold: Indicates a new term, an important word, or words that you see on screen. For example, wordsin menus or dialog boxes appear in the text like this. Here is an example: "Within Entra, click on **Show more**, then expand the **Roles & admins** dropdown, and click on **Roles & admins**."

> Note
>
> Warnings or important notes appear like this.

> Tip
>
> Tips and tricks appear like this.

Sections

In this book, you will find several headings that appear frequently (*Getting ready*, *How to do it...*, *Automating it*, *There's more...*, and *See also*).

To give clear instructions on how to complete a recipe, use these sections as follows.

Getting ready

This section tells you what to expect in the recipe and describes how to set up any software or any preliminary settings required for the recipe.

How to do it...

This section contains the steps required to follow the recipe.

Automating it

This section shows you how to leverage Microsoft PowerShell and Microsoft Graph to automate your daily tasks.

There's more...

This section consists of additional information about the recipe in order to make you more knowledgeable about it.

See also

This section provides helpful links to other useful information for the recipe.

Get in touch

Feedback from our readers is always welcome.

General feedback: If you have questions about any aspect of this book or have any general feedback, please email us at `customercare@packt.com` and mention the book's title in the subject of your message.

Errata: Although we have taken every care to ensure the accuracy of our content, mistakes do happen. If you have found a mistake in this book, we would be grateful if you reported this to us. Please visit `packt.com/submit-errata`, click **Submit Errata**, and fill in the form.

Piracy: If you come across any illegal copies of our works in any form on the internet, we would be grateful if you would provide us with the location address or website name. Please contact us at `copyright@packt.com` with a link to the material.

If you are interested in becoming an author: If there is a topic that you have expertise in and you are interested in either writing or contributing to a book, please visit `authors.packt.com/`.

Free Benefits with Your Book

This book comes with free benefits to support your learning. Activate them now for instant access (see the "*How to Unlock*" section for instructions).

Here's a quick overview of what you can instantly unlock with your purchase:

PDF and ePub Copies

Access a DRM-free PDF copy of this book to read anywhere, on any device.

Use a DRM-free ePub version with your favorite e-reader.

Next-Gen Web-Based Reader

Multi-device progress sync: Pick up where you left off, on any device.

Highlighting and notetaking: Capture ideas and turn reading into lasting knowledge.

Bookmarking: Save and revisit key sections whenever you need them.

Dark mode: Reduce eye strain by switching to dark or sepia themes.

How to Unlock

Scan the QR code (or go to packtpub.com/unlock). Search for this book by name, confirm the edition, and then follow the steps on the page.

UNLOCK NOW

Note: Keep your invoice handy. Purchases made directly from Packt don't require one

Stay Sharp in Cloud and DevOps – Join 44,000+ Subscribers of CloudPro

CloudPro is a weekly newsletter for cloud professionals who want to stay current on the fast-evolving world of cloud computing, DevOps, and infrastructure engineering.

Every issue delivers focused, high-signal content on topics like:

- AWS, GCP & multi-cloud architecture
- Containers, Kubernetes & orchestration
- Infrastructure as Code (IaC) with Terraform, Pulumi, etc.
- Platform engineering & automation workflows
- Observability, performance tuning, and reliability best practices

Whether you're a cloud engineer, SRE, DevOps practitioner, or platform lead, CloudPro helps you stay on top of what matters, without the noise.

Scan the QR code to join for free and get weekly insights straight to your inbox:

https://packt.link/cloudpro

Share your thoughts

Now you've finished *Microsoft Intune Cookbook, Second Edition*, we'd love to hear your thoughts! Scan the QR code below to go straight to the Amazon review page for this book and share your feedback or leave a review on the site that you purchased it from.

https://packt.link/r/1-805-80723-4

Your review is important to us and the tech community and will help us make sure we're delivering excellent quality content.

1

Getting Started with Microsoft Intune

Microsoft Intune is the leader in the Gartner Magic Quadrant for **unified endpoint management** (**UEM**) and is an excellent tool for managing your end user devices, especially in the modern hybrid workforce. This book is your comprehensive guide to getting you started with using and configuring Microsoft Intune with only a basic understanding of end user compute management and PowerShell (for automation and scripting).

Intune is a cloud management software service that can fully manage your entire end user computing estate wherever you are. This includes Windows, iOS, iPadOS, macOS, Android, and Linux for both corporate and personally owned devices, as well as cloud computing with Windows 365 and Azure Virtual Desktop.

You can secure corporate data on any device, and Intune follows the zero-trust security model. As well as compliance and policy management, Intune will also handle your application deployment across devices.

Before digging into the finer points of using the platform, first, we need to look at the prerequisites and have a general look at **Entra ID.** While Microsoft Intune is part of the Microsoft 365 suite, it relies on Entra ID for groups, users, conditional access policies, and more, so an understanding of how these work will make your life significantly easier. In this chapter, we will look at how we can leverage Microsoft Entra to set the foundations for a successful Intune deployment.

This chapter will include the following recipes:

- Creating a tenant
- Creating a user

- Assigning Entra ID roles
- Configuring Entra ID general device settings
- Configuring Entra ID ESR
- Creating Entra ID static groups
- Creating Entra ID dynamic groups
- Configuring Entra ID MDM/MAM scopes

Technical requirements

For this chapter, you will need a modern web browser and a **PowerShell code editor** such as **Visual Studio Code** (**VS Code**) or the PowerShell ISE.

All of the scripts referenced in this chapter can be found here: `https://github.com/PacktPublishing/Microsoft-Intune-Cookbook-Second-Edition/tree/main/Chapter-1`.

Chapter materials

Microsoft licensing can be tricky at the best of times, so we will start there.

To use Intune, you will need an Intune license, which comes in three flavors:

- **Intune Plan 1**: This includes your standard Intune functionality, including reporting and **Endpoint analytics**.
- **Intune Plan 2**: This adds **Microsoft Tunnel** for iOS and Android application-level VPNs and support for specialty devices (such as VR headsets and large conference screens).
- **Intune Suite**: This includes everything in Plans 1 and 2 plus **Remote Help**, **Endpoint Privilege Management**, **Enterprise App Management**, **Cloud PKI**, and **Advanced Endpoint Analytics** (all of which will be covered in greater depth in *Chapter 14*). Some can be purchased individually on Plan 1, but it can work out more cost-effectively to purchase the suite. I usually say at least two, ideally three, of the products to make it worthwhile, but it differs for each organization.

In 2026, Intune Suite is included in M365 E5 and parts of it will be available in M365 E3 (Remote Help, Endpoint Analytics, Intune Plan 2).

You can purchase your Intune licensing on a standalone plan or as part of the following Microsoft SKUs:

- Microsoft 365 E3 (including Remote Help, Endpoint Analytics, and Intune P2)
- Microsoft 365 E5 (Including Intune Suite)

- Microsoft 365 F1
- Microsoft 365 F3
- Microsoft 365 A3 (Education Only)
- Microsoft 365 A5
- Microsoft Business Premium
- Enterprise Mobility + Security E3
- Enterprise Mobility + Security E5

If you are purchasing Intune on a standalone plan, you will also need to purchase an **Entra Active Directory license** as well as a **Defender for Endpoint license** (if required).

These licenses are all per-user; however, Intune device-based licensing is available for some niche use cases such as multi-user kiosk machines or manufacturing facilities with non-user-assigned devices.

On top of the Intune licensing, there are some additional Windows-only features that require a Windows Enterprise license over the standard Professional (or Business) one.

This license is included in the M365 E3/E5/F3/F5/A3/A5 SKUs or can be added as an additional license.

Adding Windows Enterprise adds the following features:

- Defender for Endpoint Plan 2
- AppLocker
- Credential Guard
- Windows Virtualization Rights
- Proactive Remediations

A very useful site for referencing licensing SKUs and what each contains is `https://m365maps.com/`.

Creating a tenant

Now that we have our licensing in place, we need to create a **tenant**. This recipe will run you through the steps to create your new Microsoft 365/Intune/Azure tenant.

A tenant can be used across the full Microsoft platform, so it will apply to Microsoft 365, Azure, and Intune. If you have Active Directory set up currently, you can synchronize your users/groups/devices into Entra ID to give your users a hybrid identity (you need to ensure they do not have a `.local` suffix for this to succeed). For identity matching, the on-prem UPN has to match that of Entra.

You can synchronize multiple Active Directory forests into a single Entra tenant, but you cannot synchronize one on-premises AD domain/forest into multiple Entra tenants.

A tenant can be configured with a custom domain name rather than the *.onmicrosoft.com* one, which is automatically configured when you create your new tenant. Within a tenant, you can have multiple Azure subscriptions, but only one Intune configuration. There is also no built-in functionality to copy or migrate devices and settings between tenants using Intune.

Getting ready

We will now run through the process of purchasing a M365 Business Premium license on a 30-day trial. If you have a Visual Studio subscription, you are eligible for a M365 Development Tenant for 90 days.

> Note
>
> The licenses do not include Windows Enterprise, so you will not be able to test the chapter on Proactive Remediations.

How to do it...

To create your live tenant, first, you need to obtain your licenses. These can be purchased from any License Partner or directly from Microsoft. If you are using a developer tenant, *Steps 1* and *2* can be skipped:

1. For this book, we are going to grab a Microsoft 365 Business Premium trial license (Microsoft 365 E3 and E5 require an annual purchase); the screen will look as follows:

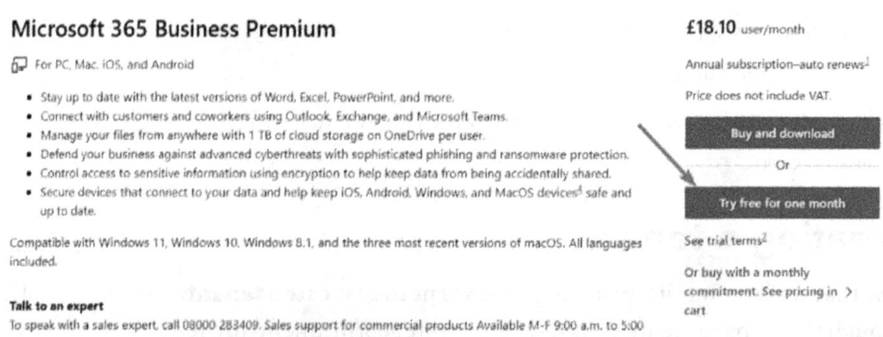

Figure 1.1 – Microsoft licensing page

After clicking the **Try free for one month** button, enter an email address to use for the tenancy. If it does not exist, it will create it for you, so long as it is on a Microsoft domain (`outlook.com`, for example).

You will also be required to verify your identity, so make sure you enter a valid telephone number.

2. Once completed, you will be taken to the **Microsoft 365 admin center**, where you can double-check your licenses in the **Licenses** menu under **Billing**.
   That is all we need to do within the Microsoft 365 admin center. Now, we must navigate to `https://entra.microsoft.com` and log in with the same account that was licensed when we set up the tenant.

   Before moving on to the next recipe, from here on, we are going to include the PowerShell and JSON code (where possible) to complete the steps both in the GUI and from a command line.

   Microsoft Graph is the technology that is used underneath most Microsoft products to handle all of the commands that are sent via the web interface. Fortunately, it includes a powerful API that we can use to automate these using PowerShell.

   To use the command-line scripts, you will need to install the **Microsoft Graph PowerShell** module and connect to Graph (we are going to set up a connection with full access so that you can reuse the connection at all stages). For this, use your preferred code editor (VS Code is a good choice and is platform agnostic) or use the built-in PowerShell ISE on a Windows device:

3. First, load up a PowerShell console and install, then import, the module:

```
Install-Module -Name Microsoft.Graph.Authentication -Scope CurrentUser -
Repository PSGallery -Force
```

4. Now, import the newly installed module:

```
import-module microsoft.graph.authentication
```

5. Finally, we need to connect:

```
Connect-MgGraph -Scopes RoleAssignmentSchedule.ReadWrite.Directory,
Domain.Read.All, Domain.ReadWrite.All, Directory.Read.All,
Policy.ReadWrite.ConditionalAccess, DeviceManagementApps.ReadWrite.All,
DeviceManagementConfiguration.ReadWrite.All,
DeviceManagementManagedDevices.ReadWrite.All, openid, profile, email,
offline_access,
Policy.ReadWrite.PermissionGrant,RoleManagement.ReadWrite.Directory,
Policy.ReadWrite.DeviceConfiguration, DeviceLocalCredential.Read.All,
DeviceManagementManagedDevices.PrivilegedOperations.All,
```

```
DeviceManagementServiceConfig.ReadWrite.All, Policy.Read.All,
DeviceManagementRBAC.ReadWrite.All, Group.ReadWrite.All,
GroupMember.ReadWrite.All
```

After pressing *Enter*, you will be prompted to log in with your new credentials and then approve the permissions for your tenant by checking the **Consent on behalf of your organization** box and then clicking **Accept**.

We now have a working tenant and a Microsoft Graph connection that we can use in the following recipes and chapters.

Creating a user

Now that our tenant has been set up, we can create our first user. This recipe will run through how to create your first user and then look at what is happening in the **Graph API** underneath.

Getting ready

Navigate to the **Microsoft Entra portal** at `https://entra.microsoft.com/#home`.

Here, you will find an overview of your tenant, including your tenant ID, which you will find yourself needing when setting up policies such as OneDrive within Intune. You cannot display it within Intune directly, so you will have to navigate back to Entra ID to find it.

Within Entra ID, click on **Users**, then **All users**; you will see the user you set up when enrolling the tenant. This user will have Global Administrator access across the whole tenant, so we will create a new user to test role assignment, license assignment, and others.

How to do it...

Follow these steps to create an additional non-admin user in your tenant. The new user screen runs across a few pages, so we will concentrate on cropped screenshots of the appropriate areas:

1. Click on **+ New user** and then **Create new user**.
2. Fill in the basic details. You will be prompted to change your password on your first login, but if you are auto-generating, click the eye icon to show the password so that you can use it to log in later:

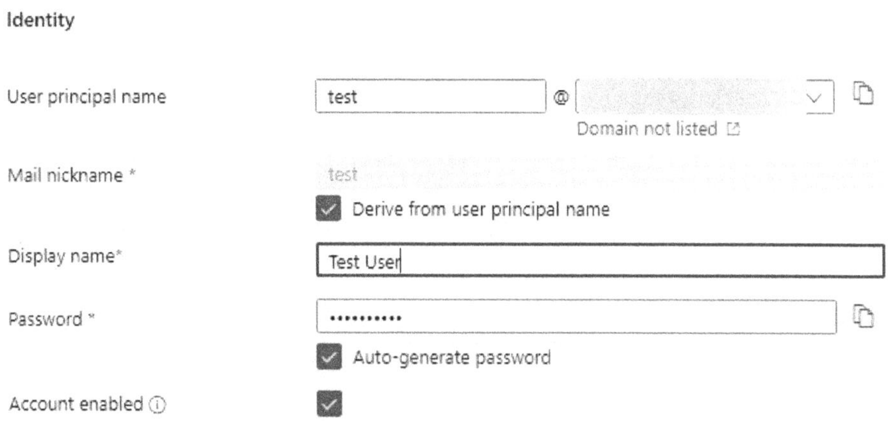

Figure 1.2 – Entra user details

3. Leave **Groups** and **Roles** empty for now; we will run through those in the *Creating Entra ID groups* recipe.
4. Add a **Usage location** value on this screen; it will not let you assign a license without one set:

Figure 1.3 – Entra user license details

5. Optionally, you can fill in **Job Info**, but this is not a requirement at this stage.
6. Finally, click **Create**.

With that, you have created your first account in your new tenant.

Automating it

Now, let's learn how to automate user creation.

You will need the PowerShell ISE or VS Code running for this, as we will be setting variables to send to Microsoft Graph.

Follow these steps in a new PowerShell script to create your user with Microsoft Graph:

1. First, create the variables to populate – in this case, this is everything we set in the GUI. Setting these as variables instead of hardcoding them within the JSON gives us the option to run within a loop and change the variables each time in the future:

```
$displayname = "User One"
$givenname = "User"
$surname = "One"
$usageLocation = "GB"
$mailNickname = "user1"
$password = "PASSWORD HERE"
$domainname = "DOMAIN HERE"
```

2. Now, populate the JSON with these variables:

```
$json = @"
{
    "accountEnabled": true,
    "displayName": "$displayname",
    "givenName": "$givenname",
    "mailNickname": "$mailNickname",
    "passwordProfile": {
        "forceChangePasswordNextSignIn": true,
        "password": "$password"
    },
    "surname": "$surname",
    "usageLocation": "$usageLocation",
    "userPrincipalName": "$mailnickname@$domainname"
}
"@
```

As you can see, the JSON is a fairly straightforward array. Watch the names of the items as they are case sensitive; as an example, `accountEnabled` will fail if it is listed as *AccountEnabled* or *accountenabled*. The error will be a standard malformed request, so it is always a good idea to start here with any troubleshooting.

You can also see that `passwordProfile` is a nested array, as it has further child items.

3. Next, tell it where to send the request. There are two versions of the Graph API – V1.0 and Beta. The Beta API receives the latest features ahead of general release. In this case,

either will work, but when creating groups, some aspects, such as being able to assign roles to them, require the beta version.

4. Next, we must point to the **Users** section of the Graph API:

```
$uri = "https://graph.microsoft.com/beta/users"
```

5. Finally, send the request to Microsoft Graph. There are different types of requests you can use; we will run through them quickly so that you understand the difference:
   - `GET`: This simply retrieves values from Graph to manipulate, export, and more
   - `POST`: This sends new values to Graph that do not currently exist (a new user, new policy, and so on)
   - `PATCH`: This updates an existing record
   - `PUT`: This is similar to `PATCH` but needs a full URL, including the ID being created
   - `DELETE`: This deletes whatever you are pointing it at

   This is a new account we are creating, and a `PUT` request is more complex than a `POST` request, so we will stick with `POST`:

```
Invoke-MgGraphRequest -Method POST -Uri $uri -Body $json -ContentType
"application/json"
```

   This command sends a `POST` request to the URL we specified earlier (in this case, `users`) to pass the JSON we wrote. The content type tells it to look for JSON.

Now that we have our user, we can assign a role to it.

Assigning Entra ID roles

Before we proceed further, we need to understand what roles are within Entra ID. A role gives user specific permissions to items within Entra Active Directory/Microsoft 365/Intune. There are numerous built-in roles, and you can also create a custom role with specific permissions applied.

It is always worth working from the principle of the least required permissions. It is better to give an admin multiple roles with strict permissions rather than going for a global administrator with keys to the kingdom.

A list of the built-in roles can be found here: `https://learn.microsoft.com/en-us/entra/identity/role-based-access-control/permissions-reference`.

As this is an Intune book, the two main roles we are interested in initially are **Intune Administrator** and **Entra Joined Device Local Administrator**. As its name suggests, Intune Administrator gives full access to everything within Intune.

Entra Joined Device Local Administrator gives users full administrative access over *all* Entra joined devices. While this is useful for support teams, if licensed, it is worth considering using **privileged identity management** (**PIM**), which you can use for role access for a limited amount of time with full reporting.

You can find out more about PIM here: `https://learn.microsoft.com/en-us/entra/id-governance/privileged-identity-management/pim-configure`.

> Note
>
> Intune also has specific **role-based access control** (**RBAC**) to restrict access within the Intune portal itself. We will cover this further in *Chapter 13*.

There are two ways to assign roles, so we will use one for each.

How to do it...

Follow these steps to assign a built-in role to your newly created user:

1. Navigate to **Entra Admin Center** within your new tenant by going to `https://entra.microsoft.com`.
2. Within Entra, expand **Entra ID**, and scroll down to **Roles & admins**:

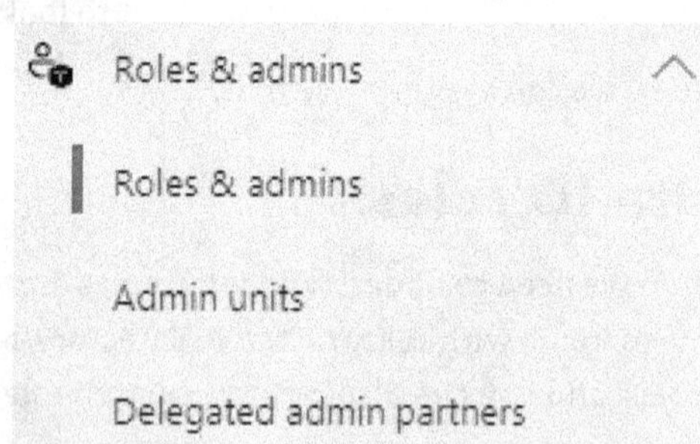

Figure 1.4 – Entra ID – Roles & admins

3. Then, click on **Roles & admins**. You will now see this screen:

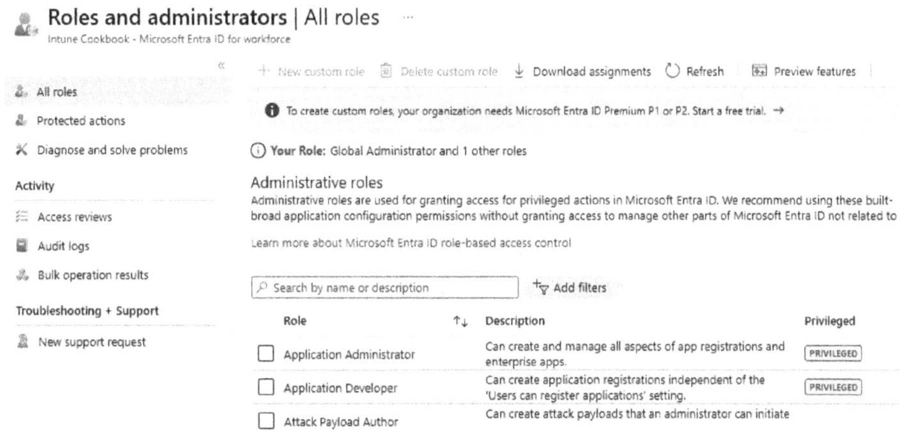

Figure 1.5 – Entra ID – Roles and administrators | All roles

For this, we will use the built-in roles, but if you need something more granular, you can create a custom role based on the exact permissions you require. This is covered in *Chapter 13*.

4. Next, select **Intune Administrator**.
5. On the screen that appears, click **+ Add Assignments** and find your new user:

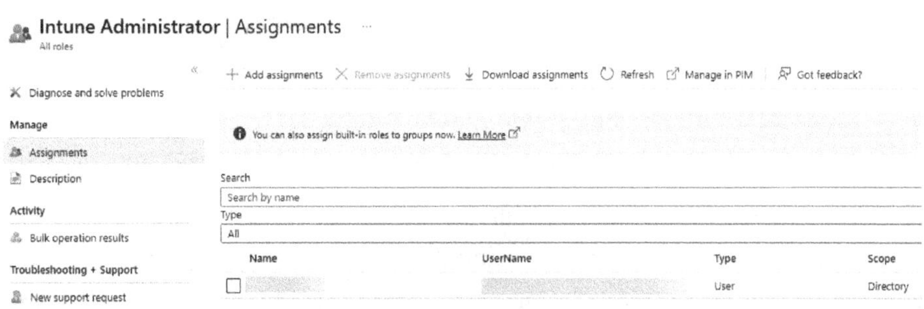

Figure 1.6 – Assigned Intune Administrator role

6. The other way we can do this is within the **Users** blade; navigate back to **Entra Active Directory** and click on **Users**, then the user you created.
7. Within the user details, click on **Assigned roles**.
8. Then, click **+ Add assignments**.
9. This time, select **Microsoft Entra Joined Device Local Administrator** and click **Add**.

Following these steps has granted your user administrative rights on your cloud-joined devices.

Automating it

By automating the assignment of roles, we can add to our previous user creation to create an automated onboarding function for user management across job roles.

Adding roles via PowerShell is slightly more complex, as we need to find the role ID to be able to assign it.

Create a new PowerShell script and follow these steps:

1. Set the variables, the role name, and the user we are assigning it to (at the time of writing, the role is still called Azure AD Joined Device Local Administrator (in 2025)):

```
$rolename = "Azure AD Joined Device Local Administrator"
$user = "test@test.onmicrosoft.com"
```

2. We need to get the ID from the **User Profile Name** (**UPN**). We are querying the Users API to the user's UPN, passing the output as `PSObject`, and then retrieving the ID from it. This can be done with two commands, one for grabbing the user details and the second for grabbing the ID from the first variable, but wrapping in brackets does the same job and runs quicker:

```
$userid = (Invoke-MgGraphRequest -Uri "https://graph.microsoft.com/beta/
users/$user" -Method Get -OutputType PSObject).id
```

   Note that we are passing `OutputType` and using a `GET` request with this first command. Setting `OutputType` allows us to use the output within PowerShell.

3. The next stage is to find the details for the role we are looking for. We can do this by grabbing all the roles and then using `where-object` to grab the role we are looking for, after which we can pass the output to a PowerShell object. We are grabbing the roles from `roleDefinitions` within the whole directory in Graph, in the `roleManagement` subsection of the API:

```
$uri = "https://graph.microsoft.com/beta/roleManagement/directory/
roleDefinitions"
$roletoassign = (((Invoke-MgGraphRequest -Uri $uri -Method Get -OutputType
PSObject).value) | where-object DisplayName -eq $rolename).id
```

4. Now that we have the role ID and the user ID, we just need to put them together and assign the role. As with the previous recipe, we will hardcode the JSON. Here, we are

setting ScopeID to "/" to cover the entire directory. We then set the URL and send a POST request:

```
$json = @'
{
"@odata.type": "#microsoft.graph.unifiedRoleAssignment",
"roleDefinitionId": "$roletoassign",
"principalId": "$userid",
"directoryScopeId": "/"
}
'@
$posturi = "https://graph.microsoft.com/beta/roleManagement/directory/
roleAssignments"
Invoke-MgGraphRequest -Uri $posturi -Method Post -Body $json -ContentType
"application/json"
```

By completing these steps, we have created our script to automate role assignment in Microsoft Entra using the Graph API.

Configuring Entra ID general device settings

The first settings we need to look at are the **general device settings**. This is where we can configure what users can and cannot do with their devices. This includes setting who can enroll devices into Intune and Entra ID, as well as the security around it.

How to do it...

While the vast majority of our device settings will be configured within Intune, there are a few within Entra ID that are worth setting up before we move on to the Intune configuration.

Following these steps will configure your Entra environment for device enrolment:

1. First, within Entra ID, expand **Devices**, click **Overview**, and then click **Device Settings**.
2. We need to ensure **Users may join devices to Microsoft Entra** is set to either **All** or **Selected**, as we need our machines to be Entra ID joined. We can restrict device types later within Intune, so it is best just to leave this one set to **All**.
   Regarding **Multi-factor authentication**, leave this set to **No** and use **Conditional Access** as recommended. This will give you much more granular control and reporting.

   The maximum number of devices is something to note here. It is also a setting within Intune, so there are two places where you can check if users have issues enrolling devices. The Entra ID setting here is for all registered devices, so it will include any personally enrolled devices that are not Intune joined. It is also worth noting that this will include any previous devices as Entra ID does not automatically clean stale devices (although this can be scripted; see the following *Automating it* section).

Unless you have a large number of devices per user, leave this set to `50` devices per user.

You can ignore the blue text link, as we configured that with the Entra ID roles earlier.

The final setting here (**Restrict non-admin users from recovering the BitLocker key(s) for their owned devices (preview)**) lets your end users retrieve their own BitLocker keys (after authenticating). This is a personal preference; changing it to **Yes** would result in additional support calls in the event of a power cut or other events that could trigger BitLocker, but it does improve your security posture. For this example, we are leaving it set to **No**.

3. Once you have configured the settings, click **Save**.

This recipe has allowed our tenant to accept Intune device enrolment.

Automating it

Again, we can use PowerShell to automate this configuration to make it more easily repeatable:

1. Set some variables and change them so that they match your environment:

```
$devicequota = 50
##Set to 0 to block Entra ID Registration
$entraregister = 1
##Set to 0 to block Entra ID Join
$entrajoin = 1
##Set to 1 to require MFA
$mfa = 0
##Set to False to block BitLocker
$bitlocker = "true"
```

While this is displayed on one screen in the GUI, this is two separate policies, so we need to create the JSON for the non-BitLocker settings. This JSON will include some nested arrays, as each section of the page is an array in itself.

2. These settings are all configured with defaults from the initial tenant configuration, so if you need to check the raw JSON values, run a `GET` request against this URL: `https://graph.microsoft.com/beta/policies/authorizationPolicy/authorizationPolicy`.

3. We are simply manipulating the retrieved values to receive our new values. You can copy and paste this script block as we set our values in *Step 1* (you may again notice

reference to Azure AD here in the JSON; this is correct – Graph is harder to change than the frontend UI):

```
$jsonsettings = @"
{
"@odata.context":"https://graph.microsoft.com/beta/$metadata#policies/
deviceRegistrationPolicy/$entity",
"multiFactorAuthConfiguration":"$mfa",
"id":"deviceRegistrationPolicy",
"displayName":"Device Registration Policy",
"description":"Tenant-wide policy that manages intial provisioning controls
using quota restrictions, additional authentication and authorization
checks",
"userDeviceQuota":$devicequota,
"azureADRegistration":{
"appliesTo":"$entraregister","allowedUsers":null,"allowedGroups":null,"isAd
minConfigurable":false
},
"azureADJoin":{
"appliesTo":"$entrajoin","allowedUsers":[],"allowedGroups":
[],"isAdminConfigurable":true
}
}
"@
```

4. Then, we manipulate the BitLocker settings:

```
$jsonbitlocker = @"
{"defaultUserRolePermissions":{"allowedToReadBitlockerKeysForOwnedDevice":
$bitlocker}}
"@
```

5. Now, set the URLs for each setting we are changing:

```
$registrationuri = "https://graph.microsoft.com/beta/policies/
deviceRegistrationPolicy"
$bitlockeruri = "https://graph.microsoft.com/beta/policies/
authorizationPolicy/authorizationPolicy"
```

6. For `deviceRegistrationPolicy`, we need to send a `PUT` request:

```
Invoke-MgGraphRequest -Method PUT -Uri $registrationuri -Body $jsonsettings
-ContentType "application/json"
```

7. For the BitLocker policy, we must send a `PATCH` request as we are amending existing settings:

```
Invoke-MgGraphRequest -Method PATCH -Uri $bitlockeruri -Body $jsonbitlocker
-ContentType "application/json"
```

These steps have configured our tenant to allow enrolment and let users view their BitLocker keys.

As we mentioned earlier, clearing out stale devices requires a script, so we will run through that quickly as well:

1. To try and keep things to just using the authentication module, we will stick with `invoke-mggraphrequests`, but that does limit us by default due to Graph pagination (100 items). Therefore, we will use a custom function to grab all results by parsing `@odata.nextlink` until we reach the end. The function is available in the GitHub repository.
2. Set the necessary variables:

```
$daystodisable = 90
$daystoremove = 120
```

   Now, we will disable anything over 90 days (or whatever the variable is set to). It is always best to do something slightly less drastic initially.

3. After setting the date we are looking for, loop through the devices and find any that have not been seen in that time, then disable them.
4. We now want to grab all devices from this URI: `https://graph.microsoft.com/beta/devices`.
   We are then filtering on devices that have not logged on in the last 90 days.

   For each of the devices we find, we are running a `PATCH` request to disable the device. We send this request to the URI of the device itself:

```
$dt = (Get-Date).AddDays(-$daystodisable)
$devicesuri = "https://graph.microsoft.com/beta/devices"
```

```
$Devices = getallpagination -url $devicesuri | Where-Object
{($_.ApproximateLastSignInDateTime -le $dt) -and ($_.AccountEnabled -eq
$true)}
foreach ($Device in $Devices) {
    $deviceuri = "https://graph.microsoft.com/beta/devices/$deviceid"
    $devicejson = @"
    {
        "@odata.type": "#microsoft.graph.device",
        "accountEnabled": false
    }
"@
Invoke-MgGraphRequest -Uri $deviceuri -Method PATCH -Body $devicejson -
ContentType "application/json"
}
```

5. Then, do the same retrieval, but look for anything older than our delete date, which is also disabled (this will stop us from deleting something we had to re-enable previously but still has not been seen for whatever reason). For these devices, remove them using a `DELETE` command against the `Devices/DeviceID` section of Graph:

```
$dt = (Get-Date).AddDays(-$daystoremove)
$Devices = Get-MgDevice -All | Where-Object
{($_.ApproximateLastLogonTimeStamp -le $dt) -and ($_.AccountEnabled -eq
$false)}
foreach ($Device in $Devices) {
    $deviceid = $Device.Id
    $deviceuri = "https://graph.microsoft.com/beta/devices/$deviceid"
    Invoke-MgGraphRequest -Uri $deviceuri -Method DELTE
}
```

This script has configured your tenant to allow enrolment and configured key device settings, as well as keeping your environment clean with device clean-up.

Configuring Entra ID ESR

Now, we will look at **Enterprise State Roaming** (**ESR**), which automatically backs up some device user preferences into Azure for a more seamless experience when moving between Windows devices.

How to do it...

The other device setting within Entra ID is ESR. This is similar to the older **User Experience Virtualization** (**UE-V**), which can be found in the **Microsoft Desktop Optimization Pack** (**MDOP**).

It backs up certain user settings within Intune and Edge and backs them up to Azure Storage (outside the subscription and without cost).

The following settings that are being backed up are currently within Windows:

- **Keyboard**: Turn on toggle keys (off by default)
- **Date, time, and region**: Country/region
- **Date, time, and region**: Region format (locale)
- **Language**: Language profile
- **Keyboard**: List of keyboards
- **Mouse**: Primary mouse button
- **Passwords**: Web credentials
- **Pen**: Pen handedness
- **Touchpad**: Scrolling direction
- **Wi-Fi**: Wi-Fi profiles (only WPA)

The following settings are backed up in Edge:

- Favorites
- Passwords
- Addresses and more (form-fill)
- Collections
- Settings
- Extensions
- Open tabs (available in Microsoft Edge version 88 or later)
- History (available in Microsoft Edge version 88 or later)

To enable ESR, follow these steps:

1. Navigate to **Entra ID** | **Devices** | **Overview** | **Device settings** and click on **Enterprise State Roaming**.

2. Change the **Users may sync settings and app data across devices** setting to **All** or **Selected**. As there is no cost regarding this, it is recommended to set it to **All**.
3. Then, click **Save**.

You have now enabled ESR across your tenant.

Automating it

This one is slightly more complicated as it does not work with the Graph API; instead, you have to access the more hidden Azure **Identity and Access Management** (**IAM**) API:

1. Set the necessary variables:

```
##Set to 2 to disable or 0 to enable
$esrstatus = 0
$tenantid = "Your-Tenant-ID"
```

2. Create the JSON. If we had set it to a select user group, it would be populated within the `syncSelectedUsers` array. As we are doing an all-or-nothing, we will simply leave the array blank:

```
$json = @"
{
    "isAdminConfigurable": true,
    "isRoamingSettingChanged": true,
    "syncSelectedUsers": [],
    "syncSetting": $esrstatus
}
"@
```

3. Set the URL (note the non-Graph setup of it):

```
$url = "https://main.iam.ad.ext.azure.com/api/RoamingSettings?ESRV2=true"
```

4. Now, create the access token and headers.
5. When you run this section, you will be presented with a hyperlink and some code that you must enter to authenticate. Click the link, enter the code, and then accept the numerous prompts.
6. Here, we are using `Invoke-Restmethod` to send a `POST` request to the `oauth2` Microsoft login URL for the tenant and requesting a token for the Entra ID IAM client ID.

As this one requires user interaction, we will add a `while` loop to wait until the request has been made and approved within the web browser. If no activity is detected, the script will stop with an error code:

```
##Create Access Token
$clientid = "1950a258-227b-4e31-a9cf-717495945fc2"
$response = Invoke-RestMethod -Method POST -UseBasicParsing -Uri "https://
login.microsoftonline.com/$tenantId/oauth2/devicecode" -ContentType
"application/x-www-form-urlencoded" -Body
"resource=https%3A%2F%2Fmain.iam.ad.ext.azure.com&client_id=$clientId"
Write-Output $response.message
$waited = 0
while($true){
    try{
        $authResponse = Invoke-RestMethod -uri "https://
login.microsoftonline.com/$tenantId/oauth2/token" -ContentType
"application/x-www-form-urlencoded" -Method POST -Body
"grant_type=device_code&resource=https%3A%2F%2Fmain.iam.ad.ext.azure.com&co
de=$($response.device_code)&client_id=$clientId" -ErrorAction Stop
        $refreshToken = $authResponse.refresh_token
        break
    }catch{
        if($waited -gt 300){
            Write-Verbose "No valid login detected within 5 minutes"
            Throw
        }
        #try again
        Start-Sleep -s 5
        $waited += 5
    }
}
$response = (Invoke-RestMethod "https://login.windows.net/$tenantId/oauth2/
token" -Method POST -Body "resource=74658136-14ec-4630-
ad9b-26e160ff0fc6&grant_type=refresh_token&refresh_token=$refreshToken&clie
nt_id=$clientId&scope=openid" -ErrorAction Stop)
    $resourceToken = $response.access_token
```

7. The previous command has given us our access token, which we can then add to the header to call out `webrequest`. The authorization section always needs to start with `"Bearer"` and then the access token (in this case, `$resourceToken`):

```
$Headers = @{
    "Authorization" = "Bearer " + $resourceToken
    "Content-type"  = "application/json"
    "X-Requested-With" = "XMLHttpRequest"
    "x-ms-client-request-id" = [guid]::NewGuid()
    "x-ms-correlation-id" = [guid]::NewGuid()
}
```

8. Finally, send the request to enable or disable ESR:

```
Invoke-RestMethod -Uri $url -Headers $Headers -Method PUT -Body $json -
ErrorAction Stop
```

This script has automated enabling ESR using the IAM API.

Creating Entra ID static groups

Now that our new user has been configured, we need a way to assign our policies to them and any machines they may use. For this, we need to configure Entra ID groups, which come in two flavors – static and dynamic.

If you are familiar with traditional Active Directory groups, these are very similar, except they include dynamic groups, where a group is populated automatically based on a particular query or filter that has been configured.

Getting ready

First, load the Entra portal, expand **Groups**, and click on **All Groups** (you can also access groups within the Intune portal, which loads the same window).

How to do it...

A **static group** is pretty straightforward to use – you manually add either users or devices to it:

1. Click on **New Group** and enter the necessary details. Set **Group type** to **Security** and enter **Group name** and **Group description** values. If you want to be able to assign roles directly to the group instead of at the user level (for example, you want a group of

Intune administrators), change the setting to **Yes**. Set **Membership type** to **Assigned**. Optionally, add any members and an owner to manage the group. Then, click **Create**.

2. Once your group has been created, click on it to look at some of the other actions you can take against it. You can also get an overview of the group membership, as well as the group ID:

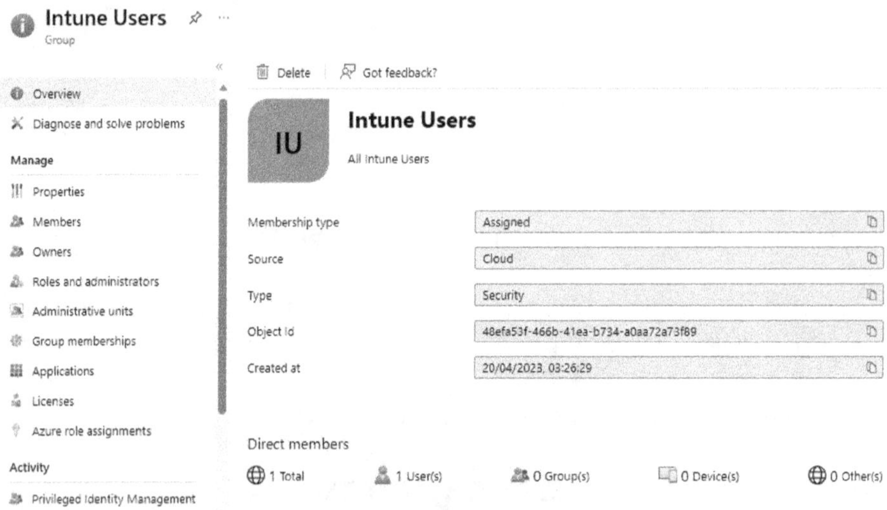

Figure 1.7 – Entra ID group menu

Members and **Owners** are pretty self-explanatory. **Administrative units** is a useful feature if you want to delegate within your environment. Say, for example, you want your service desk to be able to perform tasks against a particular group of users – you can create an administrative unit and assign users and groups to it. You can then configure a custom Azure role with specific access *only* to that administrative unit. **Group memberships** is for nested groups. Clicking the **Licenses** option allows you to assign a license at a group level rather than directly to the users. If you selected **Yes** earlier, you can also assign Azure roles to the group in the **Azure role assignments** menu.

With that, you have created a static Microsoft Entra group.

Automating it

Creating this PowerShell script will automate your Entra group creation process, which will be useful when you need to bulk-create groups during your tenant management.

This is a fairly easy one to automate:

1. As usual, let's start with the variables:

```
$groupname = "TestGroup123"
$groupdescription = "TestGroupDescription"
```

2. Convert the group name into lowercase and remove any special characters so that we can use it as the mail nickname:

```
$groupnickname = ($groupname -replace '[^a-zA-Z0-9]', '').ToLower()
```

3. Set the URL. Here, we are using the **Groups** subsection of Graph:

```
$uri = "https://graph.microsoft.com/beta/groups/"
```

4. Populate the JSON. We do not need mail for this group as it is for Entra ID and Intune membership only, and it is a security group, so we need to pass this through:

```
$json = @"
{
    "description": "$groupdescription",
    "displayName": "$groupname",
    "mailEnabled": false,
    "mailNickname": "$groupnickname",
    "securityEnabled": true
}
"@
```

5. Send the command to create the group:

```
Invoke-MgGraphRequest -Uri $uri -Method Post -Body $json -ContentType
"application/json"
```

   This can also be completed by using the `New-mgGroup` module and passing variables through if required.

You now have a script to create your static Entra groups automatically.

Creating Entra ID dynamic groups

In this recipe, we will configure Entra ID dynamic groups, where we can configure a group to automatically populate based on specified criteria. This example will cover both user and device-based queries.

Getting ready

First, load the Entra portal, expand **Groups**, and click on **All groups** (you can also access groups within the Intune portal, which loads the same window).

How to do it...

Dynamic groups are automated; you set a membership rule (the user is a member of a particular location, device prefix, and so on), and then Entra ID reviews the rules on a schedule and adds/removes members accordingly. It is worth noting that there can be a delay while Entra queries the membership rules to populate the group membership.

For this example, we will create one M365 Apps (the product formally known as Office) user group and one Autopilot device dynamic group that we can use later on.

The user group will collect any users with an Office Business license (not the Enterprise ones), while the device group will collect all of your **Autopilot devices**; we will cover this in more detail in *Chapter 4*.

Creating a dynamic Office user group

Follow these steps to create a dynamic group containing only licensed Office users:

1. Starting with the user group, click **New Group** and enter the basic details:
   - **Group type**: **Security**.
   - Enter **Group name** and **Group description** details.
   - Change the membership type to **Dynamic User**.
2. You will notice that we have to create a dynamic query. So, click **Add dynamic query**. This will take you to the **Rule Builder** interface, and this is where you can view the properties available and set them accordingly. If you already know the query, you can add it directly into the **Rule syntax** window.
   To detect Office users, we are going to check the User Assigned plans:
   - For **Property**, enter **assignedPlans**.
   - Set **Operator** to **Any**.

  - The value needs to be `(user.assignedPlans -any (assignedPlan.servicePlanId -eq "094e7854-93fc-4d55-b2c0-3ab5369ebdc1" -and assignedPlan.capabilityStatus -eq "Enabled"))`.
  - It should look like this in the syntax (sometimes, you may need to edit it to add the final closing brackets):

Figure 1.8 – Entra ID – new dynamic rule result

3. Now, click the **Validate Rules** button.
4. Add a user who has an Office license assigned and click **Select**.
5. Then, click **Validate**. Here, you can see I have only assigned the license to one of my two users:

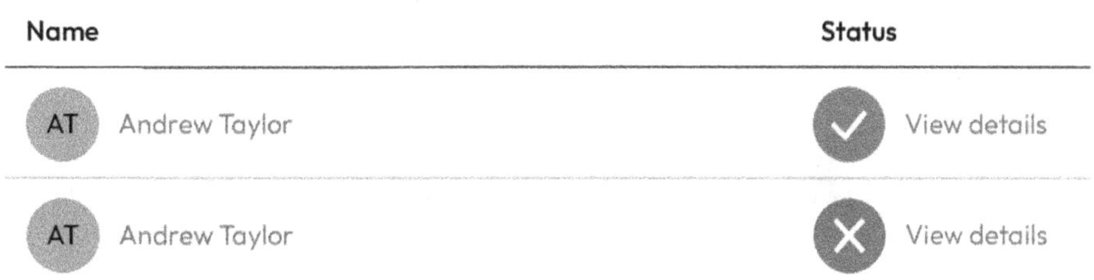

Figure 1.9 – User validation results

With that, we have created a dynamic user group for users with an Office license.

To find the `servicePlanId` value for individual products, you can use a downloadable CSV from the Microsoft site. You can use this to create any other dynamic groups: `https://learn.microsoft.com/en-us/entra/identity/users/licensing-service-plan-reference`.

Creating a dynamic Autopilot device group

When we create our Autopilot profile later, in *Chapter 4*, we can configure it to automatically pick up all users/devices. However, in a pilot or **Proof of Concept** (**PoC**), we may only want to target those devices enrolled in Autopilot. For this, we can query the device's ZTID, which is added when we import it (covered in *Chapter 4*).

Follow this process to create our dynamic group.

1. Create a **New Group** value in Entra ID, but this time, pick **Dynamic Device** as the membership type. Set **Group type** to **Security**. Then, add **Group name** and **Group description** values. Finally, click **Add dynamic query**.
2. This one is slightly more straightforward. Set **Property** to **devicePhysicalIds**, **Operator** to **Any**, and **Value** to `(_ -startsWith "[ZTDid]`:

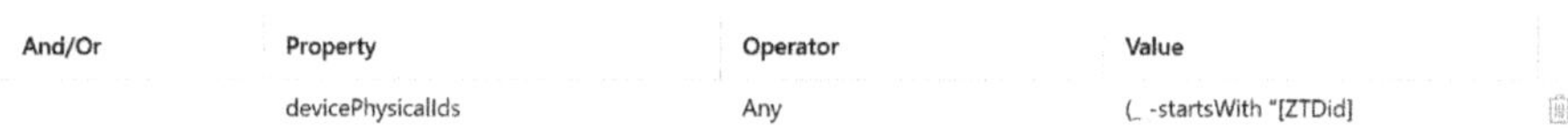

Figure 1.10 – Dynamic rule creator

3. It should look like this (sometimes, you may need to edit to add the final closing brackets). Click **OK** on this screen:

Figure 1.11– Dynamic device query

We do not need to validate this one, as we do not have any device enrolled yet anyway.

4. Now, click **Save**, then **Create** on the following screen.

With that, we have created our dynamic Autopilot devices group so that it is ready to enroll devices in *Chapter 4*.

Automating it

This script will demonstrate how we can use Graph and PowerShell to create both of our dynamic groups, demonstrating the different queries.

Dynamic Office user group

This is similar to a static group, except we must add an extra line for the dynamic rule:

1. Set the necessary variables:

```
$groupname = "TestGroup123"
$groupdescription = "TestGroupDescription"
$membershiprule = '(user.assignedPlans -any (assignedPlan.servicePlanId -eq
\"43de0ff5-c92c-492b-9116-175376d08c38\" -and assignedPlan.capabilityStatus
-eq \"Enabled\"))'
$groupnickname = ($groupname -replace '[^a-zA-Z0-9]', '').ToLower()
```

> **Note**
>
> We have single quotes around the rule because we are using double quotes in the rule and also escaping the double quotes.

2. Now, give it a URL:

```
$url = "https://graph.microsoft.com/beta/groups"
Populate the JSON
$json = @"
{
    "description": "$groupdescription",
    "displayName": "$groupname",
    "groupTypes": [
        "DynamicMembership"
    ],
    "mailEnabled": false,
    "mailNickname": "$groupnickname",
    "membershipRule": "$membershiprule",
    "membershipRuleProcessingState": "On",
    "securityEnabled": true
}
"@
```

3. Finally, submit our Graph request:

```
Invoke-MgGraphRequest -Uri $url -Method Post -Body $json -ContentType
"application/json"
```

This script will create a dynamic group for users who have an active Office license based on the SKU and license properties.

Dynamic Autopilot device group

This is the same as the user group but with a different rule. The Graph backend does not differentiate between user and device groups.

We can now create a PowerShell script to create a dynamic group:

1. Set the necessary variables:

```
$groupname = "TestGroup123"
$groupdescription = "TestGroupDescription"
```

2. Set the mail nickname:

```
$groupnickname = ($groupname -replace '[^a-zA-Z0-9]', '').ToLower()
```

3. Set the membership rule:

```
$membershiprule = '(device.devicePhysicalIDs -any (_ -contains "[ZTDID]"))'
```

4. Set the URL:

```
$url = "https://graph.microsoft.com/beta/groups"
```

5. Populate the JSON:

```
$json = @"
{
    "description": "$groupdescription",
    "displayName": "$groupname",
    "groupTypes": [
        "DynamicMembership"
    ],
    "mailEnabled": false,
    "mailNickname": "$groupnickname",
    "membershipRule": $membershiprule,
    "membershipRuleProcessingState": "On",
    "securityEnabled": true
```

```
}
"@
```

6. Finally, submit our Graph request:

```
Invoke-MgGraphRequest -Uri $url -Method Post -Body $json -ContentType
"application/json"
```

We now have a script for creating our dynamic Autopilot group.

Configuring Entra ID MDM scope

The last thing we must do before we move on to Intune is allow our users to enroll devices into **Mobile Device Management** (**MDM**) and, if required, **Mobile Application Management** (**MAM**).

MDM is for enrolling your corporate-owned devices into Intune, while MAM is for your **bring-your-own devices** (**BYODs**). Both use the same URLs; you will notice options for **Windows Information Protection (WIP)**, but this is now deprecated and can be left blank.

How to do it...

Follow these steps to configure your Entra ID MDM scope:

1. Within Microsoft Entra ID, expand **Settings** and click on **Mobility**.
2. Within the **Mobility** portal, click **Microsoft Intune**:

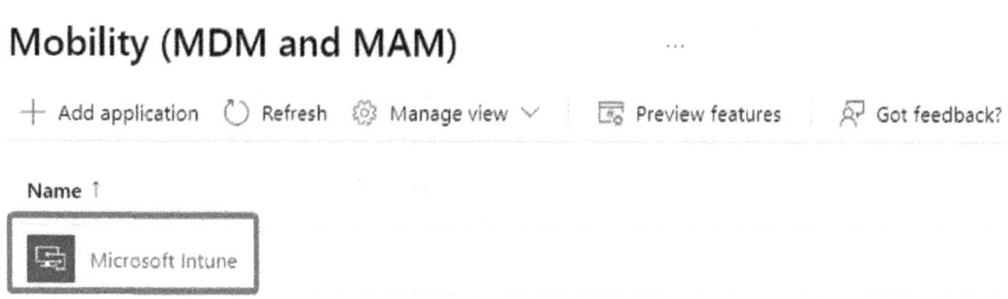

Figure 1.12 – The Mobility (MDM and MAM) screen

3. For this environment, set the MDM user scope to **All** and leave WIP as **None**. Note that you can restrict by groups – for example, only allowing users with an Intune license based on a dynamic group, or block completely. Leave the default URLs as is and then click **Save**.

With that, we have configured our Microsoft Entra environment for device enrolment.

Automating it

This is a tricky one to automate. Not only does it use the IAM API that we used for ESR, but the MDM application ID is also tenant-specific.

Let's build a PowerShell script to automate these settings:

1. First, in your browser window, look in the address bar and grab the ID:

Figure 1.13 – Address bar object ID

2. Set the necessary variables, including this ID. A setting of 2 means enabled for all, while `0` means disabled:

```
$MDMstatus = 2
$WIPStatus = 0
$policyid = "Policy ID grabbed from browser"
```

3. Populate the JSON. As with the Entra ID device settings, we are manipulating the default values so that we can retrieve the current JSON with a `GET` request. In this case, we are only changing two settings; everything else remains the same:

```
$json = @"
{
    "appCategory": "Mdm",
    "appData": {
        "complianceUrl": "https://portal.manage.microsoft.com/?
portalAction=Compliance",
        "enrollmentUrl": "https://enrollment.manage.microsoft.com/
enrollmentserver/discovery.svc",
        "mamComplianceUrl": "",
        "mamEnrollmentUrl": "https://wip.mam.manage.microsoft.com/Enroll",
        "mamTermsOfUseUrl": "",
        "termsOfUseUrl": "https://portal.manage.microsoft.com/
TermsofUse.aspx"
    },
    "appDisplayName": "Microsoft Intune",
    "appId": "0000000a-0000-0000-c000-000000000000",
    "isOnPrem": false,
    "logoUrl": null,
```

```
    "mamAppliesTo": $WIPstatus,
    "mamAppliesToGroups": [],
    "mdmAppliesTo": $MDMstatus,
    "mdmAppliesToGroups": [],
    "objectId": "$policyid",
    "originalAppData": {
        "complianceUrl": "https://portal.manage.microsoft.com/?
portalAction=Compliance",
        "enrollmentUrl": "https://enrollment.manage.microsoft.com/
enrollmentserver/discovery.svc",
        "mamComplianceUrl": "",
        "mamEnrollmentUrl": "",
        "mamTermsOfUseUrl": "",
        "termsOfUseUrl": "https://portal.manage.microsoft.com/
TermsofUse.aspx"
    }
}
"@
```

4. Set the URL:

```
$url = "https://main.iam.ad.ext.azure.com/api/MdmApplications/$policyid?
mdmAppliesToChanged=true&mamAppliesToChanged=true"
```

5. Authenticate against the IAM API:

```
##Create Access Token
$clientid = "1950a258-227b-4e31-a9cf-717495945fc2"
$response = Invoke-RestMethod -Method POST -UseBasicParsing -Uri "https://
login.microsoftonline.com/$tenantId/oauth2/devicecode" -ContentType
"application/x-www-form-urlencoded" -Body
"resource=https%3A%2F%2Fmain.iam.ad.ext.azure.com&client_id=$clientId"
Write-Output $response.message
$waited = 0
while($true){
    try{
        $authResponse = Invoke-RestMethod -uri "https://
login.microsoftonline.com/$tenantId/oauth2/token" -ContentType
"application/x-www-form-urlencoded" -Method POST -Body
"grant_type=device_code&resource=https%3A%2F%2Fmain.iam.ad.ext.azure.com&co
de=$($response.device_code)&client_id=$clientId" -ErrorAction Stop
```

```
        $refreshToken = $authResponse.refresh_token
        break
    }catch{
        if($waited -gt 300){
            Write-Verbose "No valid login detected within 5 minutes"
            Throw
        }
        #try again
        Start-Sleep -s 5
        $waited += 5
    }
}

$response = (Invoke-RestMethod "https://login.windows.net/$tenantId/oauth2/
token" -Method POST -Body "resource=74658136-14ec-4630-
ad9b-26e160ff0fc6&grant_type=refresh_token&refresh_token=$refreshToken&clie
nt_id=$clientId&scope=openid" -ErrorAction Stop)
    $resourceToken = $response.access_token
```

6. Create the headers:

```
$Headers = @{
    "Authorization" = "Bearer " + $resourceToken
    "Content-type"  = "application/json"
    "X-Requested-With" = "XMLHttpRequest"
    "x-ms-client-request-id" = [guid]::NewGuid()
    "x-ms-correlation-id" = [guid]::NewGuid()
}
```

7. Configure the policy:

```
Invoke-RestMethod -Uri $url -Headers $Headers -Method PUT -Body $json -
ErrorAction Stop
```

We now have a script to amend the MDM enrolment scope.

This brings us to the end of this recipe and the chapter. We have a tenant that is ready to start configuring and deploying to. In the next chapter, we will begin deploying the configuration for your Windows devices.

Get This Book's PDF Version and Exclusive Extras

Scan the QR code (or go to `packtpub.com/unlock`). Search for this book by name, confirm the edition, and then follow the steps on the page.

UNLOCK NOW

Note: Keep your invoice handy. Purchases made directly from Packt don't require one.

2

Configuring Your New Tenant for Windows Devices

Now that your tenant is built and we have some **Entra ID** groups and roles configured, we can start populating the Intune environment.

To do so, we use policies that are equivalent to **group policies** in a traditional Active Directory configuration. These are used to configure your devices with the settings chosen within the Intune portal. This chapter looks at the different policy options for Windows devices to configure any non-security settings.

There are a variety of ways to configure policies, which we will cover in this chapter. This chapter will include the following recipes:

- Configuring a Settings catalog policy
- Configuring a Custom policy
- Importing and ingesting an ADMX policy
- Group policy analytics
- Properties catalog (for Device Inventory)

Technical requirements

For this chapter, you will need a modern web browser and a PowerShell code editor such as **Visual Studio Code** or the **PowerShell ISE**.

All of the scripts referenced can be found here:

`https://github.com/PacktPublishing/Microsoft-Intune-Cookbook-Second-Edition/tree/main/Chapter-2`

Before following the recipes, you may first need to re-authenticate to Microsoft Graph, as covered in *Chapter 1.*

Chapter materials

Before moving on to configuring our policies, there are a couple of things to keep in mind.

Firstly, some settings can be configured in multiple places, especially when looking at security policies, so it is always worth keeping in mind what you are configuring and where to avoid making conflicting policies. Even if a setting has the same value in two different policies, it will be marked as a conflict within the GUI.

The other thing is the concept of **tattooing**. Some settings, when applied, can leave the setting configured on a device when switched to **Not Configured** within Intune. If there is a setting with the **Enabled** or **Not Configured** options, changing it to **Not Configured** does not send a signal to revert the configuration on the device; it simply tells Intune not to do anything with that particular setting and leave it to whatever happens to be set on the device already. Normally, this will just be the default Windows settings, but if it is a policy you have previously applied, it will remain at that value.

Fortunately, this is much improved in recent Intune updates, but there are still a few places where it can happen, so it is always worth being aware of.

Remember, all settings configured in Intune are ultimately just registry or file-level changes, so there is no *best* way of deploying a policy, but (as we will show in the *security* example in the next chapter) applying policies within the **Endpoint security** blade adds a few extra options on top of using a standard policy, or a baseline.

This chapter covers the most-used options when setting a new policy, but there are multiple different options available:

- **Settings catalog**: This is also known as the **Unified Settings catalog**. This contains over 25,000 settings in an easy-to-use interface and is the current direction of travel for most policies within Intune. We will cover this in the following chapter.
- **Properties catalog**: This new functionality is for setting which details to grab from devices when using **Device Inventory**. We will cover this in greater detail below.
- **BIOS configurations and other settings**: Currently only supporting Dell devices, this allows you to upload a BIOS settings file and deploy to your devices.
- **Custom**: This is for policies not currently natively supported but backed by a **Configuration Service Provider** (**CSP**), and they can be created directly. This is also covered in the following chapter.

- **Delivery optimization**: This is a way to configure devices to check machines in the local network/VPN for any files previously retrieved from Microsoft, saving bandwidth across the WAN. You can read more here: `https://learn.microsoft.com/en-gb/mem/intune/configuration/delivery-optimization-windows`.
- **Device Firmware Configuration Interface (DFCI)**: For devices that support DFCI, you can use these policies to configure **BIOS (Basic Input/Output System)** settings on your **Autopilot devices**. You can read more here: `https://learn.microsoft.com/en-gb/mem/intune/configuration/device-firmware-configuration-interface-windows`.
- **Device restrictions**: These are legacy restriction policies from when Intune was first introduced. It is worth using **Settings** catalog for these.
- **Device restrictions (Windows 10 Team)**: These are restrictions for Teams devices only.
- **Domain join**: Best avoided where possible. This is for when Autopilot is used with **hybrid Entra Join**.
- **Edition upgrade and mode switch**: This can be used to switch the Windows edition or move in or out of **S mode** (a security-streamlined Windows version).
- **Email**: Fairly self-explanatory, this sets an email server and configuration for the mail client on a machine.
- **Endpoint protection**: Another legacy policy where you can configure some basic security settings. It is recommended to use the **Endpoint security** blade covered in *Chapter 3*.
- **Identity protection**: Similar to endpoint protection, this has also been migrated to the **Security** blade.
- **Imported Administrative templates**: Covered in this chapter, this is used to import third-party ADMX policies.
- **Kiosk**: This allows you to configure devices to run in single- or multi-app kiosk mode, where devices auto-login with a local account and are restricted to running only the allowed application(s).
- **Microsoft Defender for Endpoint**: Another legacy security policy. Again, use the **Security** blade to set this.

- **Network boundary**: When using **Windows Defender Application Guard**, you can configure certain sites to be blocked by setting a network boundary. You can find out more here: `https://learn.microsoft.com/en-gb/mem/intune/protect/endpoint-protection-windows-10`.
- **Public Key Cryptography Standards (PKCS) certificate**: Configure a **Public Key Pair Certificate** for certificate-based authentication.
- **PKCS imported certificate**: Use an imported PKCS for **Secure/Multipurpose Internet Mail Extensions (S/MIME)** email encryption.
- **Simple Certificate Enrollment Profile (SCEP) certificate**: Use a SCEP for certificate-based authentication.
- **Secure assessment**: This is for educational customers to create a restricted device for exam-type scenarios.
- **Shared multi-user device**: Specific settings when dealing with shared multi-user devices, such as profile management. You can read more here: `https://learn.microsoft.com/en-us/windows/configuration/set-up-shared-or-guest-pc?tabs=intune#shared-pc-mode-concepts`.
- **Trusted certificate**: Used to import your trusted root certificate from a certificate authority.
- **VPN**: Create a VPN profile for your devices.
- **Wi-Fi**: Fairly self-explanatory – create a profile for your wireless network settings. Supports both basic and enterprise networks.
- **Windows Health Monitoring**: This configures what data is sent to Microsoft from your devices. When dealing with **Autopatch** (which we will cover in *Chapter 4*), it is a requirement.
- **Wired network**: Similar to Wi-Fi, but for wired networks.

When it comes to automating, creating some of these policies can be quite complicated, so it is worth familiarizing yourself with **Graph Explorer** (`https://cmd.ms/ge`) and also the *F12* developer tools in your browser. When creating your policies in the GUI, you can use these to see what is happening at the network level, including the URLs and payload. The **Graph Xray extension** for Chrome and Edge will also display the exact PowerShell commands you can use to recreate whatever is configured in the GUI (`https://graphxray.merill.net`).

> **Tip**
>
> A useful tip when navigating some of these policies is to use the `out-gridview` functionality in PowerShell. If you grab all of the settings for a particular policy type, this gives you a useful GUI with filtering options and search functionality, rather than having to scroll through the command-line output.

Configuring a Settings catalog policy

We will start with Settings catalog (or Unified Settings catalog) policies, which will be your primary policy type moving forward. Many of the *older* policies are being migrated to Settings catalog, and due to the nature of the Graph underneath these new policy types, this allows for significantly more available settings (there are well over 25,000 at the time of writing).

Settings catalog is also cross-platform and can be used for Windows, macOS, and iOS policies at present, with more being migrated daily. You will find the vast majority of your traditional on-premises **Group Policy Objects** (**GPOs**) here as well. If there is a setting you cannot find, there are other deployment methods, which will be covered in the following recipes.

As a Settings catalog policy can contain many thousands of policy settings, it can become more difficult to troubleshoot and slow to load and edit within a browser. Similar to when dealing with on-premises GPO, less is more; create multiple policies with fewer settings in each so that you can have a policy for each particular task (OneDrive, Office, Edge, etc.). It is also worth noting that Intune policies do not run during login and halt logins; they run while a user is logged in, so adding more policies does not impact login speed. Intune will also queue the policy deployment, based on the current activity of tasks on your tenant, and automatically deploy to Windows devices. The speed with which the policy settings are deployed, received, and configured may depend on the state of the device (is it off or on?), the network connectivity of the device, and when it was last checked into Intune for an update.

How to do it...

Now, let's move on to creating our very first policy. For this one, we will configure some OneDrive settings to make life for your users easier:

1. Within the Intune portal, navigate to **Devices**, expand **By platform**, then select **Windows**, click on **Configuration**, and finally, click **+ Create and click + New policy.**
2. Select **Windows 10 and later**, then **Settings catalog**, and click **Create**.
3. Give your policy a meaningful name and description. Remember that while you will know what the policy is doing now, in the future you may not remember as easily, or

someone else may be managing your tenant, so giving policies a sensible name and description makes future changes so much easier.

Once you have added your name and description, click **Next**.

Figure 2.1 – Initial policy creation

4. Now, we need to add some settings, so click the blue text that says **+ Add settings**. At this point, note that you can select a category or perform a search. A category can contain many settings (within sub-categories), so it is often quicker to perform a search. When searching, the UI will display all of the categories containing policies with your search term, which you can then click through to find the correct policy.
5. In our case, **OneDrive** has its own category, so we can simply scroll down and select it by clicking on it.
6. Once you have clicked on the category, you will see all of the settings available for selection. You can select all of them here, or just select individual settings. For this policy, we will configure **Files On-Demand**, **single sign-on** (**SSO**), and **known folder move** (**KFM**). Check the boxes labeled as follows:
    - **Silently move Windows known folders to OneDrive**
    - **Silently sign in users to the OneDrive sync app with their Windows credentials**
    - **Use OneDrive Files On-Demand**

Figure 2.2 – OneDrive settings selection

7. You will then see the settings in the left-hand panel with their default values (in this case, all are set as **Disabled**).

   If you decide that you do not want to set a particular policy, click on the **-** button to the right. You can also remove an entire category by clicking the blue **Remove category** text.

8. Now, we want to enable all of these policies, which is simply a case of clicking on the slider. For the first two settings, it is a simple on/off switch, but note that for KFM, more settings will appear underneath:

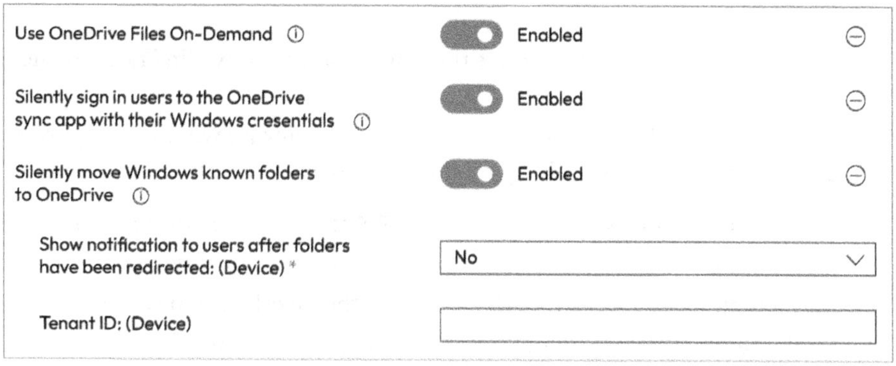

Figure 2.3 – OneDrive settings enabled

Enter your **tenant ID** here (if you do not have it to hand, load the Entra portal and navigate to **Entra Active Directory**), and optionally select whether you want your users to receive a toast notification when complete.

9. After entering your details, click **Next**.
10. We can ignore **Scope tags** for now, as this is a simple environment. They are a way to differentiate policies and settings, used with split permissions in an estate with multiple levels of administrators. They will be covered in *Chapter 13*, so click **Next**.
11. Now, we need to assign the policy. As these are user settings, we will assign the policy to the group we created earlier, containing your users. Alternatively, you could click the **Add all users** option if you want it to be deployed to everyone. You will also see the ability to filter here, which will also be covered in *Chapter 13*.
12. After selecting your group, click **Select**.
13. Once your assignments are configured, click **Next**.
14. You will now see a final screen to confirm everything you are creating in your new policy, as well as the policy details and the assignment. Once you are happy with these, click **Create**.

Here, we have learned how to configure our first Settings catalog policy to learn how the policies work and configure our OneDrive settings.

Automating it

Due to the nature of the Settings catalog and the use of categories, creating our policy via PowerShell is a little more tricky than some of the more straightforward policies, such as **Device restrictions** or **Compliance**. Here, we will configure our OneDrive policy using PowerShell and Graph:

1. Before showing you how to create this particular policy, we first need to understand exactly how the JSON is assembled.
   We need to find the category ID containing the policy we wish to configure. We can either search for it or simply list all the categories.

   Listing the categories involves running a `GET` command against one of these URLs. We are working now in the `deviceManagement` section of Graph, which is where most Intune settings reside. Within there, we will then work in `configurationCategories` for the Settings catalog. We can then filter further on the platform for the different operating systems. Security settings also use `microsoftSense` technology instead of the default `mdm`, helping to differentiate between the operating systems we are configuring:

- Windows:

```
https://graph.microsoft.com/beta/deviceManagement/
configurationCategories?=&$filter=(platforms has 'windows10') and
(technologies has 'mdm')
```

- iOS:

```
https://graph.microsoft.com/beta/deviceManagement/
configurationCategories?=&$filter=(platforms has 'iOS') and
(technologies has 'mdm' or technologies has 'appleRemoteManagement')
```

- Windows Security:

```
https://graph.microsoft.com/beta/deviceManagement/
configurationCategories?
templateCategory=True&$filter=(platforms has 'windows10') and
(technologies has 'microsoftSense')
```

- macOS:

```
https://graph.microsoft.com/beta/deviceManagement/
configurationCategories?=&$filter=(platforms has 'macOS') and
(technologies has 'mdm' or technologies has 'appleRemoteManagement')
```

> **Note**
>
> If using PowerShell, you will need to escape the **$** before **`filter`** with a backtick (**`**); otherwise, it will interpret **`$filter`** as a PowerShell variable, which we have not set to will remove it completely. Adding a backtick tells PowerShell that it is text to parse.

2. If you want to search and find the category, add this to the end of the `GET` URL:

```
&$search="SEARCH TERM HERE"
```

In your results, you need to grab the category ID.

3. Now that we have the ID, we can list the policies within it. This is another `GET` command, as we are requesting information from Graph:

```
https://graph.microsoft.com/beta/deviceManagement/configurationSettings?
&`$filter=categoryId eq 'CATEGORY ID'
```

Grab the root definition ID for the policy; you will need that later, when configuring the final JSON.

4. For a simple enable/disable policy, you then need to look in the options array within the policy and grab the `itemID` for the value you want.
For those with a further child setting, you need to look at the `Options` array and investigate the `dependedOnBy` array, which will show you which sub-settings are activated when you enable the policy.

   In the case of OneDrive KFM, this gives the following:

```
device_vendor_msft_policy_config_onedrivengscv2.updates~policy~onedrivengsc
_kfmoptinnowizard_kfmoptinnowizard_textbox
True
device_vendor_msft_policy_config_onedrivengscv2.updates~policy~onedrivengsc
_kfmoptinnowizard_kfmoptinnowizard_dropdown
True
device_vendor_msft_policy_config_onedrivengscv2.updates~policy~onedrivengsc
_kfmoptinnowizard_kfmoptinnowizard_desktop_checkbox
True
device_vendor_msft_policy_config_onedrivengscv2.updates~policy~onedrivengsc
_kfmoptinnowizard_kfmoptinnowizard_documents_checkbox
True
device_vendor_msft_policy_config_onedrivengscv2.updates~policy~onedrivengsc
_kfmoptinnowizard_kfmoptinnowizard_pictures_checkbox
True
```

This aligns with the fact there are two different Policy checkboxes for KFM within the Settings catalog. One is to enable it and supply the tenant ID, and the other is to specify which folders to redirect.

Now that we know what a Settings catalog policy is comprised of, let's have a look at the policy for OneDrive, as created in the GUI earlier.

5. First, as usual, we set our variables:

```
$policyname = "Onedrive Configuration"
$policydescription = "Configures OneDrive"
$tenantid = "TENANT ID HERE"
$groupid = "AAD GROUP ID HERE"
```

6. Then, we need the URL to create the policy:

```
$url = "https://graph.microsoft.com/beta/deviceManagement/
configurationPolicies"
```

Now, set the JSON with the policy details that we found using the methods in the previous steps. You can find the JSON here: `https://github.com/PacktPublishing/Microsoft-Intune-Cookbook-Second-Edition/blob/main/Chapter2/onedrive-settings-catalog.ps1`.

7. When creating the policy, we want the output in a variable so that we can then find the policy ID to assign it.

```
$policy = Invoke-MgGraphRequest -Method POST -Uri $url -Body $json -
ContentType "application/json" -OutputType PSObject
```

Note that we use `-OutputType` here to return the policy as a PowerShell object; otherwise, it would return raw JSON, which would involve more steps to grab the ID.

8. Find the policy ID from our created policy:

```
$policyid = $policy.id
```

9. Set the URL for assignment to include the policy ID:

```
$assignurl = "https://graph.microsoft.com/beta/deviceManagement/
configurationPolicies('$policyid')/assign"
```

10. Create the JSON with the Entra ID Group ID. This is a nested array and uses the `@odata.type` of `"#microsoft.graph.groupAssignmentTarget"`, which tells it to include that group.

```
$assignjson = @"
{
```

```
        "assignments": [
            {
                "target": {
                    "@odata.type": "#microsoft.graph.groupAssignmentTarget",
                    "groupId": "$groupid"
                }
            }
        ]
    }
    "@
```

11. Finally, assign our new policy:

```
$assign = Invoke-MgGraphRequest -Method POST -Uri $assignurl -Body
$assignjson -ContentType "application/json"
```

We have now created our OneDrive settings catalog policy using PowerShell and Graph.

There's more...

When working with Settings catalog and retrieving data, pagination is used to limit the results to more manageable amounts, which, when looking in a GUI, would display a link to show the next 25 results.

When working in Graph, obviously, there is no way to click a link, but it displays as `@odata.nextLink`.

Therefore, when retrieving data, you need to be aware of pagination and work around it. The way to do this is to run your initial `GET` request, then look for the link, and run another `GET` request against that, continuing this method until you have all of the results added to your array.

Here is some example code you can use:

```
$uri = "URL HERE"
$response = (Invoke-MgGraphRequest -uri $uri -Method Get -OutputType PSObject)
$allsettings = $response.value
$allsettingsNextLink = $response."@odata.nextLink"
while ($null -ne $allsettingsNextLink) {
$allsettingsResponse = (Invoke-MGGraphRequest -Uri $allsettingsNextLink -Method
Get -outputType PSObject)
$allsettingsNextLink = $allsettingsResponse."@odata.nextLink"
$allsettings += $allsettingsResponse.value
```

```
}
$allsettings
```

This keeps looping through until the `nextLink` value is empty, at which point it has reached the end and returns the data.

Configuring a custom policy

While the Settings catalog (and other options in the following recipes) will capture 99% of your needs in a standard environment, there may be times when you need to set CSP settings directly on machines and there is no template available.

For this recipe, we are going to use the policy that skips the **User Settings** section within the **Enrollment Status Page** (**ESP**) (there will be more on that in *Chapter 4*), which can be useful if you are happy that all of the key apps are targeted at the device setup and you do not want users to wait for the user-targeted apps to finish installing.

A custom **Open Mobile Alliance Uniform Resource Identifier** (**OMA-URI**) policy allows you to directly set the CSP settings, but you have to be careful that what you enter matches exactly what is expected, as these policies are very exact and will fail if a setting is incorrect.

Getting ready

As mentioned, for this example, we will skip the user status page, details of which can be found at the bottom of the page at the following link: `https://learn.microsoft.com/en-us/troubleshoot/mem/intune/device-enrollment/understand-troubleshoot-esp`.

The exact settings are specified, which is what you would expect when configuring a policy such as this.

How to do it...

Following these instructions will configure your custom policy:

1. First, in the Intune portal, navigate to **Devices**, expand **By platform**, then select **Windows**, click on **Configuration**, and finally, click **+ Create** and click **+ New policy**.
2. This time, you need to select **Windows 10 and later** | **Templates** | **Custom**, and then click **Create**.
3. Give your policy a name and description; remember to make it clear what the policy is doing, and future you will thank you when you need to find a specific policy. Then, click **Next**.
4. On the next screen, we want to add a setting. Some policies can have multiple OMA-URI settings, but this one is a simpler one with a single setting. Click the **Add** button.

Add a name and description for the individual setting.

5. For the **OMA-URI** value, you need to enter the following: `./Vendor/MSFT/DMClient/Provider/MS DM Server/FirstSyncStatus/SkipUserStatusPage`

   Note the dot at the front, which is important. We can see it is a vendor policy, and in this case, the vendor is Microsoft (MSFT).

   You have multiple settings available for the **Value** field, so again, check the documents carefully. In our case, it is a Boolean (`True` or `False`), and we need to set it to `True`.

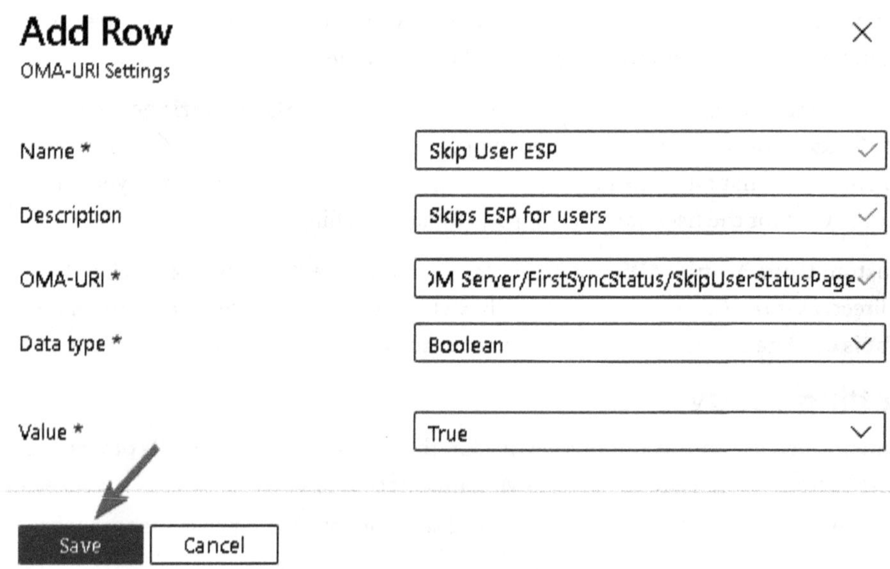

Figure 2.4 – OMA-URI settings values

Click **Save**, and as this is the only policy being configured here, we can click **Next**. Some custom policies may have multiple rows, which you would populate here before continuing.

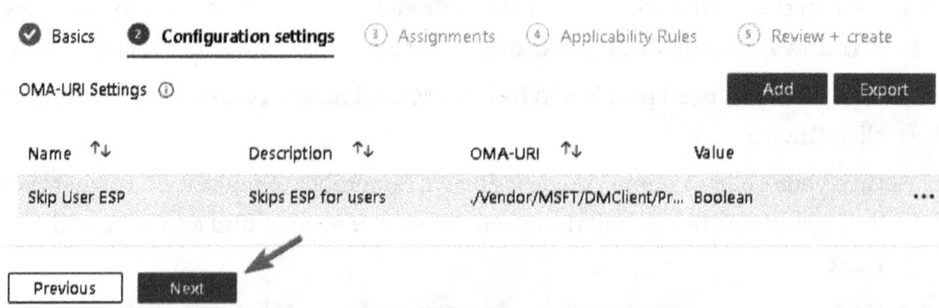

Figure 2.5 – OMA-URI settings configured

6. This is a user-targeting policy, so we will assign it to the Intune-users group we created in *Chapter 1* (or all users if required).
   We do not need any filters on this, as it should be applicable to all devices for the selected users. Therefore, click **Next**.
7. We will cover applicability rules in *Chapter 14*, but at a basic level, we could restrict this policy to only certain OS versions, which is not required for this policy, as we want it to apply to all devices without restrictions, so again, click **Next**.
8. Give everything a final sense check on the **Review + create** page, and then click **Create**.

This step configures a custom policy to skip the Account Setup screen during the **Out of Box Experience** (**OOBE**).

Automating it

Fortunately, these policies are easier to automate than the previous Settings catalog policies. We will use PowerShell and Graph to automate this policy creation:

1. As usual, we will start with our variables. For this particular policy, we will need to set the OMA-URI, the value type (Boolean, string, or integer), and the value itself. To make things easier, the script takes the type in plain text and then converts it to what the JSON needs:

```
$groupid = "00000000-0000-0000-0000-000000000000"
$name = "Skip User ESP"
$description = "Skips Enrollment Status Page Users section"
$omauri = "./Vendor/MSFT/DMClient/Provider/MS DM Server/FirstSyncStatus/
SkipUserStatusPage"
$omavalue = "true"
##Value Type can be string, integer or Boolean
$valuetype = "boolean"
```

2. Next, specify the URL. Custom policies use the `deviceConfigurations` subcategory within the `deviceManagement` area of Graph:

```
$url = "https://graph.microsoft.com/beta/deviceManagement/
deviceConfigurations"
```

3. We will let PowerShell do the clever bits with the value type, using a simple `Switch` command. This takes the value we have sent and converts it to the value that the JSON needs:

```
##Switch on the valuetype
switch ($valuetype) {
    "boolean" {
        $policytype = "#microsoft.graph.omaSettingBoolean"
    }
    "string" {
        $policytype = "#microsoft.graph.omaSettingString"
    }
    "integer" {
        $policytype = "#microsoft.graph.omaSettingInteger"
    }
}
```

4. Now that we have all of the data we need, we can create the JSON. As this is a new policy, there is no ID. If we were manipulating a current policy, we would need to pass through the ID here.
   `omaSettings` are in an array of their own, as signified by the *square brackets [ ]*:

```
$json = @"
{
    "@odata.type": "#microsoft.graph.windows10CustomConfiguration",
    "description": "$description",
    "deviceManagementApplicabilityRuleOsVersion": null,
    "displayName": "$name",
    "id": "00000000-0000-0000-0000-000000000000",
    "omaSettings": [
        {
            "@odata.type": "$policytype",
            "description": "$description",
            "displayName": "$name",
            "omaUri": "$omauri",
            "value": "$omavalue"
        }
    ],
    "roleScopeTagIds": [
        "0"
```

```
    ]
}
"@
```

5. As we are assigning the policy again, we will run the request to output to a variable. We are creating a new policy, so we use the POST command:

```
$policy = Invoke-MgGraphRequest -Method POST -Uri $url -Body $json -
ContentType "application/json" -OutputType PSObject
```

To assign it, use the same method as the previous policy, but with a slightly different URL. Obtain the policy ID to populate the URL:

```
$policyid = $policy.id
```

6. Create the URL:

```
$assignurl = "https://graph.microsoft.com/beta/deviceManagement/
deviceConfigurations/$policyid/assign"
```

7. Create the JSON:

```
$assignjson = @"
{
    "assignments": [
        {
            "target": {
                "@odata.type": "#microsoft.graph.groupAssignmentTarget",
                "groupId": "$groupid"
            }
        }
    ]
}
"@
```

8. Finally, assign the policy:

```
Invoke-MgGraphRequest -Method POST -Uri $assignurl -Body $assignjson -
ContentType "application/json"
```

We have created a new script here to disable account setup during OOBE.

Importing and ingesting an ADMX policy

A relatively new (and welcome) addition is the ability to ingest ADMX policies directly within the console. This is useful for your third-party products, which do not have policies configured within the Settings catalog and are easier to configure than custom OMA-URI policies.

Getting ready

For this example, we will use the **Mozilla Firefox** policy templates. The templates can be downloaded from this location: `https://github.com/mozilla/policy-templates/releases`.

The process is the same for any ADMX-based **Architecture Description Markup Language (ADML)**, so feel free to use others if needed.

After downloading and extracting your templates, you will need `firefox.admx` and the matching ADML for your preferred language.

How to do it...

Follow this recipe to ingest and configure a policy for Mozilla Firefox:

1. Inside the Intune portal, navigate to **Devices** | **Windows** | **Configuration profiles**. At the top, next to where it says **Policies**, you will see an **Import ADMX** text link. Click it.
2. Now, we need to click the **+ Import** button and select the ADMX and ADML files, downloaded in the *Getting ready* section.
   Before we can import the Firefox files, we need to import the Mozilla base files, as they are a prerequisite for Firefox admin templates. Click on the folder icons, and navigate to `mozilla.admx` and `mozilla.adml` from within the files downloaded in the *Getting ready* section. Then, click **Next**:

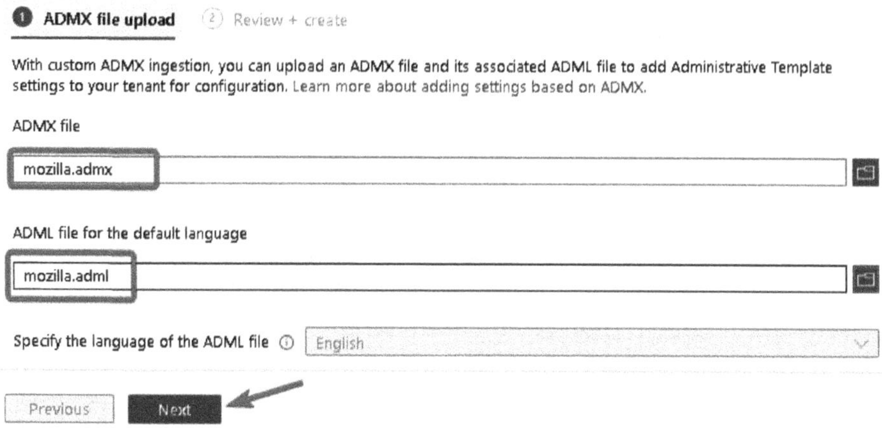

Figure 2.6 – Importing Mozilla policies

3. On the **Review + create** screen, check that the filenames are correct and click **Create**.
4. After clicking **Create** on the previous screen, we are taken to the following page, where we wait for the upload to complete:

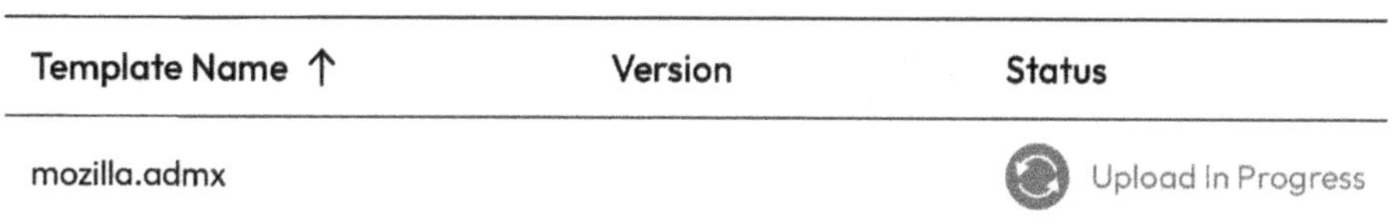

Template Name ↑	Version	Status
mozilla.admx		Upload In Progress

Figure 2.7 – The Mozilla ADMX upload in progress

After the upload has completed, we will see this screen:

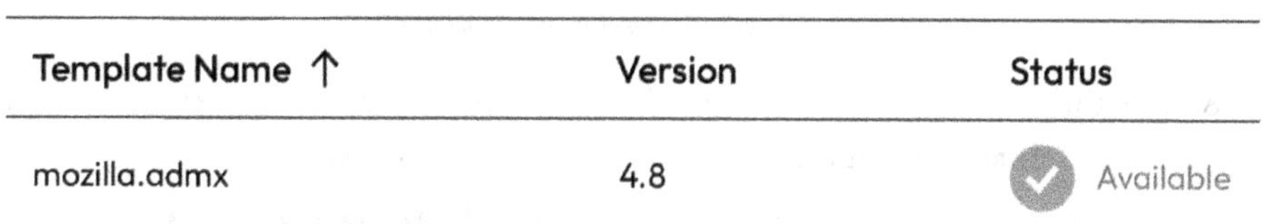

Template Name ↑	Version	Status
mozilla.admx	4.8	Available

Figure 2.8 – The Mozilla ADMX upload completed

5. Now, we can upload the Firefox-specific policies, following the same process as before. Click the folders, select the `firefox.admx` and `firefox.adml` files, and then click **Next**.

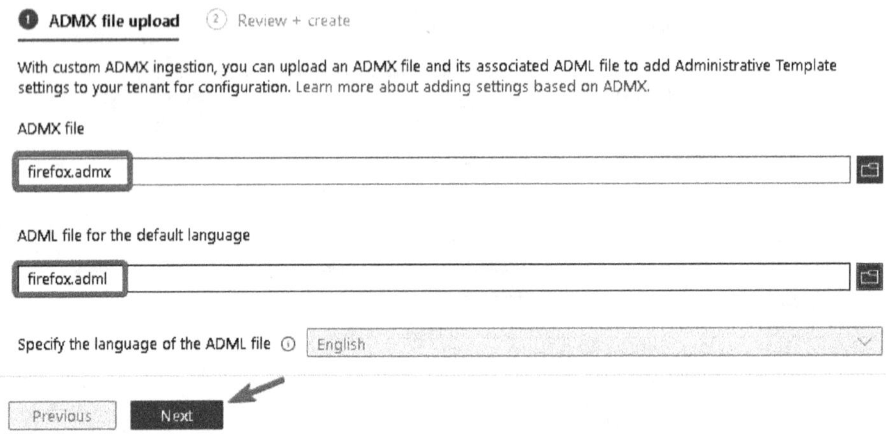

Figure 2.9 – Importing the Firefox module

6. On the **Review + create** screen, confirm the filenames are correct. and click **Create**.
7. Again, wait for the notification that the upload has completed.

   Once complete, you will see this screen:

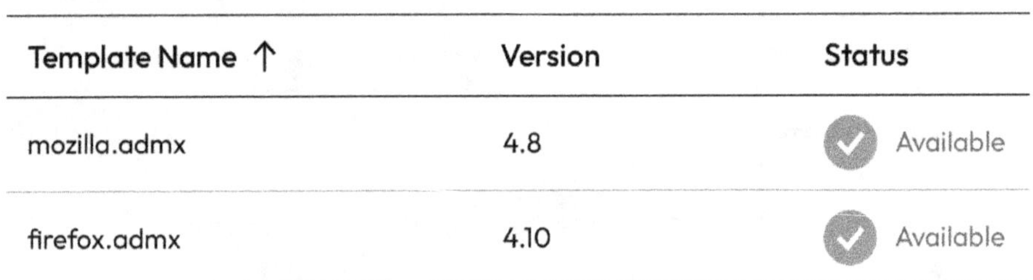

Template Name ↑	Version	Status
mozilla.admx	4.8	Available
firefox.admx	4.10	Available

Figure 2.10 – Firefox and Mozilla ADMX complete

8. Now that we have our policies available, we need to create a policy to use them. Click on the **Policies** text/button, and then click **Create profile**.
9. This time, we want to select **Windows 10 and later** | **Templates** | **Imported Administrative templates (Preview)**. Now, click **Create**.

> **Note**
>
> At the time of writing, this is in preview, and therefore, the steps may change during GA.

10. Give the new profile a name and description, and then click **Next**.

11. On the next screen, you will see the available policies for both the user and the device. I am going to keep it simple and force a start page at the device level, as this is likely to be the most used setting. For your environment, select whichever policies apply. Select **URL for Home page**:

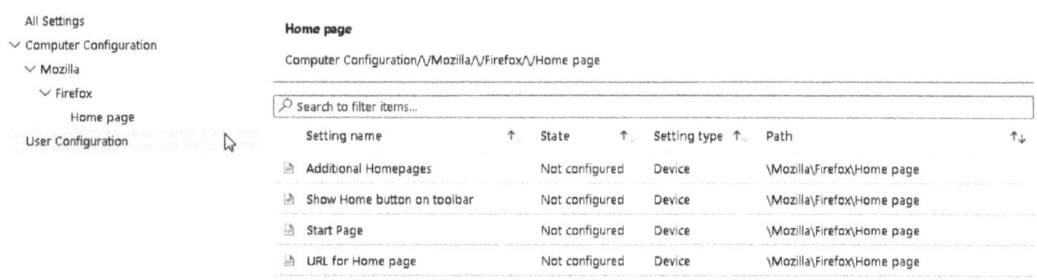

Figure 2.11 – Profile setting options

12. In the flyout, set the policy to **Enabled**, enter your homepage URL, and then click **OK**.
13. After you have configured your settings, click **Next**.
14. We do not need to target this policy at a device level, so click **Next** again to skip the scope tags.
15. At this point, you can assign to either users or devices, depending on what you have configured. For this example, we will assign to **Intune Users**. Then, click **Next**.
16. Check throughout that everything looks correct. and then click **Create**.

These steps have ingested a third-party set of administrative templates for Mozilla Firefox and used them to configure a start page for the browser.

Automating it

Now, we can create a PowerShell script to automate this using Graph.

Ingestion

Ingesting the policy files is reasonably straightforward; we need to grab the files, convert them to Base64, and then upload them to Intune:

1. First, create your variables with the file paths and ADML language.

```
$admxpath = "PATH TO ADMX FILE"
$admlpath = "PATH TO ADML FILE"
$language = "en-US"
```

2. Set the URL, this time using the `groupPolicyUploadedDefinitionFiles` subcategory:

```
$url = "https://graph.microsoft.com/beta/deviceManagement/
groupPolicyUploadedDefinitionFiles"
```

3. Grab the filenames from the paths. We will use this by splitting the path into objects and then using the `-leaf` command to grab the final value. We will need these when populating the JSON later:

```
$admxfile = Split-Path -Path $admxpath -Leaf
$admlfile = Split-Path -Path $admlpath -Leaf
```

4. Convert the files to Base64 and store them in the variables, using the .NET functionality built into PowerShell. We will grab the file, read it, and then convert it to Base64:

```
$admxcontent =
[System.Convert]::ToBase64String([System.IO.File]::ReadAllBytes($admxpath))
$admlcontent =
[System.Convert]::ToBase64String([System.IO.File]::ReadAllBytes($admlpath))
```

5. Create the JSON:

```
$json = @"
{
    "content": "$admxcontent",
    "defaultLanguageCode": "",
    "fileName": "$admxfile",
    "groupPolicyUploadedLanguageFiles": [
        {
            "content": "$admlcontent",
            "fileName": "$admlfile",
            "languageCode": "$language"
        }
    ]
```

```
}
"@
```

6. Run our newly created import JSON:

```
invoke-mggraphrequest -Method POST -Uri $url -Body $json -ContentType
"application/json"
```

This has ingested our templates into Intune, which we can now use to create a policy.

Policy creation

For imported policies, we need to create an empty policy first and then run a second POST command to add the values to it.

Similar to the Settings catalog, we first need to do some exploring to find the details to populate the JSON:

1. First, we need to get the policy definition ID by running a GET command against this URL:

```
https://graph.microsoft.com/beta/deviceManagement/groupPolicyDefinitions
```

If you want to narrow it down, you can append a search to the end of the URL:

```
?$search="SEARCH TERM"
```

2. Make a note of the ID (not groupPolicyCategoryId), as we will need this to populate the JSON. Watch for the class type field here as well, which differentiates between your user and machine policies.
3. In the JSON, we also need to add the presentation details (the ID and value), so with your ID from the previous step, add it to this URL to find the presentations:

```
https://graph.microsoft.com/beta/deviceManagement/groupPolicyDefinitions/
POLICYID/presentations
```

Here, you need the ID and the selected value. Keep an eye on the @odata.type value as well; if it is a textbox, it is safe to assume we are passing a string, but for a checkbox, it will be a Boolean value, as a checkbox can only be true or false. These will have to match in the JSON we are passing to Graph, as you will see in our example.

Now that you know how to find the details we need, we can test with the policy we created earlier in the GUI.

4. Set your variables:

```
$name = "Mozilla Firefox"
$description = "ADMX templates to configure Mozilla Firefox"
$groupid = "000000000000000"
```

5. Set the policy creation URL using the `groupPolicyConfigurations` subcategory:

```
$url = "https://graph.microsoft.com/beta/deviceManagement/
groupPolicyConfigurations"
```

6. Create the JSON for the policy:

```
$json = @"
{
    "description": "$description",
    "displayName": "$name",
    "roleScopeTagIds": [
        "0"
    ]
}
"@
```

7. Create the (empty) policy, and grab the details to use to both populate and assign it:

```
$policy = Invoke-MgGraphRequest -Method POST -Uri $url -Body $json -
ContentType "application/json" -OutputType PSObject
```

8. Now, find the policy ID:

```
$policyid = $policy.id
```

9. Create the URL to update the policy content:

```
$updateuri = "https://graph.microsoft.com/beta/deviceManagement/
groupPolicyConfigurations('$policyid')/updateDefinitionValues"
```

10. Add the JSON with the values we found earlier:

```
$updatejson = @"
{
    "added": [
        {
            "definition@odata.bind": "https://graph.microsoft.com/beta/
deviceManagement/groupPolicyDefinitions('POLICYID')",
            "enabled": true,
            "presentationValues": [
                {
                    "@odata.type":
"#microsoft.graph.groupPolicyPresentationValueText",
                    "presentation@odata.bind": "https://
graph.microsoft.com/beta/deviceManagement/
groupPolicyDefinitions('POLICYID')/presentations('PRESENTATIONID')",
                    "value": "homepage"
                }
            ]
        },
        {
            "definition@odata.bind": "https://graph.microsoft.com/beta/
deviceManagement/groupPolicyDefinitions('POLICYID')",
            "enabled": true,
            "presentationValues": [
                {
                    "@odata.type":
"#microsoft.graph.groupPolicyPresentationValueText",
                    "presentation@odata.bind": "https://
graph.microsoft.com/beta/deviceManagement/
groupPolicyDefinitions('POLICYID')/presentations('PRESENTATIONID')",
                    "value": "https://www.packtpub.com/"
                },
                {
                    "@odata.type":
"#microsoft.graph.groupPolicyPresentationValueBoolean",
                    "presentation@odata.bind": "https://
graph.microsoft.com/beta/deviceManagement/
groupPolicyDefinitions('POLICYID')/presentations('PRESENTATIONID')",
                    "value": true
                }
```

```
            ]
        }
    ],
    "deletedIds": [],
    "updated": []
}
"@
```

11. Run the update script we created to add the values:

```
Invoke-MgGraphRequest -Method POST -Uri $updateuri -Body $updatejson -
ContentType "application/json"
```

Now that we have a complete policy, we finally need to assign it.

12. Populate the URL:

```
$assignurl = "https://graph.microsoft.com/beta/deviceManagement/
groupPolicyConfigurations('$policyid')/assign"
```

13. Create the JSON:

```
$assignjson = @"
{
    "assignments": [
        {
            "id": "",
            "target": {
                "@odata.type": "#microsoft.graph.groupAssignmentTarget",
                "groupId": "$groupid"
            }
        }
    ]
}
"@
```

14. Run the JSON:

```
invoke-mggraphrequest -Method POST -Uri $assignurl -Body $assignjson -
ContentType "application/json"
```

These steps have created a PowerShell script to automate the ingestion of third-party administrative templates and the creation of a policy using them.

Group policy analytics

While it is generally recommended to create your new policies from scratch to reduce the amount of *technical debt* when migrating to Intune, you may have certain group policies configured in your on-premises Active Directory that you feel are good enough to be migrated directly to Intune. For this, we can use Group Policy analytics, which will ingest your policies, tell you which can be migrated, and also, if selected, migrate them for you.

Getting ready

The first thing we need is an XML export of the group policy we wish to inspect for compatibility with Intune. If you do not have a domain controller available, there is an example within GitHub here: `https://github.com/PacktPublishing/Microsoft-Intune-Cookbook/blob/main/Chapter2/gpreport.xml`:

1. Within **Active Directory**, navigate to **Group Policy Objects**:

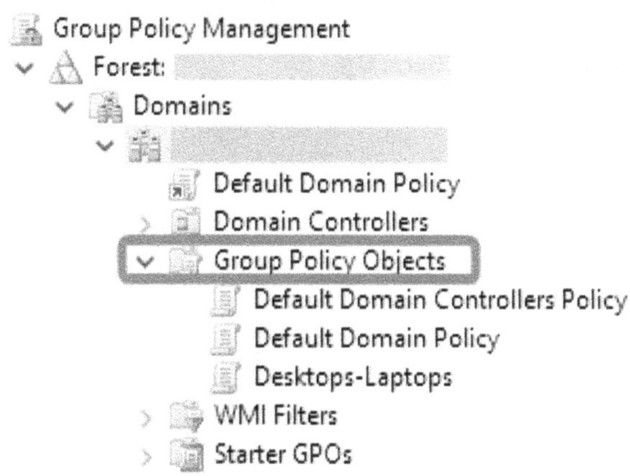

Figure 2.12 – Group Policy Objects

2. Right-click on the group policy in question and click **Back Up...**.

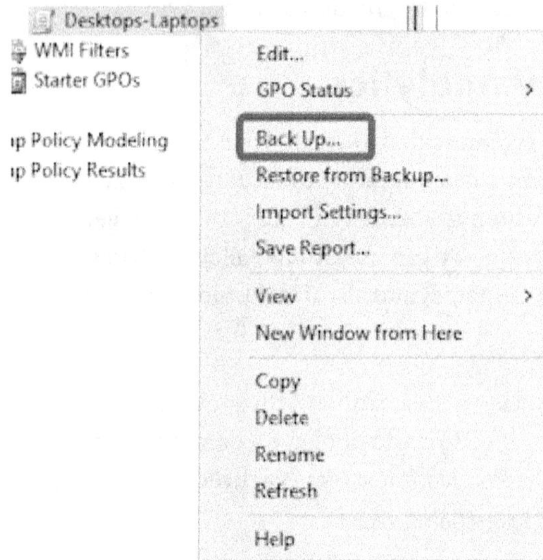

Figure 2.13 – Backing up GPO

3. Select a location and click **Back Up**:

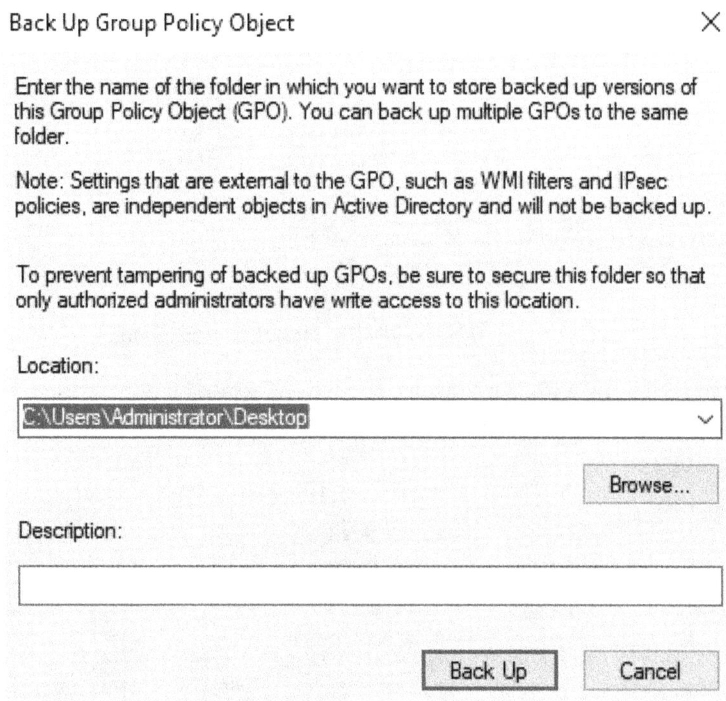

Figure 2.14 – Specifying a backup location

4. Within the export location, we will need the `gpreport.xml` file.

How to do it...

We will now ingest the XML file into Intune to check for compatibility:

1. Within the Intune console, click **Devices** and then **Group Policy analytics**.
2. Click the **Import** button.
3. Select the `GPReport` file, and click **Next**.
4. Click **Next** on the **Scope tags** page:
5. Now, click **Create**.
6. Once complete, you can see the status of the GPO:

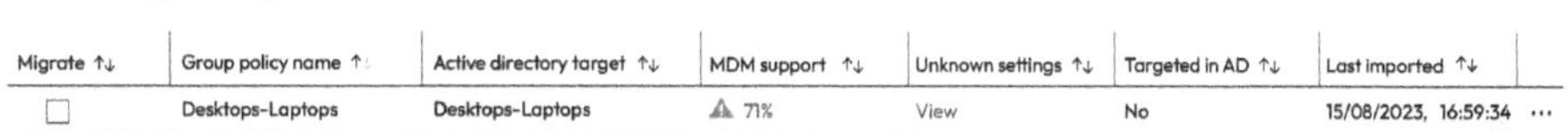

Figure 2.15 – Checking the status of the imported GPO

Clicking **MDM support** will show the objects within the policy and those that are supported:

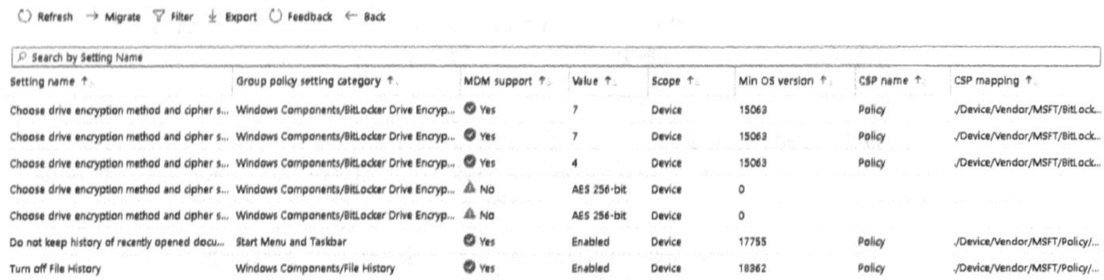

Figure 2.16 – The individual settings status

If you are happy with the settings, click the **Migrate** button at the top (*Figure 2.15*), and you will be taken to the following page, where you can select the settings you wish to migrate, and click **Next**:

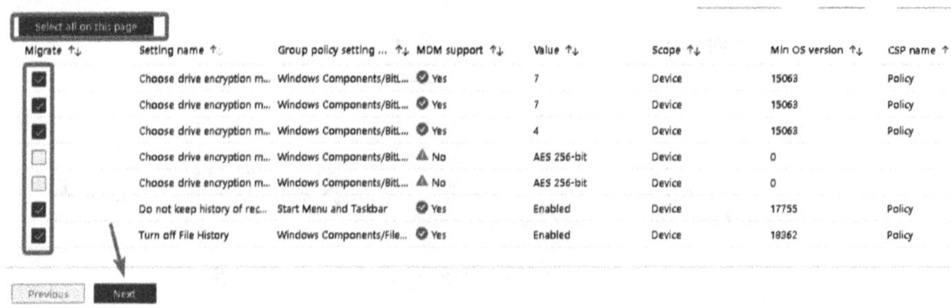

Figure 2.17 – Selecting settings to migrate

7. You will then be taken to the following screen, where you can change any settings as required in the textbox, and click **Next**:

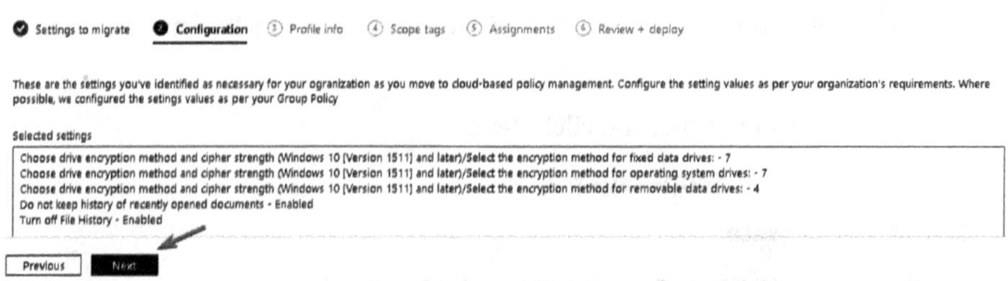

Figure 2.18 – Reviewing the settings configuration

8. Provide a name and description for the policy you will be creating, and click **Next**.

9. After clicking **Next**, assign the newly created policies as required, and click **Next**.
10. Finally, you will see a list of everything configured. Confirm that everything looks OK, and click **Deploy**.

We have now ingested an XML export of our on-premises Group Policies and used the migration functionality to create new Intune policies on the back of it.

Automating it

As the policy creation is largely dependent on the settings you require, we will only automate the ingestion of the XML here. Therefore, we will create a PowerShell script using Microsoft Graph to ingest this file automatically and then review it in the GUI:

1. First, we need to set the URL and also the path to the XML:

```
$url = "https://graph.microsoft.com/beta/deviceManagement/
groupPolicyMigrationReports/createMigrationReport"
$filepath = ""
```

2. Inside the JSON, we need to pass both the file content in the Base64 format as well as the name of the GPO itself. We could manually enter that, but why not let PowerShell extract it from the XML for us by using `Get-Content` and specifying XML:

```
$xml = [xml](Get-Content -Path "$filepath")
$policyname = $xml.gpo.name
```

3. Then, grab the Base64 contents:

```
$bytes = [System.IO.File]::ReadAllBytes($filepath)
$base64 = [System.Convert]::ToBase64String($bytes)
```

4. Populate the content and name in the JSON:

```
$json = @"
{
    "groupPolicyObjectFile": {
        "content": "$base64",
        "ouDistinguishedName": "$policyname",
        "roleScopeTagIds": [
        ]
    }
```

```
}
"@
```

5. Finally, send the POST request to ingest the Base64 contents of the XML file:

```
Invoke-MgGraphRequest -Method POST -Uri $url -Body $json -ContentType
"application/json"
```

Using this script, we have ingested an on-premises Group Policy into Intune to then review in the GUI.

Properties catalog

A relatively new feature for Microsoft Intune, you can now configure **Device Inventory** to specify additional properties to retrieve from managed devices to use in reporting.

There are two parts to this: the first is to create the Properties catalog, which we will cover here, and then there is retrieving the results themselves, which will be covered in *Chapter 9*.

How to do it...

As with other policies, we create a new one using a very similar approach:

1. Within the Intune console, click **Devices** and then **Configuration**.
2. Click **+ Create** and select **+ New Policy.**
3. In the first dropdown, select **Windows 10 and later**, then select **Properties catalog**, and then click **Create**.

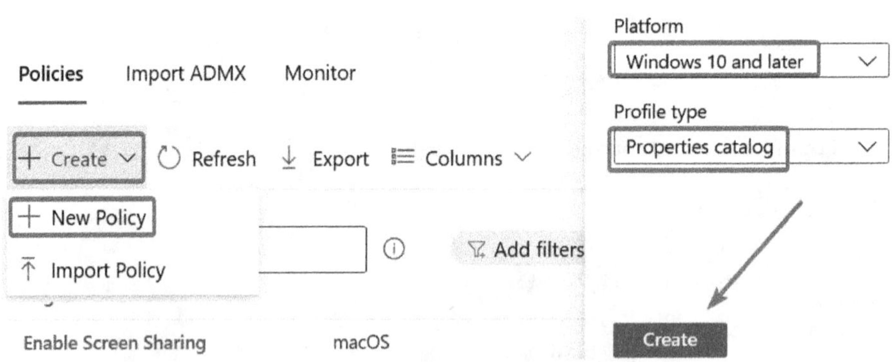

Figure 2.19 – New Properties catalog

4. Fill in **Name** and **Description** and click **Next**.
5. Click **+ Add Properties**.

6. In the flyout, select which **Windows Management Interface** (**WMI**) settings you would like to retrieve from your devices. Selecting the top-level will automatically select all sub-entries, or you can be as specific as you like. As you check them, they will show on the right-hand side, where you can also click to remove them.

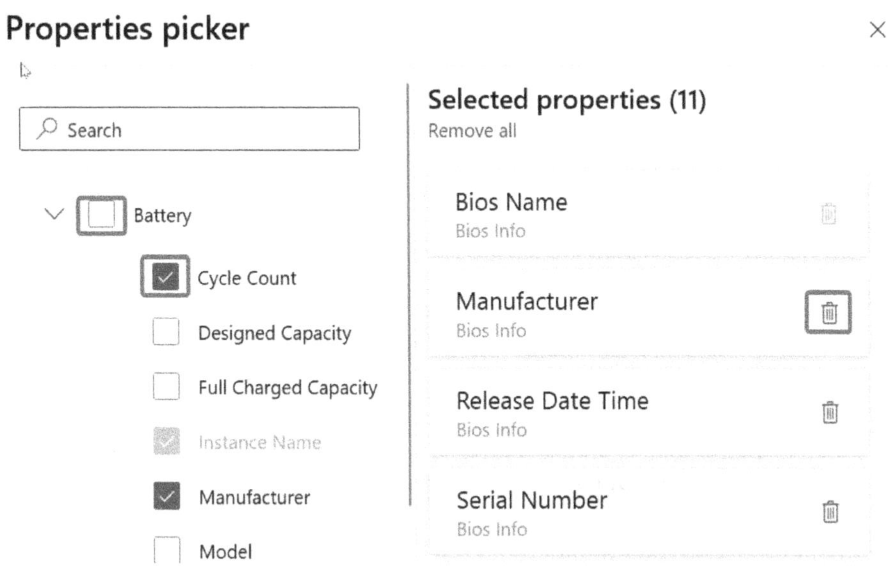

Figure 2.20 – Properties picker

7. When you have finished, click **Select** at the bottom and then click **Next**.
8. We do not require **Scope tags** at this point, so click **Next**.
9. This policy uses the new Assignments UI, so search for your group at the top and click on it. In this case, we will use the **Autopilot-Devices** group.
10. When selected, make sure it is set to **Included** and click **Next**.
11. Finally, review that all looks correct and click **Create**.

Now that we know how to create in the UI, we can look at automating it with PowerShell and Graph.

Automating it

This policy uses Settings Catalog underneath, so you will notice similarities with the previous recipe on Settings Catalog in this chapter, and for brevity, only key information will be included here. The full script is available on GitHub here: `https://github.com/PacktPublishing/Microsoft-Intune-Cookbook-Second-Edition/blob/main/Chapter-2/properties-catalog.ps1`.

1. As usual, we start with the URL. We send this to the `inventoryPolicies` endpoint:

```
$url = "https://graph.microsoft.com/beta/deviceManagement/
inventoryPolicies"
```

2. We now need the policy name and description:

```
$policyname = "Properties Catalog"
$policydescription = "Battery and BIOS Config"
```

3. We also need the group ID for assignment:

```
$EntraGroupID = "xxxxxx-xxxxxxx-xxxxxx"
```

4. Now, when we look at the policy configuration items, you will see a pattern, OS (in this case, Windows) `_deviceinventory_category(battery)_instancename_WMI setting (cyclecount)_refreshperiod(24)`:

```
{
                                    "@odata.type":
"#microsoft.graph.deviceManagementConfigurationChoiceSettingInstance",
                                    "choiceSettingValue": {
                                        "@odata.type":
"#microsoft.graph.deviceManagementConfigurationChoiceSettingValue",
                                        "children": [],
                                        "value":
"windows_deviceinventory_battery_instancename_cyclecount_24"
                                    },
                                    "settingDefinitionId":
"windows_deviceinventory_battery_instancename_cyclecount"
                                }
```

5. Populate these to the JSON and create the policy:

```
$policy = Invoke-MgGraphRequest -Method POST -Uri $url -Body $json -
ContentType "application/json" -OutputType PSObject
```

Now, we finally need to assign it.

6. Grab the policy ID:

```
$policyid = $policy.id
```

7. Feed it into the URL:

```
$assignurl = "https://graph.microsoft.com/beta/deviceManagement/
inventoryPolicies('$policyid')/assign"
```

8. Add the group to the JSON:

```
$assignjson = @"
{
    "assignments": [
        {
            "target": {
                "@odata.type": "#microsoft.graph.groupAssignmentTarget",
                "groupId": "$EntraGroupID"
            }
        }
    ]
}
"@
```

9. Send the assignment request:

```
$assign = Invoke-MgGraphRequest -Method POST -Uri $assignurl -Body
$assignjson -ContentType "application/json"
```

In this recipe, we have learned how to configure a Properties Catalog policy for use with Device Inventory.

Join us on Discord

For discussions around the book and to connect with your peers, join us on Discord at `packt.link/discordcloud` or scan the QR code below:

3

Securing Your Windows Devices with Security Policies

Chapter 2 showed you the basics of each of the core policy types, as well as what happens behind the scenes. This chapter will take that knowledge and extend it into the **Endpoint Security** blade within Microsoft Intune. You will find out how to secure your devices with the various policies and settings available.

We will configure the four policies that are most critical in a new environment: **antivirus**, **BitLocker**, **Firewall**, and **Advanced Surface Reduction** (**ASR**). These, combined with your baseline, will give you an excellent security footprint to build upon.

You can configure a lot of these security settings within standard policies as well as within Endpoint Security, but using the dedicated **Endpoint Security** blade gives you a couple of advantages:

- On the policy summary, you can see the status of your policies and devices, as well as running remedial actions where required
- With Intune's **role-based access control** (**RBAC** – covered in *Chapter 13*) roles, you can configure a separate role with restricted access to this area only so that you can provide your security team with access to review and act upon incidents, but without giving them access to everything else

This chapter will include the following recipes:

- Setting up a security baseline
- Configuring an antivirus policy
- Configuring Windows Security Experience
- Configuring Windows Firewall

- Configuring your BitLocker policy
- Deploying ASR rules
- Enrolling in Defender for Endpoint
- Deploying Windows **Local Admin Password Solution** (**LAPS**)
- Configuring Application Control

Technical requirements

For this chapter, you will need a modern web browser and a PowerShell code editor such as **Visual Studio Code** (**VS Code**) or PowerShell ISE.

All of the scripts that are referenced in this chapter can be found here: `https://github.com/PacktPublishing/Microsoft-Intune-Cookbook-Second-Edition/tree/main/Chapter-3`.

Chapter materials

Before we start configuring our policies, we should look at best practices to ensure that our Windows devices are as secure as possible. For this, there are resources available that can offer guidance.

An example of this is the NCSC Windows guidance, available at `https://www.ncsc.gov.uk/collection/device-security-guidance/platform-guides/windows`.

You can also download a CSV file including all recommended settings or preconfigure **Group Policy Objects** (**GPOs**) that you can import directly into Intune (as covered in *Chapter 2*). These files are available here: `https://github.com/ukncsc/Device-Security-Guidance-Configuration-Packs/tree/main/Microsoft/Windows`.

You can find best practice recommendations from CIS regarding their Intune baselines at `https://www.cisecurity.org/benchmark/intune`.

The CIS downloads also include GPOs that you can import into Intune directly.

> **Tip**
>
> While simply enabling every setting would provide you with a quick, secure environment, this is not necessarily the best approach, as you need to ensure you are not causing issues for your own applications or user experience. It is best to review all settings and enable those required for your environment after careful testing.

Setting up a security baseline

Security baselines are a *quick-start* group of settings selected by Microsoft to quickly secure your tenant. They are available for Windows, Edge, Windows 365, and Microsoft Defender for Endpoint.

While they do not have the granularity of using the more bespoke *settings catalog*-backed policies (covered in this chapter), they are a quick, easy, and useful way to get you up and running.

> Tip
>
> The Windows baseline in particular contains many settings, and unless you learn about every individual setting, you could find yourself dealing with unexpected issues on your devices. I usually recommend either building your own from scratch using the settings catalog, as covered in this chapter, or using one of the community baselines that have been created and tested (and are more regularly updated).

Should you decide to move to the more dedicated policies, make sure you change the associated setting in your baseline to **Not Configured**; otherwise, you will find yourself with policy conflicts. There is an example JSON extract in this book's GitHub repository that you can import (using the script found at `https://andrewstaylor.com/2022/12/07/intune-backing-up-and-restoring-your-environment-new-and-improved/`) into your environment and amend accordingly to get you started.

Microsoft also updates the baseline policies on a regular cadence to ensure that you are always receiving the latest versions. When an update is released, your current policies will continue working but will change to read-only mode within the Intune console. To make any changes, you will need to update them to their latest versions; this will be covered in this recipe.

Configuring any of the baselines follows the same process, so for this recipe, we will configure the Microsoft Edge baseline, as that is least likely to conflict with any other policy settings.

How to do it...

To set up a security baseline, please perform the following steps:

1. Navigate to the Intune console and click **Endpoint security**, then **Security baselines**.
2. Click **Security Baseline for Microsoft Edge** and then **+ Create policy**.
3. In the fly-out, click the **Create** button.

4. When adding **Name** and **Description** values, you will see the current version of the baseline that is available. Then, click **Next**.
5. On the next screen, you will see all of the available settings. Change these to suit your requirements. Pay attention to the **Control which extensions cannot be installed** setting, as, by default, this is set to **Block all extensions**. Once you have set these, click **Next**.
6. Click **Next** on the **Scope tags** page; we will cover scope tags later in *Chapter 13*.
7. While there is no right or wrong answer, assigning security policies at the device level is a good option, as they will be needed across users. So, we are going to assign this one to the **Autopilot Devices** group.
8. Click **Next** and, if you are happy that everything looks correct, click **Create**.

We have now configured our Edge baseline in the GUI and can look at doing so via automation.

Automating it

Now, let's use Graph and PowerShell to complete the same tasks.

Since Intune release 0523, security defaults have transitioned to **Settings Catalog**, so you will see a lot of similarities to the **Settings Catalog** policy created in *Chapter 2* in the first recipe.

First, we need to set our variables:

```
$groupid = "00000000000000000000"
$policyname = "Edge Baseline"
$policydescription = "Edge Baseline - Selected Defaults"
$uri = "https://graph.microsoft.com/beta/deviceManagement/configurationPolicies"
```

Next, we populate the JSON. The full code block can be found in the GitHub repository, so only a selection will be included here for brevity. You may notice the platform is still listed as Windows 10. This is to be expected, and while Windows 11 is now the supported OS, making these changes at the Graph level is a lot more complicated:

```
$json = @"
{
    "description": "$policydescription",
    "name": "$policyname",
    "platforms": "windows10",
    "roleScopeTagIds": [
        "0"
    ],
    "settings": [
```

```
        {
            "@odata.type":
"#microsoft.graph.deviceManagementConfigurationSetting",
            "settingInstance": {
                "@odata.type":
"#microsoft.graph.deviceManagementConfigurationChoiceSettingInstance",
                "choiceSettingValue": {
                    "@odata.type":
"#microsoft.graph.deviceManagementConfigurationChoiceSettingValue",
                    "children": [
                        {
                            "@odata.type":
"#microsoft.graph.deviceManagementConfigurationSimpleSettingCollectionInstance",
                            "settingDefinitionId":
"device_vendor_msft_policy_config_microsoft_edge~policy~microsoft_edge~extensions_
extensioninstallblocklist_extensioninstallblocklistdesc",
                            "settingInstanceTemplateReference": {
                                "settingInstanceTemplateId": "26c1a943-562d-4286-
b5ff-4b491b9515bc"
                            },
                            "simpleSettingCollectionValue": [
                                {
                                    "@odata.type":
"#microsoft.graph.deviceManagementConfigurationStringSettingValue",
                                    "value": "*"
                                }
                            ]
                        }
                    ],
                    "settingValueTemplateReference": {
                        "settingValueTemplateId": "e9f334db-ca88-4b09-9ccf-
d7b9b3142210"
                    },
                    "value":
"device_vendor_msft_policy_config_microsoft_edge~policy~microsoft_edge~extensions_
extensioninstallblocklist_1"
                },
                "settingDefinitionId":
"device_vendor_msft_policy_config_microsoft_edge~policy~microsoft_edge~extensions_
extensioninstallblocklist",
                "settingInstanceTemplateReference": {
```

```
                    "settingInstanceTemplateId": "fb2f16e0-2804-45a0-9982-
fe709d59fef8"
                }
            }
        }
"@
```

Send the POST request to create the policy and grab the ID, which we will need for assignment:

```
$policy = Invoke-MgGraphRequest -Method POST -Uri $uri -Body $json -ContentType
"application/json" -OutputType PSObject
$policyid = $policy.id
```

Populate the ID into the assignment URL and the group ID into the JSON, then send our final POST request to assign the policy:

```
$assignuri = "https://graph.microsoft.com/beta/deviceManagement/
configurationpolicies/$policyid/assign"
$assignjson = @"
{
    "assignments": [
        {
            "target": {
                "@odata.type": "#microsoft.graph.groupAssignmentTarget",
                "groupId": "$groupid"
            }
        }
    ]
}
"@
Invoke-MgGraphRequest -Method POST -Uri $assignuri -Body $assignjson -ContentType
"application/json"
```

This has automated the configuration of Microsoft Edge baselines. If you want to deploy defaults across all baselines, there is an additional PowerShell script in this book's GitHub repository that you can use.

There's more...

As mentioned earlier, Microsoft releases updates for its security baselines, which you need to implement to be able to make any changes to existing deployed policies.

The best thing to do is to duplicate your current policy so that you can test the changes before deploying to production. Let's take a look at how to do this:

1. Click on the baseline and click the three dots to the right of the policy. Then, click **Duplicate**.
2. Next, place a tick in the checkbox to the left of your new duplicate policy and click the **Change Version** button.
3. Here, you can select the version to update to and how you want to handle the changes. Usually, you would select the first option (**Accept baseline changes but keep my existing setting customizations**) to keep any changes you have made to the defaults.
4. Then, it is simply a case of clicking **Submit** and testing.

Once you are happy that everything is working as it should, follow the same procedure for your original policies. It is worth keeping the duplicate one to use next time there is an update.

Now that our baselines have been configured, we can start exploring the **Endpoint Security** blade and configure some other policies. There are numerous policy options here, from your standard BitLocker and Firewall to account protection and enumerating additional administrative accounts.

Configuring an antivirus policy

This recipe will run through how to configure your antivirus policy and also configure the UI on your end user devices to restrict what the user can and cannot see. If you are running the full Microsoft stack, configuring an antivirus policy will give you control over the application, when it updates, what to do with threats, and a better overview of your devices.

How to do it...

We will start with the antivirus policy:

1. Navigate to **Endpoint Security** in Intune, click **Antivirus**, and then click **+ Create Policy**.

> Note
>
> You may have noticed the **Reusable settings** tab at the top. This is currently only for firewall rules, so you can ignore it for now. We will cover it in the *Configuring Windows Firewall* recipe.

2. For the policy type, select **Microsoft Defender Antivirus** in the **Profile** dropdown and the platform, in this case **Windows**. We will cover **Security Experience** in the *Configuring Windows Security Experience* recipe.
3. Set the policy's **Name** and **Description** values.
4. Configure the settings as per your environment. If there are any you are not sure about, the lowercase **i** letter in a circle next to each field will give you further details. There are a lot of options in here, so make sure you understand what you are setting. If in doubt, select the defaults. Once your settings have been configured, click **Next**.
5. Click **Next** on the **Scope tags** page.
6. Once you have configured your settings, assign the policy to your **Autopilot Devices** group. This uses the newer assignment UI; search for the group in the box and then set **Include** or **Exclude** as required:

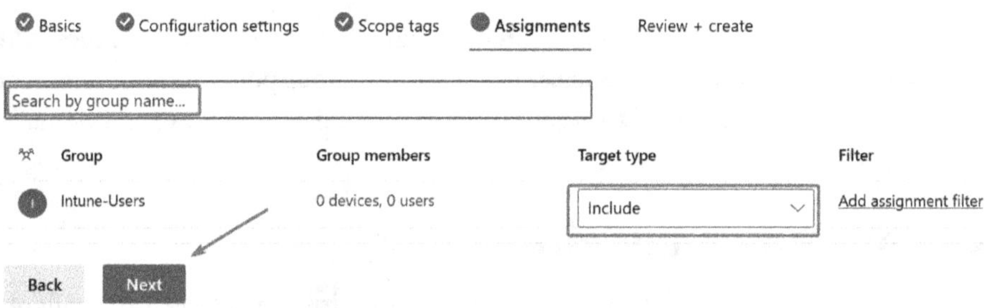

Figure 3.1 – Assignments UI

7. Review your settings (click the arrow next to **Defender** to expand them) and click **Save**.

Your policy has now been created.

Automating it

Now, we can move on to deploying the policy with PowerShell and Graph.

This policy is running from the unified **Settings Catalog**, but as well as **Mobile Device Management** (**MDM**), it has Microsoft Sense (used by Microsoft Security and Defender for Endpoint) as the second technology. So, we can use the security policies URL to list what is available with this tag, or we can just do a search and check the tag in the results:

```
https://graph.microsoft.com/beta/deviceManagement/configurationCategories?
templateCategory=True&`$filter=(platforms has 'windows10') and (technologies has
'mdm' or technologies has 'microsoftSense')
```

Since we have already learned how **Settings Catalog** works, this is the code for the policy created earlier:

1. First, set the group, name, and description:

```
$groupid = "000000000000000000000000"
$policyname = "Anti-Virus Policy"
$policydescription = "Default AV policy"
```

2. Set the URL. Note that it is in `configurationPolicies`, so it is using Settings Catalog underneath:

```
$policyurl = "https://graph.microsoft.com/beta/deviceManagement/
configurationPolicies"
```

3. Set the JSON (we are just including one setting here to save space, but the example file includes the whole code):

```
$policyjson = @"
    "description": "$policydescription",
    "name": "$policyname",
    "platforms": "windows10",
    "roleScopeTagIds": [
        "0"
    ],
    "settings": [
        {
            "@odata.type":
"#microsoft.graph.deviceManagementConfigurationSetting",
            "settingInstance": {
                "@odata.type":
"#microsoft.graph.deviceManagementConfigurationChoiceSettingInstance",
                "choiceSettingValue": {
                    "@odata.type":
"#microsoft.graph.deviceManagementConfigurationChoiceSettingValue",
                    "children": [],
                    "settingValueTemplateReference": {
                        "settingValueTemplateId": "9ead75d4-6f30-4bc5-8cc5-
ab0f999d79f0"
                    },
                    "value":
```

```
"device_vendor_msft_policy_config_defender_allowarchivescanning_1"
                },
                "settingDefinitionId":
"device_vendor_msft_policy_config_defender_allowarchivescanning",
                "settingInstanceTemplateReference": {
                    "settingInstanceTemplateId": "7c5c9cde-f74d-4d11-904f-
de4c27f72d89"
                }
            }
        }
"@
```

4. Create the policy and pass it to a variable, then grab the ID:

```
$policy = Invoke-MgGraphRequest -Method POST -Uri $policyurl -Body
$policyjson -ContentType "application/json" -OutputType PSObject
$policyid = $policy.id
```

5. Populate the URL for assignment:

```
$assignurl = "https://graph.microsoft.com/beta/deviceManagement/
configurationPolicies/$policyid/assign"
```

6. Create the JSON:

```
$assignjson = @"
{
    "assignments": [
        {
            "target": {
                "@odata.type": "#microsoft.graph.groupAssignmentTarget",
                "groupId": "$groupid"
            }
        }
    ]
```

```
}
"@
```

7. Assign it:

```
Invoke-MgGraphRequest -Method POST -Uri $assignurl -Body $assignjson -
ContentType "application/json"
```

With that, we have configured our antivirus policy using automation tools.

Configuring Windows Security Experience

This one is not quite as critical, but it is worth configuring so that users do not get bombarded with notifications. This policy is not so much for security, but more for what your end users can see and do on the devices. It is largely up to you to configure for your requirements, so this one just covers the two that are recommended for all.

How to do it...

We will now configure the **Windows Security Experience** policy to amend the end user experience when looking at the security settings within Windows:

1. Navigate back to the **Antivirus** menu in **Endpoint Security** and create a new policy, but this time, select **Windows Security Experience**.
2. Set the policy's **Name** and **Description** values and click **Next**.
3. Most of these are personal preferences, but make sure you enable **Tamper Protection**. Since this is a corporate machine, disable **Family UI**. After that, make any changes that apply to your environment.
4. Click **Next**.
5. Assign the policy to **Autopilot Devices**.
6. Then, review and click **Create**.

We have now configured Windows Security Experience for our devices.

Automating it

Let us replicate how we configured our Security Experience policy, but this time using Graph and PowerShell.

This is another one based on Settings Catalog. Again, we have cut down the policies that are listed here with just Tamper Protection, but the rest are in the example script:

1. First, set the group ID and policy URL, as well as the name and description:

```
$groupid = "000000000000000000000000"
$policyurl = "https://graph.microsoft.com/beta/deviceManagement/
configurationPolicies"
$name = "Windows Security Experience"
$description = "UI Settings"
```

2. Now, populate the JSON:

```
$policyjson = @"
{
    "description": "$description",
    "name": "$name",
    "platforms": "windows10",
    "roleScopeTagIds": [
        "0"
    ],
    "settings": [
        {
            "@odata.type":
"#microsoft.graph.deviceManagementConfigurationSetting",
            "settingInstance": {
                "@odata.type":
"#microsoft.graph.deviceManagementConfigurationChoiceSettingInstance",
                "choiceSettingValue": {
                    "@odata.type":
"#microsoft.graph.deviceManagementConfigurationChoiceSettingValue",
                    "children": [],
                    "settingValueTemplateReference": {
                        "settingValueTemplateId": "fc365da9-2c1b-4f79-aa4b-
dedca69e728f"
                    },
                    "value":
```

```
"vendor_msft_defender_configuration_tamperprotection_options_0"
                },
                "settingDefinitionId":
"vendor_msft_defender_configuration_tamperprotection_options",
                "settingInstanceTemplateReference": {
                    "settingInstanceTemplateId":
"5655cab2-7e6b-4c49-9ce2-3865da05f7e6"
                }
            }
        },
    "technologies": "mdm,microsoftSense",
    "templateReference": {
        "templateId": "d948ff9b-99cb-4ee0-8012-1fbc09685377_1"
    }
}
"@
```

Again, you can see that the technologies include Microsoft Sense.

3. Now, create the policy and grab the ID:

```
$policy = Invoke-MgGraphRequest -Method POST -Uri $policyurl -Body
$policyjson -ContentType "application/json" -OutputType PSObject
$policyid = $policy.id
```

4. Finally, populate the assignment URL with the ID and the assignment JSON with our group ID. Then, send a POST request to assign our policy:

```
$assignurl = "https://graph.microsoft.com/beta/deviceManagement/
configurationPolicies/$policyid/assign"
$assignjson = @"
{
    "assignments": [
        {
            "target": {
                "@odata.type": "#microsoft.graph.groupAssignmentTarget",
                "groupId": "$groupid"
            }
        }
    ]
}
```

```
"@
Invoke-MgGraphRequest -Method POST -Uri $assignurl -Body $assignjson -
ContentType "application/json"
```

We have now configured a Windows Security Experience policy using PowerShell and Graph.

Configuring Windows Firewall

When we look at Windows Firewall, we will be introduced to the **Reusable settings** option. An environment will often have multiple firewall policies for different user and device groups to allow a piece of software to run or to further restrict a selection of devices. The idea behind **Reusable settings** is that you can configure your specific firewall rules and then apply those across policies without needing to manually add them each time.

To give you an idea, this rule would block all Google domains:

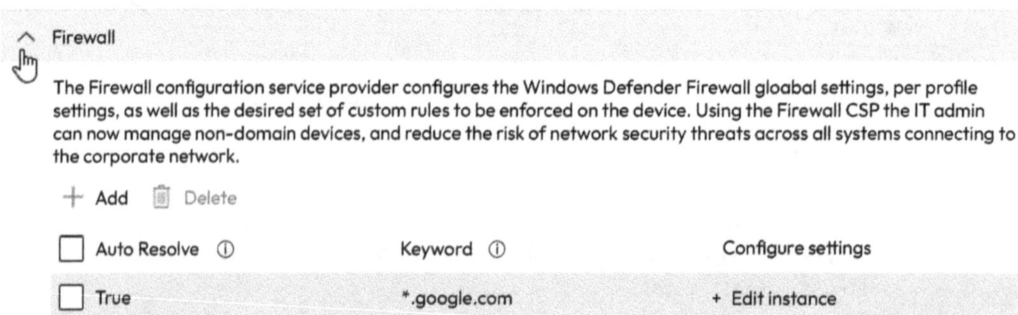

Figure 3.2 – Microsoft Defender Firewall – Reusable settings

In this recipe, we will stick with a basic firewall to block incoming traffic and allow outbound traffic as our first line of defense. In a world where users can work from anywhere, the traditional on-premises hardware firewall is often not enough for zero-trust. Therefore, having a software firewall on the device itself adds a significant layer of security.

How to do it...

Now that we have briefly covered **Reusable settings**, follow these steps to configure the standard Microsoft Defender firewall policy:

1. In the portal, navigate to **Endpoint Security**, then **Firewall**. Choose **+ Create Policy**. We want **Windows** and a **Windows Firewall** policy.
2. Set the policy's **Name** and **Description** values.
3. On the next screen, there are a *lot* of available options. If you have a dedicated networking or security team, it is always worth working with them on something like

this to ensure you have the best security available, but with your applications and services still able to function.

> **Note**
>
> Each setting has a lowercase **i** letter enclosed in a circle. You can click on it to gain thorough information about each setting. Use these if you are not sure exactly what a setting does – the last thing you want to do is enable everything and find that your machines stop working properly.

As mentioned previously, we are keeping this one simple by enabling the firewall on all profiles, blocking inbound traffic, and allowing outbound traffic.

4. Once you have configured your settings, click **Next**.
5. On the **Scope tags** page, click **Next**.

> **Note**
>
> We are using device assignment, but there may be cases where you need to assign a firewall policy to users if you have a particular application that needs custom rules. That way, you can be confident the firewall exception will apply only to machines when those users are logged in. It gives a seamless experience for users, saves time administering groups when machines are replaced, and adds a layer of security for users who do not need the exception.

6. Once assigned, check that everything looks correct and click **Create**.

With that, you have configured your firewall policies using the UI.

Automating it

Now, we can look at how to deploy our firewall policy using PowerShell.

You can find the firewall templates within the templates we used previously for BitLocker, as well as the baselines (run a `GET` command against the following URL to see them: `https://graph.microsoft.com/beta/deviceManagement/templates/c53e5a9f-2eec-4175-98a1-2b3d38084b91/categories/fae9ad7a-772f-4cae-a60b-14a10fa827f7/recommendedSettings`).

The settings we have configured in the preceding section are based on the **Unified Settings Catalog** under the `4a5e4714-00ac-4793-b0cc-5049041b0ed7` category ID.

If you run the following command, you will be able to see all of the available policy options for the firewall:

```
((Invoke-MgGraphRequest -Method GET -Uri "https://graph.microsoft.com/beta/
deviceManagement/configurationSettings?&`$filter=categoryId eq
'4a5e4714-00ac-4793-b0cc-5049041b0ed7'" -OutputType PSObject).value | select-
object name, description, '@odata.type', rootDefinitionId, options,
@{Name="Platform"; Expression={ $_.applicability | Select-Object
platform}},@{Name="technologies"; Expression={ $_.applicability | Select-Object
technologies}},valuedefinition, id) | out-gridview
```

You will notice that I have tweaked the output to make it more accessible by selecting the fields to display and also output to `gridview` to give us a UI.

When viewing the output, the policy names are the same across the different profiles. So, pay attention to `rootDefinitionID` as that will differentiate between them:

Figure 3.3 – Policy definition IDs

The `Options` field is an additional array that contains the values you can set for each policy. In the case of `InboundActions`, they are *block* (`0`) and *allow* (`1`):

```
vendor_msft_firewall_mdmstore_domainprofile_defaultinboundaction_0
vendor_msft_firewall_mdmstore_domainprofile_defaultinboundaction_1
```

Now that you know the theory behind it, let's look at our policy in action. The full code is available in this book's GitHub repository; we will just include one setting to see how it works:

1. First, as usual, set the group ID, policy details, and URL:

   ```
   $groupid = "00000000000000000000"
   $policyname = "Windows Firewall Settings"
   $policydescription = "Baseline Firewall Settings"
   $uri = "https://graph.microsoft.com/beta/deviceManagement/
   configurationPolicies"
   ```

   You will see that the URL is a standard configuration policy (Settings Catalog) rather than an intent or a template.

2. Set the JSON. Note that it has populated default values for the settings we did not change when configuring originally. This is expected behavior. This is just a small selection of the policies; the full JSON is available on GitHub:

```
$json = @"
{
    "description": "$policydescription",
    "name": "$policyname",
    "platforms": "windows10",
    "roleScopeTagIds": [
        "0"
    ],
    "settings": [
        {
            "@odata.type":
"#microsoft.graph.deviceManagementConfigurationSetting",
            "settingInstance": {
                "@odata.type":
"#microsoft.graph.deviceManagementConfigurationChoiceSettingInstance",
                "choiceSettingValue": {
                    "@odata.type":
"#microsoft.graph.deviceManagementConfigurationChoiceSettingValue",
                    "children": [],
                    "settingValueTemplateReference": {
                        "settingValueTemplateId": "559f6e01-53a9-4c10-9f10-
d09d8fe7f903"
                    },
                    "value":
"vendor_msft_firewall_mdmstore_global_disablestatefulftp_true"
                },
                "settingDefinitionId":
"vendor_msft_firewall_mdmstore_global_disablestatefulftp",
                "settingInstanceTemplateReference": {
                    "settingInstanceTemplateId":
"38329af6-2670-4a71-972d-482010ca97fc"
                }
            }
```

```
    }
"@
```

3. Now, deploy the policy, populate the URL, and assign it:

```
$policy = Invoke-MgGraphRequest -Method POST -Uri $uri -Body $json -
ContentType "application/json" -OutputType PSObject
$policyid = $policy.id
$assignuri = "https://graph.microsoft.com/beta/deviceManagement/
configurationPolicies/$policyid/assign"
$assignjson = @"
{
    "assignments": [
        {
            "target": {
                "@odata.type": "#microsoft.graph.groupAssignmentTarget",
                "groupId": "$groupid"
            }
        }
    ]
}
"@
Invoke-MgGraphRequest -Method POST -Uri $assignuri -Body $assignjson -
ContentType "application/json"
```

This completes the automation script to configure a firewall policy.

Configuring your BitLocker policy

Another important thing to consider is **BitLocker** drive encryption. While antivirus software and a firewall protect the machine when in use, this protects the data if your machine is lost or stolen. You should always use the strongest encryption possible and make it a requirement for **device compliance** and **Conditional Access** (more on those in *Chapter 8*).

There are specific settings for this policy to enable silent encryption during **Autopilot**, so you need to make sure these are set correctly.

How to do it...

The following steps will show you how to configure your **BitLocker Disk Encryption** policy:

1. Within **Endpoint Security**, click on **Disk Encryption.** Select **Windows** as the platform and **BitLocker** as the policy type. Then create a policy.

2. Set the policy's **Name** and **Description** values and click **Next**.
3. Set the **BitLocker** values as per the following screenshot; these are important for silent encryption with Autopilot. If you are fully cloud-only, the backup can just be to Azure AD (the old name for Entra ID):

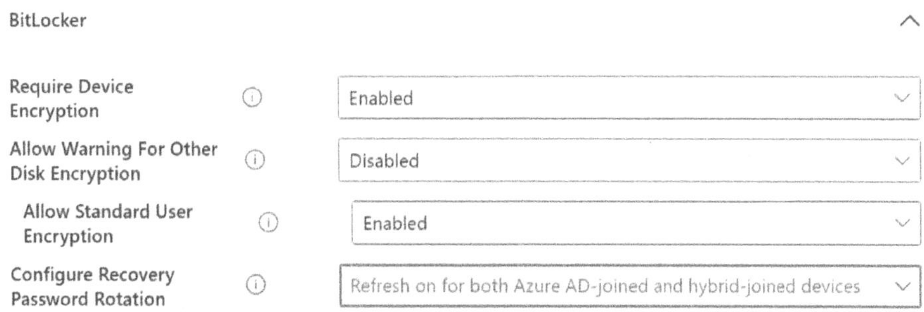

Figure 3.4 – BitLocker – Base settings

4. Set the **BitLocker** settings as per this screenshot. Note, we are using **AES** for fixed drives and **CBC** for removable:

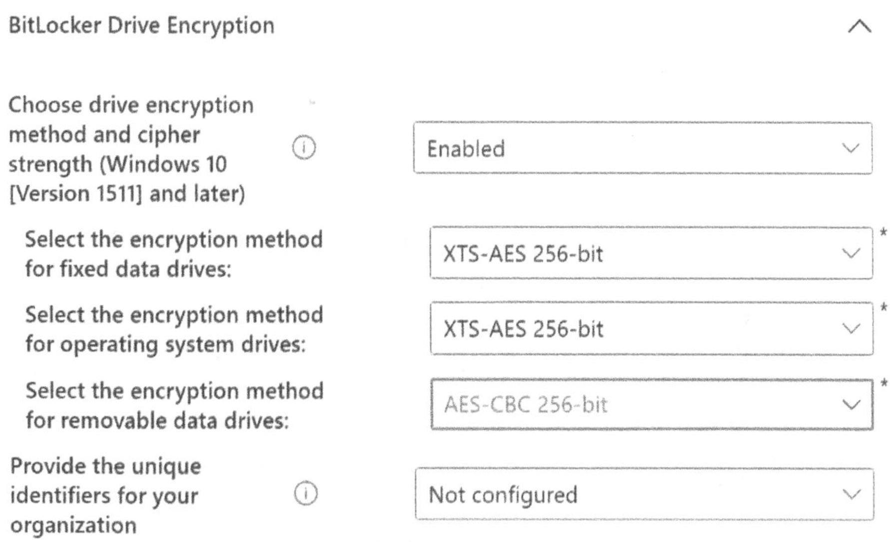

Figure 3.5 – BitLocker Drive Encryption settings

5. For **Operating System Drives** settings, the only required setting is to set the encryption method, but you may want to set **Startup authentication required** to **Yes**, especially if you are looking for CIS compliance. If you decide to set a startup PIN, keep in mind that it can interfere with Autopilot deployments:

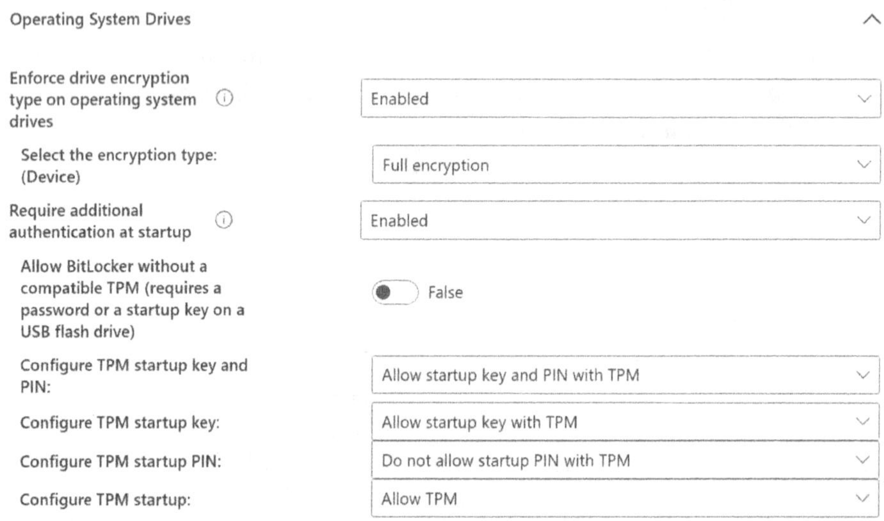

Figure 3.6 – BitLocker – Operating System Drives settings

6. Configure your **Fixed Data Drives** settings; some suggested settings are in this screenshot:

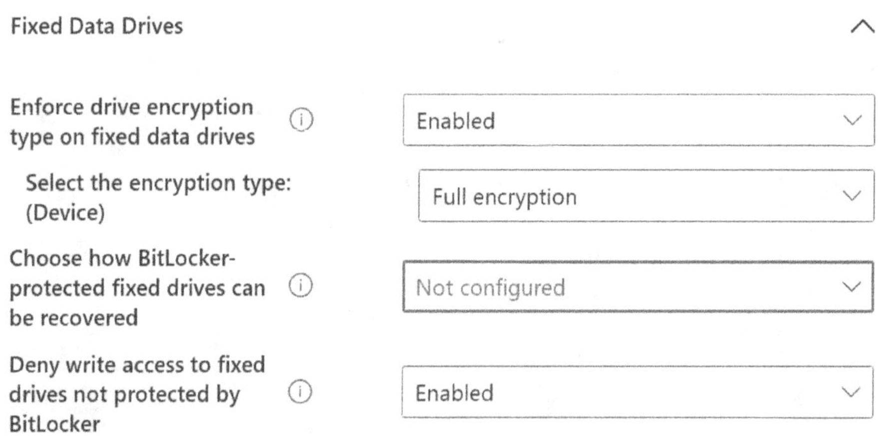

Figure 3.7 – BitLocker – Fixed Drive settings

7. **Removable Data Drives** settings are for your USB sticks. If you are blocking USB storage completely, this is less important, but it is worth setting it anyway just to be on the safe side:

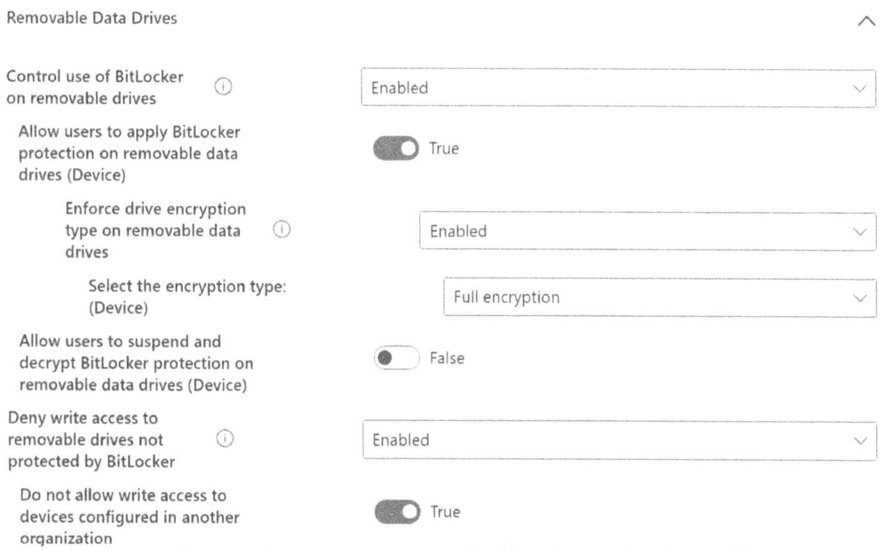

Figure 3.8 – BitLocker – Removable Data Drives settings

Click **Next**.

8. Now, assign it to **Autopilot Devices** and click **Next**.
9. Review the settings and click **Create**.

With that, we have successfully created our BitLocker policy in the UI.

Automating it

Now, let's learn how to create the same policy using Graph.

As with our previous Settings Catalog policies, the settings themselves can be found by looping through the categories using a `GET` command and then checking the recommended settings for each category: `https://graph.microsoft.com/beta/deviceManagement/templates/d1174162-1dd2-4976-affc-6667049ab0ae/categories/CATEGORY-ID/recommendedSettings`.

This is another long policy, so grab the PowerShell script from this book's GitHub repository and amend or deploy it as required. It follows the same basic principles as before, sets the URL, populates the JSON, and creates and assigns the policy.

Deploying ASR rules

There are some more well-known and documented weak points in a standard machine build that bad actors like to target. JavaScript, Office Macros, and Adobe Acrobat Reader are some examples.

Fortunately, there are built-in ASR rules that can be enabled to block these from executing. Additionally, there is the option to enable them in **Audit mode** if there are concerns about the potential impact on your application.

Getting ready

To configure these, head to the **Endpoint Security** blade, click **Attack Surface Reduction**, and choose **+ Create Policy**. Select **Windows** and then **Attack Surface Reduction Rules** from the list of options.

Once again, you will see that we have **Reusable settings** here; this is where you can specify USB and printer device IDs. These are not relevant to ASR rules; they are for some of the other policies that can be configured in this blade.

How to do it...

These steps will run you through creating your new ASR policy:

1. Set your policy's **Name** and **Description** values and then click **Next**.
2. On the **Settings** screen, check each policy and consider whether it is going to impact your environment. If you are not sure or think it might, err on the side of caution and set it to **Audit mode** initially.
   Then, review the reports, and if it is not flagging anything, enable it. **Enabled** is more secure, but the machines still have to work for the users and apps.
3. We are setting everything to **Block** in this recipe, as it is a lab environment, which means we do not have any legacy apps to worry about. When using in production, test carefully to ensure your Office add-ons and line of business applications all work as expected.
   When changing a setting, you will see **ASR Only Per Rule Exclusions** appear. This can exclude a particular application (type in the application executable) from the policy setting.

   As with other policies, clicking the lowercase **i** letter enclosed in a circle will tell you exactly what the policy is doing, but again, use **Audit** or **Warn** if in doubt.
4. Once you have configured your policy settings, click **Next**.
5. Again, on the **Scope tags** page, click **Next**.
6. On the **Assignment** screen, assign to either users or devices, depending on how your user personas look. If, for example, your finance department has an Office add-on, you may want a policy just for them that is slightly more relaxed, but not want to have to relax it across the organization.
7. Then, as usual, review and create your policy by clicking **Create**.

We have now configured our ASR rules in the UI to add extra protection to our devices.

Automating it

Now, let's learn how to create this policy using PowerShell.

As these policies are a reasonably new addition, they run entirely from Settings Catalog. If you run a query to list all of the categories in there, you will see one called **Attack Surface Reduction**. However, do not use this one – it has older settings on an ADMX-backed policy.

The settings we are looking for are in the Defender category with an ID of `e8400c82-34c8-4d6e-bbf9-85220f3205ea`.

As with the firewall, running this command will list the available policies. At this point, you can look through the `Options` array to see the available values:

```
((Invoke-MgGraphRequest -Method GET -Uri "https://graph.microsoft.com/beta/
deviceManagement/configurationSettings?`$filter=categoryId eq 'e8400c82-34c8-4d6e-
bbf9-85220f3205ea'" -OutputType PSObject).value | select-object name, description,
'@odata.type', rootDefinitionId, options, @{Name="Platform";
Expression={ $_.applicability | Select-Object platform}},@{Name="technologies";
Expression={ $_.applicability | Select-Object technologies}},valuedefinition, id)
| out-gridview
```

As an example, Adobe Reader would give you these options:

```
device_vendor_msft_policy_config_defender_attacksurfacereductionrules_blockadobere
aderfromcreatingchildprocesses_off
device_vendor_msft_policy_config_defender_attacksurfacereductionrules_blockadobere
aderfromcreatingchildprocesses_block
device_vendor_msft_policy_config_defender_attacksurfacereductionrules_blockadobere
aderfromcreatingchildprocesses_audit
device_vendor_msft_policy_config_defender_attacksurfacereductionrules_blockadobere
aderfromcreatingchildprocesses_warn
```

As most ASR rules are similar, once you know the policy name, you can work out the value to use.

The policy we created earlier is available in the repository. So, again, the code here has been condensed, with just one setting included:

1. First, set the group ID and URL:

```
$groupid = "00000000000000000000"
$uri = "https://graph.microsoft.com/beta/deviceManagement/
configurationPolicies"
```

2. Then, configure the JSON (again, there is only one setting here):

```
$json = @"
{
    "description": "Block everything",
    "name": "Attack Surface Reduction",
    "platforms": "windows10",
    "roleScopeTagIds": [
        "0"
    ],
    "settings": [
        {
            "@odata.type":
"#microsoft.graph.deviceManagementConfigurationSetting",
            "settingInstance": {
                "@odata.type":
"#microsoft.graph.deviceManagementConfigurationGroupSettingCollectionInstan
ce",
                "groupSettingCollectionValue": [
                    {
                        "children": [
                            {
                                "@odata.type":
"#microsoft.graph.deviceManagementConfigurationChoiceSettingInstance",
                                "choiceSettingValue": {
                                    "@odata.type":
"#microsoft.graph.deviceManagementConfigurationChoiceSettingValue",
                                    "children": [],
                                    "value":
"device_vendor_msft_policy_config_defender_attacksurfacereductionrules_bloc
kadobereaderfromcreatingchildprocesses_block"
                                },
```

```
                                    "settingDefinitionId":
"device_vendor_msft_policy_config_defender_attacksurfacereductionrules_bloc
kadobereaderfromcreatingchildprocesses"
                                }
                            ]
                        }
                    ],
                    "settingDefinitionId":
"device_vendor_msft_policy_config_defender_attacksurfacereductionrules",
                    "settingInstanceTemplateReference": {
                        "settingInstanceTemplateId": "19600663-e264-4c02-8f55-
f2983216d6d7"
                    }
                }
            }
        ],
        "technologies": "mdm,microsoftSense",
        "templateReference": {
            "templateId": "e8c053d6-9f95-42b1-a7f1-ebfd71c67a4b_1"
        }
}
"@
```

3. Finally, create the policy, add the ID to the URL, and assign it to the group you specified earlier:

```
$policy = Invoke-MgGraphRequest -Method POST -Uri $uri -Body $json -
ContentType "application/json" -OutputType PSObject
$policyid = $policy.id
$assignuri = "https://graph.microsoft.com/beta/deviceManagement/
configurationPolicies/$policyid/assign"
$assignjson = @"
{
    "assignments": [
        {
            "target": {
                "@odata.type": "#microsoft.graph.groupAssignmentTarget",
                "groupId": "$groupid"
            }
        }
    ]
```

```
}
"@
Invoke-MgGraphRequest -Method POST -Uri $assignuri -Body $assignjson -
ContentType "application/json"
```

That completes the steps to automate our ASR policy deployment.

There's more...

There are numerous other options for security policies available within the portal. While we will not be running through deploying them all (as they are all pretty similar), this section will briefly outline what they are and where they live within the portal:

- **Microsoft Defender Antivirus Exclusions**: Found in **Antivirus** | **Windows**. This sets your exclusions for files, locations, and more.
- **Defender Update Controls**: Found in **Antivirus** | **Windows**. This gives you more control over Defender updates so that you can configure a ring approach to their deployment, similar to Office and Windows (covered in *Chapter 4*).
- **Windows Defender Firewall Rules**: Found in **Firewall** | **Windows**. This allows you to configure individual firewall rules, similar to how you would in an on-premises scenario (or directly on the device).
- **Endpoint Privilege Management**: This is covered in **Intune Suite**; we will look at it in more detail in *Chapter 14*.
- **Endpoint Detection and Response**: Found in **Endpoint detection and response** | **Windows**. This will be covered in the next recipe.
- **App Control for Business**: This is a way to control the installation and running of applications across your estate via **Windows Defender Application Control** (**WDAC**) XML or using the built-in rules to restrict to approved applications deployed via Intune. You can find out more at `https://learn.microsoft.com/en-us/intune/intune-service/protect/endpoint-security-app-control-policy`.
- **Exploit Protection**: Found in **Attack Surface Reduction** | **Windows**. As well as blocking the ability for users to disable it, you can also upload a custom set of rules in XML format here. To learn more about creating these rules, go to `https://learn.microsoft.com/en-us/microsoft-365/security/defender-endpoint/import-export-exploit-protection-emet-xml?view=o365-worldwide`.
- **Device Control**: Found in **Attack Surface Reduction** | **Windows**. These give finer controls over the likes of Bluetooth, removable storage, and device installations. Watch for clashes with any security baselines.

- **App and Browser Isolation**: Found in **Attack Surface Reduction | Windows**. Here, you can specify details for any enterprise network settings, as well as restrictions applied to Edge and any isolated Windows environments using Application Guard.
- **Application Control**: Found in **Attack Surface Reduction | Windows**. This turns on SmartScreen and configures App Locker for Components, Store Apps, and Smart Locker.
- **Local User Group Membership**: Found in **Account Protection | Windows**. This policy allows you to specify specific users or groups to be added to or removed from user groups in the devices themselves. This should be used carefully, especially with the introduction of LAPS.
- **Account Protection**: Found in **Account Protection | Windows**. Another place to configure Device Guard and Windows Hello for Business. Again, watch for policy conflicts!

Enrolling in Defender for Endpoint

Microsoft Defender for Endpoint gives you additional controls and monitoring on your devices. It works on top of Microsoft Defender to give more advanced device protection as well as web filtering, looking for exploits, outdated applications, and a lot more. While it requires additional licensing, it is one worth considering.

Getting ready

While it is managed from within Intune, you first need to onboard your tenant and devices into the service.

> Note
>
> You need a Microsoft Defender for Endpoint P1 or P2 license to complete the following steps (a free trial can be obtained from the Microsoft admin center).

To start, we need to navigate to the **Security** portal at `https://security.microsoft.com`.

How to do it...

Now that we are in the portal, follow these settings to enroll your devices:

1. Click **Settings**.
2. Then, click **Endpoints**.
3. Now, scroll to the bottom; there should be a setting marked **Microsoft Intune connection**. Slide that to **On**.
4. Then, click **Save Preferences** and return to the Intune portal.

5. Navigate to **Endpoint Security**, then **Endpoint Detection and Response**, and create a new policy (**Windows**).
6. Set the policy's **Name** and **Description** values.
7. As we have enabled **Intune connection** within the **Security** portal, we now have the option to select the **Auto from connector** option from the **Microsoft Defender for Endpoint client configuration package type** dropdown. If it is not there, make sure **Intune connection** was enabled and saved correctly in the previous steps within the **Security** portal.
8. Set **Sample Sharing** and click **Next**.
9. On the **Scope tags** page, click **Next**.
10. Defender for Endpoint *only* works at the device level, so either assign to a device group or choose **All Devices**. This is probably one occasion where **All Devices** is worthwhile.
11. Finally, click **Create**.
12. We can now click on the **Microsoft Defender for Endpoint** link in the menu and check that everything is connected.
13. You can also find additional settings here for non-Intune managed and Android/iOS devices. Review them for your needs and enable them as required.

This recipe has enrolled your Intune tenant into Defender for Endpoint and then configured a policy to automatically enroll your devices into Defender for Endpoint.

Deploying Windows LAPS

Although it has been around for years for on-premises directories, this is a very new addition for Entra-managed devices, largely due to the inclusion of the LAPS client within Windows itself rather than needing an additional MSI and **Active Directory** (**AD**) schema update.

Before looking at deploying LAPS, it is first worth understanding what it does and why you may want to use it. LAPS is a system that rotates the local admin password on a machine to add an extra layer of security, as it ensures that no two machines have the same password; this helps prevent lateral traversal attacks.

With the introduction of Autopilot, Intune, and Entra ID, this was removed as the admin account was disabled by default. There are options available for managing these devices (such as the **Cloud Joined Device Local Admin Role** or **Local User Group Membership**), but they both have disadvantages (the role is for all devices, and the membership is one policy per device).

Windows LAPS, on the other hand, gives you a password per device that can be retrieved from the Intune or Entra portal and will automatically expire to keep your machines protected.

With the introduction of **Endpoint Privilege Management** as part of Intune Suite (covered in *Chapter 14*), this may replace a lot of the use cases for LAPS, but that is at an additional cost.

When configuring LAPS for the first time, you need to consider whether you want to use the built-in admin account and re-enable it (you can also rename it) or create your own account and leave the admin account disabled. The reasons for creating a new account are around security. Firstly, it is a well-known **security identifier** (**SID**), so even if you rename it, it can still be targeted. Secondly, the admin account will never lock out due to bad password attempts, so there is always a risk of a brute-force attack; it is extremely unlikely to work with a complex password (to give you an idea, if you set it to 20 characters, uppercase, lowercase, numbers, and special characters, it will take 42 quintillion years to crack... but reset every 30 days!).

Tip

With Windows 11 24H2, automated account management is included in the base OS. The recipe to configure the admin account is still included here for earlier operating systems, but automatic management will also be covered in the LAPS policy itself.

In this recipe, you will learn how to deploy with either option so that you are free to decide which works best for you.

Getting ready

There are some operating system version-specific requirements for this, so if you are looking to deploy it, make sure you have one of the following:

- Windows 10 20H2 or above with KB5025221 (April 2023 update)
- Windows 11 21H2 or above with KB5025224 (April 2023 update)

This recipe will move between the Entra portal (Entra ID) and the Intune portal (both **Configuration Profiles** and **Endpoint Security**).

How to do it...

Follow these steps to configure your policies and deploy Windows LAPS:

1. First, head to **Entra** | **Devices** | **Overview** | **Device Settings**.
2. Toward the bottom, there is the option for **Local administrator settings**. By default, this will be set to **No** (off), so we need to toggle it to **Yes**.
3. Then, click **Save** at the top.

Now, we need to navigate back to the Intune console and create a policy to either enable the admin or create a new account.

> **Note**
>
> You can skip these steps with Windows 11 24H2

Using the built-in account

If you want to use the built-in account, follow these steps:

1. Navigate to **Devices** | **Configuration** | **+ Create** and click **+New Policy**
2. Select **Settings catalog** from the **Profile type** dropdown.
3. Set the policy's **Name** and **Description** values and then click **Next**.
4. Now, check the boxes against these settings:
    - **Local Policy Security Options**: **Accounts Enable Administrator Account Status**
    - **Local Policy Security Options**: **Accounts Rename Administrator Account**
5. Enable the account, and if you want, change its name under **Accounts Rename Administrator Account**.
6. Now, assign the policy; this is device-level, so choose a device group or **All devices**.
7. Then, create the policy by clicking **Create**.

That completes the steps for configuring LAPS with the built-in admin account.

Creating a new account

If you want to create a new account, the only way currently is to use a custom OMA-URI, as described in *Chapter 2*. We will configure this now:

1. In the console, we want to create a new custom profile.
2. As usual, specify its **Name** and **Description** values.
3. On the next page, we need to add two new rows.

   The first one is to create the new user with an **OMA-URI** value of `./Device/Vendor/MSFT/Accounts/Users/lapsadmin/Password`, where `lapsadmin` is your username to be created.

   Data type needs to be **String**, and the value is the initial password for the account:

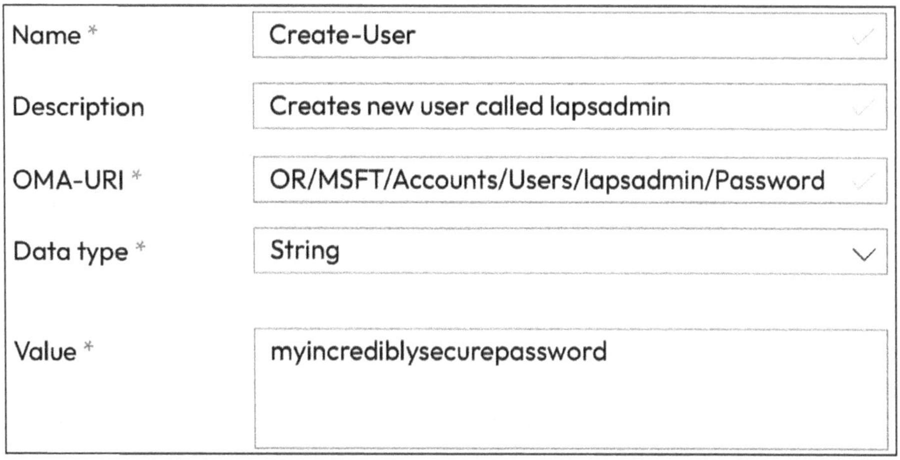

Figure 3.9 – New account policy – New user setting

4. The second row is to add the user to the administrators group on the machines. This one uses an **OMA-URI** value of `./Device/Vendor/MSFT/Accounts/Users/lapsadmin/LocalUserGroup`, where, again, `lapsadmin` is the user account.

   Set it to **Integer** with **Value** set to 2:

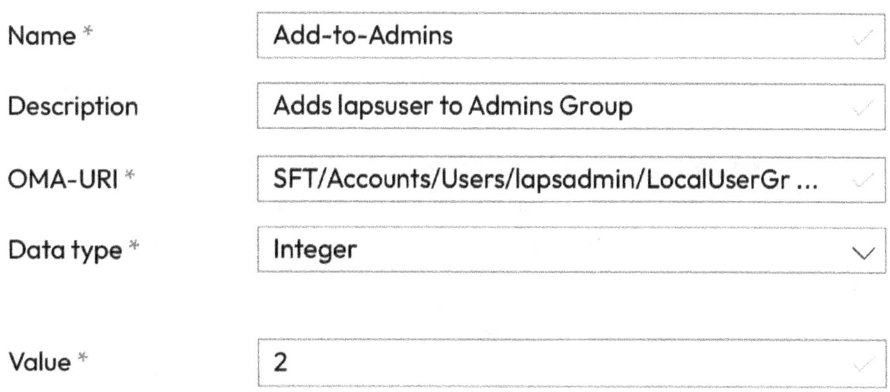

Figure 3.10 – New account policy – Admin group setting

5. Once you have added these two settings, click **Next**.
6. Now, on the **Assignment** tab, target devices, not users.
7. Click **Next** on the **Applicability Rules** page since we do not need any.
8. Review and click **Create**.

After creating our user or enabling the built-in admin, we can create the LAPS policy itself.

Creating the LAPS policy

Now that our user account has been enabled or created, we need to configure the LAPS policy itself by performing the following steps:

1. For this, navigate to **Endpoint Security** | **Account Protection** | **Create Policy**.
2. Select **Windows** and **Local admin password solution (Windows LAPS)**.
3. Set the policy's **Name** and **Description** values.
4. On the next screen, we have the following fields:
    - **Backup Directory**: We are only using AAD for our devices, so that is what we need here.
    - **Password Age Days**: This is worth setting and depends on your security posture.
    - **Administrator Account Name**: If you renamed or created a new account, configure this and enter the name of the account. Leave this off if you are using the managed account option.
    - **Password Complexity**: Always select the most complex.
    - **Password Length**: 20 or more characters makes it pretty much uncrackable.
    - **Post Authentication Actions**: You can either reset the password only, force a logoff, or force a reboot, whichever works best for your environment.
    - **Post Authentication Reset Delay**: Here, you can specify how many hours after using the password you want it to reset (defaults to **24**).
    - **Automatic Account Management Enabled**: This is the new functionality for 24H2 and above, which will automate the account creation for you. Enabling this reveals further options to configure for your environment.
5. Once configured, click **Next**.
6. On the **Scope tags** page, click **Next**.
7. Once configured, assign the policy to your devices and click **Next**.
8. Review the settings and click **Create**.

Once your machines have collected the policy, navigating to them will show the details of the current password and when it is due to rotate.

That completes the LAPS policy configuration.

Accessing and rotating passwords

Now that our devices are using LAPS, we need to be able to view and rotate the passwords. While we have not enrolled any devices in this tenant, we will use a different tenant to demonstrate this here. Follow these steps to retrieve and rotate the passwords:

1. Navigate to **Devices** | **Windows** and then select one of your devices.
2. Once you are in the device's details, click on **Local admin password**.
   Here, you can click the blue **Show local administrator password** button to view the password for the device.
3. To reset the password, click on the **Overview** option for the device.
4. Now, click the three dots on the far right-hand side of the **Actions** bar and select **Rotate local admin password**.
5. Finally, click **Yes** to rotate.

Now that we have learned how to configure and use LAPS in the UI, we can cover automating it.

Automating it

Fortunately, all of the preceding steps in this recipe can be automated using Graph alone, even the Entra ID part!

As always, the full script can be found in this book's GitHub repository.

Entra ID

Starting with Entra ID, we need to enable the LAPS setting:

1. Set the URL and grab the current settings. This one needs all the settings when amending, so we cannot send a simple command to change one setting – we have to change it in the array and then pass the array back again. Here, we are leaving Intune (the `deviceManagement` Graph category) and moving into Entra ID *policies*. The relevant settings are within the `deviceRegistrationPolicy` sub-category:

```
$checkuri = "https://graph.microsoft.com/beta/policies/
deviceRegistrationPolicy"
$currentpolicy = Invoke-MgGraphRequest -Method GET -Uri $checkuri -
OutputType PSObject -ContentType "application/json"
```

2. Set the `localAdminPassword.isEnabled` array value from `False` to `True`. To do this, we must grab the entire policy; the value we need is within a nested array. We can dig into that array by using:

   ```
   $currentpolicy.localAdminPassword.isEnabled = $true
   ```

   Setting the value within the nested array will automatically update the master array with the new settings.

3. We converted the output into a PowerShell object to manipulate. So, now, we need to convert it back into JSON:

   ```
   $policytojson = $currentpolicy | ConvertTo-Json
   ```

4. Now, we can reconfigure the settings with a `PUT` command:

   ```
   Invoke-MgGraphRequest -Method PUT -Uri $checkuri -Body $policytojson -
   ContentType "application/json"
   ```

That completes the Entra ID configuration to enable LAPS.

> **Note**
>
> If you are using the 24H2 managed account, you can skip these next two steps.

Enabling the local admin and renaming

If you went down this route, as we found earlier, it is a Settings Catalog policy under the **Local Policy Security Options** category with an ID of `914a31d0-ae3b-4ae5-bd31-504b9f0b91df`.

Looking through the settings, you can find the setting name and values in the `Options` array. In the case of enabling the account, we have `1` for enable and `0` for disable:

```
device_vendor_msft_policy_config_localpoliciessecurityoptions_accounts_enableadmin
istratoraccountstatus_1
device_vendor_msft_policy_config_localpoliciessecurityoptions_accounts_enableadmin
istratoraccountstatus_0
```

For our policy, do the following:

1. Set the account name you wish to use:

```
$accountname = ""
```

2. Set the URL:

```
$createurl = "https://graph.microsoft.com/beta/deviceManagement/
configurationPolicies"
```

3. Configure the JSON:

```
$createjson = @"
{
    "description": "Enable and Rename account",
    "name": "Enable Administrator Account",
    "platforms": "windows10",
    "roleScopeTagIds": [
        "0"
    ],
    "settings": [
        {
            "@odata.type":
"#microsoft.graph.deviceManagementConfigurationSetting",
            "settingInstance": {
                "@odata.type":
"#microsoft.graph.deviceManagementConfigurationChoiceSettingInstance",
                "choiceSettingValue": {
                    "@odata.type":
"#microsoft.graph.deviceManagementConfigurationChoiceSettingValue",
                    "children": [],
                    "value":
"device_vendor_msft_policy_config_localpoliciessecurityoptions_accounts_ena
bleadministratoraccountstatus_1"
                },
                "settingDefinitionId":
"device_vendor_msft_policy_config_localpoliciessecurityoptions_accounts_ena
bleadministratoraccountstatus"
            }
        },
```

```
        {
            "@odata.type":
"#microsoft.graph.deviceManagementConfigurationSetting",
            "settingInstance": {
                "@odata.type":
"#microsoft.graph.deviceManagementConfigurationSimpleSettingInstance",
                "settingDefinitionId":
"device_vendor_msft_policy_config_localpoliciessecurityoptions_accounts_ren
ameadministratoraccount",
                "simpleSettingValue": {
                    "@odata.type":
"#microsoft.graph.deviceManagementConfigurationStringSettingValue",
                    "value": "$accountname"
                }
            }
        }
    ],
    "technologies": "mdm"
}
"@
```

4. Create the policy:

```
$createpolicy = Invoke-MgGraphRequest -Method POST -Uri $createurl -Body
$createjson -OutputType PSObject -ContentType "application/json"
```

5. Grab the ID and assign it. In this case, we are using the **All Devices** option, which, rather than using the group ID, uses `"#microsoft.graph.allDevicesAssignmentTarget"`. For devices, it would be `"#microsoft.graph.allUsersAssignmentTarget"`:

```
$createpolicyid = $createpolicy.id
$createassignurl = "https://graph.microsoft.com/beta/deviceManagement/
configurationPolicies/$createpolicyid/assign"
$createassignjson = @"
{
    "assignments": [
        {
            "target": {
                "@odata.type":
```

```
"#microsoft.graph.allDevicesAssignmentTarget"
                }
            }
        ]
}
"@
Invoke-MgGraphRequest -Method POST -Uri $createassignurl -Body
$createassignjson -ContentType "application/json" -OutputType PSObject
```

This script will enable and rename the local admin account as the first option for using Windows LAPS. Now, we can look at the alternative – creating a new account.

Creating a new account

As this is a custom OMA-URI, the process is a bit more straightforward:

1. First, as we are setting a password, we need a quick function to generate a random secure one. There are multiple ways to do this; here, we are using built-in commands to generate one:

```
function Get-RandomPassword {
    param (
        [Parameter(Mandatory)]
        [int] $length,
        [int] $amountOfNonAlphanumeric = 1
    )
    Add-Type -AssemblyName 'System.Web'
    return [System.Web.Security.Membership]::GeneratePassword($length,
$amountOfNonAlphanumeric)
}
$password = Get-RandomPassword -Length 20
```

2. Now, set the URL:

```
$customurl = "https://graph.microsoft.com/beta/deviceManagement/
deviceConfigurations"
```

3. Populate the JSON. It is a new policy, so the ID is effectively blank:

```
$customjson = @"
{
    "@odata.type": "#microsoft.graph.windows10CustomConfiguration",
```

```
    "description": "Creates a new user to be used with LAPS",
    "displayName": "Windows-LAPS-User",
    "id": "00000000-0000-0000-0000-000000000000",
    "omaSettings": [
        {
            "@odata.type": "#microsoft.graph.omaSettingString",
            "description": "Create lapsadmin and set password",
            "displayName": "Create-User",
            "omaUri": "./Device/Vendor/MSFT/Accounts/Users/$accountname/
Password",
            "value": "$password"
        },
        {
            "@odata.type": "#microsoft.graph.omaSettingInteger",
            "description": "Add to admins",
            "displayName": "Add-to-group",
            "omaUri": "./Device/Vendor/MSFT/Accounts/Users/$accountname/
LocalUserGroup",
            "value": 2
        }
    ],
    "roleScopeTagIds": [
        "0"
    ]
}
"@
```

4. Create and assign the policy (again, all devices):

```
$policy = Invoke-MgGraphRequest -Method POST -Uri $customurl -Body
$customjson -OutputType PSObject -ContentType "application/json"
$policyid = $policy.id
$assignurl = "https://graph.microsoft.com/beta/deviceManagement/
deviceConfigurations/$policyid/assign"
$assignjson = @"
{
    "assignments": [
        {
            "target": {
                "@odata.type":
"#microsoft.graph.allDevicesAssignmentTarget"
```

```
            }
        }
    ]
}
"@
Invoke-MgGraphRequest -Method POST -Uri $assignurl -Body $assignjson -
ContentType "application/json" -OutputType PSObject
```

This script will create a new administrator account for use with LAPS. Now, we can create the policy itself.

LAPS policy

Before starting, let's look at how the script works. This runs from a template that can be found by running a GET request at `https://graph.microsoft.com/beta/deviceManagement/configurationPolicyTemplates/adc46e5a-f4aa-4ff6-aeff-4f27bc525796_1`.

A list of the settings can be found at `https://graph.microsoft.com/beta/deviceManagement/configurationPolicyTemplates/adc46e5a-f4aa-4ff6-aeff-4f27bc525796_1/settingTemplates`.

As it has several settings, check this book's GitHub repository for the full values.

There are two scripts in the repository, one for those using the 24H2 and above managed account and one for those manually managing.

This example will just include one setting:

1. First, we have the policy. Let's set its URL:

```
$lapsurl = "https://graph.microsoft.com/beta/deviceManagement/
configurationPolicies"
```

2. Set the JSON:

```
$lapsjson = @"
{
    "description": "Uses lapsadmin created via custom OMA-URI policy",
    "name": "LAPS Config",
    "platforms": "windows10",
    "roleScopeTagIds": [
        "0"
    ],
    "settings": [
```

```
        {
            "@odata.type":
"#microsoft.graph.deviceManagementConfigurationSetting",
            "settingInstance": {
                "@odata.type":
"#microsoft.graph.deviceManagementConfigurationChoiceSettingInstance",
                "choiceSettingValue": {
                    "@odata.type":
"#microsoft.graph.deviceManagementConfigurationChoiceSettingValue",
                    "children": [
                        {
                            "@odata.type":
"#microsoft.graph.deviceManagementConfigurationSimpleSettingInstance",
                            "settingDefinitionId":
"device_vendor_msft_laps_policies_passwordagedays_aad",
                            "simpleSettingValue": {
                                "@odata.type":
"#microsoft.graph.deviceManagementConfigurationIntegerSettingValue",
                                "value": 30
                            }
                        }
                    ],
                    "settingValueTemplateReference": {
                        "settingValueTemplateId": "4d90f03d-
e14c-43c4-86da-681da96a2f92"
                    },
                    "value":
"device_vendor_msft_laps_policies_backupdirectory_1"
                },
                "settingDefinitionId":
"device_vendor_msft_laps_policies_backupdirectory",
                "settingInstanceTemplateReference": {
                    "settingInstanceTemplateId": "a3270f64-
e493-499d-8900-90290f61ed8a"
                }
            }
        }
    ],
    "technologies": "mdm",
    "templateReference": {
        "templateId": "adc46e5a-f4aa-4ff6-aeff-4f27bc525796_1"
```

```
        }
    }
    "@
```

3. Create and assign the policy:

```
$lapspolicy = Invoke-MgGraphRequest -Method POST -Uri $lapsurl -Body
$lapsjson -ContentType "application/json" -OutputType PSObject
$lapspolicyid = $lapspolicy.id
$lapsassignurl = "https://graph.microsoft.com/beta/deviceManagement/
configurationPolicies/$lapspolicyid/assign"
$lapsassignjson = @"
{
    "assignments": [
        {
            "target": {
                "@odata.type":
"#microsoft.graph.allDevicesAssignmentTarget"
            }
        }
    ]
}
"@
Invoke-MgGraphRequest -Method POST -Uri $lapsassignurl -Body
$lapsassignjson -ContentType "application/json"
```

That concludes the creation of the LAPS policy. Now, let's learn how to retrieve and rotate the passwords.

Accessing and rotating passwords

Now that our LAPS policy has been configured, we need to access the passwords for real-world usage:

1. First, we can look at accessing a password. For this, we need the device ID, which we can retrieve from the address bar in the GUI:

Figure 3.11– Device ID

2. We can add this to the script:

```
$deviceid = "xxxxxxxx-xxxx-xxxx-xxxx-xxxxxxxxxxxx"
```

Or, to avoid using the GUI, we can grab all of our devices:

```
$alldevices = (Invoke-MgGraphRequest -Method GET -Uri "https://
graph.microsoft.com/beta/deviceManagement/managedDevices" -OutputType
PSObject).value
```

3. Output them into a grid view (with passthrough):

```
$selecteddevice = $alldevices | Out-GridView -PassThru -Title "Devices"
```

4. Then, select the ID:

```
$deviceid = $selecteddevice.id
```

5. Now, we need to add this to the URL. We are using the `deviceLocalCredentials` category here. The URL must be structured slightly differently, as we have both ? and $ characters, which are reserved in PowerShell. Therefore, we must split the `$deviceid` variable and add a backtick (`) before `$select` so that it treats the variable as a raw string:

```
$url = "https://graph.microsoft.com/beta/deviceLocalCredentials/" +
$deviceid + "?`$select=credentials"
```

6. Now, we can grab all the credentials and put them in a variable:

```
$lapspassword = (Invoke-MgGraphRequest -Method GET -Uri $url -OutputType
PSObject).credentials
```

The account name is straightforward:

```
$accountName = $lapspassword.accountName
```

The password is slightly trickier as it is Base64 encoded, so we need to wrap that in the `.Net` function to `base64` decode from a string:

```
$password =
[System.Text.Encoding]::UTF8.GetString([System.Convert]::FromBase64String((
$lapspassword.passwordBase64)))
```

7. Now, simply output them:

```
write-host "Account Name: $accountName"
write-host "Account Password: $password"
```

Rotating the password is more straightforward:

1. First, using the same device ID as before, add it to the URL:

```
$rotateurl = "https://graph.microsoft.com/beta/deviceManagement/
managedDevices/$deviceid/rotateLocalAdminPassword"
```

   This one uses the `managedDevices` category and calls the `rotateLocalAdminPassword` command within it.

2. While it is a `POST` command, it does not need a payload to be attached, so the command is as follows:

```
Invoke-MgGraphRequest -Method POST -Uri $rotateurl -OutputType PSObject
```

With that, we have configured, deployed, and managed LAPS using PowerShell.

Configuring Application Control

A new feature in Intune is **Application Control**, which extends the WDAC functionality but with an easier deployment.

There are two methods of deploying Application Control: via a GUI with boxes to select or using an XML file created for WDAC.

For this example, we will be using the GUI method, but if you would rather have more granular control, you can use the WDAC wizard from Microsoft to assist in creating the file.

You can read more about that here: `https://learn.microsoft.com/en-us/windows/security/threat-protection/windows-defender-application-control/wdac-wizard`.

How to do it...

Before we can create our policy, we need to activate the managed installer. This allows the Intune **Management** extension to install applications without restrictions. Follow these steps to configure it in your environment:

1. Click on **Endpoint Security** and then **App Control for Business**.
2. At the top, click the **Managed installer** tab and click **Add**.
3. In the fly-out panel, click **Add**.
4. Press **Yes** to confirm you wish to add the managed installer.
5. Now that this has been enabled, we can create our policy. Click **Application control**, then **Create Policy**. Things will look familiar now as this uses the standard unified Settings Catalog underneath.
6. Specify your policy's **Name** and **Description** values and click **Next**.
7. On the next screen, we are going to use the GUI. So, for **Configuration settings format**, select **Use built-in controls**.
   This will change the display in terms of some options (again, this will look similar to Settings Catalog):
   - **Enable app control policy to trust Windows components and Store apps**: The only options here are **Enforce** and **Audit**. Setting it to **Audit** will record events, but not block any applications from running.
   - Select additional rules for trusting apps:
     - **Trust apps with good reputation**: This approves applications trusted by Microsoft Intelligent Security Graph.
     - **Trust apps from managed installers**: This uses AppLocker to allow certain installers, such as Configuration Manager. You can read more here: .

These rules help ensure only the intended applications are trusted and installed in your environment.

In this example, we will keep everything restricted to Intune only, so leave the two additional rules empty. Once you have configured settings for your environment, click **Next**.

1. We do not need scope tags here, so click **Next**.
   While we wish to assign all security policies at the device level, this is an exception to the rule. If we assign this to all devices, *all* applications will need to be deployed via Intune, even single apps required by IT for troubleshooting or one-off installations. To

avoid this, we are going to assign at the user level so that we can add exceptions for IT support staff as required. Populate the groups as required and click **Next**.

2. Finally, review that everything looks correct and click **Create**.

With that, we have configured Application Control in the UI.

Automating it

There are two steps to automating this: enabling the installer and creating the policy.

We will start with the installer. Follow these steps to enable it:

1. To find out whether it is already enabled, we can run a `GET` command against this URL:

```
https://graph.microsoft.com/beta/deviceAppManagement/windowsManagementApp/
```

2. Check the value of `managedInstaller` in the response. If it is enabled, you do not have to complete this step.
   If it is not enabled, we simply need to send an empty payload `POST` request to a URL:

```
$posturl = "https://graph.microsoft.com/beta/deviceAppManagement/
windowsManagementApp/setAsManagedInstaller"
Invoke-MgGraphRequest -Method POST -Uri $posturl -Body $body -OutputType
PSObject
```

Now that this has been enabled, the next step will be similar – we must deploy a Settings Catalog policy. The GitHub repository contains a more complex script that configures the JSON for either a GUI or XML setup, but for this example, we will simply replicate what we have created in the web interface:

1. First, we need some variables. We are also including variables for the options we have selected:

```
$url = "https://graph.microsoft.com/beta/deviceManagement/
configurationPolicies"
$name = "Application Control"
$description = "Application Control Policy"
$groupid = "00000000000"
$managedinstallers = "false"
$trustedinstallers = "false"
$windowsappcontrol = "enable"
```

2. Now, we must add that to the JSON (the script is available on GitHub).

There is no mention of the three variables we set, as these change the layout of the JSON. Switching the first option to **Audit** changes the settings value to the following:

```
device_vendor_msft_policy_config_applicationcontrol_built_in_controls_enabl
e_app_control_1
```

If we activate either of the other two settings, new child entries will be added to the JSON, both with the same setting but with slightly different values.

3. For managed installers, use the following code:

```
        {
                "@odata.type":
"#microsoft.graph.deviceManagementConfigurationChoiceSettingValue",
                "children": [],
                "value":
"device_vendor_msft_policy_config_applicationcontrol_built_in_controls_trus
t_apps_1"
        }
```

4. For trusted installers, use the following code:

```
        {
                "@odata.type":
"#microsoft.graph.deviceManagementConfigurationChoiceSettingValue",
                "children": [],
                "value":
"device_vendor_msft_policy_config_applicationcontrol_built_in_controls_trus
t_apps_0"
        }
```

The GitHub script will automate this for you based on your selections.

With that, we have learned how to automate the process of configuring Application Control.

Get This Book's PDF Version and Exclusive Extras

Scan the QR code (or go to `http://packtpub.com/unlock`). Search for this book by name, confirm the edition, and then follow the steps on the page.

UNLOCK NOW

Note: Keep your invoice handy. Purchases made directly from Packt don't require one.

4

Setting Up Enrollment and Updates for Windows

Now that we have our security and configuration policies in place for our Windows devices, we are almost ready to enroll our first device (we will cover application deployment in *Chapter 11, Packaging Your Windows Applications*, but that is not essential for enrollment).

Before we start enrollment, we have to consider that we are working with devices directly from the manufacturer/distributor that could have been sitting in a warehouse or on a container ship for several months. Therefore, it makes sense to configure our Windows update policies ahead of enrollment so that we can sleep safely at night, knowing that even a newly provisioned device will be kept up to date.

In this chapter, we will look at configuring update rings manually and using **Windows Update for Business** (**WUfB**) as well as **Windows Autopatch**, which you can think of as *Windows updates as a service*, where Microsoft does the heavy lifting for you.

Once we have our updates in place, we can look at configuring enrollment profiles and, finally, enrolling devices.

This chapter contains the following recipes:

- Building your update rings – including feature and quality updates
- Configuring driver updates
- Enrolling and using Autopatch
- Configuring Windows Hello for Business
- Setting up Windows Autopilot enrollment profiles
- Configuring Autopilot device preparation

- Configuring an **Enrollment Status Page** (**ESP**)
- Enrolling your Windows device

Technical requirements

For this chapter, you will need a modern web browser and a PowerShell code editor such as **Visual Studio Code** (**VS Code**) or PowerShell ISE.

All of the scripts that are referenced in this chapter can be found here: `https://github.com/PacktPublishing/Microsoft-Intune-Cookbook-Second-Edition/tree/main/Chapter-4`.

Building your update rings – including feature and quality updates

With fully managed machines, the last thing you want is them updating themselves without having any control over when they receive updates and which updates they receive, and you especially do not want users opting into insider builds themselves.

While Autopatch is now available for the vast majority of licenses and makes sense to use where possible (covered in the next recipe), there may be situations where you need or want to create your own update rings instead.

Getting ready

Before building the rings, navigate to the Entra ID portal and create some Entra ID (static) groups. We will populate these with devices to assign to each of the rings.

Create four groups:

- One for preview devices.
- One for pilot devices.
- One for VIP devices.
- One for everything else (broad ring). This could be a dynamic group to save on admin overhead.

Once you have created these groups, navigate to the Intune portal; we will be using the **Update Rings**, **Feature updates**, and **Quality updates** options.

When populating the rings, make sure you add devices to the preview and pilot groups. You will often have IT staff in these groups who log in to other machines to do repairs and troubleshooting. The last thing you want is for a user to log in and switch on a broad ring device for a pre-release build! You will want some non-IT staff in your non-insider builds as well for some real-world feedback, as you may find that IT staff, especially with administrative rights, simply fix any issues themselves, which will not be an option for standard users.

How to do it...

In this recipe, we are going to create four update rings and a feature update policy. As the update rings are the same but just with different release dates, the screenshots will be combined in places to save repeating content.

Building update rings

Follow these steps:

1. Navigate to **Devices**, click **Windows**, and select **Windows updates**.
2. In the **Update rings** tab, click **Create Profile**.
3. Specify descriptive **Name** and **Description** values. This is especially important so that you can quickly differentiate the update rings.
4. Now, we need to configure our settings; a lot of these will be dependent on your environment.

   > **Tip**
   >
   > The default options are set to blue and switch to purple upon configuration. If you revert a change, it will remain purple.

   We will have a look at what they all are and the recommended settings for each of the rings:

   - **Microsoft Product updates**: This enables Windows Update. We need this to be enabled.
   - **Windows drivers**: This allows Windows Update to search for and install drivers on the machine. If you would prefer to use vendor-specific apps for this, simply block here.
   - **Quality update deferral period**: This allows you to specify the number of days after Patch Tuesday when quality updates will be installed. Check out *Table 4.1* for recommended values.
   - **Feature update deferral period**: Set this to `0` so that we can use the feature update policy. Anything other than 0 and Intune will ignore the extra policy.
   - **Upgrade Windows 10 devices to the latest Windows 11 release**: Windows 10 is no longer supported from October 2025, so enabling this is recommended. However, it depends on your upgrade readiness, so set it accordingly.

- **Set feature update uninstall period**: How many days after the update has been installed will you allow a rollback (for your deferred installations, it is the number of days after the deferral period)?
- **Enable pre-release builds**: You will need pre-release builds for your pilot and preview rings; refer to *Table 4.1*. Some details about the different channels can be found in *Figure 4.1*:

Pre-Release Channels

Channel	Dev Channel	Beta Channel	Release Preview Channel
Suggested Users	Very technical users, a few key members of IT team, ideally on test machines.	Early adopters, usually IT staff, but on non-test machines for more real-world testing	Key power-users
Group Type	Device based	Device based	Device
Description	This is the very latest Windows builds at the very early stages of the development lifecycle and should be used for testing.	These builds are more than likely going to become full releases, but may have some issues.	Access releases a few weeks early to fully test the user experience and applications. Best for key users across the estate.
Concerns	More likely to crash. Regular updates which may require restarts. Some features may appear and then be removed.	Updates are validated. More stable than dev channel.	Fully supported builds, no concerns over a standard release
Update Ring	Pilot (or earlier)	Pilot	Preview

Figure 4.1 – Pre-release channels

- **Automatic update behavior**: Here, you can set when updates are downloaded and installed, including active hours. If you select **Reset to default**, the machine will detect the active hours and install accordingly. Set this as appropriate for your environment (for example, 7:00 A.M. to 7:00 P.M. for your standard office workers).

- **Restart Checks**: Checks whether the battery life is over 40%, a user is at the machine, it is not in presentation mode, a full-screen app is being used, a user is mid-phone call or mid-game, and so on.
- **Option to pause Windows updates**: You can pause updates centrally. This happens at the user level.
- **Option to check for Windows updates**: This allows or stops users from checking for updates.
- **Use deadline settings**: This forces updates to be installed, provides a grace period, and allows auto-updates. It is usually best to turn this on so that you can force a reboot on end user devices so that they cannot constantly postpone and leave the devices at risk.

As mentioned earlier, here are some recommended settings:

Update Channel	Pilot Ring	Preview Ring	Broad Ring	VIP Ring
Service Channel	Beta	Release preview	Retail	Retail
Quality Deferral	0	7 days	10 days	30 days
Feature Deferral	0	0	0	0

Table 4.1 – Windows Update recommended settings

5. Once you have configured your settings, click **Next**.
6. Now, we need to assign the policy. For our pilot, preview, and VIP policies, it is a straightforward process – simply assign them to the groups we created earlier.
7. Once you have added your assignments, click **Next**.

   We need the broad ring to collect *everything* not assigned to the other rings so that we can ensure all of the devices are being updated. So, we will create an included assignment under **Autopilot Devices** but exclude the other rings:

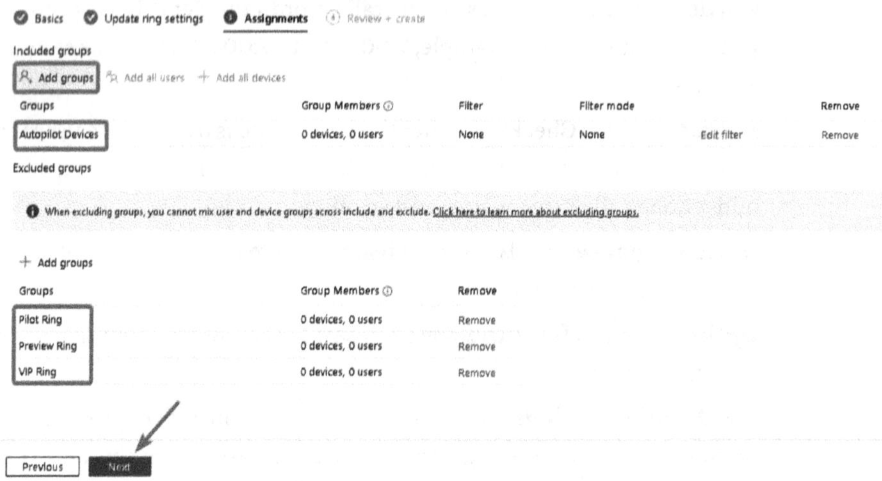

Figure 4.2 – Broad update ring assignment

As mentioned earlier, ensure that your preview/pilot groups contain devices!

8. Review your settings and click **Create**.

   VIP Ring is for your mission-critical devices (and often executive users) and is where you want full control over when they install and reboot.

   Often, it is best to disable forced reboot and set a maintenance window where someone can be present at the machine to ensure everything installs and reboots OK. All deferrals are set to the maximum as well to give the maximum time to test updates first.

Now that we have created our Windows update rings, we need to configure feature update rings that match.

Building feature updates

Now that we have the update rings in place, we need to look after the feature updates as we set all deferrals to 0 days; otherwise, the machines are all going to upgrade to Windows 11 or any new semi-annual release on the following Patch Tuesday:

1. Within the Intune portal, click **Devices** | **Windows** | **Windows Updates**, click **Feature updates** in the top bar then **+ Create** and select **Create feature update policy**.

   Generally, you want your devices to be on a fixed version across the estate, but should you have specific requirements, you can create multiple profiles here and include/exclude them accordingly.

For this example, we will set devices to the current latest Windows 11 25H2 version. This policy will bring all devices to Windows 11 25H2 and fix them there until we update the policy. When 26H2 is released, the devices will remain on 25H2 unless this policy is updated accordingly. We will also enable the setting to keep any devices that are not compatible with Windows 11 on the latest Windows 10 build:

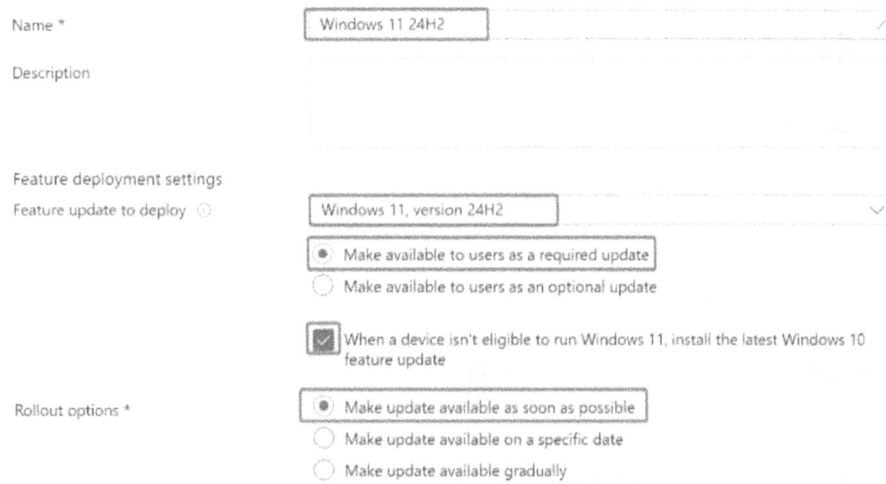

Figure 4.3 – Feature update settings

Note that the feature update list only includes operating system versions that are within their support date, so if you are running anything pre-Windows 10 21H1, your machines are going to upgrade to whatever you set here.

You can also specify the rollout options to gradually deploy for larger estates. You can also create multiple policies with specific dates and use your assignment groups to target should you want more control.

2. Once you have configured these settings, click **Next**.
3. To align everything, assign the policies to **Autopilot Devices** to capture everything in the estate. Then, click **Next**.
4. Now, review your policy and click **Create**.

Now that we have configured our update settings in the UI, we can look at how to automate the process.

Automating it

In this section, we will cover how to automate our update rings and feature updates for quicker, more reliable deployments.

Building update rings

There is a lot of repetition when creating all of these policies. So, for this example, we will use the broad ring as that is the most complex to assign.

A PowerShell script is included in this book's GitHub repository that will deploy and assign all four of the update rings; you can amend the JSON based on the knowledge you will have picked up when configuring this one. Run these scripts in a PowerShell editor of your choice; remember to connect to Microsoft Graph first:

1. As usual, start with our variables – in this case, group IDs:

```
$pilotgroupid = "xxxxxxxx-xxxx-xxxx-xxxx-xxxxxxxxxxxx"
$previewgroupid = "xxxxxxxx-xxxx-xxxx-xxxx-xxxxxxxxxxxx"
$broadgroupid = "xxxxxxxx-xxxx-xxxx-xxxx-xxxxxxxxxxxx"
$vipgroupid = "xxxxxxxx-xxxx-xxxx-xxxx-xxxxxxxxxxxx"
```

2. Now, set the URL to create the policy:

```
$url = "https://graph.microsoft.com/beta/deviceManagement/
deviceConfigurations"
```

3. Set the JSON:

```
$broadjson = @"
{
    "@odata.type":
"#microsoft.graph.windowsUpdateForBusinessConfiguration",
    "allowWindows11Upgrade": true,
    "automaticUpdateMode": "autoInstallAtMaintenanceTime",
    "autoRestartNotificationDismissal": "notConfigured",
    "businessReadyUpdatesOnly": "userDefined",
    "deadlineForFeatureUpdatesInDays": 5,
    "deadlineForQualityUpdatesInDays": 5,
    "deadlineGracePeriodInDays": 3,
    "description": "",
    "displayName": "Windows Updates - Broad Ring",
    "driversExcluded": false,
    "engagedRestartDeadlineInDays": null,
    "engagedRestartSnoozeScheduleForFeatureUpdatesInDays": null,
    "engagedRestartSnoozeScheduleInDays": null,
    "engagedRestartTransitionScheduleForFeatureUpdatesInDays": null,
```

```
        "engagedRestartTransitionScheduleInDays": null,
        "featureUpdatesDeferralPeriodInDays": 0,
        "featureUpdatesPaused": false,
        "featureUpdatesRollbackWindowInDays": 10,
        "id": "",
        "installationSchedule": {
            "@odata.type": "#microsoft.graph.windowsUpdateActiveHoursInstall",
            "activeHoursEnd": "17:00:00.0000000",
            "activeHoursStart": "08:00:00.0000000"
        },
        "microsoftUpdateServiceAllowed": true,
        "postponeRebootUntilAfterDeadline": false,
        "qualityUpdatesDeferralPeriodInDays": 10,
        "qualityUpdatesPaused": false,
        "roleScopeTagIds": [],
        "scheduleImminentRestartWarningInMinutes": null,
        "scheduleRestartWarningInHours": null,
        "skipChecksBeforeRestart": false,
        "updateNotificationLevel": "restartWarningsOnly",
        "updateWeeks": null,
        "userPauseAccess": "enabled",
        "userWindowsUpdateScanAccess": "enabled"
    }
"@
```

Here, you can see that `"allowWindows11Upgrade"` is set to `true`, so we are not blocking that one.

The preceding code also sets active hours, deadlines, notifications, and all of the other settings we configured in the GUI. Fortunately, these are all fairly well named, so you can work out what is being set and how to change it as needed.

The only thing to watch out for here is some of the double negatives. If you look at `driversExclude`, setting that to `false` will allow driver updates because we are saying no to a block. If we set `allowWindows11Upgrade` to `true`, this will allow updates

4. Now, create the policy and grab the ID:

```
$broadpolicy = Invoke-MgGraphRequest -Uri $url -Method Post -Body
$broadjson -ContentType "application/json" -OutputType PSObject
$broadpolicyid = $broadpolicy.id
```

5. Populate the ID with the assignment URL:

```
$broadassignurl = "https://graph.microsoft.com/beta/deviceManagement/
deviceConfigurations/$broadpolicyid/assign"
```

6. Then, set the JSON:

```
$broadjsonassign = @"
{
    "assignments": [
        {
            "target": {
                "@odata.type": "#microsoft.graph.groupAssignmentTarget",
                "groupId": "$broadgroupid"
            }
        },
        {
            "target": {
                "@odata.type":
"#microsoft.graph.exclusionGroupAssignmentTarget",
                "groupId": "$pilotgroupid"
            }
        },
        {
            "target": {
                "@odata.type":
"#microsoft.graph.exclusionGroupAssignmentTarget",
                "groupId": "$previewgroupid"
            }
        },
        {
            "target": {
                "@odata.type":
"#microsoft.graph.exclusionGroupAssignmentTarget",
                "groupId": "$vipgroupid"
            }
        }
    ]
}
"@
```

As you can see, we are using both included and excluded groups here. They are differentiated by `@odata.type`:

```
#microsoft.graph.groupAssignmentTarget - INCLUDED
#microsoft.graph.exclusionGroupAssignmentTarget - EXCLUDED
```

7. Finally, assign the policy:

```
Invoke-MgGraphRequest -Method POST -Uri $broadassignurl -Body
$broadjsonassign -ContentType "application/json"
```

Now that we have automated the update rings, we can look at feature updates.

Building feature updates

While this policy is smaller in terms of code, the update to deploy would normally be taken from the drop-down list in the GUI. So, to avoid having to use that, we are going to grab the options directly from Graph:

1. We still need our fixed variables first:

```
$groupid = "00000000-0000-0000-0000-000000000000"
$description = "Fixes machines on Windows 11 24H2"
$displayname = "Windows 11 24H2"
```

2. To find the available versions, we need to run a `GET` request against this URL: `https://graph.microsoft.com/beta/deviceManagement/windowsUpdateCatalogItems/microsoft.graph.windowsFeatureUpdateCatalogItem`.
   Then, we can output it in grid view format (you may need to use `out-consolegridview` on PowerShell Core for non-Windows operating systems) with passthrough enabled so that selections will be sent to our JSON:

```
$allupdatesurl = "https://graph.microsoft.com/beta/deviceManagement/
windowsUpdateCatalogItems/microsoft.graph.windowsFeatureUpdateCatalogItem"
$availablefeatures = (Invoke-MgGraphRequest -Uri $allupdatesurl -Method GET
-OutputType PSObject).value
$latest = $availablefeatures | Out-GridView -PassThru
$selected = $latest.version
```

3. Set the URL:

```
$createurl = "https://graph.microsoft.com/beta/deviceManagement/
windowsFeatureUpdateProfiles"
```

4. Create the JSON:

```
$createjson = @"
{
    "description": "$description",
    "displayName": "$displayname",
    "featureUpdateVersion": "$selected",
    "installFeatureUpdatesOptional": false,
    "installLatestWindows10OnWindows11IneligibleDevice": true,
    "roleScopeTagIds": [],
    "rolloutSettings": {
        "offerEndDateTimeInUTC": null,
        "offerIntervalInDays": null,
        "offerStartDateTimeInUTC": null
    }
}
"@
```

5. Create the policy, grab the ID, and assign it:

```
$policy = Invoke-MgGraphRequest -Method POST -Uri $createurl -Body
$createjson -ContentType "application/json" -OutputType PSObject
$policyid = $policy.id
$assignurl = "https://graph.microsoft.com/beta/deviceManagement/
windowsFeatureUpdateProfiles/$policyid/assign"
$assignjson = @"
{
    "assignments": [
        {
            "target": {
                "@odata.type": "#microsoft.graph.groupAssignmentTarget",
                "groupId": "$groupid"
            }
        }
    ]
}
```

```
"@
Invoke-MgGraphRequest -Method POST -Uri $assignurl -Body $assignjson -
ContentType "application/json" -OutputType PSObject
```

This script will create a feature update policy using PowerShell and Graph.

There's more...

There might be occasions when you need to expedite quality updates on machines that are considerably out of date.

For this, you can use the **Quality Updates** option within Intune.

Normally, your update rings will tackle quality updates without any issues. If you need to rapidly deploy expedited updates, this is configured in the same way as the feature updates we configured earlier.

There are plenty of warnings here, which is why this is for only critical situations.

You can set the minimum update level and then specify when to force an update. The maximum is two days, so you can see how urgent these updates are. Users will *not* be allowed to postpone this reboot – you have been warned!

Configuring driver updates

You can also use Intune to gain finer control over driver updates on your devices so that you can include automatic deployments or manual approval before deploying. This will allow you to test drivers for any issues before a full-scale deployment.

Intune will automatically check your estate and populate the drivers as appropriate. If you have chosen not to share telemetry with Microsoft, you will need to do so for driver updates to present themselves.

How to do it...

Follow these steps:

1. First, select **Devices** and then **Windows updates**.
2. Now, click **Driver Updates** and create a new profile.
3. Specify your profile's name and a description and click **Next**.
   Here, you must set whether you want updates to be manually approved or automatically updated. Note that you cannot change this setting after configuring it; you will need to delete the profile and create a new one.

4. In this case, we are going to manually manage drivers for greater control. Once selected, click **Next**.

   If you select **Automatic**, you will be given a second prompt to set the number of days before drivers are approved.

5. We are not setting scope tags in this example, so click **Next**.

6. Assignments are very much device-based policies, so it is best to assign to device groups until filters are available.

   In this case, we are going to assign to Autopilot devices.

7. Confirm that everything looks correct and click **Create**.

With that, we have created a driver update policy in the UI. Now, we can look at the automation process.

Automating it

This is one of the easiest policies to automate as it only has one real setting, whose options are *manual* and *automatic*.

It sends a `POST` request to `deviceManagement/windowsdDriverUpdateProfiles`. Follow these steps:

1. As usual, we will start with the basics:

```
$name = "Driver Updates"
$description = "Driver Update Management"
$groupid = "000000-0000-0000-0000-000000000000"
```

2. Now, configure the approval type:

```
$driversetting = "manual"
```

3. Set the URL:

```
$url = "https://graph.microsoft.com/beta/deviceManagement/
windowsDriverUpdateProfiles"
```

4. Populate the JSON:

```
$json = @"
{
    "approvalType": "$driversetting",
    "description": "$description",
```

```
    "displayName": "$name",
    "roleScopeTagIds": [
        "0"
    ]
}
"@
```

As mentioned earlier, if you select **Automatic**, you also need to set the number of days before approval:

```
    "approvalType": "automatic",
    "deploymentDeferralInDays": 3,
```

5. Create the profile and grab the ID:

```
$driverpolicy = Invoke-MgGraphRequest -Method POST -uri $url -body $json -
ContentType "application/json" -OutputType PSObject
$policyid = $driverpolicy.id
```

6. Populate the URL and JSON and assign them:

```
$assignurl = "https://graph.microsoft.com/beta/deviceManagement/
windowsDriverUpdateProfiles/$policyid/assign"
$assignjson = @"
{
    "assignments": [
        {
            "target": {
                "@odata.type": "#microsoft.graph.groupAssignmentTarget",
                "groupId": "$groupid"
            }
        }
    ]
}
"@
Invoke-MgGraphRequest -Method POST -uri $assignurl -body $assignjson -
ContentType "application/json" -OutputType PSObject
```

With that, you have automated your first driver deployment policy.

There's more...

After a day or two, Intune will grab your device details and show you any outstanding driver updates to review:

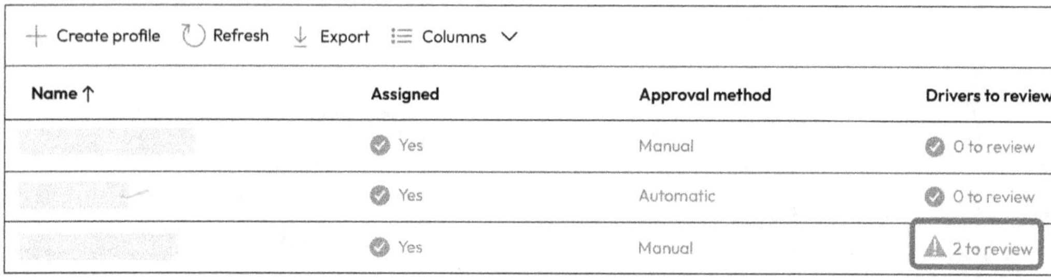

Figure 4.4 – Driver approval

Clicking the blue text link under **Drivers to review** will take you to the drivers, where you can approve or pause the updates. When approving, you can select the date for Windows Update to grab the drivers:

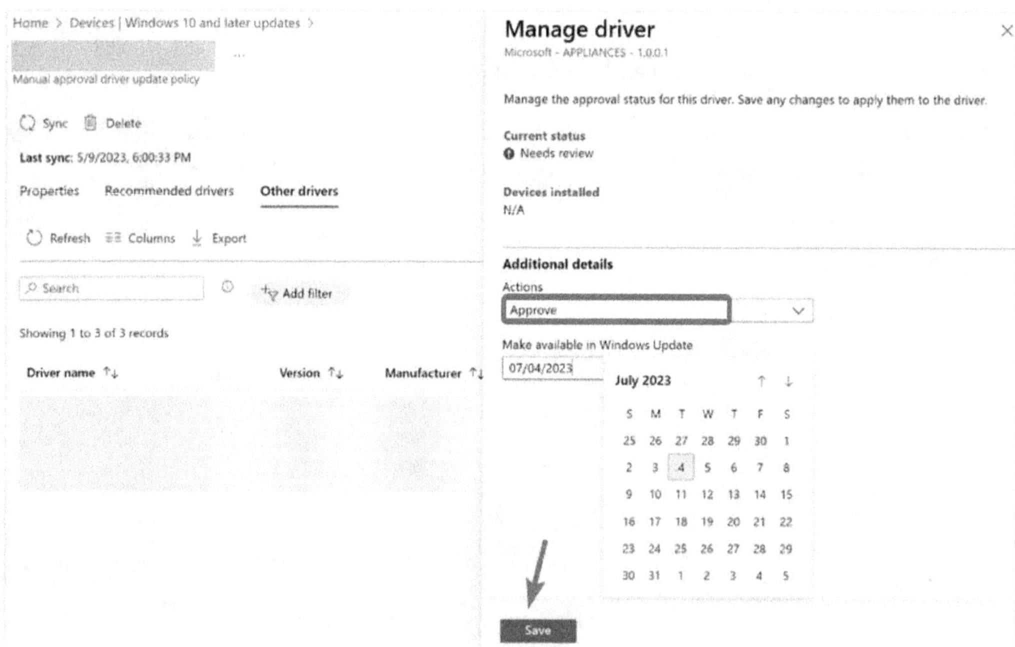

Figure 4.5 – Approving the driver

You can find out more here: `https://learn.microsoft.com/en-us/mem/intune/protect/windows-driver-updates-overview`.

We have covered how to manually configure our update rings, but is there a better way?

Enrolling and using Autopatch

If you have any of these licenses, Autopatch is available to you: M365 Business Premium, M365 E3, M365 E5, M365 A3, M365 A5, or M365 F3. Instead of manually configuring and populating your Windows update rings, you can use Windows Autopatch from Microsoft. This is a semi-managed service that automates updates for Windows, Microsoft Office, Microsoft Teams, Edge, drivers, SQL ODBC, and .NET. When using Autopatch, Microsoft can also centrally pause updates so that if it notices that a particular update is causing issues, it can block it before it is installed on your devices and then automatically resume it when the issue has been resolved.

As well as the *click-and-forget* option, you can also use Autopatch groups for more granular control over your updates. This will be covered in the *There's more...* section of this recipe.

How to do it...

Enrolling devices into Autopatch is incredibly easy and just requires setting up one of the following policies within your Windows Update settings:

- Update ring
- Quality update
- Driver update
- Feature update

For this example, we will configure a quality update policy as we have not previously covered that in depth in the previous recipes:

1. Click on **Devices** and then **Windows updates**, and then click on the **Quality Updates** tab.
2. Click **Create** and then **Windows quality update policy**.

3. Enter a name and description and click **Next**.

   Quality updates are pretty simple; you may also notice that this is where you can enable "**hotpatch**" for updating devices without a reboot.

4. You cannot disable a Windows quality update policy, so simply select whether you want to use hotpatch and click **Next**:

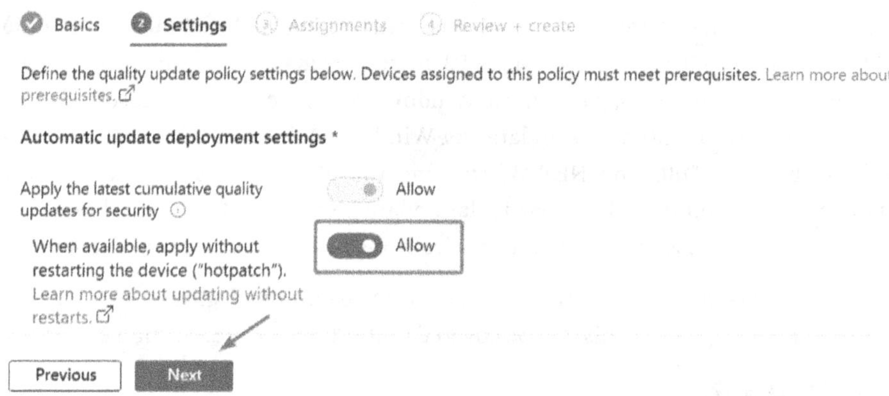

Figure 4.6 – Creating a quality update policy

5. Assign the policy to the **Intune-Users** group and click **Next**.
6. Review that the settings are correct and click **Create**:

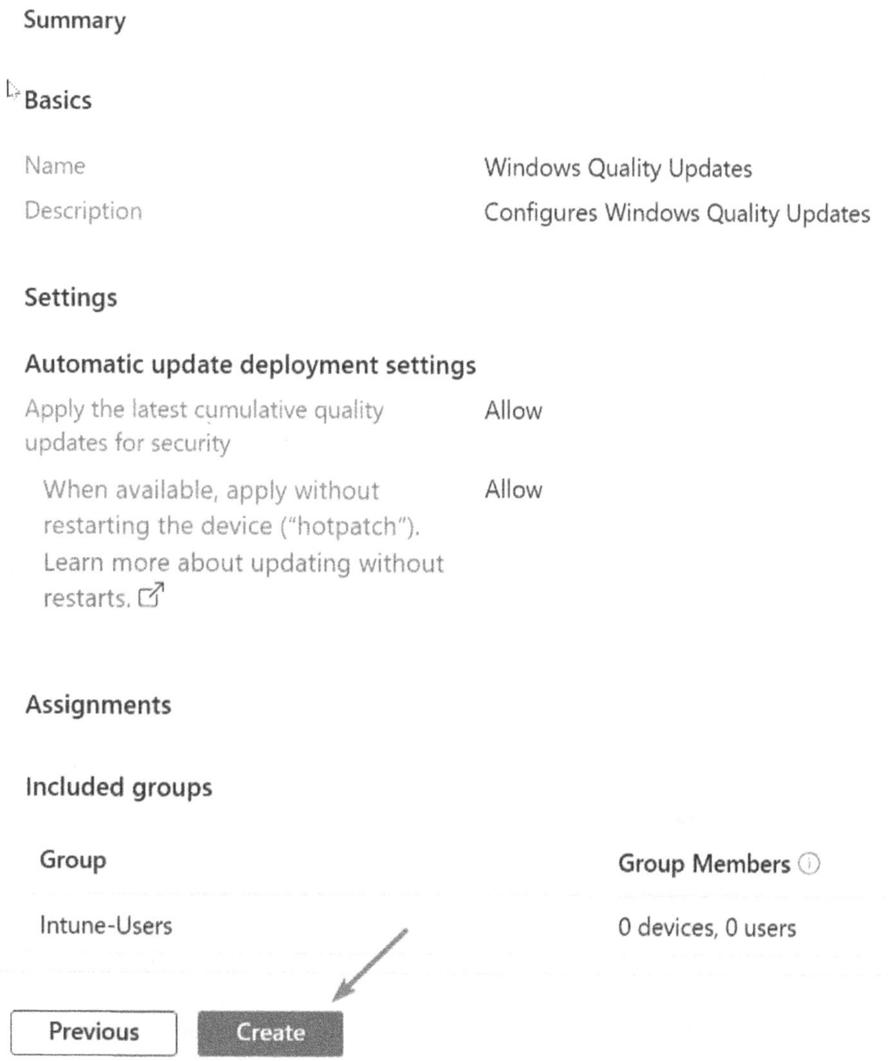

Figure 4.7 – Final quality update policy review

With this recipe, we have successfully enrolled our tenant into Windows Autopatch.

Automating it

As we have chosen a quality update policy, automating it is incredibly straightforward as we simply turn on hotpatch and push out the policy:

1. As always, we begin with the basics:

```
$name = "Windows Update Quality Policy"
$description = "Enables Quality Updates with HotPatch for Autopatch"
$groupid = "xxxxxxxx-xxxx-xxxx-xxxx-xxxxxxxxxxxx"
$url = "https://graph.microsoft.com/beta/deviceManagement/
windowsQualityUpdatePolicies"
```

2. Then, we configure the JSON, which in this case is a true/false for hotpatch:

```
$json = @"
{
    "description": "$description",
    "displayName": "$name",
    "hotpatchEnabled": true,
    "roleScopeTagIds": []
}
"@
```

3. Then we create the policy and grab the ID:

```
$updatepolicy = Invoke-MgGraphRequest -Uri $url -Method Post -Body $json -
OutputType PSObject -ContentType "application/json"
$updatepolicyid = $updatepolicy.id
```

4. Populate the assignment URL and add the group ID to the JSON request:

```
$assignurl = "https://graph.microsoft.com/beta/deviceManagement/
windowsQualityUpdatePolicies/$updatepolicyid/assign"
$assignjson = @"
{
    "assignments": [
        {
            "target": {
                "@odata.type": "#microsoft.graph.groupAssignmentTarget",
                "groupId": "$groupid"
```

```
            }
        }
    ]
}
"@
```

5. Finally, send the POST request to assign the policy:

```
Invoke-MgGraphRequest -Uri $assignurl -Method Post -Body $assignjson -
OutputType PSObject -ContentType "application/json"
```

There's more...

While for most, using Autopatch is an excellent way of letting Microsoft deal with the entire Windows Update service, including patch windows (in preview at the time of writing), in larger organizations, you may want more granular control over quality and feature updates (especially when you are planning larger operating system upgrades). For this, you can use Autopatch groups, which allow you to configure additional update rings and populate them with custom Entra ID groups.

You could use this to deploy by department or building, or use hardware-specific details such as make or manufacturer. As these are standard Entra ID groups, you can also use dynamic device queries to automate this for you.

To configure this, navigate to **Tenant Management | Windows Autopatch** and click **Autopatch groups**.

You can create up to 49 groups on top of the default one, so even larger organizations can use this for a phased rollout.

When adding groups, you can have a minimum of 2 or a maximum of 15.

To add groups, carry out the following steps:

1. Click **Create**.
2. Set **Name** and **Description** values and click **Next: Deployment rings**.
   On the next screen, you can use **static** or **dynamic** groups, but these differ from the Entra ID groups of the same name.

   For a dynamic group, you can point Autopatch to a single group; it automatically splits the devices between the rings. In this example, we will use static groups as we want as much control as possible.
3. We have created four Entra ID groups – **Test Devices**, **Ring 1**, **Ring 2**, and **Remainder**.

4. On the **Add Autopatch group** screen, click **Add deployment ring** twice to add additional rings.
5. For each ring, click **Add group to ring** and select the groups we created earlier.
6. Once you have added your groups, click **Next: Windows update settings**.
7. Here, you can click the three dots to configure the relevant settings, as covered earlier in this recipe. Once you have done so, click **Next: Review + create**.
8. Confirm that the settings are correct and click **Create**.

That completes our recipe on Windows Autopatch. Now, we can look at **Windows Hello for Business** (**WHfB**).

Configuring Windows Hello for Business

WHfB provides **multi-factor authentication** (**MFA**) on Windows devices via either PIN, biometrics (face or fingerprint), or a FIDO2 security key.

This can be configured either at a tenant level (via the device enrollment menu) or at a more granular level using the settings catalog. In this recipe, we will cover both methods, starting with the tenant level, as that needs to be left set to **Not Configured** for the settings catalog to work.

The recommended approach, however, is to use the settings catalog.

How to do it...

We will start this recipe by covering how to enable WUfB in the GUI.

Configuring at the tenant level

Follow these steps:

1. Navigate to **Devices**, then **Enrollment**, and click on the **Windows** tab. Then, click on **Windows Hello for Business**.

   This will load a fly-out window where we can configure the **Configure Windows Hello for Business** and **Use security keys for sign-in** settings.
2. Change **Configure Windows Hello for Business** from **Not Configured** to **Enabled**. This will load up further options to be configured.
3. TPM is required for Windows 11 anyway, so it makes sense to require it here as well.
4. The other settings are environment-specific; the options for **Lowercase**, **Uppercase**, and **Special characters** are **Not Allowed**, **Allowed**, and **Required**.
5. Here, you can also set a PIN expiry time and how many previous PINs are remembered before they can be reused. This requires a balance of enforcing a secure PIN setup, but

not being too complicated as this results in users either forgetting or, worse still, writing down their PIN.

One important thing to keep in mind is that this PIN is *only* set on the device. The same PIN will not work on any other devices unless the same PIN was configured while setting up WHfB. This PIN will also not work on any Microsoft 365 apps. If you are using SSO, it will access the machine, which will then send the password to Microsoft 365 apps, but the PIN itself is device-level only. Most environment attacks are remote and not on the device itself.

If a user gets the PIN wrong more than once, they will be prompted to reboot to attempt another PIN login.

6. The next option is to allow biometric authentication – that is, face or fingerprint. You will still need to set a PIN for recovery when using these options.
7. Anti-spoofing requires specific cameras and adds an extra layer of security when using facial recognition. It is worth enabling when it becomes available.
8. Finally, allow phone sign-in using a supported application on a mobile device (such as Microsoft Authenticator) to act as an authentication method for Windows.
9. The other available setting is **Use Security keys for sign-on**, which allows FIDO2 authentication keys for device login.
10. Once you have configured your settings, click **Save**.

This recipe covered how to enable WHfB at the tenant level, but you may have scenarios where you only want specific user groups to use WHfB. We will look at this next.

Configuring at the group level

As you saw on the previous fly-out, these settings are automatically applied to all users with no way of excluding users. If this does not work for your environment, you can switch the global configuration to **Not Configured** (which is the default if it was not previously configured) and use a settings catalog policy instead:

1. For this, navigate to **Devices**, then **Windows**, then **Configuration**, and click **Create Profile**.
2. Select **Windows 10 and Later**, then **Settings Catalog**, and click **+ Create** and select **+ New Policy**.
3. Specify **Name** and **Description** values and click **Next**.
4. Click **Add Settings** and find **Windows Hello for Business** toward the bottom of the categories.

   There is a mix of user and device settings in this category, so do not select all settings. Instead, select any settings that apply to your environment. In this case, we are selecting the same settings that we did at the tenant level, plus adding a few features that are only available here (such as enhanced anti-spoofing for facial features).

You could also combine the two: use the tenant-level settings for most, and add to it with a settings catalog policy; just watch out for conflicts.

5. Once you have configured your settings, click **Next**:
6. On the **Scope tags** page, click **Next**.
7. Assign permissions as required for your environment. Remember that you can duplicate settings catalog policies to quickly create near-identical policies if needed. Then, click **Next**.
8. Review the configuration and click **Create**.

Now that we know how to manually configure the settings, let's look at how to automate this from the command line.

Automating it

This section will cover how we can configure WHfB using automation.

Configuring at the tenant level

The JSON for this one is very straightforward, but the catch here is that the URL requires the policy ID of the existing WHfB configuration:

1. To do that, we need to run a `GET` request against the following URL:

```
https://graph.microsoft.com/beta/deviceManagement/
deviceEnrollmentConfigurations
```

2. This will return all of the enrollment and restriction policies, so we need to filter further on our results using `where-object` and look for the following `@odata.type`:

```
#microsoft.graph.deviceEnrollmentWindowsHelloForBusinessConfiguration
```

Let's wrap all of this so that we only retrieve the ID:

```
$policyid = ((Invoke-MgGraphRequest -Method GET -uri "https://
graph.microsoft.com/beta/deviceManagement/deviceEnrollmentConfigurations" -
OutputType PSObject).value | where-object '@odata.type' -eq
"#microsoft.graph.deviceEnrollmentWindowsHelloForBusinessConfiguration").id
```

3. Now that we have the ID, we can populate the URL:

```
$url = "https://graph.microsoft.com/beta/deviceManagement/
deviceEnrollmentConfigurations/$policyid"
```

4. Now, we can configure the JSON, which, fortunately, is straightforward and understandable:

```
$json = @"
{
    "@odata.type":
"#microsoft.graph.deviceEnrollmentWindowsHelloForBusinessConfiguration",
    "enhancedBiometricsState": "enabled",
    "pinLowercaseCharactersUsage": "allowed",
    "pinPreviousBlockCount": 3,
    "pinSpecialCharactersUsage": "allowed",
    "pinUppercaseCharactersUsage": "allowed",
    "securityDeviceRequired": true,
    "securityKeyForSignIn": "enabled",
    "state": "enabled"
}
"@
```

5. Finally, deploy it. As it is an existing policy, it is a PATCH request:

```
Invoke-MgGraphRequest -Method PATCH -Uri $url -Body $json -ContentType
"application/json" -OutputType PSObject
```

Now that we have configured WHfB at the tenant level, we can look at the granular approach.

Configuring at the group level

Here, we will use the settings catalog, which we ran through in *Chapter 2, Configuring Your New Tenant for Windows Devices*. Following on from what we learned there, we need to look at the settings within `Category ID`:

```
e7ae2b99-0479-475f-af5c-96457121fcd0
```

Some of the values will be `true` or `false`, such as **Allow Biometrics**:

```
device_vendor_msft_passportforwork_biometrics_usebiometrics_true
```

Others will have a `1/0` (enabled/disabled) value, such as **Use Security Key for Sign-In**:

```
device_vendor_msft_passportforwork_securitykey_usesecuritykeyforsignin_1
```

Those that require a numeric value simply have this set:

```
"value": 3
```

The full script is available in this book's GitHub repository, so we will only configure one setting here:

1. Set the URL as usual:

```
$settingsurl = "https://graph.microsoft.com/beta/deviceManagement/
configurationPolicies"
```

2. Configure the JSON:

```
$json = @"
{
    "description": "",
    "name": "Windows Hello for Business",
    "platforms": "windows10",
    "roleScopeTagIds": [
        "0"
    ],
    "settings": [
        {
            "@odata.type":
"#microsoft.graph.deviceManagementConfigurationSetting",
            "settingInstance": {
                "@odata.type":
"#microsoft.graph.deviceManagementConfigurationChoiceSettingInstance",
                "choiceSettingValue": {
                    "@odata.type":
"#microsoft.graph.deviceManagementConfigurationChoiceSettingValue",
                    "children": [],
                    "value":
"device_vendor_msft_passportforwork_biometrics_usebiometrics_true"
                },
                "settingDefinitionId":
```

```
"device_vendor_msft_passportforwork_biometrics_usebiometrics"
            }
        }
    ],
    "technologies": "mdm"
}
"@
Run it and output to a variable as we will need the ID for assignment:
$policy = Invoke-MgGraphRequest -Uri $settingsurl -Method Post -Body $json
-ContentType "application/json" -OutputType PSObject
$policyid = $policy.id
```

3. Set the group ID and assign it accordingly:

```
$groupid = "xxxxxxxx-xxxx-xxxx-xxxx-xxxxxxxxxxxx"
$assignurl = "https://graph.microsoft.com/beta/deviceManagement/
configurationPolicies/$policyid/assign"
$assignjson = @"
{
    "assignments": [
        {
            "target": {
                "@odata.type": "#microsoft.graph.groupAssignmentTarget",
                "groupId": "$groupid"
            }
        }
    ]
}
"@
Invoke-MgGraphRequest -Uri $assignurl -Method Post -Body $assignjson -
ContentType "application/json" -OutputType PSObject
```

That covers setting up WHfB at the group level.

Setting up Windows Autopilot enrollment profiles

Now that we have our policies in place to manage devices, we can start configuring the policies so that we can enroll and provision them. The first of these is the Windows Autopilot enrollment profile, which tells the device what to do when it hits the Autopilot service during the **out-of-the-box experience** (**OOBE**).

This recipe will cover Windows Autopilot profiles (sometimes referred to as v1); the next recipe will look at the newer Windows Autopilot device preparation policies.

You can have multiple profiles assigned to different Entra ID groups, usually using the group tag functionality, which we will cover in *Chapter 14*. By using group tags when adding devices to Autopilot, you can then add devices to Dynamic Entra ID groups and assign them to the appropriate Autopilot profile. Here are a couple of examples of why you would want multiple profiles:

- **Kiosk devices (using self-deploying mode)**: These profiles self-deploy and require no user input during provisioning. This means they can be configured to automatically sign in using a local device account. You can then configure policies to force them to run in a single application mode, often a web browser.
- **International organizations**: You specify the operating system language during Autopilot provisioning, so you could use group tags to assign a different profile based on the language required.

How to do it...

For this example, we will set up a standard user-driven deployment. Follow these steps to configure and amend the deployment as appropriate for your environment:

1. Navigate to **Devices**, then **Enrollment**. Select **Windows** and then click on **Deployment Profiles**.
2. Click **Create Profile** and select **Windows PC**.
3. Specify the profile's name and description. You also have the **Convert all targeted devices to Autopilot** option. If you target this profile at an Entra ID group containing devices not enrolled or provisioned via Autopilot, it will automatically enroll them into the service, and any future device resets will automatically go through Autopilot during the OOBE.
4. In our case, we are only targeting Autopilot devices, but there is no harm in setting it to **Yes** anyway. Then, click **Next**.

   On the next screen, we can set the basic settings during the OOBE, including the language and what users can see when they are setting up their devices.
5. In this case, **Deployment mode** needs to be user-driven, which is where the user logs in during the OOBE and configures accordingly. Self-driven is for Kiosk-type devices where there is no fixed user.
6. Leave **Join to Microsoft Entra ID as** set to **Microsoft Entra joined**. Hybrid join is possible but does not work well with Autopilot and should be avoided where possible.

As we are configuring a whole new tenant and environment, try to avoid bringing technical debt with you.

7. The best practice is to always keep **User Account Type** set to **Standard**. There are ways around providing administrative rights as required, including using the Entra ID role, which we covered in *Chapter 1*, Windows LAPS, as covered in *Chapter 3*, or Endpoint Privilege Management, as will be covered in *Chapter 14*.
   Allow pre-provisioned deployments (previously called **White Glove**). This is where an IT admin can, during the OOBE, press the Windows key five times and pre-configure all of the device-targeted policies and applications, leaving the user just needing to complete the user enrollment steps. This can be useful where you have quite a heavy deployment or users on low-bandwidth connections, but it is also worth looking at how quickly your environment changes. If you have applications with regular updates, you may find users receiving devices with out-of-date applications if the device has been pre-provisioned too far in advance.

   We are also configuring a device naming template of the serial number of the device (or `%SERIAL%`). With Intune, the device name is a lot less important than it used to be, so this is not hugely important.
8. When you have configured the settings as required for your environment, click **Next**.
9. Now, we want to assign this to our Autopilot devices group. This group is set to add devices as soon as they are enrolled onto the Autopilot service and, therefore, picks them up quicker. Add the group and click **Next**.
10. Finally, review your settings and click **Create**.

This section has covered configuring our first deployment profile. Now, we can look at automating it using PowerShell and Graph.

Automating it

Now that we know how to configure our profile in the GUI, let's learn how to automate it:

1. As usual, first, we need to set our group ID:

```
$groupid = "xxxxxxxx-xxxx-xxxx-xxxx-xxxxxxxxxxxx"
```

2. Now, we need to set the URL. This time, we will be adding to `windowsDeviceAutopilotProfiles`:

```
$autopiloturl = "https://graph.microsoft.com/beta/deviceManagement/
windowsAutopilotDeploymentProfiles"
```

3. When looking at the JSON, note that there is a nested array covering the OOBE settings. Amend the settings as required. For the description, \ adds a line break. Watch for any special characters – they will cause the deployment to fail:

```
$json = @"
{
    "@odata.type":
"#microsoft.graph.azureADWindowsAutopilotDeploymentProfile",
    "description": "User Driven\nNon Administrators\nSerial Device Name",
    "deviceNameTemplate": "%SERIAL%",
    "deviceType": "windowsPc",
    "displayName": "Autopilot Profile",
    "enableWhiteGlove": true,
    "extractHardwareHash": true,
    "hybridAzureADJoinSkipConnectivityCheck": false,
    "language": "en-GB",
    "outOfBoxExperienceSettings": {
        "deviceUsageType": "singleUser",
        "hideEscapeLink": true,
        "hideEULA": true,
        "hidePrivacySettings": true,
        "skipKeyboardSelectionPage": true,
        "userType": "standard"
    },
    "roleScopeTagIds": []
}
"@
```

4. Now, we need to deploy the profile and grab the ID to populate the assignment URL:

```
$policy = Invoke-MgGraphRequest -Method POST -Uri $autopiloturl -Body $json
-ContentType "application/json" -OutputType PSObject
$policyid = $policy.id
$assignurl = "https://graph.microsoft.com/beta/deviceManagement/
windowsAutopilotDeploymentProfiles/$policyid/assignments"
```

5. The assignment JSON is the same as it is for any other policy:

```
$assignjson = @"
{
    "target": {
        "@odata.type": "#microsoft.graph.groupAssignmentTarget",
        "groupId": "$groupid"
    }
}
"@
Invoke-MgGraphRequest -Method POST -Uri $assignurl -Body $assignjson -
ContentType "application/json" -OutputType PSObject
```

That covers your deployment profile. The next recipe covers your **Enrollment Status Page** (**ESP**).

Configuring Autopilot device preparation

One of the drawbacks of Autopilot was the requirement to harvest the hardware hash and add it to Autopilot prior to being able to enroll devices. This restricted the ability to let staff simply grab any off-the-shelf device in an emergency without needing IT support. With device preparation, all that is needed is for an admin to add the serial number into Intune, and Autopilot will handle the rest.

Getting ready

Before we can configure our policy, we need an Entra group, which Autopilot can add the devices to for Enrollment Time Grouping. This group also needs a particular owner for this to be completed:

1. Click in **Groups** and click **New group**.
2. Add a name and description and then click the blue **No owners selected** text.

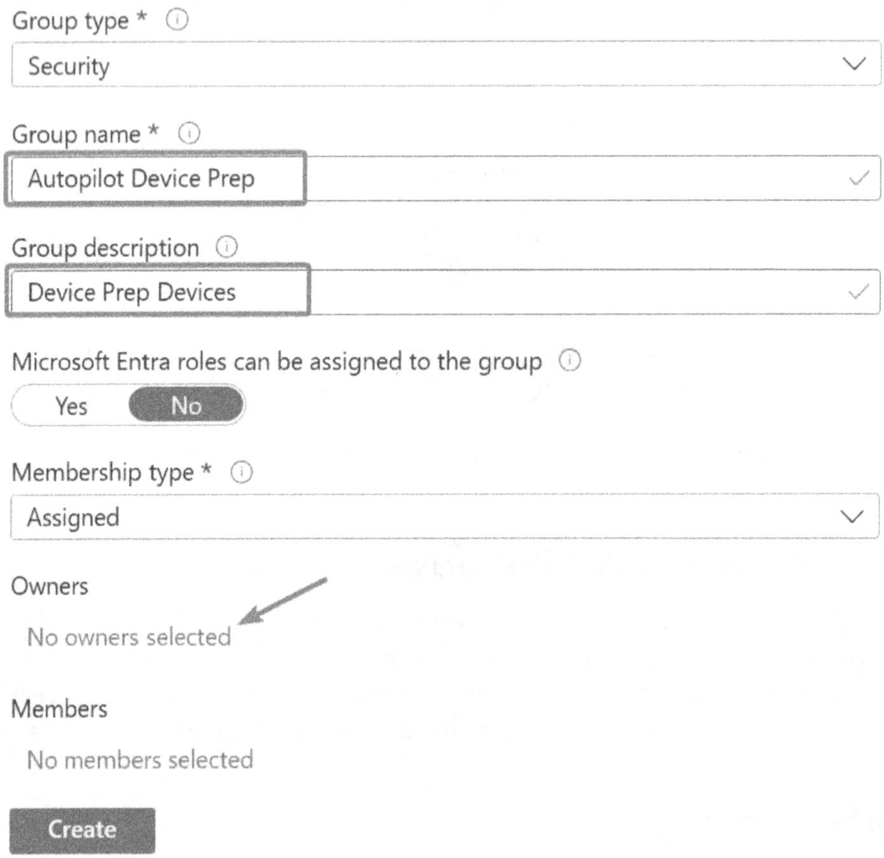

Figure 4.8 – Creating the device preparation group

3. Search for **Intune Provisioning Client** (ID `f1346770-5b25-470b-88bd-d5744ab7952c`). On some tenants, this will not exist, so run this script to add it:

```
$spid = "f1346770-5b25-470b-88bd-d5744ab7952c"
 $appregid = New-MgServicePrincipal -BodyParameter $ServicePrincipalId
```

4. Once added and selected, click **Create**.

Make a note of the group ID as we will need that for our automation.

How to do it...

These steps will walk through how to create our new Autopilot device preparation policy to start enrolling devices:

1. Now that we have our device group created, click **Devices** – **Enrollment** and click **Device Preparation Policies**.
2. Click **Create** and select **User Driven**.
   The new device preparation configuration combines the traditional Autopilot profile and the ESP into one location, so we have more options available to us here.
3. First, click **Next** on the introduction screen.
4. Add a name and description and click **Next**.
5. We now need to find the device group created earlier, search for it, and select it. Then, click **Next**
6. Now we set the ESP style settings. In **Deployment settings**, change **User account type** to **Standard user** by sliding the bar. Hybrid join is not an option here, so the other boxes have a dropdown, but no further options inside.
7. Set **Out-of-box experience settings** to suit your environment. I would suggest no more than a 120-minute time-out and let users skip after multiple failures, so at least you can troubleshoot from the desktop.
8. You can now select up to 10 apps to deploy. Note that they have to be deployed to the same device security group created earlier. While you can have 10, the fewer the better, as with the previous Autopilot; stick to those that are critical for the user to start working, or security software.
   A similar approach is required with the scripts; again, only pick scripts that are critical prior to login, security registry keys, debloat scripts, and so on.
9. Once you have configured everything, click **Next**. In this case, I will deploy Microsoft 365 apps and a debloat script to demonstrate when automating.
10. We do not need scope tags at this point. Click **Next**.
11. On the **Assignments** screen, we need to select a user-based group as this is a user-led deployment. Select **Intune-Users** and click **Next**.
12. If you are confident that everything looks correct, click **Save**.

Automating it

As you can imagine, when automating this, we need to reference a lot of IDs for groups, apps, and scripts. It is also settings catalog-based, so you can find the full script on GitHub, which will just include the important parts to watch for. As with all settings catalog policies, it is the "value" fields you are looking for:

1. The first thing we will need is the group ID we grabbed earlier, as well as the IDs of both the script and application.

   The easiest way to find these is to load them in the UI and find them in the URL:

Figure 4.9 – App ID URL

2. Start by setting the variables we need:

```
$name = " Autopilot Device Preparation Policy"
$description = "Device Preparation Policy for Autopilot"
$createurl = "https://graph.microsoft.com/beta/deviceManagement/
configurationPolicies"
$appid = "00000000-0000-0000-0000-000000000000"
$scriptid = "00000000-0000-0000-0000-000000000000"
$devicegroupid = "00000000-0000-0000-0000-000000000000"
$usergroupid = "00000000-0000-0000-0000-000000000000"
```

3. Populate them into the JSON, in this case, `appID` and `scriptID`:

```
        {
            "settingInstance": {
                "@odata.type":
"#microsoft.graph.deviceManagementConfigurationSimpleSettingCollectionInsta
nce",
                "settingDefinitionId":
"enrollment_autopilot_dpp_allowedappids",
                "settingInstanceTemplateReference": {
                    "settingInstanceTemplateId": "70d22a8a-a03c-4f62-b8df-
dded3e327639"
                },
                "simpleSettingCollectionValue": [
                    {
                        "@odata.type":
```

```
"#microsoft.graph.deviceManagementConfigurationStringSettingValue",
                        "value": "{\"id\":\"$appid\",\"type\":
\"#microsoft.graph.win32LobApp\"}"
                    }
                ]
            }
        },
        {
            "settingInstance": {
                "@odata.type":
"#microsoft.graph.deviceManagementConfigurationSimpleSettingCollectionInsta
nce",
                "settingDefinitionId":
"enrollment_autopilot_dpp_allowedscriptids",
                "settingInstanceTemplateReference": {
                    "settingInstanceTemplateId":
"1bc67702-800c-4271-8fd9-609351cc19cf"
                },
                "simpleSettingCollectionValue": [
                    {
                        "@odata.type":
"#microsoft.graph.deviceManagementConfigurationStringSettingValue",
                        "value": "$scriptid"
                    }
                ]
            }
        }
```

4. We then create the policy and grab the ID:

```
$apdppolicy = Invoke-MgGraphRequest -Uri $createurl -Method Post -Body
$json -ContentType "application/json" -OutputType PSObject
$policyid = $apdppolicy.id
```

5. The unusual step here is that we next assign the device group for Enrollment Time Grouping:

```
$settargeturi = "https://graph.microsoft.com/beta/deviceManagement/
configurationPolicies('$policyid')/setEnrollmentTimeDeviceMembershipTarget"
$settargetjson = @"
{
```

```
    "enrollmentTimeDeviceMembershipTargets": [
        {
            "targetId": "$devicegroupid",
            "targetType": "staticSecurityGroup"
        }
    ]
}
"@
Invoke-MgGraphRequest -Uri $settargeturi -Method Post -Body $settargetjson
-ContentType "application/json" -OutputType PSObject
```

6. Then, finally, comes the user assignment:

```
$assigntargeturi = "https://graph.microsoft.com/beta/deviceManagement/
configurationPolicies('$policyid')/assign"
$assignjson = @"
{
    "assignments": [
        {
            "target": {
                "@odata.type": "#microsoft.graph.groupAssignmentTarget",
                "groupId": "$usergroupid"
            }
        }
    ]
}
"@
Invoke-MgGraphRequest -Uri $assigntargeturi -Method Post -Body $assignjson
-ContentType "application/json" -OutputType PSObject
```

Configuring an Enrollment Status Page (ESP)

The final step before we can deploy a Windows device using Autopilot is to configure our ESP. This is the screen that users see after entering their credentials during the OOBE and displays the progress of their device configuration and onboarding. It also has the potential to be where you will experience most of your issues, so be sure to check out the *There's more...* section for some troubleshooting tips.

> **Note**
>
> This is not required if using Autopilot device preparation.

How to do it...

Follow these instructions:

1. First, navigate to **Devices**, then click on **Enrollment**. Select **Windows** and then **Enrollment Status Page**.

   You can have multiple pages configured that are queried according to their priority (and then also queried for group membership).

   As the ESP is used to block a device until a particular subset of applications has been installed, you may find yourself needing more than one, should different departments/regions/groups have key applications that must be installed before they can log in and use the machines.

   Note that you cannot delete the **Default** page here, and while you can edit it, we will instead create a new one.

   As we have not deployed any applications into this environment yet (this will be covered in *Chapter 11*), we have added the **Microsoft To Do** store application to demonstrate configuring an ESP.

2. Click the **Create** button.
3. Provide **Name** and **Description** values and click **Next**.
4. Now, we need to tell Intune to display an ESP. So, change the **Show app and profile configuration progress** setting to **Yes**.

   This will open up the other available settings:

   - **Show an error when installation takes longer than the specified number of minutes**: When configuring this setting, you need to look at the applications being deployed and also configure the slowest broadband connection your users could be using. If you set this too high and misconfigure an application or script, the ESP will remain on-screen until the timeout is reached, even if nothing is going to happen until the error is fixed. This is not a great user experience. Similarly, if you set the value too low and have a particularly large or complex application, you could find the ESP timing out when the configuration is completed as planned. Usually, 60–120 minutes is adequate.
   - **Show custom message when time limit or error occurs**: If you have a support desk or a particular number for users to call when configuring a new device, enter that here, along with some instructions for them. Should Autopilot fail or time out, this is the message that will be displayed.

- **Turn on log collection and diagnostics page for end users**: This is useful when troubleshooting. Should a machine fail, the users will be presented with a button to retrieve the logs from the device itself. It will not be visible before then.
- **Only show page to devices provisioned by out-of-box experience (OOBE)**: It is suggested that you set this to **No**. If you do, after provisioning a machine, any future account logins that are not done by the primary user will see the ESP when logging in for the first time. Your IT staff will not thank you for disabling this when they are logging in to a machine to troubleshoot something.
- **Block device use until all apps and profiles are installed**: This enables or disables the next three settings. If you set it to **No**, you will not be able to block until applications are installed.
- **Allow users to reset device if installation occurs**: You have three options if Autopilot fails – reset the device, allow the users to continue using it, or do nothing at all. This is the first option; it will display a **Reset** button to attempt provisioning again.
- **Allow users to use a device if installation error occurs**: This is the second option. Setting it to **Yes** will display a **Continue** button on failure, which will send the users to their desktop. Setting both to **No** is the third option.
- **Block device use until required apps are installed if they are assigned to the user/device**: If you set this to **All**, users will not be able to log in until every application is deployed as required to all users/all devices, or until any groups that the user/device is a member of complete installation. Setting this to **Selected** allows you to pick from your deployed applications. As mentioned previously, we are selecting **Microsoft To Do** for this example.
- There is also the **Only fail selected blocking apps in technician phase** option. This is used with pre-provisioning and forces your selected apps when a user enrolls a device. However, during pre-provisioning, it installs all required applications instead.

5. Once you have configured your settings, click **Next**.

   If you are only ever going to need one ESP, it can be deployed to all users or all devices. For this example, we will deploy to our Intune users group so that there are more options in the future should you want to add multiple ESP configurations for different user groups, for example.

6. Once you have selected your deployment group, click **Next**.

7. On the **Scope tags** page, click **Next**.
8. Finally, review that everything looks correct and click **Create**.

Now that we have created our ESP in the GUI, we can look at how we can automate it.

Automating it

The JSON for an ESP is a friendly one with simple true/false statements and a numerical input for the timeout. The only tricky part is the application blocking, which is a nested array. This uses the application ID, which can be grabbed from the URL or directly from Graph by performing a GET request on this URL: `https://graph.microsoft.com/beta/deviceAppManagement/mobileApps`.

Alternatively, you can install the `Install-Script -Name GetIntuneApps` script, which will list all applications and their details.

After installing it, simply run `GetIntuneApps.ps1` in a PowerShell window.

Now that we have the application ID, we can continue with the PowerShell script:

1. As usual, set our assignment group:

```
$groupid = "xxxxxxxx-xxxx-xxxx-xxxx-xxxxxxxxxxxx"
```

2. Set the URL for the ESP itself:

```
$espuri = " https://graph.microsoft.com/beta/deviceManagement/
deviceEnrollmentConfigurations"
```

3. Add our JSON:

```
$espjson = @"
{
    "@odata.type":
"#microsoft.graph.windows10EnrollmentCompletionPageConfiguration",
    "allowDeviceResetOnInstallFailure": true,
    "allowDeviceUseOnInstallFailure": false,
    "allowLogCollectionOnInstallFailure": true,
    "allowNonBlockingAppInstallation": true,
    "blockDeviceSetupRetryByUser": false,
    "customErrorMessage": "Please call IT support on xxx",
    "description": "120 minute time-out\nContinue on Error\nForce
installation of Microsoft To Do",
    "disableUserStatusTrackingAfterFirstUser": true,
```

```
    "displayName": "Standard Enrollment",
    "id": "28aa4055-b08d-41bb-b030-8c1adef7fbed",
    "installProgressTimeoutInMinutes": 120,
    "installQualityUpdates": true,
    "roleScopeTagIds": [
        "0"
    ],
    "selectedMobileAppIds": [
        "2d7531e9-a16c-43a3-b65b-7f3c550b8a4c"
    ],
    "showInstallationProgress": true,
    "trackInstallProgressForAutopilotOnly": true
}
"@
```

4. Create the policy and output it to a variable for the assignment ID. You may notice that for this one, the ID also includes `_Windows10EnrollmentCompletionPageConfiguration`. This is perfectly normal behavior:

```
$esp = Invoke-MgGraphRequest -Method POST -Uri $espuri -Body $espjson -
OutputType PSObject -ContentType "application/json"
$policyid = $esp.id
```

5. Set the URL and assign the policy:

```
$assignurl = "https://graph.microsoft.com/beta/deviceManagement/
deviceEnrollmentConfigurations/$policyid/assign"
$assignjson = @"
{
    "enrollmentConfigurationAssignments": [
        {
            "target": {
                "@odata.type": "#microsoft.graph.groupAssignmentTarget",
                "groupId": "48efa53f-466b-41ea-b734-a0aa72a73f89"
            }
        }
    ]
}
"@
```

```
Invoke-MgGraphRequest -Method POST -Uri $assignurl -Body $assignjson -
OutputType PSObject -ContentType "application/json"
```

This completes the recipe for configuring our ESP.

There's more...

While you can obtain and send logs after a device has failed, when testing your deployments, it is sometimes useful to see what is happening in the background:

1. The first step here is to press *Shift* + *F10*, which will load up an elevated command prompt. This is running in the full Windows environment, not the PE environment, which you may be used to from the SCCM/MDT days.
   From this command prompt, you can access the usual Task Manager, File Explorer, Registry, and more to establish what is happening.
2. In **Task Manager**, select **Details**.
3. Right-click on **Name** at the top and choose **Select columns**.
4. Select **Command line** and click **OK**.
   This will show you the exact command, which is especially useful with your application deployments.

Some useful troubleshooting tips can be found here: `https://learn.microsoft.com/en-us/troubleshoot/mem/intune/device-enrollment/understand-troubleshoot-esp`.

You can also deploy this script to launch some useful tools during ESP: `https://andrewstaylor.com/2022/08/16/autopilot-troubleshooting-tools-during-esp/`.

Enrolling your Windows device

We now have everything in place and can enroll our first Windows device into Intune using Autopilot. This recipe will run through the different options for adding the hardware hash into Autopilot and then provisioning a new machine.

Getting ready

For this recipe, you will need a Windows machine capable of running Windows 11. This can include a **virtual machine** (**VM**) that we will be using, but it has to have TPM enabled to pass the prerequisites for Windows 11. The machine will be wiped during the process, so please ensure there is no data on it.

To add devices, you will also need the `get-windowsautopilotinfocommunity` (a community fork with more functionality) PowerShell script: `https://www.powershellgallery.com/packages/get-windowsautopilotinfocommunity/`.

Once you have a machine ready, follow the steps to build it.

How to do it...

The first thing we need to do is add the device to the Autopilot service. We have a few options available for this, depending on whether we are using Autopilot device preparation.

Adding a device identifier

If using **Autopilot device preparation**, we simply need the serial number to be entered:

1. Navigate to **Devices** | **Enrollment** | **Corporate device identifiers**.
2. Click **Add** and then **Enter manually** (or use a CSV if you have multiple serial numbers).
3. In the dropdown, select **Serial number**.
4. In the **Identifier** field, add the serial number and then add a description in the **Details** field. Then, click **Add**.

Requesting from your hardware vendor

You can speak to your hardware supplier and ask them to add your devices to your tenant (you will need to provide them with the appropriate permissions).

JSON injection within the operating system

Another option is to inject the JSON directly into an ISO with which to build devices (known as offline enrollment).

> **Note**
>
> Due to a discovered security flaw with this process, you must have personal device enrollment enabled to enroll with this approach.

To do this, follow these steps:

1. Install and import the `WindowsAutopilotIntuneCommunity` module:

```
Install-Module WindowsAutopilotIntuneCommunity
import-module WindowsAutopilotIntuneCommunity
```

2. Then, run the following command to output the JSON (watch for the encoding – it is important):

```
Get-AutopilotProfile ConvertTo-AutopilotConfigurationJSON | Set-Content -
Encoding Ascii "c:\temp\AutopilotConfigurationFile.json"
```

3. Then, you need to add this JSON file to your build image in `c:\windows\provisioning\autopilot\path`.

   You can also use a tool such as OSDCloud to do this for you: `https://www.osdcloud.com/`.

   If you go down the offline route, you will also need to amend the dynamic rule on your Autopilot devices to the following:

```
(device.devicePhysicalIDs -any (_ -contains "[ZTDid]")) -or
(device.enrollmentProfileName -eq "PROFILENAME")
```

   Here, `PROFILENAME` is from your JSON export.

This covers using JSON injection to provision your devices. Now, let's look at further options.

CSV import

For existing devices, you can grab the hardware hash from the machines, export it to a CSV file, and then import that into Autopilot:

1. On your devices, run this command:

```
Get-WindowsAutoPilotInfocommunity.ps1 -OutputFile c:\mydevice.csv
```

2. Once you have your CSV, navigate to **Devices**, then **Enrollment**. Select **Windows** and then click on **Devices**.
3. Click on **Import**.
4. Select your CSV and click **Import**.

This covers exporting a CSV from your device and importing it directly into the console as a further provisioning option.

Online enrollment

The other option is to skip the CSV output and import directly on the device. This can be on a current machine or during the OOBE:

1. Launch an elevated command prompt (*Shift* + *F10* during the OOBE).
2. Set the script's execution:

```
Set-ExecutionPolicy Unrestricted
```

3. Install the script:

```
Install-script get-windowsautopilotinfocommunity
```

4. Run the script with the `-online` parameter:

```
get-windowsautopilotinfo.ps1 -online
```

   It will install some additional modules before prompting for credentials. Enter them into the standard Microsoft Online sign-in screen and click **Next**.

5. Consent to the permissions (you will need appropriate permissions within Azure/Entra to configure application registrations) and click **Accept**.

After enrolling our devices into the tenant, let's learn how to build the Windows operating system and configure it.

Building the device

This recipe will run through how we can build the devices we have enrolled into Autopilot using our configured ESP and settings:

1. In the portal, you should see your device under **Devices** | **Enroll Devices** | **Devices** with the profile set to **Assigned**.
   We can now continue with the build.
2. If you ran the previous command during the OOBE, within the PowerShell window, type the following:

```
C:\windows\system32\sysprep\sysprep.exe
```

   Keep the default values and click **OK**:

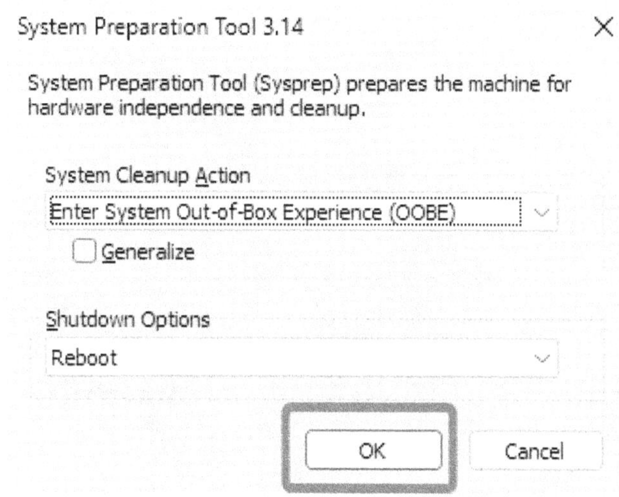

Figure 4.10 – System preparation

If you enrolled with another method, you need to rebuild the device from a Windows ISO.

3. Your machine should detect that Autopilot has been enrolled and take you to a Microsoft 365 login screen. Enter your user details and click **Next**. Enter your password and click **Sign in**.

   You may briefly see a screen that says **Please wait while we set up your device**. At this point, the ESP we configured earlier will run:

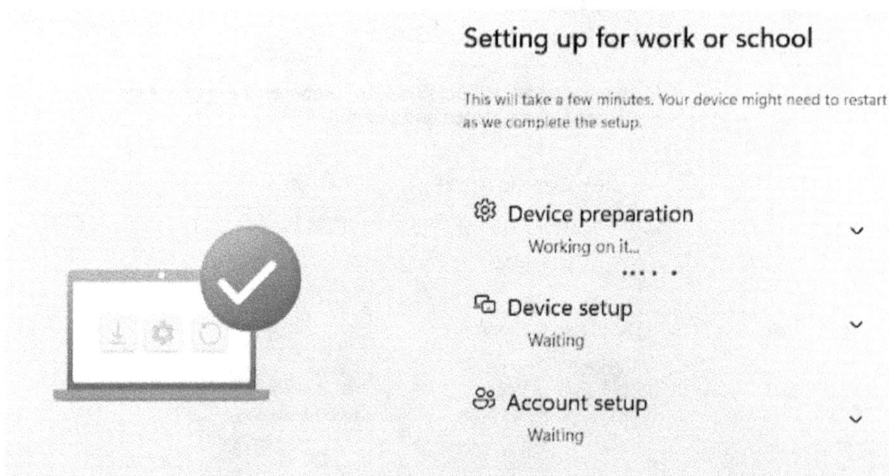

Figure 4.11 – ESP screen

4. Once completed, as we have previously configured Windows Hello, you will be prompted to configure the device. Click **OK**.
   After completion, you will be sent to the desktop, where you will see that your previous OneDrive policy has worked and that the app has automatically signed in:

Figure 4.12 – Windows 11 start screen

Congratulations – you have configured and enrolled your first Windows device into Intune and Autopilot!

There's more...

As mentioned earlier, a device can also be pre-provisioned, which pre-installs any device-targeted apps, as well as applying any policies at the device level. This can be useful for quicker deployments where some larger apps are required, or for users on lower-bandwidth connections.

It is worth remembering that if you pre-provision a device and an application is updated, it will update itself when the user logs in, so keep an eye on how long devices are left before being deployed.

> Note
>
> This requires TPM attestation, so it cannot be tested on a VM.

Follow these steps to pre-provision a device:

1. To pre-provision a machine, after adding it to Autopilot, on the login screen, press the Windows key five times; this will take you to the following screen. Click **Pre-provision with Windows Autopilot** and then **Next**:

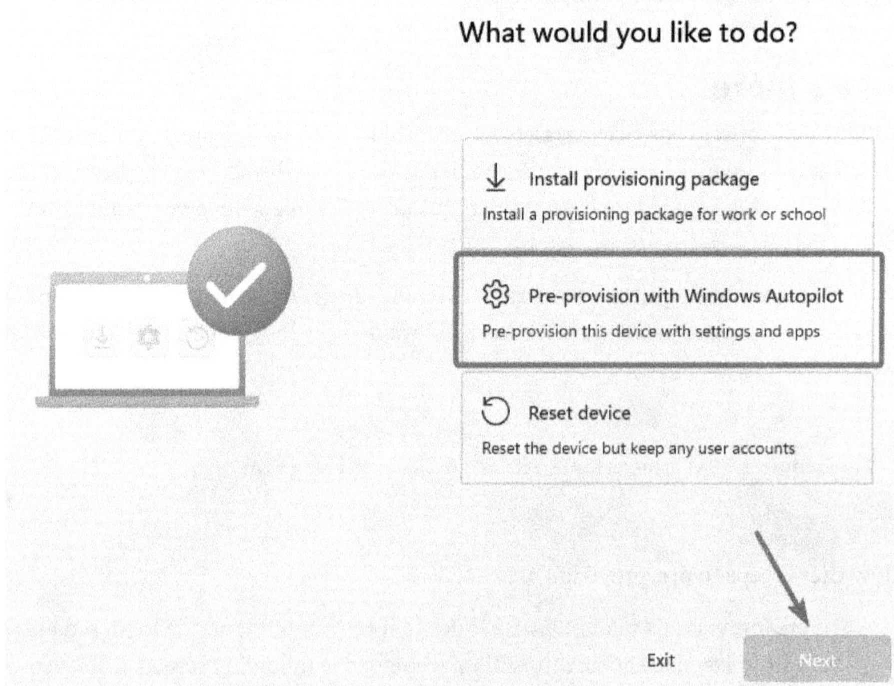

Figure 4.13 – The pre-provision menu

The device will check for updates.

2. When you are presented with the following screen, click **Next**:

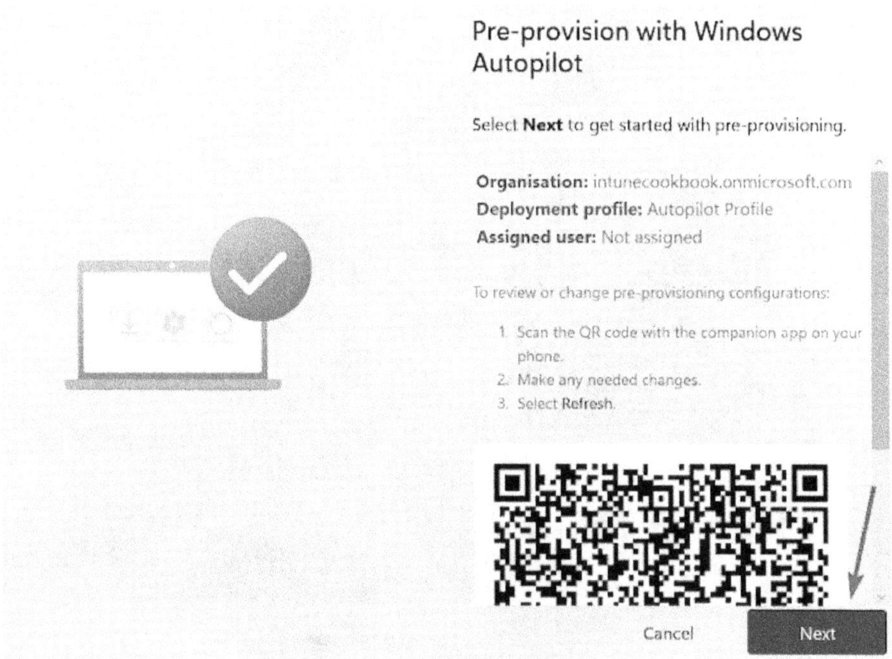

Figure 4.14 – Pre-provision check

You will now see the same ESP screen as before.

3. Once you have done this, click **Reseal**:

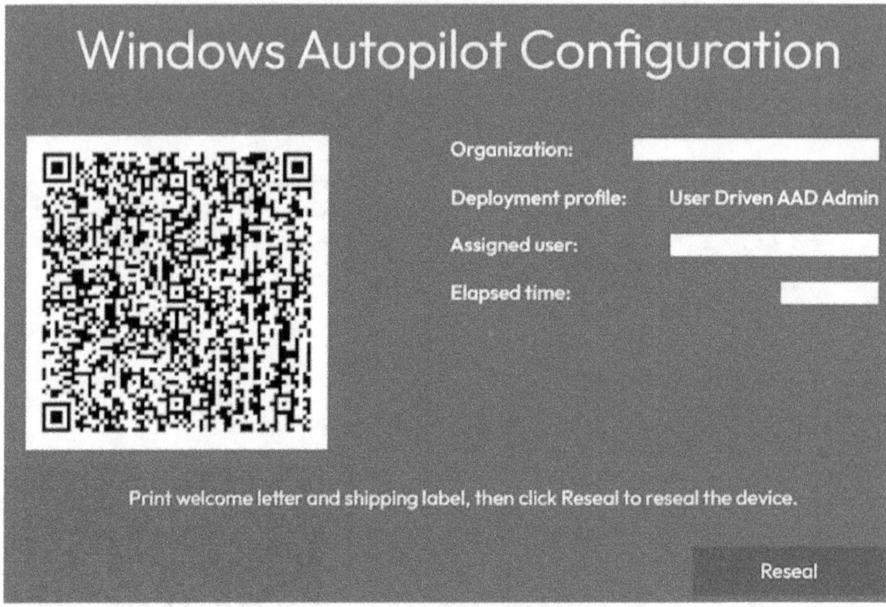

Figure 4.15 – Reseal

With that, we have enrolled our first device into Autopilot and also learned how to use pre-provisioning to pre-configure devices for our users.

Join us on Discord

For discussions around the book and to connect with your peers, join us on Discord at `packt.link/discordcloud` or scan the QR code below:

5

Android Device Management

After the excitement of enrolling and provisioning our first Windows device, we can now look at the other supported operating systems. This chapter looks at Android device management, configuring policies to manage enterprise-owned and managed devices, and then app protection policies to protect your user-owned **bring-your-own device** (**BYOD**).

It will also run through the process of configuring Intune to work with a managed Google Play account and deploying applications from the Play Store.

Finally, we will enroll both a managed device and a BYOD.

This chapter includes the following recipes:

- Setting up a managed Google Play account
- Configuring enrollment profiles
- Adding a Google Play application
- Configuring a device restrictions policy
- Configuring an OEM policy
- Configuring a Wi-Fi policy
- Adding an app protection policy
- Enrolling an Android device – managed
- Enrolling an Android device – BYOD

Chapter materials

As with *Chapter 2*, this chapter will not cover all the available policy types, so we will run through them all now to get a better understanding of what is available for Android devices. All profiles are available for creation for either corporate-owned (fully managed, dedicated, or work profile) or personally owned (work profile) devices. These profile types will be explained in the first recipe. We will also be concentrating on Android Enterprise devices; **Android Device Administrator** is now legacy and should not be used. **Android Open Source Project** (**AOSP**) is improving, but still less popular and has fewer options available.

The available profile types are as follows:

- **Settings Catalog**: The future direction of all Intune policies, but currently, for Android, it only covers password and blocking Bluetooth, which can also be configured in a *Device restrictions* policy. One for the future, but not at the time of writing.
- **OEM config**: We will cover this later in this chapter. It is for configuring manufacturer-specific OEM settings (where applicable).
- **Derived credential**: This is used for certificate authentication within apps. You can read more here: `https://learn.microsoft.com/en-gb/mem/intune/protect/derived-credentials`.
- **Device restrictions**: This is the primary configuration for Android devices; we will cover this shortly.
- **PKCS certificate**: This configures a public key pair certificate for authentication.
- **PKCS imported certificate**: This sets up an imported PKCS for S/MIME email authentication.
- **SCEP certificate**: This is used for certificate-based device authentication.
- **Trusted certificate**: This imports a trusted root certificate from an on-premises certificate authority server.
- **VPN**: This configures a VPN connection for your Android devices.
- **Wi-Fi**: This configures Wi-Fi profiles, both basic and enterprise-supported, and can be used with certification profiles where applicable.

As with our Windows security policies, there are suggested policy settings and other guidance from government agencies. Using these as a baseline will assist you in securing the devices, especially if it is required for external auditing.

The following guidance is available:

- **CIS**: `https://www.cisecurity.org/benchmark/google_android`

- **NCSC**: `https://www.ncsc.gov.uk/collection/device-security-guidance/platform-guides/android`
- **NCSC also includes baseline configurations on GitHub**: `https://github.com/ukncsc/Device-Security-Guidance-Configuration-Packs/tree/main/Google/Android`

Technical requirements

For this chapter, you will need a modern web browser and a PowerShell code editor such as **Visual Studio Code** (**VS Code**) or PowerShell ISE.

All of the scripts that are referenced in this chapter can be found here: `https://github.com/PacktPublishing/Microsoft-Intune-Cookbook-Second-Edition/tree/main/Chapter-5`.

For enrolling devices, you will need a factory-reset Android device.

> **Tip**
>
> If your device is already enabled for another MDM, you will need to remove any previous management that has been configured and then wipe the device before enrolling in Intune.

Setting up a managed Google Play account

Before we configure any Android policies or settings, we need to attach Intune to a managed Google Play account. We will then use this for enrolling devices as well as deploying applications.

Managed Google Play now supports Entra accounts, so it is best to first configure a shared account that can be used for this purpose. The account will need the *Cloud Application Administrator* and *Intune Administrator* roles, along with an Intune license for setup.

Follow this recipe to link Intune and a managed Google Play account.

How to do it...

Follow these steps:

1. First, we need to navigate to **Devices** from the Intune menu.
2. Then, click **Enrollment**.
3. Now, click the **Android** tab.
4. Click **Managed Google Play**.

5. Check the box to agree to the permissions and click the **Launch Google to connect now** button.
6. Enter your Google Play shared account details and click **Next**.
7. It will detect that the account is a Microsoft account; click on the **Sign in with Microsoft** button.
8. Accept the permissions requested.
9. It will grab details from Entra; fill in any that are missing, and click **Continue**.
10. You should not need any additional licenses, but if any apply to your organization, add as required and click **Next**.
11. Click **Agree and Continue** on the terms.
12. Finally, click **Allow and Create**, and you will be redirected to the Intune portal.

The window will now close and return you to Intune, where you can confirm that the connection has been established:

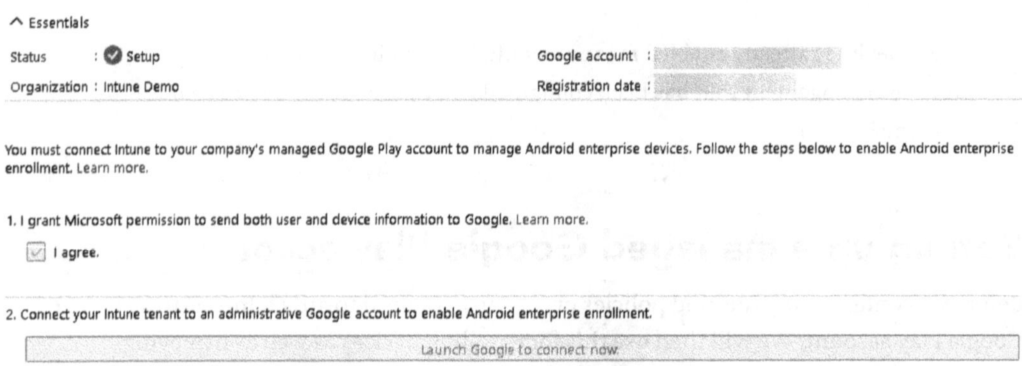

Figure 5.1 – Google Play – connection established

With that, you have successfully connected your tenant to Google Play. We can now use this to enroll our devices and deploy applications.

Configuring enrollment profiles

Now that our Google Play account has been linked, we can configure a profile to allow devices to be enrolled. This will provide us with a QR code and text code that we can use when setting up a new device.

Before we run through the process of creating a profile, we need to understand all of the options available on the Android device enrollment screen:

- **Zero-touch enrollment**: This is a way of bulk-enrolling devices into your profile without needing to configure any steps during device configuration and enrollment (similar to Apple iOS and Apple Business Manager **Automated Device Enrolment (ADE)**, which will be covered in the next chapter). It requires specific devices that have to be enrolled in the service by the distributor or service provider. Samsung Knox is a popular example that is free to configure and use, as well as Android Zero Touch for non-Samsung devices.
- **Personally-owned devices with work profile**: This button just loads an information page where nothing can be configured. When a user enrolls a personal device via Company Portal, it will add the applications to a separate profile on the device to secure the data within them. It is enabled by default.
- **Corporate-owned dedicated devices**: This is for Kiosk-style devices without a specific user assigned.
- **Corporate-owned, fully managed user devices**: These are the most common profiles for your standard users who have a corporate phone assigned to them that is fully managed. This is the profile we will be configuring in this recipe.
- **Corporate-owned devices with work profile**: This is for a corporate-owned device, but where the device is also for personal use, and the applications reside in a work profile to protect the data contained.
- **AOSP Corporate-owned, user-associated devices**: This is similar to fully managed user devices, but it is for devices running AOSP (which is Android), without Google Play services. Your hardware supplier will inform you if you have these devices. Often, they are for specific use cases, such as those manufactured by Zebra.
- **AOSP Corporate-owned userless devices**: This is for Kiosk devices not running Google Play services.
- **Android Administrator Personal and corporate-owned devices with device administrator privileges**: This is a legacy method and should not be used for new devices.

How to do it...

Now that we know what everything does, we will configure a profile for corporate-owned, fully managed user devices in this recipe:

1. First, click on **Corporate Owned, Fully Managed User Devices**.
2. Click **Create Profile**.

Creating a profile is extremely straightforward. Apart from a name and description, there are no settings to configure, and no assignment is required.

3. Enter your name and optionally a **Description** value and click **Next**.
4. There is not much to review here, but it is always best to check for errors. Once you have done that, click **Create**.
5. Now, you will see your profile in the list. It is worth noting that the tokens are valid for 90 days, after which you will need to create a new one (of course, you can use the automation steps to automate this for you in something such as an Azure runbook). Click on the newly created profile.
6. Now, click **Token**.
   Here, you will find your QR code and token, which you can provide to users to enroll their devices. You can also revoke a token, should you need to, and also export it in JSON format.

Automating it

As these tokens expire, automation can be a useful way to keep on top of device enrollments, especially in a larger organization with multiple devices. This code could be used with an Entra ID application registration process or configured to run every 90 days (or you could go one step further and check the expiry date before running), after which you can export the code to Teams, email, or anywhere else.

When creating the JSON here, the available fields are for all of the token types, so not all are applicable. In this case, you cannot set Wi-Fi networks on this enrollment type – that is, for dedicated devices:

1. First, as usual, we need our name and description:

```
$name = "Android Enrollment Profile"
$description = "Corporate Owned, Fully Managed"
```

2. Then, we need the URL we are sending the request to, which, in this case, is `androidDeviceOwnerEnrollmentProfiles`:

```
$url = "https://graph.microsoft.com/beta/deviceManagement/
androidDeviceOwnerEnrollmentProfiles"
```

3. We do not want to hard-code an expiry date here; otherwise, we will need to edit it every time the script runs. So, we will let PowerShell do the work for us. We are taking

the current date, adding 90 days, and then converting it into the format Graph is looking for (yyyy-MM-ddTHH:mm:ss.fffZ, where fff is milliseconds):

```
$tokenExpirationDateTime = (Get-
Date).AddDays(90).ToUniversalTime().ToString("yyyy-MM-ddTHH:mm:ss.fffZ")
```

4. Now, drop these values into the JSON:

```
$json = @"
{
    "configureWifi": false,
    "description": "$description",
    "displayName": "$name",
    "enrollmentMode": "corporateOwnedFullyManaged",
    "roleScopeTagIds": [],
    "tokenExpirationDateTime": "$tokenexpirationdatetime",
    "wifiHidden": false,
    "wifiPassword": "",
    "wifiSecurityType": "none",
    "wifiSsid": ""
}
"@
```

Make sure you do not use the `$profile` variable at any point here, that is reserved for PowerShell and will cause you errors.

Now, create the profile, grab the ID and populate it into the URL so we can grab the token details:

```
$androidprofile = Invoke-MgGraphRequest -Uri $url -Method Post -body $json
$profileid = $androidprofile.id
$tokenurl = "https://graph.microsoft.com/beta/deviceManagement/
androidDeviceOwnerEnrollmentProfiles/$profileid"
```

5. We need to run a `GET` command against our URL to retrieve the policy details. This one is not inside the `value` property, so we just need the full response:

```
$androidtokendetails = Invoke-MgGraphRequest -Uri $tokenurl -Method Get
```

6. The token QR code is stored within an array called `qrcodeimage` and contains the image type under `type` and the image itself, stored in Base64 format, under `value`. Therefore, we must grab the value of that array:

```
$qrbase64 = ($androidtokendetails.qrcodeimage).value
```

7. We need the image to be stored somewhere:

```
$Image = "c:\temp\AndroidQR.png"
```

8. The next step is to use the `[convert]::FromBase64String` .NET command to read and decode the value and convert it into raw bytes:

```
[byte[]]$Bytes = [convert]::FromBase64String($qrbase64)
```

9. Finally, we must export the raw bytes as the image:

```
[System.IO.File]::WriteAllBytes($Image, $Bytes)
```

It is also worth grabbing the token code in case there is a situation where the code cannot be scanned (talking a user through enrollment over the phone, for example).

10. This is stored as plain text in the `tokenvalue` field, so we simply need to retrieve that and output it to a text file. It could also be used in an email:

```
$androidtoken2 = ($androidtokendetails.tokenvalue)
$androidtoken2 | out-file "c:\temp\token.txt"
```

In this recipe, we learned how to configure a managed Google Play account and retrieve an enrollment token, both in the GUI and using PowerShell.

Adding a Google Play application

Before we look at our configuration policies, it is best to cover application deployment, as we will need applications in the tenant for both device restrictions and OEM policies.

This recipe is going to concentrate on managed Google Play applications, as they are the preferred choice for application deployment in an enterprise environment. It is worth covering the other application options so that we are aware of what is available:

- **Android Store app**: This adds applications that are effectively shortcuts to the Play Store. Users will need a Google account, and you will need your restrictions to leave the store open, which means users can install anything they want.
- **Managed Google Play app**: This adds a managed application that does not require a Google Play account. The store can be restricted to only approved applications.
- **Web link**: This deploys a web link to devices on the home screen.
- **Built-in app**: These are pre-approved and curated applications that can be deployed without using the Play Store. They are also the apps that are pre-configured for App Protection (covered later in this chapter).
- **Line-of-business app**: This was the way of deploying custom APK links to Android device administrator devices. When using Enterprise, it is best to add to the private Google Play Store. An important note is that the app package's name needs to be unique – not just in your environment but across Google Play. You can read more here: `https://learn.microsoft.com/en-us/mem/intune/apps/apps-add-android-for-work`.
- **Android Enterprise system app**: This is for deploying built-in applications, usually from the manufacturer. You need to add the exact application name (for example, `com.microsoft.word`).

Now that we understand all of the different application types, we can continue and add our first managed Google Play app.

How to do it...

Follow these steps:

1. First, click on **Apps**.

> **Note**
>
> Upon connecting to the managed Google Play Store, the applications required to enroll a device are automatically added to Intune. These are Intune Company Portal, Managed Home Screen, Microsoft Authenticator, and Microsoft Intune.

2. Then, click **Android**.
3. Click **Add** at the top.

4. Select **Managed Google Play app** from the dropdown and click **Select**. This will load the Play Store within the Intune portal.
5. Search for the application you want to deploy. We will use **Microsoft Outlook**, as that is common to most environments. Click on the application in the search results.
6. Click **Approve**.
7. Check that you are happy with the permissions that are required and click **Approve**.
8. You will now be asked what the default behavior is if those permissions change. Select what suits your environment (keep it approved when the app requests new permissions or revoke approval when the app requests new permissions) and click **Done**.
9. The app will be approved. However, you can still unapprove it or change the preferences you set before:

Figure 5.2 – Outlook options post-approval

10. Finally, click the **Sync** button at the top to add the application to Intune.
11. After a couple of minutes, the application will appear in Intune. However, note that it has not been assigned, so we need to click **Microsoft Outlook**.
12. Click **Properties**.
13. Click **Edit** next to **Assignments**.

    Here, we have a few options:

    - **Required**: This will automatically install the application on any managed and enrolled devices. It can be targeted to user or device groups (or the **All Users/All Devices** virtual group).

  - **Available for enrolled devices**: This displays the application in Company Portal for enrolled devices. As it is an available application, it can only be targeted at the user level.
  - **Available with or without enrollment**: This displays the applications in Company Portal, even if the device itself is not enrolled in Intune (a BYOD using MAM, for example). This can only be targeted at the user level, and the users must have an Intune license.
  - **Uninstall**: This removes the application without prompting. It can be targeted at either the user or device level.

14. As we are demonstrating both corporate and BYOD in this chapter, we will deploy with and without enrollment to our Intune user's Entra ID group. Clicking **Included** or **Default** under **Update Priority** lets you set whether the assignment is included or excluded, as well as increase or decrease the priority for updates. Once everything has been configured, click **Review + Save**.
15. If you are happy that everything is correct on the review screen, click **Save**.

Automating it

While you can automate adding the other application types, due to most of the work happening within the Google Play Store, adding a managed Google Play application is currently a manual process. We can, however, automate how the applications are assigned after adding them.

We can do this by finding the application ID and then assigning it:

1. First, set the name we are looking for. We will let PowerShell and Graph do the hard work for us:

```
$appname = "Microsoft Authenticator"
```

2. Now, we can run a `GET` request against all of the mobile apps in the tenant. We only want managed Google Play deployed applications using the `@odata.type` variable as `#microsoft.graph.androidManagedStoreApp`. Once we have the Play apps, we can find just those that match the name. Finally, we just want the ID (nested within `Value`):

```
$appid = ((Invoke-MgGraphRequest -Uri "https://graph.microsoft.com/beta/
deviceAppManagement/mobileApps" -Method Get -ContentType "application/json"
-OutputType PSObject).value | Where-Object {$_.'@odata.type' -eq
'#microsoft.graph.androidManagedStoreApp'} | Where-Object {$_.displayName -
eq $appname}).id
```

3. Populate the URL with `$appid`:

```
$url = "https://graph.microsoft.com/beta/deviceAppManagement/mobileApps/
$appid/assign"
```

4. Add our variables for `GroupID` and the assignment type (this can be `Required`, `Available`, `Uninstall`, or `AvailableWithoutEnrollment`):

```
$groupid = "00000000-0000-0000-0000-000000000000"
$assignmenttype = "Available"
```

5. Now, we need the JSON. We have set this to be available for `Intune-Users` with or without enrollment:

```
$json = @"
{
    "mobileAppAssignments": [
        {
            "@odata.type": "#microsoft.graph.mobileAppAssignment",
            "intent": "$assignmenttype",
            "settings": {
                "@odata.type":
"#microsoft.graph.androidManagedStoreAppAssignmentSettings",
                "androidManagedStoreAppTrackIds": [],
                "autoUpdateMode": "default"
            },
            "target": {
                "@odata.type": "#microsoft.graph.groupAssignmentTarget",
                "groupId": "$groupid"
            }
        }
    ]
}
"@
```

6. Finally, post the assignment:

```
Invoke-MgGraphRequest -Uri $url -Method Post -Body $json -ContentType
"application/json"
```

We have now covered adding our first managed Google Play application and assigning it, as well as covering the assignment in PowerShell.

Configuring a device restrictions policy

While we can now enroll a device, it will lack any configuration, and the user experience will be the same as any off-the-shelf device. For the full corporate experience, we need to configure a policy to manage them.

Android policies have yet to migrate to Settings Catalog, so for this example, we are going to configure a device restrictions policy with some basic settings to set you on your way. The PowerShell script and included JSON will contain further settings.

How to do it...

Follow these steps:

1. First, click on **Devices** in the Intune menu.
2. Then, click **Android**.
3. Now, click **Configuration Profiles**.
4. Finally, add a profile by clicking **Create profile**.
5. Select **Android Enterprise**, select **Templates** from the dropdown, and then **Device Restrictions** under **Fully Managed, Dedicated and Corporate-Owned Work-Profile**. Then, click **Create**.
6. Give your policy a name and a description and click **Next**.
   This next screen lists every setting available for Android devices. Make a note of the headers as some settings only apply to particular device types (Kiosk settings are only for dedicated devices, for example).

   A list of every setting and its descriptions can be found here: `https://learn.microsoft.com/en-us/mem/intune/configuration/device-restrictions-android-for-work`.

   For our fully managed, user-assigned devices, these are some suggested settings. For additional suggestions, review the NCSC and CIS guidance in the *Chapter materials* section:

   - **Wi-Fi access point configuration**: Block
   - **Tethering and access to hotspots**: Block
   - **USB file transfer**: Block
   - **External media**: Block

- **Factory reset protection emails**: This allows you to restrict factory reset to approved admins only
- **Factory reset**: Block
- **Notification windows**: Disable
- **Locate device**: Allow
- **Threat scan on apps**: Require
- **Enrollment profile type – fully managed**: This loads additional settings to configure the device using Microsoft Launcher. Ensure that Microsoft Launcher is a required application (covered later in this chapter)
- **Password**: Set this to whatever suits your environment. It is always recommended to disable everything from the lock screen
- **Add new users**: Block
- **User removal**: Block
- **Personal Google accounts**: Block
- **Lock screen message**: Set this to something for lost devices as an extra protection layer

7. When you have configured your settings, click **Next**.
8. Assign it to either your Intune users group or **All Users/All Devices** as required, then click **Next**.
9. Check that everything looks OK and click **Create**.

Automating it

Now that we know how to manually configure the policy, we can look at how to automate it. We have not covered device restrictions before, but it is more straightforward than a Settings Catalog policy. Most settings are configured inline with either a numeric or Boolean value, with the occasional nested array – in this case, for the likes of password settings or Microsoft Launcher:

1. As always, we start with our variables:

```
$name = "Android Device Restrictions"
$description = "Android Device Restrictions"
$groupid = "00000000-0000-0000-0000-000000000000"
```

2. Set the URL:

```
$url = "https://graph.microsoft.com/beta/deviceManagement/
deviceConfigurations"
```

3. The full JSON is available in this book's GitHub repository, so for this example, we will only add a couple of settings here to get a feel for how it looks:

```
$json = @"
{
    "@odata.type":
"#microsoft.graph.androidDeviceOwnerGeneralDeviceConfiguration",
    "alreadySetPassword": "********",
    "appsRecommendSkippingFirstUseHints": true,
    "cellularBlockWiFiTethering": true,
    "certificateCredentialConfigurationDisabled": true,
    "crossProfilePoliciesAllowDataSharing": "notConfigured",
    "description": "$description",
    "displayName": "$name",
    "enrollmentProfile": "fullyManaged",
    "factoryResetBlocked": true,
    "googleAccountsBlocked": true
}
"@
```

4. Create the profile:

```
$androidprofile = Invoke-MgGraphRequest -Method POST -Uri $url -Body $json
-ContentType "application/json" -OutputType PSObject
```

5. Grab the ID and populate the URL:

```
$androidprofileid = $androidprofile.id
$assignurl = "https://graph.microsoft.com/beta/deviceManagement/
deviceConfigurations/$androidprofileid/assign"
```

6. Add the group ID to the assignment JSON:

```
$assignjson = @"
{
    "assignments": [
```

```
            {
                "target": {
                    "@odata.type": "#microsoft.graph.groupAssignmentTarget",
                    "groupId": "$groupid"
                }
            }
        ]
    }
"@
```

7. Finally, assign the policy:

```
Invoke-MgGraphRequest -Method POST -Uri $assignurl -Body $assignjson -
ContentType "application/json" -OutputType PSObject
```

That completes this recipe, where we created our Android device restrictions policy in both the GUI and code.

Configuring an OEM policy

Most large Android manufacturers also provide the option to configure device-specific settings using a mixture of a Google Play application and a corresponding OEM policy. You can then use device filters (which we will cover in *Chapter 13*) to restrict these applications and policies to the correct devices.

For this example, we are going to configure a policy for the Microsoft Surface Duo range of devices, but some other manufacturer applications are as follows:

- **Microsoft Surface**: `https://play.google.com/store/apps/details?id=com.microsoft.surface.config`
  Settings: `https://learn.microsoft.com/en-us/surface-duo/surface-duo-2-manage-oemconfig`
- **Zebra**: `https://play.google.com/store/apps/details?id=com.zebra.oemconfig.common`
  Settings: `https://techdocs.zebra.com/oemconfig/11-5/about/`
- **Samsung**: `https://play.google.com/store/apps/details?id=com.samsung.android.knox.kpu`
  Settings: `https://docs.samsungknox.com/admin/uem/intune-configure-ksp-oemconfig-2.htm`

- **Motorola**: `https://play.google.com/store/apps/details?id=com.motorola.oemconfig.rel`
  Settings: `https://en-gb.support.motorola.com/app/answers/detail/a_id/160503/~/moto-oemconfig-guide`
- **Datalogic**: `https://play.google.com/store/apps/details?id=com.datalogic.settings.oemconfig`
  Settings: `https://datalogic.github.io/oemconfig/overview/`
- **Nokia**: `https://play.google.com/store/apps/details?id=com.hmdglobal.app.oemconfig`
  Settings: `https://solutions.hmdglobal.com/knowledgehub/what-benefits-does-the-oemconfig-app-offer`

The available settings will depend on the hardware manufacturer and have been provided here.

Getting ready

As we mentioned previously, we are using the Surface Duo OEM configuration for this example, so deploy the Microsoft Surface OEM application to your environment and assign it, as we covered previously.

Once the application has been approved and assigned, continue to the next steps to configure the policy.

How to do it...

Follow these steps:

1. First, navigate to **Devices**.
2. Then, click **Android**.
3. Then, click **Configuration Profiles**.
4. Click **Create Profile** to start the process.
5. Finally, select **Android Enterprise**, **Templates**, and **OEMConfig**, then click **Create**.
6. As usual, add a name and a description. You also need to select the **OEMConfig** app you deployed earlier by clicking the blue **Select an OEMConfig app** text.
7. Select the application and click **Select**.
8. Once configured, click **Next**.
9. On the next screen, you can decide whether to configure the settings in a GUI or by editing the JSON.

As the Microsoft settings are all user-friendly, we will continue with the configuration designer, but it is always worth checking which option is best for your manufacturer.

10. In this example, we will block Bluetooth and NFC for added security. Once you have configured the settings for your environment, click **Next**:

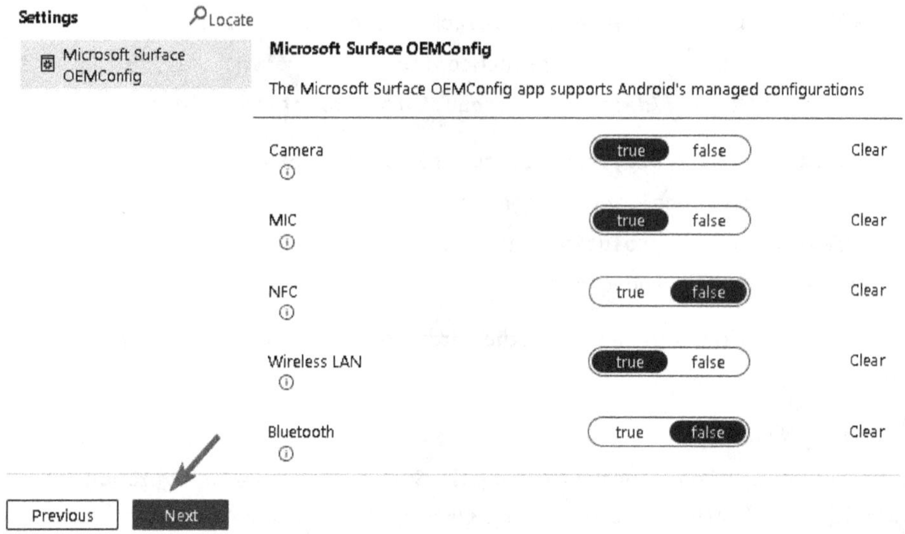

Figure 5.3 – OEM settings configuration

11. Click **Next** to skip the **Scope tags** page.
12. For assignments, choose the one that works best with a filter. So, pick **All Devices** and then filter to just your Surface devices. While we will cover this properly in *Chapter 13*, this is what a Surface filter looks like:

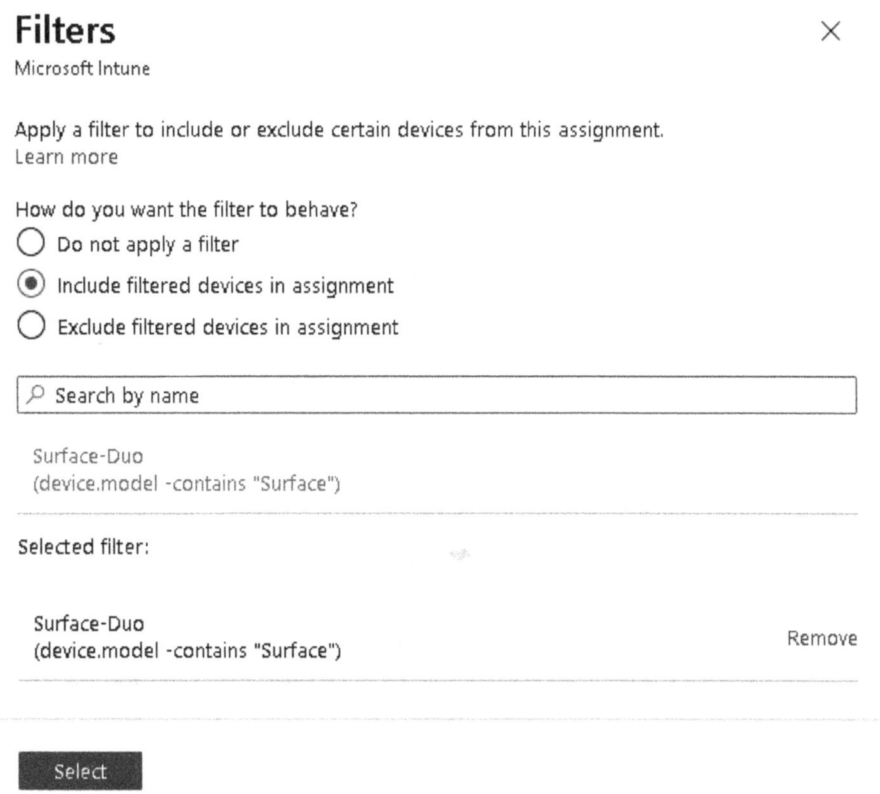

Figure 5.4 – Example Surface filter

13. For now, we will simply assign to all devices and click **Next**.
14. Check that everything looks correct and click **Create**.

Automating it

Automating an OEM policy is slightly more complicated than previous ones, as we are passing both the application details and the configuration in JSON.

As JSON can include special characters, a lot will be encoded into Base64 content before it is uploaded. A useful website for encoding and decoding Base64 is `https://www.base64decode.org/`. Follow these steps:

1. We will start with the basics, only this time, we are including the application ID, which can be found at the following Google Play Store URL:

```
$name = "Surface Duo Config"
$description = "OEMConfig policy for Surface Duo"
$packageid = "com.microsoft.surface.config"
```

2. Now, set the URL, which, in this case, is `mobileAppConfigurations`:

```
$url = "https://graph.microsoft.com/beta/deviceAppManagement/
mobileAppConfigurations"
```

3. With that, we have come to the first slightly tricky part. As well as the package ID, the payload also needs the application ID, which is specific to the application within your tenant, so we will run a command to grab it.
   This queries all `mobileApps` (that is, all apps) in the tenant, filters on the package ID, and returns the application ID (and just the ID by using the `-expandproperty` object):

```
$appid = (Invoke-MgGraphRequest -Uri "https://graph.microsoft.com/beta/
deviceAppManagement/mobileApps" -Method GET -OutputType PSObject).value |
Where-Object { $_.packageId -eq $packageid } | select-object -
ExpandProperty id
```

4. Now, we must configure the raw JSON with the values we picked earlier:

```
$configjson = @"
{
    "kind": "androidenterprise#managedConfiguration",
    "productId": "app:com.microsoft.surface.config",
    "managedProperty": [
        {
            "key": "CAM",
            "valueBool": true
        },
        {
            "key": "MIC",
```

```
                "valueBool": true
            },
            {
                "key": "NFC",
                "valueBool": false
            },
            {
                "key": "WLAN",
                "valueBool": true
            },
            {
                "key": "BT",
                "valueBool": false
            }
        ]
}
"@
```

5. As we mentioned previously, this needs to be in Base64 format, so we need to convert it:

```
$configjsonbase64 =
[Convert]::ToBase64String([System.Text.Encoding]::UTF8.GetBytes($configjson
))
```

6. Next, we must add everything we have configured to the JSON and create the policy:

```
$json = @"
{
    "@odata.type": "#microsoft.graph.androidManagedStoreAppConfiguration",
    "description": "$description",
    "displayName": "$name",
    "id": "00000000-0000-0000-0000-000000000000",
    "packageId": "com.microsoft.surface.config",
    "payloadJson": "$configjsonbase64",
    "roleScopeTagIds": [
        "0"
    ],
    "targetedMobileApps": [
        "$appid"
    ]
```

```
}
"@
$oempolicy = Invoke-MgGraphRequest -Method POST -Uri $url -Body $json -
ContentType "application/json" -OutputType PSObject
```

7. Grab the new policy ID:

```
$oempolicyid= $oempolicy.id
```

8. Add the policy to the URL. You will notice that it has an additional option to specify the application type:

```
$assignurl = "https://graph.microsoft.com/beta/deviceAppManagement/
mobileAppConfigurations/$oempolicyid/
microsoft.graph.managedDeviceMobileAppConfiguration/assign"
```

9. Finally, set our all devices target and assign it:

```
$assignjson = @"
{
    "assignments": [
        {
            "target": {
                "@odata.type":
"#microsoft.graph.allDevicesAssignmentTarget"
            }
        }
    ]
}
"@
Invoke-MgGraphRequest -Method POST -Uri $assignurl -Body $assignjson -
ContentType "application/json" -OutputType PSObject
```

With that, we have learned how to configure an OEM policy for device-specific configuration profiles, including automating how they are created.

Configuring a Wi-Fi policy

In an enterprise/office setup, you want a secure wireless network that the users both should not and cannot connect to themselves, whether this is using a certificate-based connection or just a secure code that is not shared with staff.

To do this, we need to deploy a Wi-Fi policy to our mobile devices. Remember, however, that unless you are using a zero-touch enrollment such as Samsung Knox, the devices will not pick up this new policy until *after* enrollment. Therefore, you will need an initial internet connection to enroll and set up new devices. This could be a 4G/5G connection, a guest network, or a basic enrollment network with strict security policies applied.

This example will cover a simpler WPA2 network configuration, as an Enterprise configuration will require certificate deployments. If this is more appropriate for your environment, you can follow the guide here: `https://learn.microsoft.com/en-us/mem/intune/configuration/wi-fi-settings-android-enterprise`.

Getting ready

For this recipe, you will need a secure wireless network and access to the WPA key. If you would rather use an Enterprise wireless network, you will need to configure the certificate policies beforehand:

- `https://learn.microsoft.com/en-us/mem/intune/protect/certificates-pfx-configure`
- `https://learn.microsoft.com/en-us/mem/intune/protect/certificates-profile-scep`
- `https://learn.microsoft.com/en-us/mem/intune/protect/certificates-scep-configure`

How to do it...

Follow these steps:

1. To create our policy, navigate to **Configuration profiles** within **Devices**, then **Android**.
2. Then, click **Create profile**.
3. Select **Android Enterprise**, **Templates**, and the **Wi-Fi** profile type, and click **Create**.
4. Add a name and description, then click **Next**.
5. Select your Wi-Fi type from the dropdown. Depending on your environment, you can choose **Basic** for a WEP/WPA key-based authentication or **Enterprise** for certificate-based EAP/PEAP authentication. For this example, we are deploying a **Basic** network.
6. Fill in the details as appropriate and click **Next**.
7. Now, assign the policy as appropriate. If you have one network across the estate, **All Devices** or **All Users** will be fine, but if you have different networks, it may be worth

using group-based assignments (IT could have a less restricted network). Once configured, click **Next**.

8. Review the settings and click **Create**.

Automating it

Now, let's learn how to automate this process. Fortunately, this is easier than the OEM profile and just consists of a few extra variables:

1. We will start with the normal variables:

```
$name = "Android-Wi-Fi"
$description = "Android-Wi-Fi"
$groupid = "00000000-0000-0000-0000-000000000000"
```

2. Now, add the Wi-Fi-specific settings:

```
$ssid = "mobilewifi"
$wpakey = "12345678"
```

3. Add the URL:

```
$url = "https://graph.microsoft.com/beta/deviceManagement/
deviceConfigurations"
```

4. You will notice that the JSON is the same for both **Basic** and **Enterprise**, with certain settings simply switched off. Populate our variables in the JSON:

```
$json = @"
{
    "@odata.type": "#microsoft.graph.androidDeviceOwnerWiFiConfiguration",
    "authenticationMethod": null,
    "connectAutomatically": true,
    "connectWhenNetworkNameIsHidden": false,
    "description": "$description",
    "displayName": "$name",
    "eapType": null,
    "id": "00000000-0000-0000-0000-000000000000",
    "innerAuthenticationProtocolForEapTtls": null,
    "innerAuthenticationProtocolForPeap": "none",
    "networkName": "Android-Devices",
    "outerIdentityPrivacyTemporaryValue": null,
```

```
        "preSharedKey": "$wpakey",
        "proxyAutomaticConfigurationUrl": null,
        "proxyExclusionList": null,
        "proxyManualAddress": null,
        "proxyManualPort": null,
        "proxySettings": "none",
        "roleScopeTagIds": [
            "0"
        ],
        "ssid": "$ssid",
        "trustedServerCertificateNames": [],
        "wiFiSecurityType": "wpaPersonal"
}
"@
```

5. Create the profile and grab the ID, then add it to the assignment URL:

```
$policy = Invoke-MgGraphRequest -Method POST -Uri $url -Body $json -
ContentType "application/json" -OutputType PSObject
$policyid = $policy.id
$assignurl = "https://graph.microsoft.com/beta/deviceManagement/
deviceConfigurations/$policyid/assign"
```

6. Finally, add the group ID to the JSON and assign the profile:

```
$assignjson = @"
{
    "assignments": [
        {
            "target": {
                "@odata.type": "#microsoft.graph.groupAssignmentTarget",
                "groupId": "$groupid"
            }
        }
    ]
}
"@
Invoke-MgGraphRequest -Method POST -Uri $assignurl -Body $assignjson -
ContentType "application/json" -OutputType PSObject
```

By following this recipe, we have configured a Wi-Fi profile for our Android devices, both in the UI and using PowerShell.

Adding an app protection policy

We have now configured policies for our corporate-owned devices to keep them secured and managed, but what about devices owned by users who want to access their email and other corporate apps on their personal devices? One option is to block this completely, but for most, that is not ideal, and we will just end up with a much larger list of corporate devices to purchase and manage.

Another option is to do nothing and let them add the apps completely unmanaged, but from a data protection perspective, this is a security concern, as you have no control over your corporate data.

For this, we can use app protection policies and enroll devices into **Mobile Application Management** (**MAM**) instead of **Mobile Device Management** (**MDM**). Both can be used for additional security, but this would be unusual, as it would add extra steps for the users on their devices and we can assume a managed device is secure at the device layer. We do not want users to fully enroll personal devices into the Intune tenant, so it is sensible to block personal devices; this will be covered in *Chapter 13*. We will also want to link this to an Entra Conditional Access policy to ensure unmanaged applications will not be able to access any data. Sending a **remote wipe** to these devices will also wipe corporate data from the managed apps, but not wipe the rest of the device.

We configured the MAM enrollment scopes in *Chapter 1*, so now, we need to configure the app protection policy and Entra Conditional Access policy.

App protection policies can be targeted at all applicable applications, be they Microsoft applications, core applications, or specific applications.

A list of the applications included in each is available here: `https://learn.microsoft.com/en-us/mem/intune/apps/apps-supported-intune-apps`.

How to do it...

We will start with the application protection policy and then move on to Conditional Access.

Adding an app protection policy

For this example, we will protect all Microsoft applications. If a different option is more suitable for your environment, it is a simple drop-down selection to change your choice as required:

1. First, we need to click on **Apps**.

2. Then, click **Protection**.
3. Then, click **Create**.
4. Select **Android** from the dropdown.
5. Set your name and description, and then click **Next**. You will notice that the platform has been preconfigured for you.
6. On the next screen, we can select which apps to protect. If you want to protect selected apps, you need to click **+Select Public Apps** or **+Select Custom Apps**. Otherwise, change the dropdown so that it matches your needs.
7. In this case, we will select **All Microsoft Apps** and click **Next**.

   On the next screen, we must set the data protection settings for our data protected within these applications. You can set these as per your organization's requirements. As a general rule, the following settings are good to start with:

   - **Back up org data to Android backup services**: Block (one less breach to worry about)
   - **Send org data to other apps**: Policy-managed apps (we do not want data leaving our corporate "bubble" on the device)
   - **Save copies of org data**: Block with **OneDrive** and **SharePoint** selected (it is an unmanaged device, so we do not want data on the device; select **Box** if it is approved in your environment)
   - **Transfer telecommunication data to**: Any policy-managed dialer app (again, keep things managed)
   - **Open data into org documents**: Block with **OneDrive for Business** and **SharePoint** selected (this is for copying into documents, so it can be loosened if required)
   - **Restrict cut, copy, and paste between other apps**: Policy-managed apps with paste-in (restrict within the bubble)
   - **Screen capture and Google Assistant**: Block
   - **Encrypt org data**: Require
   - **Encrypt org data on enrolled devices**: Require
   - **Sync policy-managed app data with native apps or add-ins**: Block (note that this blocks Outlook from adding to the native contacts, so be careful with this setting)

   - **Printing org data**: Block (this is a little point-restricting if they can just print it)
   - **Restrict web content transfer with other apps**: **Microsoft Edge** (this is a personal preference, but managing one browser across platforms is easier)
8. Once you have configured your settings, click **Next**.
9. The next screen (**Access Requirements**) lets you specify access requirements for the applications themselves. As you cannot force the device to require a PIN, you can force the application itself to request one. Set these as preferred; it is often best to match the corporate device PIN requirements to make it easier to explain to end users.
10. The next page (**Conditional Launch**) allows you to set further conditions for accessing the application, including the following:
    - **Max PIN attempts**: How many times an incorrect PIN can be entered. You can then either force a PIN reset or wipe the data.
    - **Offline grace period**: The number of minutes after which you block access and the number of days after which you wipe the data.
    - **Disabled account**: Block or allow access.
    - **Minimum app version**: Oldest version of the app allowed (numeric)

    You can also set restrictions on the device itself:

    - **Jailbroken/rooted devices**: Block access or wipe data.
    - **Minimum or Maximum OS version**: Warn, block, or wipe data (make sure you keep on top of this one if you are setting it).
    - **Minimum patch version**: Warn, block, or wipe data.
    - **Device manufacturer(s)**: Block or wipe anything not specified. This is an allow list, not a block list, so make sure you populate it carefully.
    - **SafetyNet device attestation**: Warn, block, or wipe data (an API will confirm whether the app and operating system are genuine).
    - **Require threat scan on apps**: Warn or block.
    - **Required SafetyNet evaluation type**: Hardware-backed key.
    - **Require Device Lock** (low, medium, or high complexity): Warn, block, or wipe data.
    - **Minimum Company Portal version** or **Maximum Company Portal age**: Warn, block, or wipe data (this is another one to keep on top of; otherwise, it will soon be useless if your minimum is out of date anyway).

- **Maximum allowed device threat level** (secured, low, medium, or high): Block or wipe data – this needs a Defender for Endpoint connection.
- **Primary MTD Service**: Either Defender for Endpoint or Mobile Threat Defense (non-Microsoft) – your device's antivirus.

11. Once you have configured your settings, click **Next**. See the following screenshot for the settings that were used in this example:

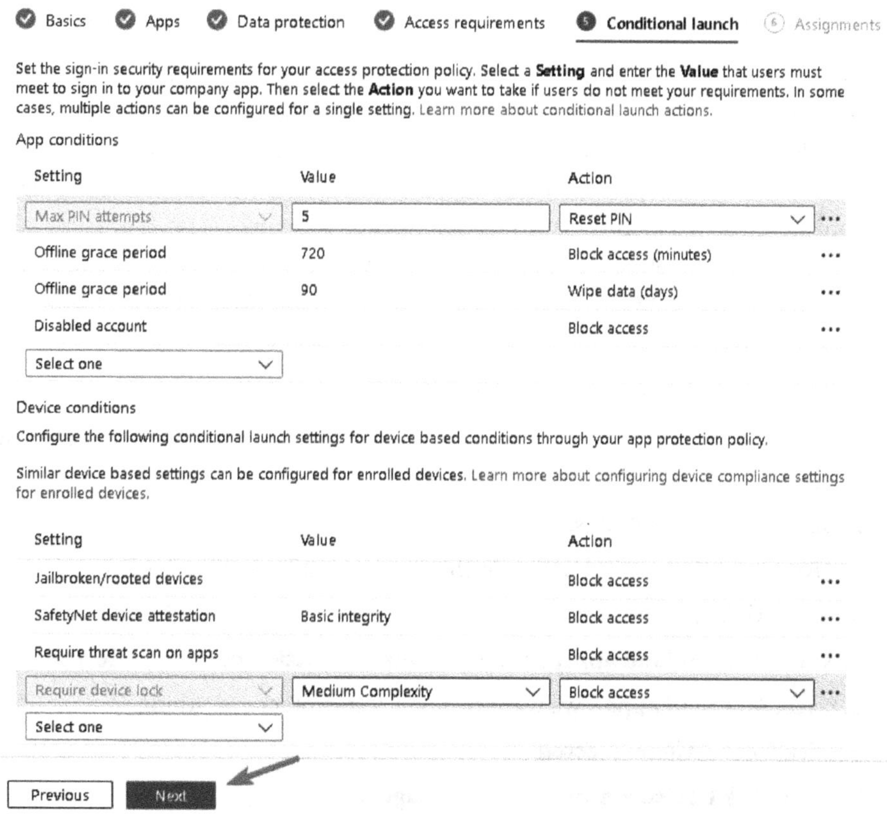

Figure 5.5 – Conditional launch settings

12. On the next screen, you will notice that we cannot assign this to the **All Users** or **All Devices** virtual groups. This is also a user-based policy, as we have no information on the devices themselves, so we will assign it to the **Intune Users** group. Then, click **Next.**
13. Finally, double-check your settings and click **Create**.

Creating the Conditional Access policy

At this point, we have our app protection policy with all of the lovely **Block access** settings, but Intune itself cannot block access to Microsoft 365 applications. For that, we need to use Conditional Access. There are new policy templates for most requirements, but in this case, we will manually create the policy so that you can understand the settings.

To find out more about Conditional Access policies, visit this page: `https://learn.microsoft.com/en-us/azure/active-directory/conditional-access/overview`.

One important thing to note is that when you are setting up Conditional Access policies, make sure you have a break-glass account configured that is excluded from all policies. If you accidentally set a policy that locks everyone out, you can use this to access the environment and fix the issue. A break-glass account should be a non-user account with a very secure password stored on paper in a secure location (ideally a fireproof safe). If possible, also link it to a FIDO2 security key stored in another safe. Remember that this account has full access to your environment without any of your Conditional Access protections, so it needs to be secured accordingly.

To access Conditional Access policies, follow these steps:

1. You can either use the Entra portal or, within **Endpoint Security**, click **Conditional Access**.
2. Click **Create New Policy**.
3. Give your policy a name and then click **0 users and groups selected**.
4. Select **All Users** under **Include** and then exclude your break-glass account.
5. Now, click **No cloud apps, actions, or authentication contexts selected**.
6. Select **All Cloud apps** – we want this policy to protect everything.
7. Click **0 conditions selected**.
8. Then, click **Device Platforms Not Configured**.
9. Set **Configure** to **Yes**. As app protection is only supported on Android, Windows, and iOS, we need to restrict the platforms for this policy. While we are currently configuring for Android, *Chapter 6* covers iOS, so it makes sense to use the same policy for both. Windows has different requirements, so that policy will be covered in *Chapter 11*.
10. Select **Android** and **iOS** and click **Done**:

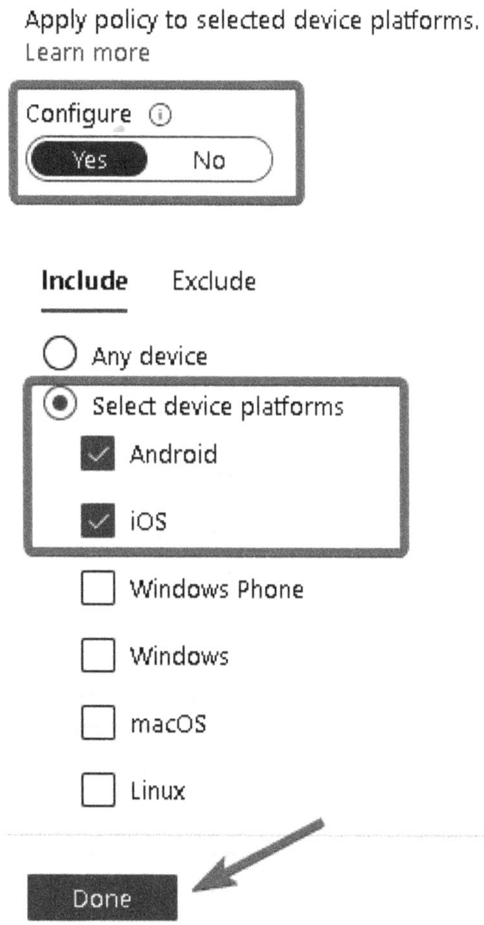

Figure 5.6 – Device platforms

11. Click **0 controls selected** underneath **Grant**.
12. Tick **Require app protection policy** and click **Select**:

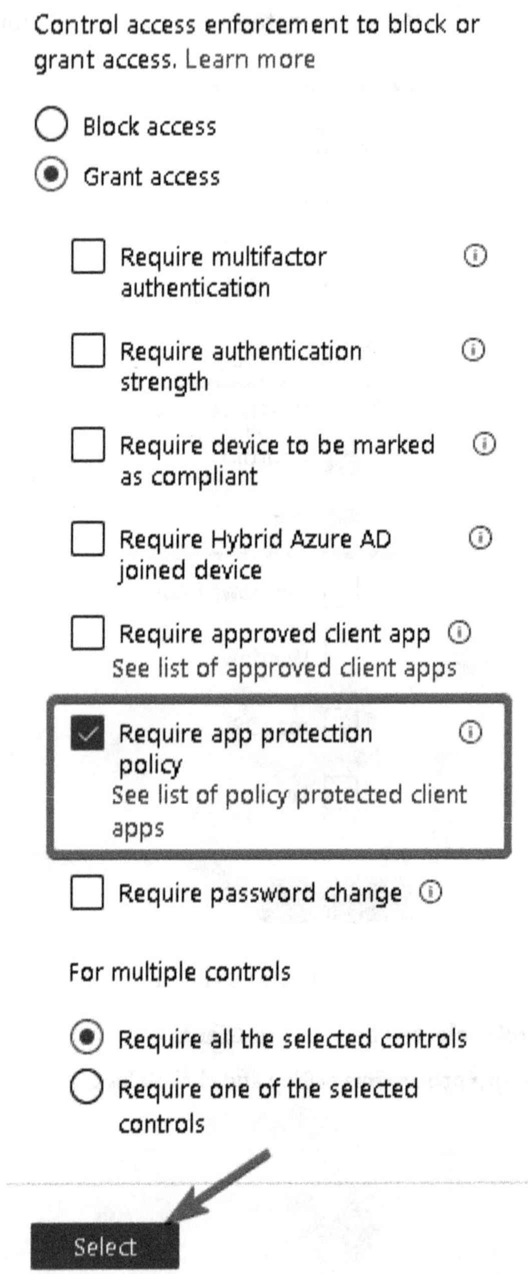

Figure 5.7 – Selecting grant controls

Session controls allow you to set a sign-in frequency and other session-based settings. We do not need those here.

13. At the bottom of the page, you can set the policy to **Off**, **Report-Only**, or **On**. For most policies, it is best to check the impact by setting it to **Report-Only**, but as this is a security-related policy, we can switch it straight to **On**, as we do not want users accessing apps that are not protected anyway. Then, click **Create**.

Let's move on to the next subsection.

Automating it

These two policies are slightly different when it comes to automation – they are still JSON, but their structure is slightly different.

App protection policy

Starting with the app protection policy, the first thing you will notice is that the assignment is part of the policy creation and not a second `POST` request afterward. It is stored in an array within the JSON.

You will also notice that all settings are available within the JSON, so in that respect, it is easier to configure and amend:

1. As usual, we will start with the name, description, and group ID:

```
$name = "Android App Protection Policy"
$description = "Microsoft Apps Only"
$groupid = "00000000-0000-0000-0000-000000000000"
```

2. Now, we need to set the URL. This one is in the `deviceAppManagement` category and `androidManagedAppProtections` sub-category:

```
$url = "https://graph.microsoft.com/beta/deviceAppManagement/
androidManagedAppProtections"
```

3. Finally, we must add the variables to the JSON with the settings we configured earlier. The full JSON is available in this book's GitHub repository, so we will just include a few settings here as an example:

```
$json = @"
{
    "@odata.type": "#microsoft.graph.androidManagedAppProtection",
    "allowedAndroidDeviceManufacturers": "",
```

```
    "allowedDataIngestionLocations": [
        "oneDriveForBusiness",
        "sharePoint"
    ],
    "allowedDataStorageLocations": [
        "oneDriveForBusiness",
        "sharePoint"
    ],
    "allowedInboundDataTransferSources": "managedApps",
    "allowedOutboundClipboardSharingExceptionLength": 0,
    "allowedOutboundClipboardSharingLevel": "managedAppsWithPasteIn",
    "allowedOutboundDataTransferDestinations": "managedApps",
    "apps": [],
    "assignments": [
        {
            "target": {
                "@odata.type": "#microsoft.graph.groupAssignmentTarget",
                "deviceAndAppManagementAssignmentFilterId": null,
                "deviceAndAppManagementAssignmentFilterType": "none",
                "groupId": "$groupid"
            }
        }
    ],
    "biometricAuthenticationBlocked": false,
    "description": "$description",
    "deviceComplianceRequired": true,
    "deviceLockRequired": false,
    "dialerRestrictionLevel": "managedApps",
    "disableAppEncryptionIfDeviceEncryptionIsEnabled": false,
    "disableAppPinIfDevicePinIsSet": false,
    "displayName": "$name",
    "encryptAppData": true
}
"@
```

4. We need to create the policy, but as we have already assigned it, we do not need the output in a variable:

```
Invoke-MgGraphRequest -Method POST -Uri $url -Body $json -ContentType
"application/json"
```

Next, we will configure our Conditional Access policy.

Conditional Access policy

Conditional Access policies also do not need to be assigned, as we select which users are applied in the policy configuration.

These use nested arrays to hold the settings for each of the areas we configured earlier (apps, session, grant, and so on):

1. First, set the name:

```
$name = "Require App Protection Policy"
```

2. Set the URL. While we accessed this through Endpoint Security, it has an Entra ID configuration underneath, so the URL is within the `identity` category:

```
$url = "https://graph.microsoft.com/v1.0/identity/conditionalAccess/
policies"
```

3. As we mentioned earlier, the full code is in this book's GitHub repository, so the code here is only to give you an example. Each category/array has an `include/exclude` option (a further array) that is configured accordingly:

```
    "conditions": {
        "applications": {
            "excludeApplications": [],
            "includeApplications": [
                "All"
            ],
            "includeAuthenticationContextClassReferences": [],
            "includeUserActions": [],
            "networkAccess": null
        },
        "clientApplications": null,
        "clientAppTypes": [
            "all"
        ],
        "clients": null,
        "devices": null,
        "locations": null,
        "platforms": {
```

```
            "excludePlatforms": [],
            "includePlatforms": [
                "android",
                "iOS"
            ]
        },
```

This policy is an *everything* policy, so no exclusions are included.

4. Finally, create the policy:

```
Invoke-MgGraphRequest -Method POST -Uri $url -Body $json -ContentType
"application/json" -OutputType PSObject
```

There's more...

Similar to the **OEMConfig** policy, you can also configure an app configuration policy via **Apps** | **App Configuration Policies**.

For supported apps, app configuration policies allow you to configure application-specific settings such as home screen settings for Microsoft Launcher or Exchange settings for Microsoft Outlook.

These can be configured using a GUI or raw JSON, as with the OEM policy we created earlier.

You have now completed this recipe and configured an app protection policy and a Conditional Access policy to protect your personally owned devices.

Enrolling an Android device – managed device

Now that our policies have been fully configured, we can start enrolling our devices, starting with fully managed corporate accounts. To do this, we will need an Android device that can be wiped for enrollment.

Getting ready

Wipe your Android device to the screen where you are prompted to enter your Gmail account and have your previously created QR code ready.

How to do it...

Follow these steps:

1. On the screen where you must enter your credentials, you have two options, depending on the age of the device. For older devices, you will need to enter `afw#setup`; on newer devices, repeatedly tap the same screen:

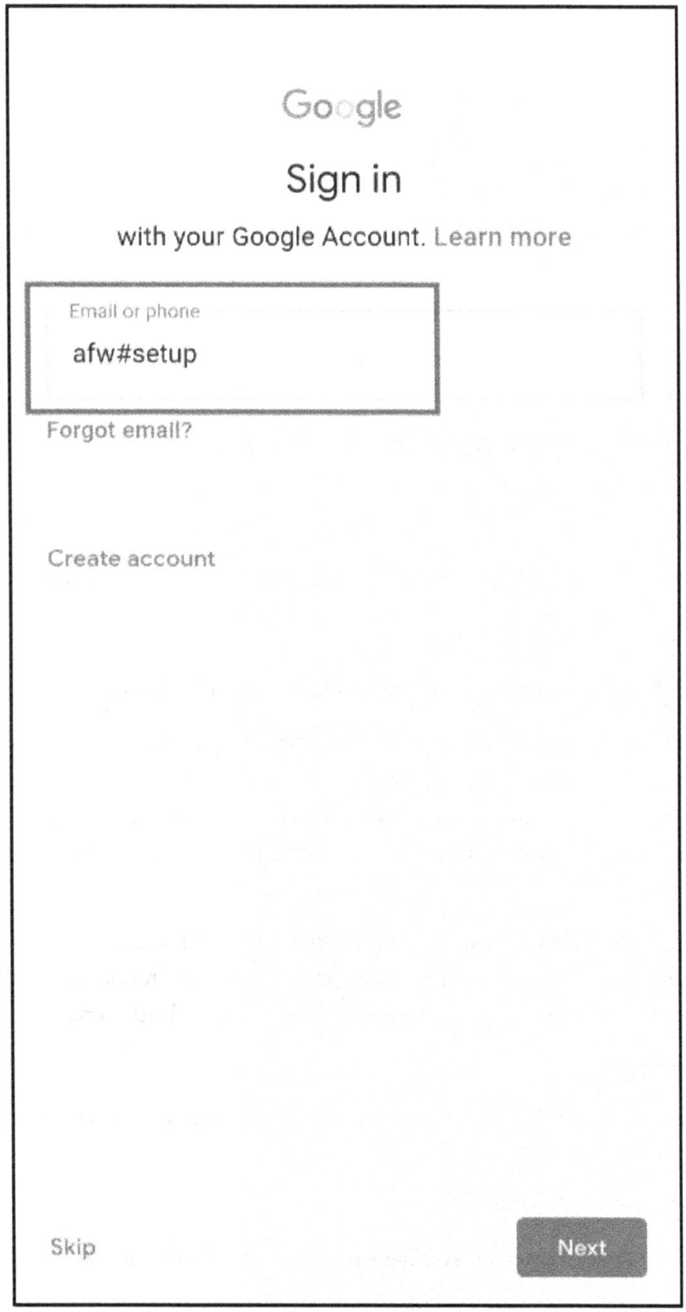

Figure 5.8 – Android's Sign in screen

Click **Accept and Continue** on the **Let's set up your work device** screen.

2. Scan your QR code (or enter it manually) and click **Accept & Continue**.
3. Click **Next** on the privacy screen.
4. Click **ACCEPT & CONTINUE** on the Chrome screen.
5. Enter your email and password to sign in.
6. Set up your screen lock.
7. Set up notification settings and click **Next**. The settings are not important here as we have configured them via policy anyway.
8. Click **Install** on the **Install work apps** screen.
9. Click **Done** to confirm the required apps (these will vary, depending on your environment).
10. Click **Set up** on the **Register your device** screen.
11. Click **Sign In** on the Intune screen.
12. Click **Done**.

You will be taken to your device's home screen. Congratulations – you have enrolled your Android device!

Enrolling an Android device – BYOD

The preceding recipe was for corporate-owned devices. However, you cannot reset and enroll a personally owned device without many complaints. So, for these devices, we will use the Company Portal app to install our deployed apps into the secure work profile. As you will recall from earlier, personally owned devices with a work profile are enabled without any further configuration.

There are two ways of doing this, depending on your configuration – you can either allow or block personal devices to enroll with a work profile (covered in *Chapter 13*). The enrollment process is slightly different for each, so we will run through both here.

Getting ready

For this recipe, you will need a current Android device with a connection to the Play Store and a signed-in account.

How to do it...

First, let's check what happens if you have personal enrollment *allowed* within your tenant.

Enrolling with personal enrollment allowed

Follow these steps:

1. Within the Google Play Store, find **Intune Company Portal** and click **Install**.
2. Once complete, click **Open**.
3. Once loaded, click **Sign In**.
4. After entering your credentials, you will be prompted to configure and activate your work profile. Click **Begin**.
5. Review the permissions settings and click **Continue**.
6. You then have another set of terms to accept and continue.
7. The phone will now configure the work profile, which can take a couple of minutes. Once it is finished, you will see the following screen; click **Next**:

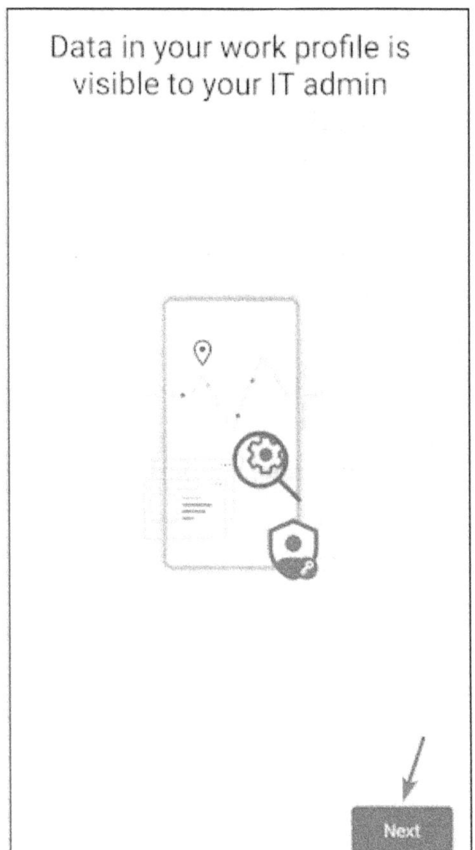

Figure 5.9 – Work profile permissions

8. This will configure and return you to Company Portal. After re-authenticating, you will be taken back to the original screen, but this time, to activate the work profile. Click **Continue**.
9. After a minute or so, you will return to the screen where everything should be configured. Click **Done**.
10. You will now be given a quick overview of how a work profile works. Click **Got It**.
11. To see the available apps, click **Open** in the notification at the bottom. Alternatively, you can click the Play Store icon with a briefcase next to it:

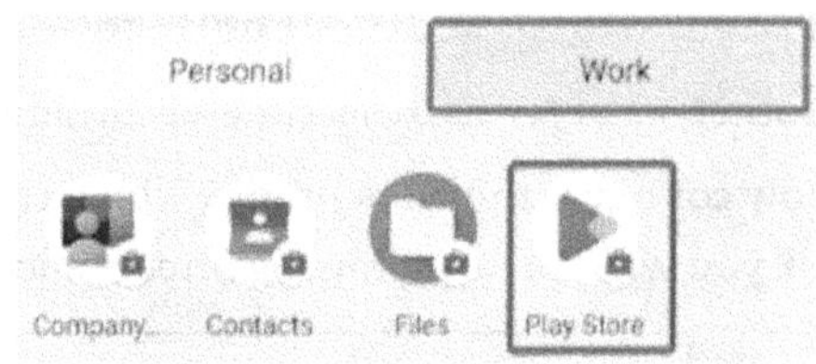

Figure 5.10 – Work profile – Play Store

As you can see, we published Outlook as an available app that now appears here. If we install this, it will be installed in the work profile, where we can control the data inside it. All work profile applications have a briefcase on the icon.

Now, let's see what happens if you have personal enrollment blocked.

Enrolling with personal enrollment blocked

This process still uses Company Portal to enforce our app protection policies. The application itself does nothing else – you cannot install applications from within it; it just serves as a broker:

1. Find and install **Microsoft Outlook** (or Word, Excel, or something else).
2. After installing it, click **Open**.
3. After logging in, you will be presented with the following screen. Click **GO TO STORE**:

Figure 5.11 – GO TO STORE

4. This will take you to Company Portal. Click **Install**.
5. After installing it, click **Open**.

You will then be taken back to Outlook to continue as normal. All data within the application is secured via the app protection policy.

That completes this recipe for enrolling your Android BYOD.

6

iOS Device Management

We have covered Windows and Android enrollment, so the next logical step is iOS devices. This chapter looks at iOS device management, configuring policies to manage enterprise-owned and managed devices, and app protection policies for protecting your user-owned **bring your own device** (**BYOD**). For our enterprise devices, we will be using Apple Business Manager (or Apple Education). Configuring this is explained in the *Technical requirements* section.

We will also run through the process of configuring Intune to work with Apple Business Manager and deploying applications using the **Volume Purchase Program** (**VPP**).

Finally, we will enroll both a managed device and a BYOD.

This chapter will include the following recipes:

- Configuring a connector between Apple and Intune
- Configuring an Apple VPP token
- Adding enrollment profile tokens
- Configuring iOS policies using the settings catalog
- Configuring iOS policies using device restrictions
- Deploying applications via Apple VPP
- Configuring iOS update settings
- Configuring an app protection policy
- Enrolling your device: corporate
- Enrolling your device: BYOD

Chapter materials

As with *Chapters 2* and *5*, this chapter will not cover all available policy types, so we will run through them all now to get a better understanding of what is available for iOS devices. You will notice more similarities with Windows profile types than with Android here, including the migration to the unified settings catalog.

The available profile types are as follows:

- **Settings catalog**: The unified settings catalog is the more modern way to deploy settings. We will cover this in the *Configuring iOS policies using the settings catalog* section.
- **Derived credentials**: This is used for certificate authentication within apps. You can read more about this at `https://learn.microsoft.com/en-gb/mem/intune/protect/derived-credentials`.
- **Device restrictions**: This is an alternative to the settings catalog for your standard restrictions. We will cover it in the *Configuring iOS policies using device restrictions* section.
- **Device features**: Device restrictions are used to protect and lock down devices. Device features provide more custom settings, such as lock-screen messages, home screen layouts, and so on.
- **Edition Upgrade and Mode Switch**: While sharing the name with the Windows profile type, this actually just sets days and times for updates to be installed.
- **Email**: This configures email settings for the built-in mail client.
- **PKCS certificate**: This configures a public key pair certificate for authentication.
- **PKCS imported certificate**: This sets up an imported PKCS for S/MIME email authentication.
- **SCEP certificate**: This is used for certificate-based device authentication.
- **Secure Assessment** (**Education**): This is used to configure student and teacher certificates for the classroom app. You can read more at `https://learn.microsoft.com/en-us/mem/intune/fundamentals/education-settings-configure-ios`.
- **Trusted Certificate**: This imports a trusted root certificate from an on-premises certificate authority server.

- **VPN**: This configures a VPN connection for your iOS devices.
- **Wi-Fi**: This configures Wi-Fi profiles, both basic and enterprise-supported, and can be used with certification profiles where applicable.

Important notes

It is important when dealing with Apple devices to keep an eye on the certificate renewal dates and to record them somewhere with a reminder. You could also use Azure Automation to automate the reminders for you. See more at `https://andrewstaylor.com/2022/06/07/alerting-when-my-apple-certificates-expire-in-intune-using-azure-automation/`. You can also use a free service such as Daily Checks at `https://dailychecks.euctoolbox.com`.

The MDM push certificate connects your devices to the Intune MDM service. If this one expires, you can contact Apple directly within 30 days of expiry to renew it. If they cannot, or if 30 days have passed, your only option is to wipe and re-enroll all your devices. *Yes, this is a full wipe, data destruction, everything*!

An enrollment token is used to enroll your devices initially. If this one expires, you must create a new enrollment profile and transfer your devices to it. It is not quite as bad as a wipe, but it can result in the devices looking less healthy within the Intune portal itself.

The Apple VPP certificate is used to deploy applications to devices. If that one expires, users will not be able to download and install any new applications until it is renewed. This is not a massive issue and they are easy to replace, but you could waste time troubleshooting an app install issue and not consider this as the issue.

When looking at your device restrictions/settings catalog policy, the settings you configure need to be tailored to your specific needs to provide the best security without ruining the end user experience. Blocking the App Store, iCloud, and so on is a good starting point.

The official CIS benchmarks for iOS can be found at `https://www.cisecurity.org/benchmark/apple_ios`.

The NCSC guidance can be found at `https://github.com/ukncsc/Device-Security-Guidance-Configuration-Packs/tree/main/Apple/iOS`.

While these should not be used as the only way to configure your settings, they are an excellent starting point, as iOS does not offer preconfigured security baselines as with Windows.

Some rough guidance to start with can be found here: `https://github.com/PacktPublishing/Microsoft-Intune-Cookbook-Second-Edition/blob/main/Chapter-6/Recommended_iOS_Config.txt`

Technical requirements

For this chapter, you will need a modern web browser and a PowerShell code editor such as Visual Studio Code or PowerShell ISE. You will also need to be connected to Microsoft Graph, as outlined in *Chapter 1*.

All of the scripts referenced can be found here: `https://github.com/PacktPublishing/Microsoft-Intune-Cookbook-Second-Edition/tree/main/Chapter-6`.

You will need an **Apple Business Manager** (**ABM**) account set up and ready to be configured with Intune. You can find instructions for setting up your ABM account at `https://www.apple.com/business/docs/site/Apple_Business_Manager_Getting_Started_Guide.pdf` and `https://www.intuneirl.com/onboarding-to-abm/`.

Your hardware supplier or service provider should be able to add your devices to ABM, but you can also use Apple Configurator on a device running macOS or iOS: `https://support.apple.com/en-gb/apple-configurator`.

Alternatively, you can follow these videos:

- `https://www.youtube.com/watch?v=G_9bPrsJHGY&t=34s`
- `https://www.youtube.com/watch?v=G-rvHUY4iA0`

For enrolling devices, you will need an iOS device enrolled in ABM and a standard iOS device for BYOD enrollment.

Configuring a connector between Apple and Intune

Before we can enroll or configure devices, we need to set up a connector to link Intune to ABM or Apple Education. We will cover that here.

Getting started

Before starting this recipe, log in to your ABM account and navigate to your account preferences. From here, we can add an MDM server.

It is worth having Intune in a different tab, as we will be switching between the two when configuring the certificates.

How to do it...

Follow these instructions:

1. In the Intune portal, navigate to **Devices** and then **iOS/iPadOS**.

2. Next, click on **Enrollment**.
3. You will notice there is only one option available here, which is **Apple MDM Push Certificate**, so click on that.
4. In the popup, tick the box and download the CSR certificate.
5. Then, click on the **Create your MDM Push Certificate** link, which will take you to the Apple portal.
6. Click **Create a certificate**.
7. Tick the box and click **Accept**.
8. Upload the CSR we downloaded from the Intune portal.
9. Make a note of the expiry date, add a reminder somewhere, and then click **Download**.

Figure 6.1 – Downloading the certificate

10. Enter your Management Apple ID (do not use a personal Apple ID), upload the certificate, and click **Upload**.
11. You should now see a success message in the same panel.

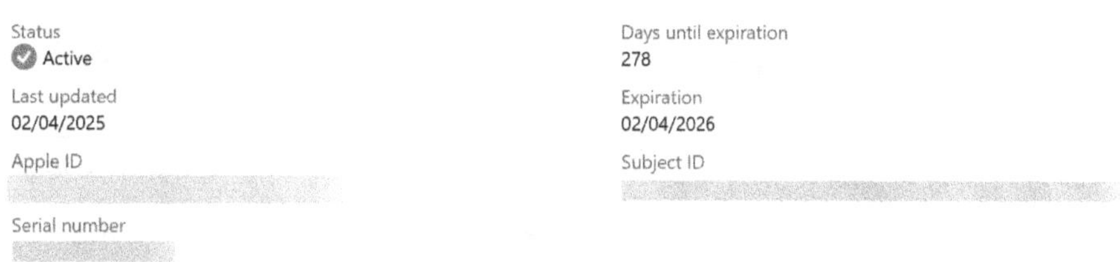

Figure 6.2 – Intune MDM certificate status

Intune is now connected to ABM, and the status should change to **Active**, as shown in *Figure 6.2*, which is the first step to deploying devices. In the next section, we will look at the Apple VPP token used to deploy applications.

Configuring an Apple VPP token

Now that we have our environments linked, we need to configure our VPP token for application deployment.

Getting started

Open two tabs, one on ABM and one in the Intune portal. We will again be switching between them for certificates.

How to do it...

Follow these instructions:

1. Within the ABM preferences, click **Payments and Billing**.
2. At the bottom of the page, download the content token.
3. Now, return to Intune, navigate to **Tenant Administration**, and click on **Connectors and Tokens**.
4. Click on **Apple VPP Tokens**.
5. Click **Create** at the top.
6. Enter a name and your Apple ID, upload the certificate from before, and click **Next**.
7. This is our only MDM server, so we can leave the top option as **No**.
8. Set the region, set the account type (usually **Business**, unless you are configuring for an education establishment), and select whether you want to allow automatic app updates. Finally, agree to the permissions and click **Next**:

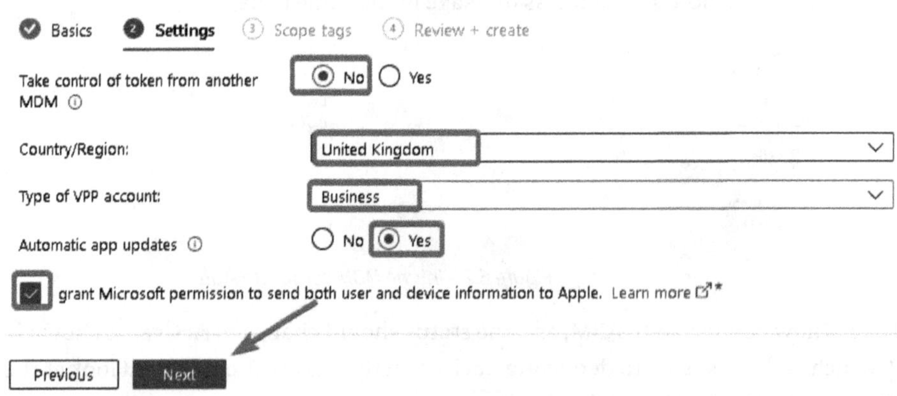

Figure 6.3 – VPP token settings

9. Click **Next** when on the **Scope tags** tab.
10. Check that everything is correct and click **Create**.

Automating it

This is the first step we can fully automate using Graph, but only after downloading the token from ABM:

1. First, we need to set our basic variables, including the path to the VPP token:

```
$url = "https://graph.microsoft.com/beta/deviceAppManagement/vppTokens"
$tokenpath = "c:\temp\vpptoken.vpp"
$appleid = "APPLEID"
$tokentype = "business"
$name = "Apple VPP"
```

2. Now, obviously, we cannot upload a file, so we need to convert it to `base64`:

```
$token =
[System.Convert]::ToBase64String([System.Text.Encoding]::UTF8.GetBytes([Sys
tem.IO.File]::ReadAllText($tokenpath)))
```

3. Populate the JSON, note the country code, and enable automatic app updates:

```
$json = @"
{
    "@odata.type": "#microsoft.graph.vppToken",
    "appleId": "$appleid",
    "automaticallyUpdateApps": true,
    "claimTokenManagementFromExternalMdm": false,
    "countryOrRegion": "gb",
    "dataSharingConsentGranted": true,
    "displayName": "$name",
    "roleScopeTagIds": [
        "0"
    ],
    "token": "$token",
    "vppTokenAccountType": "$tokentype"
```

```
}
"@
```

4. Finally, create the token:

```
Invoke-MgGraphRequest -Uri $url -Method Post -body $json -ContentType
"application/json"
```

Let us move on to the next recipe.

Adding enrollment profile tokens

The last step before we can enroll devices is to configure an enrollment profile token. We then configure ABM to use this token when deploying devices.

How to do it...

Follow these instructions:

1. Start by clicking **Devices** and then **iOS/iPadOS**.
2. Then, click **Enrollment**.
3. Click **Enrollment Program Tokens**.
4. Click **Create** at the top.
5. Check **Agree** and download the public key, as we will need that in ABM.
6. Navigate to ABM via the link:

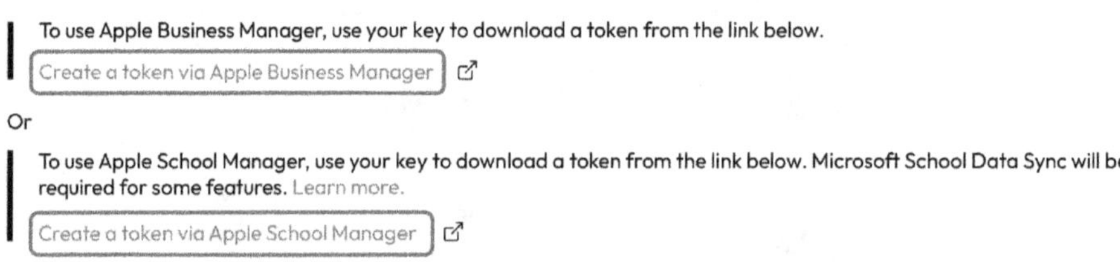

Figure 6.4: The Apple Business Manager and Apple School Manager links

7. In ABM, within your profile, click **Add** next to **Your MDM Servers**.
8. Enter a name, upload the certificate, and click **Save**.

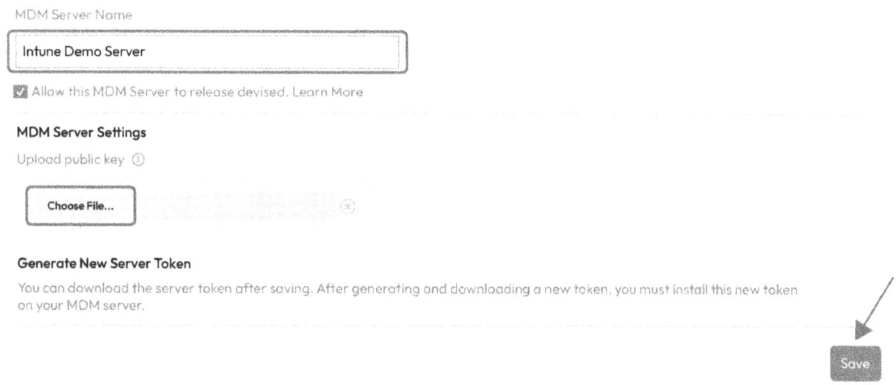

Figure 6.5 – Uploading the server token

9. Click **Download Token**.
10. Back in the Intune portal, enter the Apple ID, select the certificate just downloaded, and click **Next**:

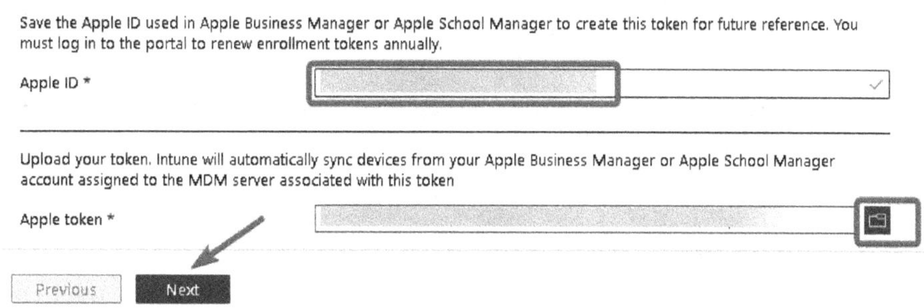

Figure 6.6 – Adding the ABM enrollment token

11. Finally, check that everything is correct and click **Create**.
12. There are now two steps to complete for enrollment. First, in the ABM portal, click **MDM Server Assignment**.
13. Click **Edit**.
14. Select your MDM server for each applicable hardware type and click **Save**.
15. Now, return to the Intune portal and click on your new enrollment program token:

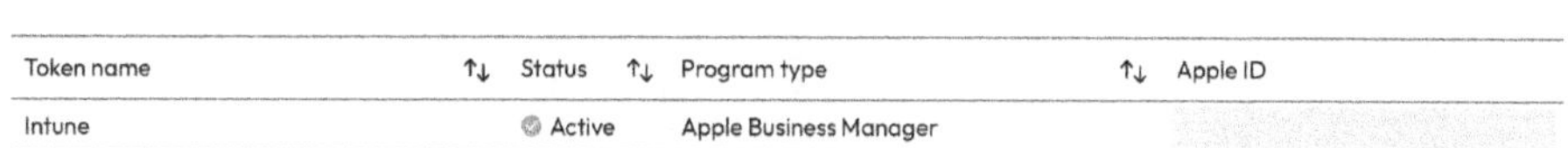

Figure 6.7 – Intune enrollment program tokens

16. Click **Profiles**.
17. Click **Create Profile** and select **iOS/iPadOS**.
18. Enter the basic details and click **Next**.

    There are options on the next screen:

    - **User affinity**: Here, you can select whether devices are enrolled to a specific user (**Enroll with User Affinity**), without a user, such as a kiosk (**Enroll without User Affinity**), or as a shared device (**Enroll with Microsoft Entra shared mode**). We are configuring a standard user device, so we select **Enroll with User Affinity**.

      This will load some new options to pick from. First is the authentication method: you can either deploy and use **Company Portal** to authenticate the users or use **Setup Assistant with modern authentication**.
    - **Setup Assistant with modern authentication** is often more reliable, so we are going to use that one for this example. This also allows required authentication using Entra ID credentials during the **out-of-box experience** (**OOBE**) prior to accessing the device's home screen. It is also a requirement for **Just-in-Time enrollment** (covered in the *Enrolling your device: corporate* section).
19. We want to use the VPP to install the app, so the user does not require an Apple ID.

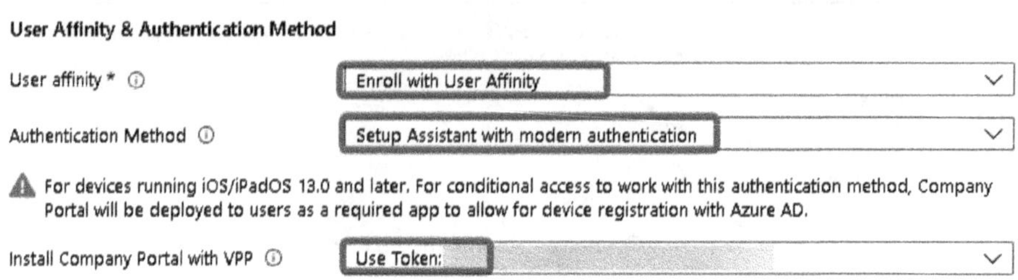

Figure 6.8 – Authentication methods

Whichever authentication method has been chosen, make sure **Supervised** is set to **Yes** to allow for more device configuration for an unsupervised device.

20. Locked enrollment stops users from removing the profile from the device. Unless you are using Apple Configurator, set **Sync with computers** to **Deny All**:

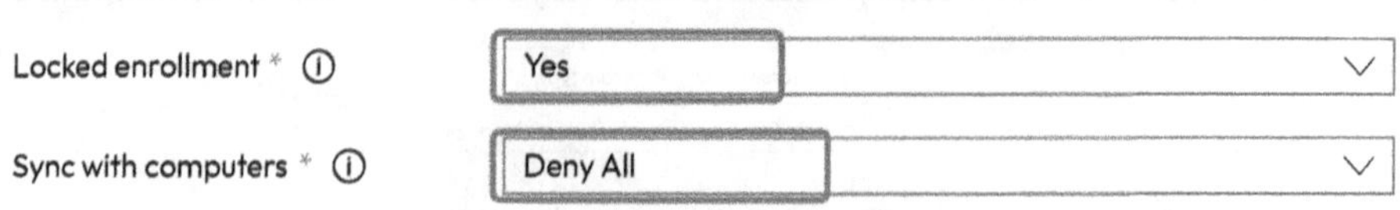

Figure 6.9 – Locked enrollment

Finally, you can set **Device Naming Template**, which supports the `{{SERIAL}}` and `{{DEVICETYPE}}` variables as well as any plain text.

21. **Activate cellular data** is for any compatible eSim devices (you will need the server URL from your carrier if you set this to **Yes**). Click **Next**.
22. On the next screen, you can select what options are available during setup and input IT contact details in case of issues.
23. It is recommended to hide as many setup screens as possible to speed up the process for your users and protect devices. Generally, just leaving **Passcode** and **Touch ID and Face ID** enabled should be all that is required.
24. Once you have configured your settings, click **Next**.
25. Now, review the settings and click **Create**.
26. Finally, click **Set default profile**.
27. Select the profile just created and click **OK**. After configuring all of these settings, any devices now added to ABM will automatically be assigned to Intune and configured with the enrollment profile token created.
28. If needed, you can assign a profile directly to a device by clicking **Devices** within the token, selecting the device, and clicking the **Assign Profile** button.

Automating it

The JSON for this is reasonably straightforward (although, as a restrictions policy contains all available settings, whether configured or not, the code is long), but first, we need to populate the URL with the ID of the Apple token:

1. First, set the variables:

```
$name = "iOS Enrollment"
$description = "Corporate Managed iOS Devices"
```

2. Now, we need to run a `GET` command to grab the ID of the token. It is within the `Value` array within the output, as with most graph objects, to allow pagination. We are looking for the ID setting:

```
$settingsurl = "https://graph.microsoft.com/beta/deviceManagement/
depOnboardingSettings/"
$tokenid = (Invoke-MgGraphRequest -Method GET -Uri $settingsurl -OutputType
PSObject).value.id
```

3. Now, we populate that into the URL:

```
$url = "https://graph.microsoft.com/beta/deviceManagement/
depOnboardingSettings/$tokenid/enrollmentProfiles"
```

4. Add the variables to the JSON. You can see that every setting is configured with either a `true` or `false` value (the full JSON is available in the GitHub repository; the following has been shortened for brevity):

```
$json = @"
{
    "@odata.type": "#microsoft.graph.depIOSEnrollmentProfile",
    "appearanceScreenDisabled": true,
    "configurationEndpointUrl": "",
    "configurationWebUrl": true,
    "description": "$description",
    "deviceNameTemplate": "{{DEVICETYPE}}-{{SERIAL}}",
    "deviceToDeviceMigrationDisabled": true,
    "diagnosticsDisabled": true,
    "displayName": "$name",
    "enabledSkipKeys": [
        "Location"
    ],
    "enableSharedIPad": false,
    "zoomDisabled": true
}
"@
```

5. Finally, create the profile. There is no need to assign this one, but we still need to store it in a variable to set as our default profile:

```
$iosprofile = Invoke-MgGraphRequest -Method POST -Uri $url -Body $json -
ContentType "application/json" -OutputType PSObject
```

6. To set the default profile, we send a `POST` request with an empty body, as the URL does the configuration for us. Grab the ID:

```
$profileid = $iosprofile.id
```

7. Now, populate the URL and send the request:

```
$defaulturl = "https://graph.microsoft.com/beta/deviceManagement/
depOnboardingSettings/$tokenid/enrollmentProfiles/$profileid/
setDefaultProfile"
Invoke-MgGraphRequest -Method POST -Uri $defaulturl -ContentType
"application/json" -OutputType PSObject
```

Let us move on to the next recipe.

Configuring iOS policies using the settings catalog

Our connection between ABM and Intune is now complete. We could enroll devices now if we wanted, but we have not configured any policies or applications yet, so we want to configure those first. Policies can be configured using either the **settings catalog** or **device restrictions**. Both configure the same settings. Using the settings catalog is more modern, but either will work. For this recipe, we will use the settings catalog, and in the next one, we will use device restrictions.

How to do it...

Follow these instructions:

1. In the Intune console, select **Devices** and then **iOS/iPadOS**.
2. Click **Configuration** and click **Create**.
3. In the fly-out menu, select **Settings catalog** and click **Create**.
4. As usual, provide a name and description and click **Next**.

   You will now see the settings picker we covered earlier during Windows profile creation (*Chapter 2*). Here, you can select the settings applicable to your environment. This list will continue to expand, so what is listed currently may increase as new settings are added. For this example, we are going to configure a couple of device restrictions to match the device restrictions policy we are setting up in the next recipe.

5. Once you have configured your settings, click **Next**:

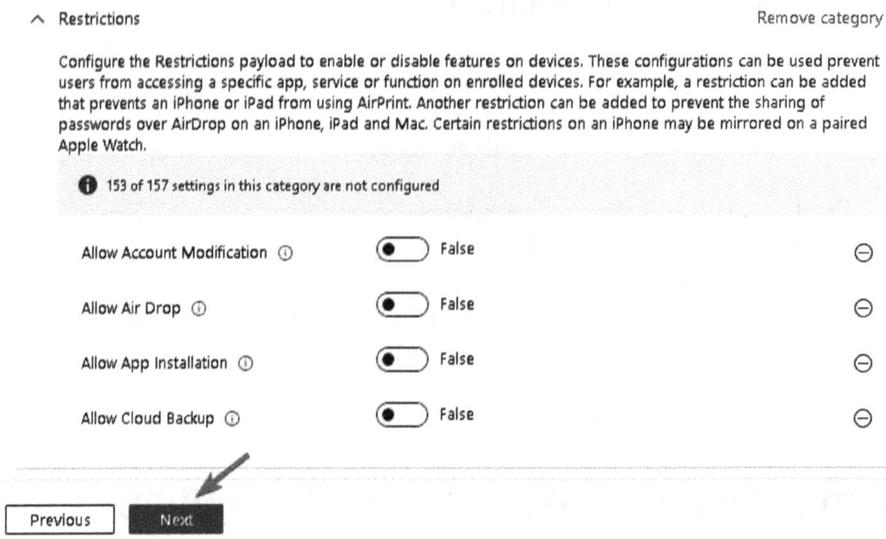

Figure 6.10 – Profile configured settings

6. We do not need scope tags, so click **Next**.

   We can assign this depending on our preference. For device restrictions, you could select all devices and filter on iOS devices, create a dynamic group, or just use a static user or device-based group. These types of settings will usually apply across the estate, so using a dynamic group or using filters will save time managing the groups and reduce the risk of a device being issued without the restrictions applied.

   If using a dynamic group, you could use `enrollmentProfileName equals xxx`, where xxx is the profile name we configured earlier, or `deviceOSType equals iOS`. For a filter, you can also use the enrollment profile name and select the filter for just iOS/iPadOS devices.

7. Click **Next** after assignment.
8. Finally, check that everything looks correct and click **Create**.

Automating it

This follows the same setup as the Windows settings catalog policies, though there are a few small differences:

1. The first difference is the category. To find all of the settings applicable to iOS, you need to run a `GET` request against this URL:

```
https://graph.microsoft.com/beta/deviceManagement/configurationCategories?
=&`$filter=(platforms has 'iOS') and (technologies has 'mdm' or
technologies has 'appleRemoteManagement')
```

You can see that not only are we looking at the platform, but we are also extending the technologies to include `appleRemoteManagement`. This is similar to how we had to expand it for the security policies.

The other important thing to note is that many of the iOS settings have dependent parent settings. You can find out whether the setting you are configuring has a dependency by looking at the **Options** field on the policy itself.

We can take `AllowNFC` as an example and expand the policy options:

```
itemId        : com.apple.applicationaccess_allownfc_false
description   :
helpText      :
name          : Disabled
displayName   : False
optionValue   :
@{@odata.type=#microsoft.graph.deviceManagementConfigurationStringSettingVa
lue; settingValueTemplateReference=; value=false}
dependentOn   :
{@{dependentOn=com.apple.applicationaccess_com.apple.applicationaccess;
parentSettingId=com.apple.applicationaccess_com.apple.applicationaccess}}
dependedOnBy : {}
```

You can see that this particular policy setting requires `com.apple.applicationaccess`.

Now, when we create our JSON, instead of jumping straight into configuring the settings as follows:

```
"settingInstance": {
                "@odata.type":
```

```
"#microsoft.graph.deviceManagementConfigurationChoiceSettingInstance",
                "settingDefinitionId": "$policysettingid",
                "choiceSettingValue": {
                    "@odata.type":
"#microsoft.graph.deviceManagementConfigurationChoiceSettingValue",
                    "value": "$selectedvalue",
                    "children": []
                }
            }
```

We instead need to use `GroupSettingsCollectionInstance` and add child items and the parent ID:

```
"settingInstance": {
    "@odata.type":
"#microsoft.graph.deviceManagementConfigurationGroupSettingCollectionInstan
ce",
    "groupSettingCollectionValue": [
        {
            "children": [
                {
                    "@odata.type":
"#microsoft.graph.deviceManagementConfigurationChoiceSettingInstance",
                    "choiceSettingValue": {
                        "@odata.type":
"#microsoft.graph.deviceManagementConfigurationChoiceSettingValue",
                        "children": [],
                        "value": "$selectedvalue"
                    },
                    "settingDefinitionId": "$policyid"
                }
            ]
        }
    ],
    "settingDefinitionId": "$dependancy"
}
```

2. Now, to look at the policy we created earlier, we set our variables, including the URL, which you will notice is the same as for any other settings catalog policy:

```
$name = "iOS Settings Catalog"
$description = "Blocks iCloud, App Store and AirDrop"
$groupid = "00000000-0000-0000-0000-000000000000"
$url = "https://graph.microsoft.com/beta/deviceManagement/
configurationPolicies"
```

3. Now, we populate the JSON using the additional parent/child settings as discussed. Unlike the Windows settings, where the value was usually a Boolean value of `0` or `1` for true or false, the iOS settings actually use the text `True` and `False` to differentiate them. Again, this has been shortened for brevity and the full JSON is available in the GitHub repository:

```
$json = @"
{
    "description": "$description",
    "name": "$name",
    "platforms": "iOS",
    "roleScopeTagIds": [
        "0"
    ],
    "settings": [
        {
            "@odata.type":
"#microsoft.graph.deviceManagementConfigurationSetting",
            "settingInstance": {
                "@odata.type":
"#microsoft.graph.deviceManagementConfigurationGroupSettingCollectionInstan
ce",
                "groupSettingCollectionValue": [
                    {
                        "children": [
                            {
                                "@odata.type":
"#microsoft.graph.deviceManagementConfigurationChoiceSettingInstance",
                                "choiceSettingValue": {
                                    "@odata.type":
"#microsoft.graph.deviceManagementConfigurationChoiceSettingValue",
```

```
                                        "children": [],
                                        "value":
"com.apple.applicationaccess_allowaccountmodification_false"
                                    },
                                    "settingDefinitionId":
"com.apple.applicationaccess_allowaccountmodification"
                                "settingDefinitionId":
"com.apple.applicationaccess_com.apple.applicationaccess"
                }
            }
    ],
    "technologies": "mdm,appleRemoteManagement"
}
"@
```

4. Now, we just need a standard policy creation and assignment, the same as with any other policy:

```
$createprofile = Invoke-MgGraphRequest -Uri $url -Method Post -body $json -
ContentType "application/json" -OutputType PSObject
$profileid = $createprofile.id
$assignurl = "https://graph.microsoft.com/beta/deviceManagement/
configurationPolicies/$profileid/assign"
$assignjson = @"
{
    "assignments": [
        {
            "target": {
                "@odata.type": "#microsoft.graph.groupAssignmentTarget",
                "groupId": "$groupid"
            }
        }
    ]
}
"@
Invoke-MgGraphRequest -Method POST -Uri $assignurl -Body $assignjson -
ContentType "application/json"
```

Let us move on to the next recipe.

Configuring iOS policies using device restrictions

The preceding recipe demonstrated how to use the newer settings catalog to create a new profile for your iOS devices, but there is also the option to use a device restrictions policy, which is similar to that used with the Android devices in the previous chapter.

This recipe will demonstrate how to configure and automate your policy using the device restrictions profile type.

How to do it...

Follow these instructions:

1. As before, in the Intune console, select **Devices** and then **iOS/iPadOS**.
2. Click **Configuration** and click **+ Create** | **+ New Policy**.
3. This time, instead of the settings catalog, pick **Templates** and then **Device restrictions**. Click **Create**.
4. As usual, populate the basic details and click **Next**.
   Here, you can find all of the device restrictions grouped, but without the useful search functionality found in the settings catalog.

   We are going to configure the same three settings as earlier to block iCloud backups (found in Cloud Storage), the App Store (found in the App Store), and AirDrop (found under **Connected devices**). Then, click **Next**:

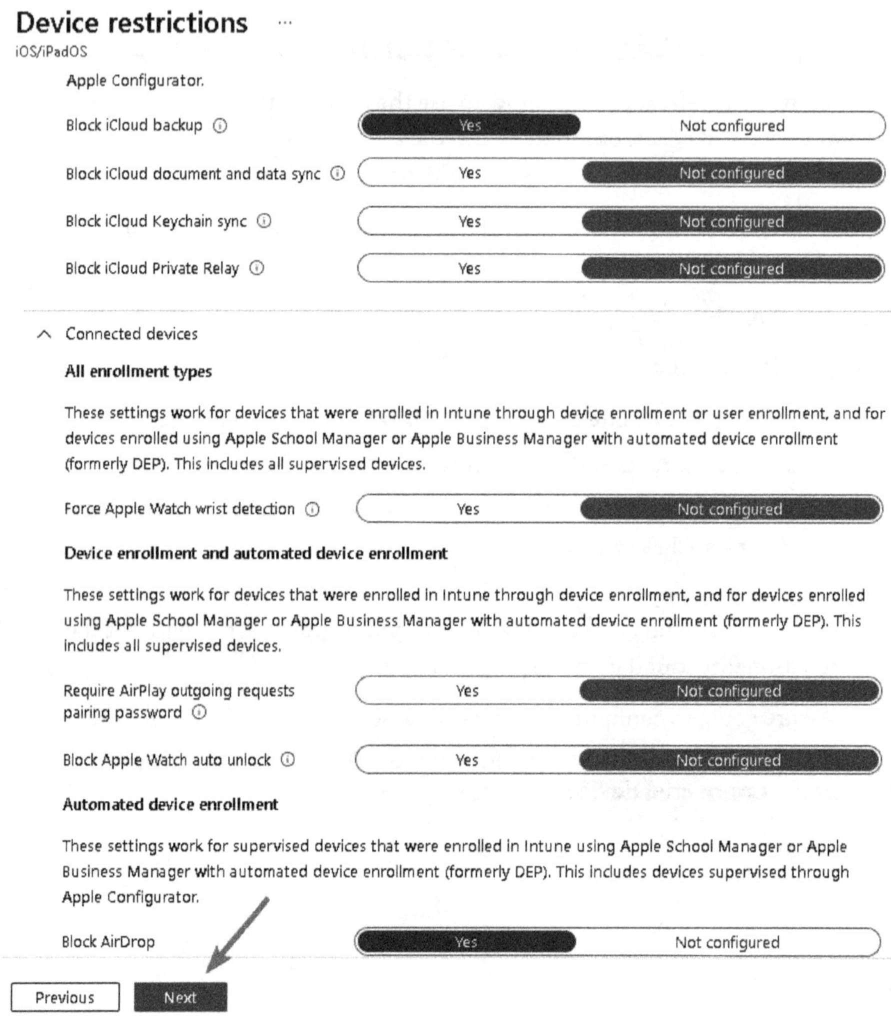

Figure 6.11: Device restrictions settings

5. You cannot set a scope tag on a device restrictions policy, so we are taken directly to the **Assignments** page. The same applies to the earlier policy. You can use filtering here as well. Once you have created the assignment, click **Next**.
6. Finally, check that everything is correct and click **Create**.

Automating it

Being a device restrictions profile, this recipe is easier than the settings catalog recipe, as it has a finite number of settings. Even if we configure all of them, the underlying JSON would be a lot more manageable. If you try to configure every settings catalog setting, especially with Windows, you will soon find it almost impossible to manage (not to mention your browser will struggle with it). Take the following steps:

1. First, we set our standard variables:

```
$name = "iOS Device Restrictions"
$description = "Block App Store, iCloud and AirDrop"
$groupid = "0000000-0000-0000-0000-000000000000"
$url = "https://graph.microsoft.com/beta/deviceManagement/
deviceConfigurations"
```

2. There are a couple of things to note with the JSON itself. First, the cellular settings can only be `True` or `False` and are required; therefore, even if we do not configure them, they will still default to `False` in the JSON. The same is true for Safari cookie settings. You will also see that the scope tags nested array is present, even though you cannot set a scope tag within the GUI itself. As with the settings catalog, these settings are largely `true/false` values with the exception of any plain text fields, such as password policy, or amending installed apps.

   As with all JSON, note the case of the settings. These are case-sensitive and always start with a lowercase letter (`camelCase`):

```
$json = @"
{
    "@odata.type": "#microsoft.graph.iosGeneralDeviceConfiguration",
    "airDropBlocked": true,
    "appStoreBlocked": true,
    "appsVisibilityListType": "none",
    "compliantAppListType": "none",
    "description": "$description",
    "displayName": "$name",
    "iCloudBlockBackup": true,
    "id": "00000000-0000-0000-0000-000000000000",
    "networkUsageRules": [
        {
            "cellularDataBlocked": false
```

```
        },
        {
            "cellularDataBlockWhenRoaming": false
        }
    ],
    "passcodeRequiredType": "deviceDefault",
    "roleScopeTagIds": [
        "0"
    ],
    "safariCookieSettings": "browserDefault"
}
"@
```

3. As usual, we now create the policy, grab the ID, and assign it:

```
$newprofile = Invoke-MgGraphRequest -Uri $url -Method Post -Body $json -
ContentType "application/json" -OutputType PSObject
$profileid = $newprofile.id
$assignurl = "https://graph.microsoft.com/beta/deviceManagement/
deviceConfigurations/$profileid/assign"
$assignjson = @"
{
    "assignments": [
        {
            "target": {
                "@odata.type": "#microsoft.graph.groupAssignmentTarget",
                "groupId": "$groupid"
            }
        }
    ]
}
"@
Invoke-MgGraphRequest -Method POST -Uri $assignurl -Body $assignjson -
ContentType "application/json"
```

Let's move on to the next recipe.

Deploying applications via Apple VPP

We now have our restrictions configured, so we know the devices are secure, but our users will not be happy if they cannot access the App Store and do not have any applications available centrally.

This recipe is going to concentrate on Apple VPP applications, as they are the preferred choice for application deployment in an enterprise environment. It is worth covering the other application options for awareness of what is available:

- **iOS store app**: This adds applications that are effectively shortcuts to the App Store. Users will need an Apple ID, and you will need your restrictions policy configured to leave the store unblocked, which obviously means users can install anything they want.
- **iOS/iPadOS Web Clip**: This adds a shortcut to a web app to the device's home screen.
- **Web link**: This deploys a web link to devices on the home screen.
- **Built-in app**: These are pre-approved and curated applications that can be deployed without using the App Store. They are also preconfigured for app protection (covered in the *Configuring an app protection policy* section later in this chapter).
- **Line-of-business apps**: These were the way to deploy custom `ipa` applications to your managed devices (up to 2 GB in size). You can find out more at `https://learn.microsoft.com/en-us/mem/intune/apps/lob-apps-ios`.

Getting started

The first step here is to log in to the ABM portal and make sure you have all of your details configured, including a payment method if you are adding any applications that are not free.

Then, click on **Apps and Books**.

Once on this screen, continue to follow the recipe.

How to do it...

First, search for your application. In this case, we are going to deploy **Microsoft Authenticator** to ensure that our users are configured for **multi-factor authentication** (**MFA**). Then, follow these steps:

1. Click on the app in the results pane.
2. Select your MDM server in the drop-down menu, enter the number of licenses you require, and click **Get**. At the top, notice that it says **Device Assignable**. This is important to note during the application assignment.

For fewer than 5,000 licenses, the application should appear almost straight away within the Intune console. Between 5,000 and 19,999 orders are processed daily at 13:00 (PST), and over 20,000 are processed at 16:00 (PST).

Just to be on the safe side, we will speed this along by giving the VPP a sync.

3. Within the Intune console, navigate to **Tenant Administration** and then **Connectors and Tokens**.
4. Click **Apple VPP Tokens**.
5. Click the three dots to the right of the token (you may have to scroll across) and then click **Sync**:

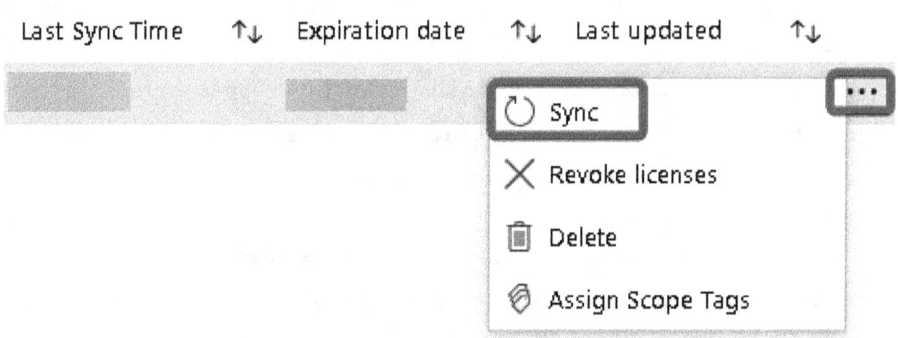

Figure 6.12 – Sync VPP token

6. Now, click on **Apps** and **iOS/iPadOS**.
7. You should see your application in the list, but not assigned. Click on the application.
8. Click **Properties**.
9. Click **Edit** next to **Assignments**.

   You will see that you do not have the **Available for Unenrolled devices** option like with Android. This is due to the licensing mentioned earlier.

   You can pick between **Required** (forced installation), **Available** (self-service), or **Uninstall**. In this case, we are going to force installation on all devices, as we want all users to have the application straight away.

10. After adding the assignment, some further options will be displayed:

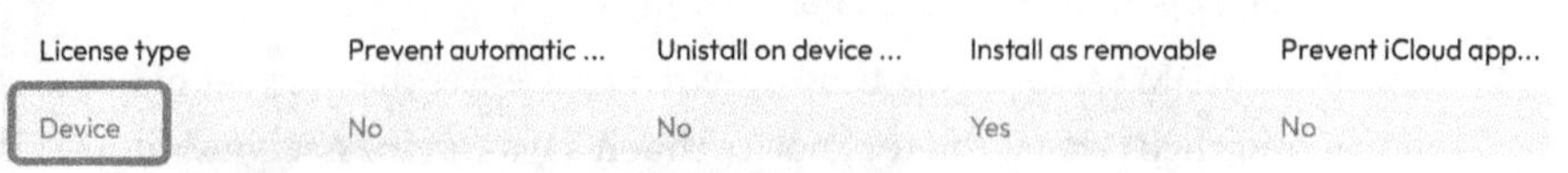

Figure 6.13 – Assignment options

The important one here is the license type. We have made it so that our users do not require an Apple ID. Therefore, we need to make sure we use **Device licensing** (as we noted during the application purchase earlier).

Clicking on any of the blue text links will load a fly-out panel with further options.

11. You can configure these settings as required. In this case, we want the application to be forced, updated, not backed up (as this stores credentials), and not deleted unless the device is removed from management. When you have configured your requirements, click **OK**:

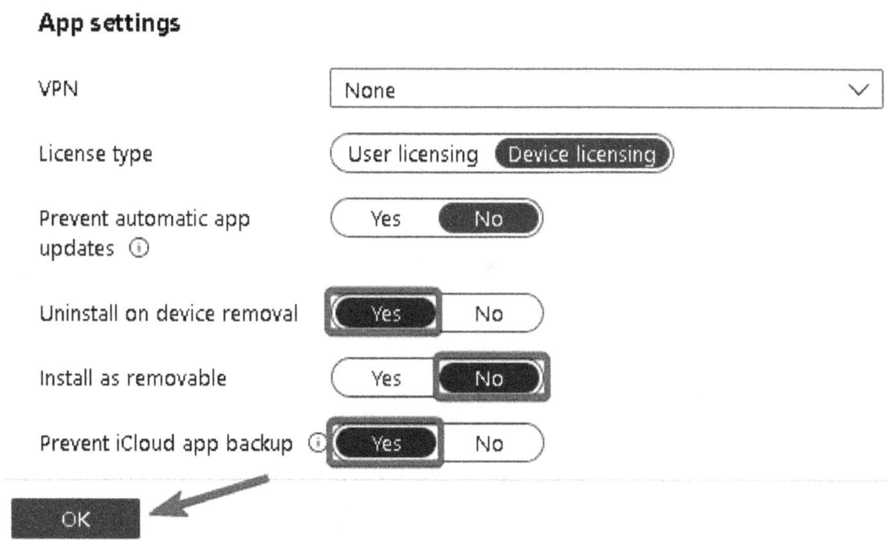

Figure 6.14 – App-specific settings

12. Now, click **Review & Save**.
13. Check that everything looks okay and click **Save**.

We click **Save** rather than **Create** because we are updating an application assignment rather than creating something new.

Automating it

While you cannot automate adding the application itself, you can automate its assignment. We do this by finding the application ID and then assigning it:

1. First, set the name we are looking for. We will let PowerShell and Graph do the hard work for us:

```
$appname = "Microsoft Authenticator"
```

2. Now, we can run a `GET` request against all of the mobile apps in the tenant. We then only want Apple VPP-deployed applications using the `@odata.type` variable, `#microsoft.graph.iosVppApp`. Once we have the VPP apps, we can find just those that match the name. Finally, we just want the ID (nested within `Value`):

```
$appid = ((Invoke-MgGraphRequest -Uri "https://graph.microsoft.com/beta/
deviceAppManagement/mobileApps" -Method Get -ContentType "application/json"
-OutputType PSObject).value | Where-Object {$_.'@odata.type' -eq
'#microsoft.graph.iosVppApp'} | Where-Object {$_.displayName -eq
$appname}).id
```

3. Populate the URL with `$appid`:

```
$url = "https://graph.microsoft.com/beta/deviceAppManagement/mobileApps/
$appid/assign"
```

4. Now, we need the JSON, which we configured for all devices earlier with the custom settings:

```
$json = @"
{
    "mobileAppAssignments": [
        {
            "@odata.type": "#microsoft.graph.mobileAppAssignment",
            "intent": "Required",
            "settings": {
                "@odata.type":
"#microsoft.graph.iosVppAppAssignmentSettings",
                "isRemovable": false,
                "preventAutoAppUpdate": false,
                "preventManagedAppBackup": true,
                "uninstallOnDeviceRemoval": true,
                "useDeviceLicensing": true,
                "vpnConfigurationId": null
            },
            "target": {
                "@odata.type":
"#microsoft.graph.allDevicesAssignmentTarget"
            }
        }
```

```
    ]
}
"@
```

5. Finally, post the assignment:

```
Invoke-MgGraphRequest -Url $url -Method Post -Body $json -ContentType
"application/json"
```

Now, we can move on to the next recipe.

Configuring iOS update settings

We may also want to manage OS updates on our iOS and iPadOS devices in a similar way to feature updates on Windows devices. This could be ensuring they are always up to date, restricting devices to a certain version, or specifying when to install an update. To do this, we use an update policy.

One important thing to note is that this does not stop users from manually searching for and installing updates, but you can set a deferral of up to 90 days using device restrictions (either in a device restrictions policy or the settings catalog).

This is accomplished using Declarative Device Management (DDM) which is configured via a Settings Catalog policy. As with Windows devices, for a large macOS estate, it is worth using deployment rings so that updates can be tested prior to large-scale deployment.

How to do it...

Follow these steps:

1. Start by clicking on **Devices** and then **macOS**.
2. Then, click **Configuration**.
3. Click **+Create** and select **+New Policy**.
4. In the fly-out, select **Settings catalog**
5. As usual, we will start with a name and description, and then click **Next**.
6. On the next screen, click **+Add settings** and expand **Declarative Device Management (DDM)**
7. Here we are looking at the settings within the following options; **Software Update**, **Software Update Enforce Latest** and **Software Update Settings**. The configuration here depends on your particular needs.

Note

For more information on the settings, the official guide can be found here:

`https://learn.microsoft.com/en-us/intune/device-updates/apple/?tabs=automatic-updates`

8. In our case, we are forcing updates, but blocking users from installing major updates to keep control and allow us to use the update rings.

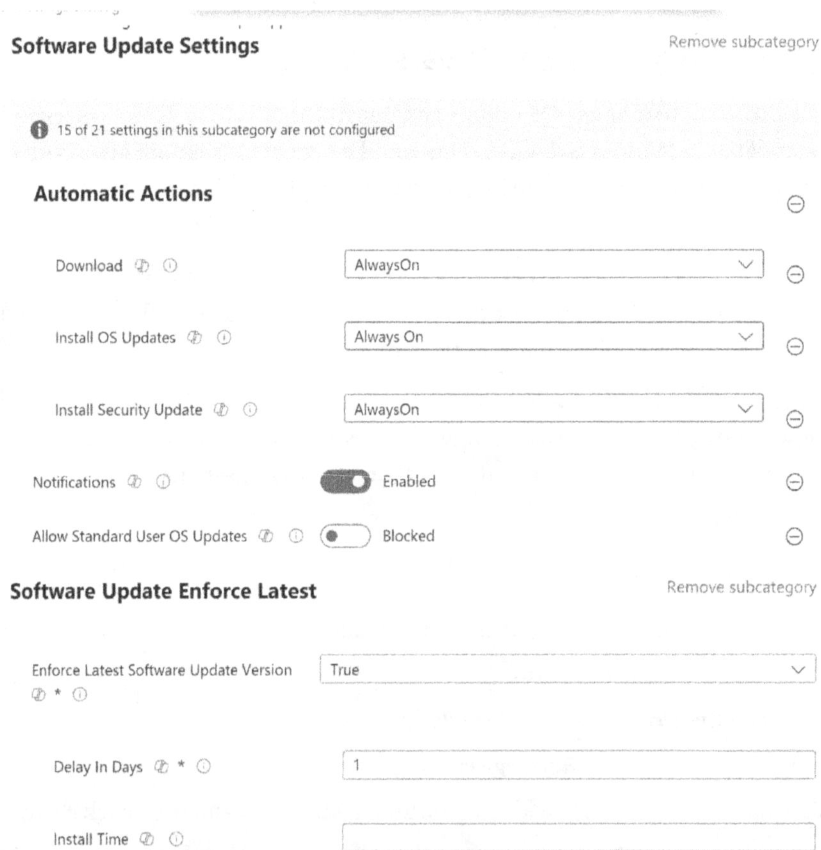

Figure 6.15 – Update policy settings

9. Once you have configured your environment, click **Next**.
10. We do not need scope tags, so again, click **Next**.

11. Now, consider your assignments, depending on what you have selected for the update policy. You may wish to create multiple policies with different settings for different user groups or device types (for example, your non-user kiosk-style devices may need different settings, or you could have shift workers).
12. In our case, we will assign to Intune users, giving us the flexibility to exclude other groups as required. Unlike Windows devices, you do not have the option to pick different deployment rings, and also note that you cannot set the OS version as with Windows and iOS.
13. Once configured, click **Next:**
14. Finally, check that everything looks correct, and then click **Create**.
15. We have now created our update policy in the Intune UI.

Automating it

As this policy is using Settings catalog, the automation is very similar to the earlier recipe covering using Settings catalog to create policies.

1. Start with the basics as usual:

```
$url = "https://graph.microsoft.com/beta/deviceManagement/
configurationPolicies"
$name = "iOS Updates"
$description = "Managed updates on iOS devices"
$groupid = "000000-0000-0000-0000-000000000000"
```

2. We then populate the JSON with the settings we have configured. For brevity, I will only include one section initially, but the full script can be found in the GitHub repository mentioned at the top of this chapter.

```
$json = @"
{
"description": "$description",
"name": "$name",
"platforms": "iOS",
"roleScopeTagIds": [
"0"
],
"settings": [
{
"@odata.type": "#microsoft.graph.deviceManagementConfigurationSetting",
"settingInstance": {
```

```
"@odata.type":
"#microsoft.graph.deviceManagementConfigurationGroupSettingCollectionInstan
ce",
"groupSettingCollectionValue": [
{
"children": [
{
"@odata.type":
"#microsoft.graph.deviceManagementConfigurationChoiceSettingInstance",
"choiceSettingValue": {
"@odata.type":
"#microsoft.graph.deviceManagementConfigurationChoiceSettingValue",
"children": [
{
"@odata.type":
"#microsoft.graph.deviceManagementConfigurationSimpleSettingInstance",
"settingDefinitionId": "ddm-latestsoftwareupdate_delayindays",
"simpleSettingValue": {
"@odata.type":
"#microsoft.graph.deviceManagementConfigurationIntegerSettingValue",
"value": 1
}
}
```

3. Finally, create and assign the policy:

```
$policy = Invoke-MgGraphRequest -Uri $url -Method Post -Body $json -
ContentType "application/json" -OutputType PSObject
$policyid = $policy.id
$assignurl = "https://graph.microsoft.com/beta/deviceManagement/
configurationPolicies/$policyid/assign"
$assignjson = @"
{
    "assignments": [
        {
            "target": {
                "@odata.type": "#microsoft.graph.groupAssignmentTarget",
                "groupId": "$groupid"
            }
        }
    ]
```

```
}
"@
Invoke-MgGraphRequest -Uri $assignurl -Method Post -Body $assignjson -
ContentType "application/json"
```

Now, we move on to the next recipe.

Configuring an app protection policy

For our BYOD devices, we cannot rely on device restrictions, as they are limited to corporate devices that have been fully enrolled. As with Android devices, which were covered in *Chapter 5*, we want to implement app protection policies to ensure that the data is securely stored on user-owned devices.

Unlike Android, iOS does not support multiple profiles, so while the data is protected in the same way, it is less segregated on the device.

Getting started

The Conditional Access policy configured in the Android app protection policy in *Chapter 5* was configured for both Android and iOS devices, so rather than run through the same steps in this recipe (if you have not configured that yet), read the Android recipe and configure the policy appropriately. This is used to force your devices to only connect if the application is policy-managed.

How to do it...

Follow these instructions:

1. First, we need to navigate to **Apps** and click **Protection**.
2. Click + **Create** and select **iOS/iPadOS** in the drop-down menu.
3. As usual, name and describe your policy. The platform is preselected based on the drop-down menu selection before. Then, click **Next**.
4. Here, we can select which apps to protect. If you want to protect selected apps, you need to click the **+Select Public Apps** or **+Select Custom Apps** text. Otherwise, change the drop-down menu to match your needs.
5. In this case, we will select **All Microsoft Apps** and click **Next**.
   On the next screen, we set the data protection settings for our data protected within these applications. You can set these as per your organization's requirements. As a general rule, these settings are good to start with:
   - **Backup org data to iTunes and iCloud backups**: Set this to **Block** (one less breach to worry about).

- **Send org data to other apps**: This should be set to **Policy managed apps** (we do not want data leaving our corporate bubble on the device). You can add exemptions here if required.
- **Save copies of org data**: Set this to **Block** with **OneDrive** and **SharePoint** selected (it is an unmanaged device, so we do not want data on the device; select **Box** if it is approved in your environment).
- **Transfer telecommunication data to**: Ideally, you should set this to **None**, but users may complain about being unable to copy and paste a telephone number, so it is worth considering this.
- **Receive data from other apps**: Either **Policy managed apps** or **All Apps with Incoming Org Data** should be set here.
- **Restrict cut, copy, and paste between other apps**: This should be set to **Policy managed apps with paste in** (restrict within the bubble).
- **Encrypt org data**: Set this option to **Require**.
- **Sync policy managed app data with native apps or add-ins**: Configure this setting to **Block** (note that this blocks Outlook from adding contacts into the native contacts application, so be careful with this setting).
- **Printing org data**: Set this to **Block** (there is little point restricting if they can just print it).
- **Restrict web content transfer with other apps**: This should ideally be set to **Microsoft Edge.** This is a personal preference, but managing one browser across platforms is easier.

6. Once you have configured your settings, click **Next**.

   The next screen lets you specify access requirements for the applications themselves. As you cannot force the device to require a PIN, you can instead force the application itself to request one. Set these as per your requirements, as it is often best to match the corporate device PIN requirements to make it easier to explain to end users. One thing to watch here is the **Work or school account credentials for access** setting. If you set this to **Require** and also **Require biometrics**, users will be prompted for both.

7. Set as required and click **Next**.

   This next page allows you to set further conditions for accessing the application, including the following:

   - **Max PIN attempts**: This is how many times an incorrect PIN can be entered. You can either force a PIN reset or wipe the data.

- **Offline grace period**: This is after how many minutes you block access, and after how many days you wipe the data.
- **Disabled account**: You can block or allow access.
- **Minimum app version**
- **Min Software Development Kit (SDK) version**

You can also set restrictions on the device itself, including the following:

- **Jailbroken/rooted devices**: You can block access or wipe data.
- **Minimum or Maximum OS version**: Either warn, block, or wipe data (make sure you keep on top of this one if you set it).
- **Minimum patch version**: Warn, block, or wipe data.
- **Device models(s)**: Block or wipe anything not specified. It is an allow list, not a block list, so make sure you populate it carefully.
- **Maximum allowed device threat level** (**Secured**, **Low**, **Medium,** or **High**): Block or wipe data. This needs a Defender for Endpoint connection.
- **Primary MTD Service**: Set to either **Defender for Endpoint** or **Mobile Threat Defense** (non-Microsoft) – your device antivirus.

8. Once you have configured your settings, click **Next**. See the following screenshot for the settings used in this example:

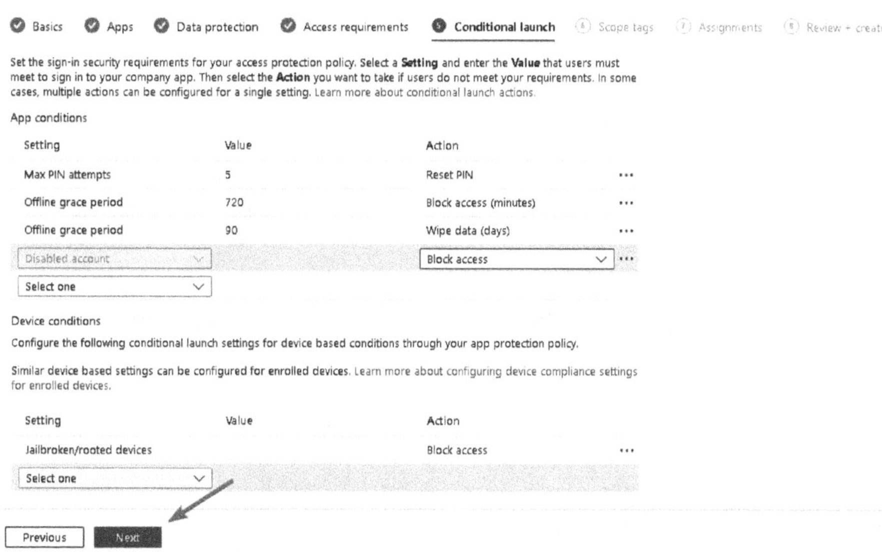

Figure 6.16 – Conditional launch settings

9. Click **Next** on the **Scope tags** page.
10. You will notice on the next screen that we cannot assign this to the **All Users** or **All Devices** virtual groups. This is also a user-based policy, as we have no information on the devices themselves. Assign it to the **Intune Users** group. Then, click **Next**.
11. Finally, check that everything looks okay. The policy will automatically have added key links to include and exclude. Then, click **Create**.

Automating it

As with the Android app protection policy, the first thing to note with this is that the assignment is included in the policy creation instead of having to be created and assigned, as was done for most recipes so far.

The JSON is fairly clear to follow, with a few nested arrays such as the allowed locations setting where we selected multiple options in the UI earlier.

Due to the large number of links included, we will not include the full JSON here, but it is, of course, available in the GitHub repository.

A list of all available settings and their relevant JSON can be found here: `https://learn.microsoft.com/en-us/graph/api/intune-shared-iosmanagedappprotection-create?view=graph-rest-beta`.

Follow these steps to create your script:

1. First, we start with the policy's name, description, and group ID:

```
$name = "iOS App Protection"
$description = "Protect Microsoft Apps"
$groupid = "00000000-0000-0000-0000-000000000000"
$url = "https://graph.microsoft.com/beta/deviceAppManagement/
iosManagedAppProtections"
```

2. Now, we populate the JSON. Remember to include the assignment inside the array here:

```
$json = @"
{
    "appActionIfDeviceComplianceRequired": "block",
    "appActionIfIosDeviceModelNotAllowed": "block",
    "appActionIfMaximumPinRetriesExceeded": "block",
    "appActionIfUnableToAuthenticateUser": "block",
    "appDataEncryptionType": "whenDeviceLocked",
```

```
    "appGroupType": "allMicrosoftApps",
    "apps": [],
    "assignments": [
        {
            "target": {
                "@odata.type": "#microsoft.graph.groupAssignmentTarget",
                "deviceAndAppManagementAssignmentFilterId": null,
                "deviceAndAppManagementAssignmentFilterType": "none",
                "groupId": "$groupid"
            }
        }
    ],
    "blockAfterCompanyPortalUpdateDeferralInDays": 0,
    "description": "$description",
    "deviceComplianceRequired": true,
    "dialerRestrictionLevel": "blocked",
    "disableAppPinIfDevicePinIsSet": false,
    "disableProtectionOfManagedOutboundOpenInData": false,
    "displayName": "$name",
    "printBlocked": true,
    "protectInboundDataFromUnknownSources": false,
    "roleScopeTagIds": [
        "0"
    ],
    "saveAsBlocked": true,
    "shareWithBrowserVirtualSetting": "anyApp",
    "simplePinBlocked": true,
    "targetedAppManagementLevels": "unspecified",
    "thirdPartyKeyboardsBlocked": false,
    "warnAfterCompanyPortalUpdateDeferralInDays": 0,
    "wipeAfterCompanyPortalUpdateDeferralInDays": 0
}
"@
```

3. As the assignment is already done, we do not need any further details after creation. We can run the Graph request without adding the output to a variable:

```
Invoke-MgGraphRequest -Method POST -uri $url -Body $json -ContentType
"application/json"
```

There's more...

You may have noticed some other settings underneath **App protection policies** in the menu, so we will cover those now for a greater understanding.

Looking at app configuration policies

App configuration policies can be applied at either the device or application level to set application-specific configurations (where supported by the application itself).

Some examples would be to configure the Outlook application or line-of-business applications. Depending on the application, you will have the choice to use a configuration designer or type in the raw text, whether that is S/MIME/XML, JSON, or something else.

For some apps, such as Outlook, the configuration designer includes comprehensive settings, while others include only text boxes. You need to be sure you know what to enter into them.

If we use Outlook as an example, the designer looks as follows:

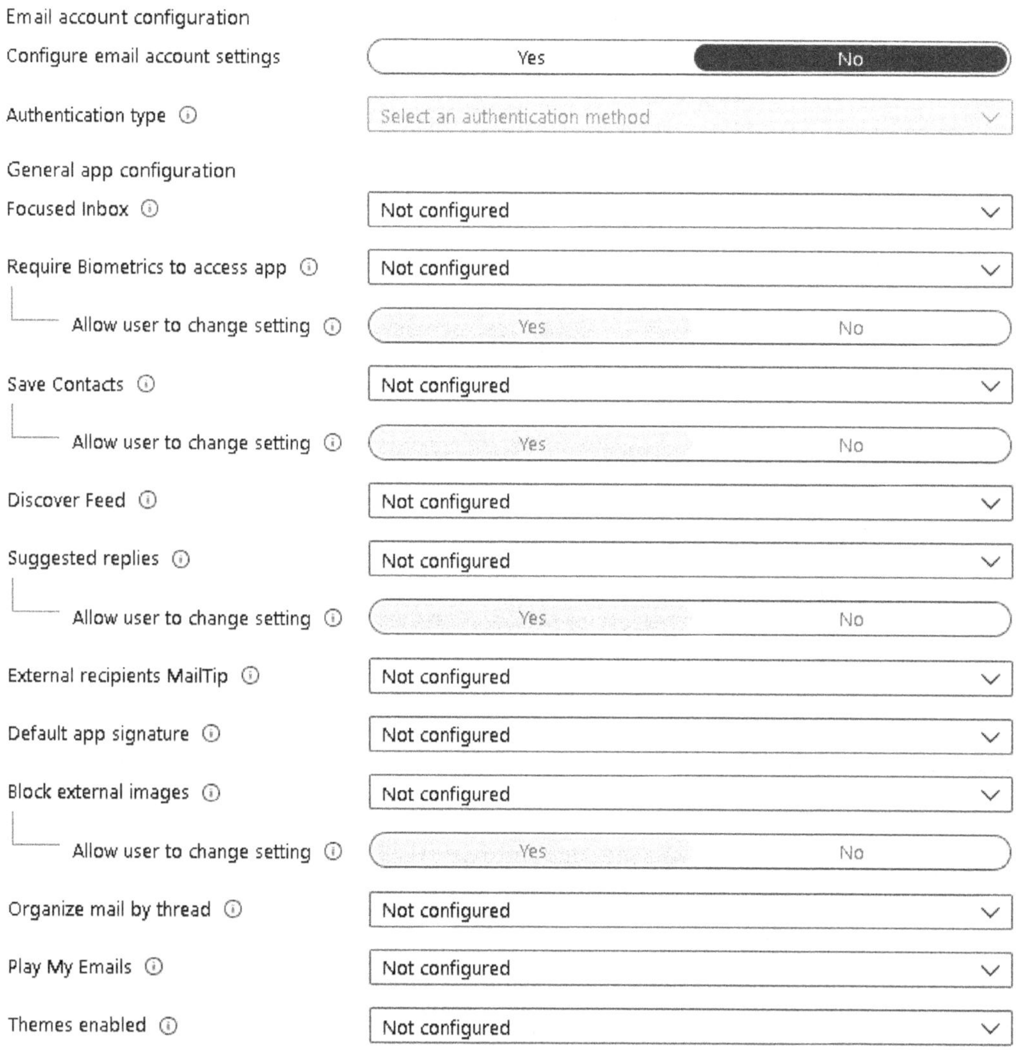

Figure 6.17 – Outlook app configuration settings

For Microsoft Word, for example, you have to enter the settings manually:

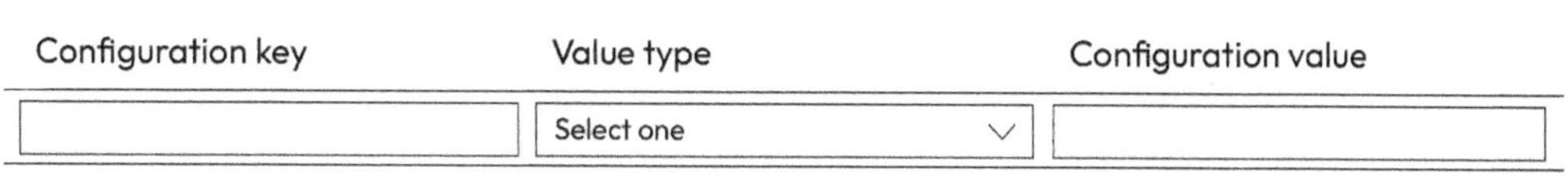

Figure 6.18 – Microsoft Word app configuration settings

Selecting the settings in Outlook simply populates the values for you:

Configuration key	Value type	Configuration value	
com.microsoft.outlook.EmailProf...	String	ModernAuth	...
com.microsoft.outlook.EmailProf...	String	{{userprincipalname}}	...
com.microsoft.outlook.EmailProf...	String	{{mail}}	...
IntuneMAMAllowedAccountsOnly	String	Enabled	...
IntuneMAMUPN	String	{{userprincipalname}}	...
com.microsoft.outlook.Mail.Focu...	Boolean	false	...
com.microsoft.outlook.Contacts....	Boolean	true	...
com.microsoft.outlook.Mail.Offic...	Boolean	false	...
com.microsoft.outlook.Mail.Sug...	Boolean	false	...
com.microsoft.outlook.Mail.Exter...	Boolean	true	...
com.microsoft.outlook.Mail.Org...	Boolean	false	...
com.microsoft.outlook.Mail.Text...	Boolean	false	...
	Select one		

Figure 6.19 – Outlook configured settings

In terms of automation, if we use the Outlook example, we are sending a `POST` request to `https://graph.microsoft.com/beta/deviceAppManagement/mobileAppConfigurations`.

The JSON would be as follows:

```
{
    "@odata.type": "#microsoft.graph.iosMobileAppConfiguration",
    "description": "",
    "displayName": "Outlook Configuration",
    "encodedSettingXml": "",
    "id": "00000000-0000-0000-0000-000000000000",
    "roleScopeTagIds": [
        "0"
    ],
    "settings": [
        {
            "appConfigKey": "com.microsoft.outlook.EmailProfile.AccountType",
            "appConfigKeyType": "StringType",
            "appConfigKeyValue": "ModernAuth"
```

```
        },
        {
            "appConfigKey": "com.microsoft.outlook.EmailProfile.EmailUPN",
            "appConfigKeyType": "StringType",
            "appConfigKeyValue": "{{userprincipalname}}"
        },
        {
            "appConfigKey": "com.microsoft.outlook.EmailProfile.EmailAddress",
            "appConfigKeyType": "StringType",
            "appConfigKeyValue": "{{mail}}"
        }
    ],
    "targetedMobileApps": [
        "40957e67-f032-44b8-9eda-3d2312b3e142"
    ]
}
```

As you can see, you will need the application ID, but we can reuse the code used when assigning an application earlier to let PowerShell automate that part for you.

Learning about iOS app provisioning profiles

App provisioning profiles are used for your line-of-business applications, which need custom configuration suppliers. You simply upload the profile supplied with the application and assign it accordingly.

You can read more about them here: `https://learn.microsoft.com/en-gb/mem/intune/apps/app-provisioning-profile-ios?WT.mc_id=Portal-Microsoft_Intune_Apps`.

Enrolling your device: corporate

We have our environment configured, so now we can start enrolling our devices, starting with the corporate-owned and managed devices.

Getting started

First, make sure you have a factory reset iOS/iPadOS device enrolled in either ABM or Apple Education Manager.

How to do it...

Follow these instructions:

1. First, set your language and region on your device.
2. On the **Quick Start** screen, click **Set Up Manually**.

3. Connect to your Wi-Fi network, if required, or use mobile data.
4. You will then see the **Remote Management** screen. Click **Next**.
5. Sign in with your credentials and click **Next**.

If your policy requires a passcode, you will be asked to set and confirm it after signing in.

Finally, after a couple of minutes, you will see your home screen with any required applications deployed.

There's more...

A recent addition to Intune is the availability of *Just-in-Time* enrollment for iOS and iPadOS. This uses the **single sign-on** (**SSO**) extension and leverages sign-in to any compatible application to trigger a compliance check and complete enrollment.

You can learn more about Just in Time enrollment, including how to configure it and a user experience video, at the following link: `https://learn.microsoft.com/en-us/intune/intune-service/enrollment/set-up-just-in-time-registration`.

Enrolling your device: BYOD

Due to the differences between Android and iOS (no work profile, VPP, and Google Play differences), there are no real advantages to be gained from allowing personal devices to be enrolled over simply using app protection policies. Therefore, in this recipe, we will just demonstrate how to enroll using app protection only.

Getting started

For this recipe, you will need an Apple iOS/iPadOS device set up and signed in with an Apple ID to access Microsoft Store applications.

How to do it...

Follow these instructions:

1. Load up the App Store and search for an application. In this case, we are using Microsoft Word. After installing, click **Open**.
2. Click **Existing Microsoft 365 Users? Sign In**.
3. Enter your email address and click **Next**.
4. Enter your password and click **Sign In**.
5. After signing in, you will see the message in *Figure 6.19*. Click **OK** to restart the app:

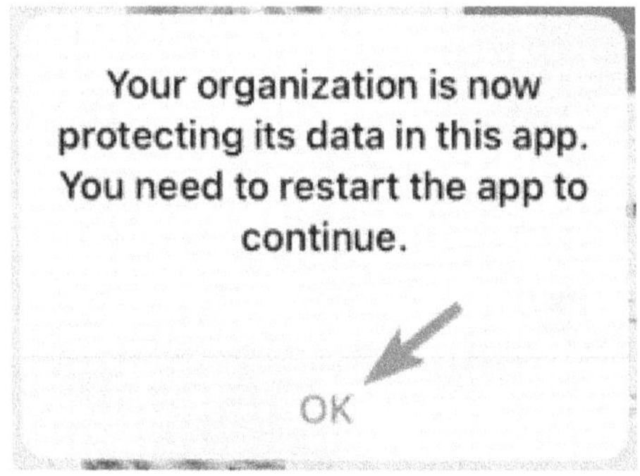

Figure 6.20 – Restart to manage

6. When you perform any action in the application (open a document, create a document, etc.), you will be prompted to set a PIN. You will also be told about any PIN restrictions set in your app protection policy.
7. Complete the same steps with any other organization apps.

This covers the chapter on iOS device management, and you can now fully manage your corporate and personal devices using Intune. In the next chapter, we will look at your macOS devices.

Join us on Discord

For discussions around the book and to connect with your peers, join us on Discord at `packt.link/discordcloud` or scan the QR code below:

7

macOS Device Management

The last of the different platforms we will cover in this book is macOS (at the time of writing, Linux and ChromeOS management are still too limited). We will look at configuring and then deploying a corporate device. For this, we will use **Apple Business Manager** (or **Apple Education**) configuration, which is explained in the *Technical requirements* section (as well as in the previous chapter on iOS).

The chapter will cover the configuration of profiles for your macOS devices, as well as their enrollment.

We will also run through the process of configuring Intune to work with **Apple Business Manager** (**ABM**) and deploy applications, using the **Volume Purchase Program**.

In this chapter, we will cover the following recipes:

- Configuring a macOS settings catalog policy
- Deploying shell scripts to macOS
- Configuring update policies for macOS
- Deploying apps to macOS
- Configuring a macOS enrollment profile
- Configuring Platform SSO for Entra integration
- Enrolling your corporate device

Chapter materials

As with *Chapters 2, 5,* and *6*, this chapter will not cover all available policy types, so we will run through them all now to ensure you have an understanding of what is available for macOS devices. As with Windows and iOS, macOS policy settings have now been largely migrated to the settings catalog.

The available profile types are as follows:

- **Settings catalog**: The unified settings catalog is a more modern way to deploy settings.
- **Custom**: This lets you upload a `.mobileconfig` file created in Profile Manager to configure settings not yet available elsewhere. We will cover this briefly in the following shell scripts recipe. Some examples can be found here: `https://github.com/microsoft/shell-intune-samples/tree/master/macOS`.
- **Device restrictions**: These are an alternative to the settings catalog for your standard restrictions.
- **Device features**: Device restrictions are used to protect and lock down devices. Device features set more custom settings, such as lock-screen messages and home screen layout.
- **Endpoint protection**: You can use this to set a firewall, FileVault, or Gatekeeper. This is now deprecated, and you should use the settings catalog instead.
- **Extensions**: This configures kernel and system extensions, both allowed and blocked. This is now deprecated and you should use the settings catalog instead.
- **Preference file**: Configure application or device preferences using a `.plist` file.
- **Public-key cryptography standards (PKCS) certificate**: This configures a public key pair certificate for authentication.
- **PKCS imported certificate**: This sets up an imported PKCS for **Secure/Multipurpose Internet Mail Extensions** (**S/MIME**) email authentication.
- **Simple Certificate Enrollment Protocol (SCEP) certificate**: This is used for certificate-based device authentication.
- **Software updates**: This is the same as an update policy, which we will cover in the following recipe.
- **Trusted certificates**: Import the trusted certificate needed for SCEP.
- **VPN**: Configure a VPN connection for your macOS devices.
- **Wi-Fi**: Configure Wi-Fi profiles, both basic and enterprise-supported. This can be used with certification profiles where applicable.
- **Wired network**: Same as a Wi-Fi profile but with a wire. Set which network adapter to use and your network settings.

Important notes

When dealing with Apple devices, there are some very important things to consider throughout the initial setup and continued management, which we will run through here.

It is important when dealing with Apple devices to keep an eye on the certificate renewal dates and record them somewhere, with a renewal reminder. You could also use Azure Automation to automate the reminders for you; see more here: `https://andrewstaylor.com/2022/06/07/alerting-when-my-apple-certificates-expire-in-intune-using-azure-automation/`.

If you would rather something a bit more set and forget, check out my free tool at `https://dailychecks.euctoolbox.com`.

The **MDM push certificate** connects your devices to the Intune MDM service. If this one expires, you can sometimes contact Apple directly if it is within 30 days of expiry to renew it. If they cannot, or 30 days have passed, your only option is to wipe and re-enroll all your devices. Yes, it is a full wipe – data destruction, everything.

The enrollment token is used to initially enroll your devices. If this one expires, you must create a new enrollment profile and transfer your devices to it. It is not quite as bad as a wipe, but it can result in the devices looking less healthy within the Intune portal itself.

The Apple VPP certificate is used to deploy applications to devices. If that one expires, users will not be able to download and install any new applications from the App Store until it is renewed. It is not a massive issue, and the certificate is easy to replace, but you could waste time troubleshooting an app installation issue and not consider this the issue.

When looking at your device restrictions/settings catalog policy, the settings you configure need to be tailored to your specific needs, providing the best security without ruining the end user experience.

The official CIS Benchmarks for macOS can be found here: `https://www.cisecurity.org/benchmark/apple_os`.

The NCSC guidance can be found here: `https://www.ncsc.gov.uk/collection/device-security-guidance/platform-guides/macos`.

While these should not be used as the only way to configure your settings, they are an excellent starting point, as macOS does not offer preconfigured security baselines like Windows.

macOS management is constantly evolving and improving with Intune. It is worth keeping an eye on the latest planned Intune developments by using the following link: https://www.microsoft.com/en-gb/microsoft-365/roadmap?rtc=3&filters=Mac%2CMicrosoft%20Intune.

If you are managing a fleet of macOS devices, the Microsoft Mac Admins community is also worth joining using the following link: https://www.intunemacadmins.com/.

Technical requirements

For this chapter, you will need a modern web browser and a PowerShell code editor, such as Visual Studio Code or PowerShell ISE.

All of the scripts referenced can be found here: https://github.com/PacktPublishing/Microsoft-Intune-Cookbook-Second-Edition/tree/main/Chapter-7.

You will need an ABM account (which requires a DUNS number, so keep this in mind) set up and ready to be configured with Intune. You can find instructions for setting up your ABM account at https://www.apple.com/business/docs/site/Apple_Business_Manager_Getting_Started_Guide.pdf, https://www.intuneirl.com/onboarding-to-abm/, and https://intunestuff.com/2024/10/09/manage-macos-with-intune-including-apple-business-manager-including-platform-sso-the-complete-guide/.

Your hardware supplier should be able to add your devices to ABM, but you can also use Apple Configurator on a device running macOS or iOS: https://support.apple.com/en-gb/apple-configurator.

Alternatively, you can watch these videos:

- https://www.youtube.com/watch?v=G_9bPrsJHGY&t=34s
- https://www.youtube.com/watch?v=G-rvHUY4iA0

To enroll devices, you will need a macOS device enrolled in ABM. If you want to use the latest Platform SSO functionality, you will need to be running macOS 13.x as a minimum, ideally 14.x.

Configuring a macOS settings catalog policy

We have looked at the different policy types available, but the most expanded option is the settings catalog, which is constantly being updated with new settings and, therefore, is the recommended method to deploy settings to your macOS device. You can now also export and import the settings catalog directly in the UI, which is a further advantage over other policy options.

Follow this recipe to find out how to configure your devices.

How to do it...

Here, we will learn how to use the settings catalog to configure our first macOS policy:

1. First, navigate to **Devices**, and then click on **macOS**.

Figure 7.1 – The Devices menu and macOS option

2. Now, click on **Configuration**, and **+ Create** and select **+ New Policy** in the drop-down.
3. Select **Settings catalog**, and click **Create**.
4. Enter a name and a description (optional), and then click **Next**.
   As with our Windows and iOS devices, we need to add settings.

   Here, you can pick the settings applicable to your environment. Adopt the same *less is more* approach that we used with Windows; it is better to have multiple smaller policies than fewer unmanageable ones. In this case, we will set some basic device restrictions, forcing encryption and enabling OneDrive **Known Folder Move** (**KFM**) and files on demand.

   Again, refer to the CIS and NCSC baselines (more details can be found by following the links in the *Important notes* section) for some general security guidance.

   Note that, in our settings, a lot of the macOS settings default to allow instead of block. Pay attention to the wording; you do not want to accidentally deploy a policy that allows everything you actually wanted to block.

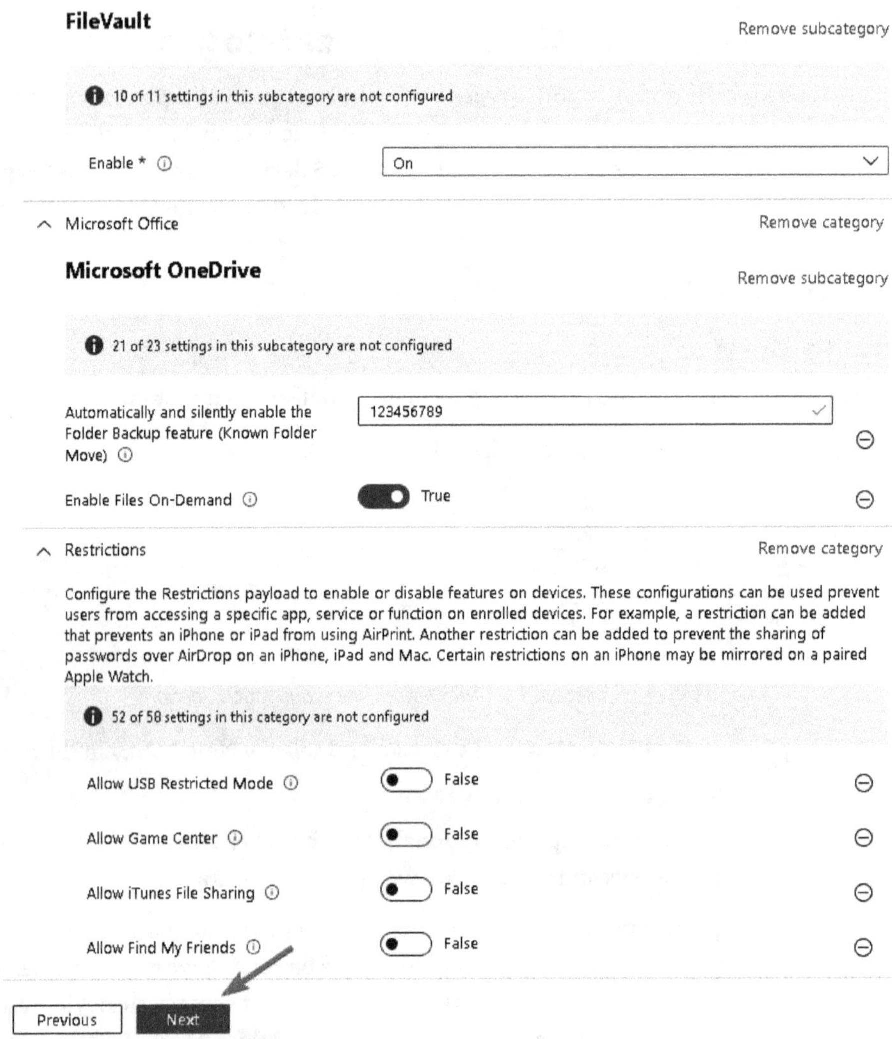

Figure 7.2 – The configured settings

5. When you have configured the settings, click **Next**.
6. Click **Next** on the **Scope tags** page.

   As this is a device restriction policy, we have picked settings that will apply to all devices without exception, so we can use the **All Devices** assignment. We could also go one step further, applying a filter to just macOS devices.

> **Note**
>
> As with any other policies, I suggest that if there are any settings that may need different configurations for different user groups, you leave these out of the baseline policies. This way, you can have a single baseline across the estate and then smaller, easier policies to handle one-off exceptions.

7. When you have configured your assignment, click **Next**.
8. Finally, check that everything looks correct, and then click **Create**.

Automating it

Now that we have learned how to configure in the UI, we can look at how to automate this policy using PowerShell.

Similar to automating iOS settings in the previous chapter, there is a mix of settings here, some of which are child items and some of which are direct assignments:

1. We can start by looking at the URL to find all of the available macOS settings:

   ```
   https://graph.microsoft.com/beta/deviceManagement/configurationCategories?
   =&`$filter=(platforms has 'macOS') and (technologies has 'mdm' or
   technologies has 'appleRemoteManagement')
   ```

   If we pick a couple of settings, we can have a look at the differences.

2. We will first run a `GET` command against the preceding URL to retrieve all of the categories available.
   Our returned ID for full disk encryption is `3f56adc1-2207-4033-a6e2-07f64c08e3ff`.

3. Now, we run a `GET` command to find the policies within the category against this URL:

   ```
   https://graph.microsoft.com/beta/deviceManagement/configurationSettings?
   &$filter=categoryId+eq+'3f56adc1-2207-4033-a6e2-07f64c08e3ff'
   ```

   In the output, we can see that this setting depends on a parent setting ID:

   ```
   "dependentOn": [
       {
           "dependentOn":
               "com.apple.mcx.filevault2_com.apple.mcx.filevault2",
           "parentSettingId":
   ```

```
            "com.apple.mcx.filevault2_com.apple.mcx.filevault2"
    }
```

This means it is a child setting and uses `groupSettingCollectionValue` with children in the JSON.

For OneDrive KFM, we will use the category ID `19ba782c-3594-45da-b829-72b54f6d45c7`.

Running a `GET` command on this URL then returns the available settings:

```
https://graph.microsoft.com/beta/deviceManagement/configurationSettings?
&$filter=categoryId+eq+'19ba782c-3594-45da-b829-72b54f6d45c7'
```

In this output, both `dependentOn` and `dependedOnBy` are empty arrays, which means the JSON for these is more standard, as found in the Windows settings catalog:

```
    "dependentOn": [],
    "dependedOnBy": []
```

4. Now, we can use this knowledge and look at the JSON for our configured policy. Set the name, description, and URL:

```
$name = "macOS Settings"
$description = "Baseline settings for macOS devices"
$url = "https://graph.microsoft.com/beta/deviceManagement/
configurationPolicies"
```

We will not include the full JSON here, as that is available on GitHub, and will instead use two of the example settings, one with a child item (OneDrive KFM) and one without (enabling FileVault):

```
$json = @"
{
    "description": "$description",
    "name": "$name",
    "platforms": "macOS",
    "roleScopeTagIds": [
        "0"
    ],
    "settings": [
```

```
        {
            "@odata.type":
"#microsoft.graph.deviceManagementConfigurationSetting",
            "settingInstance": {
                "@odata.type":
"#microsoft.graph.deviceManagementConfigurationGroupSettingCollectionInstan
ce",
                "groupSettingCollectionValue": [
                    {
                        "children": [
                            {
                                "@odata.type":
"#microsoft.graph.deviceManagementConfigurationChoiceSettingInstance",
                                "choiceSettingValue": {
                                    "@odata.type":
"#microsoft.graph.deviceManagementConfigurationChoiceSettingValue",
                                    "children": [],
                                    "value":
"com.apple.mcx.filevault2_enable_0"
                                },
                                "settingDefinitionId":
"com.apple.mcx.filevault2_enable"
                            }
                        ]
                    }
                ],
                "settingDefinitionId":
"com.apple.mcx.filevault2_com.apple.mcx.filevault2"
            }
        },
        {
            "@odata.type":
"#microsoft.graph.deviceManagementConfigurationSetting",
            "settingInstance": {
                "@odata.type":
"#microsoft.graph.deviceManagementConfigurationSimpleSettingInstance",
                "settingDefinitionId":
"com.apple.managedclient.preferences_kfmsilentoptin",
                "simpleSettingValue": {
                    "@odata.type":
"#microsoft.graph.deviceManagementConfigurationStringSettingValue",
```

```
                        "value": "123456789"
                    }
                }
            }
        }
    ],
    "technologies": "mdm,appleRemoteManagement"
}
"@
```

5. Create the policy, and copy the policy ID:

```
$policy = Invoke-MgGraphRequest -Method POST -Uri $url -Body $json -
OutputType PSObject -ContentType "application/json"
$policyid = $policy.id
```

6. Populate the URL with the ID:

```
$assignurl = "https://graph.microsoft.com/beta/deviceManagement/
configurationPolicies/$policyid/assign"
```

7. Finally, assign the ID to all devices:

```
$json = @"
{
    "assignments": [
        {
            "target": {
                "@odata.type":
"#microsoft.graph.allDevicesAssignmentTarget"
            }
        }
    ]
}
"@
Invoke-MgGraphRequest -Method POST -Uri $assignurl -Body $json -OutputType
PSObject -ContentType "application/json"
```

Deploying shell scripts to macOS

With Windows devices, you can use PowerShell scripts to make changes not currently supported by other methods, such as the settings catalog or a custom OMA-URI. We will cover these in *Chapter 12, PowerShell Scripting across Intune.*

For devices that run macOS, the alternative is shell scripts. These can be configured to run at either the system or user level, and as macOS is Unix-based, it can configure almost anything on a device.

Getting ready

There are some prerequisites and things to watch out for with shell scripts; we will start with the prerequisites:

- **Prerequisites**:
  - You must be running at least macOS 11.0
  - Your devices must have a direct connection to the internet (no proxy server)
  - Scripts must begin with `#!`
- **Considerations**:
  - Shell scripts run in parallel, so if you deploy multiple scripts, they will run at the same time
  - Scripts deployed as the signed-in user will run on *all* signed-in accounts on the device at the point that the script runs
  - A user has to be signed in to access user-level scripts
  - Users will need root access for any user-level scripts that are running elevated commands
  - While you can specify how often a script will run, should something change on the device, it may run more regularly (clearing cache, device restart, etc.)
  - A script that runs for more than 60 minutes will time out, be stopped, and be reported as failed
  - Shell scripts can be a maximum of 200 KB

Now that we have these out of the way, we can create our first shell script.

We will not be running through the process of creating shell scripts here but instead will cover how to deploy them to your devices.

Before starting this recipe, you will need a shell script in the `.sh` format. Some examples from Microsoft can be found here: `https://github.com/microsoft/shell-intune-samples/tree/master/macOS`.

In this example, we will deploy a wallpaper image using the script here: `https://github.com/microsoft/shell-intune-samples/tree/master/macOS/Config/Wallpaper`.

The two scripts used are also available on GitHub.

To gain an understanding of how to deploy a custom profile (which is used to run your script on devices), we will also include those steps.

How to do it...

We need to start by deploying the shell script itself, and then we can configure the policy to deploy it.

Deploying a shell script

Follow these steps to deploy a shell script into Intune:

1. First, we need to navigate to **Devices** and then **macOS**.
2. In **macOS policies**, click **Scripts** and **Add**, set the name and description, and then click **Next**.
3. Click the folder icon and select your script.

   This will display the script contents in the read-only editor below the script path on-screen. If you need to make changes, the file will need to be re-uploaded:

```
#!/bin/sh
# Define variables
usebingwallpaper=false
wallpaperurl="https://github.com/microsoft/shell-intune-samples/raw/master/img/M365.
wallpaperdir="/Library/Desktop"
wallpaperfile="Wallpaper.jpg"
log="/var/log/fetchdesktopwallpaper.log"
```

Figure 7.3 – The shell script content

   Below the script name, you can see the details.

4. In our case, as shown in *Figure 7.4*, we want the script to run elevated, so **Run script as signed-in user** is set to **No**.

   We do not want notifications, and we want the script to run every day so that we can update the background.

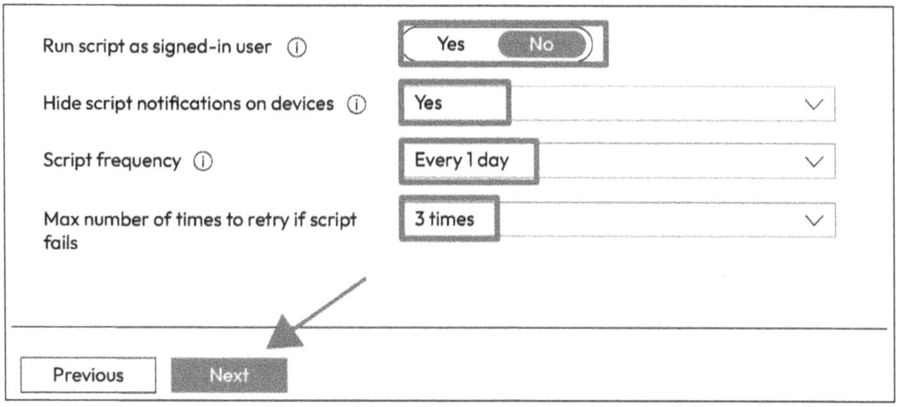

Figure 7.4 – The shell script settings

5. Once you have configured the settings for your script, click **Next**.
6. We are not setting scope tags at this point, so click **Next**.
7. Assign as appropriate; we will use Intune users so that we have the option to have different images for different user groups, but if it is a fixed corporate background, all devices with a filter will also work well. After configuring your assignments, click **Next**.
8. Finally, confirm that everything is correct, and then click **Add**.

Deploying a custom profile

The script we have just created will download the wallpaper image to the device, but we also need to tell the device to use it. To do that, we are going to deploy a custom profile:

1. Click **Configuration**, and then click **+ Create** and select **+ New Policy**.
2. In the fly-out, click **Templates** | **Custom**, and then click **Create**.
3. Give your new profile a name and description.
4. Give the setting a name, and select whether it runs in the **User** or **Device** context. This cannot be changed after the profile has been created, so if you select the wrong option here, the only option is to recreate the profile.
5. Upload your file, and it will display in the read-only editor below:

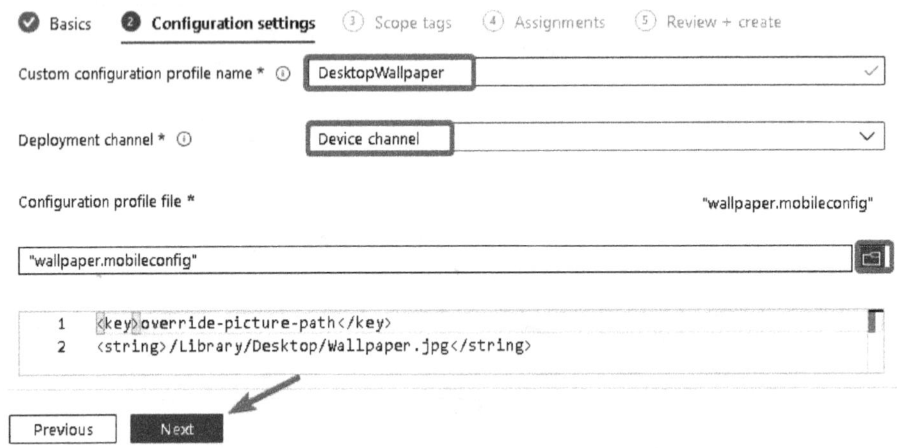

Figure 7.5 – Custom profile settings

6. In this example, the file needs to run in the device context. After configuring your settings, click **Next**.
7. Again, we do not need scope tags here, so press **Next**.
8. It is worth matching the assignment here to the custom script deployed earlier. Then, click **Next**.
9. Confirm that everything looks okay, and then click **Create**.

To take things one step further, you can then restrict users from changing the background by setting **Allow Wallpaper Modification** to **False** in the settings catalog (as covered earlier):

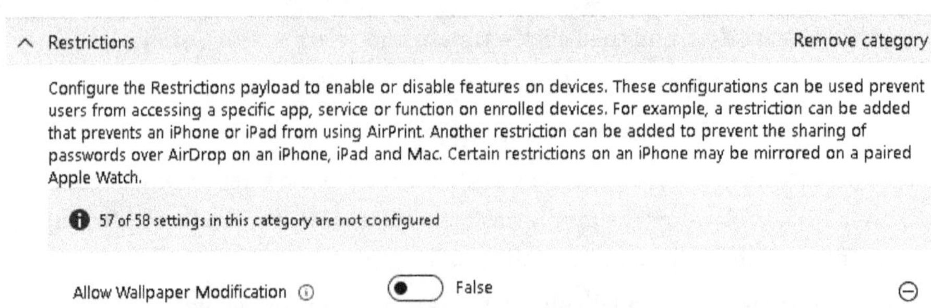

Figure 7.6 – Wallpaper modification in the settings catalog

Automating it

Now, we can look at automating both the shell script and the custom profile. As both involve a file upload, we will again let PowerShell do the heavy lifting and convert to Base64 for upload.

Deploying a shell script

Let's start with the shell script:

1. We will start with the default settings and also include the path to the script itself. We will use the `deviceShellScripts` area of Microsoft Graph for this command:

```
$url = "https://graph.microsoft.com/beta/deviceManagement/
deviceShellScripts"
$name = "Download Wallpaper Background"
$description = "Downloads the wallpaper background to be used with Custom
Profile"
$groupid = "000000-0000-0000-0000-000000000000"
$scriptpath = "c:\temp\downloadwallpaper.sh"
```

2. Now, we want to convert the script to Base64:

```
$shellscript =
[System.Convert]::ToBase64String([System.Text.Encoding]::UTF8.GetBytes([Sys
tem.IO.File]::ReadAllText($scriptpath)))
```

3. We also need to pass the filename, which we will get using the `[System.IO.Path]::GetFileName` function:

```
$filename = [System.IO.Path]::GetFileName($scriptpath)
```

4. Next, populate the JSON. Note that we can also set the retry count (up to 3) and the frequency, which in this case is `P1D` (which stands for **period one day**).
   The notifications are set via a simple `true/false` Boolean, and `runAsAccount` can be `system` or `user`:

```
$json = @"
{
    "blockExecutionNotifications": true,
    "description": "$description",
    "displayName": "$name",
    "executionFrequency": "P1D",
    "fileName": "$filename",
    "retryCount": 3,
    "roleScopeTagIds": [
        "0"
```

```
    ],
    "runAsAccount": "system",
    "scriptContent": "$shellscript"
}
"@
```

5. As usual, create the policy and grab the ID:

```
$policy = Invoke-MgGraphRequest -Uri $url -Method Post -Body $json -
ContentType "application/json" -OutputType PSObject
$policyid = $policy.id
```

6. Add the profile ID to the assignment URL, and assign it:

```
$assignurl = "https://graph.microsoft.com/beta/deviceManagement/
DeviceShellScripts/$policyid/assign"
$assignjson = @"
{
    "deviceManagementScriptAssignments": [
        {
            "target": {
                "@odata.type": "#microsoft.graph.groupAssignmentTarget",
                "groupId": "$groupid"
            }
        }
    ]
}
"@
Invoke-MgGraphRequest -Uri $assignurl -Method Post -Body $assignjson -
ContentType "application/json"
```

This has created our shell script and then added and assigned it to Intune.

Deploying a custom profile

The same applies to the custom profile, where we need to upload a file and grab the filename:

1. As usual, start with the basics. Along with the file path, we also need a name for the setting itself:

```
$url = "    https://graph.microsoft.com/beta/deviceManagement/
deviceConfigurations"
```

```
$name = "Configure Desktop Wallpaper"
$description = "Forces wallpaper to /Library/Desktop/Wallpaper.jpg\nAs
downloaded in Shell Script"
$settingname = "DesktopWallpaper"
$groupid = "000000-0000-0000-0000-000000000000"
$configpath = "c:\temp\wallpaper.mobileconfig"
```

2. Convert our image to Base64:

```
$configscript =
[System.Convert]::ToBase64String([System.Text.Encoding]::UTF8.GetBytes([Sys
tem.IO.File]::ReadAllText($configpath)))
```

3. Grab the filename:

```
$filename = [System.IO.Path]::GetFileName($configpath)
```

4. Populate the JSON. The only additional setting here is the deployment context, where you can have either `deviceChannel` or `userChannel`:

```
$json = @"
{
    "@odata.type": "#microsoft.graph.macOSCustomConfiguration",
    "deploymentChannel": "deviceChannel",
    "description": "$description",
    "displayName": "$name",
    "id": "00000000-0000-0000-0000-000000000000",
    "payload": "$configscript",
    "payloadFileName": "$filename",
    "payloadName": "$settingname",
    "roleScopeTagIds": [
        "0"
    ]
}
"@
```

5. Create the profile and grab the ID:

```
$policy = Invoke-MgGraphRequest -Uri $url -Method Post -Body $json -
ContentType "application/json" -OutputType PSObject
$policyid = $policy.id
```

6. Populate our URL with the policy ID, and assign the policy:

```
$assignurl = "https://graph.microsoft.com/beta/deviceManagement/
deviceConfigurations/$policyid/assign"

$assignjson = @"
{
    "deviceManagementScriptAssignments": [
        {
            "target": {
                "@odata.type": "#microsoft.graph.groupAssignmentTarget",
                "groupId": "$groupid"
            }
        }
    ]
}
"@
Invoke-MgGraphRequest -Uri $assignurl -Method Post -Body $assignjson -
ContentType "application/json"
```

By following this script, you have created a custom profile and added your custom script to it.

Configuring update policies for macOS

As with our Windows and iOS devices, we want to make sure they run the latest available OS version to increase security across the estate. For macOS, this is accomplished using **Declarative Device Management** (**DDM**), which is configured via a settings catalog policy. As with Windows devices, for a large macOS estate, it is worth using deployment rings so that updates can be tested prior to large-scale deployment.

How to do it...

Take the following steps:

1. Start by clicking on **Devices** and then **macOS**.
2. Then, click **Configuration**.

3. Click **+Create** and select **+New Policy**.
4. In the fly-out, select **Settings catalog**.
5. As usual, we will start with a name and description, and then click **Next**.
6. On the next screen, click **+Add settings** and expand **Declarative Device Management (DDM)**.
7. Here we are looking at the settings within the following options: **Software Update**, **Software Update Enforce Latest**, and **Software Update Settings**. The configuration here depends on your particular needs.
   For more information on the settings, the official guide can be found here: `https://learn.microsoft.com/en-us/intune/device-updates/apple/?tabs=automatic-updates`.

   In our case, we are forcing updates but blocking users from installing major updates to keep control and allow us to use the update rings.

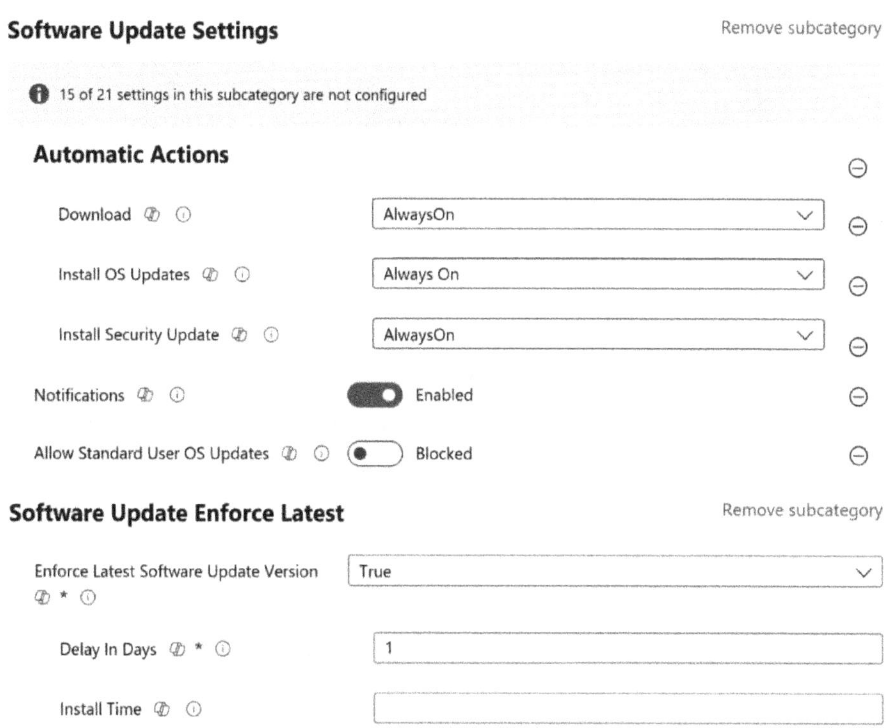

Figure 7.7 – Update policy settings

8. Once you have configured your environment, click **Next**.
9. We do not need scope tags, so again, click **Next**.

10. Now, consider your assignments, depending on what you have selected for the update policy. You may wish to create multiple policies with different settings for different user groups or device types (for example, your non-user kiosk-style devices may need different settings, or you could have shift workers).
    In our case, we will assign to Intune users, giving us the flexibility to exclude other groups as required. Unlike Windows devices, you do not have the option to pick different deployment rings. Also note that you cannot set the OS version as with Windows and iOS.
11. Once configured, click **Next**.
12. Finally, check that everything looks correct, and then click **Create**.

We have now created our update policy in the Intune UI.

Automating it

As this policy is using the settings catalog, the automation is very similar to the earlier recipe covering using the settings catalog to create policies:

1. Start with the basics as usual:

```
$url = "https://graph.microsoft.com/beta/deviceManagement/
configurationPolicies"
$name = "macOS Updates"
$description = "Managed updates on macOS devices"
$groupid = "000000-0000-0000-0000-000000000000"
```

2. We then populate the JSON with the settings we have configured. For brevity, I will only include one section initially, but the full script can be found in the GitHub repository mentioned at the start of this chapter:

```
$json = @"
{
"description": "$description",
"name": "$name",
"platforms": "macOS",
"roleScopeTagIds": [
"0"
],
"settings": [
{
"@odata.type": "#microsoft.graph.deviceManagementConfigurationSetting",
"settingInstance": {
```

```
"@odata.type":
"#microsoft.graph.deviceManagementConfigurationGroupSettingCollectionInstan
ce",
"groupSettingCollectionValue": [
{
"children": [
{
"@odata.type":
"#microsoft.graph.deviceManagementConfigurationChoiceSettingInstance",
"choiceSettingValue": {
"@odata.type":
"#microsoft.graph.deviceManagementConfigurationChoiceSettingValue",
"children": [
{
"@odata.type":
"#microsoft.graph.deviceManagementConfigurationSimpleSettingInstance",
"settingDefinitionId": "ddm-latestsoftwareupdate_delayindays",
"simpleSettingValue": {
"@odata.type":
"#microsoft.graph.deviceManagementConfigurationIntegerSettingValue",
"value": 1
}
}
```

3. Finally, create and assign the policy:

```
$policy = Invoke-MgGraphRequest -Uri $url -Method Post -Body $json -
ContentType "application/json" -OutputType PSObject
$policyid = $policy.id
$assignurl = "https://graph.microsoft.com/beta/deviceManagement/
configurationPolicies/$policyid/assign"
$assignjson = @"
{
    "assignments": [
        {
            "target": {
                "@odata.type": "#microsoft.graph.groupAssignmentTarget",
                "groupId": "$groupid"
            }
        }
    ]
```

```
}
"@
Invoke-MgGraphRequest -Uri $assignurl -Method Post -Body $assignjson -
ContentType "application/json"
```

We have now created and assigned an update policy for our macOS devices using PowerShell and Graph.

Deploying apps to macOS

We have configured and protected our devices, but the end users are going to want to have some applications deployed as well. Within Intune, there are a number of options available:

- **Microsoft 365 Apps**: A GUI to deploy Microsoft 365 apps (covered later)
- **Microsoft Edge**: To deploy Edge V77 and later (Chromium) (covered later)
- **Microsoft Defender for Endpoint**: To protect your devices (covered later)
- **Web link**: Deploy a URL to the desktop
- **Line-of-business app**: Deploy a custom PKG application
- **macOS app (DMG)**: Upload and deploy a DMG-based application (covered later)
- **macOS app (pkg)**: Upload and deploy a PKG-based application (covered later)
- **App Store app**: Similar to iOS, this deploys a VPP app from the App Store (covered later)

Getting ready

For this recipe, make sure you have a DMG file available to deploy, and also access to either ABM or Apple Education to deploy applications from the App Store.

How to do it...

All of these instructions will be carried out after going to **Apps** and then **macOS apps** in the Intune portal.

App Store

Take the following steps:

1. Within ABM, click **Apps and Books**.
2. Search for the application you want, and make sure it is a macOS app. In this case, we will use **GarageBand**:

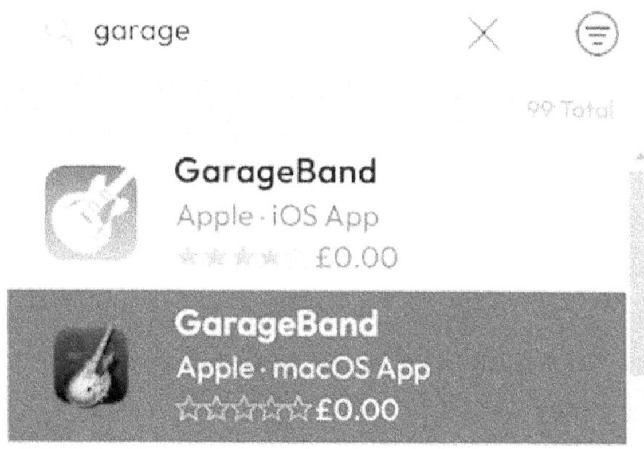

Figure 7.8 – App selection

3. After clicking on the application, purchase licenses for your MDM, and then click **Get**:

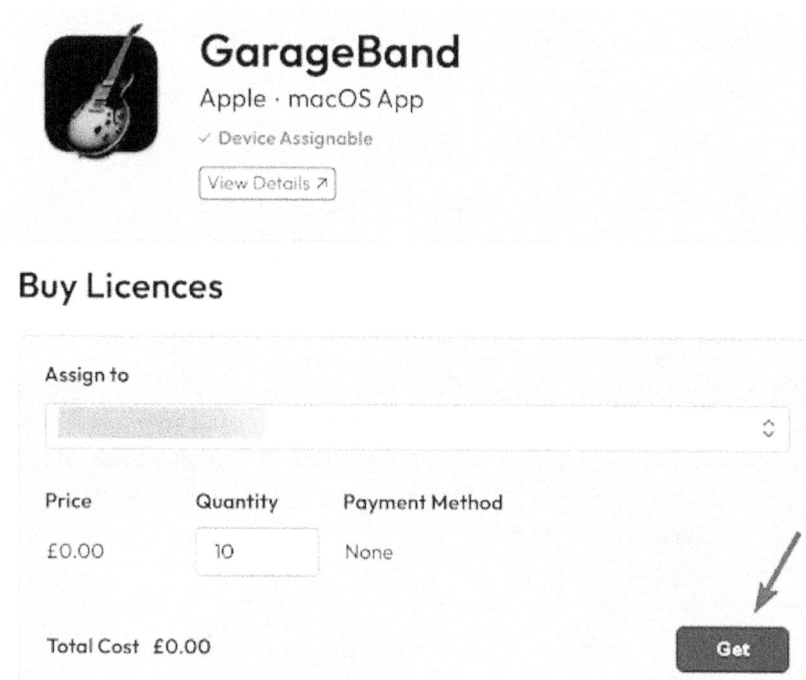

Figure 7.9 – Getting an app

4. This application should appear almost instantly in Intune, but you can follow the application instructions in *Chapter 6, iOS Device Management*, to force a sync if not.

5. Back in the Intune portal, you can see the application, which is unassigned. Click on it to configure assignments:

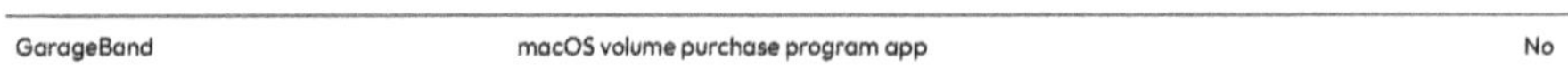

Figure 7.10 – The app in Intune

6. Click **Properties**, and under **Assignments**, click **Edit**.
7. Assign the application as required. For an application such as this, it is normally suggested to create application-specific install and uninstall groups, which is what we have done here. For a standard app such as Microsoft 365 or Edge, the assignments can be broader. You can also set the application as a forced install (**Required**) or self-service (**Available**).

   For free applications that do not require a license, one option is to force an installation on members of the group (those who need it for their role) and allow it as self-service for others to install as required.
8. After adding the assignment, some further options will be displayed:

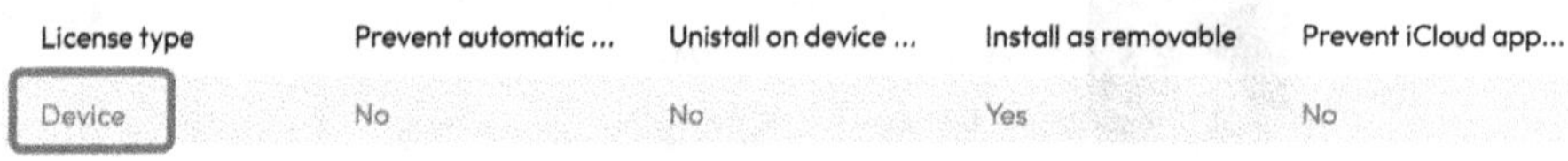

Figure 7.11 – Assignment options

   The important option here is the license type. We do not want our users to need an Apple ID to install applications, and therefore, we need to make sure we choose **Device** licensing.
9. Clicking on any of the blue text links will load a fly-out panel with further options. You can configure these settings as required; in this case, we want the application to be forced, updated, and not backed up, as it stores credentials and should not be deleted unless the device is removed from Intune management. When you have configured your requirements, click **OK**:

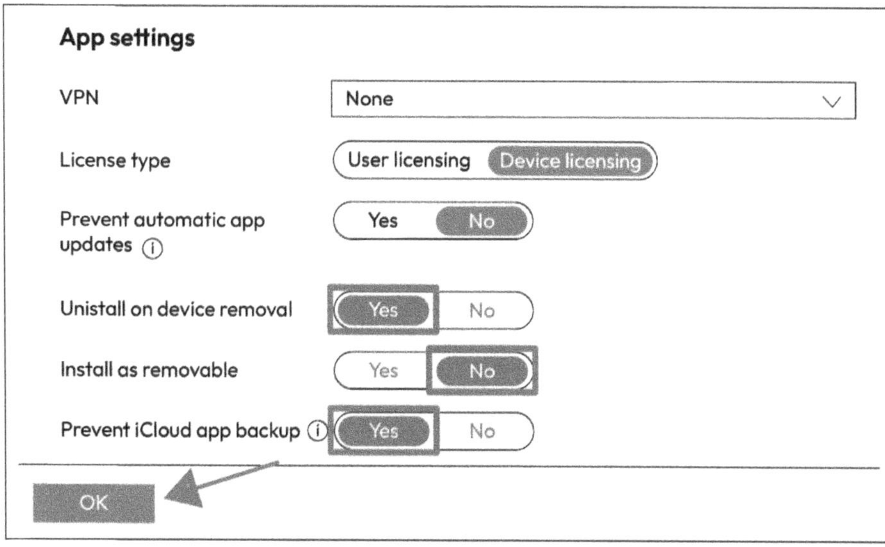

Figure 7.12 – Further app settings

10. Once you have configured your assignments and settings, click **Review and Save**. We are editing an existing application, which is why there is no **Create or Add** option.
11. Check that everything looks acceptable, and then click **Save**.

DMG applications

When Intune first supported macOS, you had to wrap applications in the `.intunemac` format, similar to Windows Win32 apps and the `intunewin` packaging. Fortunately, in early 2022, the ability to deploy `.dmg` files directly was added.

To follow this recipe, you will need a DMG file to deploy to your devices; in this example, we will use Adobe Acrobat Reader, available at the following link (if you are downloading from a Windows machine, click **More Options** to select the macOS version): `https://get.adobe.com/uk/reader/`.

Now, take the following steps:

1. Return to the Intune portal in Apps/macOS, and then click **Add**.
2. In the fly-out, select **macOS App (DMG)**, and then click **Select**.
3. Click **Select app package file**.
4. In the fly-out, select the DMG file downloaded earlier, and click **OK**.
5. Complete the application details. If you are allowing this for self-service, supplying an image and category will make the company portal easier for end users to navigate.

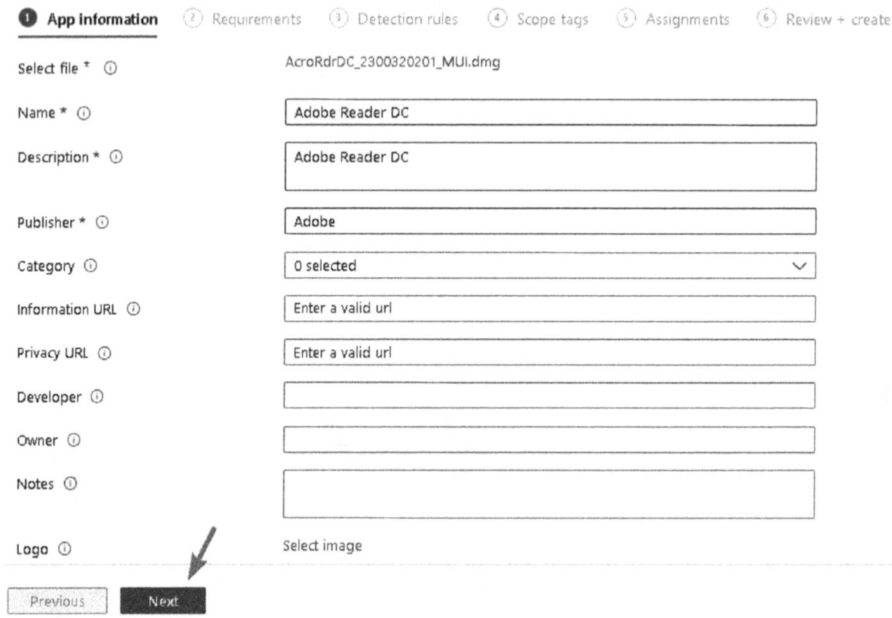

Figure 7.13 – The application details

6. Once you have entered the necessary information, click **Next**.
7. On the next screen, you can specify a minimum OS version for the software to install on. In this case, the installer works on all of the available options, so we will select the oldest OS version.
8. If you have a mixed estate, you can deploy multiple versions of the same application, and then when assigning, simply use device filters to only install on applicable devices. Once you have selected a version, click **Next**.
9. We now have to look at application detection. The first thing is to check or ignore the app version. If the application automatically updates, you want to leave **Ignore app version** as **Yes** so that the application continues to be detected after an update.
10. When you set **Ignore app version** as **No**, the app bundle ID and version must match before the application is uninstalled (when a user/device is added to the uninstall group). If it is set to **Yes**, Intune only checks the bundle ID and ignores the version. To find the bundle ID, install the application on a test machine, and run the following command in Terminal (replace `Adobe Acrobat Reader` with the exact name of the application):

```
osascript -e 'id of app "Adobe Acrobat Reader"'
```

Note that the app list is case-sensitive, so pay close attention to the name.

11. We need to enter an app version, but it will not actually be used, as we have **Ignore app version** set to **Yes**. Once configured, click **Next**.

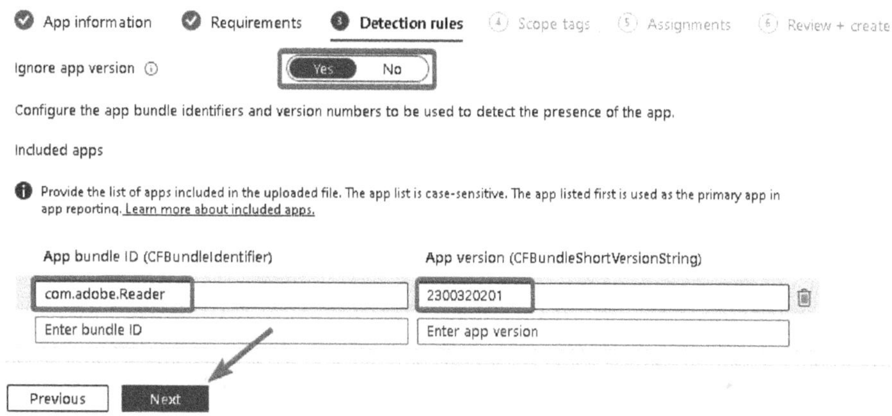

Figure 7.14 – App detection rules

12. We can skip past the **Scope tags** page, so click **Next**.
    As with the store application, we are going to use groups for **Required** and **Uninstall** assignment. There is no self-service option for DMG-deployed applications. Once you have added your groups, click **Next**.
13. Finally, check that everything looks okay, and click **Create**.

PKG applications

Another release in 2022, Intune now also supports the deployment of PKG applications to further increase the support of different applications.

For this example, we will be using Adoptium Temurin, an open source Java JDK that can be downloaded from `https://adoptium.net/en-GB/temurin/releases/?os=any&arch=any&version=21`. Follow these steps:

1. Navigate to the Intune portal. Click on **Apps**, then **macOS**, and then click **Add**.
2. In the fly-out, select **macOS App (PKG)**, and then click **Select**.
3. Click **Select app package file**.
4. In the fly-out, select the PKG file downloaded earlier, and click **OK**.
5. Enter any missing details, or update any included as required. Optionally, add a logo and click **Next**.

6. If you have any pre- or post-install scripts, you can add them here. When completed, click **Next**.
7. Select the minimum operating system and click **Next**.
8. It should automatically detect your detection rules, but if you want to add more or change them, you can do so here. If the app auto-updates, make sure you ignore the application version or the detection will fail when updated. When completed, click **Next**.
9. Assign the policy as required in your organization, then click **Next**.
10. Finally, confirm that all looks correct and click **Create**.

Microsoft 365 apps

Now that we have covered the more complex applications, we can look at the simpler GUI-driven ones for your key Microsoft applications. For Windows devices, we will look at something similar in *Chapter 11*, but it is often preferred to deploy Microsoft 365 apps as a Win32 application packaged with the **Office Deployment Tool** (**ODT**), due to the way applications and policies are processed.

On macOS, however, the GUI works well and does not have the same drawbacks:

1. Within macOS apps, create a new application, select **macOS** under **Microsoft 365 Apps**, and then click **Select**.
2. On the next screen, you have the familiar application details; conveniently, it is all pre-populated for you.
   With Windows deployments, you have more options to select here, but for macOS, it is a simple configuration.
3. Make any changes to your environment and click **Next**.
4. We do not need scope tags at this point, so again, click **Next**.
5. Assign the application as required. Generally, these apps are required by everyone, but you could also create a dynamic group to include only users who have an Office desktop apps license with this dynamic rule:

```
(user.assignedPlans -any (assignedPlan.servicePlanId -eq "43de0ff5-
c92c-492b-9116-175376d08c38" -and assignedPlan.capabilityStatus -eq
"Enabled"))
```

6. The deployment options here are either required or available. There is no uninstall option, but you can utilize self-service with available assignments, unlike with a DMG application.

7. In our case, we are going to use the **Intune-Users** group, and then click **Next**.
8. Finally, confirm everything is correct, and then click **Create**.

Microsoft Edge

Another Microsoft app you may want to deploy to your macOS devices is Microsoft Edge, for easier management, cross-platform continuity, and integration with Defender for Endpoint.

Fortunately, this is another straightforward GUI configuration:

1. Create a new application. This time, in the dropdown, select **macOS** under **Microsoft Edge, version 77 and later** (version 77 was the switch to the new Edge Chromium version). Then, click **Select**.
2. Note that, as with Microsoft 365 apps, the details here are pre-populated, but this time, there is no option to add or change the image. This is because the image is selected depending on which channel is chosen on the next screen. Change anything if needed, and then click **Next**.
3. On the next screen, you can select which version of Edge to deploy: **Dev**, **Beta**, or **Stable**. While you should use **Stable** as the default for the majority of your users, it is worth deploying both the **Dev** and **Beta** versions to test users, similar to how we handle OS updates. This gives you a chance to confirm that all web-based applications work correctly before updates are applied. It also gives you advance notice of any UI changes that you may want to notify your users about.
   You can find out more about the different Edge channels here: `https://learn.microsoft.com/en-us/deployedge/microsoft-edge-channels`.
4. In this case, we are going to deploy the **Stable** version:

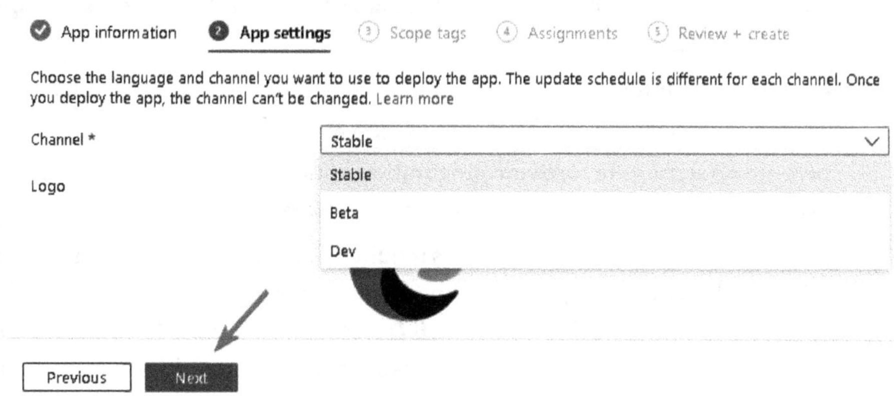

Figure 7.15 – Edge app settings

5. As usual, press **Next** on the **Scope tags** screen.
6. While this is an application that you will undoubtedly want to have across your entire estate and could potentially use for all users or devices, as mentioned earlier, you may prefer to utilize deployment rings for testing purposes. Therefore, assigning the application to a group gives you greater control.
   Note that, again, there is no uninstall group option, but you can add it for self-service along with a standard **Required** installation.

   In our case, we are going to use the **Intune-Users** group.
7. Finally, check that everything looks okay, and then click **Create**. Note that the logo has now been added to match the channel chosen earlier.

Microsoft Defender for Endpoint

The final application we may wish to deploy is Microsoft Defender for Endpoint. We can use this to both protect against malware and, if licensed, use some of the extra features, such as web filtering:

> Note
>
> There are prerequisites that need to be deployed to your environment before deploying the application. You can find out what they are and how to deploy them at the following link: `https://learn.microsoft.com/en-us/microsoft-365/security/defender-endpoint/mac-install-with-intune?view=o365-worldwide`.

1. As with the other Microsoft applications, it also has a simple GUI. Create a new application, and this time, select **macOS** under **Microsoft Defender for Endpoint**. Then, click **Select**.
2. Again, all of the information is pre-populated, including the image (which you cannot change). Click **Next** after making any changes as required.
3. There are no settings or further configuration options for Defender for Endpoint, so we are taken straight to the **Scope tags** page. Click **Next**.
4. Again, we have the option to deploy as required or available, but there is no uninstall option. As this is a security application, we really want to be sure it is installed everywhere, so we are going to select **All Devices**. As mentioned earlier, you could add a filter to only include macOS devices in order to keep things tidier. Once you have added your assignment, click **Next**.
5. Finally, confirm that everything looks correct, and then click **Create**.

Automating it

Now that we have added our application to the UI, we can look at which parts can be automated.

App Store

While you cannot automate adding the application itself, you can automate its assignment. We do this by finding the application ID and then assigning it:

1. First, we set the name we are looking for. We will let PowerShell and Graph do the hard work for us:

```
$appname = "GarageBand"
```

2. Now, we can run a `GET` request against all of the mobile apps in the tenant. We then only want Apple VPP-deployed applications, using the `@odata.type` variable as `#microsoft.graph.macOSVppApp`. Once we have the VPP apps, we can find just those that match the name, and finally, we just want the ID (nested within the `Value` attribute):

```
$appid = ((Invoke-MgGraphRequest -Uri "https://graph.microsoft.com/beta/
deviceAppManagement/mobileApps" -Method Get -ContentType "application/json"
-OutputType PSObject).value | Where-Object {$_.'@odata.type' -eq
'#microsoft.graph.macOSVppApp'} | Where-Object {$_.displayName -eq
$appname}).id
```

3. Populate the URL with `$appid`:

```
$url = "https://graph.microsoft.com/beta/deviceAppManagement/mobileApps/
$appid/assign"
```

4. Now, we need the JSON, which you can see that we have configured with the `Required`, `Uninstall`, and `Available` assignments:

```
$json = @"
{
    "mobileAppAssignments": [
        {
            "@odata.type": "#microsoft.graph.mobileAppAssignment",
            "intent": "Required",
```

```
            "settings": {
                "@odata.type":
"#microsoft.graph.macOsVppAppAssignmentSettings",
                "preventAutoAppUpdate": false,
                "preventManagedAppBackup": false,
                "uninstallOnDeviceRemoval": false,
                "useDeviceLicensing": true
            },
            "target": {
                "@odata.type": "#microsoft.graph.groupAssignmentTarget",
                "groupId": "$installgroupid"
            }
        },
        {
            "@odata.type": "#microsoft.graph.mobileAppAssignment",
            "intent": "Available",
            "settings": {
                "@odata.type":
"#microsoft.graph.macOsVppAppAssignmentSettings",
                "preventAutoAppUpdate": false,
                "preventManagedAppBackup": false,
                "uninstallOnDeviceRemoval": false,
                "useDeviceLicensing": true
            },
            "target": {
                "@odata.type":
"#microsoft.graph.allLicensedUsersAssignmentTarget"
            }
        },
        {
            "@odata.type": "#microsoft.graph.mobileAppAssignment",
            "intent": "Uninstall",
            "settings": {
                "@odata.type":
"#microsoft.graph.macOsVppAppAssignmentSettings",
                "useDeviceLicensing": true
            },
            "target": {
                "@odata.type": "#microsoft.graph.groupAssignmentTarget",
                "groupId": "$unistallgroupid"
            }
```

```
        }
    ]
}
"@
```

5. Finally, send a POST request to add the assignment:

```
Invoke-MgGraphRequest -Uri $url -Method Post -Body $json -ContentType
"application/json"
```

DMG applications

At present, DMG applications cannot be added using Graph and PowerShell, as the file encryption information seems to be hidden during the Azure Blob upload process.

PKG applications

As with DMG applications, PKG applications cannot be added using Graph and PowerShell, as the file encryption information seems to be hidden during the Azure Blob upload process. A community tool is available here should you want to automate in a CI/CD pipeline: `https://github.com/almenscorner/intune-uploader`.

Microsoft 365 apps

Deploying Microsoft 365 apps is as straightforward using PowerShell as it is via the GUI. This is more of a policy than an application, so the JSON just contains references to the applications rather than having to deal with file uploads or finding app information from the store:

1. As usual, we will start with the basics, that is, the name, description, URL, and group ID:

```
$url = "https://graph.microsoft.com/beta/deviceAppManagement/mobileApps/"
$appname = "Microsoft 365 Apps"
$appdesc = "Microsoft 365 Apps for Enterprise"
$groupid = "00000000-0000-0000-0000-000000000000"
```

2. As this is a preconfigured application, the JSON already includes the Base64 code for the image, but if you want to add a custom image, you can just grab a file and convert it using this code, and then reference the variable in the JSON:

```
$imagepath = "c:\temp\yourimage.jpg"
$imagebase64 =
```

```
[System.Convert]::ToBase64String([System.Text.Encoding]::UTF8.GetBytes([Sys
tem.IO.File]::ReadAllText($imagepath)))
```

For our Microsoft 365 apps, the JSON is as follows:

```
$json = @"
{
    "@odata.type": "#microsoft.graph.macOSOfficeSuiteApp",
    "description": "$appdesc",
    "developer": "Microsoft",
    "displayName": "$appname",
    "informationUrl": "https://products.office.com/explore-office-for-
home",
    "isFeatured": false,
    "largeIcon": {
        "type": "image/png",
        "value":
"iVBORw0KGgoAAAANSUhEUgAAAF0AAAAeCAMAAAEOZNKlAAAAAXNSR0IArs4c6QAAAARnQU1BAA
Cxjwv8YQUAAAJhUExURf////7z7/i9qfF1S/KCW/i+qv3q5P/9/
PrQwfOMae1RG+s8AOxGDfBtQPWhhPvUx/759/zg1vWgg+9fLu5WIvKFX/rSxP728/nCr/
FyR+tBBvOMaO1UH+1RHOs+AvSScP3u6f/+/v3s5vzg1+xFDO9kNPOOa/i7pvzj2/
vWyes9Af76+Pzh2PrTxf/
6+f7y7vOGYexHDv3t5+1SHfi8qPOIZPvb0O1NFuxDCe9hMPSVdPnFs/3q4/vaz/
STcu5VIe5YJPWcfv718v/9/e1MFfF4T/F4TvF2TP3o4exECvF0SexIEPONavzn3/
vZze1QGvF3Te5dK+5cKvrPwPrQwvKAWe1OGPexmexKEveulfezm/BxRfamiuxLE/apj/
zf1e5YJfSXd/OHYv3r5feznPakiPze1P7x7f739f3w6+xJEfnEsvWdf/
Wfge1LFPe1nu9iMvnDsfBqPOs/BPOIY/WZevJ/V/zl3fnIt/
vTxuxHD+xEC+9mN+5ZJv749vBpO/KBWvBwRP/8+/SUc/etlPjArP/7+vOLZ/F7UvWae/
708e1OF/aihvSWdvi8p+tABfSZefvVyPWihfSVde9lNvami+9jM/
zi2fKEXvBuQvOKZvaliffF5UPJ/WPSPbe9eLfrKuvvd0uxBB/7w7Pzj2vrRw/rOv+1PGfi/q/
eymu5bKf3n4PnJuPBrPf3t6PWfgvWegOxCCO9nOO9oOfaskvSYePi5pPi2oPnGtO5eLPevlvKDX
frNvv739Pzd0/70O9gL+9lNfJ9VfrLu/OPbPnDsPBrPus+A/
nArfarkQAAAGr5HKgAAADLdFJOU////////////////////////////////////////////////
///////////////////////////////////////////////////////////////////////////
///////////////////////////////////////////////////////////////////////////
///////////////////////////////////////////////////////////////////////
8AvuakogAAAAlwSFlzAAAOwwAADsMBx2+oZAAAAz5JREFUOE+tVTtu4zAQHQjppmWzwIJbEVCzp
TpjbxD3grQHSOXKRXgCAT6EC7UBVAmp3KwBnmvfzNCyZTmxgeTZJsXx43B+HBHRE34ZkXgkerXF
TheeiCkRrbB4UXmp4wSWz5raaQEMTM5TZwuiXoaKgV+6FsmkZQcSy0kA71yMTMGHanX+AzMMGLA
QCxU1F/ZwjULPugazl82GM0NEKm/U8EqFwEkO3/EAT4grgl0nucwlk9pcpTTJ4VPA4g/
Rb3yIRhhp507e9nTQmZ1OS5RO4sS7nIRPEeHXCHdkw9ZEW2yVE5oIS7peD58Avs7CN+PVCmHh21
```

```
oOqBdjDzIs+FldPJ74TFESUSJEfVzy9U/
dhu+AuOT6eBp6gGKyXEx8euO450ZE4CMfstMFT44broWw/
itkYErWXRx+fFArt9Ca9os78TFed0LVIUsmIHrwbwaw3BEOnOk94qVpQ6Ka2HjxewJnfyd6jUtG
DQLdWlzmYNYLeKbbGOucJsNabCq1Yub0o92rtR+i30V2dapxYVEePXcOjeCKPnYyit7BtKeNlZq
Hbr+gt7i+AChWA9RsRs03pxTQc67ouWpxyESvjK5Vs3DVSy3IpkxPm5X+wZoBi+MFHWW69/
w8FRhc7VBe6HAhMB2b8Q0XqDzTNZtXUMnKMjwKVaCrB/CSUL7WSx/
HsdJC86lFGXwnioTeOMPjV+szlFvrZLA5VMVK4y+41l4e1xfx7Z88o4hkilRUH/
qKqwNVlgDgpvYCpH3XwAy5eMCRnezIUxffVXoDql2rTHFDO+pjWnTWzAfrYXn6BFECblUpWGrvP
ZvBipETjS5ydM7tdXpH41ZCEbBNy/
+wFZu71QO2t9pgT+iZEf657Q1vpN94PQNDxUHeKR103LV9nPVOtDikcNKO+2naCw7yKBhOe9Hm7
9pe8C4/CfC2wDjXnqC94kEeBU3WwN7dt/
2UScXas7zDl5GpkY+M8WKv2J7fd4Ib2rGTk+jsC2cleEM7jI9veF7B0MBJrsZqfKd/
81q9pR2NZfwJK2JzsmIT1Ns8jUH0UusQBpU8d2JzsHiXg1zXGLqxfitUNTDT/
nUUeqDBp2HZVr+Ocqi/Ty3Rf4Jn82xxfSNtAAAAAElFTkSuQmCC"
    },
    "notes": "",
    "owner": "Microsoft",
    "privacyInformationUrl": "https://privacy.microsoft.com/
privacystatement",
    "publisher": "Microsoft",
    "roleScopeTagIds": []
}
"@
```

The important thing to note here is `@odata.type`, which tells Graph which app to deploy. For Microsoft 365 apps, it is `#microsoft.graph.macOSOfficeSuiteApp`.

3. We then need to create the application and grab the ID:

```
$mobileapp = Invoke-MgGraphRequest -Url $url -Method Post -Body $json -
ContentType "application/json" -OutputType PSObject
$mobileappid = $mobileapp.id
```

4. Finally, we populate the URL and send our `POST` command with the JSON to assign it:

```
$assignurl = "https://graph.microsoft.com/beta/deviceAppManagement/
mobileApps/$mobileappid/assign"

$assignjson = @"
{
    "mobileAppAssignments": [
```

```
            {
                "@odata.type": "#microsoft.graph.mobileAppAssignment",
                "intent": "Required",
                "settings": null,
                "target": {
                    "@odata.type": "#microsoft.graph.groupAssignmentTarget",
                    "groupId": "$groupid"
                }
            }
        ]
}
"@
Invoke-MgGraphRequest -Uri $assignurl -Method Post -Body $assignjson -
ContentType "application/json"
```

Microsoft Edge

This is very similar to Microsoft 365 apps; the only differences are the different `#odata.type` `"#microsoft.graph.macOSMicrosoftEdgeApp"` attributes and the option to select the channel. The Base64 code for this application is quite substantial, so it has been removed from the JSON here, but it is available in the script within the GitHub repository:

1. First, we need to set the URL and group ID for assignment and the channel to deploy. The name and description are preconfigured, but you could replace these with variables if you wanted:

```
$url = https://graph.microsoft.com/beta/deviceAppManagement/mobileApps/
$channel = "stable"
$groupid = "00000000-0000-0000-0000-000000000000"
```

2. Now, populate the JSON:

```
$json = @"
{
    "@odata.type": "#microsoft.graph.macOSMicrosoftEdgeApp",
    "channel": "$channel",
    "description": "Microsoft Edge is the browser for business with modern
and legacy web compatibility, new privacy features such as Tracking
prevention, and built-in productivity tools such as enterprise-grade PDF
support and access to Office and corporate search right from a new tab.",
    "developer": "Microsoft",
```

```
    "displayName": "Microsoft Edge for macOS",
    "informationUrl": "https://www.microsoft.com/windows/microsoft-edge",
    "isFeatured": false,
    "largeIcon": {
        "type": "image/png",
        "value": BASE64 HERE
},
    "notes": "",
    "owner": "",
    "privacyInformationUrl": "https://privacy.microsoft.com/
privacystatement",
    "publisher": "Microsoft",
    "roleScopeTagIds": []
}
"@
```

3. No doubt you have guessed what is coming next – send the `POST` request to create the application, grab the ID, and assign it:

```
$mobileapp = Invoke-MgGraphRequest -Url $url -Method Post -Body $json -
ContentType "application/json" -OutputType PSObject

$mobileappid = $mobileapp.id

$assignurl = "https://graph.microsoft.com/beta/deviceAppManagement/
mobileApps/$mobileappid/assign"

$assignjson = @"
{
    "mobileAppAssignments": [
        {
            "@odata.type": "#microsoft.graph.mobileAppAssignment",
            "intent": "Required",
            "settings": null,
            "target": {
                "@odata.type": "#microsoft.graph.groupAssignmentTarget",
                "groupId": "$groupid"
            }
        }
    ]
}
```

```
"@
Invoke-MgGraphRequest -Uri $assignurl -Method Post -Body $assignjson -
ContentType "application/json"
```

Microsoft Defender for Endpoint

This is another simple deployment, only without the channel we saw with Edge.

Again, `@odata.type` is the main difference here, which in this case is `#microsoft.graph.MacOSMicrosoftDefenderApp` (note the capital `M` found on `MacOS` here, which is not present in the previous examples).

The Base64 image is also quite large, so it has been removed from the example but is still available in the GitHub script:

1. This time, we only need to set the URL and group ID, unless you want to change any of the text:

```
$url = "https://graph.microsoft.com/beta/deviceAppManagement/mobileApps/"
$groupid = "00000000-0000-0000-0000-000000000000"
```

2. Set the JSON, which is fairly standard:

```
$json = @"
{
    "@odata.type": "#microsoft.graph.MacOSMicrosoftDefenderApp",
    "description": "Microsoft Defender for Endpoint is a unified platform
for preventative protection, post-breach detection, automated
investigation, and response. Microsoft Defender for Endpoint protects
endpoints from cyber threats; detects advanced attacks and data breaches,
automates security incidents and improves security posture.",
    "developer": "Microsoft",
    "displayName": "Microsoft Defender for Endpoint (macOS)",
    "informationUrl": "https://docs.microsoft.com/en-us/windows/security/
threat-protection/microsoft-defender-atp/microsoft-defender-advanced-
threat-protection",
    "isFeatured": false,
    "largeIcon": {
        "type": "image/png",
        "value":
},
    "notes": "",
    "owner": "Microsoft",
```

```
    "privacyInformationUrl": "https://docs.microsoft.com/en-us/windows/
security/threat-protection/microsoft-defender-atp/mac-privacy",
    "publisher": "Microsoft",
    "roleScopeTagIds": []
}
"@
```

3. Again, create and assign:

```
$mobileapp = Invoke-MgGraphRequest -Url $url -Method Post -Body $json -
ContentType "application/json" -OutputType PSObject
$mobileappid = $mobileapp.id
$assignurl = "https://graph.microsoft.com/beta/deviceAppManagement/
mobileApps/$mobileappid/assign"
$assignjson = @"
{
    "mobileAppAssignments": [
        {
            "@odata.type": "#microsoft.graph.mobileAppAssignment",
            "intent": "Required",
            "settings": null,
            "target": {
                "@odata.type": "#microsoft.graph.groupAssignmentTarget",
                "groupId": "$groupid"
            }
        }
    ]
}
"@
Invoke-MgGraphRequest -Uri $assignurl -Method Post -Body $assignjson -
ContentType "application/json"
```

We have now deployed the Microsoft Defender for Endpoint application using PowerShell and Graph.

Configuring a macOS enrollment profile

Before we enroll our first macOS device, we have one last task to complete – we need to configure an enrollment profile, the same as we did in the previous chapter for iOS.

Getting ready

For this recipe, you will need your Intune instance to be linked to ABM with an enrollment token configured. If you did not do this in *Chapter 6*, complete the following recipes in that chapter before continuing:

- *Configuring a connector between Apple and Intune*
- *Adding enrollment profile tokens*

How to do it...

Take the following steps:

1. First, select **Devices** and then **macOS**.
2. Click **Enrollment**.
3. Now, click on **Enrollment Program Tokens**.
4. Click on the token created in *Chapter 6*:

Token name ↑↓	Status ↑↓	Program type ↑↓
Intune	Active	Apple Business Manager

Figure 7.16 – An Apple token

5. Next, click on **Profiles**. If you set up an iOS profile earlier, you should see it here now.
6. Select the drop-down arrow next to **Create profile**, and choose **macOS**.
7. Enter a name and description, and then click **Next**.
8. Similar to our iOS profiles, we need to set a couple of settings:
   - **User affinity**: This is whether the device will be associated with a user. For non-kiosk devices, you need to select **Enroll with user affinity**.
   - After selecting this, you will see an additional option for **Authentication method**. We want to select **Setup Assistant with modern authentication** here.
   - **Locked Enrollment** specifies whether the user has the ability to remove the profile. For corporate devices, you want this set to **Yes** to stop users from unenrolling their devices.
9. Once you have set this, click **Next**.
10. On the next screen, you can specify what is and is not available on the setup screen. Unless there are any you particularly need, you can just toggle all of them to **Hidden**. You do need to set the department details at the top. Once configured, click **Next**.

11. We now create a local primary account with the details of the user kicking off the enrollment. Simply set **Create a local primary account** to **Yes** and leave the rest as defaults. Then, click **Next**.
12. Now, we need to review and create the profile. Check that everything is okay, and then click **Create**.

    Now, we need to set it as our default profile, which will default all new macOS devices imported from ABM to use it.
13. Back on your profiles screen, select **Default Profile**.
14. Select your newly created profile under **macOS Enrollment profile**, and then click **OK**.

We have created our first macOS profile within Intune using the UI.

Automating it

The JSON for this is reasonably straightforward (although with all of the available settings, it runs to many lines of code), but first, we need to populate the URL with the ID of the Apple token. If you have completed the recipes in the previous chapter, it is basically the same but with a slightly different JSON set:

1. First, set the variables:

```
$name = "macOS Enrollment"
$description = "Corporate Managed macOS Devices"
```

2. Now, we need to run a GET command to grab the ID of the token. It is nested within the Value array within the output, as with most Graph objects, which allows for pagination. We are looking for the ID setting:

```
$settingsurl = "https://graph.microsoft.com/beta/deviceManagement/
depOnboardingSettings/"
$tokenid = (Invoke-MgGraphRequest -Method GET -Uri $settingsurl -OutputType
PSObject).value.id
```

3. Now, we populate that in the URL:

```
$url = "https://graph.microsoft.com/beta/deviceManagement/
depOnboardingSettings/$tokenid/enrollmentProfiles"
```

4. Add the variables to the JSON. You can see that every setting is configured with either a `true` or `false` value, plus our account information is specified:

```
$json = @"
{
    "@odata.type": "#microsoft.graph.depMacOSEnrollmentProfile",
    "accessibilityScreenDisabled": true,
    "appleIdDisabled": true,
    "applePayDisabled": true,
    "autoUnlockWithWatchDisabled": true,
    "chooseYourLockScreenDisabled": true,
    "configurationEndpointUrl": "",
    "configurationWebUrl": true,
    "description": "$description",
    "diagnosticsDisabled": true,
    "displayName": "$name",
    "displayToneSetupDisabled": true,
    "dontAutoPopulatePrimaryAccountInfo": false,
    "enableAuthenticationViaCompanyPortal": false,
    "enabledSkipKeys": [
        "Location",
        "TOS",
        "Biometric",
        "Payment",
        "Siri",
        "Privacy",
        "AppleID",
        "DisplayTone",
        "ScreenTime",
        "Diagnostics",
        "Restore",
        "TermsOfAddress",
        "Intelligence",
        "Registration",
        "FileVault",
        "iCloudDiagnostics",
        "iCloudStorage",
        "Appearance",
        "Accessibility",
        "UnlockWithWatch",
        "EnableLockdownMode",
```

```
        "Wallpaper"
    ],
    "enableRestrictEditing": true,
    "fileVaultDisabled": true,
    "iCloudDiagnosticsDisabled": true,
    "iCloudStorageDisabled": true,
    "id": "",
    "isMandatory": true,
    "locationDisabled": true,
    "primaryAccountFullName": "{{username}}",
    "primaryAccountUserName": "{{partialupn}}",
    "privacyPaneDisabled": true,
    "profileRemovalDisabled": true,
    "registrationDisabled": true,
    "requireCompanyPortalOnSetupAssistantEnrolledDevices": false,
    "requiresUserAuthentication": true,
    "restoreBlocked": true,
    "screenTimeScreenDisabled": true,
    "siriDisabled": true,
    "skipPrimarySetupAccountCreation": false,
    "supervisedModeEnabled": true,
    "supportDepartment": "IT Department",
    "supportPhoneNumber": "IT Department",
    "termsAndConditionsDisabled": true,
    "touchIdDisabled": true,
    "waitForDeviceConfiguredConfirmation": true
}
"@
```

5. Finally, create the profile; there is no need to assign this one, but we still need to store it in a variable to set it as our default profile:

```
$macosprofile = Invoke-MgGraphRequest -Method POST -Uri $url -Body $json -
ContentType "application/json" -OutputType PSObject
```

6. To set the default profile, we send a `POST` request but with an empty body, as the URL does the configuration for us. Grab the ID:

```
$profileid = $macosprofile.id
```

7. Now, populate the URL and send the request:

```
$defaulturl = "https://graph.microsoft.com/beta/deviceManagement/
depOnboardingSettings/$tokenid/enrollmentProfiles/$profileid/
setDefaultProfile"
Invoke-MgGraphRequest -Method POST -Uri $defaulturl -ContentType
"application/json" -OutputType PSObject
```

This script has used PowerShell and Graph to automate the configuration and assignment of our macOS profile.

Configuring Platform SSO for Entra integration

Platform SSO is a reasonably new functionality to replace directory binding and enables passwordless SSO and sign-in via your Entra account.

For more information, you can refer to the official documentation here: `https://learn.microsoft.com/en-us/intune/intune-service/configuration/platform-sso-macos`.

Or you can check out this excellent guide from Intune MVP Joery Van den Bosch: `https://intunestuff.com/2024/10/09/manage-macos-with-intune-including-apple-business-manager-including-platform-sso-the-complete-guide/`.

How to do it...

Platform SSO simply requires setting up one settings catalog policy. We are going to use the **Secure Enclave** configuration as it offers the most security:

1. Click on **Devices**, then **macOS**, and then click **Configuration**.
2. Click **Create** and **New Policy** from the dropdown.
3. In the fly-out, select **Settings Catalog** and then click **Create**.

4. Give your policy a name and description and click **Next**.
5. Click **Add settings**, expand **Authentication**, and select **Extensible Single Sign On (SSO)**.
6. Select these settings:
    - **Extension Identifier** (set to **com.microsoft.CompanyPortalMac.ssoextension**)
    - **Platform SSO | Authentication method** (set to **UserSecureEnclaveKey**)
    - **Platform SSO | Use Shared devices keys** (set to **Enabled**)
    - **Registration Token** (set to **{{DEVICEREGISTRATION}}**)
    - **Screen Locked Behaviour** (set to **Do Not Handle**)
    - **Platform SSO | Token to user mapping | Account Name** (set to **preferred_username**)
    - **Platform SSO | Token to user mapping | Full Name** (set to **name**)
    - **Team Identifier** (set to **UBF8T346G9**)
    - **Type** (set to **Redirect**)
    - **URLS** (enter these on separate lines):
        - `https://login.microsoftonline.com`
        - `https://login.microsoft.com`
        - `https://sts.windows.net`

    The following figure illustrates how the Platform SSO settings should appear in your environment.

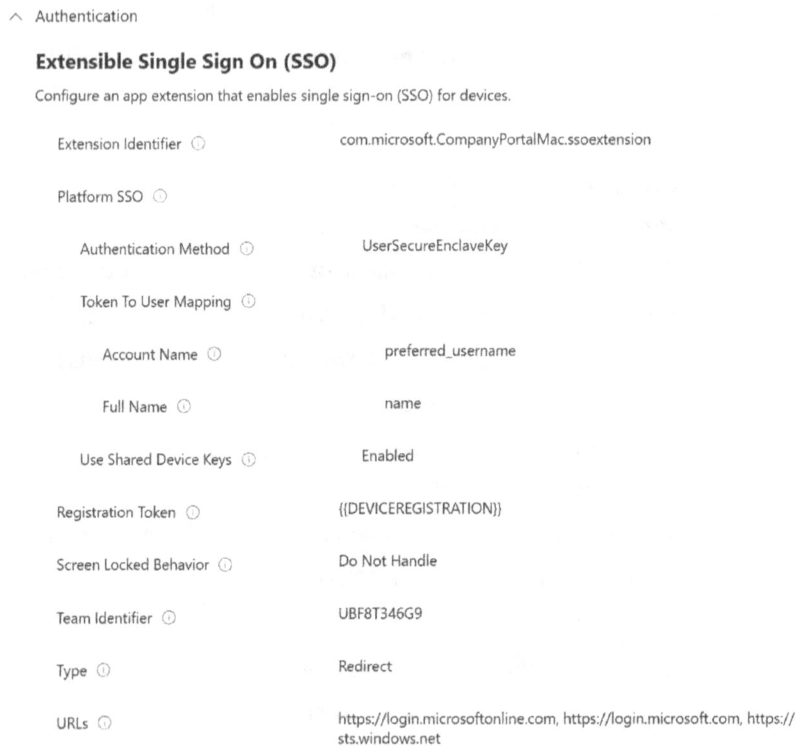

Figure 7.17 – Platform SSO configuration

7. Once configured, click **Next**.
8. We do not require scope tags, so click **Next**.
9. Assign as required. For this example, we are using the **Intune-Users** group. Click **Next**.
10. Check that all looks correct and click **Create**.

Automating it

As this is a settings catalog-backed policy, the process is much the same as when we configured the firewall earlier in the chapter:

1. We start by setting our basics:

```
$name = "Platform SSO"
$description = "Platform SSO"
$groupid = "00000000-0000-0000-0000-000000000000"
$posturl = "https://graph.microsoft.com/beta/deviceManagement/
configurationPolicies"
```

2. We then populate these into the JSON. For brevity, the script is available in the GitHub repository, rather than including it all here.
3. Once we have our JSON, we need to create the policy and grab the ID:

```
$policy = Invoke-MgGraphRequest -Method POST -Uri $posturl -Body $json -
ContentType "application/json" -OutputType PSObject
$policyid = $policy.id
```

4. We then populate our assignment URL:

```
$assignurl = "https://graph.microsoft.com/beta/deviceManagement/
configurationPolicies('$policyid')/assign"
```

5. Finally, add the group ID to the JSON and send the assignment to Graph:

```
$assignjson = @"
{
    "assignments": [
        {
            "target": {
                "@odata.type": "#microsoft.graph.groupAssignmentTarget",
                "groupId": "$groupid"
            }
        }
    ]
}
"@
Invoke-MgGraphRequest -Method POST -Uri $assignurl -Body $assignjson -
ContentType "application/json" -OutputType PSObject
```

Enrolling your corporate device

Now, we have our environment configured to support and manage macOS devices, and we can enroll our first device. As these are generally corporate-owned machines, this recipe will only cover full ABM enrollment, and it is suggested to turn off personal enrollment of macOS devices.

If, however, you need to allow **bring your own device** (**BYOD**) for macOS, you can find instructions here: `https://learn.microsoft.com/en-us/mem/intune/user-help/enroll-your-device-in-intune-macos-cp`.

Getting ready

For this recipe, you will need a factory reset device that is already enrolled in either ABM or Apple Education and connected to the internet. If you wish to use Apple Configurator on an iPhone to register your applications, use the guide at the following link: `https://support.apple.com/en-gb/guide/apple-configurator/apd65c9ff558/ios`.

A special thanks to Joery Van den Bosch for providing the screenshots.

You can also find a video demonstrating enrollment here: `https://www.youtube.com/watch?v=Jk7kPtUW2p4`.

How to do it...

Use the following steps:

1. Upon booting your device, you will first be presented with a screen to select your language. Select as appropriate, and click **Continue**:

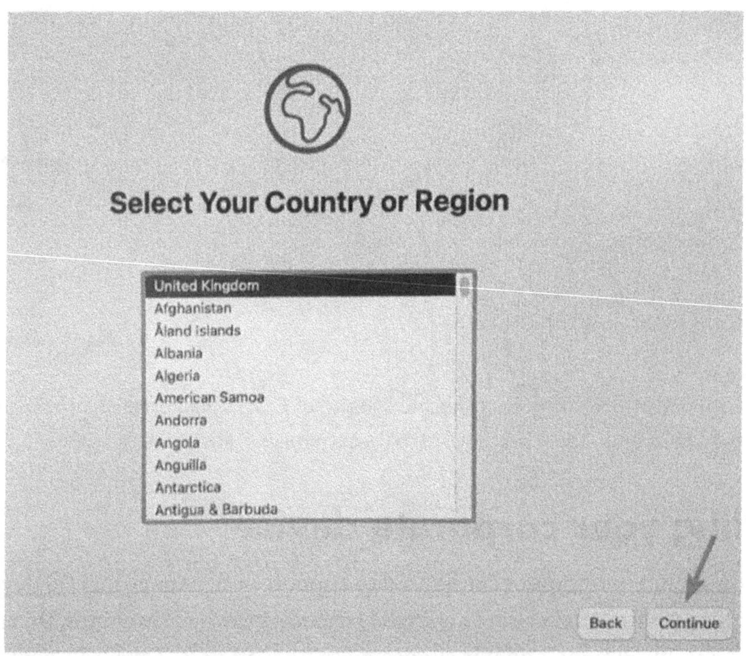

Figure 7.18 – Selecting an OS country or region

2. macOS will now configure the language settings according to your country selection, but if necessary, click **Customize Settings** and change them accordingly. Then, click **Continue**.

Figure 7.19 – Setting a language

3. Depending on the settings used in your enrollment profile, you may see other screens here, such as **Accessibility**:

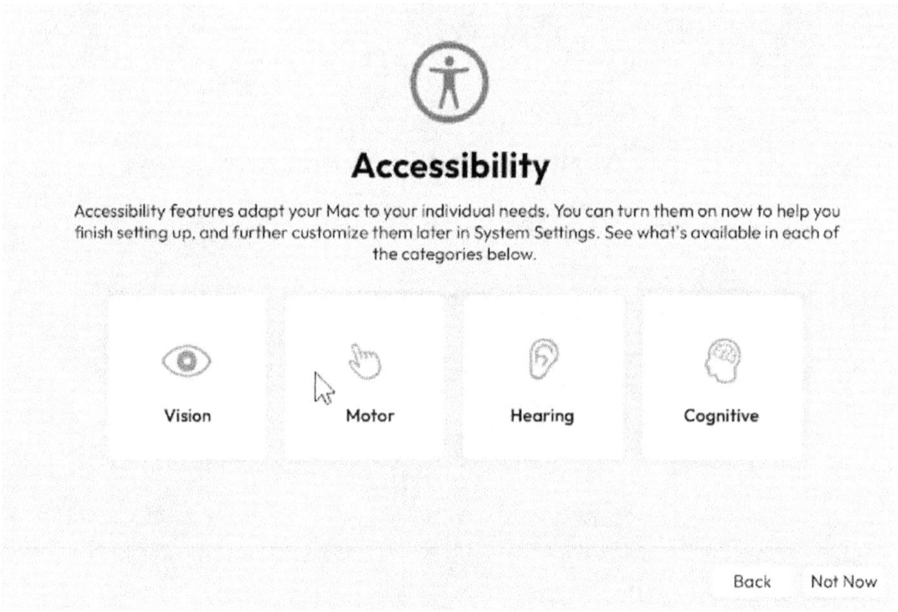

Figure 7.20 – Accessibility options

4. Once you have completed any additional settings, you will be prompted to connect to a wireless network (unless the device has a hardwired connection). Select your network, enter the password, and click **Continue**.

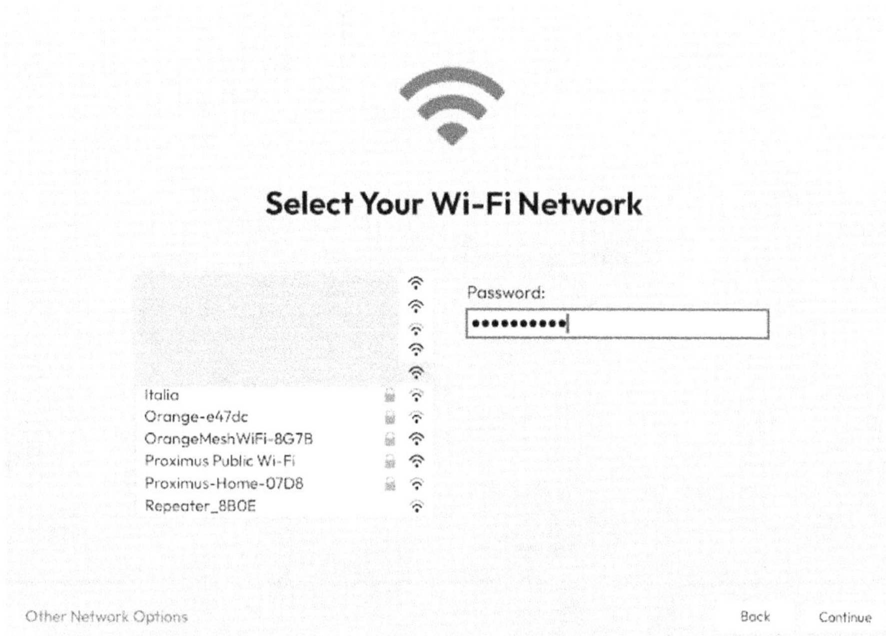

Figure 7.21 – Connecting to a wireless network

5. Click **Continue** on the **Data & Privacy** screen:

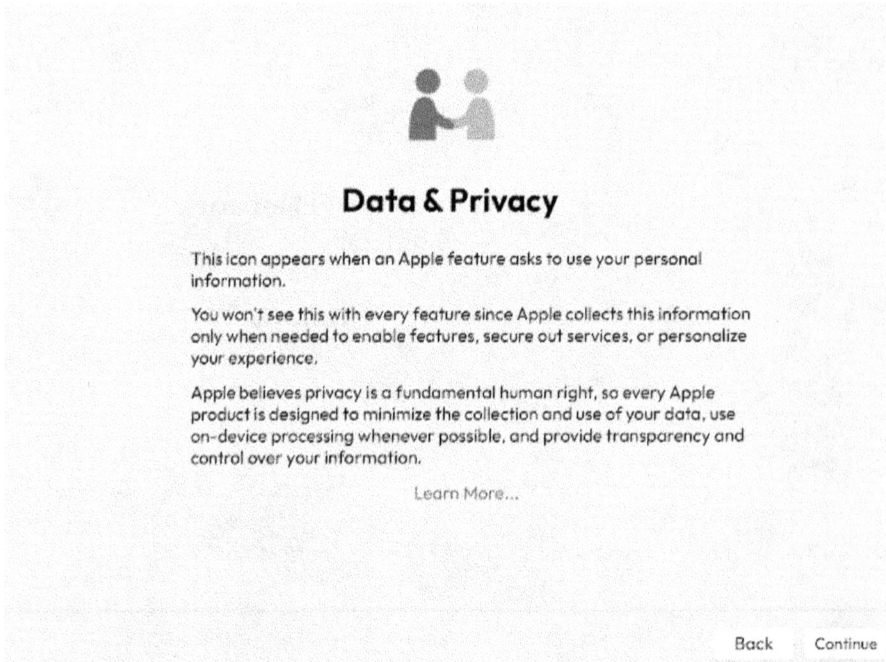

Figure 7.22 – Data & Privacy

6. This is where setup differs from an unmanaged device; you will be prompted to enable remote management. Click **Continue**.

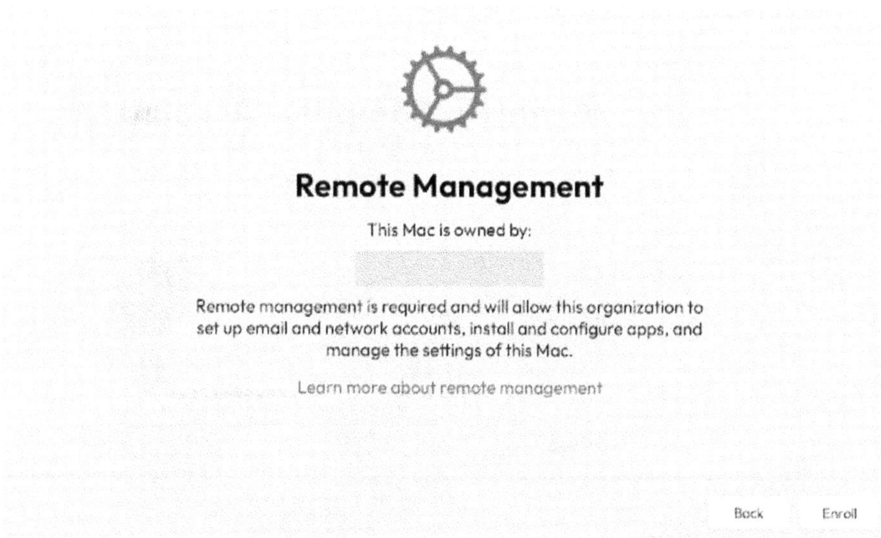

Figure 7.23 – Enabling remote management

7. Enter your Microsoft credentials (username and password).

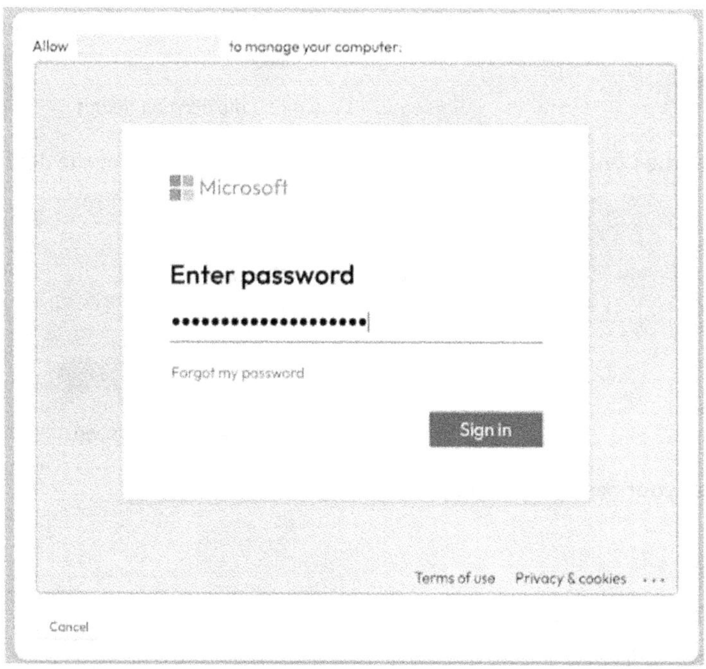

Figure 7.24 – Enter credentials

8. Enter your details to create an account:

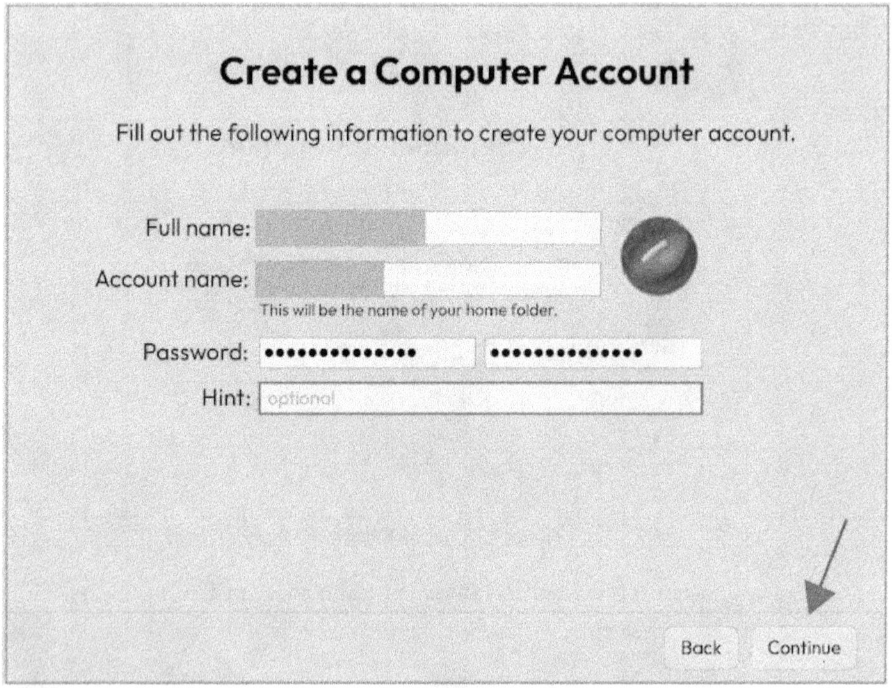

Figure 7.25 – Confirming the account details

9. Click the Company Portal message in the top-right corner of the desktop:

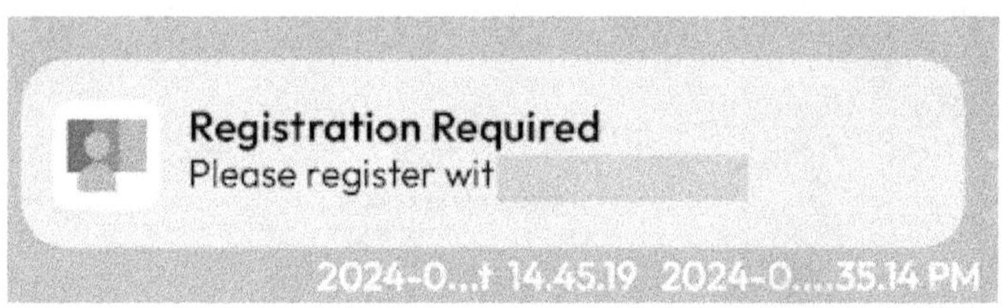

Figure 7.26 – Registration Required message

10. Enter your password (or use Touch ID):

Figure 7.27 – Login

11. Enter your Microsoft 365 credentials:

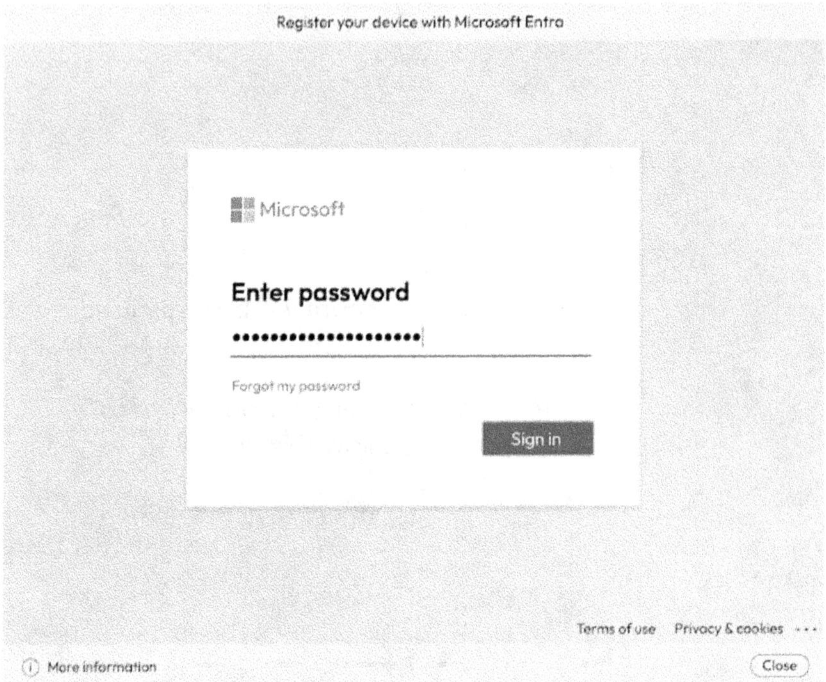

Figure 7.28 – Entra credentials

12. Wait for your device to finish preparation:

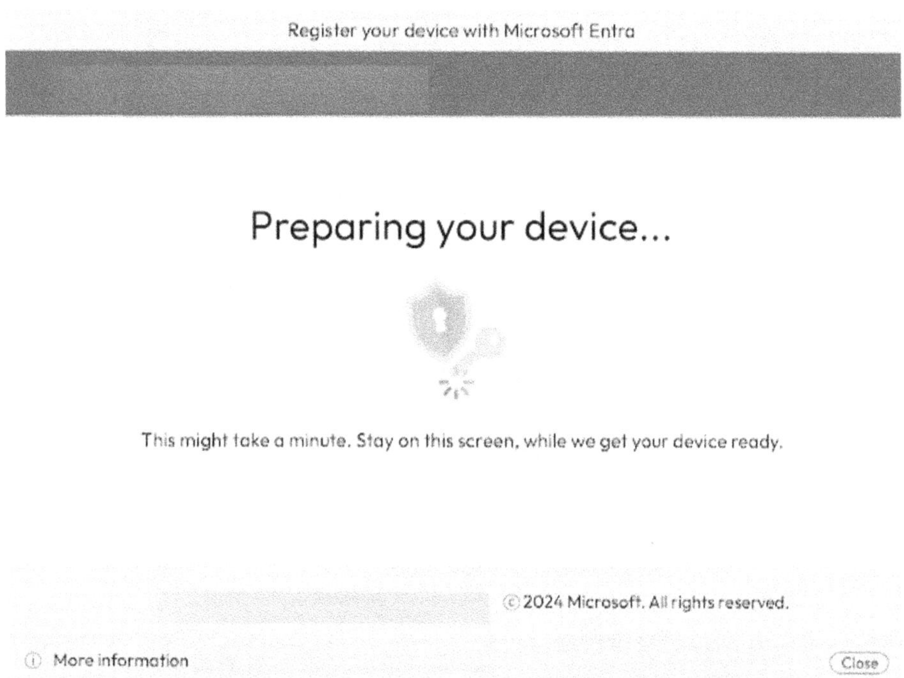

Figure 7.29 – Preparing your devices

13. Turn on **Company Portal** and click **Open System Settings**:

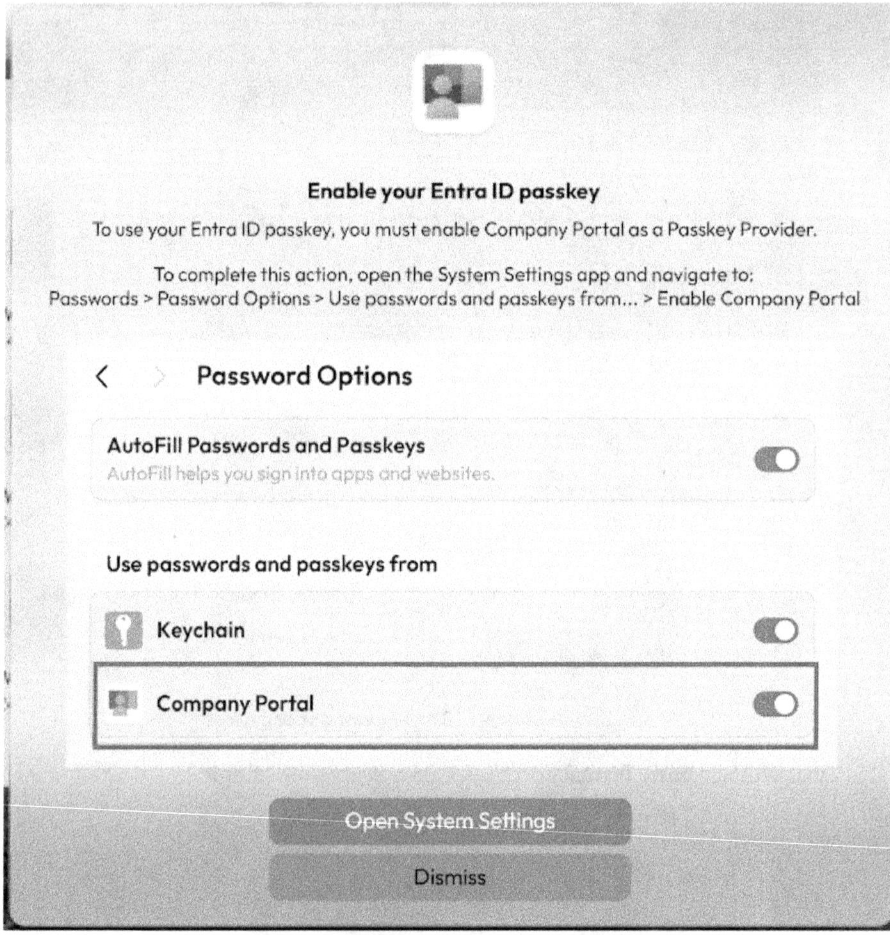

Figure 7.30 – Enable Entra ID passkey

14. Enable **Company Portal** and click **Close**:

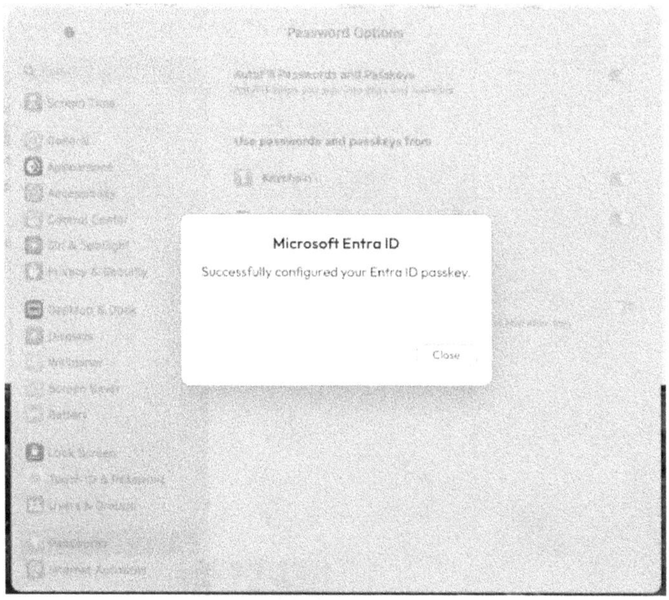

Figure 7.31 – Enable Company Portal

15. Launch **Company Portal** and click **Sign In**:

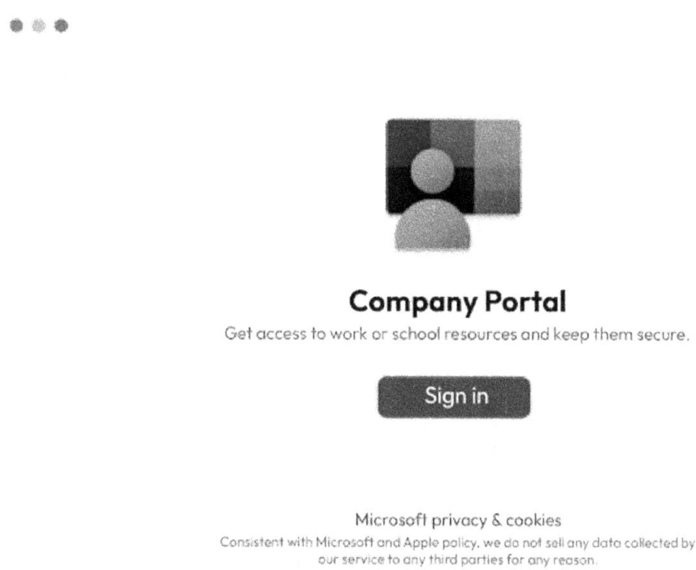

Figure 7.32 – Company Portal sign-in

16. Finally, select your account and click **Continue**:

Figure 7.33 – Complete Company Portal SSO

Congratulations! You have enrolled your first macOS device on Intune.

Get This Book's PDF Version and Exclusive Extras

Scan the QR code (or go to `packtpub.com/unlock`). Search for this book by name, confirm the edition, and then follow the steps on the page.

UNLOCK NOW

Note: Keep your invoice handy. Purchases made directly from Packt don't require one.

8

Setting Up Your Compliance Policies

Now that we have successfully enrolled devices from all of the major platforms (Windows, macOS, iOS, and Android), we need a method of ensuring they are always managed, updated, and compliant with our own requirements. For that, we can use **compliance policies**. These allow us to configure a set of requirements that devices must meet to be classed as compliant within the environment. Then, we can add a **Conditional Access** policy on top to restrict access to corporate data from any devices that do not meet the criteria. This increases our security posture and also gives us the ability to quickly monitor our estate for any major issues.

In addition to showing you how to deploy these policies, we will also look at what each of the settings requires on the device. We will also cover the more advanced custom compliance policy for Windows.

Finally, we will look at how to restrict access from non-compliant machines using conditional access.

In this chapter, we will cover the following recipes:

- Configuring notification templates
- Deploying a Windows compliance policy
- Deploying an Android compliance policy
- Deploying an iOS compliance policy
- Deploying a macOS compliance policy
- Deploying a Linux compliance policy
- Configuring and deploying a Windows custom compliance policy
- Using conditional access to restrict access based on compliance

Technical requirements

For this chapter, you will need a modern web browser and a PowerShell code editor such as Visual Studio Code or the PowerShell ISE.

All of the scripts that will be referenced in this chapter can be found here: `https://github.com/PacktPublishing/Microsoft-Intune-Cookbook-Second-Edition/tree/main/Chapter-8`.

If you wish to test the policies, you will need a corporate-managed device running each device platform for testing. For Linux, it will need to be running Ubuntu.

Chapter materials

Before we begin configuring our policies, there is one setting that we want to configure for the tenant that tells Intune what to do with devices that do not have any compliance policies assigned.

For this, navigate to **Devices** and then **Compliance**. Then, click on the **Compliance settings** tab.

We have two settings here:

- **Mark devices with no compliance policy assigned as**: A device without a policy assigned is a potential security risk as it could potentially be non-compliant with multiple settings. The best practice is always to set this to **Not Compliant**.
- **Compliance status validity period (days)**: This sets how long you will accept a prior status report – put another way, if a device has not checked into Intune, after how many days should it be flagged as non-compliant? At a very basic level, consider Windows updates; if a machine has not been seen for 30 days or more, assume it is missing at least one set of updates, possibly including antivirus updates and definitions.
  In our case, we are leaving the second setting set as **30 days** and setting devices without a policy to **Not Compliant**. Once these have been set, click **Save**.

There is also one configuration that applies to all compliance policies, and that is the action to take on non-compliant devices.

Actions for non-compliance

After configuring the compliance settings, we also need to tell Intune what to do when it detects devices that do not meet the criteria:

- **Mark device non-compliant**: Set the number of days before a device is marked as non-compliant. As mentioned earlier, setting it to **Immediately** may cause issues with some attestation rules, but setting it too long increases the security risk.
- **Send email to end user**: Here, you can also set the number of days after which an email is sent to the user informing them that the device is not compliant. You can configure the message that is sent and also send a copy elsewhere, such as to your IT department. You could set multiple templates here with different warnings to the user before you simply block access. We will look at this in the first recipe.
- **Add device to retire list**: After the number of days has been selected, the device will be added to a retirement list. Nothing will happen until the administrator retires the devices via the **Retire noncompliant devices** menu within **Compliance Policies**:

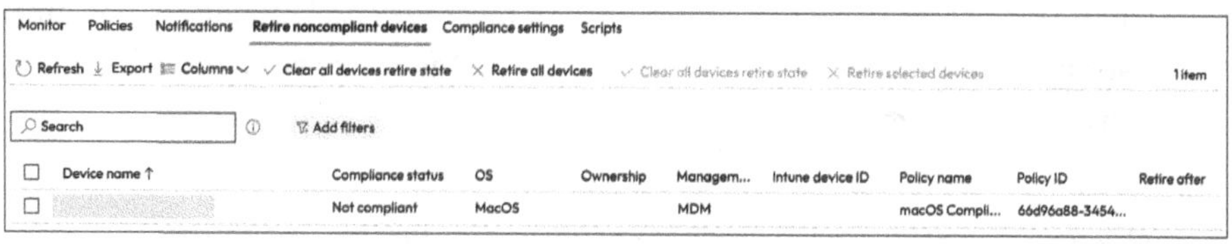

Figure 8.1 – Retire noncompliant devices

- **Send push notification to end user (Android and iOS only)**: This is similar to email, but the message appears on-screen and cannot be customized.
- **Remotely lock the non-compliant device (iOS and Android only)**: This option locks the user out of the device:

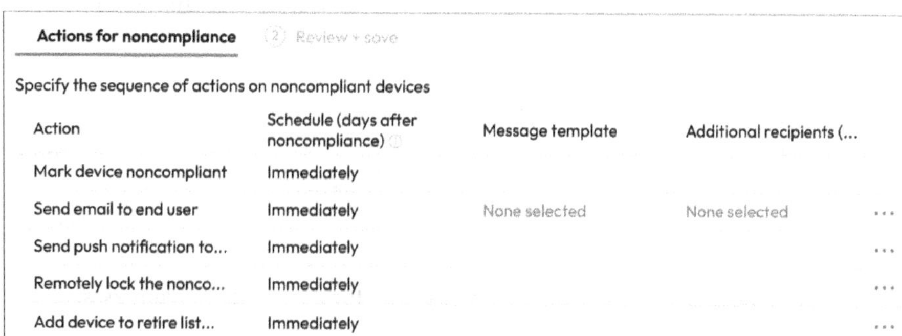

Figure 8.2 – Actions for noncompliance

Configuring notification templates

All supported platforms can send an email to the end user (and copy it to any other distribution lists), informing them that they are using a non-compliant device. This can be used to provide warnings before the device is blocked.

As these are cross-platform, this first recipe will cover how to create your template.

How to do it...

Follow these steps:

1. First, navigate to **Devices** and then **Compliance**.
2. Then, click on **Notifications** and click **+Create notification**.
3. First, you must set a name for the template and select how corporate you want it to look. The corporate details are grabbed from **Tenant details**, which we will cover in *Chapter 13*. Once selected, click **Next**.
4. On the next screen, you can configure your message and language. If you are multinational, you can have multiple notifications. One has to be set as the default before you can click **Next** to continue.
5. Click **Next** to progress past **Scope tags**.
6. Finally, check that everything looks correct and click **Create**.

Automating it

Now that we have created a template, we can look at how to automate this process.

Creating notification templates is an unusual one to automate as while we do not have to assign it, it is still a two-step process:

1. First, though, we need to set the subject and message. Note that any line breaks need `\n` in the code:

```
$subject = "First Warning"
$message = "Your device is now showing as non-compliant. Please contact IT
to resolve the issue.\nYour access will be blocked in xx days"
$displayname = "First Alert"
```

   All these notifications use the following URL for `POST` and `GET` requests:

   `https://graph.microsoft.com/beta/deviceManagement/notificationMessageTemplates`

2. Now, we need to set the URL:

```
$createnotificationurl = "https://graph.microsoft.com/beta/
deviceManagement/notificationMessageTemplates"
```

3. Next, we need to create the initial policy with the display name and the corporate branding settings, which are simply comma-separated values in the setting:

```
$createnotificationjson = @"
{
    "brandingOptions":
"includeCompanyLogo,includeCompanyName,includeContactInformation",
    "displayName": "$displayname",
    "roleScopeTagIds": [
        "0"
    ]
}
"@
$createnotification = invoke-mggraphrequest -uri $createnotificationurl -
json $createnotificationjson -method post -contenttype "application/json" -
outputtype PSObject
```

4. We have output the policy creation as we still need the policy ID for the next step:

```
$createnotificationid = $createnotification.id
```

5. Add the policy ID to the URL:

```
$createnotificationmessageurl = "https://graph.microsoft.com/beta/
deviceManagement/notificationMessageTemplates/$createnotificationid/
localizedNotificationMessages"
```

6. Now, we can populate the JSON and add the template to the policy:

```
$createnotificationmessagejson = @"
{
    "isDefault": true,
    "locale": "en-GB",
    "messageTemplate": "$message",
    "subject": "$subject"
}
```

```
"@
$createnotificationmessage = invoke-mggraphrequest -uri
$createnotificationmessageurl -json $createnotificationmessagejson -method
post -contenttype "application/json" -outputtype PSObject
```

If you have multiple templates for different languages, then each template is a separate `POST` request, not a nested array.

Deploying a Windows compliance policy

There are two ways to configure compliance policies for Windows devices. Both will be covered in this chapter, but we will start with the easier of the two, which is GUI-driven.

Getting ready

As mentioned earlier, before we start creating our policy, we should look at the settings available and what they do.

Compliance settings

We will start with the available compliance settings.

Custom compliance

We will cover this in a later recipe (*Configuring and deploying a Windows custom compliance policy*), but to summarize, you can deploy a custom PowerShell script to monitor anything on the device and feed it into a compliance policy.

Device Health

Device health rules use the **Device Health Attestation** service. One important thing to note is that they require a reboot to report back as they are querying the BIOS, among other things. Therefore, if you set these settings, make sure you do not set devices as non-compliant immediately; otherwise, your fresh devices will lose access. Let us run through the available settings under **Device Health**:

- **BitLocker**: Checks that drives are encrypted using BitLocker
- **Secure Boot**: Checks that Secure Boot is enabled within UEFI
- **Code integrity**: Checks drivers and firmware for signs of corruption or malicious activity

Device Properties

Under the **Device Properties** sub-heading, we have the following options:

- **Minimum OS version**: The operating system version in `major.minor.build.revision` format. For example, if we wanted the Windows 11 25H2 January 2026 release, it would be `10.0.26200.7705`.

> **Note**
>
> You can check which versions are available at `https://support.microsoft.com/en-us/topic/windows-11-version-25h2-update-history-99c7f493-df2a-4832-bd2d-6706baa0dec0`.

- **Maximum OS version**: The same as **Minimum OS version**, but if you want to restrict to non-preview builds, for example, you can also set a maximum version.
- **Minimum and Maximum OS version for mobile devices**: This is for Windows Mobile, so it can be ignored.
- **Valid operating system builds**: You can use this to specify multiple minimum and maximum builds. For example, if you want to support Windows 10 and Windows 11, but only on supported versions, you could add one entry for each with the minimum set to the last supported revision.

Configuration Manager compliance

If you are running in a co-managed environment with Configuration Manager, setting this to **Require** will force devices to use the device compliance set within Configuration Manager.

System Security

Under the **System Security** heading, we have these options:

- **Require a password to unlock mobile devices**: Unlike mobile devices, this one is actually for Windows and is related to the PIN for Windows Hello for Business.
- **Simple passwords**: This will block simple PINs such as `1234` or `0000`.
- **Password type**: The password type can be one of the following:
  - **Device Default**: Password, numeric PIN, or alphanumeric PIN
  - **Numeric**: Password or numeric PIN only
  - **Alphanumeric**: Password or alphanumeric only

  The recommended option is alphanumeric to add some extra complexity.

- **Minimum password length**: The number of digits for the PIN (make sure this follows company policy and matches your other PIN configuration policies).
- **Maximum minutes of activity before password is required**: This can be anything from **Not Configured** to 8 hours, down to 1 minute. 15 minutes is recommended for a good balance between security and user experience.
- **Password expiration**: After how many days the user will need to reset the password (1–730).
- **Number of previous passwords to prevent reuse**: How many passwords must have been used before an old one can be reused (1–24).
- **Require password when device returns from idle state**: This is only for Windows Mobile and Holographic.

These configurations will not force the settings; they will simply check whether the device is compliant with them. If you do not have additional policies (settings catalog and so on) configured, a user could still, for example, set a simple four-digit PIN, but the device would be marked as non-compliant.

Encryption

Under the **Encryption** heading, we have the **Require encryption of data storage on device** setting. This is a simpler encryption check compared to the **Require BitLocker** option but does not require a reboot.

Device Security

Our next heading is **Device Security**, which contains the following settings:

- **Firewall**: Requires Windows Firewall to be enabled and monitoring traffic.
- **Trusted Platform Module (TPM)**: Requires a TPM to be present (this is a prerequisite for Windows 11 installations anyway, so it is only applicable for Windows 10 devices).
- **Antivirus**: Requires antivirus software to be present. This can be Windows Defender or a third party, so long as it is registered and recognized by Security Center. If you are using a third party, a custom compliance policy may give you more options.
- **Antispyware**: The same as **Antivirus** but for anti-spyware.

Defender

Under the **Defender** heading, we have the following settings:

- **Microsoft Defender Antimalware**: Checks that the Antimalware service is enabled and running.

- **Microsoft Defender Antimalware minimum version**: The minimum version of the antimalware product – for example, 4.11.0.0. This can be found here: `https://www.microsoft.com/en-us/wdsi/defenderupdates`.
- **Microsoft Defender Antimalware security intelligence up-to-date**: Checks that the signatures have been updated.
- **Real-time protection**: Checks that the real-time protection service is enabled and running.

Microsoft Defender for Endpoint

Note that to use this setting, you will require licensing for Defender for Endpoint. Double-check you have the correct licenses before enabling this option:

- **Require the device to be at or under the machine risk score**: The options are as follows:
    - **Not Configured**: No setting will be applied
    - **Clear**: The device cannot have any threats at all
    - **Low**: The device can only have low-level threats
    - **Medium**: The device can have low or medium-level threats
    - **High**: This allows all threat levels

  You can find out more about these risk levels at `https://learn.microsoft.com/en-us/microsoft-365/security/defender-endpoint/alerts-queue?view=o365-worldwide`.

How to do it...

Now that we know what all of the settings do, we can create our policy. For this example, we will keep it fairly simple, but amend it as appropriate for your environment:

1. First, navigate to **Devices** and then **Compliance**.
2. Within **Policies**, click **Create policy**.
3. In the fly-out, select **Windows 10 and Later** and **Windows 10/11 compliance policy**, then click **Create**.
4. As with any other policy/profile, we start with **Name** and **Description** values and click **Next**.
5. Now, we need to configure our settings based on the information we covered earlier. In this example, we are going to require all **Device Health** options, as well as **Antivirus**, **Microsoft Defender Antimalware**, **Firewall**, and **TPM** (listed under the **System Security** section).

6. Once configured, click **Next**.
7. Now for the non-compliance actions. As mentioned earlier, our device health rules require a restart, so we will set that to `0.5` days. We are going to assume that a machine not seen for 180 days no longer exists and add it to the retire list. Once configured for your environment, click **Next**.

> Note
>
> Adding a device to the retire list does not retire it; this is only for reporting. To retire these devices, follow the steps in the *This chapter's materials* section.

8. We do not want to set **Scope tags**, so click **Next**.

> Note
>
> When looking at assignments, for user-based devices, it is important to assign the policy to a user group. If assigned to a device group, the policy will run against both the user and system account, and if either flags as non-compliant, the device will fail compliance.
>
> Device-based assignment should only be used for non-user-based machines, such as kiosks.

9. In our case, we are going to use the **Intune-Users** group. Once set, click **Next**.
10. Finally, check that everything looks correct and click **Create**.

With that, we have configured a Windows compliance policy in the UI.

Automating it

Now, we can look at using PowerShell and Graph to automate our Windows compliance configuration.

The first thing to note when automating compliance policies is that the `POST` requests are sent to the same URL for all device platforms:

```
https://graph.microsoft.com/beta/deviceManagement/deviceCompliancePolicies
```

The difference between them is the `@odata.type` field, which for this Windows policy is as follows:

```
#microsoft.graph.windows10CompliancePolicy
```

At the time of writing, compliance policies use the settings catalog, so the JSON is a simpler setting: value configuration, with the values being either Boolean or plain text.

The non-compliance actions are also a nested array within the main settings. Let's take a look:

1. As usual, start with the basics:

```
$name = "Windows Compliance Policy"
$description = "Windows Compliance Policy using GUI settings"
$groupid = "0000000-0000-0000-0000-000000000000"
$url = "https://graph.microsoft.com/beta/deviceManagement/
deviceCompliancePolicies"
```

2. Now, let's look at the JSON:

```
$json = @"
{
    "@odata.type": "#microsoft.graph.windows10CompliancePolicy",
    "activeFirewallRequired": true,
    "antiSpywareRequired": true,
    "antivirusRequired": true,
    "bitLockerEnabled": true,
    "codeIntegrityEnabled": true,
    "defenderEnabled": true,
    "description": "$description",
    "deviceThreatProtectionEnabled": false,
    "deviceThreatProtectionRequiredSecurityLevel": "unavailable",
    "displayName": "$name",
    "id": "00000000-0000-0000-0000-000000000000",
    "passwordRequiredType": "deviceDefault",
    "roleScopeTagIds": [
        "0"
    ],
    "rtpEnabled": true,
    "scheduledActionsForRule": [
        {
            "ruleName": "PasswordRequired",
            "scheduledActionConfigurations": [
                {
                    "actionType": "block",
                    "gracePeriodHours": 12,
                    "notificationMessageCCList": [],
```

```
                "notificationTemplateId": ""
            },
            {
                "actionType": "retire",
                "gracePeriodHours": 4320,
                "notificationMessageCCList": [],
                "notificationTemplateId": ""
            }
        ]
    }
],
"secureBootEnabled": true,
"signatureOutOfDate": true,
"tpmRequired": true
}
"@
```

Anything not configured is not included in the JSON, so the majority are true. The `deviceThreatProtectionRequiredSecurityLevel` setting is `unavailable` in this case as the tenant does not have licensing for Defender for Endpoint, so there is no risk of non-compliance when licensing is not in place.

3. We covered notification templates in the previous recipe, but to find the ID, simply run a `GET` request against this URL: `https://graph.microsoft.com/beta/deviceManagement/notificationMessageTemplates`.
4. Finally, we need to create the policy and assign it:

```
$compliance = invoke-mggraphrequest -uri $uri -json $json -method post -
contenttype "application/json" -outputtype PSObject
$complianceid = $compliance.id
$assignurl = "https://graph.microsoft.com/beta/deviceManagement/
deviceCompliancePolicies/$complianceid/assign"
$assignjson = @"
{
    "assignments": [
        {
            "target": {
                "@odata.type": "#microsoft.graph.groupAssignmentTarget",
                "groupId": "527ee8b8-b3e7-4bbf-9abf-45bdced10a0d"
            }
```

```
            }
        ]
    }
    "@
    invoke-mggraphrequest -uri $assignurl -json $assignjson -method post -
    contenttype "application/json" -outputtype PSObject
```

That concludes this recipe on deploying a Windows compliance policy using PowerShell and Graph.

Deploying an Android compliance policy

Now, we can look at our Android corporate devices. While BYOD is handled by app protection policies (as we have no control over the device itself), we can force our managed devices to remain compliant to access corporate data. In this recipe, we are only going to be looking at corporate-owned and managed devices. Settings for other device types can be found here: `https://learn.microsoft.com/en-gb/mem/intune/protect/compliance-policy-create-android-for-work#system-security-settings`.

Getting ready

As with the Windows policy, we will start by looking at the available options and what they do.

Compliance settings

We can run through the various compliance settings for our Android devices.

Microsoft Defender for Endpoint

Note that for this setting, you will require licensing for Defender for Endpoint. Double-check whether you have the correct licenses before enabling it. It also requires the application to be deployed to and running on the device:

- **Require the device to be at or under the machine risk score**: The options are as follows:
    - **Not Configured**: Take no action
    - **Clear**: The device cannot have any threats at all
    - **Low**: The device can only have low-level threats
    - **Medium**: The device can have low- or medium-level threats
    - **High**: This allows all threat levels

You can find out more about these risk levels at `https://learn.microsoft.com/en-us/microsoft-365/security/defender-endpoint/alerts-queue?view=o365-worldwide`.

Device Health

Under the **Device Health** heading, we have the following settings:

- **Rooted**: Allows you to block rooted devices from accessing company resources.
- **Require the device to be at or under the Device Threat Level**: The options are as follows:
  - **Not Configured**
  - **Secured**
  - **Low**
  - **Medium**
  - **High**

  This uses a Mobile Threat Defense partner and feeds back into Intune. If you do not use Mobile Threat Defense, leave this as **Not Configured**. A list of partners can be found here: `https://learn.microsoft.com/en-us/mem/intune/protect/mobile-threat-defense#mobile-threat-defense-partners`.
- **Play Integrity Verdict**: The options are as follows:
  - **Not configured**
  - **Check basic integrity**: The application has not been tampered with
  - **Check basic integrity & device integrity**: The application and device have not been tampered with

  These leverage the Google Play API. More information can be found here: `https://support.google.com/googleplay/android-developer/answer/11395166?hl=en-GB`.

Device Properties

Under **Device Properties**, we have the following settings:

- **Minimum and Maximum OS version**: These are self-explanatory. Remember that these are just for compliance and will not force a version or restrict enrollment (we will cover this in *Chapter 13*). A list of version numbers can be found here: `https://source.android.com/docs/setup/about/build-numbers`.
- **Minimum security patch level**: Similar to Windows updates, Android has security patches as well as larger operating system updates. These are generally released each

month, and you can use a compliance policy to specify a minimum version allowed. This can be useful in the case of any zero-day exploits. It has to be in YYYY-MM-DD format. To find the version numbers, check the bulletin here: `https://source.android.com/docs/security/bulletin/asb-overview`.

System Security

We have the following settings under **System Security**:

- **Require a password to unlock mobile devices**: Enable this to require users to configure a password. Remember, this will not force a password, and if you do nothing with your non-compliant devices, they can continue to use a device without a password.
- **Required password type**: The options are as follows:
    - **Device default**: This cannot be used to evaluate compliance, so it is not recommended.
    - **Password required, no restrictions**: Any password can be set; you cannot set further restrictions.
    - **Weak biometric**: More information can be found at `https://android-developers.googleblog.com/2018/06/better-biometrics-in-android-p.html`.
    - **Numeric**: The password can only contain numbers. It also presents the option for a minimum length (4–16).
    - **Numeric complex**: The password can only contain numbers and there cannot be patterns. It also presents the option for a minimum length (4–16).
    - **Alphabetic**: The password can only contain letters in the alphabet. It also presents the option for a minimum length (4–16).
    - **Alphanumeric**: The password can contain uppercase letters, lowercase letters, and numbers only. It also presents the option for a minimum length (4–16).
    - **Alphanumeric with symbols**: The password can contain uppercase letters, lowercase letters, numeric characters, punctuation marks, and symbols. This also presents options for the minimum password length (4–16), number of characters required (1–16), number of lowercase characters required (1–16), number of uppercase characters required (1–16), number of non-letter characters required (1–16), number of numeric characters required (1–16), and number of symbol characters required (1–16).

- **Maximum minutes of inactivity before password is required**: Try to balance security and usability here. The value can be 1 minute to 8 hours.
- **Number of days until password expires**: This is an optional field. The values can be set to 1–365 days or left blank so that it is disabled.
- **Number of passwords required before user can reuse a password**: This is also optional and can be set to 1–24 previous passwords if required. Again, consider security implications as well as potential user issues.

Encryption

Under the **Encryption** heading, we have the **Require encryption of data storage on device** setting. Android Enterprise forces encryption on enrollment, so this is not necessarily required, but an extra layer of protection is not a bad thing.

Device Security

Finally, we have a single setting under **Device Security**: **Intune app runtime integrity**. This checks that Intune App (previously Company Portal) has the default runtime environment installed, is correctly signed, and is not in debug mode.

How to do it...

Now that we understand the settings, we can configure the policy. In this example, we will set a few key settings:

1. First, click **Devices** and then **Android**.
2. Click **Compliance**.
3. Now, click **Create Policy**.
   In the fly-out, select **Android Enterprise** and **Fully managed, dedicated and corporate-owned work profile**.
4. Once selected, click **Create**.
5. Set **Name** and **Description** values and click **Next**.
6. Configure your settings as required and click **Next**. In this example, we have configured the following:
   - **Play Integrity Verdict**: Check basic integrity and device integrity
   - **Required password type**: **Alphanumeric With Symbols**
   - **Length** = **6**, **Characters** = **6**, and one of each of the available options
   - **Require encryption of data storage on device**: Require
   - **Intune app runtime integrity**: Require

7. Now, we need to set the non-compliance actions, as covered at the beginning of this chapter. As this is a mobile device, we have a few extra options that we will enable. After configuring them, click **Next**.
8. We do not need scope tags in this example, so click **Next**.
9. Set your assignments. As with Windows, for non-kiosk devices, it is sensible to configure with user-based assignment. In this case, we are using Intune users, but you could also use **All Users** and an Android filter. You may wish to have different policies, depending on the devices. Once set, click **Next**.
10. Finally, confirm that everything looks correct and click **Create**.

With that, we have configured our Android compliance policy in the UI.

Automating it

Now, we can look at replicating the previous steps but automating them in PowerShell and Graph.

As with Windows, the JSON is similar, and we are sending a `POST` request to the same URL with a different `@odata.type`. In this case, this is as follows:

```
#microsoft.graph.androidDeviceOwnerCompliancePolicy
```

This book's GitHub repository contains an example with all the settings configured, but for this example, we will use the policy we created previously.

Follow these steps:

1. As usual, we start with the standard variables:

```
$name = "Android-Compliance-FullyManaged"
$description = "Android Compliance Policy for Fully Managed Devices"
$groupid = "000000-0000-0000-0000-000000000000"
$url = "https://graph.microsoft.com/beta/deviceManagement/
deviceCompliancePolicies"
```

2. Now, populate the JSON. Again, it is mostly Boolean and string values, and the non-compliance actions are included in a nested array. As this is a new policy, the ID is clear. If we were updating another policy, the ID would be included and we would be running a `PATCH` command:

```
$json = @"
{
```

```
    "@odata.type": "#microsoft.graph.androidDeviceOwnerCompliancePolicy",
    "advancedThreatProtectionRequiredSecurityLevel": "unavailable",
    "deviceThreatProtectionEnabled": false,
    "deviceThreatProtectionRequiredSecurityLevel": "unavailable",
    "displayName": "$name",
    "description": "$description",
    "id": "00000000-0000-0000-0000-000000000000",
    "localActions": [],
    "passwordMinimumLength": 6,
    "passwordMinimumLetterCharacters": 6,
    "passwordMinimumLowerCaseCharacters": 1,
    "passwordMinimumNonLetterCharacters": 1,
    "passwordMinimumNumericCharacters": 1,
    "passwordMinimumSymbolCharacters": 1,
    "passwordMinimumUpperCaseCharacters": 1,
    "passwordRequired": true,
    "passwordRequiredType": "alphanumericWithSymbols",
    "roleScopeTagIds": [
        "0"
    ],
    "scheduledActionsForRule": [
        {
            "ruleName": "PasswordRequired",
            "scheduledActionConfigurations": [
                {
                    "actionType": "block",
                    "gracePeriodHours": 0,
                    "notificationMessageCCList": [],
                    "notificationTemplateId": ""
                },
                {
                    "actionType": "pushNotification",
                    "gracePeriodHours": 120,
                    "notificationMessageCCList": [],
                    "notificationTemplateId": ""
                },
                {
                    "actionType": "remoteLock",
                    "gracePeriodHours": 240,
                    "notificationMessageCCList": [],
                    "notificationTemplateId": ""
```

```
                }
            ]
        }
    ],
    "securityBlockJailbrokenDevices": true,
    "securityRequiredAndroidSafetyNetEvaluationType": "basic",
    "securityRequireIntuneAppIntegrity": true,
    "securityRequireSafetyNetAttestationBasicIntegrity": null,
    "securityRequireSafetyNetAttestationCertifiedDevice": true,
    "storageRequireEncryption": true
}
"@
```

3. Create the policy and grab the ID:

```
$androidpolicy = Invoke-MgGraphRequest -uri $url -Method Post -Body $json -
ContentType "application/json" -OutputType PSObject
$androidpolicyid = $androidpolicy.id
```

4. Now, populate the URL and assign the policy:

```
$assignurl = "https://graph.microsoft.com/beta/deviceManagement/
deviceCompliancePolicies/$androidpolicyid/assign"
$assignjson = @"
{
    "assignments": [
        {
            "target": {
                "@odata.type": "#microsoft.graph.groupAssignmentTarget",
                "groupId": "$groupid"
            }
        }
    ]
}
"@
Invoke-MgGraphRequest -uri $assignurl -Method Post -Body $assignjson -
ContentType "application/json" -OutputType PSObject
```

This completes the steps to automate the creation of our Android compliance policy.

Deploying an iOS compliance policy

After setting up our Android policy, we can now look at iOS devices. As with other policies, we will start by looking at the available settings and what they require before looking at configuring the policy and how it works.

Getting ready

We will start by looking at all of the available settings and what they require.

Compliance settings

Let's run through all of the settings available for iOS devices.

Email

We will start with the single setting under the **Email** heading: **Unable to set up email on the device**. The device must use a managed account configured via Intune. Any accounts that were manually added previously will need to be removed before the device can be marked as compliant.

Device Health

Now, we can review the options for **Device Health**:

- **Jailbroken devices**: Any jailbroken devices will be blocked on iOS 8.0 and above.
- **Require the device to be at or under the Device Threat Level**: The options are as follows:
    - **Not Configured**
    - **Secured**
    - **Low**
    - **Medium**
    - **High**

  This uses a Mobile Threat Defense partner and feeds back into Intune. If you do not use Mobile Threat Defense, leave this as **Not Configured**. A list of partners can be found here: `https://learn.microsoft.com/en-us/mem/intune/protect/mobile-threat-defense#mobile-threat-defense-partners`.

Device Properties

Under **Device Properties**, we have these options:

- **Minimum and Maximum OS version**: These are self-explanatory. Remember that these are just for compliance and will not force a version or restrict enrollment (we will cover this in *Chapter 13*). A list of version numbers can be found here: `https://iosref.com/ios`.

- **Minimum and Maximum OS build version**: Here you can set the build versions and, optionally, the supplemental build number. Apple security updates can be found here: `https://support.apple.com/en-us/HT201222`.

Microsoft Defender for Endpoint

Note that this setting requires licensing for Defender for Endpoint. Double-check that you have the correct licenses before enabling it. It also requires the application to be deployed to and running on the device:

- **Require the device to be at or under the machine risk score**: The options are as follows:
    - **Not Configured**
    - **Clear**: The device cannot have any threats at all
    - **Low**: The device can only have low-level threats
    - **Medium**: The device can have low or medium-level threats
    - **High**: This allows all threat levels

  You can find out more about the risk levels here: `https://learn.microsoft.com/en-us/microsoft-365/security/defender-endpoint/alerts-queue?view=o365-worldwide`.

System Security

Onto the **System Security** options. We have the following:

- **Password**:
    - **Require a password to unlock mobile devices**: This marks a device as non-compliant if no password of any sort is set. The next settings only apply to devices enrolled using Apple Business Manager or Apple School Manager and do not apply to BYOD. These will also force the setting rather than just reporting on it, so be extra careful:
        - **Simple passwords**: Block sequences such as 1111 or 1234
        - **Minimum password length**: 4–14 digits; digits or characters
        - **Required password type**: Can be **Not Configured**, **Numeric**, or **Alphanumeric**
        - **Number of non-alphanumeric characters in password**: Can be set to **Not Configured** or between 0 and 4 characters

- **Maximum minutes after screen lock before password is required**: Can be set to one of the following options:
  - **Immediately**
  - **1 minute**
  - **5 minutes**
  - **15 minutes**
  - **1 hour**
  - **4 hours**

  As the screen is locked, **Immediately** is the safest option and should not cause too much disruption.
- **Maximum minutes of inactivity until screen locks**: Can be anything from **Immediately** up to **15 minutes**. While **Immediately** is the most secure, that may cause disruption for your users. 2–3 minutes should be a good balance of security and usability.
- **Password expiration (days)**: Can be 1 to 730 days. Depending on your password complexity, pick the most balanced for your environment.
- **Number of previous passwords to prevent reuse**: 1–24 passwords. Again, if you set it to 24, users are going to struggle to think of a new password and will just add numbers to old ones, or worse still, write it down.

• **Device Security**:
- **Restricted apps**: A list of apps that, if detected, will be marked as non-compliant. The policy will take no action; just mark it as non-compliant. You can configure a **Device Restrictions** policy to remove these apps.

How to do it...

Now that we have covered the settings, we can set up our policy:

1. First, navigate to **Devices** and then **Compliance**.
2. Click **Policies** and then **Create Policy**.
3. In the fly-out, select **iOS/iPadOS** and click **Create**.
4. Specify your policy's name and description, then click **Next**.
5. Configure your settings as required. In this case, we are blocking user-configured email and jailbroken devices and configuring the password settings. Once you have configured your environment, click **Next**.

6. Now, set the actions for non-compliant devices. Again, as with Android, you can specify push notifications as well as email.
7. We are not setting scope tags in this example, so click **Next**.
8. Again, we are using a user-based assignment for a better experience, and in this example, we are using the **Intune-Users** group we created in *Chapter 1*. Often, your executive users will have iOS devices, so you may find yourself needing different compliance policies for different user groups. Once you have configured everything, click **Next**.
9. Finally, check that everything looks correct and click **Create**.

We have configured our iOS compliance policy in the UI and can now look at automating it using PowerShell and Graph.

Automating it

As with our Android policy, for this example, we will cover the preceding settings, but in this book's GitHub repository, there is an example with all the settings configured: `https://github.com/PacktPublishing/Microsoft-Intune-Cookbook-Second-Edition/blob/main/Chapter-8/create-ios-compliance-allsettings.ps1`.

This is similar to previous policies, only with `@odata.type` set to the following:

```
#microsoft.graph.iosCompliancePolicy
```

Again, the MDE components are marked as unavailable due to licensing:

1. First, we will start with the basics, including the standard compliance policy URL:

```
$name = "iOS Compliance"
$description = "iOS Compliance Policy"
$groupid = "00000-00000-00000-00000"
$url = "https://graph.microsoft.com/beta/deviceManagement/
deviceCompliancePolicies"
```

2. Now, we must populate the JSON. Note that again, the actions are nested JSON within the primary policy:

```
$json = @"
{
    "@odata.type": "#microsoft.graph.iosCompliancePolicy",
    "advancedThreatProtectionRequiredSecurityLevel": "unavailable",
    "description": "$description",
```

```
    "deviceThreatProtectionEnabled": false,
    "deviceThreatProtectionRequiredSecurityLevel": "unavailable",
    "displayName": "$name",
    "id": "00000000-0000-0000-0000-000000000000",
    "managedEmailProfileRequired": true,
    "passcodeBlockSimple": true,
    "passcodeExpirationDays": 30,
    "passcodeMinimumCharacterSetCount": 1,
    "passcodeMinimumLength": 6,
    "passcodeMinutesOfInactivityBeforeLock": 0,
    "passcodeMinutesOfInactivityBeforeScreenTimeout": 2,
    "passcodePreviousPasscodeBlockCount": 3,
    "passcodeRequired": true,
    "passcodeRequiredType": "alphanumeric",
    "roleScopeTagIds": [
        "0"
    ],
    "scheduledActionsForRule": [
        {
            "ruleName": "PasswordRequired",
            "scheduledActionConfigurations": [
                {
                    "actionType": "block",
                    "gracePeriodHours": 0,
                    "notificationMessageCCList": [],
                    "notificationTemplateId": ""
                },
                {
                    "actionType": "pushNotification",
                    "gracePeriodHours": 48,
                    "notificationMessageCCList": [],
                    "notificationTemplateId": ""
                },
                {
                    "actionType": "remoteLock",
                    "gracePeriodHours": 120,
                    "notificationMessageCCList": [],
                    "notificationTemplateId": ""
                },
                {
                    "actionType": "retire",
```

```
                    "gracePeriodHours": 720,
                    "notificationMessageCCList": [],
                    "notificationTemplateId": ""
                }
            ]
        }
    ],
    "securityBlockJailbrokenDevices": true
}
"@
```

3. Create the policy and grab the ID:

```
$iospolicy = Invoke-MgGraphRequest -uri $url -Method Post -Body $json -
ContentType "application/json" -OutputType PSObject
$policyid = $iospolicy.id
```

4. Populate the URL and JSON, then assign the policy:

```
$assignurl = "https://graph.microsoft.com/beta/deviceManagement/
deviceCompliancePolicies/$policyid/assign"
$assignjson = @"
{
    "assignments": [
        {
            "target": {
                "@odata.type": "#microsoft.graph.groupAssignmentTarget",
                "groupId": "$groupid"
            }
        }
    ]
}
"@
Invoke-MgGraphRequest -uri $assignurl -Method Post -Body $assignjson -
ContentType "application/json" -OutputType PSObject
```

That completes this recipe on deploying an iOS compliance policy.

Deploying a macOS compliance policy

Now that we have looked at Apple devices, we can look at making sure our corporate-managed macOS device is compliant.

> Note
>
> One important thing to note with macOS is that unlike our other policies (except iOS), if you configure the PIN setting within a macOS compliance policy, it will enforce the setting on the device rather than just reporting on it.

Getting ready

As with the other recipes, we will start by looking at the settings available to us.

Compliance settings

Now, let's run through the settings available for macOS devices.

Device Health

We will start with the single setting available under **Device Health**: **Require system integrity protection**. This stops protected files and folders from being changed by malicious software and was introduced in the El Capitan release. More information can be found here: `https://support.apple.com/en-gb/HT204899`.

Device Properties

Now, we will look at the settings under **Device Properties**:

- **Minimum and Maximum OS Version**: In standard format, which can be found here: `https://support.apple.com/en-gb/HT201260`
- **Maximum and Minimum OS Build Version**: These are the build numbers and rapid response numbers, as found in brackets on the page linked here: `https://developer.apple.com/news/releases/`

System Security

Within **System Security**, we have the following settings:

- **Password**: Our password options are as follows:
    - **Require a password to unlock mobile devices**: Marks a device as non-compliant if no password of any sort is set. We have the following options underneath this:
        - **Simple passwords**: Block sequences such as 1111 or 1234
        - **Minimum password length**: 4–14 digits; digits or characters
        - **Required password type**: Can be **Not Configured**, **Numeric**, or **Alphanumeric**
        - **Number of non-alphanumeric characters in password**: Can be set to **Not Configured** or from 0 to 4 characters
    - **Maximum minutes of inactivity before password is required**: Can be set to one of the following values:
        - **1 minute**
        - **5 minutes**
        - **15 minutes**
        - **1 hour**
        - **4 hours**

      As with your Windows devices, you want a balance of security and usability here. Anything more than 15 minutes is going to leave you more open to security issues.
    - **Password expiration (days)**: Can be 1 to 730 days. Depending on the password complexity, pick the most balanced option for your environment.
    - **Number of previous passwords to prevent reuse**: Can be 1–24 passwords. Again, if you set it to 24, users are going to struggle to think of a new password and will just add numbers to old ones, or worse still, write it down.
- **Encryption**: Our encryption compliance option is as follows:
    - **Require encryption of data storage on device**: This will mark machines not encrypted with FileVault as non-compliant
- **Device Security**: Here, we have the following options:
    - **Firewall**: Requires the firewall to be enabled.

    - **Incoming connections**: This will block any connections that are not required for basic internet services. This includes blocking sharing services.
    - **Stealth Mode**: This blocks ping requests or connection attempts from closed TCP or UDP networks.
- **Gatekeeper**: Under **Gatekeeper**, we have these options:
    - **Allow apps downloaded from these locations**: This restricts application installations to trusted software. The options are as follows:
        - **Not Configured**
        - **Mac App Store**
        - **Mac App Store and identified developers**
        - **Anywhere**

More information can be found here: `https://support.apple.com/en-gb/guide/security/sec5599b66df/web`.

Keep in mind that if you deploy apps via Company Portal that are not identified developers, the installation will be blocked unless set to **Anywhere**, so it is worth reviewing your application requirements before configuring this setting.

How to do it...

Now that we have covered the settings, we can set up our policy:

1. Start with **Devices** and then **Compliance**.
2. Click **Policies** and then **Create policy**.
3. In the fly-out, select **macOS** and click **Create**.
4. Add **Name** and **Description** values and click **Next**.
5. Configure the settings as required using the preceding details as a reference point. Once configured, click **Next**.
6. Next, set the actions for non-compliance. We still have the option to remotely lock the device, but as this is not iOS or Android, we cannot send a push notification.
7. As usual, we are not setting any scope tags in this example, so click **Next**.
8. As mentioned in other recipes, assigning to users gives better results, so we are assigning to our **Intune-Users** group.
9. Finally, check that everything looks correct and click **Create**.

That completes this recipe on how to configure a macOS compliance policy in the UI. Now, let's automate it.

Automating it

When looking at automating this policy, it is very similar to the recipes we covered earlier. Again, we have included an example with all the settings configured in this book's GitHub repository: `https://github.com/PacktPublishing/Microsoft-Intune-Cookbook-Second-Edition/blob/main/Chapter-8/create-macos-compliance-allsettings.ps1`.

The `@odata.type` property that is used for a macOS compliance policy is as follows:

```
#microsoft.graph.macOSCompliancePolicy
```

Follow these steps:

1. As with all the other scripts, we will start with the basic variables:

```
$name = "macOS Compliance"
$description = "Compliance Policy for macOS Devices"
$groupid = "00000000-0000-0000-0000-000000000000"
$url = "https://graph.microsoft.com/beta/deviceManagement/
deviceCompliancePolicies"
```

2. Then, populate the JSON. Again, the non-compliance actions are a nested array within the main JSON with everything else as string or Boolean values:

```
$json = @"
{
    "@odata.type": "#microsoft.graph.macOSCompliancePolicy",
    "description": "$description",
    "displayName": "$name",
    "firewallEnabled": true,
    "firewallEnableStealthMode": true,
    "gatekeeperAllowedAppSource": "macAppStoreAndIdentifiedDevelopers",
    "id": "00000000-0000-0000-0000-000000000000",
    "passwordBlockSimple": true,
    "passwordExpirationDays": 41,
    "passwordMinimumCharacterSetCount": 1,
    "passwordMinutesOfInactivityBeforeLock": 5,
    "passwordPreviousPasswordBlockCount": 3,
    "passwordRequired": true,
    "passwordRequiredType": "alphanumeric",
    "roleScopeTagIds": [
        "0"
```

```
    ],
    "scheduledActionsForRule": [
        {
            "ruleName": "PasswordRequired",
            "scheduledActionConfigurations": [
                {
                    "actionType": "block",
                    "gracePeriodHours": 0,
                    "notificationMessageCCList": [],
                    "notificationTemplateId": ""
                },
                {
                    "actionType": "remoteLock",
                    "gracePeriodHours": 480,
                    "notificationMessageCCList": [],
                    "notificationTemplateId": ""
                },
                {
                    "actionType": "retire",
                    "gracePeriodHours": 1080,
                    "notificationMessageCCList": [],
                    "notificationTemplateId": ""
                }
            ]
        }
    ],
    "storageRequireEncryption": true,
    "systemIntegrityProtectionEnabled": true
}
"@
```

3. Assign the policy and grab the ID:

```
$assignpolicy = Invoke-MgGraphRequest -Uri $url -Method POST -Body $json -
ContentType "application/json" -OutputType PSObject
$policyid = $assignpolicy.id
```

4. Add the ID to the URL:

```
$assignurl = "https://graph.microsoft.com/beta/deviceManagement/
deviceCompliancePolicies/$policyid/assign"
```

5. Populate the JSON and assign our policy:

```
$assignjson = @"
{
    "assignments": [
        {
            "target": {
                "@odata.type": "#microsoft.graph.groupAssignmentTarget",
                "groupId": "$groupid"
            }
        }
    ]
}
"@
Invoke-MgGraphRequest -Uri $assignurl -Method POST -Body $assignjson -
ContentType "application/json" -OutputType PSObject
```

That completes the automated process of creating our macOS compliance policy.

Deploying a Linux compliance policy

This is a relatively new addition to Intune. While we cannot currently deploy configuration or applications to Linux devices, we can configure compliance policies, primarily for Ubuntu-based devices, to ensure that any devices accessing corporate data meet the same standards across platforms.

Getting ready

Again, we will start by looking at the available settings. One of the first things to note is that Linux compliance uses the settings catalog to configure as it is a much newer addition.

Allowed Distributions

Under **Allowed Distributions**, we have the **Type** option. At the time of writing, the only options are **Ubuntu** or **RHEL**, but you can set minimum and maximum versions. The version numbers can be found here: `https://wiki.ubuntu.com/Releases`.

Custom Compliance

Under **Custom Compliance**, we have the **Require custom compliance** setting. This will be covered in greater depth in the next recipe, but instead of using PowerShell to capture the settings, it uses Bash. An example policy is available here: `https://github.com/petripaavola/Intune/tree/master/Linux`.

Device Encryption

Under **Device Encryption**, we have the **Require device encryption** option. It requires Ubuntu 22.04/20.04 LTS or RHEL Enterprise 8/9 **Full Disk Encryption** (**FDE**). Any encryption that uses `dm-crypt` is recognized, and the following directories are ignored:

- Read-only files
- Pseudosystem files
- Boot partitions

Password Policy

Finally, under **Password Policy**, which forces specific password formats, we have the following options:

- **Minimum uppercase**
- **Minimum lowercase**
- **Minimum length**: The total length of the password
- **Minimum digits**: Numeric digits in the password

How to do it...

Now that we know about the different settings, we can create our policy. This should all be familiar as it is a settings catalog policy, which we covered in *Chapter 2*:

1. First, navigate to **Devices** and then **Compliance**.
2. Click on **Policies** and then **Create policy**.
3. In the fly-out, select **Linux**. Select **Settings Catalog**. Then, click **Create**.
4. As usual, start with **Name** and **Description** values, then click **Next**.
5. Click **Add Settings**.
6. Add your settings as required. If you are looking at versions, check the Ubuntu version URL and see which are currently in support and exclude those that are out of support as a start. In this recipe, we require encryption and will only set a password.
7. In the non-compliance options, we can only email the user. The devices are not fully managed, so you cannot retire them, and Linux does not support push notifications. In

our case, we will simply mark it as not compliant and let the conditional access policy sort the rest.

8. As usual, we are skipping **Scope tags** in this example, so click **Next**.
9. As with other policies, we are assigning at the user level. Compliance is less of a risk with a Linux device, but often, you will find these are used by developers and other IT staff, so you may need slightly different policies accordingly. In this case, we are using our **Intune-Users** Entra group. When you have selected your assignment, click **Next**.
10. Finally, check that everything looks correct and click **Create**.

Automating it

As with the previous recipe, we are only creating the Linux compliance policy here, but this book's GitHub repository contains a policy example with all the settings configured: `https://github.com/PacktPublishing/Microsoft-Intune-Cookbook-Second-Edition/blob/main/Chapter-8/create-linux-compliance-allsettings.ps1`.

Unlike the others, however, this policy uses the settings catalog underneath, so the JSON is different.

When setting the variables, you can see that the URL is still the same as it was for the previous policies:

```
https://graph.microsoft.com/beta/deviceManagement/compliancePolicies
```

To find the available categories, we need to run a `GET` request against this URL: `https://graph.microsoft.com/beta/deviceManagement/complianceCategories?$filter=technologies eq 'linuxMdM'`.

As an example, the allowed distributions fall under the category ID:

```
f2c81665-b10b-4fa2-b177-7781b8650292
```

The individual settings can be found here: `https://graph.microsoft.com/beta/deviceManagement/compliancesettings`.

For allowed distributions, go to `https://graph.microsoft.com/beta/deviceManagement/compliancesettings?$filter=categoryId eq 'f2c81665-b10b-4fa2-b177-7781b8650292'`.

Now, let's get back to our example:

1. As usual, we start with the basics:

```
$name = "Linux Compliance"
$description = "Linux Compliance, non-custom"
$url = "https://graph.microsoft.com/beta/deviceManagement/
compliancePolicies"
$groupid = "00000000-0000-0000-0000-000000000000"
```

2. Populate the newly discovered JSON (reduced for brevity; the full code is available on GitHub):

```
$json = @"
{
    "description": "$description",
    "name": "$name",
    "platforms": "linux",
    "roleScopeTagIds": [
        "0"
    ],
    "settings": [
        {
            "@odata.type":
"#microsoft.graph.deviceManagementConfigurationSetting",
            "settingInstance": {
                "@odata.type":
"#microsoft.graph.deviceManagementConfigurationChoiceSettingInstance",
                "choiceSettingValue": {
                    "@odata.type":
"#microsoft.graph.deviceManagementConfigurationChoiceSettingValue",
                    "children": [],
                    "value": "linux_deviceencryption_required_true"
                },
                "settingDefinitionId": "linux_deviceencryption_required"
            }
        }
    ],
    "technologies": "linuxMdm"
}
"@
```

3. Create the policy and grab the ID:

```
$linuxpolicy = Invoke-MgGraphRequest -uri $url -Method POST -Body $json -
ContentType "application/json" -OutputType PSObject
$policyid = $linuxpolicy.id
```

4. Update the URL and assign the policy:

```
$assignurl = "https://graph.microsoft.com/beta/deviceManagement/
compliancePolicies/$policyid/assign"
$assignjson = @"
{
    "assignments": [
        {
            "target": {
                "@odata.type": "#microsoft.graph.groupAssignmentTarget",
                "groupId": "$groupid"
            }
        }
    ]
}
"@
Invoke-MgGraphRequest -uri $assignurl -Method POST -Body $assignjson -
ContentType "application/json" -OutputType PSObject
```

That completes this recipe on automating a Linux compliance policy.

Configuring and deploying a Windows custom compliance policy

Sometimes, you will find that your compliance may not meet what is available with the built-in settings. For example, you may have third-party products that you need to monitor or want to block machines with particular software installed. You could also restrict your environment to a specific hardware type, manufacturer, and amount of RAM – anything that can be detected by PowerShell can be used for compliance.

Once the script has been configured, you can set a JSON policy within Intune that looks at the output from PowerShell and compares it to the settings we specified in the JSON and their values. If the expected value meets the actual value, that setting is compliant. If not, it is non-compliant.

One non-compliant setting is enough to mark a device as non-compliant.

Now that we know how it works, we can configure our scripts.

Getting ready

Before we create the policy, we need to create the two files we will use in them. These scripts are both available in this book's GitHub repository:

- Compliance JSON: `https://github.com/PacktPublishing/Microsoft-Intune-Cookbook-Second-Edition/blob/main/Chapter-8/custom-compliance-json.json`
- Compliance PowerShell: `https://github.com/PacktPublishing/Microsoft-Intune-Cookbook-Second-Edition/blob/main/Chapter-8/custom-compliance-script.ps1`

You can also find some preconfigured compliance templates at `https://github.com/JayRHa/Custom-Compliance-Scripts`.

PowerShell script

First, we need the PowerShell script so that we can set the output we will be looking for within the JSON.

The most important thing here is the export, which must be in this format:

```
return $hash | ConvertTo-Json -Compress
```

What `$hash` contains is up to you, but it must be returned as compressed JSON.

The JSON supports these operators:

- `IsEquals`
- `NotEquals`
- `GreaterThan`
- `GreaterEquals`
- `LessThan`
- `LessEquals`

It also supports these data types:

- `Boolean`
- `Int64`
- `Double`
- `String`

- `DateTime`
- `Version`

The options here are vast, so in this example, we will demonstrate them with a few settings.

First, we can query the device manufacturer:

```
$biosinfo = Get-CimInstance -ClassName Win32_ComputerSystem
$manufacturer = $biosinfo.Manufacturer
```

Now, we can return `$manufacturer` to query in the JSON.

We will also check whether the domain firewall is enabled:

```
$domainfirewall= ((Get-NetFirewallProfile | select Name, Enabled | where-object
Name -eq Domain | select Enabled).Enabled).ToString()
```

Notice that we are converting that into a string value so that we can query it later.

We will also check for malware:

```
$noactivemalware = Get-MpThreatDetection
if ($null -eq $noactivemalware) {
    $noactivemalware = "True"
}
else {
    $noactivemalware = "False"
}
```

Finally, we will check whether BitLocker is enabled and the drive is encrypted:

```
$bitlockerprotected = (get-bitlockervolume).ProtectionStatus
$bitlockerencryption = (get-bitlockervolume).VolumeStatus
if (($bitlockerprotected -eq "On") -and ($bitlockerencryption -eq
"FullyEncrypted")) {
    $bitlocker = "True"
}
else {
    $bitlocker = "False"
}
```

As mentioned previously, we need to add these to `$hash`. In this case, we will use an array:

```
$hash = @{
    Manufacturer = $manufacturer
    DomainFirewall = $domainfirewall
    NoActiveMalware = $noactivemalware
    Bitlocker = $bitlocker
}
```

We need to make note of the headings that are passed through to the `$hash` array as these are what are queried in the JSON.

Then, we must take our array and return it as compressed JSON:

```
return $hash | ConvertTo-Json -Compress
```

JSON file

Now that we have our PowerShell script, we need to write the JSON to query it. We covered the data types and operators earlier. We must configure rules for each setting, telling them what to look for, and also an error message if the value is not found. This is multi-language if required as well.

We can also use the `{ActualValue}` option in the error message so that the user knows not only if the device is non-compliant, but also why.

More information about the JSON composition can be found here: `https://learn.microsoft.com/en-us/mem/intune/protect/compliance-custom-json`.

For our example, the JSON looks like this:

```
{
"Rules":[
    {
        "SettingName":"Manufacturer",
        "Operator":"IsEquals",
        "DataType":"String",
        "Operand":"Dell",
        "MoreInfoUrl":"https://www.google.com",
        "RemediationStrings":[
            {
                "Language":"en_US",
                "Title":"This machine is not a Dell.",
```

```
            "Description": "We only support Dell devices, please contact us for
more information. You are on an {ActualValue}"
          }
        ]
    },
    {
      "SettingName":"DomainFirewall",
      "Operator":"IsEquals",
      "DataType":"String",
      "Operand":"True",
      "MoreInfoUrl":"https://support.microsoft.com/en-us/windows/turn-microsoft-
defender-firewall-on-or-off-ec0844f7-aebd-0583-67fe-601ecf5d774f",
      "RemediationStrings":[
        {
          "Language": "en_US",
          "Title": "Domain Firewall is Off",
          "Description": "Your domain firewall is switched off, please re-
enable."
        }
      ]
    },
    {
      "SettingName":"NoActiveMalware",
      "Operator":"IsEquals",
      "DataType":"String",
      "Operand":"True",
      "MoreInfoUrl":"https://support.microsoft.com/en-us/windows/stay-protected-
with-windows-security-2ae0363d-0ada-c064-8b56-6a39afb6a963",
      "RemediationStrings":[
        {
          "Language": "en_US",
          "Title": "Active Malware Detected",
          "Description": "Active Malware detected, please remediate."
        }
      ]
    },
    {
      "SettingName":"Bitlocker",
      "Operator":"IsEquals",
      "DataType":"String",
      "Operand":"True",
```

```
        "MoreInfoUrl":"https://support.microsoft.com/en-us/windows/turn-on-device-encryption-0c453637-bc88-5f74-5105-741561aae838",
        "RemediationStrings":[
            {
                "Language": "en_US",
                "Title": "Unencrypted",
                "Description": "Your device is not fully encrypted, please encrypt."
            }
        ]
    }
  ]
}
```

We are grabbing `SettingName` from the PowerShell array, telling it what to look for, which in our case is `Equals`, and that all items that have been converted into strings to make `DataType` easier, and then simply what we are looking for in the operand.

Then, we provide a URL for more information and the error message to display on non-compliant devices.

How to do it...

We now have our scripts so that we can create the policy. This has been split into two parts – one for the PowerShell script and one for the policy itself.

PowerShell script

The first part is to create and upload our PowerShell script to Intune. Follow these steps to do this:

1. First, click **Devices** and then **Compliance**.
2. Then, select **Scripts**, click **Add**, and select **Windows 10 and later**.
3. Set your name and description. There is also a **Publisher** field, which you can configure to your name or organization name if required. Then, click **Next**.
4. Paste your script into the box (there is no upload functionality here). We have not signed the script, so we need to leave that set to **No**. We also want this to run at the system level as we are querying to the BIOS. Finally, while 32/64-bit should not make a difference for our queries, it is best to leave it set to **Yes**. Then, click **Next**.
5. Now, confirm that everything looks correct and click **Create**.

Compliance policy

Now that we have the script, we can create the policy (the JSON is added in the policy section):

1. Click the **Policies** tab and then click **Create Policy**.
2. In the fly-out, select **Windows 10 and later** and click **Create**.
3. Enter **Name** and **Description** values and click **Next**.
4. Now, we can see the familiar settings we covered earlier. This time, we are just setting **Custom compliance**.
5. Expand **Custom compliance**, click **Require**, and then click the blue text labeled **Click to select** to select the script.
6. Pick your script from the list and click **Select**.
7. Now, select your JSON; you will see that it populates not only the script (this box is read-only) but also what it is looking for. Click **Next** if you are sure that everything looks correct.
8. Set your non-compliance actions, as we covered in the earlier recipe (*Actions for non-compliance*), then click **Next**.
9. We are not setting scope tags in this example, so click **Next**.
10. As with other policies, we want to assign at the user level to avoid issues. In this case, we are using **Intune-Users**. Once you have configured your assignment, click **Next**.
11. Finally, review your policy and click **Create**.

That completes the configuration of our custom Windows compliance policy in the UI.

Automating it

Now that we have created the policy in the UI, we can look at creating our custom policy using PowerShell and Graph.

While two different UI areas were required to create it graphically, when automating, we can run both steps within the same script, including embedding the PowerShell and JSON scripts within the same file.

As we already know the content of these scripts, they are not included in this example but are available on GitHub (links can be found in this recipe's *How to do it...* section).

We will start by creating the PowerShell script:

1. First, configure the settings. Here, we are also including the run-as context (`system` or `user`) and whether to run in the 32-bit context (`true` or `false`):

```
$name = "Windows Custom Compliance"
$description = "Checks Manufacturer, Firewall, Malware and Bitlocker"
$publisher = "Publisher"
$loggedonuser = "system"
$runas32 = "false"
```

2. Now, set the URL for the script upload:

```
$url = "https://graph.microsoft.com/beta/deviceManagement/
deviceComplianceScripts"
```

3. At this point, we can add the PowerShell script (a cut-down version has been provided here to give you an idea):

```
$psscript = @'
$biosinfo = Get-CimInstance -ClassName Win32_ComputerSystem
$manufacturer = $biosinfo.Manufacturer
'@
```

4. We need to convert this into Base64 so that we can upload it:

```
$scriptcontent = [System.Text.Encoding]::UTF8.GetBytes($psscript)
$scriptcontent = [System.Convert]::ToBase64String($scriptcontent)
```

5. Populate the configured variables into the JSON to upload the script:

```
$json = @"
{
    "description": "$description",
    "detectionScriptContent": "$scriptcontent",
    "displayName": "$name",
    "enforceSignatureCheck": false,
    "id": "",
    "publisher": "$publisher",
    "runAs32Bit": $runas32,
    "runAsAccount": "$loggedonuser"
```

```
}
"@
```

6. Upload and grab the ID; we will need this later:

```
$psscript = Invoke-MgGraphRequest -Uri $url -Method Post -Body $json -
ContentType "application/json" -OutputType PSObject
$scriptid = $psscript.id
```

7. Now, we can move on to the policy itself, starting with the standard basics:

```
$policyname = "Windows Custom Compliance"
$policydescription = "Custom Compliance ONLY"
$groupid = "000000-0000-0000-0000-000000000000"
```

8. As with the PowerShell script, we include the JSON here (again, this has been reduced):

```
$compliancejson = @'
{
    "Rules":[
        {
            "SettingName":"Manufacturer",
            "Operator":"IsEquals",
            "DataType":"String",
            "Operand":"Dell",
            "MoreInfoUrl":"https://www.google.com",
            "RemediationStrings":[
                {
                    "Language":"en_US",
                    "Title":"This machine is not a Dell.",
                    "Description": "We only support Dell devices, please
contact us for more information. You are on an {ActualValue}"
                }
            ]
        }
    ]
    }
'@
```

9. This needs to be Base64 as well:

```
$jsoncontent = [System.Text.Encoding]::UTF8.GetBytes($compliancejson)
$jsoncontent = [System.Convert]::ToBase64String($jsoncontent)
```

10. Set the URL:

```
$policyurl = "https://graph.microsoft.com/beta/deviceManagement/
deviceCompliancePolicies"
```

11. Populate the JSON, including not only the JSON in Base64 but also the script ID:

```
$policyjson = @"
{
    "@odata.type": "#microsoft.graph.windows10CompliancePolicy",
    "description": "$policydescription",
    "deviceCompliancePolicyScript": {
        "deviceComplianceScriptId": "$scriptid",
        "rulesContent": "$jsoncontent",
    },
    "deviceThreatProtectionEnabled": false,
    "deviceThreatProtectionRequiredSecurityLevel": "unavailable",
    "displayName": "$policyname",
    "id": "00000000-0000-0000-0000-000000000000",
    "passwordRequiredType": "deviceDefault",
    "roleScopeTagIds": [
        "0"
    ],
    "scheduledActionsForRule": [
        {
            "ruleName": "PasswordRequired",
            "scheduledActionConfigurations": [
                {
                    "actionType": "block",
                    "gracePeriodHours": 0,
                    "notificationMessageCCList": [],
                    "notificationTemplateId": ""
                }
            ]
        }
    ]
```

```
}
"@
```

12. Now, let's get back to normal – create the policy, grab the ID, populate the URL, and assign the policy to our Entra group:

```
$compliancepolicy = Invoke-MgGraphRequest -Uri $policyurl -Method Post -
Body $policyjson -ContentType "application/json" -OutputType PSObject
$policyid = $compliancepolicy.id
$assignmenturl = "https://graph.microsoft.com/beta/deviceManagement/
deviceCompliancePolicies/$policyid/assign"
$assignmentjson = @"
{
    "assignments": [
        {
            "target": {
                "@odata.type": "#microsoft.graph.groupAssignmentTarget",
                "groupId": "$groupid"
            }
        }
    ]
}
"@
Invoke-MgGraphRequest -Uri $assignmenturl -Method Post -Body
$assignmentjson -ContentType "application/json" -OutputType PSObject
```

This completes our recipe on configuring a custom compliance script for Windows using PowerShell and Graph.

Using conditional access to restrict access based on compliance

There is one final step when using compliance policies. While we have some non-compliance settings configured to lock mobile devices, we are mostly just warning users that their device is not compliant, but this does not stop them from using them. We do not want devices that do not meet our criteria to access corporate data, unencrypted devices, devices with active malware, and more. For that, we need to set up a conditional access policy.

Note

This conditional access policy is just for restricting non-compliant devices. For full tenant security, you will need to deploy further policies. Common policies from Microsoft can be found at the following link: `https://learn.microsoft.com/en-us/microsoft-365/security/office-365-security/zero-trust-identity-device-access-policies-common?view=o365-worldwide`.

You can also use some preconfigured templates directly from Entra, as covered here: `https://learn.microsoft.com/en-us/entra/identity/conditional-access/concept-conditional-access-policy-common?tabs=secure-foundation`.

Getting ready

Before we set up this policy, make sure you have a break-glass account configured so that we can exclude it from any conditional access policies. This will give you access to the environment in case there is an issue with a policy that blocks all access.

How to do it...

Follow these steps to configure a conditional access policy to protect the environment from non-compliant devices:

1. Start by navigating to **Endpoint Security**, then **Conditional access**.
2. Click **Create new policy**.
3. Give the policy a name and click **0 users and groups selected**.
4. Under **Include**, select **All Users**.
5. Click the **Exclude** tab and exclude your break-glass account. Also, consider your IT staff, who may need to access these machines to make them compliant again. In this case, we are going to add the **Local Device Administrators** role to the exclusion as well.
6. Now, click **No target resources selected**.
7. We do not want these machines accessing anything, so click **All cloud apps** under the **Include** tab.

Note

We also do not want an exclusion in this policy, but when looking at future policies, consider the *Microsoft Intune Enrollment* application for exclusion if you want to allow device provisioning on occasions where a conditional access policy would normally block it (such as location-based).

We need to ensure that we do not block personal non-enrolled devices using MAM as they will not be compliant as they are not enrolled at all. For this, we will use **Device Based Filtering** under **Conditions**.

8. Click **0 conditions selected** and then **Not configured** under **Filter for devices**.
9. Set the rule to **DeviceOwnership Equals Company**. This will restrict the policy so that it can only be applied to corporate-owned devices. We created an additional policy in this book to restrict our BYOD devices to require app protection. These policies are in addition to, not instead of, MFA; each is an additional layer of security. Now, click **Done**:

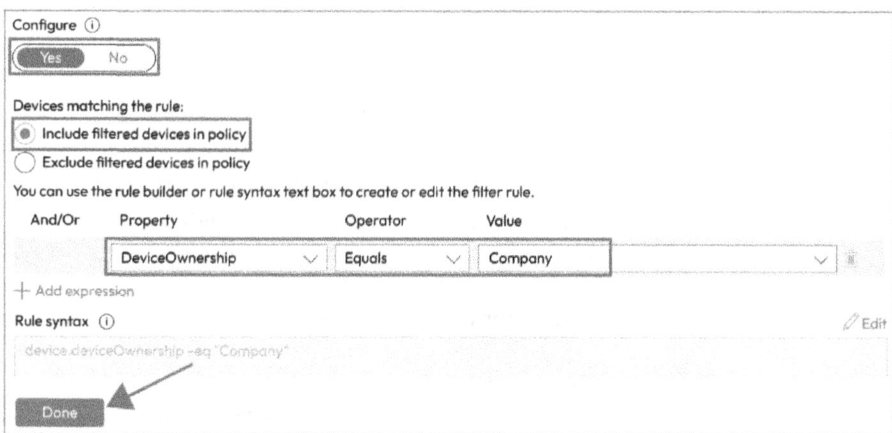

Figure 8.3 – Restricting a policy to corporate devices

10. Click **0 controls selected** under **Access controls**.
11. Select **Grant access** as this is an allow rather than a block policy, and tick the box for **Require device to be marked as compliant**.
    If you configure more than one setting here, you can specify whether the requirement is any or all of the options. Once configured, click **Select**.

12. We do not require any session controls, so we can leave that option unconfigured.
13. The final consideration is the status of the policy, which depends on the status of your environment. If you have a large number of non-compliant devices, setting this to **On** will cause calls to your IT support line as users are blocked from accessing corporate data. In this case, set it to **Report-only** so that you can monitor who will be blocked and fix the issue. As soon as your devices are mostly compliant, switch the policy on and add your security.
    In this example, we will switch the policy on.

This completes our conditional access policy configuration in the UI.

Automating it

We can now look at configuring our policy using Graph and PowerShell.

Conditional access policies require a single `POST` command as no assignment is required. All settings are contained within a nested array in the main JSON:

1. First, the only variables we need here are the name and URL:

```
$url = "https://graph.microsoft.com/v1.0/identity/conditionalAccess/
policies"
$name = "Block Non-Compliant Devices"
```

2. Then, we must configure the JSON with the values configured. For the user/role configuration, you need to use the ID rather than the display name.
   For users, this can be obtained by running a `GET` request against this URL: `https://graph.microsoft.com/v1.0/users`.

   We are grabbing this in the script with the following query:

```
$breakglassname = "Azure BreakGlass Account"
$breakglassid = (Invoke-MgGraphRequest -Uri "https://graph.microsoft.com/
v1.0/users?`$filter=displayName eq '$breakglassname'" -Method Get -
ContentType "application/json" -OutputType PSObject).value.Id
```

   The same applies to the role ID, which comes from this URL: `https://graph.microsoft.com/v1.0/directoryRoles`.

   Again, we will include this in the script:

```
$rolename = "Azure AD Joined Device Local Administrator"
$roleid = (Invoke-MgGraphRequest -Uri "https://graph.microsoft.com/v1.0/
```

```
directoryRoles?`$filter=displayName eq '$rolename'" -Method Get -
ContentType "application/json" -OutputType PSObject).value.Id
```

3. Now, we must populate the JSON:

```
$json = @"
{
    "conditions": {
        "applications": {
            "excludeApplications": [],
            "includeApplications": [
                "All"
            ],
            "includeAuthenticationContextClassReferences": [],
            "includeUserActions": [],
            "networkAccess": null
        },
        "clientApplications": null,
        "clientAppTypes": [
            "all"
        ],
        "clients": null,
        "devices": {
            "deviceFilter": {
                "mode": "include",
                "rule": "device.deviceOwnership -eq \"Company\""
            },
            "excludeDevices": [],
            "includeDevices": []
        },
        "locations": null,
        "platforms": null,
        "servicePrincipalRiskLevels": [],
        "signInRiskDetections": null,
        "signInRiskLevels": [],
        "times": null,
        "userRiskLevels": [],
        "users": {
            "excludeGroups": [],
            "excludeGuestsOrExternalUsers": null,
            "excludeRoles": [
```

```
                "$roleid"
            ],
            "excludeUsers": [
                "$breakglassid"
            ],
            "includeGroups": [],
            "includeGuestsOrExternalUsers": null,
            "includeRoles": [],
            "includeUsers": [
                "All"
            ]
        }
    },
    "displayName": "$name",
    "grantControls": {
        "authenticationStrength": null,
        "builtInControls": [
            "compliantDevice"
        ],
        "customAuthenticationFactors": [],
        "operator": "AND",
        "termsOfUse": []
    },
    "sessionControls": null,
    "state": "enabled"
}
"@
```

4. Finally, create the policy. We do not need to do anything further, so we can run the request without grabbing the output:

```
Invoke-MgGraphRequest -Method POST -Uri $url -Body $json -ContentType
"application/json" -OutputType PSObject
```

With that, we have created our conditional access policy via automation.

Join us on Discord

For discussions around the book and to connect with your peers, join us on Discord at `packt.link/discordcloud` or scan the QR code below:

9

Monitoring Your New Environment

One of the best aspects of modern device management is that a well-configured environment can free up staff resources to work on being more proactive, spotting and resolving issues before the end users find them. For that, we are going to use the tools included in Intune, starting in this chapter with a look at monitoring tools, and then continuing the theme in the next chapter when we will look at reporting.

In this chapter, we will cover the following recipes:

- Monitoring applications
- Monitoring device configuration
- Monitoring device compliance
- Monitoring device enrollment
- Monitoring updates across platforms
- Monitoring device actions
- Using device query
- Reviewing audit logs

Technical requirements

For this chapter, you will need a modern web browser and a PowerShell code editor such as Visual Studio Code or PowerShell ISE.

All the scripts referenced can be found here: `https://github.com/PacktPublishing/Microsoft-Intune-Cookbook-Second-Edition/tree/main/Chapter-9`.

If you wish to test the policies, you will need a corporate-managed device running each supported platform (Windows, iOS, macOS, Linux, and Android). For Linux, it will need to be running the Ubuntu OS.

Monitoring applications

In this recipe, we will be looking at application monitoring. There are a few options within this category, so we will cover each of them and then look at how to grab the same information via Graph. As these reports are all output-only, there is nothing to create, but we will cover the export functionality.

Getting ready

For all of the monitoring reports covered here, we need to navigate to **Apps** and then click on **Monitor**.

How to do it...

We will start by looking at monitoring application licenses and then run through the others in the order they appear within Intune:

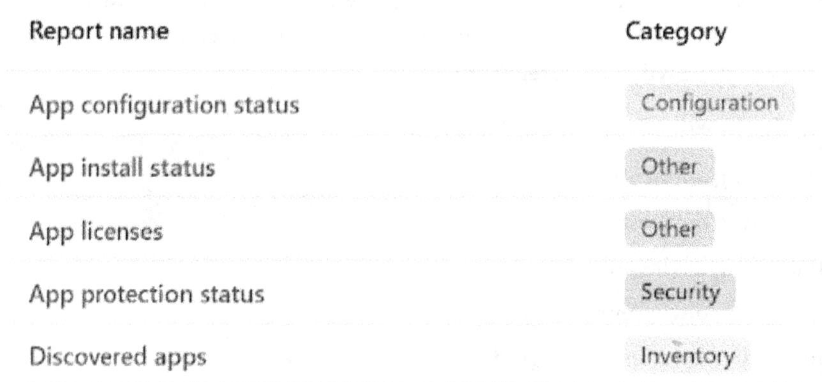

Report name	Category
App configuration status	Configuration
App install status	Other
App licenses	Other
App protection status	Security
Discovered apps	Inventory

Figure 9.1 – Monitor apps menu

App configuration status

The first application monitoring report is the **App configuration status** report.

This is for any application configuration policies you have deployed to managed devices or managed applications (MDM and MAM) and covers both Android and iOS device types at the device level.

As with other reports in this chapter, you can refresh and export as well as search here.

It also includes the ability to sort by header.

Again, there is a lot of content here, so use the scroll bar, but fortunately, most of the important settings are earlier on.

While this usually will not have any significant security issues, it is worth monitoring for an optimal user experience.

App install status

Next on the list is the **App install status** option for all apps across platforms.

As with the other reports available in Intune, you have the option to filter, search, and export.

This blade also adds the option to sort on the columns, though, which is a welcome addition.

Clicking on the app name will take you to the main application details page. Clicking **Device** and **User Failures** will take you directly to **Device install status** and **User install status**, respectively.

This is a very useful place to keep an eye on and spot any troublesome or mispackaged apps before you start seeing support calls. Sorting by **Install Failure** will cover both device and user installation and give you the best idea of what is causing issues in your estate.

App licenses

The next option is **App licenses**.

This is for store-based applications only (Apple, Microsoft, and Google Play Store). As we covered in *Chapter 6*, when deploying an application using Apple **Volume Purchase Program** (**VPP**), you select the number of licenses to make available for each application. If you have free applications, you can just order more than required, but for paid applications, you may want to restrict the licenses.

When you reach the license limit for any application, it will stop deploying; therefore, checking on license usage is a valuable thing to do.

At the top, you have the option to add additional columns (although most will not have any data), refresh, export to CSV, and, usefully, kick off a VPP sync.

Clicking the three dots also gives you the option to delete the application, which can be useful.

Unfortunately, the apps are listed alphabetically with no option to sort, but you can filter with the free text field at the top. To sort (which is much more useful), be sure to check out the automation, as that utilizes the `Out-GridView` command to give a similar display, but with better control.

Clicking on an application will take you to the application details.

App protection status

An important one for any security team is to check the status of protected applications on personal and corporate devices.

As in **App install status**, you can export, search, and sort on the headers.

There are a lot of columns here, so watch for the scroll bar across the bottom, as some of the most important fields are toward the end, where you can see **App Protection** and **Compliance Status**.

As these are MAM devices, there is no further clickthrough enabled.

While Conditional Access will protect your corporate data, monitoring your app protection status will help diagnose the issue when users are blocked from accessing resources.

Discovered apps

Finally, we can look at the **Discovered apps** report.

This report is for all applications and lists every application found on Intune-managed devices, whether deployed by Intune or not. It is a powerful tool, but as each version is a separate entry, it can be unmanageable (a small tenant could have 1,000+ entries).

Again, we can export using the button at the top and search, but there is no option to sort.

The script available at the following URL will extend the functionality to list the devices with the application installed: `https://andrewstaylor.com/2022/11/08/quick-and-easy-application-inventory-with-intune/`.

Clicking on an application takes you to the application details page, where you can look further at the install lists.

As with app licenses, the script will give more sorting options.

Automating it

When automating these reports, we will again be dealing with Graph pagination for any larger results, so the scripts all include the following function, which takes in a URL and exports all data across multiple pages:

```
function getallpagination () {
[cmdletbinding()]
param
(
    $url
)
```

```
    $response = (Invoke-MgGraphRequest -uri $url -Method Get -OutputType PSObject)
    $alloutput = $response.value
    $alloutputNextLink = $response."@odata.nextLink"
    while ($null -ne $alloutputNextLink) {
        $alloutputResponse = (Invoke-MGGraphRequest -Uri $alloutputNextLink -
Method Get -outputType PSObject)
        $alloutputNextLink = $alloutputResponse."@odata.nextLink"
        $alloutput += $alloutputResponse.value
    }
    return $alloutput
    }
```

We will also add a simple pop-up box to select whether to view or export the output using the Windows Forms functionality:

```
Add-Type -AssemblyName System.Windows.Forms
$form = New-Object System.Windows.Forms.Form
$form.Text = "Export or View"
$form.Width = 300
$form.Height = 150
$form.StartPosition = "CenterScreen"
$label = New-Object System.Windows.Forms.Label
$label.Text = "Select an option:"
$label.Location = New-Object System.Drawing.Point(10, 20)
$label.AutoSize = $true
$form.Controls.Add($label)
$exportButton = New-Object System.Windows.Forms.Button
$exportButton.Text = "Export"
$exportButton.Location = New-Object System.Drawing.Point(100, 60)
$exportButton.DialogResult = [System.Windows.Forms.DialogResult]::OK
$form.AcceptButton = $exportButton
$form.Controls.Add($exportButton)
$viewButton = New-Object System.Windows.Forms.Button
$viewButton.Text = "View"
$viewButton.Location = New-Object System.Drawing.Point(180, 60)
$viewButton.DialogResult = [System.Windows.Forms.DialogResult]::Cancel
$form.CancelButton = $viewButton
$form.Controls.Add($viewButton)
$result = $form.ShowDialog()
```

Now that we have covered the repeatable code blocks, we can look at the automation of the reports covered earlier.

App configuration status

This report uses one of the newer Intune reporting endpoints (they keep changing); these work well from the UI, but are much harder to automate.

They work from a `POST` request to the endpoint, but then you have to receive the response (which is paginated) and add that into an array. We can run through it here.

Follow these steps to create your script:

1. First, we need somewhere to output the data:

```
$exportpath = "c:\temp\appconfigstatus.csv"
```

2. Then, we set the URL:

```
$url = "https://graph.microsoft.com/beta/deviceManagement/reports/
getMobileApplicationManagementAppConfigurationReport"
```

3. Now, we have to populate the values we are retrieving in the `POST` request:

```
$json = @"
{
    "filter": "",
    "orderBy": [],
    "select": [
        "AADDeviceID",
        "App",
        "AppInstanceId",
        "AppVersion",
        "DeviceType",
        "Email",
        "LastSync",
        "_Platform",
        "Policy",
        "User",
        "DeviceName",
        "DeviceManufacturer",
        "DeviceModel",
        "AndroidSecurityPatchVersion",
```

```
            "MDMDeviceID",
            "PlatformVersion",
            "iOSSdkVersion"
        ]
}
"@
```

4. While the data returned is technically JSON, it lacks the headers to identify it as such, so we have to bump the output into a temporary file and then read that file to store it for use later:

```
$tempfilepath = $env:TEMP + "\appconfigstatus.txt"
```

5. Now, we send our request:

```
Invoke-MgGraphRequest -Method POST -Uri $url -Body $json -ContentType
"application/json" -OutputFilePath $tempfilepath
```

6. Next, we import from our `temp` file and count the total number of records. We need this for our pagination:

```
$parsedData = get-content $tempfilepath | ConvertFrom-Json
$fullvalues = $parsedData.Values
$allrows = $parsedData.TotalRowCount
```

7. Now, we need to loop through all of the records to retrieve the report content. We are using a `while` loop with a counter to stop when we reach the total number of results. As the output has to be stored in a text file, we are also adding a variable to the filename to avoid over-writing:

```
$n = 0
while ($n -lt $allrows) {
$n += 50
$tempfilepath2 = $env:TEMP + "\appconfigstatus-$n.txt"
$url = "https://graph.microsoft.com/beta/deviceManagement/reports/
getMobileApplicationManagementAppConfigurationReport"
$json = @"
{
"filter": "",
"orderBy": [],
```

```
"select": [
"AADDeviceID",
"App",
"AppInstanceId",
"AppVersion",
"DeviceType",
"Email",
"LastSync",
"_Platform",
"Policy",
"User",
"DeviceName",
"DeviceManufacturer",
"DeviceModel",
"AndroidSecurityPatchVersion",
"MDMDeviceID",
"PlatformVersion",
"iOSSdkVersion"
],
"skip": $n,
"top": 50
}
"@
Invoke-MgGraphRequest -Method POST -Uri $url -Body $json -ContentType
"application/json" -OutputFilePath $tempfilepath2
$tempdata = get-content $tempfilepath2 | ConvertFrom-Json
$fullvalues += $tempdata.Values
}
```

8. We now use this data to make a more structured array with titles, so we can view and manipulate it later:

```
$outputarray = @()
foreach ($value in $fullvalues) {
$platform = $value[15]
$aaddeviceid = $value[0]
$app = $value[2]
$appinstanceid = $value[3]
$appversion = $value[4]
$devicemodel = $value[6]
$devicename = $value[7]
```

```
$devicetype = $value[5]
$email = $value[8]
$lastsync = $value[9]
$platformversion = $value[11]
$policyname = $value[12]
$iossdkversion = $value[13]
$user = $value[14]

$objectdetails = [pscustomobject]@{
Platform = $platform
AADDeviceID = $aaddeviceid
App = $app
AppInstanceID = $appinstanceid
AppVersion = $appversion
ComplianceState = $compliancestate
DeviceModel = $devicemodel
DeviceName = $devicename
DeviceType = $devicetype
Email = $email
LastSync = $lastsync
PlatformVersion = $platformversion
PolicyName = $policyname
iOSSDKVersion = $iossdkversion
User = $user
}
$outputarray += $objectdetails
}
```

9. After using the UI covered previously to either output or export the data, we want to clean up our environment to remove all of those `temp` files:

```
Remove-Item $tempfilepath
$allrows = $parsedData.TotalRowCount
$n = 0
while ($n -lt $allrows) {
$n += 50
$tempfilepath2 = $env:TEMP + "\appconfigstatus-$n.txt"
Remove-Item $tempfilepath2
}
```

App install status

This follows the same endpoint as **App configuration status**, with the changes being the URL and the objects we are looking for:

1. We will start with the easy part, the export path and URL:

```
$exportpath = "c:\temp\appinstallstatus.csv"
$url = "https://graph.microsoft.com/beta/deviceManagement/reports/
getAppsInstallSummaryReport"
```

2. Then, we need to set the variables:

```
$json = @"
{
    "filter": "",
    "orderBy": [],
    "select": [
        "DisplayName",
        "Publisher",
        "Platform",
        "AppVersion",
        "FailedDevicePercentage",
        "FailedDeviceCount",
        "FailedUserCount",
        "ApplicationId"
    ],
}
"@
```

3. Send the request, noting the all-important `-OutputFilePath`:

```
$tempfilepath = $env:TEMP + "\appinstallstatus.txt"
Invoke-MgGraphRequest -Method POST -Uri $url -Body $json -ContentType
"application/json" -OutputFilePath $tempfilepath
```

4. Next, we need to read that JSON into a variable:

```
$parsedData = get-content $tempfilepath | ConvertFrom-Json
```

5. We also need the total rows:

```
$allrows = $parsedData.TotalRowCount
```

6. Also, we need the values for the first 50 results, which we are storing inside an array to use later:

```
$fullvalues = $parsedData.Values
```

7. Now, we need to loop through and send a request incrementing every 50 results until we hit the total count. Each time we run, we export to a `.txt` file with an incremented name and then drop the values into our array:

```
$n = 0
while ($n -lt $allrows) {
    $n += 50
    $tempfilepath2 = $env:TEMP + "\appinstallstatus-$n.txt"
    $url = "https://graph.microsoft.com/beta/deviceManagement/reports/
getAppsInstallSummaryReport"
    $json = @"
{
    "filter": "",
    "orderBy": [],
    "select": [
        "DisplayName",
        "Publisher",
        "Platform",
        "AppVersion",
        "FailedDevicePercentage",
        "FailedDeviceCount",
        "FailedUserCount",
        "ApplicationId"
    ],
    "skip": $n,
    "top": 50
}
"@
    Invoke-MgGraphRequest -Method POST -Uri $url -Body $json -ContentType
"application/json" -OutputFilePath $tempfilepath2
    $tempdata = get-content $tempfilepath2 | ConvertFrom-Json
```

```
        $fullvalues += $tempdata.Values
    }
```

8. Once that is done, we have a lot of `.txt` files and a very messy, unorganized array. Now, we need to loop through that, grab the values, clean them, and drop them into a new array.

   Let's create a new array:

```
$outputarray = @()
```

9. Loop through each item, add it to a custom PowerShell object with a useful title, and then populate the array:

```
foreach ($value in $fullvalues) {
    $id = $value[0]
    $version = $value[1]
    $appname = $value[2]
    $devicefailure = $value[3]
    $installfailure = $value[4]
    $userfailure = $value[5]
    $platform = $value[7]
    $publisher = $value[8]
    $objectdetails = [pscustomobject]@{
        ID = $id
        Version = $version
        AppName = $appname
        DeviceFailure = $devicefailure
        InstallFailurePercent = $installfailure
        UserFailure = $userfailure
        Platform = $platform
        Publisher = $publisher
    }
    $outputarray += $objectdetails
}
```

10. Now, we use the same popup as earlier and either display or export the data:

```
if ($result -eq [System.Windows.Forms.DialogResult]::OK) {
    $outputarray | export-csv $exportpath -NoTypeInformation
} elseif ($result -eq [System.Windows.Forms.DialogResult]::Cancel) {
```

```
    $outputarray | Out-GridView
}
```

11. Finally, clean up those `.txt` files:

```
Remove-Item $tempfilepath
$allrows = $parsedData.TotalRowCount
$n = 0
while ($n -lt $allrows) {
    $n += 50
    $tempfilepath2 = $env:TEMP + "\appinstallstatus-$n.txt"
    Remove-Item $tempfilepath2
}
```

That completes the recipe for **App install status**. Now, we can look at reporting on app licenses on iOS/macOS.

App licenses

Now, we can look at the **App licenses** report, which uses the earlier reporting endpoint, so it is a simpler `GET` request compared to the earlier, more complex post and retrieve.

The full script, including the preceding code, is available on GitHub here: `https://github.com/PacktPublishing/Microsoft-Intune-Cookbook-Second-Edition/blob/main/Chapter-9/get-applicenses.ps1`.

Follow the subsequent steps to create this report for your environment:

1. For our app licenses, we are going to present the option to either view or export the output, so the first thing to do is to set a path for the exported file:

```
$exportpath = "c:\temp\applicenses.csv"
```

2. Now, we need to set our URL, which filters the app types that are added from any of the stores. We then use this URL with our function to retrieve the results:

```
$url = "https://graph.microsoft.com/beta/deviceAppManagement/mobileApps?
`$filter=isof('microsoft.graph.macOsVppApp') or
isof('microsoft.graph.iosVppApp') or
isof('microsoft.graph.microsoftStoreForBusinessApp') or
isof('microsoft.graph.androidManagedStoreApp') or
```

```
isof('microsoft.graph.androidManagedStoreWebApp')"
$allapps = getallpagination -url $url
```

3. Now, this simply dumps the entire application data, which is not much use for quickly checking the licenses. It also only includes total licenses and used licenses, but there is no option to see what is available. While we can do the sums ourselves, it would be nice to be able to sort on those running out of licenses, so we will add the calculation into the `select-object` query:

```
$applist = $allapps | select-object DisplayName, totalLicenseCount,
usedLicenseCount,
@{Name="availableLicenseCount";Expression={$_.totalLicenseCount -
$_.usedLicenseCount}}
```

4. Now, we grab the result of the popup. For export, simply save it as CSV, or for view, output with `gridview`, which gives you the option to both filter and sort:

```
if ($result -eq [System.Windows.Forms.DialogResult]::OK) {
    $applist | export-csv $exportpath
} elseif ($result -eq [System.Windows.Forms.DialogResult]::Cancel) {
    $applist | Out-GridView
}
```

That completes the script for **App licenses**. We can now look at the very important **App protection status** report.

App protection status

This report uses the same process as earlier reports using the newer `POST`/retrieve endpoint, so rather than copying the entire code, we will just look at the differences.

The full script is available on GitHub here: `https://github.com/PacktPublishing/Microsoft-Intune-Cookbook-Second-Edition/blob/main/Chapter-9/get-appprotectionstatus.ps1`.

Follow these steps to create a script to review your app protection status:

1. First, set the export path:

```
$exportpath = "c:\temp\appprotectstatus.csv"
```

2. This also has a different URL, which we need to set:

```
$url = "https://graph.microsoft.com/beta/deviceManagement/reports/
getMobileApplicationManagementAppRegistrationSummaryReport"
```

3. Again, we are grabbing the total number of results and then looping through into temporary text files. The JSON request is different, though, with more items to select. This has been shortened for brevity (the full JSON can be found on GitHub):

```
$json = @"
{
    "filter": "",
    "orderBy": [],
    "select": [
        "User",
        "Email"     ]
}
"@
```

4. The array also changes accordingly (again, shortened):

```
$outputarray = @()
foreach ($value in $fullvalues) {
    $platform = $value[0]
    $objectdetails = [pscustomobject]@{
        Platform = $platform
    }
    $outputarray += $objectdetails
}
```

5. Then, either output or export the data:

```
if ($result -eq [System.Windows.Forms.DialogResult]::OK) {
    $outputarray | export-csv $exportpath -NoTypeInformation
} elseif ($result -eq [System.Windows.Forms.DialogResult]::Cancel) {
```

```
    $outputarray | Out-GridView
}
```

6. Clean up the `.txt` files we have created during our loop:

```
Remove-Item $tempfilepath
$allrows = $parsedData.TotalRowCount
$n = 0
while ($n -lt $allrows) {
    $n += 50
    $tempfilepath2 = $env:TEMP + "\appinstallstatus-$n.txt"
    Remove-Item $tempfilepath2
}
```

Now that we have learned how to programmatically view **App protection status** reports, we will look at discovered apps on your devices.

Discovered apps

Now, we can move on to the **Discovered apps** report.

The full script can be found on GitHub here: `https://github.com/PacktPublishing/Microsoft-Intune-Cookbook-Second-Edition/blob/main/Chapter-9/get-discoveredapps.ps1`.

Follow these steps to create your script for discovered apps:

1. This follows the simpler `GET` requests. As usual, we need to start with the output path:

```
$exportpath = "c:\temp\discoveredapps.csv"
```

2. We will use the same pagination function, so we need to provide it with a URL:

```
$url = "https://graph.microsoft.com/beta/deviceManagement/detectedApps"
$allapps = getallpagination -url $url
```

3. There is less data retrieved here, but we only need a few fields:

```
$applist = $allapps | select-object DisplayName, version, devicecount
```

4. Like before, run the popup and export or display as required:

```
if ($result -eq [System.Windows.Forms.DialogResult]::OK) {
    $applist | export-csv $exportpath
} elseif ($result -eq [System.Windows.Forms.DialogResult]::Cancel) {
    $applist | Out-GridView
}
```

This completes the application monitoring recipe. We can now look at device monitoring.

Monitoring device configuration

Now that we know how to monitor our applications, we can look at monitoring the devices themselves, starting with the configuration profiles applied to them.

How to do it...

There are three available monitoring options for device configuration, which we will run through one at a time. To find them, click on **Devices** and then **Configuration** (under **Manage devices**).

In the new experience, you will then be taken to the **Monitor** tab, where you can find our options, which we will now run through.

Devices with restricted apps

This option works alongside any **device restriction** policies across operating systems. You can configure a policy to block certain applications, and any device with these applications discovered will be flagged in the report.

In this case, we have a macOS restrictions profile configured to restrict the use of Apple Calculator (to ensure that it triggers):

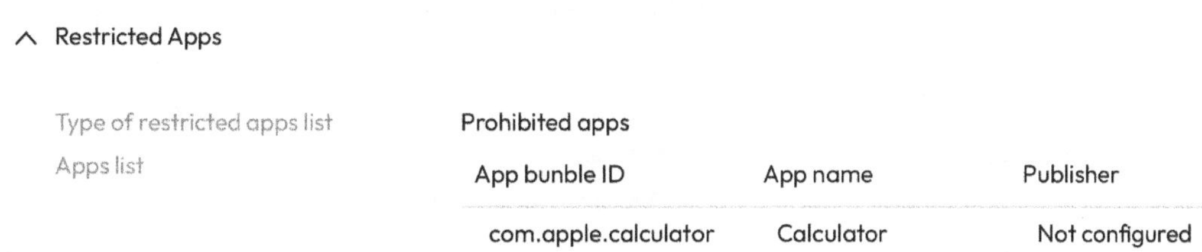

Figure 9.2 – Device restrictions – restricted apps policy

When looking at the monitoring output, the device is flagged as having a prohibited app:

Email address ↑↓	Device name ↑↓	Program type ↑↓	Platform ↑↓	State ↑↓
[illegible]	[illegible] Macbook Air	macOS Restrictions	macOS	Prohibited apps

Figure 9.3 – Monitor devices with restricted apps

Clicking on the row will tell you which apps have been discovered.

At the top, you have the usual **Export** button, search functionality (although this only searches on user email address), and the useful ability to sort on column headers.

Encryption report

This is an important one to keep an eye on, although hopefully, you have well-curated compliance policies backed by Conditional Access to at least offer some protection. While that protects these devices from accessing M365 data, if an unencrypted device is lost or stolen with locally stored files, there is still a risk. Therefore, monitoring your unencrypted devices is a very important task.

It is worth noting that this only applies to Windows and macOS devices, so do not expect to see any Android or iOS devices present.

Frustratingly, you cannot sort on the column headers here, and the search is only on either device or username, so finding your unencrypted devices is not as straightforward in a large environment (use the script in the automation section instead). You can, however, use the filter button at the top to restrict the results accordingly.

One useful header available is **Readiness**, which will quickly tell you whether a device is not encrypted and whether the issue is at the policy or device level. If the device is not ready and without an active TPM, it would suggest a hands-on look at the hardware itself rather than a hands-off remote session.

We can now move on to our next report, monitoring certificates.

Certificates

The final monitoring option for device configuration is certificates. This is only relevant if you are pushing certificates to your devices via Intune for authentication, app packaging, and so on.

There are a large number of headings available, and again, the most important two are right at the end, **Certificate expiry** and **Certificate status**, so if you are on a smaller screen, you may want to press the **Columns** button to remove some you do not need, or drag to reorder.

As well as the ability to search (free text too), you can export and sort by column heading, but you will notice that this comes at the expense of the filter button. Sorting by **Expiry** should be your go-to view for general monitoring, and then you can use the search for any additional troubleshooting.

After reviewing our certificates, we can move on to the hidden assignment failures report.

Assignment failures

While not listed with the other three monitoring options, there is one more option available when looking at device configuration, **Assignment failures**, which looks at failures at the policy level.

To get to this, navigate to **Devices** and click the blue text labeled **Configuration profile assignment failures**.

This will take you to a new screen where you can quickly look at your policies that have errors or conflicts across your devices.

You can sort by column headers here to quickly spot any policies with significant failures, as well as be able to search on the profile name. There is also a more advanced filter to restrict by platform, profile type, or profile source.

Clicking on the profile name will take you to a second screen where you can see which devices are having issues with the profiles.

While in an ideal world, this report would be clear, there will always be issues with individual devices. When looking at this, start with devices with conflict, as these are not device faults, but policy configuration or scoping faults where you have two conflicting policies on the same device (keep in mind that a policy can be in conflict even if the setting is the same across policies).

Once you have cleared your conflicting policies, you can then start on the errors. As a general rule, if the value is more than about one-third of your total estate, it is an issue with the policy itself (assuming a larger estate) rather than an issue with the device.

Automating it

After covering these reports within the UI, we can now look at each in turn and how we can automate them.

Devices with restricted apps

Fortunately, automating this one is reasonably straightforward, as it is a simple `GET` request. As with our previous exports, we will be using the `getallpagination` function to grab all results as they will be paginated on a large estate. To save an additional click, we will also list the prohibited apps in the first output.

Follow these steps to automate your report:

1. As usual, we start with the output path and the URL we are grabbing:

   ```
   $exportpath = "c:\temp\restrictedapps.csv"
   $url = "https://graph.microsoft.com/beta/deviceManagement/
   deviceConfigurationRestrictedAppsViolations"
   ```

2. Then, run the function against the URL to grab all of the values (the function is in the script on GitHub):

   ```
   $allapps = getallpagination -url $url
   ```

3. The `appID` attribute is within a nested array called `restrictedApps`, so in our next command, we want to expand that array to grab the data from it. We then run a second `select-object` to remove some of the output, such as `userID` or `deviceConfigurationID`, which do not add any real value:

   ```
   $applist = $allapps | select-object * -ExpandProperty restrictedapps |
   select-object userName, deviceName, managedDeviceID,
   deviceConfigurationName, platformType, restrictedAppsState, appId
   ```

4. As with our other scripts, we will use forms to provide a popup for the option to export or view the results.
5. We then look at the button clicked and take action appropriately with either `export-csv` or `Out-GridView`:

   ```
   if ($result -eq [System.Windows.Forms.DialogResult]::OK) {
       $applist | export-csv $exportpath
   ```

```
} elseif ($result -eq [System.Windows.Forms.DialogResult]::Cancel) {
    $applist | Out-GridView
}
```

This completes the script covering reporting on devices with restricted apps.

Encryption report

Automating the encryption report is one of the trickier ones, similar to **App configuration status** in the last recipe. It uses a POST request, and the output is not in a readable JSON format, so it needs exporting and re-importing again. We use the following steps:

1. First, we need the output path and URL:

   ```
   $exportpath = "c:\temp\encryptionreport.csv"
   $url = "https://graph.microsoft.com/beta/deviceManagement/reports/
   getEncryptionReportForDevices"
   ```

   The JSON is slightly simpler as there are fewer options to retrieve:

   ```
   $json = @"
   {
       "filter": "",
       "orderBy": [],
       "select": [
           "DeviceId",
           "DeviceName",
           "DeviceType",
           "OSVersion",
           "TpmSpecificationVersion",
           "EncryptionReadinessState",
           "EncryptionStatus",
           "UPN"
       ]
   }
   "@
   ```

2. We want to export the raw results into a temporary text file to grab the total number of rows and also the first 50 records by saving and then ingesting the data:

   ```
   $tempfilepath = $env:TEMP + "\encryptionreport.txt"
   Invoke-MgGraphRequest -Method POST -Uri $url -Body $json -ContentType
   ```

```
"application/json" -OutputFilePath $tempfilepath
$parsedData = get-content $tempfilepath | ConvertFrom-Json
$fullvalues = $parsedData.Values
$allrows = $parsedData.TotalRowCount
```

3. Now, we loop through the total number of rows, each time incrementing by 50, saving each to a new text file that we then ingest and add to the master array:

```
$n = 0
while ($n -lt $allrows) {
    $n += 50
    $tempfilepath2 = $env:TEMP + "\encryptionreport-$n.txt"
    $url = "https://graph.microsoft.com/beta/deviceManagement/reports/
getEncryptionReportForDevices"
    $json = @"
{
    "filter": "",
    "orderBy": [],
    "select": [
        "DeviceId",
        "DeviceName",
        "DeviceType",
        "OSVersion",
        "TpmSpecificationVersion",
        "EncryptionReadinessState",
        "EncryptionStatus",
        "UPN"
    ],
    "skip": $n,
    "top": 50
}
"@
    Invoke-MgGraphRequest -Method POST -Uri $url -Body $json -ContentType
"application/json" -OutputFilePath $tempfilepath2
    $tempdata = get-content $tempfilepath2 | ConvertFrom-Json
    $fullvalues += $tempdata.Values
}
```

4. Add these to a new array to use in the output with meaningful headers. By default, the TPM reports either a version number or nothing at all, so we are also changing the blank to something a bit more useful (unknown to match the GUI):

```
$outputarray = @()
foreach ($value in $fullvalues) {
    $deviceid = $value[0]
    $devicename = $value[1]
    $OSType = $value[3]
    $readiness = $value[5]
    $encryption = $value[7]
    $OSVersion = $value[8]
    $TPMversion2 = $value[9]
    $username = $value[10]
    if ($TPMversion2 -eq "") {
        $TPMversion = "Unknown"
    }
    else {
        $TPMversion = $TPMversion2
    }
    $objectdetails = [pscustomobject]@{
        DeviceID = $deviceid
        DeviceName = $devicename
        OSVersion = $OSVersion
        OS = $OSType
        TPMVersion = $TPMversion
        EncryptionReadiness = $readiness
        EncryptionStatus = $encryption
        Username = $username
    }
    $outputarray += $objectdetails
}
```

5. Then, after the popup, export or view the data retrieved:

```
if ($result -eq [System.Windows.Forms.DialogResult]::OK) {
    $outputarray | export-csv $exportpath -NoTypeInformation
} elseif ($result -eq [System.Windows.Forms.DialogResult]::Cancel) {
```

```
        $outputarray | Out-GridView
    }
```

6. Finally, clean up those text files:

```
Remove-Item $tempfilepath
$allrows = $parsedData.TotalRowCount
$n = 0
while ($n -lt $allrows) {
    $n += 50
    $tempfilepath2 = $env:TEMP + "\appconfigstatus-$n.txt"
    Remove-Item $tempfilepath2
}
```

This completes our script to view encryption reports programmatically.

Certificates

This is another export and import with a POST request, so rather than entering the same content here, we will just include the different URL and JSON. The full script is, of course, available on GitHub.

The URL for certificates is as follows:

```
$url = "https://graph.microsoft.com/beta/deviceManagement/reports/
getAllCertificatesReport"
```

The fields we are looking for are the following:

```
$json = @"
{
    "filter": "",
    "orderBy": [],
    "select": [
        "DeviceName",
        "UPN",
        "Thumbprint",
        "SerialNumber",
        "SubjectName",
        "IssuerName",
        "KeyUsage",
        "EnhancedKeyUsage",
```

```
            "ValidFrom",
            "ValidTo",
            "CertificateStatus",
            "PolicyId"
        ]
    }
    "@
```

After automating our certificates report, we can now cover assignment failures.

Assignment failures

Follow these steps to create your script:

1. This report is another `POST` request. Export and ingest the `.txt` files using this URL and JSON:

```
$url = "https://graph.microsoft.com/beta/deviceManagement/reports/
getConfigurationPolicyNoncomplianceSummaryReport"
$json = @"
{
    "filter": "",
    "orderBy": [],
    "select": [
        "PolicyName",
        "UnifiedPolicyType",
        "ProfileSource",
        "UnifiedPolicyPlatformType",
        "NumberOfNonCompliantOrErrorDevices",
        "NumberOfConflictDevices",
        "PolicyId",
        "PolicyBaseTypeName"
    ]
}
"@
```

2. To take this one step further, when using the view option, we want the ability to drill down as we can on the web portal.

For that, we are using the -PassThru parameter on Out-GridView and sending it to a variable:

```
    $selecteditems = $outputarray | Out-GridView -Title "Pick a policy to
drill-down" -PassThru
```

3. We then want to loop through the selected policy to do another export and ingest, only using these options, not the policy ID within the JSON:

```
    $url = "https://graph.microsoft.com/beta/deviceManagement/reports/
getConfigurationPolicyNonComplianceReport"
$json = @"
{
    "filter": "((PolicyBaseTypeName eq
'Microsoft.Management.Services.Api.DeviceConfiguration') or
(PolicyBaseTypeName eq 'DeviceManagementConfigurationPolicy') or
(PolicyBaseTypeName eq
'Microsoft.Management.Services.Api.DeviceManagementIntent')) and (PolicyId
eq '$policyid2')",
    "orderBy": [],
    "select": [
        "DeviceName",
        "UPN",
        "PolicyStatus",
        "PspdpuLastModifiedTimeUtc",
        "UserId",
        "IntuneDeviceId",
        "PolicyBaseTypeName",
        "UnifiedPolicyPlatformType"
    ],
    "skip": 0,
    "top": 50
}
"@
```

4. Then, we want to display the output of this second array in a second grid view:

```
$outputarray2 = @()
foreach ($value in $fullvalues2) {
$devicename = $value[0]
$deviceid = $value[1]
```

```
$policybasetype = $value[2]
$policystatus = $value[3]
$lastmodified = $value[4]
$policytype = $value[5]
$user = $value[6]
$userid = $value[7]

    $objectdetails = [pscustomobject]@{
        DeviceName = $devicename
        DeviceID = $deviceid
        PolicyBaseType = $policybasetype
        PolicyStatus = $policystatus
        LastModified = $lastmodified
        PolicyType = $policytype
        User = $user
        UserID = $userid
    }
    $outputarray2 += $objectdetails
}
}
$outputarray2 | Out-GridView
```

As always, the full script is on GitHub here: `https://github.com/PacktPublishing/Microsoft-Intune-Cookbook/blob/main/Chapter-9/get-noncompliantpolicies.ps1`.

That completes the scripts to monitor application reports, so now, we can look at device compliance.

Monitoring device compliance

After monitoring device configuration, we also need to keep an eye on device compliance, especially as this is going to cause the most complaints once users are restricted to non-compliant devices.

Getting ready

To access these reports, click on **Devices** and then **Compliance**.

You will then be taken to the **Monitor** tab, where we can access our next two reports.

You may notice the blue text labeled **Device compliance status**; this simply takes us to the same report as **Non-compliant devices**.

How to do it...

We will start by looking at non-compliant devices and then run through the other available reports.

Non-compliant devices

Starting with non-compliant devices, this report is fairly self-explanatory and displays any devices across all platforms (including Linux) that are failing any compliance policy applied. If a device has multiple policies, a single failure will send the whole device into non-compliance.

You have the standard columns and **Export** button, along with a search option to search device name, device ID, username, user email, user ID, IMEI, or serial number.

There is also the ability to filter on **Compliance Status**, **OS**, **Ownership type**, and **Device type**, as well as being able to sort on the individual headings.

Clicking on a device will take you to the device details page rather than directly to the **Device Compliance** panel within it.

If you have Conditional Access set to block non-compliant devices, this is one you should regularly monitor so you can proactively resolve issues before the user becomes blocked and calls to complain.

Policies with non-compliant and error devices

Unlike the previous reports, which look at the device level, this one drills down to the policy level.

It displays all of your policies and the number of devices either non-compliant or in an error state against them.

As with other reports, you can search, export, and change the column display.

Clicking on the policy name takes you to a further report, which lists the devices, UPN, compliance status, and when the state was last updated. You cannot, however, drill any further from here.

Automating it

After covering these reports in the UI, we can look at how to automate them.

Non-compliant devices

This works in the same way as the previous automations in this chapter, with a `POST` request. Grab the output, save it to a `.txt` file, and then re-ingest it.

The full script is on GitHub at the following URL: `https://github.com/PacktPublishing/Microsoft-Intune-Cookbook-Second-Edition/blob/main/Chapter-9/get-noncompliantdevices.ps1`.

Follow these steps to create your non-compliant devices script:

1. Here, we will again stick to just the URL and JSON:

```
$url = "https://graph.microsoft.com/beta/deviceManagement/reports/
getDeviceNoncomplianceReport"
$json = @"
{
    "filter": "",
    "orderBy": [],
    "select": [
        "DeviceName",
        "UPN",
        "ComplianceState",
        "OS",
        "OSVersion",
        "OwnerType",
        "LastContact",
        "ManagementAgents",
        "IntuneDeviceId"
    ]
}
"@
```

2. We then work out the total number of rows, loop through to grab everything into a new array, and then tidy this into an output array.

> **Note**
>
> The array values do not necessarily match, so during the `foreach` loop, it is best to do a simple `write-output` for each array item to check what it corresponds to, for example, `write-output $value[0]` will show the first value in the array.

3. In our case, the final array looks like this:

```
$outputarray = @()
foreach ($value in $fullvalues) {
$compliancestate = $value[1]
$devicename = $value[2]
$intunedeviceid = $value[3]
$lastcontact = $value[4]
$os = $value[7]
$osversion = $value[9]
$owner = $value[11]
$username = $value[12]
$objectdetails = [pscustomobject]@{
    ComplianceState = $compliancestate
    DeviceName = $devicename
    DeviceID = $intunedeviceid
    LastContact = $lastcontact
    OS = $os
    OSVersion = $osversion
    OwnerType = $owner
    Username = $username
}
$outputarray += $objectdetails
}
```

4. As with the other recipes, we send a pop-up question, then export or output as required, and clean up the environment, removing all of the .txt files created:

```
if ($result -eq [System.Windows.Forms.DialogResult]::OK) {
    $outputarray | export-csv $exportpath -NoTypeInformation
} elseif ($result -eq [System.Windows.Forms.DialogResult]::Cancel) {
    $outputarray | Out-GridView
}
Remove-Item $tempfilepath
$allrows = $parsedData.TotalRowCount
$n = 0
while ($n -lt $allrows) {
    $n += 50
    $tempfilepath2 = $env:TEMP + "\appconfigstatus-$n.txt"
```

```
    Remove-Item $tempfilepath2
}
```

We will now move on to finding any devices without a compliance policy assigned.

Policies with non-compliant and error devices

Automating this is almost identical to the assignment failures script we created in the previous recipe. Again, it uses a `POST` request with JSON, which we have to retrieve into a temporary text file and then ingest. Follow these steps to create your script:

1. We are looping through this URL with JSON attached:

```
$url = "https://graph.microsoft.com/beta/deviceManagement/reports/
getPolicyNoncomplianceSummaryReport"
$json = @"
{
    "filter": "((PolicyBaseTypeName eq
'Microsoft.Management.Services.Api.DeviceCompliancePolicy') or
(PolicyBaseTypeName eq 'DeviceManagementCompliancePolicy'))",
    "orderBy": [],
    "select": [
        "PolicyName",
        "UnifiedPolicyPlatformType",
        "NumberOfNonCompliantDevices",
        "NumberOfErrorDevices",
        "PolicyBaseTypeName",
        "PolicyId"
    ]
}
"@
```

2. The values are then transferred into this array (we need `policyBaseType` for the passthrough):

```
$outputarray = @()
foreach ($value in $fullvalues) {
$numberoferrordevices = $value[0]
$NumberOfNonCompliantDevices = $value[1]
$PolicyBaseTypeName = $value[2]
$policyid = $value[3]
$policyname = $value[4]
```

```
$unifiedpolicyplatformtype = $value[5]
    $objectdetails = [pscustomobject]@{
        PolicyName = $policyname
        NumberOfErrorDevices = $numberoferrordevices
        NumberOfNonCompliantDevices = $NumberOfNonCompliantDevices
        UnifiedPolicyPlatformType = $unifiedpolicyplatformtype
        PolicyBaseTypeName = $PolicyBaseTypeName
        PolicyID = $policyid
    }
    $outputarray += $objectdetails
}
```

3. We then export our report data or passthrough in the UI:

```
if ($result -eq [System.Windows.Forms.DialogResult]::OK) {
    $outputarray | export-csv $exportpath -NoTypeInformation
} elseif ($result -eq [System.Windows.Forms.DialogResult]::Cancel) {
    $selecteditems = $outputarray | Out-GridView -Title "Pick a policy to
drill-down" -PassThru
foreach ($selected in $selecteditems) {
    $policyid2 = $selected.PolicyID
    $PolicyBaseTypeName2 = $selected.PolicyBaseTypeName
    $url = "https://graph.microsoft.com/beta/deviceManagement/reports/
getPolicyNoncomplianceReport"
$json = @"
{
    "filter": "((PolicyBaseTypeName eq '$PolicyBaseTypeName2') and
(PolicyId eq '$policyid2'))",
    "orderBy": [],
    "select": [
        "DeviceName",
        "UPN",
        "PolicyStatus",
        "PspdpuLastModifiedTimeUtc",
        "UserId",
        "IntuneDeviceId"
    ],
    "skip": 0,
    "top": 50
```

```
}
"@
```

4. And finally, we display our drill-down array in a second grid view:

```
$outputarray2 = @()
foreach ($value in $fullvalues2) {
$devicename = $value[0]
$deviceid = $value[1]
$policystatus = $value[2]
$lastmodified = $value[3]
$user = $value[4]
$userid = $value[5]
    $objectdetails = [pscustomobject]@{
        DeviceName = $devicename
        DeviceID = $deviceid
        PolicyStatus = $policystatus
        LastModified = $lastmodified
        User = $user
        UserID = $userid
    }
    $outputarray2 += $objectdetails
}
}
$outputarray2 | Out-GridView
```

This completes the recipe to view non-compliant policies.

This completes our recipe for monitoring device compliance both in the UI and when using PowerShell and Graph.

Monitoring device enrollment

While we can now monitor our device compliance and configuration, that is of no use if the devices have failed to enroll. For that, we need to use the device enrollment monitoring options. These are especially useful when users are self-enrolling devices to look for any errors and to assist in troubleshooting.

Getting ready

To access these reports, click on **Devices** and then **Enrollment**, and click on the **Monitor** tab.

Here, you can find the available options, which we will now cover in more detail.

How to do it...

We will start by looking at enrollment failures and then run through each report available.

Enrollment failures

We start with enrollment failures, which is a cross-platform report on all failed enrollments using any supported enrollment method. It also includes error details, which are especially useful.

The first thing to check is the powerful filter available here, which can look at the platform, error type, enrollment type, and date/time of the enrollment. This will help significantly to spot any spikes or repeated failures.

There is also the ability to export the output to CSV.

Another feature specific to this option is to select either a specific user (**Select user**) or display for all users. This is a very useful troubleshooting tool, should a user have enrollment issues.

While you cannot sort by header, the powerful filter should negate that requirement.

Finally, there is the option to view a graphical representation, which is useful for a regular check to spot any enrollment failure spikes that could be caused by a firewall change or an outage somewhere.

Windows Autopilot deployments

This option is just for Windows devices and shows details of all Autopilot deployments for the previous 30 days: successes and failures.

As with the other reports covered, it includes another powerful filter.

Unlike the others, you also have the option to sort by header and even search, but there is no option to export data (you will have to use the automation for that).

Clicking on a device will show the Autopilot device details.

As Autopilot is usually a user-led enrollment, monitoring these events is always useful to keep an eye on. The last thing you want is a device being deployed with an incomplete deployment. You can also check the total time to see how the user experience is and whether there is anything that could be done to improve it.

Autopilot device preparation deployment status

One of the advantages of the new **Autopilot device preparation** functionality is that it has improved reporting over the previous version. This report will display all devices enrolled with device preparation, how long the process took (whether successfully or not), and the last phase completed. You can also see the serial number and UPN of the user who enrolled the device.

The phase is especially useful for failed deployments, as you can see exactly where it failed to help with troubleshooting.

Automating it

After reviewing these reports in the UI, we can now look at how to automate them.

Enrollment failures

This is a fairly easy one to automate as it is a `GET` request to one of two URLs, depending on the user selection. To keep things comparable, we will do the same here.

The full script can be found on GitHub at the following URL: `https://github.com/PacktPublishing/Microsoft-Intune-Cookbook-Second-Edition/blob/main/Chapter-9/get-userenrollmentfailures.ps1`.

These steps will run through the key aspects:

1. As usual, start with the CSV path:

```
$exportpath = "c:\temp\userenrollmentfailures.csv"
```

2. Now, we quickly grab all users into an array to store for later:

```
$allusersurl = "https://graph.microsoft.com/beta/users"
$allusers = getallpagination -url $allusersurl
```

3. After sending the popup, we then filter the URL on the response:
   - For all users, the URL runs at the tenant level:

```
$url = "https://graph.microsoft.com/beta/deviceManagement/
troubleshootingEvents"
```

   - If users have been selected, we need to pop up a list of users to make a selection. We then grab the user ID and populate the URL, which, in this case, is at the user level:

```
    $selecteditems = $allusers | select-object userPrincipalName, id
| Out-GridView -Title "Pick a user to drill-down" -PassThru
    foreach ($selected in $selecteditems) {
        $userid = $selected.id
        $url = "https://graph.microsoft.com/beta/users/$userid/
```

```
        deviceManagementTroubleshootingEvents"
    }
```

4. Then, we are back to a normal script. Grab all of the data for the new URL:

```
$fulloutput = getallpagination -url $url
$selectedoutput = $fulloutput | select-object *
```

5. After a second popup, either display the output or export the data to CSV:

```
if ($result -eq [System.Windows.Forms.DialogResult]::OK) {
    $selectedoutput | export-csv $exportpath
} elseif ($result -eq [System.Windows.Forms.DialogResult]::Cancel) {
$selectedoutput | Out-GridView
}
```

This completes the automation of the enrollment failures report. We will now look at incomplete user enrollments.

Windows Autopilot deployments

This is another `GET` request, but in the URL, we are adding the date to check from. Unlike the previous script, this simply retrieves all data from the date specified rather than between a range of dates.

We will also drill down to pass through the device details:

1. As usual, we start with the export file:

```
$exportpath = "c:\temp\policycompliance.csv"
```

2. Now, create the date to use (today minus 30 days):

```
$lastmonthdate = (Get-Date).AddDays(-30).ToString("yyyy-MM-
ddTHH:mm:ss.fffZ")
```

3. Populate the URL with the date:

```
$url = "https://graph.microsoft.com/beta/deviceManagement/autopilotEvents?
`$filter=microsoft.graph.DeviceManagementAutopilotEvent/
enrollmentStartDateTime ge $lastmonthdate"
```

4. Grab the output:

```
$fulloutput = getallpagination -url $url
$selectedoutput = $fulloutput | select-object *
```

5. After the popup, look for **Export** or **View**. If **View** is selected, pass the `deviceid` variable through to a new URL to grab the specific device details. Then, output those into a second `gridview` UI:

```
if ($result -eq [System.Windows.Forms.DialogResult]::OK) {
    $selectedoutput | export-csv $exportpath
} elseif ($result -eq [System.Windows.Forms.DialogResult]::Cancel) {
    $selection = $selectedoutput | Out-GridView -PassThru
    foreach ($item in $selection) {
        $deviceid = $item.deviceid
        $url = "https://graph.microsoft.com/beta/deviceManagement/
managedDevices('$deviceid')/logCollectionRequests"
        $fulloutput = getallpagination -url $url
        $selectedoutput = $fulloutput | Out-GridView
    }
}
```

Autopilot device preparation enrollments

Being a new report, it uses the update Graph reporting endpoint, as found in earlier recipes, with the `POST` request, grab to txt, and then read back.

The full script can be found on GitHub at the following URL: `https://github.com/PacktPublishing/Microsoft-Intune-Cookbook-Second-Edition/blob/main/Chapter-9/get-autopilotdeviceprepdeployments.ps1`.

Follow these steps:

1. Set the export file:

```
$exportpath = "c:\temp\autopilotdeviceprep.csv"
```

2. Then, point to the new endpoint:

```
$url = "https://graph.microsoft.com/beta/deviceManagement/reports/
getAutopilotDeploymentStatus"
```

3. Set the JSON; you will notice there are no fields to retrieve, it just grabs them all and exports to a `.txt` file:

```
$json = @"
{
    "orderBy": [
        "EnrollmentTimeInUtc desc"
    ],
    "top": 50
}
"@
$tempfilepath = $env:TEMP + "\autopilotdeviceprep.txt"
Invoke-MgGraphRequest -Method POST -Uri $url -Body $json -ContentType
"application/json" -OutputFilePath $tempfilepath
```

4. Now, count the number of rows so we can loop accordingly:

```
$parsedData = get-content $tempfilepath | ConvertFrom-Json
$fullvalues = $parsedData.Values
$allrows = $parsedData.TotalRowCount
```

5. Run the same JSON request, but increment the skip accordingly. Record each batch to a new `.txt` file:

```
$n = 0
while ($n -lt $allrows) {
    $n += 50
    $tempfilepath2 = $env:TEMP + "\autopilotdeviceprep-$n.txt"
    $url = "https://graph.microsoft.com/beta/deviceManagement/reports/
getAutopilotDeploymentStatus"
    $json = @"
{
        "orderBy": [
        "EnrollmentTimeInUtc desc"
    ],
    "skip": $n,
    "top": 50
}
"@
    Invoke-MgGraphRequest -Method POST -Uri $url -Body $json -ContentType
```

```
"application/json" -OutputFilePath $tempfilepath2
    $tempdata = get-content $tempfilepath2 | ConvertFrom-Json
    $fullvalues += $tempdata.Values
}
```

6. Then, create an object with all of the values from each loop:

```
$outputarray = @()
foreach ($value in $fullvalues) {
    $DeviceId                         = $value[0]
    $EnrollmentTimeInUtc              = $value[1]
    $CurrentProvisioningPhase         = $value[2]
    $DeploymentStatus                 = $value[3]
    $DeploymentDurationTimeInSeconds  = $value[4]
    $Phase                            = $value[5]
    $ResultCode                       = $value[6]
    $DeviceName                       = $value[7]
    $SerialNumber                     = $value[8]
    $UPN                              = $value[9]

    $objectdetails = [pscustomobject]@{
        DeviceId                        = $DeviceId
        EnrollmentTimeInUtc             = $EnrollmentTimeInUtc
        CurrentProvisioningPhase        = $CurrentProvisioningPhase
        DeploymentStatus                = $DeploymentStatus
        DeploymentDurationTimeInSeconds = $DeploymentDurationTimeInSeconds
        Phase                           = $Phase
        ResultCode                      = $ResultCode
        DeviceName                      = $DeviceName
        SerialNumber                    = $SerialNumber
        UPN                             = $UPN
    }
    $outputarray += $objectdetails
}
```

7. We can then export or display the results. The script also does a cleanup to ensure that the text files are removed.

That completes the recipe. Now, we will look at monitoring device updates.

Monitoring updates across platforms

One key requirement for most environments is keeping your devices updated with the latest security patches. While Intune has systems to do the updating for you, there is always the chance that some devices will have issues installing the updates. To check these, we have the functionality to check the update status for Windows, iOS, and macOS (no Android at present).

Getting ready

To access these reports, we need to navigate to **Devices** in the Intune menu. Each is in a different location, which will be covered for each individual report.

How to do it...

We will start this recipe by looking at Windows updates before moving on to iOS and macOS.

Windows updates

Within **Devices**, click on **Windows updates** and click **Monitor**.

This then gives you an overview of the following:

- **Autopatch Groups Membership**: This shows the devices enrolled into Autopatch, as well as those discovered but not enrolled, and the reason for it. If you are using Autopatch (which, if licensed, you absolutely should be), this will quickly flag up any issues with your estate.
- **Deployment status per Windows update ring**: This shows any devices that have issues with the update ring policies themselves, not at the individual update level.
- **Feature update policies with alerts**: This displays the number of devices across your policies having issues deploying feature updates.
- **Expedited quality update policies with alerts**: Same as before, but for expedited updates. This is one to keep a close eye on, as expedited updates are often for urgent security issues.
- **Driver update policies with alerts**: If driver updates are enabled, this will show any devices with failed drivers.

Within the report, you can then click on rows to drill down further as required and to export your data.

Use the overview page as a general indication of the estate and then the individual reports to troubleshoot and repair issues. Start with policy errors; if a policy is not applied to a device, there is a chance that it is not receiving any updates. Once they are resolved, expedited updates are the next most important to look at.

The next chapter includes a look at reports that give further insight into your Windows updates.

iOS update status

This option can be found within **Devices**, then **iOS/iPadOS**. Then, click on **Monitor**. Finally, click on **iOS update installation failures**.

Here, you will find a familiar layout with a list of your iOS devices that have installation failures. It will only list those with issues, as Apple does not report on healthy devices.

As well as the option to export, there is a powerful filter that can look at both a date range and the installation status, which is a comprehensive list.

The headers are sortable, and there is also a free-text search.

With such a large selection of reasons why an update could fail, including receiving a telephone call, this is always worth keeping an eye on, especially as iOS devices are often used by C-level executives.

macOS update status

This one is accessed via **Devices** | **macOS** | **Monitor** | **macOS update installation failures**.

Clicking on it takes us to another report screen, similar to that for iOS but slightly less feature-rich.

The filter adds support for minimum and maximum OS versions, but there are fewer update status options.

As well as the usual **Export** button, there is a search box that queries the main items, but the headers here cannot be clicked and sorted.

While not as thorough as that for Windows and iOS, there is enough data in here to spot any devices with issues and allow you to troubleshoot.

Automating it

After reviewing these reports within the portal, we can now cover the automation of them.

Windows updates

While in the web interface, this looks straightforward, if you study the network logs, you will see it is sending a batch request. This means it is sending multiple requests (either `POST` or `GET`) in a single request and then grabbing the information back.

In this case, there are four different requests being sent. Three of them use the `POST`, export, and ingest method, but fortunately, with the same JSON and output. The fourth, however, is a `GET` request with different fields.

There is no automation for the Autopatch Groups report, as the Autopatch API is not available for public use.

Therefore, we will combine the first three into a single output and split the expedited updates into a different output.

The full script is available on GitHub here: `https://github.com/PacktPublishing/Microsoft-Intune-Cookbook-Second-Edition/blob/main/Chapter-9/get-windowsupdatestatus.ps1`.

As there is a lot of repetition of `POST` requests in these reports, we have to run the same loop three times:

1. First, we need the first export path. We are also creating our empty array at the top, as we are going to populate it with all three loops:

```
$exportpath = "c:\temp\windowsupdates.csv"
$outputarray = @()
```

2. Set the URL and JSON (this is for the policy status):

```
$url = "https://graph.microsoft.com/beta/deviceManagement/reports/
getWindowsUpdateAlertSummaryReport"
$json = @"
{
    "filter": "",
    "orderBy": [],
    "select": [
        "PolicyName",
        "NumberOfDevicesWithErrors",
        "PolicyId"
    ]
}
"@
```

3. Grab the data into a `.txt` file and ingest it. Count the total rows and loop through 50 at a time, exporting into a `.txt` file and then re-importing into our array. We are also clearing out the `.txt` files during the loops here, so the files are removed for the next report:

```
$tempfilepath = $env:TEMP + "\summaryreport.txt"
Invoke-MgGraphRequest -Method POST -Uri $url -Body $json -ContentType
```

```
"application/json" -OutputFilePath $tempfilepath
$parsedData = get-content $tempfilepath | ConvertFrom-Json
$fullvalues = $parsedData.Values
Remove-Item $tempfilepath
$allrows = $parsedData.TotalRowCount
$n = 0
while ($n -lt $allrows) {
    $n += 50
    $tempfilepath2 = $env:TEMP + "\summaryreport-$n.txt"
    $url = "https://graph.microsoft.com/beta/deviceManagement/reports/
getWindowsUpdateAlertSummaryReport"
    $json = @"
{
    "filter": "",
    "orderBy": [],
    "select": [
        "PolicyName",
        "NumberOfDevicesWithErrors",
        "PolicyId"
    ],
    "skip": $n,
    "top": 50
}
"@
    Invoke-MgGraphRequest -Method POST -Uri $url -Body $json -ContentType
"application/json" -OutputFilePath $tempfilepath2
    $tempdata = get-content $tempfilepath2 | ConvertFrom-Json
    $fullvalues += $tempdata.Values
    Remove-Item $tempfilepath2
}
```

4. When adding to the output array, we have added an item to mark exactly which report it is from:

```
foreach ($value in $fullvalues) {
$numberoferrordevices = $value[0]
$policyid = $value[1]
$policyname = $value[2]
$type = "Policy Errors"
    $objectdetails = [pscustomobject]@{
        ReportType = $type
```

```
        PolicyName = $policyname
        ErrorDevices = $numberoferrordevices
        PolicyID = $policyid
    }
    $outputarray += $objectdetails
}
```

For quality updates and driver updates, the process is the same, only with these URLs:

- **Quality updates**: This is the URL required for quality updates:

  ```
  $url = "https://graph.microsoft.com/beta/deviceManagement/reports/
  getWindowsQualityUpdateAlertSummaryReport"
  ```

- **Driver updates**: If using driver updates, you require this URL:

  ```
  $url = "https://graph.microsoft.com/beta/deviceManagement/reports/
  getWindowsDriverUpdateAlertSummaryReport"
  ```

5. Then, after a popup, display or export the data retrieved from Graph:

```
if ($result -eq [System.Windows.Forms.DialogResult]::OK) {
    $outputarray | export-csv $exportpath -NoTypeInformation
} elseif ($result -eq [System.Windows.Forms.DialogResult]::Cancel) {
    $outputarray | Out-GridView
}
```

For expedited updates, this is a single `GET` request. It has no pagination options, and the output is not nested within the `value` array, so we have no need for the usual pagination function.

Therefore, we simply set the export path and URL and then grab the exact values:

```
$exportpath2 = "c:\temp\featureupdates.csv"
$url = "https://graph.microsoft.com/beta/deviceManagement/
softwareUpdateStatusSummary"
$fulloutput = Invoke-MGGraphRequest -Uri $url -Method Get -outputType
PSObject
$selectedoutput = $fulloutput | select-object *
```

Finally, again, export or view after a popup:

```
if ($result -eq [System.Windows.Forms.DialogResult]::OK) {
    $selectedoutput | export-csv $exportpath2 -NoTypeInformation
} elseif ($result -eq [System.Windows.Forms.DialogResult]::Cancel) {
    $selectedoutput | Out-GridView
}
```

This completes the automation of Windows update reporting. We can now cover iOS updates.

iOS update status

This is very straightforward to automate, as it is a simple paginated `GET` request:

1. First, set the output path:

```
$exportpath = "c:\temp\iosupdatestatus.csv"
```

2. Set the URL and grab the data:

```
$url = "https://graph.microsoft.com/beta/deviceManagement/
iosUpdateStatuses"
$fulloutput = getallpagination -url $url
$selectedoutput = $fulloutput | select-object *
```

3. The only change after this is that the output could be completely clear, which will block any export or grid view from displaying. Therefore, we inspect the output first, and if it is `null`, we simply output that to the screen:

```
if ($result -eq [System.Windows.Forms.DialogResult]::OK) {
    if ($null -eq $selectedoutput) {
       write-host "Nothing to display"
    }
    else {
        $selectedoutput | export-csv $exportpath
    }
} elseif ($result -eq [System.Windows.Forms.DialogResult]::Cancel) {
    if ($null -eq $selectedoutput) {
       write-host "Nothing to display"
    }
    else {
    $selectedoutput | Out-GridView
```

```
    }
}
```

After reviewing iOS updates, we will now cover macOS updates.

macOS update status

This is exactly the same as the preceding iOS script, only with a different export path and URL. The full script is on GitHub, but these are the only values changed to grab macOS values:

```
$exportpath = "c:\temp\masosupdatestatus.csv"
$url = "https://graph.microsoft.com/beta/deviceManagement/
macOSSoftwareUpdateAccountSummaries"
```

It also uses pagination and has the possibility of a `null` result, so it includes the same `if` statement.

That completes the recipe for monitoring updates. We will now look at device actions.

Monitoring device actions

As an Intune administrator, especially in a larger organization, it is essential to have an audit trail, as there are buttons within the console that can have serious effects. Imagine someone accidentally clicks **Wipe** on the wrong device, and you need to find out what happened for an incident report. Fortunately, these are all logged in **Device actions**, which we will cover now.

Getting ready

To access these logs, click on **Devices**, then **Overview**, and finally, click on the **Device actions** box.

How to do it...

On this screen, you will be presented with a list of all actions taken against all devices (cross-platform), including what was performed, when, and by whom.

There is no search functionality, and you cannot sort on the headers (use the automated script to add this functionality), but it does have a powerful filter that includes every possible action across all device types.

It is strictly view-only (or exportable if clicking the **Export** button). There is no functionality to drill down.

Hopefully, this is a report that is rarely required, but think of it as your insurance policy.

Automating it

This is a simple GET request, although if you watch the network in your browser, you will see that, by default, the request only selects the first 25 entries, so clearly we are going to need pagination here. Follow these steps to create your script:

1. As usual, we start with the export path and URL:

```
$exportpath = "c:\temp\deviceactions.csv"
$url = "https://graph.microsoft.com/beta/deviceManagement/
remoteActionAudits"
```

2. We will use the same function as covered at the start of the chapter to grab all data:

```
$fulloutput = getallpagination -url $url
$selectedoutput = $fulloutput | select-object *
```

3. After presenting our popup, export or display the data. While it is unlikely the report will be completely empty, there is the possibility of such, so we will include the extra `if` statement and the associated output:

```
if ($result -eq [System.Windows.Forms.DialogResult]::OK) {
    if ($null -eq $selectedoutput) {
       write-host "Nothing to display"
    }
    else {
        $selectedoutput | export-csv $exportpath
    }
} elseif ($result -eq [System.Windows.Forms.DialogResult]::Cancel) {
    if ($null -eq $selectedoutput) {
       write-host "Nothing to display"
    }
    else {
    $selectedoutput | Out-GridView
    }
}
```

This completes the recipe reviewing device actions. We will now look at the all-important audit logs.

Using device query

Device query is a way to query your devices in real time to grab key information (CPU usage, TPM information, etc.). It can be run against a single machine or multiple, depending on your use case. A full list of what is available can be found here: `https://learn.microsoft.com/en-us/intune/analytics/device-query`.

Device query requires a license including Intune Advanced Analytics (covered in *Chapter 14* on Intune Suite).

All queries are in **Kusto Query Language** (**KQL**), so I would also recommend learning the basics of this where possible. Here are some resources to get you started:

- `https://learn.microsoft.com/en-us/azure/data-explorer/kql-learning-resources`
- `https://www.systanddeploy.com/2025/01/learn-kql-in-one-month-book-2025-edition.html`

There is also this website, which includes many queries for you to grab and use: `https://www.kqlsearch.com/devicequery`. Just watch the **Copy** button as it includes the use case and details; you just need the text after **Query:**.

Getting ready

Before using device query, we need to configure a **Properties catalog** policy to tell it what to retrieve from the devices:

1. To do that, navigate to **Devices** | **Windows** | **Configuration** and click **Create** – **New Policy**.
2. Select the **Platform** option as **Windows 10 and later**, and then set **Profile type** as **Properties catalog** and click **Create**:

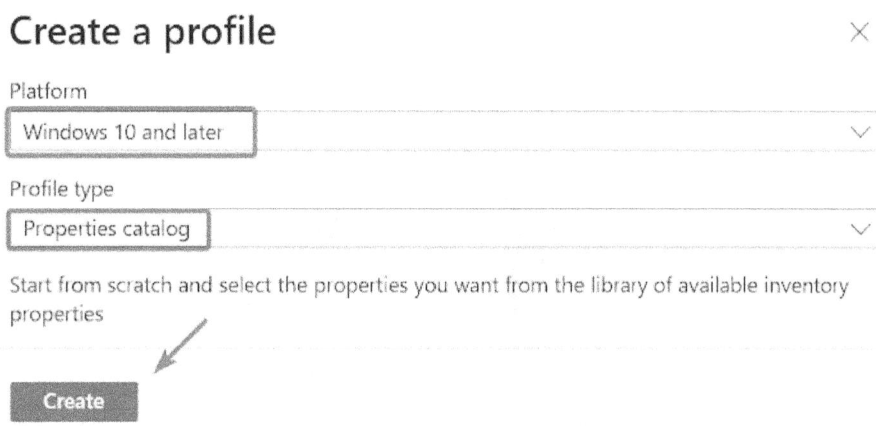

Figure 9.4 – Create Properties catalog

3. Give your policy a **Name** and **Description** value and click **Next**.
4. Click **Add properties** and select those required for your environment, then click **Select**:

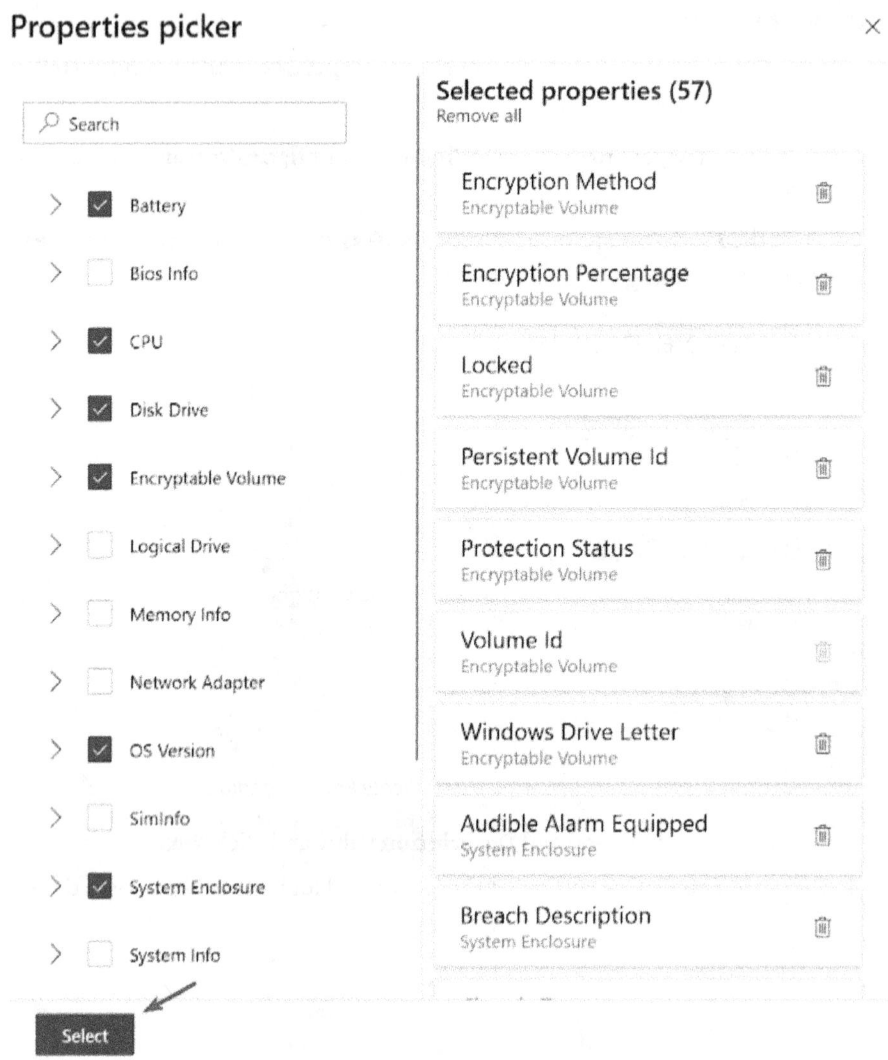

Figure 9.5 – Properties for device query

5. You will see your selections displayed. If they look correct, click **Next**.
6. We do not require scope tags at this point, so click **Next**.
7. Assign our new policy as required; usually, **All Users** or **All Devices** will work for a policy such as this, but it could be that you need different properties for different user groups. Once assigned, click **Next**.
8. Finally, check that all looks okay and click **Create**.

Now that we have our policy in place, we can look at how to query our devices. If you want to automate this, the script is available in the GitHub repository here: `https://github.com/PacktPublishing/Microsoft-Intune-Cookbook-Second-Edition/tree/main/Chapter-9`.

> **Note**
>
> The devices will need at least 24 hours before they start sending data after the policy has been created.

How to do it...

As device query can be run against a single device (for live data) or multiple devices using cached data, there are two ways of retrieving the data. We will start with multiple devices.

Multiple devices

1. Navigate to **Devices** and then click **Device query**.
   Here, you will see all of the properties available to you on the left-hand side and the space to build your KQL query. If you are licensed for **Copilot** within Intune (covered fully in *Chapter 15*), you will also have a text box where you can use natural language to create a query.

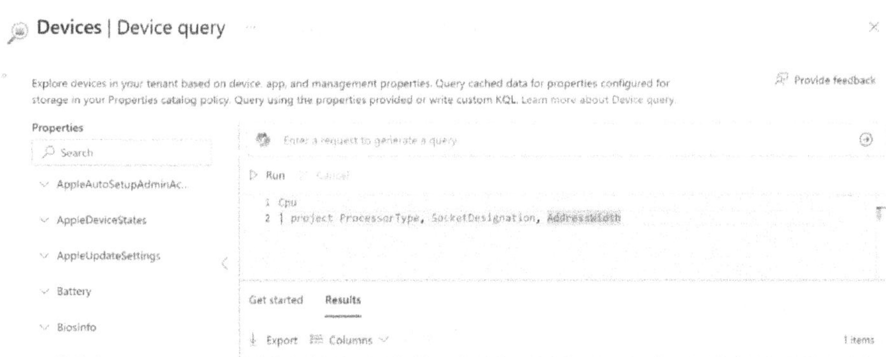

Figure 9.6 – Device query for multiple devices

   As well as typing in the box, you can also click on a property, and it will add it for you to avoid the risk of a typo. Either option requires a knowledge of KQL, as you need to structure it correctly.

2. After entering your query, simply click the **Run** button, and your results will display below.
   You also have the option to export, should you need the information.

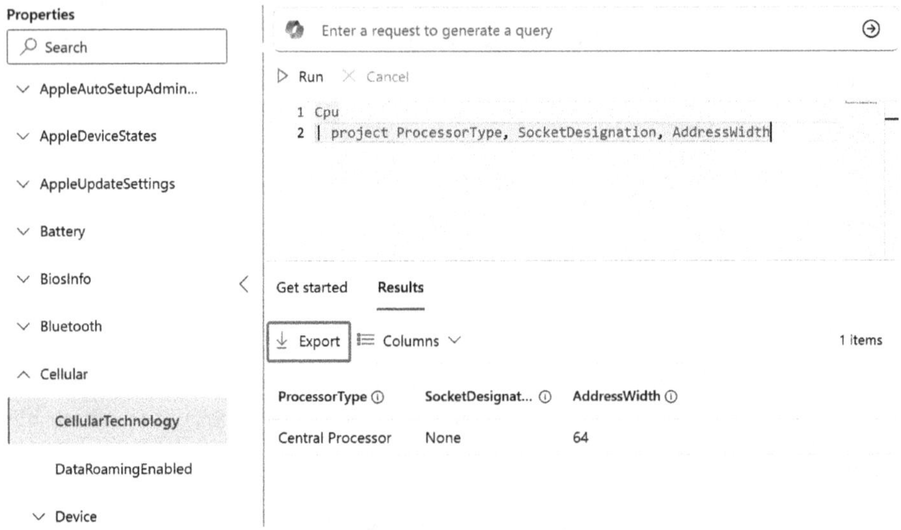

Figure 9.7 – Results for multiple devices

Single devices

Now, for single devices, where you have the option of retrieving live data, here are the steps:

1. Click on **Devices**, select a device, and then click **Device query**.

   Again, you will see the same familiar panel, but obviously, the queries are single-device only in here. There are also examples at the bottom to get started.

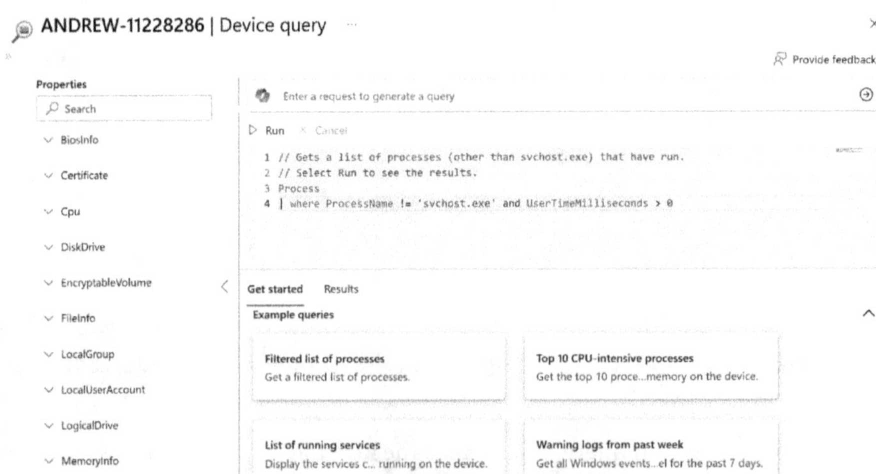

Figure 9.8 – Device query for a single device

2. Enter your query and click **Run**; your results will appear in the **Results** tab.

That is the limit of device query; if you want more control, such as working with the output, check out Explorer in *Chapter 15*.

Automating it

Unfortunately, the API endpoints for both single- and multi-device queries are currently locked. Should the API be unlocked in the future, I have included the calls from the UI in two scripts within the GitHub repository for the future.

Reviewing audit logs

In the last recipe, we covered auditing actions taken directly on devices, which, while they can have a high impact, are on an individual device level, so less likely to cause significant issues. If, however, policies are amended, deleted, or created, there is a far greater chance of issues at a larger level. To monitor for such changes, we need to delve into the audit logs.

Getting ready

To access audit logs, click on **Tenant administration** | **Audit logs**.

How to do it...

Once you are on the **Audit logs** page, you will be presented with a familiar report-type screen. Again, there is a powerful filter option at the top, including the ability to filter on the activity. Be warned, however, that this is a long list and does not have any search functionality built in, so make sure you are selecting the correct option when using it.

The search box allows you to find the person who made the change, and you can also sort by date and activity (but not the other headers).

The export here just exports exactly what is onscreen and not the further information you can grab.

Clicking on a row shows further information about exactly what was changed, including the new and old value set, which is incredibly useful if you need to revert a change but do not have the previous value recorded anywhere (or use a backup/restore tool).

While the logs within the UI are comprehensive, they are much more manageable in Graph, which we will cover now.

Automating it

The basic view is easy to automate here as it is a basic `GET` request, but there is a lot more information available. So, in this script, we will amend the output to remove some unwanted settings and also provide the ability to drill down for further information:

1. We start with our export path:

```
$exportpath = "c:\temp\auditlog.csv"
```

2. We then want to grab all results, expand the nested array called `Actor`, and remove some unwanted items via two `select-object` commands:

```
$uri = "https://graph.microsoft.com/beta/deviceManagement/auditEvents"
$eventsvalues = getallpagination -url $uri
$eventsvalues =  $eventsvalues | select-object * -ExpandProperty Actor
$eventsvalues =  $eventsvalues | select-object resources,
userPrincipalName, displayName, category, activityType, activityDateTime,
activityOperationType, id
```

3. Then, we drop these into our first array, which we will use to export or view the returned data:

```
$listofevents = @()
$counter = 0
foreach ($event in $eventsvalues)
{
    $counter++
    $id = $event.id
    Write-Progress -Activity 'Processing Entries' -CurrentOperation $id -
PercentComplete (($counter / $eventsvalues.count) * 100)
    $eventobject = [pscustomobject]@{
        changedItem = $event.Resources.displayName
        changedBy = $event.userPrincipalName
        change = $event.displayName
        changeCategory = $event.category
        activityType = $event.activityType
        activityDateTime = $event.activityDateTime
        id = $event.id
    }
```

```
    $listofevents += $eventobject
}
```

4. If we have selected export, we need a simple `export-csv` command here:

```
$listofevents | export-csv $exportpath
```

5. If we have selected `view`, we will present a `gridview` output, but we want to add the ability to look at individual items, so we are using the `-PassThru` parameter:

```
$selected = $listofevents | Out-GridView -PassThru
```

6. Create a new array to store this information in:

```
$selectedevents = @()
```

7. We then grab the ID of the selected item and retrieve the data associated with it:

```
$selectedid = $item.id
$uri = "https://graph.microsoft.com/beta/deviceManagement/auditEvents/
$selectedid"
$changedcontent = (Invoke-MgGraphRequest -Uri $uri -Method GET -ContentType
"application/json" -OutputType PSObject)
```

8. Add the item details to our array:

```
$eventobject = [pscustomobject]@{
    change = $changedcontent.displayName
    changeCategory = $changedcontent.category
    activityType = $changedcontent.activityType
    activityDateTime = $changedcontent.activityDateTime
    id = $changedcontent.id
    activity = $changedcontent.activity
    activityResult = $changedcontent.activityResult
    activityOperationType = $changedcontent.activityOperationType
    componentName = $changedcontent.componentName
    type = $changedcontent.actor.type
    auditActorType = $changedcontent.actor.auditActorType
    userPermissions = $changedcontent.actor.userPermissions
    applicationId = $changedcontent.actor.applicationId
```

```
        applicationDisplayName = $changedcontent.actor.applicationDisplayName
        userPrincipalName = $changedcontent.actor.userPrincipalName
        servicePrincipalName = $changedcontent.actor.servicePrincipalName
        ipAddress = $changedcontent.actor.ipAddress
        userId = $changedcontent.actor.userId
        remoteTenantId = $changedcontent.actor.remoteTenantId
        remoteUserId = $changedcontent.actor.remoteUserId
        resourcedisplayname = $changedcontent.resource.displayName
        resourcetype = $changedcontent.resource.type
        auditResourceType = $changedcontent.resource.auditResourceType
        resourceId = $changedcontent.resource.resourceId
    }
```

The items changed within a policy could be basically unlimited, so we still have one array left to present, which is `modifiedproperties` nested within `resources`.

To grab these and add them to the array, we need to make sure they all have different names, so we will use a numerical loop and append this to the name:

1. Start with setting our value:

```
$i = 0
```

2. Loop through the array, and on each loop, add one to the value and append that to the name. Then, add this to our master array:

```
foreach ($resource in $changedcontent.resources.modifiedproperties) {
    $name = "Name" + $i
    $oldvalue = "OldValue" + $i
    $newvalue = "NewValue" + $i
    $eventobject | Add-Member -MemberType NoteProperty -Name $name -Value
$resource.displayName
    $eventobject | Add-Member -MemberType NoteProperty -Name $oldvalue -
Value $resource.oldValue
    $eventobject | Add-Member -MemberType NoteProperty -Name $newvalue -
Value $resource.newValue
```

```
        $i++
    }
```

3. Finally, add all looped items into the same array and output it:

```
$selectedevents += $eventobject
$selectedevents | Out-GridView
```

This gives you a fully filtered, searchable list of audit events, as well as the ability to quickly check exactly what has been changed, when, and by whom.

This completed the recipe for reviewing audit logs.

10

Looking at Reporting

After looking at the more basic monitoring in the last chapter, we will now continue to look at the out-of-the-box reports available. We will then extend that to demonstrate how to export the data to use in **Power BI** and **Azure**, and look at the more advanced Windows Update reporting available using **Log Analytics**.

Reporting is an important part of any Intune environment for a **point-in-time** (**PIT**) snapshot of where you stand, especially if requested by executive members of the organization. This chapter will show you the reports available within Intune, how to run them manually, and how to automate them.

In this chapter, we will cover the following recipes:

- Checking device management reports
- Reviewing endpoint security reports
- Reviewing endpoint analytics reports
- Using Intune Data Warehouse with Power BI
- Checking Windows updates via reporting
- Expanding Windows Update reporting
- Exporting diagnostics to Azure

Technical requirements

For this chapter, you will need a modern web browser and a PowerShell code editor such as Visual Studio Code or **PowerShell Integrated Scripting Environment** (**PowerShell ISE**).

All scripts referenced can be found here: `https://github.com/PacktPublishing/Microsoft-Intune-Cookbook-Second-Edition/tree/main/Chapter-10`.

If you wish to test the policies, you will need a corporate-managed device running each device platform for testing. For Linux, it will need to be running the Ubuntu operating system.

Checking device management reports

We will start our review of available reports with those covering all aspects of device management.

> Note
>
> These reports are also available within the individual policies in Intune.

Getting ready

To access the device management reports, click the **Reports** button in the menu. We can find all these under **Device management**.

Now that we have access to the reports, we can review each in turn.

How to do it...

Here, we will run through the large selection of reports available and the data within them.

Reviewing device compliance

We will use the following steps to review device compliance:

1. For device compliance reports, click on the **Device Compliance** option and then click the **Reports** tab at the top.
   We will start by running through what each of the following reports offers and then how to run them. Apart from device compliance trends, they all have the same mechanism, so the guide to run the reports will apply to all of them:
   - **Device compliance**: This displays a list of all devices and their compliance state. This will be a useful report that most executives will be interested in. You can export it, but you cannot click through to find out why devices are not compliant. It does have search functions as well as some good filtering.
   - **Device compliance trends**: This is a simple graph that displays device compliance over the last 60 days. It gives you the option to filter, but not to export or click through.
   - **Noncompliant devices and settings**: This report gives more depth to your **Device compliance** report from earlier, and in most cases, is the most useful report. It displays the device name and then which particular setting(s) in the compliance policy (or policies) is causing the non-compliance. If you have a

custom policy, this can look at each individual setting within it. It also reports whether the setting is simply non-compliant or if there is an error. It features filtering, search functionality, and the ability to sort on headings.

- **Devices without compliance policy**: This is a reasonably straightforward report that simply lists any devices that do not have any compliance policies assigned. This should ideally be empty, so it is always worth monitoring, more so if you have configured devices not listed as compliant (it will tell you what these are set to and how to change them). You can filter on OS and ownership, as well as sorting and searching on the device name. For a simple report, this should be more than sufficient.
- **Setting compliance**: This report lists all compliance settings across all policies and platforms and the compliance/non-compliance figures for each setting. As well as filtering and searching, all columns can be selected for sorting, and you can click through to find out which devices are compliant or non-compliant for each setting. This is a useful report for spotting trends across the estate, especially if you find a lot of non-compliant devices and want to look for any similarities.
- **Policy compliance**: Similar to the previous report, but rather than looking at individual settings, this looks at the policy level and shows device compliance and non-compliance per policy. Again, if you suddenly find numerous devices being blocked for non-compliance, you can use this to see which policy is triggering it. It is especially useful for estates with larger numbers of policies to help drill down into which report a particular setting is in. As with the others, you can search, filter, and sort by column.
- **Windows hardware attestation report**: This report is used for compliance policies using device health and shows devices that have completed attestation. There are numerous filters, and you can search for devices.

2. With the exception of **Device compliance trends**, running these reports is simply a matter of clicking the **Generate report** (or **Generate again**) button.
   It can take a few minutes to process, but the portal will inform you when the report is ready.
3. For the **Device compliance trends** report, you simply click the **Refresh** button to run it.

We have now reviewed and created our device compliance reports.

Checking device configuration

Now, we can look at the device configuration report to check the status of the policies assigned:

1. This report is accessed by clicking **Reports**, then **Device Configuration**, and then the **Reports** tab at the top. Then, click on **Profile configuration status**.
2. Click **Generate report**, or click **Generate again** if you have previously run the report.
3. Once completed, you will receive this notification:

Figure 10.1 – Report success notification

This report displays a list of all profiles across operating systems, as well as a count of each status for every profile, showing **Success**, **Error**, or **Conflict** totals for the profiles.

As well as exporting, you can filter on OS and profile type, as well as the ability to search on the profile name or sort on any header. Sorting is especially useful for spotting any trends in conflicting policies or policies with errors. Those with large success figures are of less concern.

> **Tip**
>
> None of the rows can be clicked on, so there is no way to drill down from within this report; it is view only.

That covers device configuration. We can now look at Group Policy analytics.

Reviewing Group Policy analytics

This report is used alongside **Group Policy analytics**, as covered in *Chapter 2*, and simply displays the output of all of your imported group policies and the status of the settings within them. The **Summary** screen initially displayed will give an overview of the settings detected and their readiness for importing into Intune.

Follow these instructions to create your report:

1. To access it, navigate to **Reports** and then **Group Policy analytics**. Once there, click the **Reports** tab and click **Group Policy migration readiness**.

2. Once in the report, click **Generate** or **Generate again**, depending on whether you have run this before.
3. After the report has been generated, as well as the usual **Export** button, you have a useful overview and a fairly powerful filter:

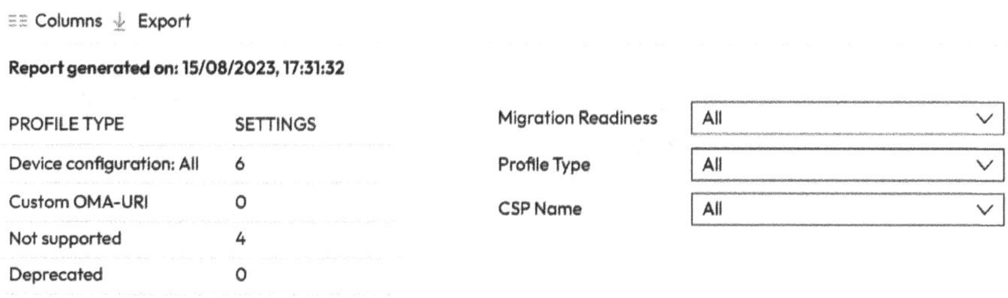

Figure 10.2 – Group Policy analytics filter

You can also search on just about anything, as well as sorting on each header.

Nothing can be clicked through here, but this report gives us an overview of what can and cannot be migrated. To perform any further steps, you would need to go back to the **Group Policy analytics** page within **Devices**.

While bulk importing settings is never the best approach, this report will at least give an indication of any settings that may need to be reviewed and either replaced or configured using an alternative method such as policy ingestion, custom policy, or PowerShell scripting:

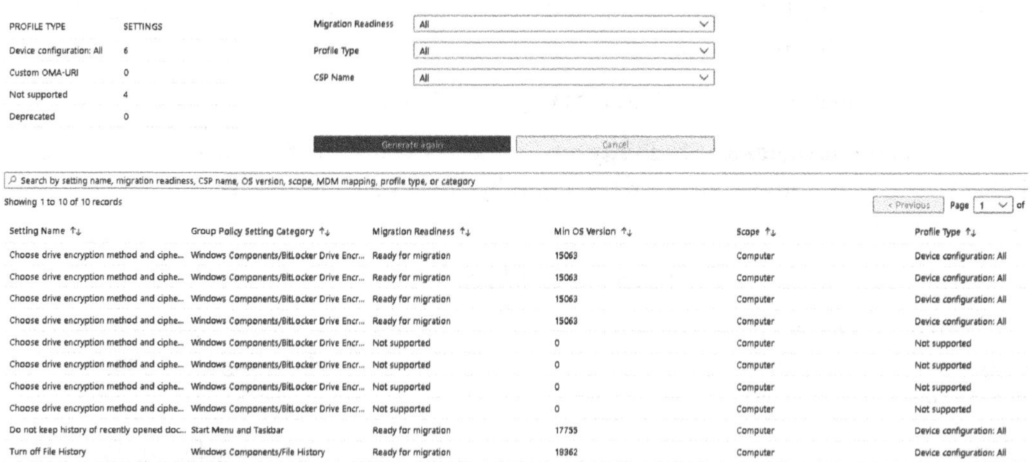

Figure 10.3 – Analytics report output

We have now reviewed the Group Policy analytics reports and can look at what is available for co-managed devices.

Cloud-attached devices

The **Co-Management Eligibility** and **Co-Managed Workloads** reports are only for environments currently using Configuration Manager and looking at co-management.

You can find out more about co-management here: `https://learn.microsoft.com/en-us/mem/configmgr/comanage/overview`

To access these reports, within the Intune portal, navigate to **Reports** | **Cloud Attached Devices** and then click on the **Reports** tab.

Now, we can look at the content of these reports.

Co-Management Eligibility

This report shows the status of cloud-attached devices and whether they are eligible for co-management.

Run the report by clicking **Generate report** or **Generate again**.

Once run, this will show basic details about the devices and the eligibility status of each one. You can filter, export, search, and sort on the headers, as with the other reports.

Co-Managed Workloads

When configuring co-management, you can select which workloads are handled by Intune and which workloads Configuration Manager handles.

Running this report will list your devices and which workloads are configured on a per-device basis. This is a useful troubleshooting tool should you encounter any issues.

As with the previous report, click **Generate Report** or **Generate Again**.

As with the **Co-Management Eligibility** report, there is a powerful filter to quickly check for individual settings. You can only search and sort by device name and device ID, however, so use the filters instead.

Reviewing Device Attestation Status

A new addition to Intune reporting, but a fairly important one, this will show the status of all of your machines so you can quickly spot those causing issues (and if using with compliance, before the users complain).

After running the report, not only can you see the status, but also the reason for any failures.

There are filters available before generating a report, which is especially useful for large environments.

As with the previous report, click **Generate Report** or **Generate Again**.

You can search and sort, as well as clicking on the devices to drill down further. Even better, you can select devices and trigger a restart or attestation in bulk to quickly remediate issues.

That completes our overview of the information available in device management reports and how to run these. We can now look at how to automate these.

Automating reports

After learning about these reports in the GUI, we can now move on to automating them.

Reviewing device compliance

As with the *How to do it...* section, there are two different approaches here: one for **Device compliance trends** and one for the other reports.

As the **Device compliance trends** report is a more graphical experience, automating it will just produce numerical output that does not offer any value over the other reports available here, so we will concentrate on automating the reports that offer a more thorough output of device details, as they all have a similar configuration.

The other reports all use a very similar method underneath, so we can get more clever here and have them all within the same script (you can, of course, split these if needed).

Some of these code blocks have been shortened for brevity. You can find the full script at the following link: `https://github.com/PacktPublishing/Microsoft-Intune-Cookbook-Second-Edition/blob/main/Chapter-10/compliance-reports.ps1`.

Follow these steps to make your master report builder:

1. We start with the output path as usual:

```
$exportpath = "c:\temp\userenrollmentfailures.csv"
```

2. Next, we are going to create an array with the different reports and their Graph API name. We use this in an `Out-GridView` cmdlet to select the value:

```
$reporttypes = @()
    $reporttypes += "DeviceCompliance"
    $reporttypes += "NoncompliantDevicesAndSettings"
    $reporttypes += "DevicesWithoutCompliancePolicy"
    $reporttypes += "SettingComplianceAggReport"
    $reporttypes += "PolicyComplianceAggReport"

$selectedreport = $reporttypes | Out-GridView -PassThru -Title "Select
Report"
```

3. We add the selected array object to the full policy name:

```
$fullreport = $selectedreport + "_00000000-0000-0000-0000-000000000001"
```

4. Now we have our policy name, we need to send a POST request to generate the report:

```
$generateurl = "https://graph.microsoft.com/beta/deviceManagement/reports/
cachedReportConfigurations"
        $json = @"
        {
            "filter": "",
            "id": "$fullreport",
            "metadata": null,
            "orderBy": [
                "PolicyName asc"
            ],
            "select": []
        }
"@
Invoke-MgGraphRequest -Method POST -Uri $generateurl -Body $json -
ContentType "application/json"
```

As you can see, we use the ID to tell Graph which report to create.

5. We do not want to grab our results until the report is ready, so we run a GET request against a URL populated with the ID:

```
$url = "https://graph.microsoft.com/beta/deviceManagement/reports/
cachedReportConfigurations('$fullreport')"
```

6. We are looking for a status of `Completed`, so we grab the output and use a `while` loop to wait for the output to match:

```
$reportcheck = (Invoke-MgGraphRequest -uri $url -Method Get -OutputType
PSObject).status
while ($reportcheck -ne "Completed") {
    $reportcheck = (Invoke-MgGraphRequest -uri $url -Method Get -OutputType
PSObject).status
    Start-Sleep -Seconds 5
}
```

7. Now we can continue to grab the data, which uses the same format as the last chapter. We need to grab the output into a text file and, due to pagination, loop through to grab all values.

   Before doing so, the JSON for each `POST` command is slightly different, so we are using the `SWITCH` command within PowerShell to check the output from the earlier selection and populate it accordingly:

```
switch ($selectedreport) {
    "DeviceCompliance" {
        $jsonselection = @"
        "Select": [
            "DeviceName",
            "ComplianceState"
        ],
"@
    }
    "NoncompliantDevicesAndSettings" {
        $jsonselection = @"
        "Select": [
            "DeviceName",
            "SettingName"
        ],
"@
    }
    "DevicesWithoutCompliancePolicy" {
        $jsonselection = @"
        "Select": [
            "DeviceId"
        ],
"@
    }
    "SettingComplianceAggReport" {
        $jsonselection = @"
        "Select": [
        ],
"@
    }
    "PolicyComplianceAggReport" {
        $jsonselection = @"
        "Select": [
```

```
        ],
"@
    }
}
```

8. We then use this data to populate our final JSON:

```
$reportjson = @"
{
    "filter": "",
    "Id": "$fullreport",
    "OrderBy": [],
    "Search": "",
$jsonselection
    "Skip": 0,
    "Top": 50
}
"@
```

9. Grab the first set of results into a `.txt` file and then re-ingest it:

```
$tempfilepath = $env:TEMP + "\compliance-report.txt"
Invoke-MgGraphRequest -Method POST -Uri $reporturl -Body $reportjson -
ContentType "application/json" -OutputFilePath $tempfilepath
$parsedData = get-content $tempfilepath | ConvertFrom-Json
$fullvalues = $parsedData.Values
```

10. Now, count the number of rows so that we can loop through accordingly:

```
$allrows = $parsedData.TotalRowCount
```

11. Set our variable and loop until we hit our total. We are doing the same grab and retrieve, only setting a filename with a number at the end to avoid overwriting the original file:

```
$n = 0
while ($n -lt $allrows) {
    $n += 50
    $tempfilepath2 = $env:TEMP + "\compliancereport-$n.txt"
    $json = @"
{
```

```
    "filter": "",
    "Id": "$fullreport",
    "OrderBy": [],
    "Search": "",
$jsonselection
    "skip": $n,
    "top": 50
}
"@
    Invoke-MgGraphRequest -Method POST -Uri $reporturl -Body $json -
ContentType "application/json" -OutputFilePath $tempfilepath2
    $tempdata = get-content $tempfilepath2 | ConvertFrom-Json
    $fullvalues += $tempdata.Values
}
```

12. As we need to create a legible array and have different JSON requests, we need to use another `SWITCH` command to populate our array depending on the selection:

```
switch ($selectedreport) {
    "DeviceCompliance" {
        $outputarray = @()
        foreach ($value in $fullvalues) {
            $objectdetails = [pscustomobject]@{
                DeviceName = $value[2]
            }

            $outputarray += $objectdetails
        }
    }
    "NoncompliantDevicesAndSettings" {
        $outputarray = @()
        foreach ($value in $fullvalues) {
            $objectdetails = [pscustomobject]@{
                DeviceName = $value[1]
            }
            $outputarray += $objectdetails
        }
    }
    "DevicesWithoutCompliancePolicy" {
        $outputarray = @()
        foreach ($value in $fullvalues) {
```

```
                $objectdetails = [pscustomobject]@{
                    DeviceId = $value[1]
                }
                $outputarray += $objectdetails
            }
        }
        "SettingComplianceAggReport" {
            $outputarray = @()
            foreach ($value in $fullvalues) {
                $objectdetails = [pscustomobject]@{
                setting = $value[3]
                }
                $outputarray += $objectdetails
            }
        }
        "PolicyComplianceAggReport" {
            $outputarray = @()
            foreach ($value in $fullvalues) {
                $objectdetails = [pscustomobject]@{
                }
                $outputarray += $objectdetails
            }
        }
}
```

13. Then, as with all previous scripts, we send a popup, which is available in the main script within the GitHub repository. Depending on the response, either display or export the report:

```
if ($result -eq [System.Windows.Forms.DialogResult]::OK) {
    # Export code here
    $outputarray | export-csv $exportpath -NoTypeInformation
} elseif ($result -eq [System.Windows.Forms.DialogResult]::Cancel) {
    # View code here
    $outputarray | Out-GridView
}
```

14. Finally, we will clean up our files:

```
Remove-Item $tempfilepath
$allrows = $parsedData.TotalRowCount
```

```
$n = 0
while ($n -lt $allrows) {
    $n += 50
    $tempfilepath2 = $env:TEMP + "\compliancereport-$n.txt"
    Remove-Item $tempfilepath2
}
```

If selecting to view the output, an example would be this:

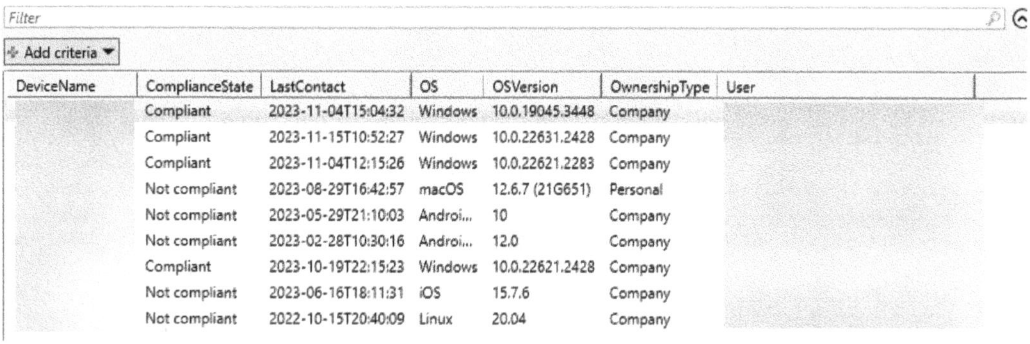

DeviceName	ComplianceState	LastContact	OS	OSVersion	OwnershipType	User
	Compliant	2023-11-04T15:04:32	Windows	10.0.19045.3448	Company	
	Compliant	2023-11-15T10:52:27	Windows	10.0.22631.2428	Company	
	Compliant	2023-11-04T12:15:26	Windows	10.0.22621.2283	Company	
	Not compliant	2023-08-29T16:42:57	macOS	12.6.7 (21G651)	Personal	
	Not compliant	2023-05-29T21:10:03	Androi...	10	Company	
	Not compliant	2023-02-28T10:30:16	Androi...	12.0	Company	
	Compliant	2023-10-19T22:15:23	Windows	10.0.22621.2428	Company	
	Not compliant	2023-06-16T18:11:31	iOS	15.7.6	Company	
	Not compliant	2022-10-15T20:40:09	Linux	20.04	Company	

Figure 10.4 – Device compliance report

That completes the script for retrieving device compliance reports; we can now look at device configuration.

Reviewing device configuration

This one is very similar to the previous report, but as it is a single report, we do not need the array and associated `SWITCH` query. Follow these steps to automate the device configuration report:

1. First, we start with the `.csv` file:

```
$exportpath = "c:\temp\profileconfigurationreport.csv"
```

2. Next, set the report name and populate the URL:

```
$selectedreport = "ConfigurationPolicyAggregate"
$fullreport = $selectedreport + "_00000000-0000-0000-0000-000000000001"
$generateurl = "https://graph.microsoft.com/beta/deviceManagement/reports/
cachedReportConfigurations"
```

3. Set the JSON and generate the report:

```
        $json = @"
        {
            "filter": "",
            "id": "$fullreport",
            "metadata": null,
            "orderBy": [
            ],
            "select": [
                "PolicyName",
                "UnifiedPolicyType",
                "UnifiedPolicyPlatformType",
                "NumberOfCompliantDevices",
                "NumberOfNonCompliantOrErrorDevices",
                "NumberOfConflictDevices"
                ]
        }
"@
Invoke-MgGraphRequest -Method POST -Uri $generateurl -Body $json -
ContentType "application/json"
```

4. As before, we need to run a `GET` request and wait for the status to be marked as `Completed`:

```
$url = "https://graph.microsoft.com/beta/deviceManagement/reports/
cachedReportConfigurations('$fullreport')"
$reportcheck = (Invoke-MgGraphRequest -uri $url -Method Get -OutputType
PSObject).status
while ($reportcheck -ne "Completed") {
    $reportcheck = (Invoke-MgGraphRequest -uri $url -Method Get -OutputType
PSObject).status
    Start-Sleep -Seconds 5
}
```

5. Once that is done, we run our command to grab the data, export to text, import back from JSON and count, then loop through the counted objects:

```
$url = "https://graph.microsoft.com/beta/deviceManagement/reports/
cachedReportConfigurations('$fullreport')"
```

```
$reportcheck = (Invoke-MgGraphRequest -uri $url -Method Get -OutputType
PSObject).status
while ($reportcheck -ne "Completed") {
    $reportcheck = (Invoke-MgGraphRequest -uri $url -Method Get -OutputType
PSObject).status
    Start-Sleep -Seconds 5
}
$reporturl = "https://graph.microsoft.com/beta/deviceManagement/reports/
getCachedReport"
$reportjson = @"
{
    "filter": "",
    "Id": "$fullreport",
    "OrderBy": [],
    "Search": "",
    "Select": [
        "PolicyName",
        "UnifiedPolicyType",
        "UnifiedPolicyPlatformType",
        "NumberOfCompliantDevices",
        "NumberOfNonCompliantOrErrorDevices",
        "NumberOfConflictDevices"
        ],
    "Skip": 0,
    "Top": 50
}
"@
$tempfilepath = $env:TEMP + "\configreport.txt"
Invoke-MgGraphRequest -Method POST -Uri $reporturl -Body $reportjson -
ContentType "application/json" -OutputFilePath $tempfilepath
$parsedData = get-content $tempfilepath | ConvertFrom-Json
$fullvalues = $parsedData.Values
$allrows = $parsedData.TotalRowCount
$n = 0
while ($n -lt $allrows) {
    $n += 50
    $tempfilepath2 = $env:TEMP + "\configreport-$n.txt"
    $json = @"
{
    "filter": "",
    "Id": "$fullreport",
```

```
        "OrderBy": [],
        "Search": "",
        "Select": [
            "PolicyName",
            "UnifiedPolicyType",
            "UnifiedPolicyPlatformType",
            "NumberOfCompliantDevices",
            "NumberOfNonCompliantOrErrorDevices",
            "NumberOfConflictDevices"
            ],
        "skip": $n,
        "top": 50
}
"@
    Invoke-MgGraphRequest -Method POST -Uri $reporturl -Body $json -
ContentType "application/json" -OutputFilePath $tempfilepath2
    $tempdata = get-content $tempfilepath2 | ConvertFrom-Json
    $fullvalues += $tempdata.Values

}
```

6. Now we have our array of values, we need to add them to an object so that we can tidy it to view or export:

```
        $outputarray = @()
        foreach ($value in $fullvalues) {
            $objectdetails = [pscustomobject]@{
                PolicyName = $value[3]
                PolicyType = $value[5]
                Platform = $value[4]
                CompliantDevices = $value[0]
                NonCompliantDevices = $value[2]
                ConflictDevices = $value[1]
            }
            $outputarray += $objectdetails
        }
```

7. After running the popup, either export or display the content:

```
if ($result -eq [System.Windows.Forms.DialogResult]::OK) {
    # Export code here
```

```
    $outputarray | export-csv $exportpath -NoTypeInformation
} elseif ($result -eq [System.Windows.Forms.DialogResult]::Cancel) {
    # View code here
    $outputarray | Out-GridView
}
```

8. Finally, clean everything up:

```
Remove-Item $tempfilepath
$allrows = $parsedData.TotalRowCount
$n = 0
while ($n -lt $allrows) {
    $n += 50
    $tempfilepath2 = $env:TEMP + "\configreport-$n.txt"
    Remove-Item $tempfilepath2
}
```

An example output for this report would look like this:

Filter

Add criteria

PolicyName	PolicyType	Platform	CompliantDevices	NonCompliantDevices	ConflictDevices
Audacity	Windows10	Windows10	2	1	0
Background and Lockscreen	Windows10	Windows10	0	3	0
Base Android Config	AndroidForWork	AndroidForWork	1	0	0
Baseline Device Restrictions	iOS	IOS	0	0	1
Baseline iOS Features	iOS	IOS	1	0	0
Browser Homepage	Windows10	Windows10	3	0	0
Cloud Site List	Windows10	Windows10	6	0	0
Cloud Trust	Windows10	Windows10	6	0	0
Command Prompt	Windows10	Windows10	2	1	0
Config Refresh	Windows10	Windows10	6	0	0
Configure Desktop Wallpaper	MacOS	MacOS	1	0	0
Elevation Settings	Windows10	Windows10	3	1	0

Figure 10.5 – Device configuration report

Now that we have completed automating our device configuration reports, we can look at Group Policy analytics.

Reviewing Group Policy analytics

This works in exactly the same way as the previous script, so we will just call out the differences in JSON and URL (the full script is in the GitHub repository): `https://github.com/PacktPublishing/Microsoft-Intune-Cookbook-Second-Edition/blob/main/Chapter-10/group-policy-analytics.ps1`.

1. First, we need to set the path:

```
$exportpath = "c:\temp\gpanalyticsreport.csv"
```

2. Set the report name itself:

```
$selectedreport = "GPAnalyticsSettingMigrationReadiness"
```

3. Add that to the full report name:

```
$fullreport = $selectedreport + "_00000000-0000-0000-0000-000000000001"
```

4. Run the initial `POST` request to generate the data output:

```
$generateurl = "https://graph.microsoft.com/beta/deviceManagement/reports/
cachedReportConfigurations"
        $json = @"
        {
            "filter": "",
            "id": "$fullreport",
            "metadata": null,
            "orderBy": [
            ],
            "select": [
                "SettingName",
                "SettingCategory",
                "MigrationReadiness",
                "OSVersion",
                "Scope",
                "ProfileType"
                ]
        }
"@
```

5. Using the same JSON, we wait for completion and then loop through all returned rows, incrementing 50 at a time.
6. Finally, we need to add these to our array:

```
$outputarray = @()
foreach ($value in $fullvalues) {
    $objectdetails = [pscustomobject]@{
        SettingName = $value[5]
        SettingCategory = $value[4]
        MigrationReadiness = $value[0]
        OSVersion = $value[1]
        Scope = $value[3]
        ProfileType = $value[2]
    }
    $outputarray += $objectdetails
}
```

7. Then, we do the usual display/export and cleanup:

```
if ($result -eq [System.Windows.Forms.DialogResult]::OK) {
    # Export code here
    $outputarray | export-csv $exportpath -NoTypeInformation
} elseif ($result -eq [System.Windows.Forms.DialogResult]::Cancel) {
    # View code here
    $outputarray | Out-GridView
}
Remove-Item $tempfilepath
$allrows = $parsedData.TotalRowCount
$n = 0
while ($n -lt $allrows) {
    $n += 50
    $tempfilepath2 = $env:TEMP + "\gpanalytics-$n.txt"
    Remove-Item $tempfilepath2
}
```

The output of this script should look like this:

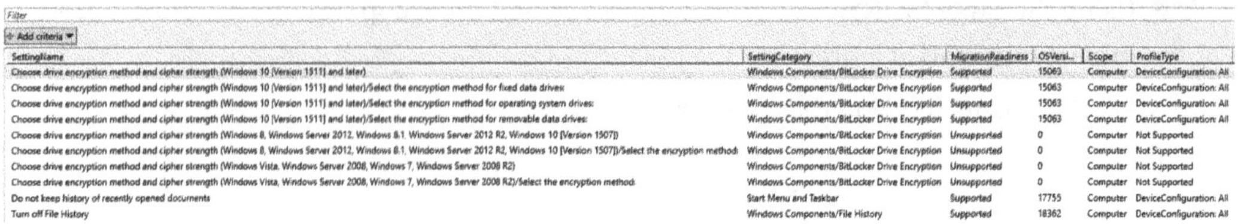
Filter

Add criteria

SettingName	SettingCategory	MigrationReadiness	OSVersi...	Scope	ProfileType
Choose drive encryption method and cipher strength (Windows 10 [Version 1511] and later)	Windows Components/BitLocker Drive Encryption	Supported	15063	Computer	DeviceConfiguration: All
Choose drive encryption method and cipher strength (Windows 10 [Version 1511] and later)/Select the encryption method for fixed data drives:	Windows Components/BitLocker Drive Encryption	Supported	15063	Computer	DeviceConfiguration: All
Choose drive encryption method and cipher strength (Windows 10 [Version 1511] and later)/Select the encryption method for operating system drives:	Windows Components/BitLocker Drive Encryption	Supported	15063	Computer	DeviceConfiguration: All
Choose drive encryption method and cipher strength (Windows 10 [Version 1511] and later)/Select the encryption method for removable data drives:	Windows Components/BitLocker Drive Encryption	Supported	15063	Computer	DeviceConfiguration: All
Choose drive encryption method and cipher strength (Windows 8, Windows Server 2012, Windows 8.1, Windows Server 2012 R2, Windows 10 [Version 1507])	Windows Components/BitLocker Drive Encryption	Unsupported	0	Computer	Not Supported
Choose drive encryption method and cipher strength (Windows 8, Windows Server 2012, Windows 8.1, Windows Server 2012 R2, Windows 10 [Version 1507])/Select the encryption method:	Windows Components/BitLocker Drive Encryption	Unsupported	0	Computer	Not Supported
Choose drive encryption method and cipher strength (Windows Vista, Windows Server 2008, Windows 7, Windows Server 2008 R2)	Windows Components/BitLocker Drive Encryption	Unsupported	0	Computer	Not Supported
Choose drive encryption method and cipher strength (Windows Vista, Windows Server 2008, Windows 7, Windows Server 2008 R2)/Select the encryption method:	Windows Components/BitLocker Drive Encryption	Unsupported	0	Computer	Not Supported
Do not keep history of recently opened documents	Start Menu and Taskbar	Supported	17755	Computer	DeviceConfiguration: All
Turn off File History	Windows Components/File History	Supported	18362	Computer	DeviceConfiguration: All

Figure 10.6 – Group Policy analytics output

That completes the automation of the Group Policy analytics report. We will now look at cloud-attached devices.

Cloud-attached devices

Both the **Co-Management Eligibility** and **Co-Managed Workloads** reports use the same basic functionality as the previous recipes, so we will look only at the URL, JSON, and output array here. The full scripts are available on GitHub:

- `https://github.com/PacktPublishing/Microsoft-Intune-Cookbook-Second-Edition/blob/main/Chapter-10/co-managed-workloads.ps1`
- `https://github.com/PacktPublishing/Microsoft-Intune-Cookbook-Second-Edition/blob/main/Chapter-10/co-management-eligibility.ps1`

Co-Management Eligibility

We will start with the **Co-Management Eligibility** report.

1. First, this is the code for the URL and required variables:

```
$selectedreport = "ComanagementEligibilityTenantAttachedDevices"
$fullreport = $selectedreport + "_00000000-0000-0000-0000-000000000001"
$generateurl = "https://graph.microsoft.com/beta/deviceManagement/reports/
cachedReportConfigurations"
```

2. The JSON looks like this:

```
$json = @"
{
    "filter": "",
    "id": "$fullreport",
    "metadata": null,
    "orderBy": [
    ],
    "select": [
```

```
                "DeviceName",
                "DeviceId",
                "Status",
                "OSDescription",
                "OSVersion"
                ]
        }
"@
```

3. The output array looks like this:

```
        $outputarray = @()
        foreach ($value in $fullvalues) {
            $objectdetails = [pscustomobject]@{
                DeviceID = $value[0]
                DeviceName = $value[1]
                OSDescription = $value[2]
                OSVersion = $value[3]
                Status = $value[4]
            }
            $outputarray += $objectdetails
        }
```

Now, we can look at the **Co-Managed Workloads** report for cloud-attached devices.

Co-Managed Workloads

These extracts will differentiate between the **Co-Management Eligibility** and **Co-Managed Workloads** report.

1. For this report, this is the code for the URL and variables:

```
$selectedreport = "ComanagedDeviceWorkloads"
$fullreport = $selectedreport + "_00000000-0000-0000-0000-000000000001"
$generateurl = "https://graph.microsoft.com/beta/deviceManagement/reports/
cachedReportConfigurations"
```

2. The JSON looks like this:

```
        $json = @"
        {
            "filter": "",
            "id": "$fullreport",
```

```
            "metadata": null,
            "orderBy": [
            ],
            "select": [
                "DeviceName",
                "DeviceId",
                "CompliancePolicy",
                "ResourceAccess",
                "DeviceConfiguration",
                "WindowsUpdateforBusiness",
                "EndpointProtection",
                "ModernApps",
                "OfficeApps"
                ]
        }
"@
```

3. This is the code for the output array:

```
        $outputarray = @()
        foreach ($value in $fullvalues) {
            $objectdetails = [pscustomobject]@{
                CompliancePolicy = $value[0]
                DeviceConfiguration = $value[1]
                DeviceID = $value[2]
                DeviceName = $value[3]
                EndpointProtection = $value[4]
                ModernApps = $value[5]
                OfficeApps = $value[6]
                ResourceAccess = $value[7]
                WindowsUpdateforBusiness = $value[8]
            }
            $outputarray += $objectdetails
        }
```

Reviewing Device Attestation Status

This uses the now familiar reporting endpoint where we send the request, wait for a response, and then grab the output.

The full script is available on GitHub here: `https://github.com/PacktPublishing/Microsoft-Intune-Cookbook-Second-Edition/blob/main/Chapter-10/device-attestation.ps1`

The key differences (apart from filenames) are the URL:

```
$selectedreport = "TpmAttestationStatus"
$fullreport = $selectedreport + "_00000000-0000-0000-0000-000000000001"
$generateurl = "https://graph.microsoft.com/beta/deviceManagement/reports/
cachedReportConfigurations"
```

And, of course, the JSON request:

```
        $json = @"
        {
            "filter": "",
            "id": "$fullreport",
            "metadata": null,
            "orderBy": [
            ],
            "select": [
                "DeviceName",
                "DeviceId",
                "UPN",
                "EnrolledByUser",
                "AttestationStatus",
                "AttestationStatusDetail",
                "OS",
                "OSVersion",
                "Ownership",
                "LastCheckin",
                "EnrollmentDate",
                "TpmVersion",
                "TpmManufacturer",
                "Model"
                ]
        }
"@
```

That completes the automation of device reports. Now, we will look at endpoint security reports.

Reviewing endpoint security reports

We will now move on to look at all-important security reports. Even if you do not monitor these yourself, you may have security teams or a **security operations center** (**SOC**) that need to keep an eye on the security status of your machines. Ideally, everything monitored here will be picked up in a compliance policy, but it is always useful to have reports to fall back on.

How to do it...

All endpoint security report references in this recipe are available under **Reports** and then **Endpoint Security**.

Once we have accessed the **Reports** menu in the UI, we can run through each report.

Reviewing Microsoft Defender Antivirus

Within the **Endpoint security reports** section, click on **Microsoft Defender Antivirus** and then click the **Reports** tab, where you will find our two available reports. Here, we will cover them both in further detail.

Antivirus Agent Status

This report shows the full status of all aspects of the antivirus agent on all devices across your estate. You can use it to quickly spot any at-risk machines, find out exactly which component is at fault, and remediate the issue.

To generate the report, click **Generate report** or **Generate again**.

After running the report, you have a useful chart that should hopefully be mostly, if not all, green to show the status of your devices.

There is a good filter, as well as basic search functionality, and the ability to sort by header:

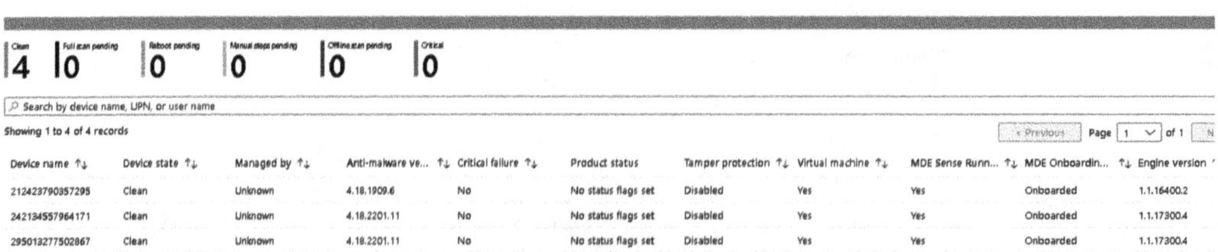

Figure 10.7 – Antivirus report

> **Note**
>
> There is a lot of data to process with a large scroll bar at the bottom, so make sure it is all checked, especially if a device is reporting issues.

Detected Malware

This report lists any infected devices (or devices that have previously been infected), as well as details about the malware found and the number of instances.

As usual, click **Generate report** or **Generate again**.

After running, you have filter, search, and sort by header options, and a useful graph to show the overall status. This report is a pretty critical one, so that you can keep on top of infected devices or repeat offenders.

After reviewing antivirus reports, the next logical step is firewall reports.

Reviewing firewall reports

The firewall report shows the status of Windows Firewall across your devices. It is a simple but useful report. Follow these steps to generate the report:

1. To access this report, click **Firewall** and then click **MDM Firewall status for Windows 10 and later**. You will notice there are no tabs within this report.
2. Click **Generate report** or **Generate again**.

After generating, you will see a similar screen to before, with a chart showing the overall status, a filter that is powerful enough, and the ability to search and sort on any column. Realistically, you will only be interested in those with the firewall disabled, so that you can either filter or sort; either will have the same ultimate result.

By following these instructions, we have generated and reviewed endpoint security reports. Now, we can look at automating them.

Automating the reports

Endpoint security reports, especially antivirus reports, are often requested for a security review of the tenant, so automating them is a good option. We can now run through how to do so.

Reviewing Microsoft Defender Antivirus

Both Microsoft Defender Antivirus and Firewall reports use the same format as our previous scripts. The full content is available on GitHub; as with the others, we will just list the URLs, JSON, and arrays here.

Now, we can look at the individual reports themselves.

Antivirus Agent Status

You can find the full script on GitHub here, as the code blocks shown next have been shortened: `https://github.com/PacktPublishing/Microsoft-Intune-Cookbook-Second-Edition/blob/main/Chapter-10/antivirus-status.ps1`

We start with the antivirus agent status report to check for any devices without active antivirus software.

1. First, we set the report name:

```
$selectedreport = "DefenderAgents"
$fullreport = $selectedreport + "_00000000-0000-0000-0000-000000000001"
```

2. Then, we configure the URL, which in this case looks like this:

```
$generateurl = "https://graph.microsoft.com/beta/deviceManagement/reports/
cachedReportConfigurations"
```

3. Next, we add the JSON to tell Graph which fields we want to retrieve:

```
        $json = @"
        {
            "filter": "",
            "id": "$fullreport",
            "metadata": null,
            "orderBy": [
            ],
            "select": [
                "DeviceName",
                "DeviceState",
                "_ManagedBy",
                "AntiMalwareVersion"
                ]
        }
"@
```

4. We also want to configure the array to return the results in a readable format:

```
        $outputarray = @()
        foreach ($value in $fullvalues) {
            $objectdetails = [pscustomobject]@{
                _ManagedBy = $value[0]
                DeviceName = $value[4]
                DeviceState = $value[6]
            }
```

```
        $outputarray += $objectdetails
    }
```

Detected Malware

Now, we can look at the **Detected Malware** report. Again, the full script can be found on GitHub: `https://github.com/PacktPublishing/Microsoft-Intune-Cookbook-Second-Edition/blob/main/Chapter-10/detected-malware.ps1`.

1. First, as with the previous report, set the ID and URL:

```
$selectedreport = "Malware"
$fullreport = $selectedreport + "_00000000-0000-0000-0000-000000000001"
$generateurl = "https://graph.microsoft.com/beta/deviceManagement/reports/
cachedReportConfigurations"
```

2. Set the JSON to retrieve from Graph:

```
        $json = @"
        {
            "filter": "",
            "id": "$fullreport",
            "metadata": null,
            "orderBy": [
            ],
            "select": [
                "DeviceName",
                "_ManagedBy",
                "DetectionCount",
                "ExecutionState",
                "Severity",
                "MalwareName",
                "MalwareCategory",
                "State"
                ]
        }
"@
```

3. Set the output array:

```
        $outputarray = @()
        foreach ($value in $fullvalues) {
```

```
        $objectdetails = [pscustomobject]@{
            _ManagedBy = $value[0]
            DetectionCount = $value[1]
            DeviceName = $value[2]
            ExecutionState = $value[3]
            MalwareCategory = $value[4]
            MalwareName = $value[5]
            Severity = $value[6]
            State = $value[7]
        }
        $outputarray += $objectdetails
    }
```

Let's move on to do this for the firewall report now.

Firewall report

As with all of the other reports, the report uses the same structure, and the full script is available on GitHub: `https://github.com/PacktPublishing/Microsoft-Intune-Cookbook-Second-Edition/blob/main/Chapter-10/firewall-status.ps1`

For brevity, we will just run through the differences here.

1. For this, we need to first set the report name and URL:

```
$selectedreport = "FirewallStatus"
$fullreport = $selectedreport + "_00000000-0000-0000-0000-000000000001"
$generateurl = "https://graph.microsoft.com/beta/deviceManagement/reports/
cachedReportConfigurations"
```

2. This is the different JSON we will be using:

```
    $json = @"
    {
        "filter": "",
        "id": "$fullreport",
        "metadata": null,
        "orderBy": [
        ],
        "select": [
            "DeviceName",
            "FirewallStatus",
            "_ManagedBy",
```

```
                    "UPN"
                ]
        }
"@
```

3. Finally, the output array will look like this:

```
$outputarray = @()
foreach ($value in $fullvalues) {
    $objectdetails = [pscustomobject]@{
        _ManagedBy = $value[0]
        DeviceName = $value[1]
        FirewallStatus = $value[2]
        UPN = $value[3]
    }
    $outputarray += $objectdetails
}
```

By following these steps, we have automated the creation and output of endpoint security reports.

Reviewing endpoint analytics reports

Endpoint analytics is a veritable treasure trove of information that displays not only information for your estate but also a baseline against similar-sized organizations.

As all of the endpoint analytics reports are display-and-export-type reports, which we have covered in the previous recipes in this chapter, rather than providing instructions on how to run them, we will instead cover what each individual report does and how it can help you.

We will then create a single automation script to grab the output from any of the reports quickly and easily.

Getting ready

To find these reports, navigate to **Reports** and click on **Endpoint analytics**.

Click on **Settings** and make sure the **Intune data collection policy** setting is showing as **Connected**.

Now that we know where to find our endpoint analytics reports, we can run through what they all display.

Startup performance

This selection of reports looks at the startup performance, from pressing the button to a usable desktop. It then reviews this against an industry baseline to give an initial representation of how your devices and configuration compare.

Within here, you can drill down on:

- **Model performance**: All models within the tenant (minimum of 10 devices).
- **Device performance**: All devices within the tenant. This and the model performance also include drive type, which is an excellent way of viewing both the performance increases with an **SSD (Solid State Drive)/NVMe (nonvolatile memory express)** compared with an old spinning HDD (to help with any business cases), but it can also help spot any drives that may be beginning to fail.
- **Startup processes**: A list of all discovered startup processes, including the number of devices discovered and how much time they are adding to the startup.
- **Restart frequency**: This is a particularly useful one as it lists the cause of restarts as well as trends over the last 30 days. If you release a software or driver update, this would be a good place to check for any spikes in reboots that could be caused by that. You could also look at **Anomaly Detection** in **Advanced Endpoint analytics**, which we cover in *Chapter 14*.

After reviewing startup performance, we can now review application reliability.

Application reliability

This set of reports digs down to the application level and looks at application crashes. The initial screen shows the reliability score compared to the baseline, as well as the main offenders over the last 14 days.

The reports include the following:

- **App performance**: A look at all discovered applications, how many devices use them (and for how long), and then how many times they have crashed in the last 14 days. This is a useful report as it includes usage figures, so an application that has crashed often but is heavily used is less of a concern than one that is rarely used but crashes each time.
- **Model performance**: This looks at application performance per device model to look for trends in application crashes that could potentially be linked to hardware issues, particularly useful for your more intensive apps, such as **CAD (Computer-Aided Design)** or graphical packages.

- **Device performance**: This drills down even further to the device level and lists application crashes per machine, including the health status of the device itself. You may find this one useful when a user complains about device performance or application crashes. If you have one device with statistics that are considerably worse than others, it could also point to hardware issues.
- **OS versions performance**: A useful report when upgrading the OS. Use this to monitor performance after deploying to your preview and pilot rings to see if there is any obvious performance degradation before deploying to the larger estate. Similarly, a noticeable performance improvement may help when convincing users to upgrade.

Our next reports to review are **Work from anywhere** reports.

Work from anywhere

These reports mainly look at the cloud management of your devices, whether they are Intune joined (or co-managed) or Autopilot builds. However, there is one important report here that displays the readiness of your devices for Windows 11, looking at all of the hardware requirements.

The reports include the following:

- **Model performance**: A count of each model and the results of the cloud management and Windows compatibility. This is a quick way to review which of your models will not support Windows 11 and to obtain the number of devices that will need replacing. You can obtain exact numbers in the Windows report.
- **Device performance**: As per the previous report, but at the individual device level. This is probably of less use, though, as the next reports look at the settings individually.
- **Windows**: An all-important report that looks at every discovered device and lists compatibility with Windows 11. As well as a pass/fail status, it will also list the reason for the failure in case it is something that can be more easily resolved. The key columns here are the last two, so make sure you scroll across.
- **Cloud identity**: This will show devices and their management type (Microsoft Entra Joined or Microsoft Entra hybrid joined). Probably less useful than other reports.
- **Cloud management**: This displays the management tool for devices (Intune, Configuration Manager) as well as the compliance policy assigned. For a split environment, it can be a quick way to grab metrics or for basic troubleshooting.
- **Cloud provisioning**: This shows your devices and the Autopilot details associated. It does give slightly more information than the **Device Enrollment** screen and has filtering, which may be useful.

That completes the **Work from anywhere** reports. We can now look at **Resource performance** reports.

Resource performance

These two reports are for Windows 365 Cloud PCs to check how your assigned devices are running and whether you may need to increase the device spec with a higher license, or if the devices are underutilized, save money and run a lower license.

The available reports are as follows:

- **Model performance**: CPU and RAM score by device model. If you see one model struggling more, you may need to look at a license uplift across the estate.
- **Device performance**: This looks at each device so that you can look for any devices that may be struggling or underused and re-license as appropriate. To manage your costs, this is the one most worth keeping an eye on, as you can always scale up again if required. It is often best to start with a lower spec and see how the users manage, especially as Windows 365 runs on the Microsoft network, so performance on web-based applications will be significantly improved.

After reviewing the Windows 365 **Resource performance** reports, we now have another Windows 365 report: **Remoting connection**.

Battery Health

Obviously, only useful for estates with laptops, but critical for those, here, you can see the status of your batteries across the entire organization.

It includes the following reports:

- **Model performance**: Displays the battery performance per model (minimum of 10 required) so you can spot those with poorer batteries or quicker degradation.
- **Device performance**: Similar to the above, but on an individual device level.
- **OS Performance**: This looks at how the batteries are performing on different operating systems (minimum of 10 devices per OS). Probably less useful with the new wave of operating systems being similar underneath, but should there be an update causing issues, you can see it here.
- **Impact**: Probably the most useful report; shows which apps are causing the most battery drain.

That completes our review of endpoint analytics reports. Now, we can look at how to automate them.

How to do it...

All of the reports in **Endpoint analytics** run automatically on loading, but we can still look at how to automate them.

Automating the reports

As mentioned earlier, all of these reports run a similar `GET` request, so rather than creating numerous scripts, we can concentrate on creating a single script with a simple menu to select which report to run.

The first important thing is that it uses pagination, so we will again be using the `getallpagination` function, as used in other scripts. Some code blocks have been shortened for brevity; therefore, the full script, including the function, is available on GitHub at the following link: `https://github.com/PacktPublishing/Microsoft-Intune-Cookbook-Second-Edition/blob/main/Chapter-10/all-analytics-reports.ps1`.

Follow these steps to create a single script for all of the reports in **Endpoint analytics**:

1. As usual, we start with the output path:

```
$exportpath = "c:\temp\analytics-report.csv"
```

2. Then, we are going to create an array containing all available reports:

```
    $outputarray = @()
    $outputarray += "Startup Performance - Model Performance"
    $outputarray += "Startup Performance - Device Performance"
    $outputarray += "Startup Performance - Startup Processes"
```

3. Now, display the array in a `gridview` output with the all-important `-PassThru` parameter so that we can grab the output:

```
$selectedreport = $outputarray | Out-GridView -Title "Select a report to 
export" -PassThru
```

4. Next, we need to run a `SWITCH` command on the selected report to populate the URL:

```
switch ($selectedreport) {
    "Startup Performance - Model Performance" {
        $url = "https://graph.microsoft.com/beta/deviceManagement/
userExperienceAnalyticsDevicePerformance/
summarizeDevicePerformanceDevices(summarizeBy=microsoft.graph.userExperienc
```

```
eAnalyticsSummarizedBy'model')?dtFilter=all&`$expand=*"
    }
    "Startup Performance - Device Performance" {
        $url = "https://graph.microsoft.com/beta/deviceManagement/
userExperienceAnalyticsDevicePerformance?dtFilter=all"
    }
    "Startup Performance - Startup Processes" {
        $url = "https://graph.microsoft.com/beta/deviceManagement/
userExperienceAnalyticsDeviceStartupProcessPerformance?dtFilter=all"
    }
}
```

Note

Watch for the $ signs in the URLs, which are escaped with the ` backtick.

5. Grab the data from the URL:

```
$allanalytics = getallpagination -url $url
```

6. After the usual popup, either display or export the report data. We are also adding some logic here to deal with empty reports:

```
if ($result -eq [System.Windows.Forms.DialogResult]::OK) {
    # Export code here
    if ($null -eq $allanalytics) {
       write-host "Nothing to display"
    }
    else {
        $allanalytics | export-csv $exportpath
    }
} elseif ($result -eq [System.Windows.Forms.DialogResult]::Cancel) {
    # View code here
    if ($null -eq $allanalytics) {
       write-host "Nothing to display"
    }
    else {
    $allanalytics | Out-GridView
    }
}
```

That completes the automation of endpoint analytics reports.

Using Intune Data Warehouse with Power BI

Anyone experienced with Power BI will know that it is a very powerful reporting tool that adds a lot of extra functionality and the ability to customize what you can get out of the box with Intune.

Fortunately, you can use Power BI with **Intune Data Warehouse**, and, better still, there are preconfigured templates to get you started.

How to do it...

Follow these steps to configure Data Warehouse with your tenant:

1. Navigate to **Reports** and click on **Data warehouse**.
   On this screen, you can grab the URL for manual data ingestion, but in this example, we will use the preconfigured template instead.

   At the end of this section, we will include some links to useful blog posts and a video for more of a deep dive into the functionality.
2. For now, click on the **Get Power BI app** link.
3. In the **Intune Compliance (Data Warehouse)** application window, click **Get it now**.
4. This will transfer you to Power BI, and after a few minutes, it will display in your list of apps:

Figure 10.8 – Intune app

5. Click on the newly added application.
6. Now, click on **Compliance Overview**. This is using sample data, so do not be alarmed.
7. Click **Connect your data**.
8. On the **Connect to Intune Compliance (Data Warehouse)** screen, click **Next**, as we do not have any parameters in this application.
9. Set the **Privacy Level** type and click **Sign in and connect**.
10. When prompted, authenticate in the pop-up window (you may need to allow popups). After a minute, you will see the initial data that is pre-populated replaced with live data from your tenant.

Now your data is connected, you can manipulate it as required.

The following are useful links for getting started with Power BI and Intune Data Warehouse:

- `https://www.petervanderwoude.nl/post/super-easy-start-with-reporting-and-the-intune-data-warehouse/`
- `https://jannikreinhard.com/2022/07/10/build-powerbi-dashboard-based-on-intune-data-warehouse/`
- `https://www.youtube.com/watch?v=2ICPKRBIews`

By following the preceding steps, you have connected your Intune tenant to Data Warehouse.

Checking Windows updates via reporting

Windows Update reports are likely to be the most useful and most used reports within Intune, as tracking the status of Windows updates is key to security across the estate. We will start by looking at the built-in reports, and then, in the next recipe, will take things further and introduce Log Analytics for finer control.

Due to the extra selections required to generate these reports, the inputs do not lend themselves to automation, as it would be a similar number of textboxes and clicks to achieve the same result. Therefore, in this recipe, we will not cover automating them. If, however, this is of interest, it uses the same export/import `POST` requests as with many of the earlier reports here.

Getting ready

Within the Intune portal, click on **Reports**, then click **Windows updates**, and finally, click the **Reports** tab.

How to do it...

There are multiple reports available here, so we will start by looking at how to run them, and then we will cover what each report contains.

1. Select any of the reports available. In this case, we will use **Windows Feature Update Report**:

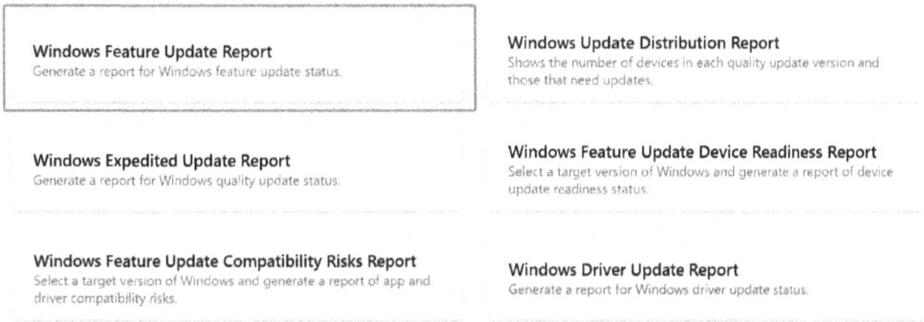

Figure 10.9 – Windows Update report options

2. In each report, you will have to make a selection to report on by clicking the blue text on the right-hand side. For this example, we need to click an update ring via the appropriate profile.
3. After making the selection, a **Generate report** button becomes available; click that.
4. You will be notified when the report is available to view.

Now we know how to run the reports, let us look at what each one displays:

- **Windows Feature Update Report**: As the name implies, when deploying feature updates such as 22H2, this will display the status of the update for all devices in the selected policy/ring.
- **Windows Update Distribution Report**: Quickly see how many devices you have on each quality update and which are outdated.
- **Windows Expedited Update Report**: Similar to the previous report, but for **Quality updates** (if configured, as these do need additional licensing).
- **Windows Feature Update Device Readiness Report**: This report also needs additional licensing and license verification enabled, which you can find at the following link: `https://learn.microsoft.com/en-gb/mem/intune/protect/windows-update-compatibility-reports#prerequisites`

  Once enabled, you can select a **target OS** version, and it will report the readiness state of your devices to receive the update. This is a very useful report to use when planning updates.
- **Windows Feature Update Compatibility Risks Report**: Another extremely useful report when planning updates. This one will list any applications or drivers that are not

compatible with the selected operating system. It also requires the same licensing and prerequisites as before.

- **Windows Driver Update Report**: If you are using the new driver update functionality, this will display the installation status of the selected driver across your estate.

There's more...

If you are licensed for **Windows Autopatch**, you also have additional reports available to you.

Navigate to **Reports** – **Windows Autopatch**, which contains the following:

- **Windows quality updates** – click **Reports** and you will find the following:
    - **Quality update status**: Displays all devices so you can quickly spot those that are outdated
    - **Quality update trending**: Shows a chart of the update status of all devices
    - **Hotpatch quality updates**: Similar to the above, but for hotpatch updates
- **Windows feature updates** – click **Reports** and you will find the following:
    - **Feature update status**: Displays all devices, the current OS, the target OS, the update status, and any alerts
    - **Feature update trending**: Similar to that for quality updates, a quick overview of the feature update status of your estate

Now that we have learned what is in the built-in Windows update reports, we can look at improving this further by utilizing Log Analytics.

Expanding Windows Update reporting

While the built-in Intune reports are excellent, we can take this one step further by leveraging Log Analytics to give us further data, manipulation, and real-time analytics.

Getting ready

For this recipe, we will need to create a Log Analytics workspace within Azure (there is no charge for Windows Update data, though).

How to do it...

Follow these steps to configure Windows Update for Business reports:

1. Navigate to `https://portal.azure.com` and search for **Log Analytics workspaces**.
2. Click **Create**.
3. Select your **Subscription** type and either select or create a new **Resource group** type.
4. Then, name your workspace and click **Review and Create**.

5. If all looks OK, click **Create**.
6. Back in the Azure portal, click **Monitor**.
7. Then, click on **View** under **Workbooks**.
8. Scroll down to **Insights** and select **Windows Update for Business Reports**.
9. Click **Get Started**.
10. Select your subscription and the workspace we created earlier, and then click **Save settings**.
11. Click **Save** to confirm.
12. You will be notified when this has been completed.

After a few days (provided the devices are switched on with an active internet connection), the workbook will contain data that you can manipulate and export.

To find out more, check out this Microsoft documentation: `https://learn.microsoft.com/en-gb/windows/deployment/update/wufb-reports-workbook`

These steps have onboarded the tenant into Windows Update for Business reports.

Exporting diagnostics to Azure

The final recipe in this chapter also uses Azure, but this time to store Intune logs and diagnostic data in a variety of locations, listed as follows:

- A Log Analytics workspace
- Azure Blob storage
- An event hub – you can learn more about this at the following URL: `https://learn.microsoft.com/en-gb/azure/azure-monitor//partners?WT.mc_id=Portal-Microsoft_Azure_Monitoring`
- A partner solution – learn more about this at the following URL: `https://learn.microsoft.com/en-us/azure/partner-solutions/overview`

In this example, we are going to use a Log Analytics workspace as it offers a greater feature set than Blob storage.

Getting ready

Again, for this one, we are going to need a Log Analytics workspace. This one will incur costs, though, so make sure you set up a cost warning if you deploy and then forget you have done so.

In the Azure portal, select **Log Analytics workspace** and click **Create new**. Create your workspace and make a note of the name.

In this example, we have created a workspace called `intunealerts` within the `rg-loganalytics` resource group.

Now that we have our workspace, we can configure the diagnostics to export into it.

How to do it...

Follow these steps to configure the diagnostics to export:

1. Back in the Intune console, click **Reports** and then **Diagnostic Settings**.
2. Click **Add diagnostic setting**.
3. On the next screen, you can pick what to send to the workspace. Remember that there are data charges, so decide how much data you want in there and weigh this up against the potential costs. You can include the following data in your workspace:
    - **Audit Logs**: Anything amended or added within the Intune portal, such as new policies, deleted policies, and so on
    - **Operational Logs**: User and device enrollment, as well as non-compliant devices
    - **DeviceComplianceOrg**: Reports on device compliance and lists non-compliant devices
    - **Devices**: Device inventory and status

    You can find out more about exporting Intune logs here: `https://learn.microsoft.com/en-us/mem/intune/fundamentals/review-logs-using-azure-monitor`
4. After selecting the reports, check **Send to Log Analytics workspace**, and then select the workspace created earlier.
5. Once selected, click **Save**.
6. After a while, your logs will appear within **Log Analytics** under **Logs**.

That completes the recipe for configuring Intune diagnostic data exports.

Join us on Discord

For discussions around the book and to connect with your peers, join us on Discord at `packt.link/discordcloud` or scan the QR code below:

11

Packaging Your Windows Applications

We have configured our Windows policies and enrolled our devices, but in most environments, we are going to need to deploy some applications.

In this chapter, we are going to run through the different application types that are available and how to deploy them into your environment.

When managing Windows devices, applications are critical, and packaging them correctly will ensure a smooth experience for end users. By following this chapter, you will learn how to package and deploy applications to your devices using the modern methods supported by Intune.

In this chapter, we will cover the following recipes:

- Using the Microsoft Store integration
- Packaging into MSIX
- Packaging Win32 applications
- Managing app supersedence and dependencies
- Deploying Office applications
- Updating Office applications
- Windows app protection

Chapter materials

Before starting, we will not be covering **MSI line-of-business** applications, as it is best practice to wrap these into a Win32 application, which is extremely straightforward. There are a couple of reasons for this:

- MSI line-of-business applications execute using the standard `msiexec` service, whereas Win32 uses the **Intune Management Extension** (**IME**) to deploy. This means that neither is aware of the other, which can lead to clashes during Autopilot provisioning, where the installer service is busy on the other application.
- Win32 applications give significantly more functionality around requirements, detection, and supersedence, none of which are available with an MSI line-of-business deployment.

Assigning applications

We also need to look at assignment options as they are the same across all app types. We have the following three options:

- **Required**: This will force an install and will only appear in the Company Portal under **Installed Applications**.
- **Available for enrolled devices**: This displays the application within the Company Portal for user self-service.
- **Uninstall**: This removes the application.

Assignments depend on the application, but as a general rule, if the application is not required across the estate, configure Microsoft Entra groups for both installation and uninstallation. This gives added flexibility after deployment and is especially useful if you need to quickly remove an application, as the group is already assigned and ready to use.

During assignment, you can also specify an installation deadline, a grace period for any restarts, and the ability to display or suppress the install/uninstall notifications.

A further consideration is around *user* versus *device* context, especially when deploying Win32 applications.

System context

Applications in the system context are run via the system user (you can test this on a standard device with the `psexec` tool by running the `psexec.exe -I -s cmd.exe` command). Your installations will have full administrative permissions to everything, but will not have user profiles. You can access the logged-in user with PowerShell scripts such as the one at `https://andrewstaylor.com/2023/11/07/enumerating-the-logged-on-user-when-running-as-system-with-azure-ad-entra-joined-devices/`.

You can also use `serviceui.exe` to provide user-level interaction with scripts and applications running at the system level.

In terms of paths and environmental variables, they are as follows:

- `Temp` points to `C:\Windows\Temp`
- Local app data: `C:\WINDOWS\system32\config\systemprofile\AppData\Local`
- App data: `C:\WINDOWS\system32\config\systemprofile\AppData\Roaming`
- User profile: `C:\users\Public`

This is most suitable for your standard Win32 applications, which you would traditionally require someone with elevated rights to install.

User context

These installations run at the level of the logged-in user, so they can only access files and folders the user can access during their day-to-day work, including the user profile and HKEY's current user registry hive. If your users do not have administrative rights, there is no access to program files, Windows, or anything that requires elevation.

In terms of paths and variables, they are as follows:

- `Temp` points to `C:\users\username\AppData\Local\Temp`
- Local app data: `C:\users\username\AppData\Local`
- App data: `C:\users\username\AppData\Roaming`
- User profile: `C:\users\username`

This is best suited for applications that target the user context, such as Teams, Visual Studio Code, OneDrive, which lives in `%LocalAppData%`, MSIX, AppX, and some MSI installers. Store apps also fall into this category as these are AppX or MSIX packages, although these can now be deployed in the system context, as covered in the first recipe (*Using the Microsoft Store integration*).

Note

If you are wrapping MSI into Win32, you might come across occasions where the MSI itself is hard-coded and forces the user context. If you find one of these, you can either edit the MSI with something such as Orca or wrap it with an installation script, after which it will unlock the option to choose.

Technical requirements

For this chapter, you will need a modern web browser and a PowerShell code editor such as Visual Studio Code or PowerShell ISE.

All the scripts that will be referenced can be found here: `https://github.com/PacktPublishing/Microsoft-Intune-Cookbook-Second-Edition/tree/main/Chapter-11`.

If you wish to test the policies, you will need a corporate-managed device running each device platform for testing. For Linux, it will need to be running Ubuntu.

Using the Microsoft Store integration

We start by looking at the **Microsoft Store integration**. This is how Windows applications such as Notepad and Calculator are deployed and updated.

Note

Store apps that are deployed via Intune will continue to receive updates even if the Windows Store is blocked for end users via a policy.

Fortunately, this change has also reduced the number of steps to deploy an application!

How to do it...

Follow these steps to deploy your first Windows Store application:

1. To start, click **Apps** and then **Windows**.
2. Click **+Create**.
3. In the flyout, select **Microsoft Store app (new)** (it may just be called **Microsoft Store app** in the future), and click **Select**.
4. Click **Search the Microsoft Store app (new)**.
5. In the flyout, search for the application you are looking for.

> **Note**
>
> It is worth noting that, due to Intune being extensively used in education, it will only search for applications with a rating suitable for children, so some apps may not be displayed.
>
> For these applications, find them in the Microsoft Store online and make a note of the app ID (highlighted with a red rectangle in the following screenshot):
>
> 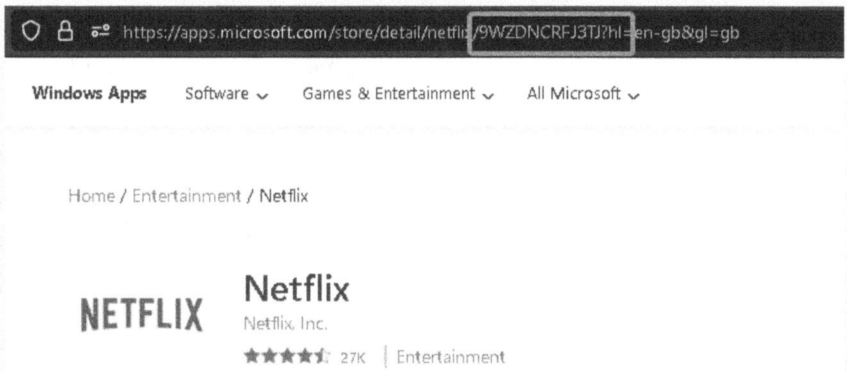
>
>
> *Figure 11.1 – App Store app ID*
>
> Now, search within Intune for that ID:
>
> 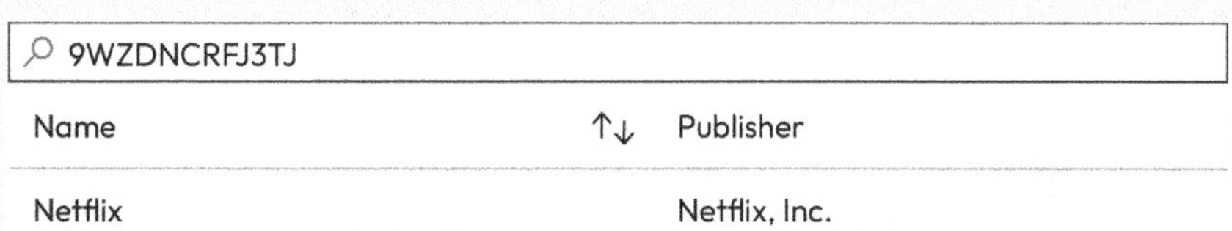
>
>
> *Figure 11.2 – Search by app ID*

6. In this example, we will keep things simple and deploy **Company Portal**, as we will need this for the demonstration later. Click **Select**.
   You will notice that the type is listed as **UWP**. This is a **Universal Windows Platform** application (APPX, MSIX, and so on), which means it is a traditional store app.

   There are also a handful of Win32 apps available that can be pushed out this way instead of being packaged into a Win32 `intunewin` application.

7. The details will now be prepopulated for you (except the logo, at the time of writing). If you want to add a logo, click **Select image** and upload one.

You can edit any of the information on here, as this is what will be displayed to the user if they self-service deploy.

Among the options available, these three are worth paying attention to:

- **Show this as a featured app in Company Portal**: This will pin the application to the home screen of the **Apps** page within **Company Portal**.
- **Install behavior**: If you want to block ESP until this app has been installed, change this to **System**; otherwise, **User** will work fine.

> **Note**
>
> Mixing **User** and **System** in the same application can cause issues in your environment, so make sure you select them early in your deployments.

- **Category**: If you have a large number of applications available, categorizing them may assist you when your users are finding the correct app to deploy.

8. Once you have confirmed the details, click **Next**.
9. Click **Next** on the **Scope tags** page.
10. Now, let's look at the assignment, which we covered at the start of this chapter. This application is one we want all users to have installed, so we are going to add the **Intune Users** group as a **Required** installation. Once configured, click **Next**.
11. Finally, check that everything looks correct and click **Create**.

With that, we have deployed a Microsoft Store app using the UI.

Automating it

When automating the deployment of store apps, we have to replicate the functionality of the GUI. So, while the actual deployment is a straightforward JSON request, we have to find the application details with which to populate. Follow this script to automate the deployment of **Company Portal**:

1. The first thing we need to do is set the application we are looking for and our install scope, as well as the assignment group ID:

```
$appname = "Company Portal"
$scope = "user" ##Can be user or system
$groupid = "000-000-000-000"
```

2. Then, we need to search the store for that application and return the details:

```
$storeSearchUrl = "https://storeedgefd.dsx.mp.microsoft.com/v9.0/
manifestSearch"
$body = @{
    Query = @{
        KeyWord   = $appName
        MatchType = "Substring"
    }
} | ConvertTo-Json
$appSearch = Invoke-RestMethod -Uri $storeSearchUrl -Method POST -
ContentType 'application/json' -body $body
$exactApp = $appSearch.Data | Where-Object { $_.PackageName -eq $appName }
```

   This creates a JSON array with the query to pass to the store, where we are looking for our app name. Then, we grab the output and restrict it to just the application we are looking for.

3. Now, we need to grab the application information by adding the **Package Identifier** to a store URL:

```
$appUrl = "https://storeedgefd.dsx.mp.microsoft.com/v9.0/packageManifests/
{0}" -f $exactApp.PackageIdentifier
```

4. Running a `GET` request will return an array containing all of the application information:

```
$app = Invoke-RestMethod -Uri $appUrl -Method GET
```

5. We can grab the values that are returned with the application details:

```
$appId = $app.Data.PackageIdentifier
$appInfo = $app.Data.Versions[-1].DefaultLocale
$appInstaller = $app.Data.Versions[-1].Installers
```

6. One advantage of scripting is that we can also grab the image directly from the Microsoft Store by grabbing the image on the store web page using the

System.Net.WebClient functionality. Then, we can download and convert the file into Base64 format:

```
$imageUrl = "https://storeedgefd.dsx.mp.microsoft.com/v9.0/products/$
($appId)?market=US&locale=en-US&deviceFamily=Windows.Desktop"
$image = Invoke-RestMethod -Uri $imageUrl -Method GET -ContentType
'application/json'
$imgurl = $image.payload.images[3].url
$wc = New-Object System.Net.WebClient
$wc.DownloadFile($imgurl, "./temp.jpg")
$base64string = [Convert]::ToBase64String([IO.File]::ReadAllBytes('./
temp.jpg'))
```

7. As the details include escape characters, we want to tidy up before we populate our JSON. You can also set `Featured` to `$true` here if required:

```
$appdescription = ($appInfo.Shortdescription).ToString()
$appdescription2 = $appdescription.replace("`n"," ").replace("`r","
").replace("\n"," ").replace("\\n"," ")
$appdeveloper = $appInfo.Publisher
$appdisplayName = $appInfo.packageName
$appinformationUrl = $appInfo.PublisherSupportUrl
$apprunAsAccount = $scope
$appisFeatured = $false
$apppackageIdentifier = $appId
$appprivacyInformationUrl = $appInfo.PrivacyUrl
$apppublisher = $appInfo.publisher
```

8. Populate the JSON and send the `POST` request to the `MobileApps` part of Graph:

```
$deployUrl = "https://graph.microsoft.com/beta/deviceAppManagement/
mobileApps"
$json = @"
{
    "@odata.type": "#microsoft.graph.winGetApp",
    "categories": [],
    "description": "$appdescription2",
    "developer": "$appdeveloper",
    "displayName": "$appdisplayName",
    "informationUrl": "$appinformationUrl",
```

```
    "installExperience": {
        "runAsAccount": "$apprunAsAccount"
    },
    "isFeatured": false,
    "largeIcon": {
        "@odata.type": "#microsoft.graph.mimeContent",
        "type": "string",
        "value": "$base64string"
        },
    "notes": "",
    "owner": "",
    "packageIdentifier": "$apppackageIdentifier",
    "privacyInformationUrl": "$appprivacyInformationUrl",
    "publisher": "$apppublisher",
    "repositoryType": "microsoftStore",
    "roleScopeTagIds": []
}
"@
$appDeploy = Invoke-mggraphrequest -uri $deployUrl -Method POST -Body $json
-ContentType "application/JSON"
```

9. The assignment uses fairly typical JSON with a few added options for deadline, notification, and restart grace periods:

```
$appdeployid = $appDeploy.id
$JSON = @"
{
    "mobileAppAssignments": [
        {
            "@odata.type": "#microsoft.graph.mobileAppAssignment",
            "intent": "Required",
            "settings": {
                "@odata.type":
"#microsoft.graph.winGetAppAssignmentSettings",
                "installTimeSettings": null,
                "notifications": "showAll",
                "restartSettings": null
            },
            "target": {
                "@odata.type": "#microsoft.graph.groupAssignmentTarget",
                "groupId": "$groupid"
```

```
                }
            }
        ]
    }
"@
$uri = "https://graph.microsoft.com/Beta/deviceAppManagement/mobileApps/
$appdeployid/assign"
Invoke-MgGraphRequest -Uri $uri -Method Post -Body $JSON -ContentType
"application/json"
```

That completes this recipe on deploying a Microsoft Store application in Intune.

Packaging into MSIX

MSIX operates by monitoring an application installation, grabbing any changes to the filesystem, registry, and so on, and then wrapping them into a single file that can be installed at the user level. One advantage of MSIX is that you can use it as **AppAttach** on Azure Virtual Desktop environments to make applications available on a per-user level rather than having to install it directly onto the host machine in a multi-user environment.

> Note
>
> An MSIX can be reverted by the end user; do not package any applications that have a database included, as reverting will wipe any additions that have been made. Client-server apps are fine, but not those with databases built into them.

Getting ready

There are some prerequisites for MSIX packages:

- **Code signing certificate**: All packages have to be signed before deployment. You have two options here: you can either purchase a public code signing certificate, which will be trusted by all devices automatically, or you can create a self-signing certificate and deploy it to your devices either via a **certificate authority** (**CA**) or using Intune. If you are using Intune, navigate to **Tenant administration** and click on **Connectors** and **Tokens**.
  Within **Windows enterprise certificate**, select your certificate and upload it.
- **Packaging machine**: As MSIX monitors an installation, you will need a virtual machine to package on. Ideally, this should be as clear as possible to avoid any additional

processes adding themselves to your final package. Make sure you enable snapshots/checkpoints as well so that you can quickly reuse them for the next package.

If you have Hyper-V available on a Windows 10 or 11 machine, you can use **Quick Create**, which will configure the machine for you:

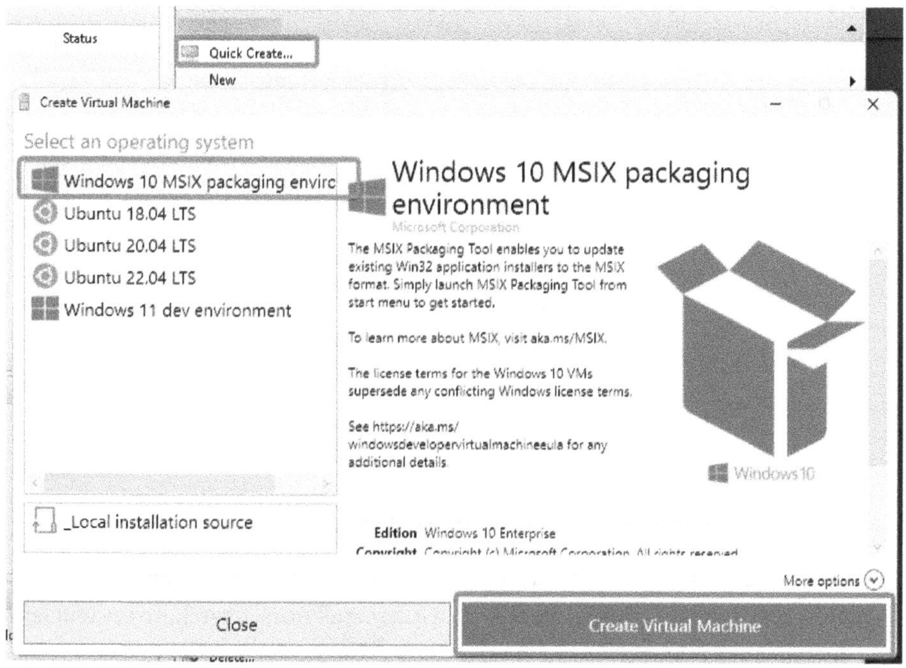

Figure 11.3 – Create Virtual Machine

Now that we have our prerequisites in place, we can start the recipe.

How to do it...

We will start by packaging the application itself and then look at deploying it.

Packaging

Now that we have a packaging machine and a certificate, we can run through the packaging and deployment process. In this example, we will use Notepad++. Follow these steps to package your first MSIX:

1. Start **MSIX Packaging Tool** and click **Application Package**.
2. Select **Create package on this computer** and click **Next**.
3. Your machine will run some checks. Disable anything suggested by ticking the checkbox next to the item that has been flagged and clicking **Disable selected** (see *Figure 11.4*) for the best packaging experience. Then, click **Next**:

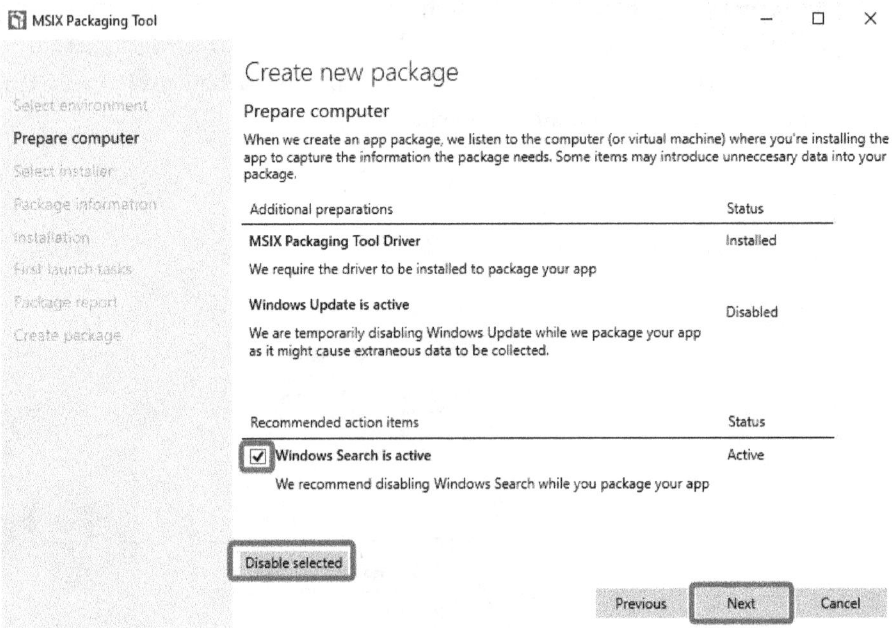

Figure 11.4 – Create new package

4. If you know the exact installation commands, you can enter them on the next screen. However, in this example, we will do a full install from scratch, so we will leave the installer boxes empty.

   We need to sign our application here.

5. Select **Sign with a certificate (.pfx)**, point at the certificate you created, and enter the password.

> **Note**
>
> The **Time stamp server URL** field is important. If you leave this blank, when your certificate expires, you will need to renew your packages with an updated certificate.
>
> If you specify a timestamp server, so long as the certificate was valid when the application was created and stamped, it will remain valid after the certificate has expired.
>
> One free server is `https://ca.signfiles.com/TSAServer.aspx`.

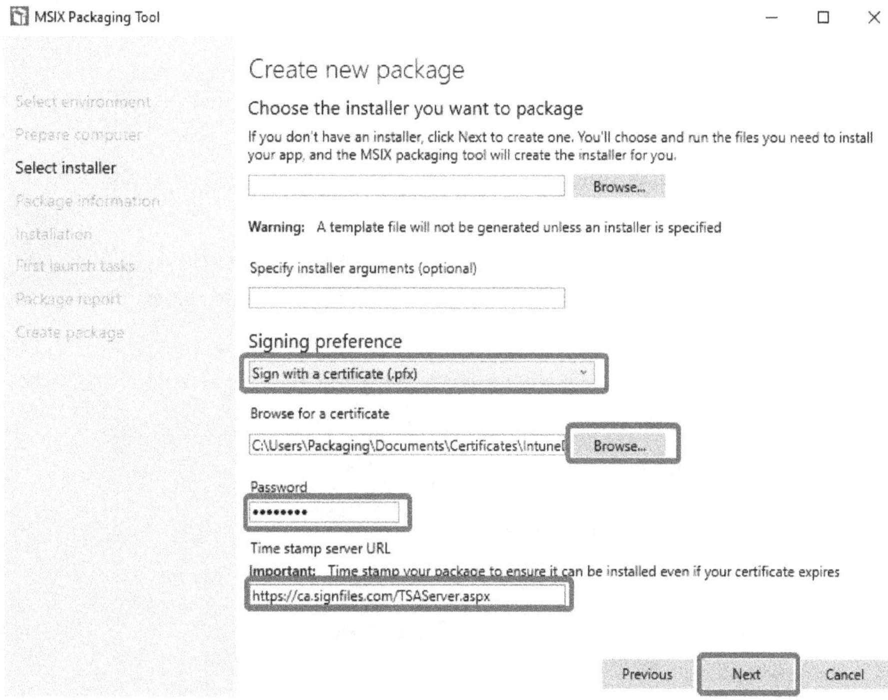

Figure 11.5 – The Select installer screen

6. After filling in the details, as shown in the previous screenshot, click **Next**.
7. On the next screen (**Package information**), you need to enter the package details. As a naming convention, app name, platform, and version are usually a good start (for example, `Notepad++_x64_8.5.8_001`). Enter **Package name**, **Package display name**, and **Package description** details; these will be displayed in **Company Portal**. Also, choose your publisher display name and version. Then, click **Next**.
8. On the **Create new package** screen, install your application. If it needs to be restarted, click the button marked **Restart machine**; the sequencer will reload on startup.
   If possible, it is a good idea to turn off auto updates, as users can revert a package, which will wipe out any updates.
9. Once installed, click **Next**.
10. The next screen shows the executables that have been detected. Running the main installer will detect any first-run modifications so that it can disable updates, hints and tips, and so on.
    You can also remove any stubs to executables you do not want users to see, such as `uninstall.exe`.

If any are missing, you can click **Browse** and manually add them here. Once you have set this up, click **Next**.

11. As this is the last monitoring step, you need to confirm that you want to stop monitoring the device here. Click **Yes, move on**.
12. If the sequencer has detected any services, you can choose to exclude them here. Once you are done, click **Next**.
13. Finally, select a location to save the package and click **Create**. You can also access the package editor here, should you wish to check the files and registry keys or make further amendments.

You can find out more about the package editor here: `https://learn.microsoft.com/en-us/windows/msix/packaging-tool/package-editor`.

Now, we need to take the MSIX file and deploy it.

Deploying our MSIX package

Now that we have packaged the application, we can deploy it to Intune:

1. Within Intune, select **Apps** and then **Windows**.
2. Click **+ Create**.
3. Choose **Line of business app** and click **Select**.
4. Click **Select app package file** and pick the MSIX file you created in the previous subsection. Then, click **OK**.
5. Amend any details and add an image if required, then click **Next**.
6. Click **Next** on the **Scope tags** page.
7. This is an application that lends itself to self-service, so we will set up **Required** and **Uninstall** groups for those who need or do not need the application, and then make them available for everyone else. You can also switch between installing in the user and device context here. Once configured, click **Next**.
8. Finally, check that everything looks correct and click **Create**.

That completes this recipe on packaging an MSIX application. Now, we can look at Win32 applications.

Packaging Win32 applications

Packaging into Win32 will be your primary method of application deployment, so this recipe is an important one to follow.

Getting ready

Before we do any packaging, we need to keep our application source code tidy so that we can easily work out what is what when we need to update that weird and wonderful application in two years!

> **Note**
>
> The packaging tool will grab *every* file in the `Source` directory you point it to, so make sure that the directory *only has source files in it*. If you point it at your `Downloads` folder, for example, you will find yourself wondering why a 2 MB installer is showing as 45 GB when packaged!

The packaging tool creates an `intunewin` file, which is effectively an encrypted ZIP file that uploads with a manifest into Azure Blob storage. When installing, your computer downloads, decrypts, and runs the installation specified.

This is entirely personal preference, but this folder layout works well:

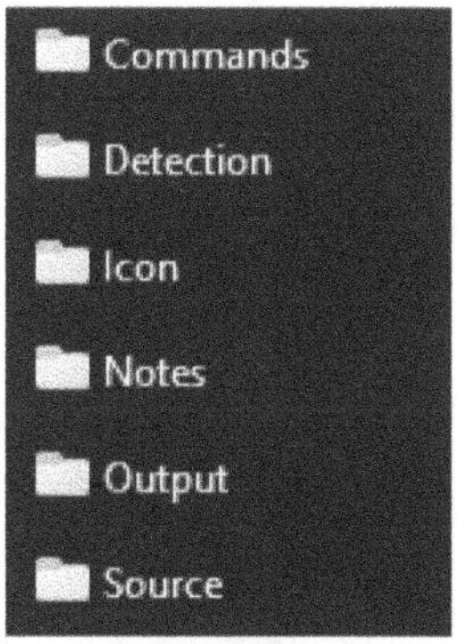

Figure 11.6 – Recommended folder structure

The `Source` folder contains the `raw`, `installer`, and `config` files, and more.

`Output` is where we will store the `intunewin` file.

The rest are pretty self-explanatory.

Once you have added your `intunewin` file to Intune, you cannot retrieve it, so always keep a copy of any `Source` files.

Now, we need to look at the different ways of creating an installer.

Calling MSI/exe directly

If it is a simple install, we could simply package up the MSI or executable on its own and then, in Intune, set the `install` command to run the file:

```
msiexec.exe /i myinstaller.msi /qn
myinstaller.exe /silent
```

This is perfectly acceptable, but does not allow for any customization pre- or post-installation.

It is also worth noting that if the MSI has been written to install in the user context, Intune may force it to do the same, and you will notice that the context is grayed out. If you want one of these to install in the system context, you will need to edit the MSI or wrap it using a method.

Batch script

While PowerShell is infinitely more powerful and modern, using a batch script will still work when you are packaging. If this is what you are more comfortable with, that is fine. In the long term, look at moving to PowerShell or **PowerShell Application Deployment Toolkit** (**PSADT**, covered later in this recipe), but for the time being, this will be more than adequate.

Simply create your installation batch script. When packaging, this is your install file:

```
For example:
rem Delete file
del c:\temp\myfile.txt
rem Stop Service
net stop myservice
rem Install App
my-installer.exe /verysilent /allusers /noreboot
rem Delete Shortcut
del %public%\desktop\myshortcut.lnk
```

Let's cover a few handy hints if you are using a batch script.

In a command prompt, type `SET` to get a list of variables on the machine. These can be referenced within `%`, as we have done with the public user environment, `%public%`.

If you want to reference the current directory, use `%~dp0` but *do not* add a backslash as it will look at the root of the machine drive rather than the launch location:

```
%~dp0myinstaller.exe
```

Within Intune, simply set your install command to `install.bat` or whatever you have called your batch script.

PowerShell script

PowerShell scripts take installation one step further, as you have greater control over the machine (and for something complex, it is just easier). You can put logic in and look at the underlying hardware – anything is available at this point.

As an example, for a PowerShell script to run an MSI, you must run the following code:

```
    $MSIArguments = @(
    "/i"
    ('"{0}"' -f $filelocation)
    "/qn"
    "/norestart"
    "/L*v"
)
Start-Process "msiexec.exe" -ArgumentList $MSIArguments -Wait -NoNewWindow
```

Of course, when using PowerShell, you can also add/remove features for apps that do not have an MSI.

Here, we are using .NET as an example:

```
Enable-WindowsOptionalFeature -Online -FeatureName 'NetFx3' -Source .\sxs\ -
NoRestart -LimitAccess
```

The installation command within Intune would be as follows:

```
powershell.exe -ExecutionPolicy Bypass -file myinstaller.ps1
```

Note

You can now select a PowerShell script when creating an application to split the script from the `intunewin` file. This gives you greater control over smaller changes and updates without having to repackage the whole installer each time:

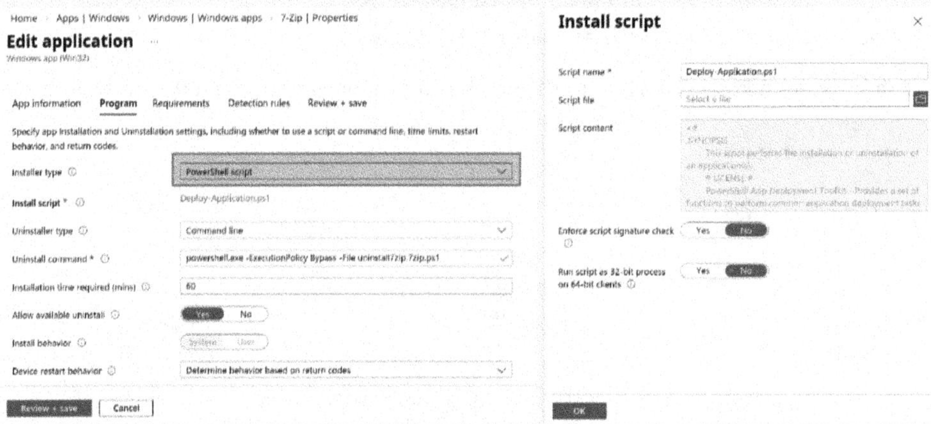

Figure 11.7 – PowerShell Script in Win32 apps

PSADT

PSADT (`https://psappdeploytoolkit.com/`) is a very powerful tool that leverages PowerShell but gives many built-in functions to take this process one step further.

For example, you could check whether applications are running and prompt the user to close them, run a particular file in the user context and have the rest in the system context, or add pre/post-installation commands.

A full list of the functions can be found at `https://psappdeploytoolkit.com/#functions-logic`.

Note

If you are deploying via Intune and you want user interaction, you will need to use the `ServiceUI` executable from the **Microsoft Deployment Tools** (**MDT**) toolkit with PSADT version 3. With v4, this functionality is included.

When deploying a PSADT packaged application, for user interaction, the install command would be as follows (v3):

```
.\ServiceUI.exe -Process:explorer.exe Deploy-Application.exe
```

Or it would be the following for v4:

```
%SystemRoot%\System32\WindowsPowerShell\v1.0\PowerShell.exe -ExecutionPolicy
Bypass -NoProfile -File Invoke-AppDeployToolkit.ps1
```

> **Note**
>
> If we just call `powershell.exe` in our install command, that will default to the 32-bit version and therefore install in the 32-bit context. For native 64-bit, we are specifically launching the PowerShell executable (you can also replace `System32` with `sysnative`).

Now that we have covered the different ways we can install an application, we can look at packaging one.

How to do it...

Now that we have our source files and installer, we need to package them using `IntuneWinAppUtil` from Microsoft, which is available here: `https://github.com/microsoft/Microsoft-Win32-Content-Prep-Tool/blob/master/IntuneWinAppUtil.exe`.

This takes the source files, encrypts and compresses them, and gives us our `intunewin` file.

Follow these steps to package your application into the `intunewin` format:

1. First, we must load the application (for ease, we are using 7-Zip). We will be prompted with **Please specify the source folder**. Point it to the `Source` folder we created earlier, which contains your installation media and setup file.
2. Then, enter the installation file's name (setup file).
3. Finally, tell `IntuneWinAppUtil` where to put the `intunewin` file (the `Output` folder).

After packaging the application, we need to find out how Intune can detect that the installation has been completed successfully.

Application detection

Before adding to Intune, it is worth grabbing the detection type so that it knows that the installation has been completed correctly. We can follow these steps to find our detection and then configure it within Intune:

1. For most applications, we can use Windows Sandbox as a temporary machine to look for a file or registry key to use for detection. However, if you have an MSI application, you can quickly grab the product code using this PowerShell script:

```
$path = "PATH TO MSI"
$comObjWI = New-Object -ComObject WindowsInstaller.Installer
$MSIDatabase =
$comObjWI.GetType().InvokeMember("OpenDatabase","InvokeMethod",$Null,
$comObjWI,@($Path,0))
$Query = "SELECT Value FROM Property WHERE Property = 'ProductCode'"
$View = $MSIDatabase.GetType().InvokeMember("OpenView","InvokeMethod",
$null,$MSIDatabase,($Query))
$View.GetType().InvokeMember("Execute", "InvokeMethod", $null, $View,
$null)
$Record = $View.GetType().InvokeMember("Fetch","InvokeMethod",$null,$View,
$null)
$Value = $Record.GetType().InvokeMember("StringData","GetProperty",$null,
$Record,1)
write-host "Your MSI code is $Value" -ForegroundColor Green
```

   This script will output the MSI code you can use for both detection and uninstallation.

2. Now that we have our file, we need to add it to Intune. Within the Intune portal, click on **Apps** and then **Windows**. Then, click **Add**.
3. In the flyout, select **Windows app (Win32)** and click **Select**.
4. Click on the blue **Select app package file** text.
5. Now, browse to the `Intunewin` file we created earlier and click **OK**.
6. As we have packaged an executable, it will only populate the filename, so, at a minimum, we need to add a publisher, but ideally a name, description, version, and logo. Once populated, click **Next**.
7. We have a few options to set on this next screen. First, populate the `Install` and `Uninstall` commands, depending on how the application was packaged. This could be a batch or PowerShell script, or simply point to the file. If the application is an MSI, both fields should auto-populate for you.

8. You can also specify how long before the installation times out as failed. This is more useful for larger or more complex applications. For 7-Zip, the default of 60 minutes will be more than adequate.
9. **Allow available uninstall** is for applications that are available for users to self-service install within **Company Portal**. Setting this to **Yes** will also give them the ability to uninstall the application themselves.
10. The install behavior for this application needs to be set to **System**. However, some apps may be user-based, so change this as required.
11. You can also specify what restart action to take if necessary.
12. Finally, if the application has unusual return codes, add them here. Generally, the default codes will be fine.
13. Once set, click **Next**.
14. Now, we need to set the minimum requirements for the application to be installed. If a device does not meet these requirements, the installation will not continue.
    You can specify finer details at the device level, including RAM and processor speed, for some more complex applications such as CAD software.

    If you want to take this further, you can also add a custom requirements script. For example, if you only want to install on laptops (for a VPN client), you could query the device chassis using **Windows Management Interface** (**WMI**) and query that here.
15. In the case of 7-Zip, we just want to check that the machine is 64-bit, as that is the version we have packaged. Once configured, click **Next**.
16. The next step is to configure the detection rule, which is what Intune will use to check whether the application has been installed correctly.
    We have a few options here:
    - **MSI**: For any straight MSI files, this will auto-populate. You can also add the MSI **globally unique identifier** (**GUID**), which will look for the presence of that ID.
    - **File**: Look for a specific file, file date, file version, or file size (these are useful for upgrades). For example, you could point it to the executable that is launched. Note the 32/64-bit option here; if you set it to **Yes**, it will look in the 32-bit context on 64-bit machines (such as `Program Files (x86)`).

- **Registry**: Look for a specific key, string, version, or integer in the registry. The same applies to 32/64-bit.
- **Requirements script**: This lets you look for almost anything, be it a running service or a combination of different methods. Here, the key is for a successful detection, so the script must exit with an exit code of `0`. An example of this is shown here:

```
$service = get-service -name "MozillaMaintenance"
if ($service.Status -eq "Running") {
    write-output "MozillaMaintenance detected and running, exiting"
    exit 0
}
else {
   exit 1
}
```

For 7-Zip, we are going to look for the presence of the 7z executable using a **File Rule** type with the path and file set accordingly.

17. Once we have configured the detection, click **Next**.
18. We will cover **Dependencies** and **Supersedence** in the next recipe, so we can press **Next** on both of these for now.
19. Click **Next** on the **Scope tags** page.
20. Now, we need to assign the application. As this is free software, once again, we will set **Available for enrolled devices** for **All users** (or **All devices**), but with specific groups for **Required** and **Uninstall** for better overall management. Once configured, click **Next**:

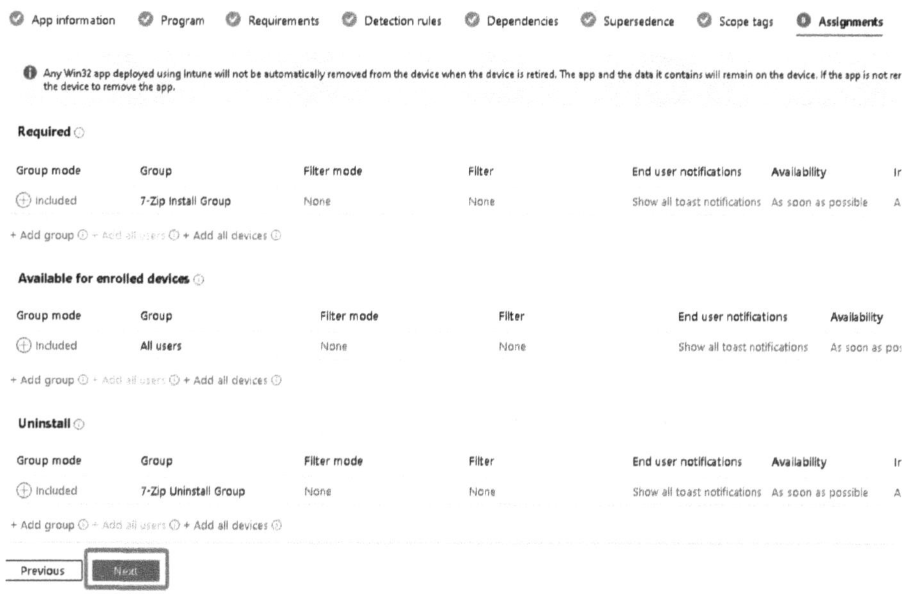

Figure 11.8 – Assignments

21. Give everything a final check and click **Create**.

With that, we have demonstrated how to create and upload a Win32 application to Microsoft Intune.

Automating it

Now that we know how to add an application in the GUI, let's look at automating this process using PowerShell and Graph.

This is a particularly complicated one to automate as it creates an application stub in Intune, then uploads the `intunewin` file and connects them.

Grab the script from this book's GitHub repository (`https://github.com/PacktPublishing/Microsoft-Intune-Cookbook-Second-Edition/blob/main/Chapter-11/create-deploy-win32.ps1`). Here, we will run through what it is doing and what each function runs rather than displaying the whole script:

1. We start by setting a temporary directory that we can use to store files and scripts (we will create a sub-folder later):

```
$path = "c:\temp\"
```

2. Specify the app name (used in the description) and the app ID (used in the group short name):

```
$appname = "Remote Help"
$appid = "RemoteHelp"
```

3. Now, we must specify the URL to the file we wish to package and where we wish to save it:

```
$appdownloadurl = "https://aka.ms/downloadremotehelp"
$appoutput = $apppath + "\remotehelpinstaller.exe"
```

4. The detection rule looks for a file, so we need to specify what we are looking for. If in doubt, install it on a temporary machine such as Windows Sandbox and install the application to check the file paths:

```
$filepath = "C:\Program Files\Remote Help\RemoteHelp.exe"
```

5. Next, set the `install` and `uninstall` strings; these will be used on the client device:

```
$installstring = "&.\remotehelpinstaller.exe /quiet acceptTerms=1"
$uninstallstring = "&.\remotehelpinstaller.exe /uninstall /quiet
acceptTerms=1"
```

6. Finally, we need to download the `IntuneWinAppUtil` executable:

```
$intuneapputilurl = "https://github.com/microsoft/Microsoft-Win32-Content-
Prep-Tool/raw/master/IntuneWinAppUtil.exe"
$intuneapputiloutput = $path + "IntuneWinAppUtil.exe"
Invoke-WebRequest -Uri $intuneapputilurl -OutFile $intuneapputiloutput
```

Now that we have set our variables, we can run through creating, deploying, and assigning the application:

1. First, we need to create a temporary location for the files:

```
$apppath = "$path\$appid"
new-item -Path $apppath -ItemType Directory -Force
```

2. Download the installer:

```
Invoke-WebRequest -Uri $appdownloadurl -OutFile $appoutput
```

3. Create the `Install` and `Uninstall` groups. This involves calling a function (`new-aadgroups`) that populates the JSON and sends a `POST` request via `Invoke-MgGraphRequest`.

   The `GroupType` variable is used to distinguish the group name and description:

```
$installgroup = new-aadgroups -appid $appid -appname $appname -grouptype
"Install"
$uninstallgroup = new-aadgroups -appid $appid -appname $appname -grouptype
"Uninstall"
```

4. Next, we need to create our script to install the application. The following code creates a simple PowerShell script containing the `install` string we set earlier and uses the `new-installscript` function. Then, we must export the script's content into a PowerShell file so that we can wrap it in our `IntuneWin` file:

```
    $installscript = new-installscript -appid $appid -appname $appname -
installstring $installstring
    $installfilename = "install$appid.ps1"
    $installscriptfile = $apppath + "\" + $installfilename
    $installscript | Out-File $installscriptfile -Encoding utf8
```

5. We must do the same for the `uninstall` script:

```
$uninstallscript = new-uninstallscript -appid $appid -appname $appname -
uninstallstring $uninstallstring
$uninstallfilename = "uninstall$appid.ps1"
$uninstallscriptfile = $apppath + "\" + $uninstallfilename
$uninstallscript | Out-File $uninstallscriptfile -Encoding utf8
```

6. The final script we need is the detection script. This takes the `filepath` value we set earlier and uses the `new-detectionscriptinstall` function to run a simple `Test-Path` on `filepath` and return an exit code of `0` if the application is detected, or an exit code of

1 if the application has not been detected. Again, we output the script's content to a PowerShell script file:

```
$detectionscript = new-detectionscriptinstall -appid $appid -appname
$appname -filepath $filepath
$detectionscriptfile = $apppath + "\detection$appid.ps1"
$detectionscript | Out-File $detectionscriptfile -Encoding utf8
```

7. Now for the important part: we need to create our `IntuneWin` file using the installer and scripts we have created. For that, we will be using the `new-intunewinfile` function, which calls the executable with the parameters required, passing various details such as the filename and output location:

```
$intunewinpath = $apppath + "\install$appid.intunewin"
new-intunewinfile -appid "$appid" -appname "$appname" -apppath "$apppath" -
setupfilename "$installscriptfile"
```

As we do not want to continue until this has been completed, we need to add a pause here. The following code uses a loop that sleeps for the duration set (in seconds). As we are using a small application, 10 seconds is fine, but for larger applications, this may need to be increased:

```
$sleep = 10
foreach ($i in 0..$sleep) {
Write-Progress -Activity "Sleeping for $($sleep-$i) seconds" -
PercentComplete ($i / $sleep * 100) -SecondsRemaining ($sleep - $i)
Start-Sleep -s 1
        }
```

8. Now for the complicated part: when a new application is created, it runs through a few stages to create an application stub, upload it to Azure Storage, and then link the two together. For this, we have a variety of nested functions.
`new-win32app` is the primary function and is where we specify the application details, `install` commands, `uninstall` commands, and detection rules:

```
$installcmd = "powershell.exe -ExecutionPolicy Bypass -File
$installfilename"
        $uninstallcmd = "powershell.exe -ExecutionPolicy Bypass -File
$uninstallfilename"
        new-win32app -appid $appid -appname $appname -appfile
```

```
$intunewinpath -installcmd $installcmd -uninstallcmd $uninstallcmd -
detectionfile $detectionscriptfile
```

1. First, this function calls `new-detectionrule`, which creates the appropriate JSON for the selected rule, which, in this case, is PowerShell. This JSON is nested in an array.
2. After creating the rules, it grabs the return codes using the `Get-DefaultReturnCodes` function.
3. The detection rule and return codes are then combined with the other information passed in the `new-win32app` command to the `Invoke-UploadWin32Lob` function.
4. This function tests that the source file path is valid with `Test-SourceFile`. Then, it uses `Get-IntuneWinXML` to read the `detection.xml` file that was created with `IntuneWinAppUtil`. This is used to grab the filename and filepath, as well as the extension.
5. If the extension is an MSI, it populates the JSON of the application with the details from the file using the `Get-Win32AppBody` function. If it is an executable, it simply uses the details passed to it.
6. Then, it adds the detection rule and return codes to the JSON containing the application details.
7. Next, it creates the application stub within Intune, which, if you look in the GUI, will say the application is not ready as the files are still uploading.
8. As the `IntuneWin` file is encrypted, the next step is to grab the encryption keys from the `detection.xml` file.
9. At this point, it extracts the file using this information (and the `Get-IntuneWinFile` function) to detect the file size. This information is then sent to Graph to create a new file reference for the application.
10. This can take a while, so the `Start-WaitForFileProcessing` function loops until the operation is complete.
11. Next, the file itself is uploaded to Azure using the URL given from Graph when the file is created, using the `UploadFileToAzureStorage` function.

12. Once uploaded, it removes the `IntuneWin` file.
13. Finally, the application needs to be committed after being uploaded via a Graph `POST` request. Again, this can take a while, so use both the `Start-WaitForFileProcessing` and `sleep` commands.

9. Now that our application has been created and uploaded, we simply need to assign it. For that, we can use the `grant-win32app` function, passing the application name and group details. This function simply grabs the application ID and populates the JSON for application assignment:

```
grant-win32app -appname $appname -installgroup $installgroup -
uninstallgroup $uninstallgroup
```

That is it – we have successfully packaged, uploaded, and assigned an application using only PowerShell and Graph.

Managing app supersedence and dependencies

This recipe looks at the functionality around application supersedence and application dependencies. As it involves amending existing applications, we will not be looking at automating, but instead at why you would use these and how to implement them.

Application supersedence

When a new version of an application is released, you have a few available options:

- Replace the `IntuneWin` file with a new one and amend the detection method so that it matches the newer version
- Create a new application and swap the assignments
- Use application supersedence

Everything will work fine, but supersedence gives you the option to remove the previous version before installing, or just do a straight update. It also makes things easier to manage as you do not have to worry about duplicate assignments or monitoring multiple applications.

Dependencies

One drawback of Intune/Autopilot is their inability to sequence applications like Configuration Manager can. Therefore, traditionally, if you had an application that needed a particular application or runtime (.NET, Java, VC Libraries, and so on) to launch, you could not guarantee it would be installed in time. Before the introduction of dependencies, this meant you had to package both into one application and then install it to use the `install` script. This worked well, but at every application update, you had to repackage both, even if only one of the two had been updated.

This is where you use a dependency: you select the runtime or application that is required and set it as a dependency on the primary application. Intune will then check whether the application is installed; if not, it will trigger an installation of the dependency before deploying the primary application.

Getting ready

To follow this recipe, you will need the following:

- Two versions of the same application for supersedence
- An application that has a dependency

How to do it...

We can now look at the steps involved in configuring these settings, starting with application supersedence.

Configuring application supersedence

For this example, we will be using 7-Zip, replacing version 19.00 with 23.00. Follow these steps to configure application supersedence within the application configuration:

1. First, click on **Apps**, then **Windows**.
2. Find your application in the list. You need the new version so that you can replace the old one – in our case, **7-Zip 23.00**. Click on it.
3. Click **Properties**.
4. Scroll down to **Supersedence** and click **Edit**.
5. Click **+ Add** to add the app it is replacing.
6. Find the application in the flyout and click **Select**.
7. If your application requires a full uninstall before you can install the new version, change **Uninstall** to **Yes**. Once set as appropriate, click **Review + save**.
8. Finally, click **Save** to confirm the changes.

This can also be configured during the initial application deployment if you are happy that the new version does not require any additional testing. Configuring it after deployment, however, allows you to test the new version for any issues before deploying it.

Now that we have covered supersedence, let's learn how to configure application dependency.

Configuring application dependency

While it is not a requirement, we will be setting the Visual C++ 2013 Redistributable package as a dependency for our new 7-Zip 23.00 version. Follow these steps to configure the application dependency for our application:

1. First, click on **Apps** and then **Windows**.
2. Find your application in the list – in our case, **7-Zip 23.00** – and click on it.
3. Click **Properties**.
4. Scroll down to **Dependencies** and click **Edit**.
5. Click **+ Add** to load the flyout with the application list.
6. Find and click on your application in the list, and click **Select**.
7. Here, you can decide whether you want the application to automatically install when the parent application is installed, or whether you want to manually deploy. In most cases, automatic is the better option. Once configured, click **Review + Save**.
8. If you have configured any supersedence, you will be prompted to confirm these here. We already know that these are correct, so click **Review + Save** once more.
9. Finally, confirm your application changes by clicking **Save**.

We have now learned what application supersedence and application dependencies are and how to configure them against applications in the tenant.

Deploying Office applications

The **Microsoft Office Suite of Applications** (now known as **Microsoft 365 apps**) is more than likely one of the most important applications required on your devices. For that reason, we need to be sure they are deployed correctly, reliably, and ideally forced on the **Enrollment Status Page** (**ESP**).

Getting started

Within Intune, there are three different ways to deploy Microsoft 365 apps, one of which is a lot more consistent than the other. The best method is to wrap it as a Win32 application using the **Office Deployment Tool** (**ODT**). We will cover this in this recipe, as we can then control the deployment of it during the ESP. We also know it will be installed using the IME, which prevents applications from clashing.

Before we look at how to deploy as a Win32 application, we should look at the other options available within the portal – that is, using the **graphical user interface** (**GUI**) with either configuration designer selections or by entering XML:

1. First, click on **Apps**, then **Windows**.
2. Click **+ Create** and select **Microsoft 365 Apps – Windows 10 and later**, then click **Select**.
3. Click **Next** on the initial screen to be taken to the **Configure app suite** screen.

The **Configuration Designer** tool lets you quickly configure your application package without needing to amend any XML or package any applications. It is a quick way to deploy the applications, but as you have no further control, you cannot specify applications that are not to be installed, such as Skype for Business, and the control is quite limited.

Switching to **Enter XML data** lets you use custom XML created by the Office Customization Tool, which we will be using for the Win32 application. The downside of using the built-in Microsoft 365 application configuration is that it is deployed more as a policy than an application, so there is the chance it might clash with another running installation. You also lose all control over detection, custom requirements, and supersedence and dependencies (which are useful if you have applications that install Office plugins).

How to do it...

Now that we have looked at the methods we should not use, let's learn how to configure, package, and deploy an application as a Win32 application. Follow these instructions to deploy Office as a Win32 application:

1. The first thing we need to do is configure our XML file to tell the ODT which components to install, what languages it should use, and so on. To do that, navigate to the Office Customization Tool: `https://config.office.com/deploymentsettings`. Here, you can specify which Office version to install, any applications to remove, change language packs, and more.

   We will be configuring the `update` channel using Intune in the next recipe, so when specifying the `update` channel here, ideally, it should match your **Broad ring** to save users from downgrading after installation. You can also specify which version to install, should you have specific application requirements.

2. In the **Installation** options, it is advisable to set **Show installation to user** to **No**, as this will be deployed in the system context anyway.
3. Also, set **Shut Down running applications** to **Yes** if you are deploying during Autopilot to avoid any timeout issues if something is already running. If you are

deploying after initial configuration, it may be better to use PSADT and prompt the users to close the applications themselves as you cannot control exactly when the application will be deployed.

4. In **Upgrade Options**, watch out for **Uninstall any MSI versions of Office, including Visio and Project**, as this will remove any detected Office applications. If you are deploying the full suite, this is less likely to be an issue, but if you are deploying apps individually, such as Visio or Project, you will want to make sure this is set to **No**; otherwise, it will uninstall everything except the single app selected for installation.
5. When looking at **Licensing and Activation**, first, change **Automatically Accept the EULA** to **Yes** to save your end users from having to accept it themselves.
   Now, let's move on to licensing. Here, we have three main options:
   - **User based**: All users have a license assigned to them and can have a maximum of five installations before they are prompted to remove a licensed installation in the Office portal.
   - **Shared Computer**: This option is better for environments where staff may use a large number of different devices, such as hot-desks or hospital environments. When a device is set in **Shared Computer** mode, it will not use one of the five available licenses for the users. If you wish to use this option, ensure that your licenses support it.
   - **Device based**: For machines with multiple unlicensed users, the machine itself is licensed. This needs special licenses.
6. In **Application Preferences**, you can configure anything that can be controlled via Group Policy or Intune Policy. For one-off configurations, this is perfectly acceptable, although using Intune policies will give you greater control and allow you to amend without having to repackage applications.
7. After configuring your settings, click **Export**.
8. Select your document format and click **OK**, then save the XML.
9. Now that we have our XML file, we need a way to use it to deploy the Office applications. For this, we will be using the ODT, which can be downloaded here: `https://www.microsoft.com/en-US/download/details.aspx?id=49117`.
10. Download the executable and run it to extract the files into a folder.
11. Now, we need to create our Win32 folder structure, as per *Figure 11.6*.
12. Copy the downloaded XML and `setup.exe` file from the ODT into the `Source` folder.

13. Also, create an `uninstall.xml` file with the following content:

```
<Configuration>
<Display Level="None" AcceptEULA="True" />
<Property Name="FORCEAPPSHUTDOWN" Value="True" />
<Remove>
<Product ID="O365ProPlusRetail">
</Product>
</Remove>
</Configuration>
```

14. Wrap it using the `IntuneWinAppUtil` tool, specify `setup.exe` as the installer, and save `intunewin` in the `Output` folder.

Now that we have our `IntuneWin` file, we can add it to Intune.

1. Within the Intune portal, navigate to **Apps**, then **Windows**.
2. Click **+ Add**, select **Win32**, and click **Select**.
3. Click the folder icon, grab your `intunewin` file, and click **OK**.
4. As this is a Win32 app from an executable, we need to populate all of the details, including the icon. Once configured, click **Next**.
5. Now, we need to set our `install` and `uninstall` commands.

   For your `install` command, you need the following:

   ```
   setup.exe /configure Configuration.xml
   ```

   For `uninstall`, you need this:

   ```
   setup.exe /configure uninstall.xml
   ```

6. Configure any other settings and click **Next**.
7. We have set our installation to 64-bit, so set that as the requirement, along with the lowest operating system version in your estate. Then, click **Next**.
8. Detection rules can be trickier for Office applications as they first install the `Click-To-Run` application, which installs the files themselves. In this case, we will check for a registry key, which will confirm that the `Click-To-Run` tool has finished running. Our configured registry keys are as follows:
   - **Key Path**: `HKEY_LOCAL_MACHINE\SOFTWARE\Microsoft\Office\ClickToRun\`

   - **Value**: `LastScenarioResult`
   - **Detection**: `Exists`

   As we are deploying the 32-bit version, we do not want to associate it with a 32-bit application; otherwise, it will look into `WOW6432Node` and fail the detection process. Set **Associated with a 32-bit app on 64-bit clients** to **No**.

9. Once configured, click **OK** and then **Next**.
10. We do not have any dependencies, supersedence, or scope tags for this application as it is a core application that is required across the estate, so click **Next** on all three screens.
11. When looking at **Assignments**, you will no doubt want this installed on all devices, so you can select **All users**, **All devices**, or deploy to a group. In our case, we will use the group we created in *Chapter 1* and deploy it to any users with an Office license. Once selected, click **Next**.
12. Finally, confirm that everything we have configured matches on the **Review + Create** screen and click **Create**.

That completes this recipe on the Microsoft 365 application deployment. Now, let's learn how to keep the applications updated.

Updating Office applications

Now that we have deployed our Office applications, we need to make sure they remain updated. As these are core apps, it is recommended to use a similar ring approach as what we used with Windows updates, both to check for any potential issues with the line of business and also to look for any significant UI changes that may need communicating with the organization.

Getting ready

Before running through the preferred approach, there are different ways to handle Office updates. We will have a look at the two main options now and then run through the configuration.

Office portal

One option is to use the Office admin portal itself, which can be accessed at `https://config.office.com`.

Here, you can configure Office policies to set any configuration setting via **Policy Management** and also use the **Cloud Updates** menu to handle updates and version deployment.

This is a good option, but it falls outside of the Intune portal. It is another portal to manage, and also increases the risk of conflicts, with the same setting potentially being configured in two different places.

Settings catalog

By using **Settings catalog**, we can configure any ADMX-backed settings directly on the devices and use our existing update groups, or create new ones. This is what we will do in this recipe.

How to do it...

Follow these steps to configure a Settings catalog policy to handle Office updates:

1. As with all previous Settings catalog-based recipes, navigate to **Devices**, click on **Windows**, then click on **Configuration profiles**.
2. At the top, click **Create**, select **New Policy**, select **Windows 10 and later**, then select **Settings catalog** from the fly-out window. Finally, click **Create**.
3. Give your new profile **Name** and **Description** values. For most environments, you will want at least three different profiles for the different rings, so name them accordingly. Then, click **Next**.
4. On the **Settings** page, click **Add settings** and find **Microsoft Office 2016 (Machine)** in the list. Click **Updates**. The Office 2016 policies are the most recent and are fully compatible with Microsoft 365 apps.
   Selecting the machine policies writes the keys to **HKEY Local Machine** (**HKLM**) and not the **HKEY Current User** (**HKCU**) hive, so users cannot change their update cadence.
5. For updates, we need two settings:
   - **Enable Automatic Updates**: Set to **Enabled**.
   - **Update Channel**: Set to **Enabled**. Set **Channel** according to the ring being configured.

   The available options for **Update Channel** can be found here: `https://learn.microsoft.com/en-us/deployoffice/updates/overview-update-channels`.

   You can also configure **Update Deadline** within the **Settings** category if required.
6. Once you have selected the appropriate channel, click **Next**.
7. Click **Next** to move past the **Scope tags** page.
8. Now, assign the application in a similar manner to the Windows Updates we covered in *Chapter 4*. The user/device set may be different for Office updates, so you may wish to include some heavy Office app users in one of the earlier rings to quickly find any issues

before they deploy to the larger estate. If you have users who regularly move between machines (such as IT staff), it may be worth using device groups here to stop Office versions from upgrading and downgrading as different users log in – just remember not to mix device and user groups when including and excluding groups.

9. Once you have configured your assignments, click **Next**.
10. Finally, review that everything looks correct and click **Create**.

That completes the steps for configuring Office updates in the UI.

Automating it

Of course, as this is a Settings catalog policy, we can deploy it via Graph, as covered in *Chapter 2*.

The first thing we need to consider is the update ring being deployed, as the actual values differ from the display name in the portal:

- **Current**: `current`
- **Semi Annual**: `deferred`
- **Monthly**: `monthlyenterprise`
- **Semi Annual (Preview)**: `firstreleasedeferred`
- **Current Preview**: `firstreleasecurrent`
- **Beta**: `insiderfast`

Follow these steps to create a script that will automate the update profile creation process in Intune:

1. Start by setting the name, description, and URL:

```
$name = "Update Ring"
$description = "Office Updates for Monthly Enterprise"
$url  = "https://graph.microsoft.com/beta/deviceManagement/
configurationPolicies"
```

2. Now, configure the channel and group ID for assignment:

```
$groupid = "xxxxxxxx-xxxx-xxxx-xxxx-xxxxxxxxxxxx"
$channel = "monthlyenterprise"
```

3. When configuring the JSON, the first setting is simply to enable automatic updates. The second setting is where we set the update ring by passing the channel value directly

into the JSON, which you can find here: `https://github.com/PacktPublishing/Microsoft-Intune-Cookbook-Second-Edition/blob/main/Chapter-11/add-office-updatepolicy.ps1`.

4. Now, create the new profile and grab the ID for assignment:

```
$updateprofile = Invoke-MgGraphRequest -Uri $url -Method POST -Body $json -
ContentType "application/json" -OutputType PSObject
$profileid = $updateprofile.id
```

5. Update the URL so that it includes the policy ID:

```
$updateurl = "https://graph.microsoft.com/beta/deviceManagement/
configurationPolicies/$profileid/assign"
```

6. Now, we need to add the group ID to the JSON and, finally, send the request to assign the profile to our group:

```
$updatejson = @"
{
    "assignments": [
        {
            "target": {
                "@odata.type": "#microsoft.graph.groupAssignmentTarget",
                "groupId": "$groupid"
            }
        }
    ]
}
"@
Invoke-MgGraphRequest -Method POST -Uri $updateurl -ContentType
"application/json" -Body $updatejson
```

With that, we have configured Office updates using Settings catalog policies, including automating their creation.

Windows app protection

With more users accessing corporate data from personal devices, application protection is more important than ever. Traditionally, this has been restricted to mobile devices running Android and iOS/iPadOS, but has recently been expanded to include Windows.

At the time of writing, Windows **Mobile Application Management** (**MAM**) still only supports the Microsoft Edge browser. For that reason, we are going to configure MAM in this recipe and then also add **Conditional Access** policies to block anything that is not Microsoft Edge for personal devices.

Getting ready

The first thing to watch here is that personal devices are not allowed to enroll in Microsoft Intune; otherwise, they will bypass the Conditional Access rules. This will be covered in *Chapter 13, Tenant Administration*.

How to do it...

Follow these steps to configure Windows application protection:

1. The first step is to enable MAM across the tenant. This only has to be done once.
2. In **Tenant administration**, click on **Connectors and tokens** and then **Mobile Threat Defense**.
3. Add a connector for **Windows Security Center**.

> **Note**
>
> Do not worry if it displays as unavailable; it will update when used.

4. Next, click on **Apps** and then click **App protection policies**.
5. Click **Create New** and select **Windows** (not **Windows Information Protection**).
6. Give your policy **Name** and **Description** values and click **Next**.
7. On the **Apps** screen, click the blue **+ Select Apps** test and select **Microsoft Edge**. Click **Select** and then click **Next**.
8. Configure your data protection settings – that is, whether you want data to be copied into or out of the application and whether to block printing. Then, click **Next**.

9. On the **Health Checks** screen, you can configure more protection around the data, including how many days after which to wipe the data, and you can also add minimum application versions. Under **Device conditions**, you can specify the minimum operating system versions to block any unsupported Microsoft installations.

> Note
>
> One health check setting worth adding here is **Disabled Account**. Set it to **Block Access** so that you can be sure any ex-employees are blocked at the personal device level.

10. Once you have configured everything, click **Next**.
11. Click **Next** on the **Scope tags** page, as this is a global policy.
12. Assign as appropriate. Remember that this is happening at the user level, as it is applying to devices not enrolled into Intune or Entra ID, so the group needs to contain users. There is currently no option to select all users, but you could create a dynamic group containing all members with a valid Intune license. Once configured, click **Next**.
13. Finally, check that the settings look correct and click **Create**.

Now that we have completed the Intune side, we need to add extra security for Conditional Access:

1. Navigate to **Endpoint Security** and click on **Conditional Access**.
   We need to block non-corporate devices from accessing anything but the web app by requiring compliance. While you should do this for all devices, this policy is only for BYOD, so we will also use a device filter to exclude corporate-owned machines.
2. First, select **All users** (excluding your break-glass account) and target **All resources (formally 'All cloud apps')**, as we do not want any data escaping unprotected.
3. As this is a Windows-only configuration, configure the device platforms to only **Windows**; we do not want this policy applied to other platforms:

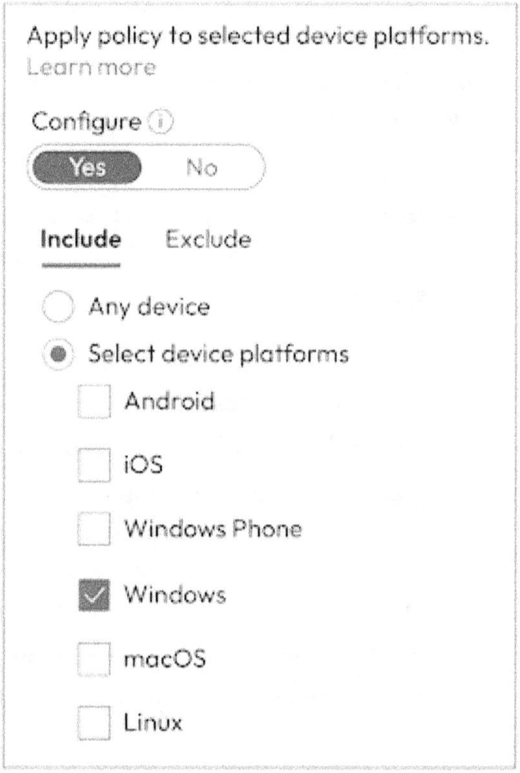

Figure 11.9 – Device platforms

4. We want to let the browser through on this one, and we will protect that in the next policy. Therefore, apply this policy to everything excluding **Browser**:

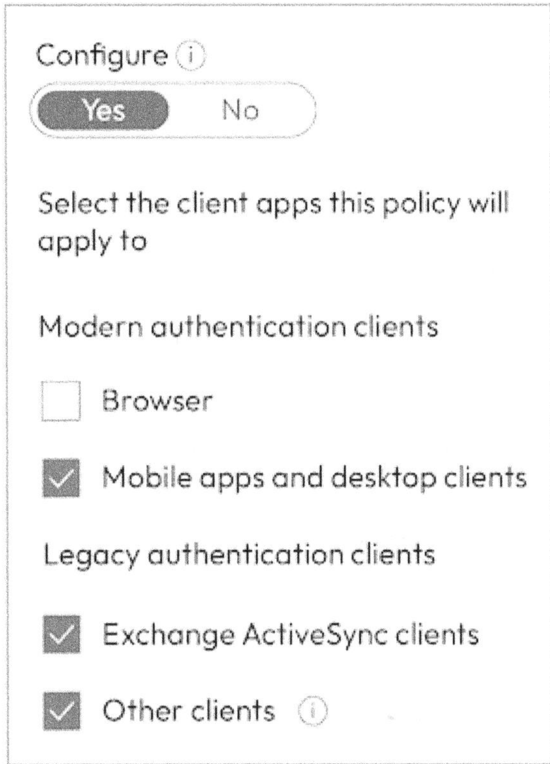

Figure 11.10 – Application clients

5. As mentioned previously, we will exclude corporate devices using the following filter, as seen in the figure that follows:

```
device.deviceOwnership -eq "Company"
```

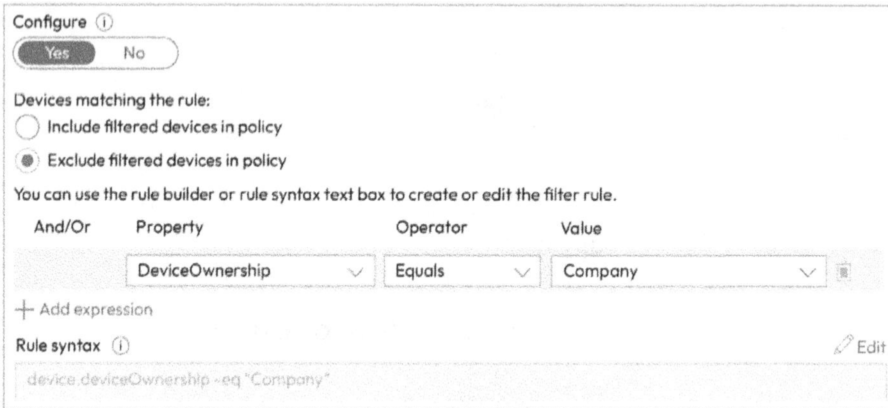

Figure 11.11 – Conditional Access filter

6. Then, we need to require compliance, which will automatically block non-corporate devices. To do this, select **Require device to be marked as compliant** within **Grant access**:

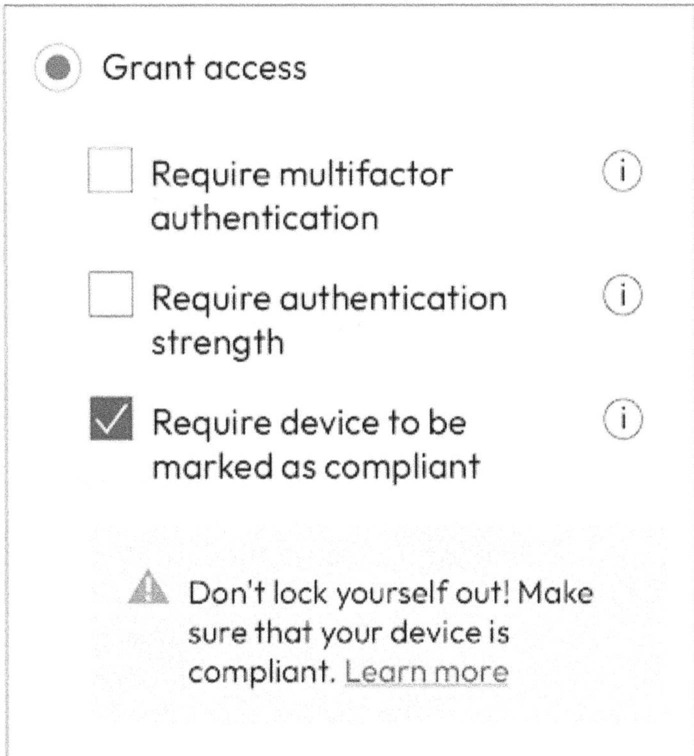

Figure 11.12 – Grant access

This has locked down our non-browser access. Now, we want to lock down browser access with a second Conditional Access policy.

7. Again, we want to target all users and all cloud apps, and also include only **Windows** devices.
8. We only want to apply this policy to **Browser**; selecting anything else will cause it to fail:

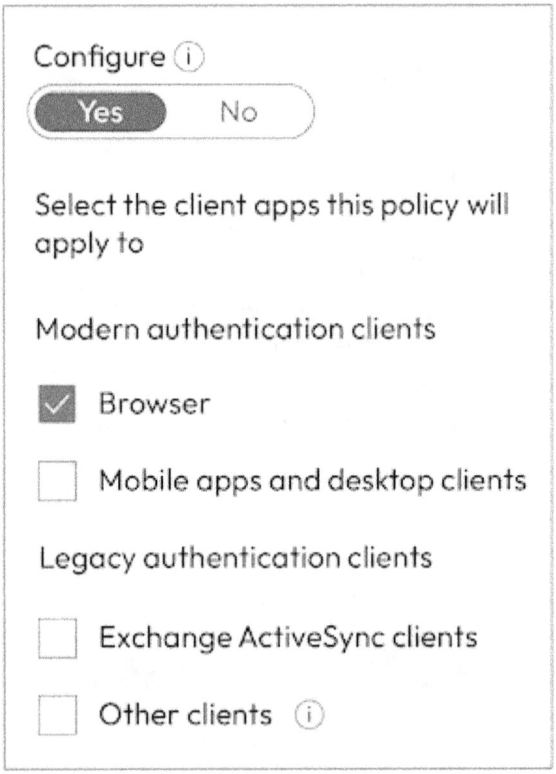

Figure 11.13 – Application client apps applicability

9. Again, ignore corporate devices with the same filter, as shown in *Figure 11.10*.
10. Most important of all, we need to select **Require app protection policy** under **Grant access**:

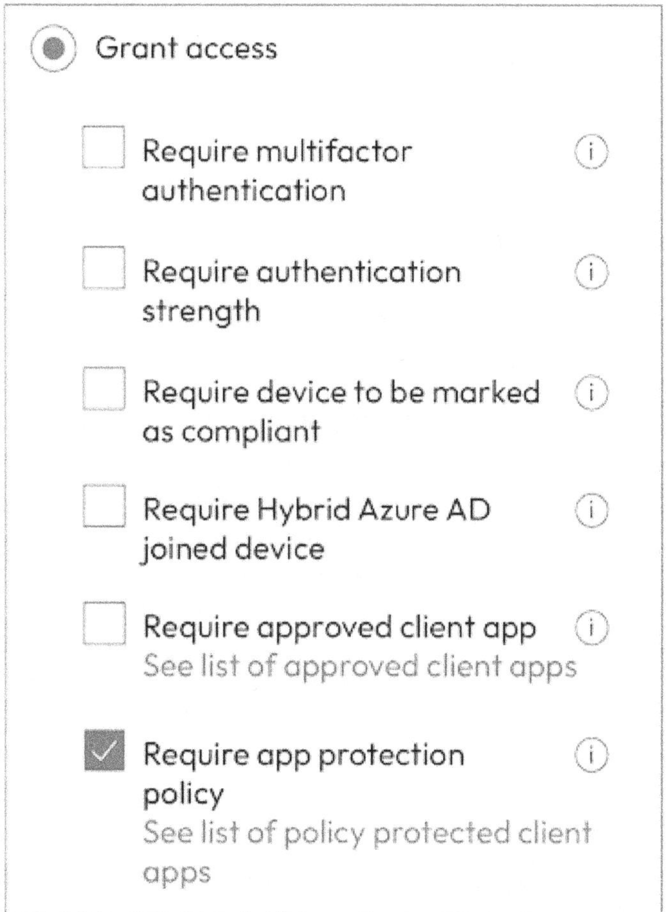

Figure 11.14 – Require app protection policy

As an extra layer of security, you can also select **Block downloads (Preview)** using **Use Conditional Access App Control** in the **Session** controls:

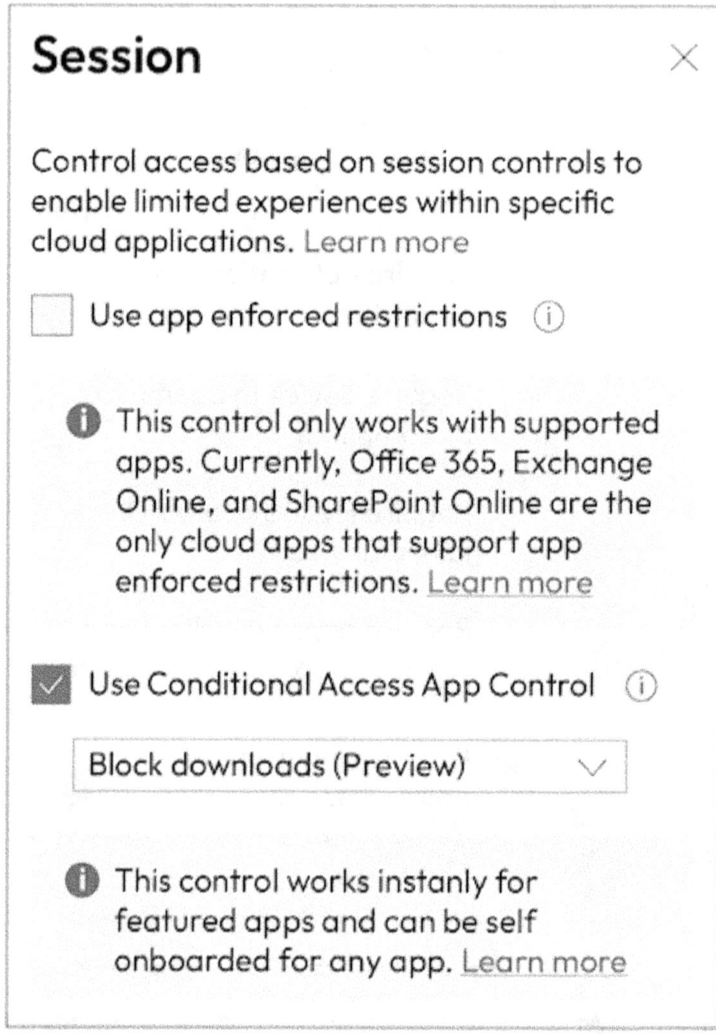

Figure 11.15 – Block downloads (Preview)

We have now secured our data within the Edge browser on personal devices and blocked access via any other methods on Windows.

Automating it

This is split into four different parts: one to enable the connector, one to add the policy, and then two Conditional Access policies. We will do everything with PowerShell and Microsoft Graph API. Follow these steps to create your policies:

1. Enabling the connector involves sending a simple request to set the value to `true`:

```
$url = "https://graph.microsoft.com/beta/deviceManagement/
mobileThreatDefenseConnectors"
$threatjson = @"
{
    "windowsMobileApplicationManagementEnabled": true
}
"@
Invoke-MgGraphRequest -Method POST -Uri $url -Body $threatjson -ContentType
"application/json" -OutputType PSObject
```

2. Now, we need to configure our policy. The JSON includes every available setting, even if they were not configured in the GUI, where they are simply set to `null`. The assignment is also included in this JSON rather than a separate command after creation. You can find the JSON in the script here: `https://github.com/PacktPublishing/Microsoft-Intune-Cookbook-Second-Edition/blob/main/Chapter-11/windows-MAM.ps1`.
3. Then, we need to create our Conditional Access policies using the same process as in *Chapter 5*.
   First, we must configure our policy so that it requires app protection. The policy can be found here: `https://github.com/PacktPublishing/Microsoft-Intune-Cookbook-Second-Edition/blob/main/Chapter-11/windows-mam-conditional-access.ps1`.

That completes this recipe on automating Windows MAM within the tenant using both Intune and Conditional Access policies.

Get This Book's PDF Version and Exclusive Extras

Scan the QR code (or go to `packtpub.com/unlock`). Search for this book by name, confirm the edition, and then follow the steps on the page.

Note: Keep your invoice handy. Purchases made directly from Packt don't require one.

12

PowerShell Scripting Across Intune

An important and often overlooked part of Intune is its ability to run scripts on devices, whether as one-off deployments (**platform scripts**) or more regularly via **Remediations** (previously called **Proactive Remediations**).

> **Note**
>
> Remediations require Windows Enterprise licensing, so they are not available on Business Premium.

With Windows 10 and Windows 11, PowerShell has become increasingly more powerful to the point where almost anything can be done on devices with a script.

In Intune, we can use PowerShell scripts to configure properties not yet available in the settings catalog, copy files, add registry keys, or even run a script to remove unwanted Windows bloatware for a cleaner build.

Platform scripts are run as configurations for simple configuration settings or anything required during device setup. Remediations, on the other hand, are repeatable scripts with logic that only runs when required.

Throughout this chapter, we will learn how to deploy PowerShell scripts and remediations, but also how to write the scripts themselves and provide some example scripts to get you started. This will include not only Remediations and platform scripts, but also the usage of scripts within application deployments.

In this chapter, we will cover the following recipes:

- Deploying platform scripts
- Configuring Remediations
- Using custom detection scripts in apps
- Using custom requirements scripts in apps

Technical requirements

For this chapter, you will need a modern web browser and a PowerShell code editor such as Visual Studio Code or PowerShell ISE.

All the scripts that are referenced in this chapter can be found here: `https://github.com/PacktPublishing/Microsoft-Intune-Cookbook-Second-Edition/tree/main/Chapter-12`.

Deploying platform scripts

We will start with the original option, which has been available in Intune for longer than the rest. Platform scripts run once on the device and can run in the system or user context. By default, they run in 32-bit mode, but this can be changed on deployment. This is important to note as environmental variables will differ accordingly for both System/User and 32/64-bit.

To find out more about User/System targeting, go to `https://andrewstaylor.com/2022/11/22/intune-comparing-system-vs-user-for-everything/`.

When running during Autopilot, there is no labeled step where scripts run – they run when it says **Preparing apps** in **User** or **Device** setup. If you hit a time-out issue here, it is more than likely a failed PowerShell script that has not reported a success code in time.

To troubleshoot and view the output of a script, retrieve the script ID from the address bar in the Intune portal. The output will be in the following location under a subkey with the respective ID:

```
HKLM:\Software\Microsoft\IntuneManagementExtension\Policies
```

Ideally, you should add logging in the script itself for more thorough and easily accessible output.

Getting ready

In this example, we will deploy a simple script to add a registry key and remove an in-built Windows AppX application.

In your editor of choice, create a new PowerShell script and enter the following code:

```
Get-AppxPackage -allusers -Name Microsoft.BingNews| Remove-AppxPackage -AllUsers
$Search = "HKLM:\SOFTWARE\Policies\Microsoft\Windows\Windows Search"
If (!(Test-Path $Search)) {
    New-Item $Search
}
If (Test-Path $Search) {
    Set-ItemProperty $Search AllowCortana -Value 0
}
```

This will remove Bing News and stop Cortana from appearing in the search box. You can see we are adding the `-allusers` switch on the `AppXPackage` command; this searches at the system level and clears the full package, rather than just for the logged-in user. If you were to run this script at the user level, unless the users are administrators (which we would hope not), it would fail as the users would not have permissions to all packages or the HKLM registry. In this case, you would remove `-allusers` and switch to HKCU.

How to do it...

Now that we have written our script, follow these steps to deploy it:

1. Within the Intune portal, navigate to **Devices**, click on **Windows**, and then click **Scripts and remediations**.
2. By default, you will be taken to **Remediations**, which we will cover in the next recipe (*Configuring Remediations*). Click on the **Platform scripts** tab at the top, then click **Add**.
3. As usual, specify your script's name and description. Once added, you will not be able to see the script's content within the portal (there is a way to download and decode it via Graph if needed), so it is advisable to make the descriptions thorough and keep a copy of the source files. Once you have configured these, click **Next**.
4. On the script **Settings** page, select the script you added earlier. Beneath that, we have a few options:
    - **Run this script using the logged on credentials**: Setting this to **Yes** runs the scripts in the user context so that they can access the user's profile. However,

unless your users have administrative rights, they cannot do anything beyond that.

- **Enforce script signature check**: Setting this to **Yes** means the script will only run if it is signed correctly. In most cases, for homemade scripts, this needs to be set to **No**. If it is required for security purposes, make sure you sign each script before uploading it.
- **Run script in 64 bit PowerShell Host**: By default, this is set to **No**, so any registry keys you write will go to `WOW6432Node`, and files will go to `Program Files (x86)`. Changing this to **Yes** will write the script files and output to the primary locations.

5. In the preceding script, we need to run it at the system level as we are writing to **HKEY Local Machine** (**HKLM**), and also need to run it in the 64-bit host. Our script is unsigned, so the setting needs to be **No** for the signature check:

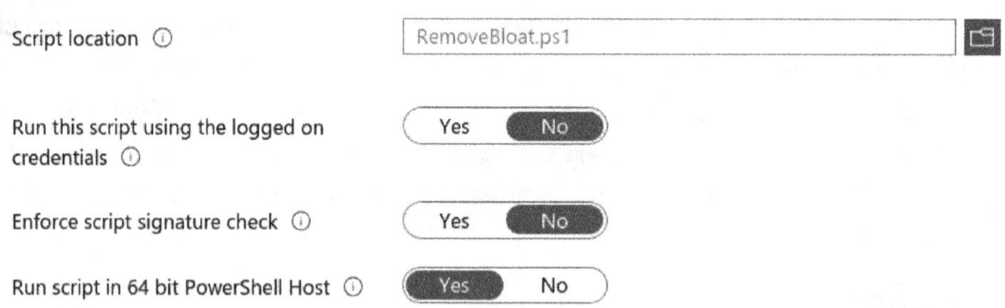

Figure 12.1 – Platform script details

Once configured, click **Next**.

6. We do not require **Scope tags** for this, so again, click **Next**.
7. Now, it is a case of assigning the script. If you want it to run during the Device phase of Autopilot, deploy to a device group; for the User phase, deploy to a user group. In this case, it is a device clean script, so we will run it in the device context so that we know it has been completed before a user logs in. Once configured, click **Next**.
8. Finally, on the **Review + Add** screen, confirm all of your settings and click **Add**.

With that, you have created, uploaded, and added a PowerShell platform script to Intune.

Automating it

When adding in the interface, you may have noticed that there is a brief notification while the file is uploaded into Intune. Fortunately, when automating, we can convert to Base64 format within our script and remove that step.

Follow these steps to deploy our platform script using Graph:

1. As usual, we will start with our name, description, group ID, and URL:

```
$name = "PowerShell Device Script"
$description = "Removes Bing News AppX package and stops Cortana running in
search box"
$groupid = "xxxxxxxx-xxxx-xxxx-xxxx-xxxxxxxxxxxx"
$url = "https://graph.microsoft.com/beta/deviceManagement/
deviceManagementScripts"
```

2. Next, we want to add the script itself within a variable. Note that we are using a single quote around it so that it fully escapes everything in the code:

```
$scriptcontent = @'
Get-AppxPackage -allusers -Name Microsoft.BingNews| Remove-AppxPackage -
AllUsers
$Search = "HKLM:\SOFTWARE\Policies\Microsoft\Windows\Windows Search"
If (!(Test-Path $Search)) {
    New-Item $Search
}
If (Test-Path $Search) {
    Set-ItemProperty $Search AllowCortana -Value 0
}
'@
```

3. Now, we need to convert the script content into Base64 format:

```
$base64encoded =
[System.Convert]::ToBase64String([System.Text.Encoding]::Unicode.GetBytes($
scriptcontent))
```

4. Next, we must populate the JSON. This is straightforward when using standard `true/false` options for the 32/64-bit, User/System, and Signed options. We have also added our Base64 encoded script:

```
$json = @"
{
    "description": "$name",
    "displayName": "$description",
    "enforceSignatureCheck": true,
```

```
    "fileName": "platform-script.ps1",
    "roleScopeTagIds": [
        "0"
    ],
    "runAs32Bit": false,
    "runAsAccount": "system",
    "scriptContent": "$base64encoded"
}
"@
```

5. Now, send a POST request to add the script to Intune and grab the script ID so that it can be assigned:

```
$addscript = Invoke-MgGraphRequest -Uri $url -Method Post -Body $json -
ContentType "application/json" -OutputType PSObject
$scriptid = $addscript.id
```

6. Populate the URL with the ID and assign it to our group:

```
$assignurl = "https://graph.microsoft.com/beta/deviceManagement/
deviceManagementScripts/$scriptid/assign"
$assignjson = @"
{
    "deviceManagementScriptAssignments": [
        {
            "target": {
                "@odata.type": "#microsoft.graph.groupAssignmentTarget",
                "groupId": "$groupid"
            }
        }
    ]
}
"@
Invoke-MgGraphRequest -Uri $assignurl -Method Post -Body $assignjson -
ContentType "application/json" -OutputType PSObject
```

You have now created your first PowerShell platform script using PowerShell and Graph.

Configuring Remediations

While platform scripts are excellent for run-once scenarios, such as when you are provisioning a device, PowerShell is incredibly powerful, and there may be situations where you want something to run more than once, or you want to view the output in the console itself.

This is where Remediations (formerly Proactive Remediations) come into play. They can be set to run on a schedule, but as they work with a detection and remediation configuration, the script itself will only run if required.

Remediation is split into two scripts: a **detection script** and a **remediation script**.

The detection script is arguably the most important of the two, as this decides whether the remediation script needs to run. The key output here is the **exit code**. An exit code of `0` means the device is compliant with the check, and no further action is needed. If the exit code is `1`, it causes the remediation to run.

There are no restrictions on the content of the scripts, so long as the two exit codes are set. We will run through an example in this recipe, but a good repository of pre-curated scripts can be found here: `https://github.com/JayRHa/EndpointAnalyticsRemediationScripts`.

> Note
>
> A remediation script is not a hard requirement here; you can just deploy the detection script to view the output (covered in the *There's more...* section of this recipe) or to remediate at the same time. Only the detection script is a fixed requirement.

Getting ready

For this recipe, we will add a Remediation that should be helpful in most environments and trigger disk cleanup if our disk space is low.

To start, we need to create two scripts (for detection and remediation). In your preferred editor, create the following PowerShell scripts:

- `Detect.ps1`:

```
$storageThreshold = 15
$utilization = (Get-PSDrive | Where {$_.name -eq "C"}).free
if(($storageThreshold *1GB) -lt $utilization){
    write-output "Storage is fine, no remediation needed"
    exit 0}
else{
    write-output "Storage is low, remediation needed"
    exit 1}
```

- `Remediate.ps1`:

```
$cleanupTypeSelection = 'Temporary Sync Files', 'Downloaded Program Files',
'Memory Dump Files', 'Recycle Bin'
foreach ($keyName in $cleanupTypeSelection) {
    $newItemParams = @{
        Path         = "HKLM:
\SOFTWARE\Microsoft\Windows\CurrentVersion\Explorer\VolumeCaches\$keyName"
        Name         = 'StateFlags0001'
        Value        = 1
        PropertyType = 'DWord'
        ErrorAction  = 'SilentlyContinue'
    }
    New-ItemProperty @newItemParams | Out-Null
}
Start-Process -FilePath CleanMgr.exe -ArgumentList '/sagerun:1' -
NoNewWindow -Wait
```

The detection script simply inspects the free space on the `C` drive. If it is less than 15 GB, it sends `Exit code 0`, which triggers the remediation to run. The other thing to consider here is the output that is sent with the exit code. You can view the detection output after running it within the Intune console, so adding `write-output` with something useful will help you when you are reviewing the device's status later on. We will cover this in the *There's more...* section of this recipe.

The remediation then runs the disk cleanup utility to clear out temp files, downloaded program files, memory dump files, and the recycle bin (change as appropriate for your environment). No exit code is needed for the remediation script.

How to do it...

Now that we have created our scripts, follow these steps to add them to Intune:

1. Navigate to **Devices**, click on **Windows**, and then click **Scripts**. It will default to **Remediations** at the top, so click **Create**.
2. As with the previous recipe, add **Name** and **Description** values. You can also add an author here; it will auto-populate the logged-in user, but it is a free-text field. While it is good practice to add a good description, remediations can be viewed in the portal once they have been added if needed. Once configured, click **Next**.
3. On the **Settings** screen, add your **Detection** and **Remediation** scripts. You have the same options as with PowerShell scripts to set the context – that is, 32/64-bit, system, and signing. In this example, we need a system context, 64-bit, and unsigned. Once configured, click **Next**:

Figure 12.2 – Remediation script settings

4. We do not need **Scope tags** for a site-wide remediation such as this, so click **Next**.
5. Now, assign the Remediation as required. You will see that you also have the option to add **All Devices** or **All Users**, as this uses the newer assignments UI. Once you have selected your group, click the text marked **Daily**; a flyout will appear where you can select the schedule for the remediation to run. The options are **Daily** (with the ability to

select how many days and at what time), **Hourly**, and **Once** (fixed date/time). You also have the option to run on demand, which we will cover in the *There's more...* section of this recipe. In this case, we are going to run it hourly as the detection script will not impact the devices significantly. Once configured, click **Next**:

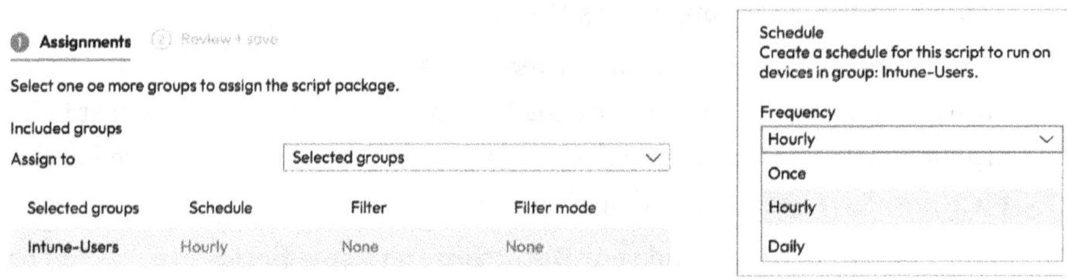

Figure 12.3 – Remediation assignments

6. Finally, ensure that everything looks correct and click **Create**. You will notice that **Version** is listed as **No Version**. This was a text field on the first screen that could not be changed. It will automatically increment as you update the scripts.

Now that we have added our remediation to the portal, we can look at automating it to quickly deploy future scripts.

Automating it

Remediations are slightly trickier to automate as we have different options when assigning, depending on the schedule that is selected. However, we simply need to make a change in the assignment JSON. We can deal with this using an `if` statement.

Follow these steps to automate your first remediation deployment:

1. To make things easier, we will add more variables at the start, including `Publisher`, `RunAs`, `32-bit`, `64-bit`, and the schedule itself:

```
$DisplayName = "Clean Disk Space"
$Description = "Clears if less than 15Gb free"
$Publisher = "Your Name Here"
##RunAs can be "system" or "user"
$RunAs = "system"
##True for 32-bit, false for 64-bit
$RunAs32 = "true"
##Daily or Hourly
$ScheduleType = "Daily"
##How Often
$ScheduleFrequency = "1"
```

```
##Start Time (if daily)
$StartTime = "01:00"
$groupid = "xxxxxxxx-xxxx-xxxx-xxxx-xxxxxxxxxxxx"
$url = "https://graph.microsoft.com/beta/deviceManagement/
deviceHealthScripts"
```

2. Once our variables have been set, we need to add the detection script and then convert it to Base64:

```
$detectionscriptcontent = @'
$storageThreshold = 15
$utilization = (Get-PSDrive | Where {$_.name -eq "C"}).free
if(($storageThreshold *1GB) -lt $utilization){exit 0}
else{exit 1}
'@
$detectionbase64encoded =
[System.Convert]::ToBase64String([System.Text.Encoding]::Unicode.GetBytes($
detectionscriptcontent))
```

3. We need to do the same with the remediation script, so set the script's content and encode it:

```
$remediationscriptcontent = @'
$cleanupTypeSelection = 'Temporary Sync Files', 'Downloaded Program Files',
'Memory Dump Files', 'Recycle Bin'
foreach ($keyName in $cleanupTypeSelection) {
    $newItemParams = @{
        Path         = "HKLM:
\SOFTWARE\Microsoft\Windows\CurrentVersion\Explorer\VolumeCaches\$keyName"
        Name         = 'StateFlags0001'
        Value        = 1
        PropertyType = 'DWord'
        ErrorAction  = 'SilentlyContinue'
    }
    New-ItemProperty @newItemParams | Out-Null
}
Start-Process -FilePath CleanMgr.exe -ArgumentList '/sagerun:1' -
NoNewWindow -Wait
'@
$remediationbase64encoded =
```

```
[System.Convert]::ToBase64String([System.Text.Encoding]::Unicode.GetBytes($
remediationscriptcontent))
```

4. The final JSON here is very similar to a standard PowerShell script, which we covered in the previous recipe, just with extra fields available to us:

```
$json = @"
{
    "description": "$description",
    "detectionScriptContent": "$detectionbase64encoded",
    "displayName": "$displayname",
    "enforceSignatureCheck": false,
    "publisher": "$publisher",
    "remediationScriptContent": "$remediationbase64encoded",
    "roleScopeTagIds": [
        "0"
    ],
    "runAs32Bit": $runas32,
    "runAsAccount": "$runas"
}
"@
```

5. Now, we need to create our script and grab the ID for assignment:

```
$addscript = Invoke-MgGraphRequest -Uri $url -Method Post -Body $json -
ContentType "application/json" -OutputType PSObject
$scriptid = $addscript.id
```

6. Now comes the interesting part – we need to check on the schedule as `Daily` and `Hourly` using different `@odata.type` options. `Daily` also has an extra option. For that, run `if` against `$ScheduleType`, which you set earlier, and set a variable accordingly:

```
if($ScheduleType -eq "Daily"){
    $Schedule = @"
    "runSchedule": {
        "@odata.type": "#microsoft.graph.deviceHealthScriptDailySchedule",
        "interval": $scheduleFrequency,
        "time": "$startTime",
        "useUtc": false
    },
```

```
"@
}
else{
    $Schedule = @"
    "runSchedule": {
        "@odata.type": "#microsoft.graph.deviceHealthScriptHourlySchedule",
        "interval": $interval
    },
"@
}
```

7. Finally, we must populate this into the `Assignment` JSON and send a `POST` request to assign the remediation:

```
$assignurl = "https://graph.microsoft.com/beta/deviceManagement/
deviceHealthScripts/$scriptid/assign"
$assignjson = @"
{
    "deviceHealthScriptAssignments": [
        {
            "runRemediationScript": true,
            $schedule
            "target": {
                "@odata.type": "#microsoft.graph.groupAssignmentTarget",
                "groupId": "$groupid"
            }
        }
    ]
}
"@
Invoke-MgGraphRequest -Uri $assignurl -Method Post -Body $assignjson -
ContentType "application/json" -OutputType PSObject
```

We have created our first remediation using Graph.

There's more...

As mentioned earlier, remediations provide us with some additional functionality beyond scheduling that is not available with platform scripts. Let's take a look.

Viewing output

A hidden but very useful feature is to be able to view the script's output within the console rather than having to access the device itself. To do so, follow these steps:

1. In the Intune portal, click on **Devices**, then **Windows**, then **Scripts**. In your list of scripts, click on the script in question.
2. Now, click **Device Status** in the left-hand menu under **Monitor**.
   The standard status is cut down so that it fits on the screen, but click on **Columns**, and you will see additional options. Tick **Pre-remediation detection output** and **Post-remediation detection output**, and click **Apply**:

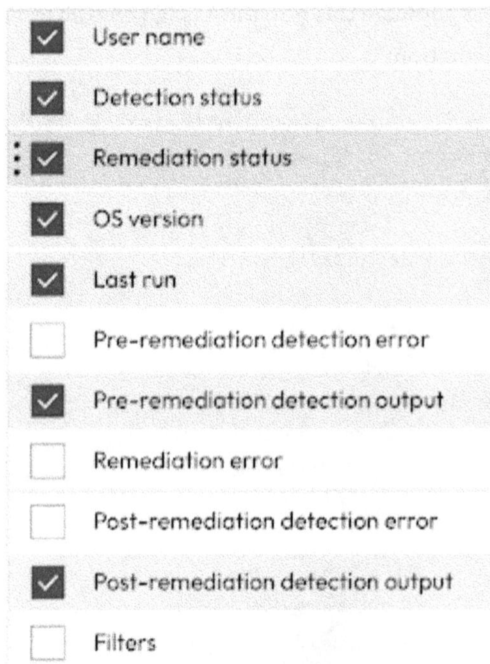

Figure 12.4 – Remediation output columns

This will now show the output that is returned by the detection script before remediation and after remediation. The output here is only as good as the `write-output` that you configured in your detection script. This is worth keeping in mind when you are creating your scripts.

Now that we have learned how to view the output, we can look at running remediations on demand.

Running remediations on demand

If you need to quickly run a remediation, another useful feature is running remediations on demand. This is especially useful for any urgent security fixes or when you are troubleshooting a device. You could run a remediation with standard troubleshooting steps and then, in the detection script, output any common errors so that you know where to start. Follow these steps to run a remediation on demand against a device:

1. To run on demand, navigate to **Devices**, then click on **Windows** and click on your device in the list.
2. Now, click the three dots (**...**) and select **Run remediation (preview)**:

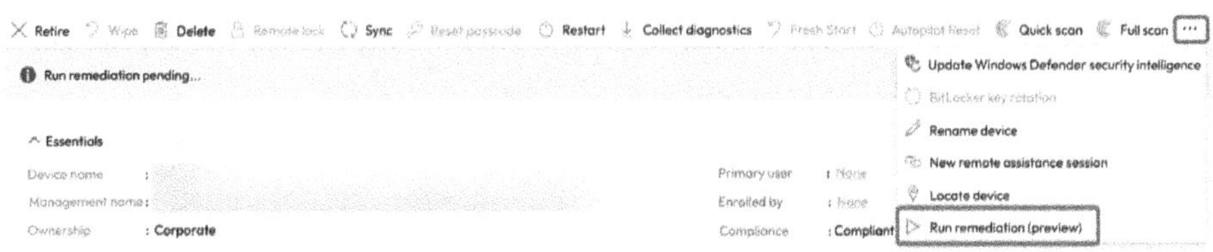

Figure 12.5 – Run remediation (preview)

3. You will be presented with a list of deployed remediations in the tenancy. Select the one you wish to run (you can only select one) and click **Run remediation**.

If you want to run remediation against multiple devices at once, you can use Graph. An example script can be found here: `https://github.com/andrew-s-taylor/public/blob/main/Powershell%20Scripts/Intune/bulk-run-remediation-ondemand.ps1`.

Running remediation on demand using Graph simply requires a basic `POST` request, including the remediation ID to a URL and the device ID:

```
$deviceid = "DeviceID"
$remediationid = "RemediationID"
$json = @"
{
    "ScriptPolicyId": "$remediationid",
}
"@
    $url = "https://graph.microsoft.com/beta/deviceManagement/
managedDevices('$deviceID')/initiateOnDemandProactiveRemediation"
    Invoke-MgGraphRequest -uri $url -Method Post -Body $json -ContentType
"application/json"
```

Using custom detection scripts in apps

While we covered this briefly in *Chapter 11*, detection scripts work slightly differently from a PowerShell platform or remediation script, so this recipe will cover how they work and include some working examples.

How to do it...

The important thing to note with a custom detection script is that it requires *both* an exit code (`0`) and a **standard output** (**STDOUT**). Sending an exit code of `1`, or not including the STDOUT, will flag the installation as failed.

Before searching the STDOUT, the script must return an output. So, the following code will suffice and mark the installation as successful:

```
Write-output "App found"
Exit 0
```

Now, let's use and deploy a custom detection script:

1. To use a custom detection script, you must add the script during packaging or after deploying. For post-deployment, click on **Apps**, then **Windows**. Find the application in question and click on it.
2. Now, click on **Properties** and click **Edit** next to **Detection Rules**.
3. In the dropdown, select **Use a custom detection script** and find the detection script you created (some options will be mentioned shortly).

> **Note**
>
> You cannot select system versus user context. One annoyance here is that custom detection scripts run exclusively in the *system* context, even if the application is at the user level. If you need to query files or registry keys in the user context, you are going to need to use your script to discover the logged-in user and add that to `c:\users\` or `HKCU\`. There is a function in the GitHub repository for this chapter that will return the logged-in user's SID and username.

4. Set the 32/64-bit settings as appropriate. This is going to be especially important for applications, as often, you will be looking for registry keys or files in the `Program Files` directory, and you want to make sure the script queries the correct location.

5. Finally, enable or disable **Enforce script signature check and run script silently**. If your scripts are unsigned, set this to **No**. Do not worry about the **run script silently** part – unsigned scripts will also run in the background as they are deploying in the *system* context.
6. Once configured, click **Review + save**.
7. Finally, confirm that everything looks correct and click **Save**.

That completes this recipe on how to use and deploy a custom detection script. Now, we can look at some real-world examples.

Examples of application detection scripts

Here are a few examples to give you an idea of how app detection scripts work. It is often easier to see a working script to fully understand the output requirements:

- This script will perform a simple registry check for 7-Zip:

```
$Path = "HKLM:\SOFTWARE\7-Zip"
$Name = "Path"
$Type = "STRING"
$Value = "C:\Program Files\7-Zip\"

Try {
    $Registry = Get-ItemProperty -Path $Path -Name $Name -ErrorAction Stop
| Select-Object -ExpandProperty $Name
    If ($Registry -eq $Value){
        Write-Output "Detected"
       Exit 0
    }
    Exit 1
}
Catch {
    Exit 1
}
```

- This script uses file detection for an application:

```
$File = "C:\windows\system32\notepad.exe"
if (Test-Path $File) {
    write-output "Notepad detected, exiting"
    exit 0
}
```

```
else {
    exit 1
}
```

> **Tip**
>
> Realistically, you would probably do these detections with the GUI tools, so we will cover some use cases that go beyond that ability.

- This example script will check that a service has been created and is running. It is useful for those apps that will not run without a running service:

```
$service = get-service -name "MozillaMaintenance"
if ($service.Status -eq "Running") {
    write-output "MozillaMaintenance detected and running, exiting"
    exit 0
}
else {
   exit 1
}
```

- If you want to ensure that the latest version has been installed but do not trust the vendor versioning within the application, you can query the last time the file was updated:

```
$filedate = (Get-Item "C:\Windows\System32\notepad.exe").LastWriteTime
if ($filedate -gt (Get-Date).AddDays(-1)) {
    write-output "Detected"
    exit 0
}
else {
    exit 1
}
```

That completes configuring detection scripts using the UI and some examples. Now, let's look at how to automate this process.

Automating it

Follow these steps to configure a custom detection script using automation:

Note

Whether you are configuring during initial deployment or afterward, the change is within the JSON that is passed when the application stub is created. The only difference is that a new application uses a POST request, whereas an update runs a PATCH request against the existing application.

1. First, similar to a platform script, we need to take the script's content:

```
$script = @'
$Path = "HKLM:\SOFTWARE\7-Zip"
$Name = "Path"
$Type = "STRING"
$Value = "C:\Program Files\7-Zip\"
Try {
    $Registry = Get-ItemProperty -Path $Path -Name $Name -ErrorAction Stop
| Select-Object -ExpandProperty $Name
    If ($Registry -eq $Value){
        Write-Output "Detected"
       Exit 0
    }
    Exit 1
}
Catch {
    Exit 1
}
'@
```

2. We must convert this into Base64:

```
$base64script =
[Convert]::ToBase64String([System.Text.Encoding]::Unicode.GetBytes($script)
)
```

3. Then, we must add it to the rules section of the JSON:

```
$json = @"
    "rules": [
        {
```

```
            "@odata.type":
"#microsoft.graph.win32LobAppPowerShellScriptRule",
            "comparisonValue": null,
            "displayName": null,
            "enforceSignatureCheck": false,
            "operationType": "notConfigured",
            "operator": "notConfigured",
            "ruleType": "detection",
            "runAs32Bit": false,
            "runAsAccount": null,
            "scriptContent": "$base64script"
        }
    ],
"@
```

Note that `@odata.type` changes to `PowerShellScriptRule` here.

You can also see that the `runAsAccount` option is present, but it is set to `null`. If you try to set this to anything else, the request will fail with the following error:

```
The RunAsAccount property may not be set for Win32LobAppPowerShellScriptRule
instances used for app detection
```

You would then populate the rest of the Win32 script and upload it accordingly.

That completes this recipe on custom application detection scripts.

Using custom requirements scripts in apps

Another PowerShell option is using custom requirements scripts. While the requirements rules are reasonably comprehensive, you may want to take these a step further – for example, only deploy an application if the device is manufactured by a particular company.

One particularly useful application for these is when you are updating *available* applications. As these are user-installed, when you deploy an update to them, the user has to manually install the latest version from the company portal (providing you have the detection rules set correctly to notice it needs re-installing). This is far from ideal, especially when you are dealing with a zero-day exploit.

In this situation, you can deploy an application *as required* to everyone and then set a requirements rule that it must detect whether the application is already present on the device to install.

These work differently and are closer to **compliance scripts** than remediation or detection scripts. We do not need an exit code since Intune reads the output of the script, which must match the condition that has been set within the application requirements rule.

As with the previous recipe, we will include some examples to demonstrate this further.

How to do it...

In this example, we will set a requirement that the application will only be installed if the device is manufactured by ACME (the manufacturer that was created for this example). Follow these steps to configure and deploy the requirements script:

1. The first thing we need to do is create our script. In your editor of choice, create a new PowerShell script with the following code:

   ```
   $Manufacturer = Get-WmiObject -Class Win32_ComputerSystem | Select-Object -
   ExpandProperty Manufacturer
   $Manufacturer
   ```

   This is simply grabbing the manufacturer's name from the machine's WMI and returning it.

2. Now, we need to add this to an application. Navigate to **Apps**, click on **Windows**, and find the application in question. Click on it and click **Properties**.
3. Now, click **Edit** next to **Requirements**.
4. Click **+ Add** at the bottom.
5. In the flyout, under **Requirement type**, select **Script**.
6. Now, select the script we have just created, which will also auto-populate the **Name** field; you can change this if required.
7. Set the standard options for 32/64-bit, user/system context, and whether the script must be signed.
8. Now for the important part – we need to tell it what data to look for.
   You have several options here, and you must select the correct one. Otherwise, your requirements script will fail, even if the device meets them:

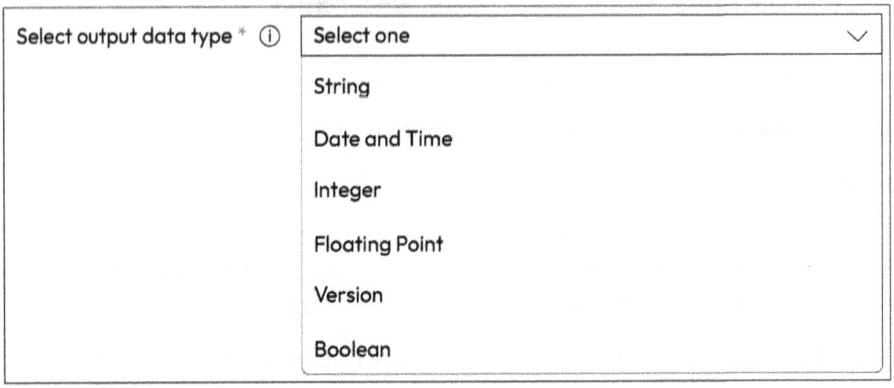

Figure 12.6 – Output data types

If you are unsure which one you need, within your script, type the variable followed by `.GetType()`.

In our case, this would look like this:

```
$manufacturer.GetType()
```

This will return the details of the output and the name you are looking for – in this case, `String`:

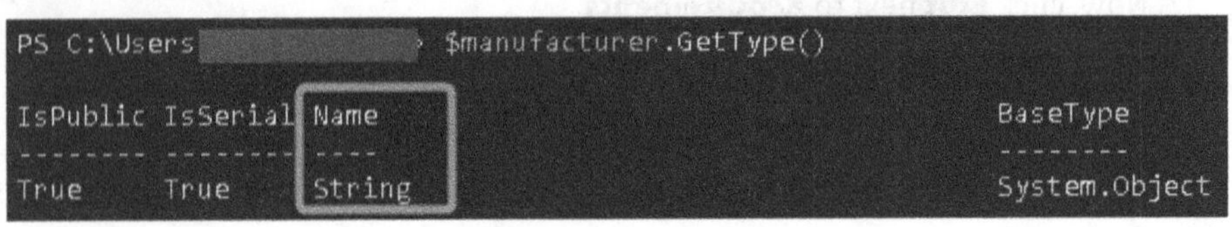

Figure 12.7 – The GetType output

To check for a numeric value, run the following code:

```
$test = 1
$Test.gettype()
```

The result will be an integer:

Figure 12.8 – Integer output

9. Select the appropriate data type from the dropdown.
10. Now, set your operator, which is either **Equals** or **Not Equal to** for a string. For the other data types, you have more options.

    We only want a particular result, so we are going to set this to **Equals**.
11. Finally, set the value we are looking for, which, in our case, is `ACME`:

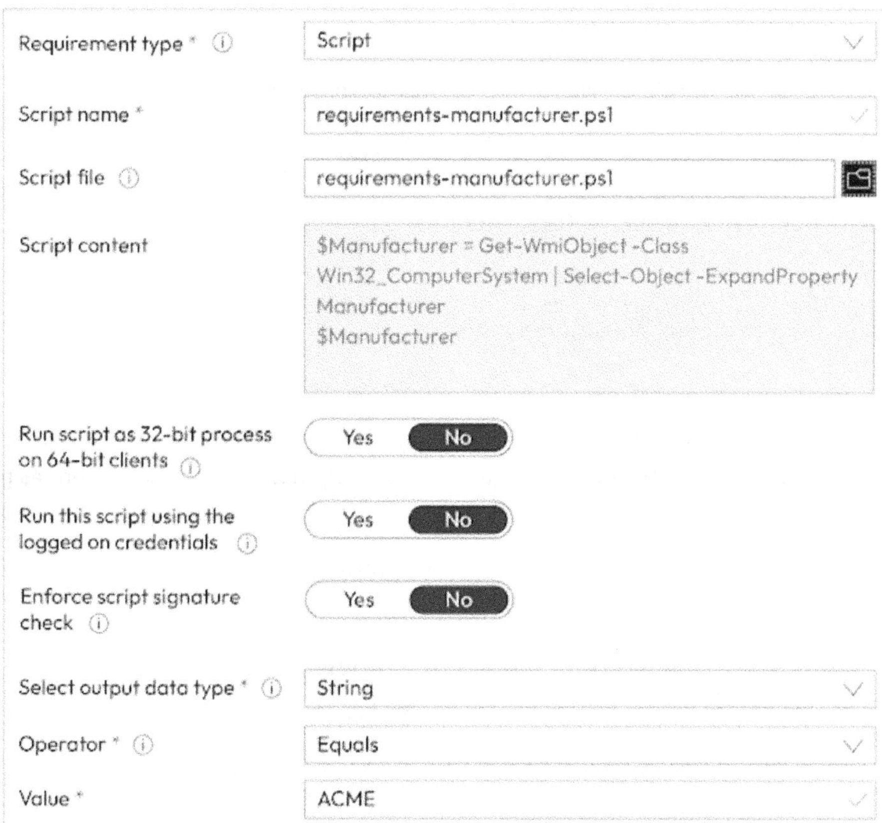

Figure 12.9 – Script requirements configuration

12. Now, click **OK**.

13. Back on the **Requirements** page, click **Review + save**.
14. Confirm that everything looks okay and click **Save**.

That completes the steps to add a custom requirements script. Now, let's look at some real world examples.

Examples of custom requirements scripts

These examples will show use cases for custom requirements scripts in application deployment:

- This script will detect and return the manufacturer:

```
$Manufacturer = Get-WmiObject -Class Win32_ComputerSystem | Select-Object -
ExpandProperty Manufacturer
$Manufacturer
```

- This script will check whether an application is installed:

```
$File = "C:\windows\system32\notepad.exe"
if (Test-Path $File) {
    write-output "Notepad detected"
}
else {
write-output "Notepad Not Detected"
}
```

In the GUI, you would be looking for a data type of **String** with an operator of **Equals** and a value of `Notepad detected` within the requirements configuration (as per *Figure 12.9*).

- This script will look for a particular hotfix on a device:

```
$hotfixid = "KB5030219"
$hotfix = Get-HotFix | where-object HotFixID -eq $hotfixid
if ($hotfix) {
    write-output "Hotfix detected"
}
else {
write-output "Hotfix Not Detected"
}
```

For this one, we need the `Hotfix detected` string.

Now that we have looked at some examples, let's learn how to automate this process.

Automating it

The automation we need to do here works the same as the custom detection scripts we covered in the previous recipe, only instead of setting the `Rules` section of the JSON, we must set the `requirementRules` section.

Follow these steps to configure our requirements script:

1. First, we need to add our script:

```
$script = @'
$Manufacturer = Get-WmiObject -Class Win32_ComputerSystem | Select-Object -
ExpandProperty Manufacturer
$Manufacturer
'@
```

2. Then, convert the script's content to Base64:

```
$base64script =
[Convert]::ToBase64String([System.Text.Encoding]::Unicode.GetBytes($script)
)
```

3. Then, populate the JSON with the converted script's content:

```
$json = @"
"requirementRules": [
    {
        "@odata.type":
"#microsoft.graph.win32LobAppPowerShellScriptRequirement",
        "operator": "equal",
        "detectionValue": "ACME",
        "displayName": "requirements-manufacturer.ps1",
        "enforceSignatureCheck": false,
        "runAs32Bit": false,
        "runAsAccount": "system",
        "scriptContent": "$base64script",
        "detectionType": "string"
    }
],
"@
```

Again, it uses the same `@odata.type` but adds our additional values, where we specify what we are looking for in the output. `runAsAccount` is also now open for amendment.

At this point, you would populate your Win32 JSON with the added requirements script and deploy it as required.

That completes this recipe on custom requirements scripts for Win32 applications.

Join us on Discord

For discussions around the book and to connect with your peers, join us on Discord at `packt.link/discordcloud` or scan the QR code below:

13

Tenant Administration

After completing the main configuration of our new environment, we can look at its administration. The items available within **Tenant Administration** are tenant-wide and cover a variety of options, from user experience to administrative tasks for you as an admin.

This chapter will cover all of the main items and, where possible, how to access them via Graph.

It is important to understand all of the options that are available for an Intune administrator to ensure a smooth service for your end users, as well as to make your day-to-day tasks as time-efficient as possible. By following this chapter, you will be in a better position to maintain your tenant in the long run.

In this chapter, we will cover the following recipes:

- Reviewing your connectors
- Adding filters
- Configuring Intune roles
- Using scope tags
- Customizing the end user experience
- Deploying custom notifications
- Setting up terms and conditions
- Configuring multi-admin approval
- Checking your tenant version
- Using Intune's troubleshooting tools
- Enrollment notifications
- Configuring device restrictions

- Configuring quiet time policies
- Reviewing admin tasks

Technical requirements

For this chapter, you will need a modern web browser and a PowerShell code editor such as Visual Studio Code or PowerShell ISE.

All the scripts that are referenced in this chapter can be found here: `https://github.com/PacktPublishing/Microsoft-Intune-Cookbook-Second-Edition/tree/main/Chapter-13`.

Reviewing your connectors

We will start by looking at an important aspect you must keep an eye on – third-party connectors such as the **Apple VPP connector**, which we covered in *Chapter 6, iOS Device Management*. A large selection is available, but not all of them will be used in every environment, so you need to monitor the ones that are important to you.

Getting ready

Here, we will learn about the various connectors that are available.

In the Intune portal, navigate to **Tenant Administration** and select **Connectors and Tokens**.

This will take you to a new section consisting of many different options. Let's take a look at what is available:

- **Windows enterprise certificate**: If you are using a code-signing certificate with MSIX packages, this is where you upload it to your tenant. After adding it, this page will show you the status of the certificate and, more importantly, its expiry date.
- **Microsoft Endpoint Configuration Manager**: If you are using Co-Management with Configuration Manager, this is where you can see the status of the Intune connector and its last successful sync.
- **Windows 365 partner connectors**: This is for estates using Windows 365 alongside either Citrix or VMware to add the connector and then view its status. To access this screen, you will need a Windows 365 license.
- **Windows data**: There are two settings here. The first is to enable sending diagnostic data (which is a requirement for Autopatch, among other things). The other option is license confirmation. Setting this to **Yes** tells Intune you have an Enterprise, Education, or AVD license (E3, E5, F3, F5), which unlocks SKU-specific features such as Remediations.

- **Apple VPP Tokens**: This is an important one if you are managing Apple devices, as it is where you add your VPP tokens for application purchasing and management, but also where you monitor their expiry dates and renew them. If you need to quickly add a purchased application to Intune, this is also where you will find the Sync button.
- **Managed Google Play**: Here, you can see the status of the Managed Google Play connector and also optionally add a scope tag to any new applications that have been added for role-based assignment.
- **Chrome Enterprise**: This is for configuring and monitoring your ChromeOS devices that have been synchronized from your Chrome Enterprise domain.
- **Firmware over-the-air update**: At the time of writing, this option is for Zebra devices only and lets you configure a connector between Intune and Zebra Lifeguard.
- **Microsoft Defender for Endpoint**: Here, you can view the status of your MDE connector and configure tenant-wide, cross-platform settings. Remember that MDE needs appropriate licensing.
- **Mobile Threat Defense**: This option lets you add a connector for third-party antivirus products and then view their status. It is also a requirement for Windows MAM, as covered in *Chapter 11*.
- **Partner device management (JAMF)**: If you are using JAMF to manage your macOS devices and want to use JAMF compliance with Conditional Access, you can use this option to set up a connector between the two.
- **Partner compliance management**: This is similar to JAMF but is for more platforms, such as MobileIron, VMware, and Blackberry, and also cross-platform options (Android, iOS, and macOS).
- **TeamViewer connector**: If you use TeamViewer for remote support, configuring the connector here adds Intune integration.
- **ServiceNow connector**: This one requires a license for Remote Help or Intune Suite. Configuring the connector adds details of ServiceNow incidents directly within the user's **Troubleshooting + support** pane in Intune.
- **Certificate connectors**: This is where you can add your SCEP and NDES certificates for device-based authentication.
- **Derived Credentials**: This option is for configuring certificates so that they can be used with smart card authentication across platforms.

Now that we know what these are all for, let's learn how to check their statuses using Graph.

How to do it...

To view the status of these connectors, simply click on them in the portal. As no real instructions are required here, we will look at the automation process instead.

Automating it

When you wish to automate connectors and tokens, fortunately, all menu options are available by using a `GET` request to a specific URL. This means we can build a custom menu using a PowerShell array and the `out-gridview` command. Follow these steps to create an automation script:

> **Note**
>
> Some of these code blocks have been shortened. The full code can be found here: `https://github.com/PacktPublishing/Microsoft-Intune-Cookbook-Second-Edition/blob/main/Chapter-13/connectors-and-tokens.ps1`.

1. The first thing we need to do is create our array:

```
$connectors = @(
    "Windows enterprise certificate",
    "Microsoft Endpoint Configuration Manager",
    "Windows 365 Partner connectors",
    "Windows data",
    "Apple VPP Tokens",
    "Managed Google Play",
    "Chrome Enterprise",
    "Firmware over-the-air (Zebra)",
    "Microsoft Defender for Endpoint",
    "Mobile Threat Defense",
    "Partner device management (JAMF)",
    "Partner compliance management",
    "TeamViewer connector",
    "ServiceNow connector",
    "Certificate connectors",
    "Derived Credentials"
)
```

2. Then, add `out-gridview` with the `passthru` command to grab the option we have selected:

```
$selectedconnector = $connectors | Out-GridView -Title "Select a connector
to check" -PassThru
```

3. We need to take this and pass it to a `switch` command to find the corresponding URL. This has been shortened for brevity; please see the link in the preceding *Note* box for the full code:

```
switch ($selectedconnector) {
    "Apple VPP Tokens" {
        $url = "https://graph.microsoft.com/beta/deviceAppManagement/
vppTokens"
    }
    "Managed Google Play" {
        $url = "https://graph.microsoft.com/beta/deviceManagement/
mobileThreatDefenseConnectors?
`$select=id,lastHeartbeatDateTime,partnerState,androidEnabled,iosEnabled,wi
ndowsEnabled,macEnabled,androidMobileApplicationManagementEnabled,iosMobile
ApplicationManagementEnabled,windowsMobileApplicationManagementEnabled"
    }
    default {
        Write-Output "Invalid connector selected."
        Exit 1
    }
}
```

4. Next, we want to run our GET request against this URL:

```
$output = Invoke-MgGraphRequest -Uri $url -Method Get -OutputType PSObject
```

5. As the output for some arrays is inside a nested value array, but some are direct, we need to add some logic to retrieve the information required from inside the array:

```
if ($output.value) {
    $output = $output.value
}
else {
```

```
    $output = $output
}
```

6. Finally, display the output in a GUI:

```
$output | Out-GridView
```

By following these steps, you have created a script to quickly check the status of any connectors.

Adding filters

As mentioned in a few of the previous chapters, **filters** are an excellent (and quicker) way to use the **All users** or **All devices** assignment but restrict who it applies to. At the time of writing, it is also the only way to add device filtering to user assignments.

Filters are only applicable to devices and apps (Android and iOS); for user-based queries, you need to use a dynamic Entra group.

To use filters during assignment, you must create them. This is what we will be covering in this recipe.

The following filter options are available:

- **Managed apps**:
  - App version
  - Device management type – unmanaged, Apple Business Manager, Kiosk, Android Enterprise, and so on
  - Device manufacturer
  - Device model
  - Operating system version
- **Managed devices**:
  - Device name
  - Manufacturer
  - Model
  - Device category
  - Operating system version
  - Is rooted (iOS, Android)
  - Device ownership – personal or corporate

- Enrollment profile name
- Device trust type (Windows) – hybrid or cloud-only
- Operating system SKU (Windows)

Now that we understand what filters are for and which options are available, we can create our own.

How to do it...

Follow these steps to create your first filter:

1. Navigate to **Tenant Administration** and click on **Assignment filters**. Click **Create** and select **Managed devices** or **Managed apps**. In this example, we will be using a device filter.
2. Enter **Name** and **Description** values, select the **Platform** attribute the filter will apply to, and click **Next**.
3. On the **Rules** screen, use the rule builder to add the queries needed for your rule. In this example, we only want devices manufactured by ACME, so set **Property** to **manufacturer**, **Operator** to **Equals**, and **Value** to **ACME**. You can also manually edit the rule by clicking the **Edit** button next to **Rule syntax**:

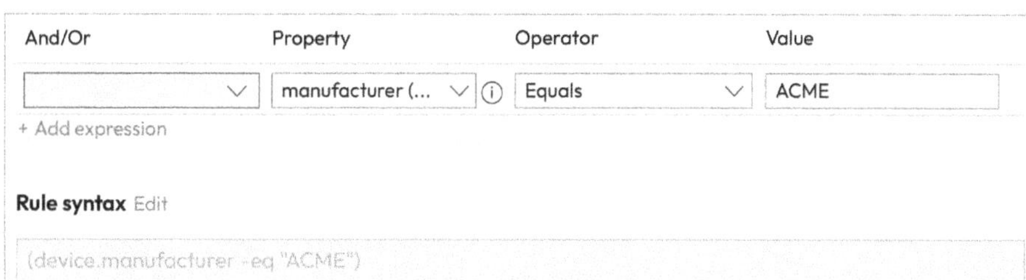

Figure 13.1 - Filters rule builder

4. Once you have set the rule, you can click **Preview** to see which devices will be detected by it. This is a good way of ensuring that you have the filter configured correctly before using it during assignment.
5. Once you are happy with the rule, click **Next**.
6. We will be covering **Scope tags** later in this chapter, so click **Next** for now.
7. Finally, review that everything looks correct and click **Create**.

You have now created your first filter. Next, we will look at how to automate it.

Automating it

We have established that filters are easy to configure within the GUI, but if you want to quickly deploy many of them, Graph and PowerShell will let you accomplish this more quickly, easily, and with less risk of error. Let's learn how to do so by following these steps:

1. First, we must start with the name and description:

```
$name = "ACME Only"
$description = "ACME Only Devices"
```

   Since all the filters post to the same location in Graph, we need to set the platform. The available options are as follows:

   - `Windows10AndLater`
   - `iOS` (iOS device)
   - `Android` (Android device administrator)
   - `AndroidForWork` (Android Enterprise)
   - `AndroidAOSP`
   - `MacOS`
   - `AndroidMobileApplicationManagement`
   - `iOSMobileApplicationManagement`

2. In this example, we are using Windows 10 and later:

```
$platform = "Windows10AndLater"
```

3. Now, add the rule itself; watch the escape characters for any quotation marks:

```
$rule = @"
(device.deviceOwnership -eq \"Corporate\")
"@
```

4. Add the URL to send the `POST` request to the following:

```
$url = "https://graph.microsoft.com/beta/deviceManagement/
assignmentFilters"
```

5. Populate the JSON with our settings:

```
$json = @"
{
    "description": "$description",
    "displayName": "$name",
    "platform": "$platform",
    "roleScopeTags": [
        "0"
    ],
    "rule": "$rule"
}
"@
```

6. Finally, send our `POST` request to create the filter:

```
Invoke-MgGraphRequest -Uri $url -Method Post -body $json -ContentType
"application/json"
```

That completes this recipe on filter creation, including a script to automate the creation of them.

Configuring Intune roles

While we have configured our environment using the Intune *Administrator* role, you may want to use different roles for different administrators within the tenant, giving admins the least privileges required for their job function. To do this, you can either use the built-in roles or create a custom role with the permissions individually selected. In this recipe, we will run through how to configure a custom role using both the GUI and PowerShell.

How to do it...

Follow these steps to configure a new Intune role:

1. Navigate to **Tenant Administration** and then **Roles**.

> Note
>
> Before creating a role, you can click on **My Permissions** to see the current permissions you have in the tenant.
>
> Back in **All Roles**, clicking on any of the built-in roles will take you to the page for that role. If you click **Properties**, you can view the permissions that have been assigned to that role. Clicking **Assignments** after will let you assign them to administrators.

2. To create a custom role, click on **All Roles**, then **+ Create**, and select **Intune Role** (or **Windows 365/Autopatch role** as required).
3. Specify your role's name and description, and then click **Next**. In this example, we are creating a basic level role that can rotate BitLocker keys and the LAPS password, as well as both sync and reboot a machine.
4. On the **Permissions** page, select the permissions required for the role you are creating and then click **Next**.
5. For our example, the options we need are under **Remote Tasks** and are labeled **Sync devices**, **Rotate BitLockerKeys**, **Reboot now**, and **Rotate Local Admin Password**. If you are unsure what a certain permission includes, click on the **i** icon to receive further details.

> Note
>
> This is one time where you may wish to assign scope tags, should you need to delegate certain permissions to only certain devices – for example, you may want the administrator of a particular office to be able to run tasks against the machines within that office, but not across the whole tenant. We will cover scope tags in the next recipe.

6. In our example, we are creating this tenant-wide. Once configured, click **Next**.
7. Finally, review that all the settings are correct and click **Create**.

8. Now that we have created our role, we need to assign it. First, click on the newly created role and click on **Assignments**.
9. Click **+ Assign**.
10. Specify your assignment's name and description and click **Next**.
11. Now, select an Entra group you want to assign this role to. All members of the group will then receive the role. Once selected, click **Next**.
12. If you want these admins to manage only a subset of users, you can set this on the **Scope Groups** screen. You can select **All Devices/All Users** to give them access everywhere or specify a group containing devices or users. If a group is selected, the admins will only be able to perform tasks against the members of that group. Once added, click **Next**.
13. Now, let's look at **Scope tags**. For the policy we have configured here, we are targeting device actions, so scope tags are less important than scope groups. If, however, you have a custom role with the ability to view or edit policies, you may want to lock those down so that different admins can only edit their subset of policies. In this situation, you would specify the scope tag that is used when creating the policy here.
14. Once configured, click **Next**.
15. As usual, confirm that everything looks correct and click **Create**.

You have now configured and assigned your first custom role in the UI.

How it works...

Now that we have created and assigned our role, we can see how that looks in PowerShell and Graph.

While configuring roles covers two screens within the portal, we can save effort here and run both parts in a single script. Follow these steps to create your role using PowerShell and Graph:

1. First, we need to configure the name, description, and our two group IDs for the admin group and scope group:

```
$name = "ServiceDesk"
$description = "Able to view Bitlocker Keys, Rotate LAPS password, Sync and 
Reboot"
$admingroupid = "xxxxxxxx-xxxx-xxxx-xxxx-xxxxxxxxxxxx"
$scopegroupid = "xxxxxxxx-xxxx-xxxx-xxxx-xxxxxxxxxxxx"
```

2. Next, we need the URL for the role creation itself:

```
$url = "https://graph.microsoft.com/beta/deviceManagement/roleDefinitions"
```

3. That is the basic options set, but now, we need to tell it which permissions we want in there. While we could look them up and manually type them in, we can use Graph to do the hard work for us. All permissions are listed at `https://graph.microsoft.com/beta/deviceManagement/resourceOperations`.

4. Therefore, we can run a `GET` request against this URL and send the output to `gridview`. We only need the ID for our policy, but we can include the name and description here to make them easier to select:

```
$allpermissions = (Invoke-MgGraphRequest -uri "https://graph.microsoft.com/
beta/deviceManagement/resourceOperations" -Method GET -OutputType
PSObject).value
$listpermissions = $allpermissions | Select-Object -Property
id,resourceName,description | Out-GridView -Title "Select Permissions" -
PassThru
```

5. This will give us an array containing our selected permissions. We need to convert it into JSON using the `convertto-json` parameter:

```
$selectedpermissions = ($listpermissions | Select-Object -ExpandProperty
id) | convertto-json
```

6. Then, add all of this to our final JSON:

```
$json = @"
{
    "description": "$description",
    "displayName": "$name",
    "id": "",
    "rolePermissions": [
        {
            "resourceActions": [
                {
                    "allowedResourceActions": $selectedpermissions
                }
            ]
        }
```

```
    ],
    "roleScopeTagIds": [
        "0"
    ]
}
"@
```

7. Create the role and grab its ID – we will need this to assign the role:

```
$role = Invoke-MgGraphRequest -uri $url -Method Post -Body $json -
ContentType "application/json" -OutputType PSObject
$roleid = $role.id
```

8. Now, set the assignment URL and add our role and group details to the JSON:

```
$assignurl = "https://graph.microsoft.com/beta/deviceManagement/
roleAssignments"
$assignjson = @"
{
    "description": "$description",
    "displayName": "$name",
    "id": "",
    "members": [
        "$adminGroupId"
    ],
    "resourceScopes": [
        "$scopeGroupId"
    ],
    "roleDefinition@odata.bind": "https://graph.microsoft.com/beta/
deviceManagement/roleDefinitions('$roleId')"
}
"@
```

9. Finally, send the `POST` request to assign our role:

```
Invoke-MgGraphRequest -uri $assignurl -Method Post -Body $assignjson -
ContentType "application/json" -OutputType PSObject
```

That completes the steps required to create and assign a custom role.

Using scope tags

We have seen scope tags throughout this book when we created various policies or applications. Now, it is time to learn what they are used for and how to create them.

First, we will clear up the differences between scope groups and scope tags.

Scope groups are configured within an Intune role and specify which users or devices an administrator can perform actions against when roles have actions configured. They are similar to administrative units within Entra ID, where administrators can be locked out from accessing all devices and users in the tenant.

Scope tags are configured on individual items within the tenant and can be used to allow or restrict access to these items. For example, you could configure a subset of your policies with a specific scope tag and allow only certain administrators to amend this policy. For larger organizations with multiple administrative teams, this can be useful to give the local admins some freedom, but only on their own devices and policies. When looking at iOS applications, the scope tag will be inherited from the VPP token by default.

When dealing with large, distributed estates, scope tags are an essential part of your **role-based access control** (**RBAC**) policy of least privileged access.

They work especially well alongside group tags. If you add group tags to your machines during Autopilot enrollment, you can then create an Entra group based on that group tag and assign the group to the scope tag.

Now that we know how they work and what they are for, we can create our first scope tag.

How to do it...

Follow these steps to configure a new scope tag:

1. Navigate to **Tenant Administration** and click on **Roles**.
2. From the left-hand menu, click **Scope tags** and click **+ Create**.
3. Specify your scope tag's name and description, and click **Next**.
4. Now, simply select the groups you want this tag to be assigned to. In this case, we are using a static group containing devices from a remote office. Once configured, click **Next**.
5. Review that your scope tag has been configured correctly and click **Create**.

As you can see, scope tags are straightforward to configure in the UI, but we can also automate them to make this process even quicker.

Automating it

While in the portal, you cannot create a tag without assigning it. Within Graph, it is still a two-step process, even if the first step is just adding a name and description!

Follow these steps to create your scope tag using automation:

1. We will start with the basics, including the group for assignment, which we will need in the next step:

```
$name = "Office-1"
$description = "Devices within Office 1"
$groupid = "xxxxxxxx-xxxx-xxxx-xxxx-xxxxxxxxxxxx"
```

2. Add our URL. Since scope tags live within roles in the portal, the URL also includes a role:

```
$url = "https://graph.microsoft.com/beta/deviceManagement/roleScopeTags"
```

3. Now, populate the JSON, which, in this case, is just `name` and `description`:

```
$json = @"
{
    "description": "$description",
    "displayName": "$name"
}
"@
```

4. Create the scope tag and grab the ID:

```
$scopetag = Invoke-MgGraphRequest -Method POST -Uri $url -Body $json -
ContentType "application/json" -OutputType PSObject
$scopetagid = $scopetag.id
```

If you decide to add this scope tag to policies in the future via Graph, this is the ID you would add to the array. Here is an example:

```
    "roleScopeTagIds": [
        "0",
        "2"
    ]
```

5. Now, add the ID to the assignment URL:

```
$assignurl = "https://graph.microsoft.com/beta/deviceManagement/
roleScopeTags/$scopetagid/assign"
```

6. Add the group ID to the JSON:

```
$assignjson = @"
{
    "assignments": [
        {
            "target": {
                "@odata.type": "#microsoft.graph.groupAssignmentTarget",
                "groupId": "$groupid"
            }
        }
    ]
}
"@
```

7. Finally, send the POST request to assign the group to the scope tag:

```
Invoke-MgGraphRequest -Method POST -Uri $assignurl -Body $assignjson -
ContentType "application/json" -OutputType PSObject
```

That completes this recipe on scope tags.

Customizing the end user experience

We have spent all of this time and effort to make the user experience as straightforward as possible, packaged the apps for self-service installation, and configured settings for the ultimate experience. However, there is one thing we have not done – that is, making the Company Portal and the general sign-in experience look better.

This recipe will concentrate primarily on the Intune side of things and configuring custom settings for the Company Portal. However, in the *There's more...* section, we will run through how to customize the sign-in experience within Entra and the Microsoft 365 admin portal.

How to do it...

Follow these steps to customize your environment for a better end user experience:

1. Navigate to **Tenant Administration** and click **Customization**.

2. Here, we can either edit the default settings or, right at the bottom of the page, configure multiple policies with group assignments, should different groups of users have different requirements (for example, a single tenant but with multiple sub-companies running from it). In this example, we are going to amend only the default settings, so click **Edit** next to **Settings**.

> **Tip**
>
> To view your changes, simply navigate to
>
> `https://portal.manage.microsoft.com/`.

There are numerous settings here, so we will go through them by section:

- **Branding**: This is all fairly straightforward – add your logos for dark and light backgrounds, set colors and organization names, and whether you wish to display just the logo or the logo and its name.
- **Support information**: This is the information that is displayed within the Company Portal's help desk. The **Additional Information** field is useful for providing the hours when support is available, out-of-hours contact details, or a physical location if you allow drop-ins.
- **Configuration**: This is where you can specify what can and cannot be done within the Company Portal:
    - **Device enrollment**: You can set whether to allow the **Enroll** button itself.
    - **Privacy statement URL**: You can provide a link to your publicly available statement.
    - **Privacy message**: If you want to change the default iOS/iPadOS privacy message, you can do so here.
    - **Device categories**: If you have categories configured, you can block the option for the users to select a category themselves.
    - **App sources**: These are additional applications to display on the Company Portal. You can choose to include any Enterprise applications registered in Entra, all of the applications added to your Office portal, and any Configuration Manager applications if they are co-managed.

The first two options can quickly clutter the Company Portal, so be careful with these.

- **Hide features**: Select which options you do not want your users to see. On Windows and iOS/iPadOS devices, you can hide the **Remove** button to stop users from unenrolling their devices, as well as the **Reset** button, which will cause more complaints as users blindly click buttons without thinking of the consequences.

3. Once you have configured your settings as required, click **Review + Save**.
4. Check that everything looks correct and click **Save**.

Now that we have looked at the customization settings within the UI, let's learn how to automate them.

Automating it

While this is often a set-and-forget configuration, if you configure multiple tenants, you may wish to automate it. Follow these steps to configure a PowerShell script to do so:

1. When configuring via PowerShell and Graph, we must start with the text field options:

```
$companyname = "Test"
$contactTelephone = "1234"
$contactEmail = "help@help"
$contactname = "IT Helpdesk"
$contactWebsite = "https://microsoft.com"
$websitename = "Name"
$privacyUrl = "https://microsoft.com"
$additionalinfo = "More Here"
```

2. Then, we need to convert the image into Base64 format:

```
$imagepath = "PATH HERE"
$imagebase64 = [System.Convert]::ToBase64String((Get-Content $imagepath -
Encoding Byte))
```

3. As this is an edit rather than us creating something, we will be sending a `PATCH` request, which means we need to find the ID of the current policy settings. For this, we need to send a `GET` request to the following URL: `https://graph.microsoft.com/beta/deviceManagement/intuneBrandingProfiles`.

This will return all policies that have been created. We are just editing the primary one, so we need to amend the URL to filter on only the default. Then, we need to grab the ID within the `value` array:

```
$customid = (Invoke-MgGraphRequest -uri "https://graph.microsoft.com/beta/
deviceManagement/intuneBrandingProfiles?`$filter=isDefaultProfile eq true"
-method GET -OutputType PSObject).value.id
```

4. Add the ID to the URL:

```
$url = "https://graph.microsoft.com/beta/deviceManagement/
intuneBrandingProfiles('$customid')"
```

Now, populate the JSON, which is available here: `https://github.com/PacktPublishing/Microsoft-Intune-Cookbook/blob/main/Chapter-13/customizations-intune.ps1`.

5. Finally, send the `PATCH` request to change the settings:

```
Invoke-MgGraphRequest -Method PATCH -Uri $url -Body $json -ContentType
"application/json" -OutputType PSObject
```

That completes the script for customizing your tenant within Intune.

There's more...

As we mentioned previously, so far, we have only configured the Company Portal. For a better experience, we also want to configure the sign-in screen options in Entra and the Microsoft 365 portal. We will look at these next.

Customizations in Microsoft Entra

The first place we can add customizations is within Entra, where we can add branding to the sign-in experience. This is especially useful when using Autopilot, as you will know that the correct profile has been applied when the standard Microsoft branding has been replaced with your own.

To do this, within **Entra ID**, expand **User Experiences** and click on **Company Branding** or go to `https://entra.microsoft.com/#view/Microsoft_AAD_UsersAndTenants/CompanyBrandingOverview.ReactView`.

Here, you can configure the branding across Entra and, most importantly, on the sign-in screen:

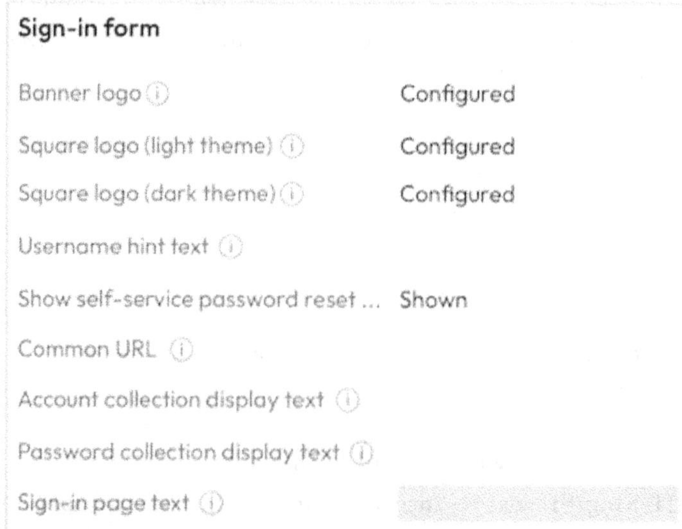

Figure 13.2 – Entra sign-in settings

Now that we have configured Entra, let's look at the Microsoft 365 portal.

Customizing the Microsoft 365 portal

The other customization option is in the Microsoft 365 admin center under **Settings** | **Org Settings** | **Custom Themes**. Alternatively, you can go to `https://admin.microsoft.com/#/Settings/OrganizationProfile/:/Settings/L1/CustomThemes`.

Clicking on **Default Theme** will let you set colors and logos on the Microsoft 365 estate. You can also add additional themes for user groups, should you have a multi-organization tenancy.

Deploying custom notifications

For Android and iOS devices, you can send custom notifications, which will be displayed in the **Notifications** area on the device.

Depending on your security configuration, these may display on a lock screen, so please double-check your settings before sending any confidential information via this method.

How to do it...

Follow these steps to configure a custom notification within your environment:

1. Click on **Tenant Administration**, then **Custom Notifications**.
2. Add **Title** and **Content** values for your message, then click **Next**.

3. Assign as required. Again, it is *user-only*, and you cannot select **All Users** here. Once assigned, click **Next**.
4. Finally, review that everything looks correct and click **Create**.

Automating it

These are equally as simply to automate.

1. First we set our variables:

```
groupid = "xxxxxxxx-xxxx-xxxx-xxxx-xxxxxxxxxxxx"
$Title = "Test Message"
$Body = "Alert! Alert! That is all"
```

2. Then populate the URL:

```
$url = "https://graph.microsoft.com/beta/deviceManagement/
sendCustomNotificationToCompanyPortal"
```

3. Add the variables to the JSON:

```
$json= @"
{
"groupsToNotify": [
"$groupid"
],
"notificationBody": "$body",
"notificationTitle": "$title"
}
"@
```

4. Send the request:

```
write-host "Creating Custom Notification"
Invoke-MgGraphRequest -uri $url -Method Post -Body $json -ContentType
"application/json"
```

Setting up terms and conditions

When enrolling a device, you want users to agree to organizational terms, especially if they are enrolling at home or using BYOD.

There are two options to do this: **Terms and Conditions** within Intune and **Terms of Use** within **Entra Conditional Access**. Terms of use are significantly more powerful and give you more flexibility, but we will cover both options here to give you the full picture.

You can learn about the differences between the two here: `https://techcommunity.microsoft.com/t5/intune-customer-success/choosing-the-right-terms-solution-for-your-organization/ba-p/280180`.

Now that we have seen our options, let's learn how to configure them.

How to do it...

We will start with Intune's terms and conditions, which give a very simplified set of terms for the user to accept.

Setting up terms and conditions

Follow these steps to configure your Intune terms and conditions:

1. First, navigate to **Tenant Administration**, then **Terms and Conditions**. Click **+ Create**.
2. Specify your policy's name and description and click **Next**.
3. Now, enter the details for the policy itself – that is, its title, summary of terms, and the actual terms and conditions. These are plain text only; for pictures, hyperlinks, and so on, we need the terms and conditions within Entra.
4. Once you have filled in your details, click **Next**.
5. If you need to delegate permissions, add your scope tags. Otherwise, simply click **Next**.
6. Now, we have to look at the term's assignment. It is worth sticking to user assignments here so that you can catch as much as possible. You can assign to all users as well, if required. Now, click **Next**.
7. Finally, review that everything looks correct and click **Create**.

That completes the steps for Intune terms and conditions. Now, let's look at those offered in Entra.

Configuring Entra's Terms of Use

Now, let's look at the more powerful **Terms of Use** available within Entra Conditional Access. For this one, we will need a PDF containing the terms of use. If you want to set multiple languages, create one for each. Follow these steps to configure **Terms of Use** within Conditional Access:

1. While these are Entra settings, we can access them within the Intune portal. Navigate to **Endpoint Security** and click **Conditional Access**.
2. Click on **Terms of Use** under **Manage** in the menu and click **+ New Terms**.

3. Set **Name**, **Title**, and **Language** values and add your PDF.
4. We have a few options available here:
   - **Require users to expand the terms of use**: Users must expand and read the Terms of Use
   - **Require users to consent on every device**: Users can either consent once for everything, or you can prompt per device
   - **Expire consents**: Enforce these terms immediately and clear out any previous consent
   - **Duration before re-acceptance required (days)**: This is how long before a user needs to re-accept
5. Finally, you can create a new policy to enforce these terms or select **Create conditional access policy later**, where you can add to an existing policy in the **Grant access** section. In this case, we will use an existing policy:

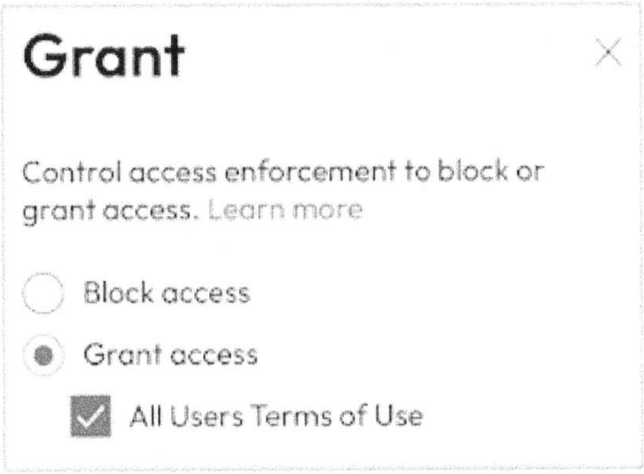

Figure 13.3 – All Users Terms of Use under Grant

6. Now, click **Create**. If you have chosen to create a new policy, you will be redirected to the familiar Conditional Access policy screen, where you can configure it accordingly.

That completes this recipe on creating our terms in the UI. Now, let's learn how to automate this process.

Automating it

Again, we will start with the terms and conditions.

Terms and conditions

Follow these steps to automate terms and conditions within Intune:

1. First, along with the usual name and description, we also need to add the details for the terms:

```
$name = "Default Terms"
$description = "Default Intune Terms and Conditions"
$title = "Terms and Conditions"
$summary = "Summary Here"
$bodyText = "Policy Here"
```

2. We also need the group ID for assignment:

```
$groupid = "xxxxxxxx-xxxx-xxxx-xxxx-xxxxxxxxxxxx"
```

3. Then, set the URL for the `POST` request:

```
$url = "https://graph.microsoft.com/beta/deviceManagement/
termsAndConditions"
```

4. Populate the JSON with our details:

```
$json = @"
{
    "acceptanceStatement": "$summary",
    "bodyText": "$bodyText",
    "description": "$description",
    "displayName": "$name",
    "roleScopeTagIds": [
        "0"
    ],
    "title": "$title",
    "version": 1
}
"@
```

5. Now, we need to send a POST request to create the policy and grab the ID, which we can use for assignment:

```
$terms = Invoke-MgGraphRequest -Uri $url -Method Post -Body $json -
ContentType "application/json" -OutputType PSObject
$termsid = $terms.id
```

6. Populate the assignment URL with the ID:

```
$assignurl = "https://graph.microsoft.com/beta/deviceManagement/
termsAndConditions/$termsid/assignments"
```

7. Add the group ID to the assignment JSON and send the request to assign the policy:

```
$assignjson = @"
{
    "@odata.type": "microsoft.graph.termsAndConditionsAssignment",
    "target": {
        "@odata.type": "#microsoft.graph.groupAssignmentTarget",
        "groupId": "$groupid"
    }
}
"@
Invoke-MgGraphRequest -Method POST -uri $assignurl -Body $assignjson -
ContentType "application/json"
```

That completes the script for terms and conditions. Next, we will look at Entra's Terms of Use.

Terms of Use

To automate Entra's Terms of Use, follow these steps:

1. Here, we must specify the display name, as well as the name of the file that contains the PDF:

```
$displayname = "All Users Terms of Use"
$filename = "PATH TO PDF HERE"
```

2. Now, we want both the Base64 content of the file and the name of the file itself. We can let PowerShell sort these for us:

```
$filenamebase64 =
[System.Convert]::ToBase64String([System.IO.File]::ReadAllBytes($filename))
$filenameonly = [System.IO.Path]::GetFileName($filename)
```

3. Next, we must set the URL:

```
$url = "https://graph.microsoft.com/beta/agreements"
```

4. Now, we must populate the JSON. Here, you can change your language for the PDF and also change the options for the **Yes/No** settings from before, where required:

```
$json = @"
{
    "displayName": "$displayname",
    "file": {
        "localizations": [
            {
                "displayName": "$displayname",
                "fileData": {
                    "data": "$filenamebase64",
                },
                "fileName": "$filenameonly",
                "isDefault": true,
                "language": "en-GB"
            }
        ]
    },
    "isPerDeviceAcceptanceRequired": false,
    "isViewingBeforeAcceptanceRequired": false,
    "userReacceptRequiredFrequency": null
}
"@
```

5. Finally, send the `POST` request to create the Terms of Use policy:

```
Invoke-MgGraphRequest -uri $url -method post -body $json -ContentType
"application/json"
```

That completes this recipe on automating terms in both Intune and Entra Conditional Access.

Configuring multi-admin approvals

Multi-admin approval is a new feature that you can implement to provide an extra layer of security when you are making changes to an environment. At the time of writing, the following Intune components are supported by multi-admin approval. When making changes to any of these, if activated, will require a second administrator to approve the change before it deploys:

- PowerShell script
- Application (you can also specify Windows, non-Windows, or both)
- Device delete
- Device retire
- Device wipe
- Role
- Tenant configuration

How to do it...

Follow these steps to set up multi-admin approvals in your tenant:

1. Navigate to **Tenant Administration** and click on **Multi Admin Approval**.
   Here, you can see any current requests (**Received Requests**), any requests you have submitted (**My Requests**), and the policies that have been configured (**Access Policies**).
2. Click on **Access Policies** and click **+ Create**.
3. Specify your policy's name and description, and select what it is being used for. You can only select one action per policy. If selecting **App**, you have additional sliders at the bottom to specify whether the policy applies to only Windows devices, only non-Windows devices, or both. Once you have made your selection, click **Next**.
4. On the **Approvers** screen, you need to select a group that contains administrators who can approve requests. Once added, click **Next**.
5. Finally, check that everything looks correct and click **Create**.
6. Now, we will look at the process of using them. When adding a new application or script, you will be prompted to provide a business justification. Instead of there being a **Create** button, we have a **Submit for approval** button.
7. We can then see the request in **Multi-Admin Approvals**:

Figure 13.4 – Viewing approvals

8. Logging on with an approver and clicking on **Business justification** will load the details of the request in a flyout, including details of the script's content and why it was submitted.
9. At the bottom of the flyout, enter some notes and then choose either **Approve request** or **Reject request**.
10. The originator then has to complete the request in the **Multi-Admin Approvers** portal, which will then add the application or script so that it is ready to be assigned. When you click the **Create** button, it grabs the details from the **payload** in the request and submits that back into Graph.

That completes this recipe on both configuring and using multi-admin approvals within Intune.

Automating it

Multi-admin approvals are very straightforward to automate so that you can create policies, as well as approve them.

Automating the policy creation process

Follow these steps to automate the multi-admin approval policy:

1. To create the policy, we need its name, description, and group ID:

```
$name = "Script Approvals"
$description = "Require Approvals for Scripts"
$groupid = "xxxxxxxx-xxxx-xxxx-xxxx-xxxxxxxxxxxx"
```

2. Then, we need to set the policy type, which can be one of the following:
   - `apps`
   - `scripts`
   - `deviceDelete`
   - `deviceRetire`
   - `deviceWipe`

  - `role`
  - `tenantConfiguration`

```
$policytype = "scripts"
```

3. If selecting app, you also need to select the policy platform.

   For Windows, this is as follows:

```
$policyplatform = "windows10AndLater, windows81AndLater, windows10X"
```

   For non-Windows, use this:

```
$policyplatform = "macOS, iOSiPadOS, androidEnterprise,
androidDeviceAdministrator"
```

   For both, use this:

```
$policyplatform = "notApplicable"
```

4. Configure the URL for our `POST` request:

```
$url = "https://graph.microsoft.com/beta/deviceManagement/
operationApprovalPolicies"
```

5. Populate the JSON with our configured variables:

```
$json = @"
{
    "approverGroupIds": [
        "$groupid"
    ],
    "description": "$description",
    "displayName": "$name",
    "policyType": "$policytype"
}
"@
```

6. If deploying an app policy, use the following:

```
$json = @"
{
    "approverGroupIds": [
        "$groupid"
    ],
    "description": "$description",
    "displayName": "$name",
    "policyPlatform": "$policyplatform",
    "policyType": "$policytype"
}
"@
```

7. Then, send the POST request to create the policy. We do not need to do anything further, so we do not need to grab the output of the request:

```
Invoke-MgGraphRequest -uri $url -Method Post -Body $json -ContentType
"application/json"
```

That completes the script for creating the policy. Now, let's learn how to approve the request programmatically.

Automating the request approval process

Follow these steps to approve a request within PowerShell:

1. For approval, we need to find the ID of the request itself. We can do this by sending a GET request to the following URL and grabbing the value. As the number of requests could grow in a large environment, we will use the `getallpagination` function to retrieve everything:

```
$requests = getallpagination -url "https://graph.microsoft.com/beta/
deviceManagement/operationApprovalRequests"
```

2. Now, we only want those not completed, so we are going to use `where-object` on the `Status` column and then output to `out-gridview` with the `passthru` parameter:

```
$selecectedrequest = $requests | where-object status -ne "completed" | Out-
GridView -PassThru
```

3. Next, we need the ID of the request we are approving/rejecting:

```
$requestid = $selecectedrequest.id
```

4. Populate the request ID you retrieved in the URL:

```
$url = "https://graph.microsoft.com/beta/deviceManagement/
operationApprovalRequests('$requestid')/approve"
```

5. Set the approval or rejection, which can be `Approved` or `Denied`:

```
$approval = "Approved"
```

6. Now, add the JSON and send the `POST` request to reply to the request:

```
$json = @"
{
    "justification": "$approval"
}
"@
Invoke-MgGraphRequest -uri $url -Method Post -Body $json -ContentType
"application/json"
```

With that, we have learned how to approve or deny admin approvals using PowerShell and Graph.

Checking your tenant version

Intune has regular updates with monthly major service updates. At the time of writing, these are in *YYMM* format – for example, November 2025 would be 2511.

You can follow all of the new features here: `https://learn.microsoft.com/en-us/mem/intune/fundamentals/whats-new`.

As Intune is globally distributed across multiple data centers worldwide, when a new version is released, it may not necessarily update your tenant straight away. For that, we can check out the tenant version.

How to do it...

Follow these brief steps to check the tenant version in your environment:

1. Navigate to **Tenant Administration** and click on **Tenant status**.

2. In the first tab, you can view your tenant details, including the tenant version and location:

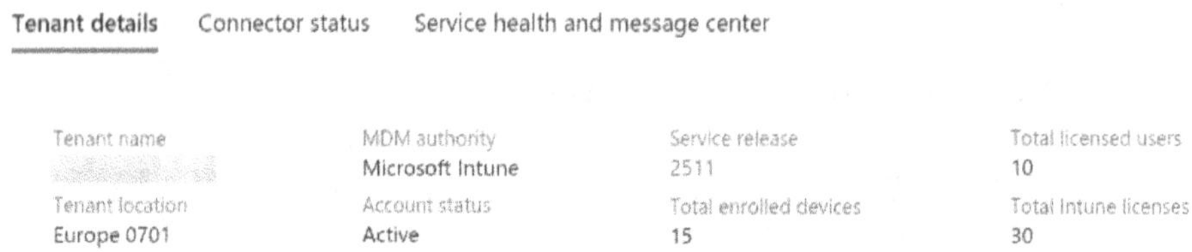

Figure 13.5 – Tenant details

3. The **Connector status** tab will show a quick overview of the connectors that have been configured. If you see any issues here, you can follow the recipe from earlier to diagnose further (*Reviewing your connectors*).
4. Finally, the **Service health and message center** area will show any central issues with Microsoft, any active incidents in your tenant that you need to take action on, and any messages, which are usually around new changes, functionality, and so on.

With that, we have learned how to check the service release and other key details about our tenant.

Using Intune's troubleshooting tools

We have created our tenant using best practices, carefully packaged our applications, and tested everything to ensure it is working. However, we all know that users are users and things will go wrong. For that, we need to be able to troubleshoot issues. Fortunately, Intune has excellent troubleshooting tools where we can quickly review what issues a user may be having.

How to do it...

Follow these steps to troubleshoot your devices:

1. Click on **Troubleshooting + support**. Then, from the menu, click **Troubleshoot**.
2. Select a user from the list; all their information will be grabbed automatically.
   The first thing we must do is look under **User status** to rule out anything basic, such as a disabled or unlicensed user.

   The **Summary** screen gives an overview of everything for the user across devices, policies, compliance, applications, and more.

   The following tabs are available:

   - **Devices**: All devices for the user, including Intune compliance, Entra compliance, and app life cycle status (failed app installs).

- **Groups**: Entra groups that the user is a member of.
- **Policy**: The policies that have been applied to the user.
- **Applications**: Cross-platform applications that have been assigned to the user and the number of devices applicable for each.
- **App protection policy**: The policies that have been assigned to the user and their status.
- **Updates**: The update policies that have been applied to the user's devices.
- **Enrollment restrictions**: The platform restrictions and limits that apply to this user. Comparing this to the **Devices** tab will show us whether the user has hit the limit and cannot enroll any further devices.
- **Diagnostics**: The output of any diagnostics requested.

3. To request diagnostics, navigate to the device in question and press the **Collect Diagnostics** button. After a while, a ZIP file will be exported containing all key diagnostics for the machine.
   A full list of what is collected can be found here: `https://learn.microsoft.com/en-us/mem/intune/remote-actions/collect-diagnostics#data-collected`.

With that, we have learned how to troubleshoot our user and device configurations.

Enrollment notifications

Introduced in release 2301 (January 2023), enrollment notifications alert a user when a new device has been added to Intune from their account. Annoyingly, it only alerts the user, and there is no way of alerting admins without exchanging mail forwarding rules.

How to do it...

Follow these steps to configure enrollment notifications for your users:

1. First, click on **Devices**, then click on **Enrollment**. Select the tab for the platform you wish to set the notifications for. You will need one policy per platform.
2. Click on **Enrollment notifications** and click **+ Create notification**.
3. Specify your notification's name and description and click **Next**.
4. On the **Notification Settings** screen, you can select which type of notification to send – that is, **Push notification** or **Email notification** (or both).
   For a push notification, you simply need the title and text to include:

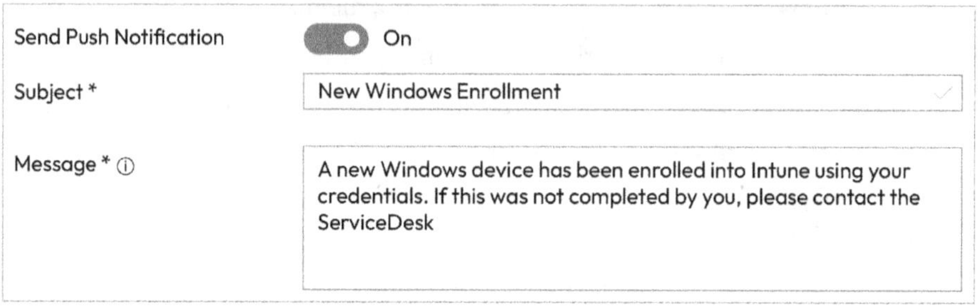

Figure 13.6 – Enrollment notifications

For an email notification, you have more options available:

- You can set the email's subject and message (with the ability to include HTML by switching on the raw HTML editor).
- You can include a header using the image we set when we customized the tenant in an earlier recipe (*Customizing the end user experience*).
- You can also include the company name, contact information, and a link to the Company Portal, where a user can see their enrolled devices. These details are all retrieved from the **Customization** settings within **Tenant Administration**. A very useful option is the ability to include the device details in the footer so that the user can check which device was enrolled and whether there are queries that supply the information when reporting it.

5. Once configured, click **Next**.
6. If you want to delegate access to the notifications, add a **Scope tag** value. If not, click **Next**.
7. **Assignment** has to be at the user level, as the device will not exist until after enrollment. Therefore, either select a user-based group or deploy to all users. Then, click **Next**.
8. Finally, review that everything looks correct and click **Create**.

This completes the instructions for configuring enrollment notifications in the UI.

Automating it

In terms of automating this process, there are two separate Graph POST requests we can use – one for push notifications and one for email notifications after creating the policy itself. Follow these steps to automate your enrollment notifications:

1. First, we need to set the name and description of the policy:

```
$policyname = "Windows Enrollment"
$policydescription = "Windows Enrollment Policy"
```

2. Then, we need the subject title and content for the notifications themselves:

```
$emailsubject = "New Windows Device Enrolled"
$pushsubject = "New Windows Enrollment"
$emailcontent = "A new Windows device has been enrolled using your
credentials. (see device details)\r\nIf this was not completed by you,
please contact us on the details below.\r\n\r\nTo view a list of your
devices, click on the link to Company Portal."
$pushcontent = "A new Windows device has been enrolled into Intune using
your credentials. If this was not completed by you, please contact the
ServiceDesk"
```

3. Now, we must create the policy itself. So, add the URL:

```
$notificationurl = "https://graph.microsoft.com/beta/deviceManagement/
deviceEnrollmentConfigurations"
```

4. Populate the JSON. You will see the platform type as well as the on/off options for the email template here. These can be amended as required:

```
$notificationurl = "https://graph.microsoft.com/beta/deviceManagement/
deviceEnrollmentConfigurations"
$notificationjson = @"
{
    "@odata.type":
"#microsoft.graph.deviceEnrollmentNotificationConfiguration",
    "brandingOptions":
"includeCompanyLogo,includeCompanyName,includeCompanyPortalLink,includeCont
actInformation,includeDeviceDetails",
    "defaultLocale": "en-US",
```

```
    "description": "$policydescription",
    "displayName": "$policyname",
    "notificationTemplates": [
        "email_00000000-0000-0000-0000-000000000000",
        "push_00000000-0000-0000-0000-000000000000"
    ],
    "platformType": "windows",
    "roleScopeTagIds": [
        "0"
    ]
}
"@
```

5. Now, create the policy with a `POST` request. We need the output of this to find the message templates that will be used:

```
$notificationpolicy = Invoke-MgGraphRequest -Uri $notificationurl -Method
Post -Body $notificationjson -OutputType PSObject -ContentType
"application/json"
```

Each enrollment notification creates new templates containing the notification data itself. These are stored in the same location in Graph as the custom compliance notifications we covered in *Chapter 8*: `https://graph.microsoft.com/beta/deviceManagement/notificationMessageTemplates`.

Fortunately, these template IDs are stored in an array within our policy output, and the ID starts with the notification type (`Email_PolicyID` or `Push_PolicyID`).

We can use PowerShell to retrieve these for us from the policy output:

```
$emailtemplateid = ($notificationpolicy.notificationtemplates | Where-
Object { $_ -like "Email*" }).split("_")[1]
$pushtemplateid = ($notificationpolicy.notificationtemplates | Where-Object
{ $_ -like "Push*" }).split("_")[1]
```

For each one, we are finding the appropriate template, splitting on "_", and grabbing the second value, which is the ID. When working with arrays, the first value is `[0]`, so the second value will be `[1]`.

6. Finally, we must populate these into the URLs, populate the JSON, and send a `POST` request with the content for each of them.

Now that we have created the policy, we must create the email templates themselves.

Email templates

For email templates, we are using the following URL and JSON to create the template:

```
$emailurl = "https://graph.microsoft.com/beta/deviceManagement/
notificationMessageTemplates/$emailtemplateid/localizedNotificationMessages"
$emailjson = @"
{
    "isDefault": true,
    "locale": "en-US",
    "messageTemplate": "$emailcontent",
    "subject": "$emailsubject"
}
"@
Invoke-MgGraphRequest -Uri $emailurl -Method Post -Body $emailjson -OutputType
PSObject -ContentType "application/json"
```

We will move on to push templates now.

Push templates

Alternatively, for push templates, we need the following URL and JSON:

```
$pushurl = "https://graph.microsoft.com/beta/deviceManagement/
notificationMessageTemplates/$pushtemplateid/localizedNotificationMessages"
$pushjson = @"
{
    "isDefault": true,
    "locale": "en-US",
    "messageTemplate": "$pushcontent",
    "subject": "$pushsubject"
}
"@
Invoke-MgGraphRequest -Uri $pushurl -Method Post -Body $pushjson -OutputType
PSObject -ContentType "application/json"
```

That completes this recipe on configuring enrollment notifications both in the UI and using automation.

Configuring device restrictions

Device restrictions are an often-overlooked yet critical part of managing your Intune environment. With the inclusion of MAM across platforms, the first step is to block the enrollment of personal devices, which can only be performed within Intune.

You can also specify device limits, as well as operating system versions and even manufacturers and models of devices!

How to do it...

There are two different settings to configure here: device limit restrictions and device platform restrictions. We will look at device limit restrictions first.

Device limit restrictions

To set up device limit restrictions, follow these steps:

1. Click on **Devices**, then **Enrollment**.
2. Select any platform and click **Device Limit Restrictions**.

   Here, you can create new restrictions or edit the default restriction, which applies to all. The restrictions are queried in numerical order, with the highest number being queried first. When it finds the restriction that applies to the user, it stops reviewing any further policies.

   If you need different groups of users to have different restrictions, create additional policies. If, however, you want a blanket approach, simply edit the default policy.

   In this example, we are going to add a new policy to allow more granular control.
3. Click **+ Create restriction**.
4. Specify the policy's name and description.
5. Under **Device limit**, select a limit. This can be between 1 and 15 devices.

   > Note
   >
   > Keep your device clean-up rules in mind here. If you set it to 1 and a user replaces their machine, you will need to manually remove the old one before they will be able to enroll a new device. If you have personal devices disabled, there should not be any risk of having this as a higher number, as the devices will all be corporate-owned anyway.
6. Once configured, click **Next**.

7. If you wish to delegate this policy, add a **Scope tag** value here. If not, click **Next**.
8. On the **Assignments** screen, assign the policy as required. You cannot select **All Users**, as that is the assignment for the default policy, so you will need to select a user group here. Once selected, click **Next**.
9. Finally, review that your restriction limit and assignment look correct and click **Create**.

This completes setting device limit restrictions. Now, let's look at device platform restrictions.

Device platform restrictions

When we look at our platform restrictions, things are more granular. You can either edit the default policy, which is applied to all platforms, or create individual policies for each platform.

As we want to block BYOD enrollment across platforms, in this example, we are going to edit the default policy.

Follow these steps to configure device platform restrictions:

1. Click on **Devices**, then **Enrollment**.
2. Select any platform and click **Device platform restrictions**.
3. Now, click the blue text labeled **All Users**.
4. Click **Properties** and then click the **Edit** text next to **Platform Restrictions**.

   Here, you can set which platforms you want to allow entirely, minimum and maximum operating system versions, personal devices, and manufacturers (Android only).

   If you decide to block at the version level, make sure you continuously review the settings as new versions are released and older ones are put out of support; otherwise, you may find yourself either blocking new devices or allowing anything.

   As **Android device administrator** is reaching its end of support, we are going to block that, as well as block all personally owned devices:

Figure 13.7 – Enrollment restrictions

5. Once configured, click **Review + Save**.

There are no assignment or scope tags here, as this is the default policy at the tenant level. If you need to have different settings for different groups or wish to delegate access, create individual policies to layer on top of the default.

6. Finally, review that everything looks correct and click **Save**.

With that, we have configured enrollment restrictions in the UI.

Automating it

As with the interactive configuration, we will split this into two parts, starting with automating the device limit restrictions.

Device limit restrictions

Creating a device limit restrictions policy is one of the more straightforward options in PowerShell and Graph, as it is cross-platform and the only field is numerical. Follow these steps to configure it in your tenant using PowerShell:

1. First, set the name and description:

```
$name = "New device restriction limit"
$description = "Set to 10 devices"
```

2. Next, set the device limit:

```
$limit = 10
```

3. Add the group ID for the assignment:

```
$groupid = "xxxxxxxx-xxxx-xxxx-xxxx-xxxxxxxxxxxx"
```

4. Set the URL to send the `POST` request to:

```
$url = "https://graph.microsoft.com/beta/deviceManagement/
deviceEnrollmentConfigurations"
```

5. Populate the JSON with the details:

```
$json = @"
{
    "@odata.type": "#microsoft.graph.deviceEnrollmentLimitConfiguration",
    "description": "$description",
    "displayName": "$name",
```

```
    "limit": $limit,
    "roleScopeTagIds": [
        "0"
    ]
}
"@
```

6. Send the request to create the policy and then retrieve the ID:

```
$restrictionpolicy = Invoke-MgGraphRequest -uri $url -Method POST -Body
$json -ContentType "application/json" -OutputType PSObject
$policyid = $restrictionpolicy.id
```

7. Add the ID to the assignment URL:

```
$assignurl = "https://graph.microsoft.com/beta/deviceManagement/
deviceEnrollmentConfigurations/$policyid/assign"
```

8. Add the group ID to the JSON and send the POST request to assign the new policy:

```
$assignjson = @"
{
    "enrollmentConfigurationAssignments": [
        {
            "target": {
                "@odata.type": "#microsoft.graph.groupAssignmentTarget",
                "groupId": "$groupid"
            }
        }
    ]
}
"@
Invoke-MgGraphRequest -uri $assignurl -Method POST -Body $assignjson -
ContentType "application/json" -OutputType PSObject
```

This completes the script for device enrollment limits. Now, we can look at platform restrictions.

Device platform restrictions

As we are amending the default settings, the first step is to grab the ID of the policy so that we can send a `PATCH` request to it. Follow these steps to configure it accordingly:

1. We know that the priority is going to be `0`, so the first thing we can do is filter the URL on that: `https://graph.microsoft.com/beta/deviceManagement/deviceEnrollmentConfigurations?$filter=priority eq 0`.
2. This will return the device limit restrictions, the platform restrictions, and the **Windows Hello for Business** (**WHfB**) settings, so we need to query `@odata.type` to return only the correct policy. Within that, we only want the ID:

   ```
   $policyid = (((Invoke-MgGraphRequest -Method GET -Uri "https://
   graph.microsoft.com/beta/deviceManagement/deviceEnrollmentConfigurations?
   `$filter=priority eq 0" -OutputType PSObject).value) | where-object
   '@odata.type' -eq
   "#microsoft.graph.deviceEnrollmentPlatformRestrictionsConfiguration").id
   ```

   Note the backtick (`) to pass through `$filter` in the URL by escaping the special character.
3. Now, we must add the policy ID to the URL:

   ```
   $url = "https://graph.microsoft.com/beta/deviceManagement/
   deviceEnrollmentConfigurations/$policyid"
   ```

   Add our JSON with the restrictions added, which are all Boolean values. The JSON can be found here: `https://github.com/PacktPublishing/Microsoft-Intune-Cookbook-Second-Edition/blob/main/Chapter-13/update-deviceplatformrestrictions.ps1`.
4. Then, send a `PATCH` request to update the policy with these new values:

   ```
   Invoke-MgGraphRequest -Uri $url -Method PATCH -Body $json -ContentType
   "application/json"
   ```

That completes this recipe on device platform restrictions.

Configuring quiet time policies

Introduced in the 2305 release of Intune (May 2023), quiet time policies give admins a way to mute Outlook and Teams notifications on devices centrally, either by day of the week or for specific date ranges on Android and iOS devices (only).

This can be used to stop notifications out of hours, such as on weekends, for a standard Monday to Friday user. The date-specific option is useful should you want to add public holidays in addition to the standard weekly quiet times.

How to do it...

Follow these steps to configure your quiet time policies:

1. To configure quiet time policies, click on **Apps**, then **Quiet time**.
2. Click **+ Create**.
3. In the flyout, select the **Policy type** value you wish to set and click **Create**.
4. Specify your policy's name and description and click **Next**.
5. The first option you have here is giving the user the ability to change the settings. Unless you have strict requirements, leave this set to **Yes**.
6. In the **Certain Hours** section, you can set notifications to be muted at certain times of the day. Set these around your expected staff working hours; remember, they can always change this. If you plan on blocking notifications on a weekend, untick **Saturday** and **Sunday** from this section, as we will configure that shortly.
7. Now, in the **All day** section, select **Saturday** and **Sunday**, or whatever your days off are (it should auto-select those when set to **Require** and **Configured**).
8. Once configured, click **Next**.
9. If you want to delegate access, add a **Scope tag** value here. If not, click **Next**.
10. When considering your assignments, look at the organization as a whole. If you have staff who work on-call (IT staff, for example), make sure you exclude them from the policy. You may also find that some executive staff work longer hours and do not want to have to manually change the settings so often that they may be worth excluding. If you run shift work, consider creating multiple policies to reflect the different shift times, although you would probably need some HR system integration to manage the group memberships for each user's shift patterns.

    Once you have configured your assignments, click **Next**.

11. Finally, review that everything looks correct and click **Create**.
12. If you are configuring a **Date Range** policy, the basic settings are all the same, but **Configuration settings** is a simple date range selection.

With that, we have learned how to configure quiet time policies in the UI. Now, let's learn how to automate them.

Automating it

Quiet time policies run on the *Unified Settings Catalog*, as covered in *Chapter 2*. This helps to standardize policy settings across the platform, but makes the PowerShell script significantly more complicated. Follow these steps to configure quiet time policies using PowerShell and Graph:

1. First, we start with our usual name, description, and group ID:

```
$name = "Quiet Time - Evenings Weekends"
$description = "Turn off notifications evenings and weekends"
$groupid = "xxxxxxxx-xxxx-xxxx-xxxx-xxxxxxxxxxxx"
```

2. Then, add the URL:

```
$url = "https://graph.microsoft.com/beta/deviceManagement/
configurationPolicies"
```

3. In the JSON, we start with the basic details, including the platform:

```
$json = @"
{
    "description": "$description",
    "name": "$name",
    "platforms": "android,iOS",
    "roleScopeTagIds": [
        "0"
    ],
```

4. Now, we move on to the settings themselves, which are split into different sections:

```
    "settings": [
```

5. First, we must set the all-day quiet time for Saturday and Sunday (days 6 and 0).

The all-day setting uses the following template ID:

```
c19aaaf1-afe1-4c49-a6b1-80b51ccdf5ec
```

The individual days are under the following ID:

```
4f48386d-2faa-4f1b-bd23-a75b0f513e42
```

We will now be referencing code blocks within the script listed on GitHub at `https://github.com/PacktPublishing/Microsoft-Intune-Cookbook-Second-Edition/blob/main/Chapter-13/new-quiettime-policy.ps1`.

6. Combining these gives us this section of the settings (lines 18–53 in the script):

```
    ],
    "settings": [
        {
            "@odata.type":
"#microsoft.graph.deviceManagementConfigurationSetting",
            "settingInstance": {
                "@odata.type":
"#microsoft.graph.deviceManagementConfigurationChoiceSettingInstance",
                "choiceSettingValue": {
                    "@odata.type":
"#microsoft.graph.deviceManagementConfigurationChoiceSettingValue",
                    "children": [
                        {
                            "@odata.type":
"#microsoft.graph.deviceManagementConfigurationChoiceSettingCollectionInsta
nce",
                            "choiceSettingCollectionValue": [
                                {
                                    "@odata.type":
"#microsoft.graph.deviceManagementConfigurationChoiceSettingValue",
                                    "children": [],
                                    "value":
"device_vendor_msft_policy_config_quiettime_mutenotificationsallday_daysoft
heweek_0"
                                },
                                {
                                    "@odata.type":
```

```
"#microsoft.graph.deviceManagementConfigurationChoiceSettingValue",
                                    "children": [],
                                    "value":
"device_vendor_msft_policy_config_quiettime_mutenotificationsallday_daysoft
heweek_6"
                                }
                            ],
                            "settingDefinitionId":
"device_vendor_msft_policy_config_quiettime_mutenotificationsallday_daysoft
heweek"
                        }
                    ],
                    "settingValueTemplateReference": {
                        "settingValueTemplateId": "4f48386d-2faa-4f1b-bd23-
a75b0f513e42"
                    },
                    "value":
"device_vendor_msft_policy_config_quiettime_mutenotificationsallday_1"
                },
                "settingDefinitionId":
"device_vendor_msft_policy_config_quiettime_mutenotificationsallday",
                "settingInstanceTemplateReference": {
                    "settingInstanceTemplateId": "c19aaaf1-afe1-4c49-
a6b1-80b51ccdf5ec"
                }
            }
        },
```

7. Next, we must set the out-of-hours quiet times for days 1 to 5 (lines 54–59):

```
        {
            "@odata.type":
"#microsoft.graph.deviceManagementConfigurationSetting",
            "settingInstance": {
                "@odata.type":
"#microsoft.graph.deviceManagementConfigurationChoiceSettingInstance",
                "choiceSettingValue": {
                    "@odata.type":
"#microsoft.graph.deviceManagementConfigurationChoiceSettingValue",
                    "children": [
```

8. We start with the start time (lines 61–68):

```
                    {
                            "@odata.type":
"#microsoft.graph.deviceManagementConfigurationSimpleSettingInstance",
                            "settingDefinitionId":
"device_vendor_msft_policy_config_quiettime_mutenotificationsdaily_starttim
e",
                            "simpleSettingValue": {
                                "@odata.type":
"#microsoft.graph.deviceManagementConfigurationStringSettingValue",
                                "value": "18:00:00"
                            }
                        },
```

9. Then, we add the days individually (lines 69–99).
10. Then, we must specify the end time (lines 100–106):

```
                        {
                            "@odata.type":
"#microsoft.graph.deviceManagementConfigurationSimpleSettingInstance",
                            "settingDefinitionId":
"device_vendor_msft_policy_config_quiettime_mutenotificationsdaily_endtime"
,
                            "simpleSettingValue": {
                                "@odata.type":
"#microsoft.graph.deviceManagementConfigurationStringSettingValue",
                                "value": "07:00:00"
                            }
                        }
```

Now, we must close off these settings with the template details (lines 108–119):

```
                ],
                "settingValueTemplateReference": {
                    "settingValueTemplateId": "ce97e111-08b3-4fa2-
bf1e-837771a6aa61"
                },
                "value":
"device_vendor_msft_policy_config_quiettime_mutenotificationsdaily_1"
            },
```

```
                "settingDefinitionId":
"device_vendor_msft_policy_config_quiettime_mutenotificationsdaily",
                "settingInstanceTemplateReference": {
                    "settingInstanceTemplateId": "a9c35a12-
ed79-40f9-89bb-7b5bc3718d9b"
                }
            }
        },
```

11. At this point, we must allow users to change the setting and close off the device management part of the `settings` array (lines 120–137):

```
        {
            "@odata.type":
"#microsoft.graph.deviceManagementConfigurationSetting",
            "settingInstance": {
                "@odata.type":
"#microsoft.graph.deviceManagementConfigurationChoiceSettingInstance",
                "choiceSettingValue": {
                    "@odata.type":
"#microsoft.graph.deviceManagementConfigurationChoiceSettingValue",
                    "children": [],
                    "settingValueTemplateReference": {
                        "settingValueTemplateId": "c018501f-5efb-49ee-8da0-
b472c212d9f4"
                    },
                    "value":
"device_vendor_msft_policy_config_quiettime_allowusertochangesetting_1"
                },
                "settingDefinitionId":
"device_vendor_msft_policy_config_quiettime_allowusertochangesetting",
                "settingInstanceTemplateReference": {
                    "settingInstanceTemplateId": "3c68cbb1-
bf32-405b-92d8-65070f55b8c5"
                }
            }
        }
    ],
```

12. Finally, we must add the template to `ExchangeOnline` (lines 139–145):

```
    "technologies": "exchangeOnline",
    "templateReference": {
        "templateDisplayName": "Days of the week",
        "templateId": "2479e1bb-612c-4b98-96b0-157f334143dd_1"
    }
}
"@
```

13. Now that we have our JSON, we can send a `POST` request to create the policy and grab the ID for assignment:

```
$quiettime = Invoke-MgGraphRequest -Method POST -Uri $url -Body $json -
ContentType "application/json" -OutputType PSObject
$quiettimeid = $quiettime.id
```

14. Populate the assignment URL:

```
$assignurl = "https://graph.microsoft.com/beta/deviceManagement/
configurationPolicies('$quiettimeid')/assign"
```

15. Add the group ID to the JSON and assign it with another `POST` request:

```
$assignjson = @"
{
    "assignments": [
        {
            "target": {
                "@odata.type": "#microsoft.graph.groupAssignmentTarget",
                "groupId": "$groupid"
            }
        }
    ]
}
"@
Invoke-MgGraphRequest -Method POST -Uri $assignurl -Body $assignjson -
ContentType "application/json" -OutputType PSObject
```

That completes this recipe on configuring a quiet time policy.

Reviewing admin tasks

Admin tasks are a very new addition to Intune (still in private preview as I write this), so things could well change as it develops. This is a one-stop location to look at pressing tasks that you need to carry out, and at present covers the following:

- **Endpoint Privilege Management (EPM)** requests (we cover those in *Chapter 14*)
- Microsoft Defender Security tasks (those listed in **Endpoint security** – **Security tasks**)
- Multi-admin approval (covered earlier in this chapter)

How to do it...

Now we know what it does, we can look at how to use it. Within the Intune portal, select **Tenant administration** and then click on **Admin tasks** (it is currently labeled as **preview**):

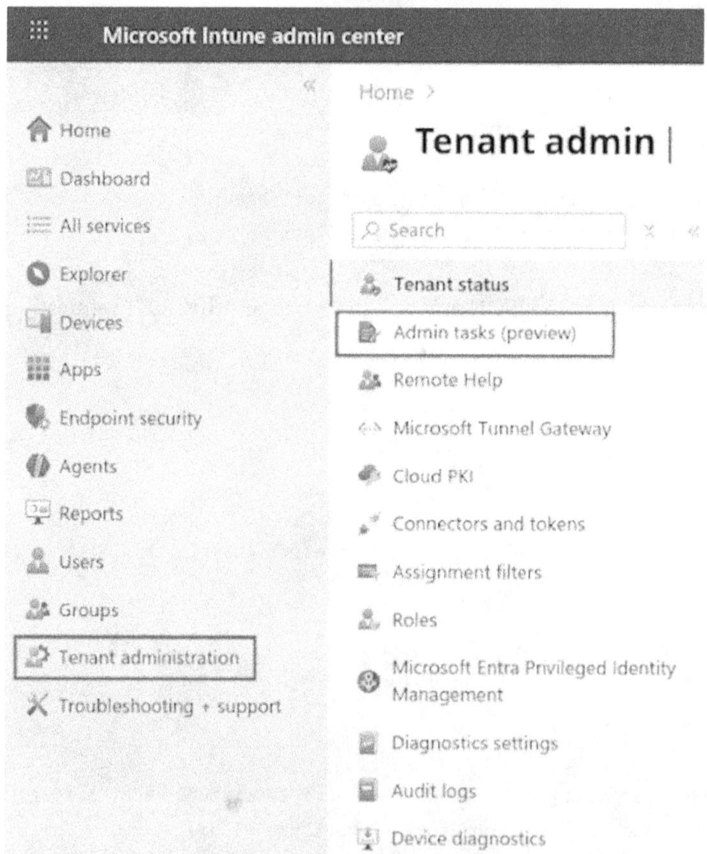

Figure 13.8 – Admin tasks

Here, you can see a list of the tasks outstanding for you:

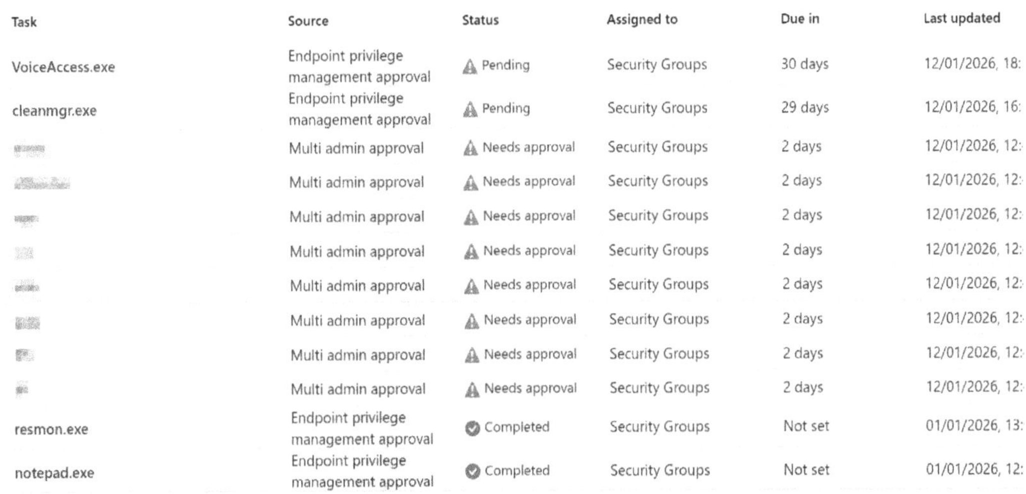

Task	Source	Status	Assigned to	Due in	Last updated
VoiceAccess.exe	Endpoint privilege management approval	Pending	Security Groups	30 days	12/01/2026, 18:
cleanmgr.exe	Endpoint privilege management approval	Pending	Security Groups	29 days	12/01/2026, 16:
[illegible]	Multi admin approval	Needs approval	Security Groups	2 days	12/01/2026, 12:
[illegible]	Multi admin approval	Needs approval	Security Groups	2 days	12/01/2026, 12:
[illegible]	Multi admin approval	Needs approval	Security Groups	2 days	12/01/2026, 12:
[illegible]	Multi admin approval	Needs approval	Security Groups	2 days	12/01/2026, 12:
[illegible]	Multi admin approval	Needs approval	Security Groups	2 days	12/01/2026, 12:
[illegible]	Multi admin approval	Needs approval	Security Groups	2 days	12/01/2026, 12:
[illegible]	Multi admin approval	Needs approval	Security Groups	2 days	12/01/2026, 12:
[illegible]	Multi admin approval	Needs approval	Security Groups	2 days	12/01/2026, 12:
resmon.exe	Endpoint privilege management approval	Completed	Security Groups	Not set	01/01/2026, 13:
notepad.exe	Endpoint privilege management approval	Completed	Security Groups	Not set	01/01/2026, 12:

Figure 13.9 – Outstanding tasks

Clicking on a task loads the details with the actions you can take. In this case, it is an EPM elevation request with the details you would usually find and an approve/deny button (we will be covering EPM in further detail in the next chapter).

For a multi-admin approval, you can see all of the details with the option to complete or cancel the request.

Automating it

Accessing via the UI is pretty straightforward, but what about within Graph?

The first thing to point out is that in a large organization, these requests could soon mount up, so I am using the `getallpagination` function, which you can find in *Chapter 1*'s GitHub repository, to be sure we grab all available tasks.

1. The first step is to grab all of the outstanding tasks:

```
$tasksurl = "https://graph.microsoft.com/beta/devicemanagement/
administrativetasks"
$alltasks = getallpagination -url $tasksurl | Where-Object Status -ne
"completed" | out-gridview -passthru
```

   We are removing any that are completed and passing them through to select whichever we require.

From there, we are just using the same code to approve/deny requests, as covered both in this chapter and in the following chapter for EPM requests.

2. We run a `foreach` loop in case more than one item has been selected, and grab the ID and type:

```
foreach ($task in $alltasks) {
$type = $task.source
$taskid = $task.id
```

3. Then, we switch on the type and action accordingly:

```
switch ($type) {
"multiAdminApproval" {
##Set URL
$url = "https://graph.microsoft.com/beta/deviceManagement/
operationApprovalRequests('$taskid')/approve"
##Approval can be Approved or Denied
$approval = "Approved"
##Set JSON
$json = @"
{
"justification": "$approval"
}
"@

##Send request
write-host "Sending request"
Invoke-MgGraphRequest -uri $url -Method Post -Body $json -ContentType
"application/json"
write-host "Request sent"
}
```

That brings this very useful chapter on tenant administration to a close, and we can now start looking at some of the add-ons available in Intune Suite (or now as part of your E3 and E5 subscription).

Get This Book's PDF Version and Exclusive Extras

Scan the QR code (or go to `packtpub.com/unlock`). Search for this book by name, confirm the edition, and then follow the steps on the page.

UNLOCK NOW

Note: Keep your invoice handy. Purchases made directly from Packt don't require one.

14

Looking at Intune Suite

Intune Suite is a set of add-ons for Microsoft Intune. For those on Business Premium licensing, they are a paid addition, but some are included in M365 E3, and all are included in M365 E5; I have highlighted which are included in each. In this chapter, we will learn about the currently available features of Intune Suite, how to deploy them, how to use them, and, more importantly, how to automate them.

At the time of writing, the date these will be available for E3 and E5 has not yet been announced, but the official blog post from Microsoft can be found here: `https://www.microsoft.com/en-us/microsoft-365/blog/2025/12/04/advancing-microsoft-365-new-capabilities-and-pricing-update/`.

In this chapter, we will cover the following recipes:

- Deploying and using Remote Help (included in E3 and £5)
- Learning about Microsoft Tunnel for Mobile Application Management (E5 only)
- Reviewing device anomalies (E3 and E5)
- Configuring Endpoint Privilege Management (E5 only)
- Deploying certificates with Cloud PKI (E5 only)
- Making app packaging easier with Enterprise App Management (E5 only)

I am not going to go into a huge deep dive into any of these tools, but I will cover the basics of getting started and your base configurations. For an in-depth look into these tools, there is an excellent book available here: `https://www.packtpub.com/en-gb/product/mastering-endpoint-management-using-microsoft-intune-suite-9781806021949`.

Technical requirements

For this chapter, you will need a modern web browser and a PowerShell code editor such as Visual Studio Code or PowerShell ISE.

All the scripts referenced can be found here: `https://github.com/PacktPublishing/Microsoft-Intune-Cookbook-Second-Edition/tree/main/Chapter-14`.

Chapter materials

At the time of writing, the suite includes the following:

- **Advanced Endpoint Analytics**: This uses machine learning to improve the Endpoint Analytics offering and look for themes and trends across the estate by detecting anomalies for proactive monitoring. It also includes advanced scope tags and an improved device timeline.
- **Endpoint Privilege Management**: Also available as a standalone add-on, this is used to elevate specified applications without users needing administrative rights.
- **Microsoft Tunnel for Mobile Application Management**: Also included in Intune Plan 2, this is a VPN tunnel for mobile applications on iOS and Android.
- **Remote Help**: This is a remote assistance tool for Windows, macOS, and Android, and is also available as a standalone add-on.
- **Specialized devices management**: This allows for the management of devices such as HoloLens and Surface Hub, and is also included in Intune Plan 2.
- **Enterprise Application Management**: This includes pre-packaged applications for easier deployment and updating.
- **Microsoft Cloud PKI**: This gives you the ability to manage and deploy certificates directly from Intune.

For those on licenses where it is not included, Intune Suite can be purchased as a trial under **Tenant administration** and clicking **Intune Add-Ons**. One thing worth noting is that each item can have different licensing requirements, so look into that before purchasing.

Deploying and using Remote Help

Remote Help is a remote assistance tool available for Windows, macOS, and Android. It allows connections to unenrolled devices and can be fully managed with granular **role-based access control** (**RBAC**) and custom Intune roles.

Getting started

There are multiple parts required for using Remote Help. This recipe will cover configuring the policies and RBAC, but you also need to have the applications deployed to your devices.

- For Windows devices, the installer can be found here and packaged following the instructions in *Chapter 11, Packaging Your Windows Applications*: `https://aka.ms/downloadremotehelp`.
- For Android, the application can be found here and deployed using the Managed Google Play Store, as covered in *Chapter 5, Android Device Management*: `https://play.google.com/store/apps/details?id=com.microsoft.intune.remotehelp`.
- macOS runs entirely in the web browser, so there is no requirement for application deployment.

How to do it...

We will now run through enabling Remote Help in the tenant and configuring an RBAC role to allow selected admins to use it:

1. To enable Remote Help, navigate to **Tenant administration** and click **Remote Help**.
2. Click **Settings** and then **Configure**.
3. In the flyout, change **Enable Remote Help** to **Enabled**. Here, you can also allow or block chat, as well as enable Remote Help for unenrolled devices.
4. Once configured for your needs, click **Save**.
5. Now, we can configure our new role. Click on **Tenant administration** and then click **Roles**.
6. Click **Create** and select **Intune role**.
7. Set your name and description and click **Next**.
8. In the roles, scroll down to **Remote Help App** and select your access for the role. You can select from the following:
    - **View screen**: Simple view-only access
    - **Elevation**: Allows the admin to UAC elevate on the machine
    - **Unattended control**: Does not require the end user to grant access
    - **Take full control**: Allows the admin to control the machine rather than just viewing it

   You may want to create different roles for different admin levels.
9. Once configured, click **Next**.

10. If you wish to set the roles to a particular business unit, you can add your scope tags on the next screen. Once completed, click **Next**.
11. Finally, check that everything looks correct and click **Create**.

In this recipe, we have enabled Remote Help and configured a custom role to allow admins to use it. We will now look at how we can complete this using PowerShell and Graph.

Automating it

When scripting the steps of this recipe, we can combine both enabling the connector and configuring the role itself into one PowerShell script to speed up deployment further:

1. The first step is to set a name and description to use when creating the role:

```
$rolename = "Remote Help Admins"
$roledescription = "Access to Remote Help"
```

2. We then want to start by enabling Remote Help in the tenant, so we want to configure the URL to send our POST request:

```
$enableuri = "https://graph.microsoft.com/beta/deviceManagement/
remoteAssistanceSettings"
```

3. When setting the JSON, look for any double negatives, as one of the settings is an *enable* while the other is a *block*, so pay close attention to the setting name when setting the value:

```
$json = @"
{
    "allowSessionsToUnenrolledDevices": true,
    "blockChat": false,
    "remoteAssistanceState": "enabled"
}
"@
```

4. There is no assignment required for this, as it is at the tenant level, so we are sending a basic POST request without needing to retrieve the output of the request:

```
Invoke-MgGraphRequest -Method PATCH -Uri $enableuri -Body $json
```

5. After enabling Remote Help, we want to configure our role. Again, we start with the URL:

```
$roleurl = "https://graph.microsoft.com/beta/deviceManagement/
roleDefinitions"
```

6. The JSON for the role is similar to that in *Chapter 13, Tenant Administration*. The settings do not have a value; any enabled roles are added to the `"allowedResourceActions"` list:

```
$rolejson = @"
{
    "description": "$roledescription",
    "displayName": "$rolename",
    "id": "",
    "rolePermissions": [
        {
            "resourceActions": [
                {
                    "allowedResourceActions": [
                        "Microsoft.Intune_RemoteAssistanceApp_ViewScreen",
                        "Microsoft.Intune_RemoteAssistanceApp_Elevation",
                        "Microsoft.Intune_RemoteAssistanceApp_Unattended",

"Microsoft.Intune_RemoteAssistanceApp_TakeFullControl"
                    ]
                }
            ]
        }
    ],
    "roleScopeTagIds": [
        "0"
    ]
```

```
}
"@
```

7. Again, there is no assignment required here, so we also need to send a `POST` request with our JSON without needing to retrieve the output:

```
Invoke-MgGraphRequest -Method POST -Uri $roleurl -Body $rolejson -
ContentType "application/json"
```

We have now configured Remote Help and assigned it to a custom role using PowerShell.

Learning about Microsoft Tunnel for Mobile Application Management

Microsoft Tunnel for **Mobile Application Management** (**MAM**) is a way to require applications to connect to an on-premises VPN solution on an unmanaged device running Android or iOS.

Getting ready

Microsoft Tunnel for MAM extends the existing Tunnel VPN functionality. Therefore, a prerequisite is for the Microsoft Tunnel connection to be active and connected to your on-premises environment.

More information about setting up Microsoft Tunnel can be found here: `https://learn.microsoft.com/en-us/mem/intune/protect/microsoft-tunnel-configure`.

For devices running Android, both the Company Portal and the Microsoft Defender for Endpoint apps need to be deployed to them. There are no app requirements for iOS.

How to do it...

Configuring Microsoft Tunnel for MAM is a setting configured within app protection policies. We covered the creation of these in *Chapter 5, Android Device Management*, and *Chapter 6, iOS Device Management*. Follow these steps to configure Microsoft Tunnel for your mobile apps:

1. Navigate to **Apps** and select **App Protection Policies**.
2. Either create a new policy or amend a policy we created earlier.
3. On the **Data Protection** screen, scroll to the bottom and set **Start Microsoft Tunnel connection on app-launch** to **True**.
4. Finally, save or create the policy depending on whether you have edited a previous policy or created a new one.

This completes the recipe to configure Microsoft Tunnel for MAM.

Reviewing device anomalies

Advanced Endpoint Analytics is another feature of the Intune Suite, and it is split into three components:

- **Device anomaly detection**: This uses machine learning to look for trends across your estate and alert you of any potential issues. This is what we will be covering in this recipe.
- **Custom device scopes**: This allows you to add scope tags to the Endpoint Analytics reports to give different permissions to different groups of administrators. For example, you could provide business unit access to only review reports for their particular devices. You can find out more about this at `https://learn.microsoft.com/en-us/mem/analytics/device-scopes`.
- **Enhanced device timeline**: This expands the history of events for any particular device to give a more thorough view of what has been happening. You can learn more about this feature at `https://learn.microsoft.com/en-us/mem/analytics/enhanced-device-timeline`.

You can then leverage anomaly detection with Azure Automation to trigger automated alerts via email or Teams when issues are detected.

Now that we understand the components, we can learn how to review our device anomalies.

How to do it...

We can now look at how to review device anomalies within Intune:

1. To start, click on **Reports** and then click **Endpoint analytics**.
2. On the overview screen, click on **Anomalies** at the top.

   Here, you can see all of the anomalies detected on your devices. By default, they are sorted by severity, but you can sort on any of the columns.

   Clicking on a title will drill down into further details, including the affected devices and any similarities between the devices and the detected anomaly (**device correlation groups**).

Device anomaly detection is an incredibly useful tool for being proactive in your device support and can also add extra weight to any issues that need to be escalated to a hardware supplier.

Now that we have looked at how to review our anomalies in the UI, we can cover how to retrieve them using Graph and PowerShell.

Automating it

In this section, we will look at using PowerShell and Graph to grab these details automatically. This uses the same functionality as we looked at in *Chapter 10, Looking at Reporting*:

1. Start by setting a path, should we wish to export the data:

```
$exportpath = "c:\temp\anomalies.csv"
```

2. Then, as this uses a simple Graph `GET` request, we can use the pagination function, so we need to add that early in the script:

```
function getallpagination () {
[cmdletbinding()]
param
(
    $url
)
    $response = (Invoke-MgGraphRequest -uri $url -Method Get -OutputType
PSObject)
    $alloutput = $response.value
    $alloutputNextLink = $response."@odata.nextLink"
    while ($null -ne $alloutputNextLink) {
        $alloutputResponse = (Invoke-MGGraphRequest -Uri $alloutputNextLink
-Method Get -outputType PSObject)
        $alloutputNextLink = $alloutputResponse."@odata.nextLink"
        $alloutput += $alloutputResponse.value
    }
    return $alloutput
    }
```

3. The function requires a URL to be passed, so we now need to set that. We will add a parameter to sort by severity to match that in the UI, but this is not required. Note the backtick escape character as well to pass $ directly:

```
$url = "https://graph.microsoft.com/beta/deviceManagement/
userExperienceAnalyticsAnomaly?=&`$orderBy=severity asc"
```

4. Now, we grab all of the output, ready to work with it further:

```
$fulloutput = getallpagination -url $url
$selectedoutput = $fulloutput | Select-Object *
```

5. We then pop up a window with options to decide whether to export or view in a UI using a Windows form:

```
Add-Type -AssemblyName System.Windows.Forms
$form = New-Object System.Windows.Forms.Form
$form.Text = "Export or View"
$form.Width = 300
$form.Height = 150
$form.StartPosition = "CenterScreen"
$label = New-Object System.Windows.Forms.Label
$label.Text = "Select an option:"
$label.Location = New-Object System.Drawing.Point(10, 20)
$label.AutoSize = $true
$form.Controls.Add($label)
$exportButton = New-Object System.Windows.Forms.Button
$exportButton.Text = "Export"
$exportButton.Location = New-Object System.Drawing.Point(100, 60)
$exportButton.DialogResult = [System.Windows.Forms.DialogResult]::OK
$form.AcceptButton = $exportButton
$form.Controls.Add($exportButton)
$viewButton = New-Object System.Windows.Forms.Button
$viewButton.Text = "View"
$viewButton.Location = New-Object System.Drawing.Point(180, 60)
$viewButton.DialogResult = [System.Windows.Forms.DialogResult]::Cancel
$form.CancelButton = $viewButton
$form.Controls.Add($viewButton)
$result = $form.ShowDialog()
```

6. Now, run an `if` query to check what was selected. If we selected **Export**, simply send the data to `export-csv`. As the report can potentially be empty, we will do a check first for data and report back if there is none, because if we do not, the script will just exit:

```
if ($result -eq [System.Windows.Forms.DialogResult]::OK) {
    # Export code here
    if ($null -eq $selectedoutput) {
```

```
            write-host "Nothing to display"
        }
        else {
            $selectedoutput | export-csv $exportpath
        }
}
```

7. If **View** is selected in the popup, after looking for an empty dataset, we display the output in `GridView`, but here, we add the `Passthru` parameter so we can drill down further:

```
elseif ($result -eq [System.Windows.Forms.DialogResult]::Cancel) {
    # View code here
    if ($null -eq $selectedoutput) {
        write-host "Nothing to display"
    }
    else {
    $allanomalies = $selectedoutput | Out-GridView -PassThru
```

   The `passthru` parameter populates our `$allanomalies` variable with the details of the anomaly selected.

8. We need the ID of that anomaly to grab further details:

```
$anomalyid = $allanomalies.id
```

9. Add the ID to the URL. Run another `GET` request against this URL, send the details to the UI via `Out-GridView`, and close the loops:

```
$anomalydetailsurl = "https://graph.microsoft.com/beta/deviceManagement/
userExperienceAnalyticsAnomaly/$anomalyid"
    $anomalydetails = Invoke-MgGraphRequest -Uri $anomalydetailsurl -Method
Get -OutputType PSObject
    $anomalydetails | Out-GridView
    }
}
```

We have now learned how to retrieve and manipulate anomalies using Graph and PowerShell.

Configuring Endpoint Privilege Management

Endpoint Privilege Management (**EPM**) is a mechanism for elevating particular applications for end users without granting them administrative rights across the device. This could be for a particular line-of-business application that requires elevation or for your helpdesk to be able to run particular tools on devices. We can configure rules for EPM to allow automatic elevation or have it require approval first.

This recipe will demonstrate how to configure EPM and then add a file rule to allow a particular application to run elevated.

How to do it...

First, we will run through how to configure EPM in the UI:

1. Navigate to **Endpoint Security** and click on **Endpoint Privilege Management**.
2. We need to start with a settings policy, so click **Create** and then, in the flyout, select **Windows 10 and later** and **Elevation settings policy**. Then, click the **Create** button.
3. Give your policy a name and description and click **Next**.
4. On this screen, the first thing we need to do is enable EPM. We can then specify the diagnostics data to report on (**Diagnostic data only**, **Diagnostic data and all endpoint elevations**, or **Diagnostic data and managed endpoint elevations only**). You can also set **Default elevation response** (**Not configured**, **Deny all requests**, or **Require user confirmation**). We also want to add a setting to require support approval. We can use this to allow users to request that the application be elevated. This is covered in the *There's more...* section.
5. Once configured for your requirements, click **Next**:

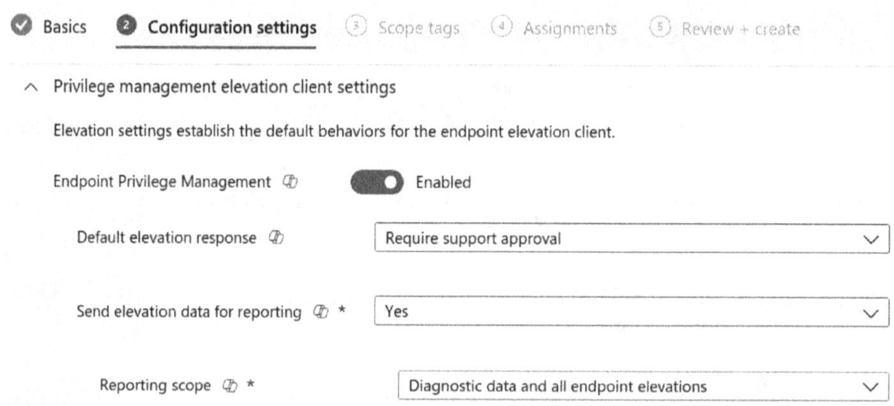

Figure 14.1 – EPM tenant settings

6. If you need to delegate permissions to a particular group of administrators, add your scope tags on the next screen. If not, simply click **Next**.
7. Assign the policy as required. If you are not using scope tags, this is a tenant-wide setting, so applying to all users or all devices would be a sensible choice. Once assigned, click **Next**.
8. Finally, check that everything looks correct and click **Create**.

Now that we have EPM configured at the tenant level, we can add our first rule to allow an application to be elevated:

1. Within the same **Endpoint Security** > **Endpoint Privilege Management** menu blade, click **Create Policy**, and, in the fly-out panel, select **Windows 10 and later** and then **Elevation rules policy**. Then, click **Create**.
2. Give your policy a name and description. Remember that you may end up with multiple rules policies for different applications, so a good naming convention will be useful here. Then, click **Next**.
3. On the **Configuration settings** screen, you can add multiple applications by clicking the **Add** button. You will notice there is already an item in there, so click **+ Edit instance** to edit this one:

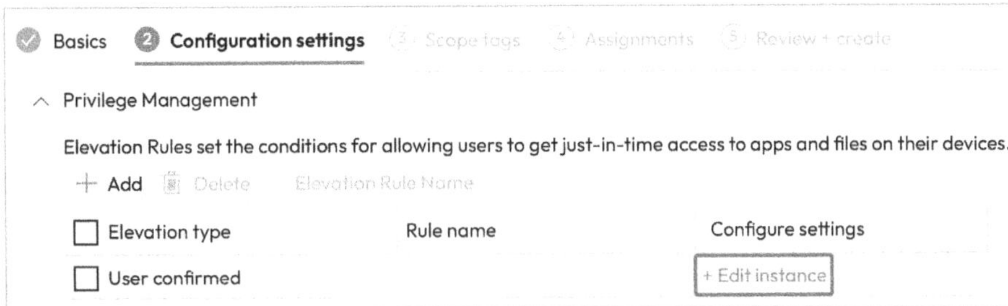

Figure 14.2 – EPM file settings

4. In the flyout, enter a rule name and description.
5. In **Elevation Conditions**, you can select whether this application will automatically approve for elevation or whether it requires the user to confirm with a selected reason (**Business justification**) or with credentials (**Windows authentication**). These are useful for auditing, so they are worth considering.

   You can also select the action for child processes. You can either allow them automatically, deny them automatically, or have them require their own rule. For example, if you elevate the Command Prompt application and the user tries to launch Notepad, you can specify in which context Notepad will be launched.
6. Next, we move on to the file information, which Intune and Windows use to decide whether the application can be elevated. You have two options for configuring the application here. You can use `filehash`, which can be retrieved by running the following PowerShell command:

   ```
   Get-filehash -path "path to executable"
   ```

   Alternatively, you can upload a certificate for the file to use instead.

   A certificate can be exported using the following PowerShell command:

   ```
   Get-AuthenticodeSignature -FilePath "path to executable"
   ```

   If you have multiple applications from the same publisher, you can reuse the same certificate using the **Reusable settings** option.

   You must also enter a filename here. You can also optionally add **File path**, **Minimum version**, **File description**, **Product name**, and **Internal name** information.
7. Once configured, click **Save** and then **Next**.
8. On the **Scope tags** screen, if you need to delegate, do so here, then click **Next**.

9. Assign the rule as required for your environment. Work according to the least privilege model here, so keep the assignments to a minimum, especially if allowing child processes. Once configured, click **Next**.
10. Finally, check that everything looks correct and click **Create**.

That completes the configuration and deployment of our first EPM policy within the Intune UI.

Automating it

After learning how to configure in the UI, we can now learn how to set up EPM using PowerShell to automate further. While we could combine both policies into one script because one is a one-off, tenant-level configuration, and the other could be used multiple times, in this case, we will split them into two. The second script, however, will automate a lot of the previous manual steps for us.

Both of these use the unified settings catalog underneath, so the code will look familiar to that covered in *Chapter 2, Configuring Your New Tenant for Windows Devices*:

1. Starting with the tenant-wide policy, we start with our name, description, and URL:

```
$name = "Elevation Settings Policy"
$description = "Elevation Settings Policy"
$policyuri = "https://graph.microsoft.com/beta/deviceManagement/
configurationPolicies"
```

When looking at the policy JSON, the drop-down options from the UI are set in the `value` code block with a numerical value after the name, rather than `enabled/disabled`, as this allows for more options, as in this example:

`device_vendor_msft_policy_elevationclientsettings_reportingscope_2`.

2. We need to populate the JSON with our preceding variables, and this example uses the same settings we configured in the UI (*Figure 14.2*):

```
$policyjson = @"
{
"description": "$description",
"name": "$name",
"platforms": "windows10",
"roleScopeTagIds": [
"0"
],
"settings": [
```

```
{
"@odata.type": "#microsoft.graph.deviceManagementConfigurationSetting",
"settingInstance": {
"@odata.type":
"#microsoft.graph.deviceManagementConfigurationChoiceSettingInstance",
"choiceSettingValue": {
"@odata.type":
"#microsoft.graph.deviceManagementConfigurationChoiceSettingValue",
"children": [
{
"@odata.type":
"#microsoft.graph.deviceManagementConfigurationChoiceSettingInstance",
"choiceSettingValue": {
"@odata.type":
"#microsoft.graph.deviceManagementConfigurationChoiceSettingValue",
"children": [],
"value":
"device_vendor_msft_policy_elevationclientsettings_defaultelevationresponse
_2"
},
"settingDefinitionId":
"device_vendor_msft_policy_elevationclientsettings_defaultelevationresponse
"
},
{
"@odata.type":
"#microsoft.graph.deviceManagementConfigurationChoiceSettingInstance",
"choiceSettingValue": {
"@odata.type":
"#microsoft.graph.deviceManagementConfigurationChoiceSettingValue",
"children": [
{
"@odata.type":
"#microsoft.graph.deviceManagementConfigurationChoiceSettingInstance",
"choiceSettingValue": {
"@odata.type":
"#microsoft.graph.deviceManagementConfigurationChoiceSettingValue",
"children": [],
"value":
"device_vendor_msft_policy_elevationclientsettings_reportingscope_2"
},
```

```
"settingDefinitionId":
"device_vendor_msft_policy_elevationclientsettings_reportingscope"
}
],
"value": "device_vendor_msft_policy_elevationclientsettings_senddata_1"
},
"settingDefinitionId":
"device_vendor_msft_policy_elevationclientsettings_senddata"
}
],
"settingValueTemplateReference": {
"settingValueTemplateId": "a13cc55c-307a-4962-aaec-20b832bf75c7"
},
"value": "device_vendor_msft_policy_elevationclientsettings_enableepm_1"
},
"settingDefinitionId":
"device_vendor_msft_policy_elevationclientsettings_enableepm",
"settingInstanceTemplateReference": {
"settingInstanceTemplateId": "58a79a4b-ba9b-4923-a7a5-6dc1a9f638a4"
}
}
}
],
"technologies": "mdm,endpointPrivilegeManagement",
"templateReference": {
"templateId": "e7dcaba4-959b-46ed-88f0-16ba39b14fd8_1"
}
}
"@
```

3. Then, send a `POST` request to create the policy, grab the ID, and use it to populate the assignment URL:

```
$addpolicy = Invoke-MgGraphRequest -method POST -Uri $policyuri -Body
$policyjson -ContentType "application/json" -OutputType PSObject
$policyid = $addpolicy.id
$policyassignuri = "https://graph.microsoft.com/beta/deviceManagement/
configurationPolicies/$policyid/assign"
```

4. We are assigning this policy to all users, so there is no group ID to populate here. Simply send a POST request with the JSON:

```
$policyassignjson = @"
{
    "assignments": [
        {
            "target": {
                "@odata.type":
"#microsoft.graph.allLicensedUsersAssignmentTarget"
            }
        }
    ]
}
"@
Invoke-MgGraphRequest -Method POST -Uri $policyassignuri -Body
$policyassignjson -ContentType "application/json"
```

When moving on to the settings rule, the JSON is complex, so we will run through the key aspects here, which you can run through with the code from the GitHub repository (`https://github.com/PacktPublishing/Microsoft-Intune-Cookbook-Second-Edition/blob/main/Chapter-14/create-epm-rule.ps1`). We are going to combine both policy configurations into one script and let PowerShell do the work, whether for a file hash or certificate.

5. The first thing to set is the elevation type, which can be `User` or `Auto` (the user must request elevation, or the application automatically elevates). The setting here will change the JSON passed to the request. We also want a description and, of course, the group ID for the assignment:

```
$elevationtype = "Auto"
$typedescription = "Automatically approved"
$groupid = "xxxxx-xxxxx-xxxxx-xxxx"
```

6. Now, we need to decide whether to use the file hash or certificate method by setting `$authtype` to either `hash` or `cert`. Of course, we also need the path to the executable, which needs to be available on the machine we are running the script from:

```
$authtype = "hash"
$filepath = "C:\windows\System32\cmd.exe"
```

7. From the file path, we want to grab the name and path so we can populate the JSON with them:

```
$filename = $filepath | Split-Path -Leaf
$pathonly = ($filepath | Split-Path) -replace '\\','\\'
```

Now, we want to query whether it is a file hash or a certificate and take appropriate action. We do this with an `if` statement.

For a file hash, we simply use the `get-filehash` command and grab the output:

```
if ($authtype -eq "hash") {
$hash = Get-FileHash -Path $filepath
$hash = $hash.Hash
}
```

For a certificate, we have to upload the contents of the `.cer` file in Base64 content, so for this, we need to export it, grab the details, and delete it:

```
if ($authtype -eq "cert") {
    $cerpath = "$env:temp\$filename.cer"
    Get-AuthenticodeSignature -FilePath $filepath | Select-Object -
ExpandProperty SignerCertificate | Export-Certificate -Type CERT -FilePath
$cerpath
    ##Convert to $cerpath to base64
    $bytes = Get-Content -Path $cerpath -Encoding Byte
$base64 = [System.Convert]::ToBase64String($bytes)
##Delete cert
remove-item $cerpath
}
```

8. Before setting the JSON, we also need the URL for our request:

```
$addurl = "https://graph.microsoft.com/beta/deviceManagement/
configurationPolicies"
```

9. Next, we split the JSON into multiple sections so we can select whichever is appropriate for our earlier selections.

10. After adding the JSON, we run further queries to populate a variable with the appropriate selections:

```
if ($authtype -eq "hash") {
    $json1 = $jsonhash
}
else {
    $json1 = $jsoncert
}
if ($elevationtype -eq "Auto") {
   $finaljson = $json + $json1 + $json2auto + $json3
}
else {
    $finaljson = $json + $json1 + $json2user + $json3
}
```

11. Finally, we send our POST request with this final JSON:

```
$addpolicy = Invoke-MgGraphRequest -method POST -Uri $addurl -Body
$finaljson -ContentType "application/json"
```

12. As usual, we need the policy ID to populate the assignment URL:

```
$policyid = $addpolicy.id
$assignurl = "https://graph.microsoft.com/beta/deviceManagement/
configurationPolicies('$policyid')/assign"
```

13. Finally, add the group ID to the assignment JSON and submit our final POST request:

```
$jsonassign = @"
{
    "assignments": [
        {
            "target": {
                "@odata.type": "#microsoft.graph.groupAssignmentTarget",
                "groupId": "$groupid"
            }
        }
    ]
}
"@
```

```
Invoke-MgGraphRequest -method POST -Uri $assignurl -Body $jsonassign -
ContentType "application/json"
```

This completes our recipe on configuring EPM, but there is even more functionality available, which we will look at now to make it easier to configure the rules policies.

There's more...

Rather than relying on finding the correct file details, certificate, or path, a better option may be to use the **Support Approved** functionality built into EPM. This allows your end users to request elevated access to a particular file.

When a user tries to elevate a file, they are prompted to justify the request:

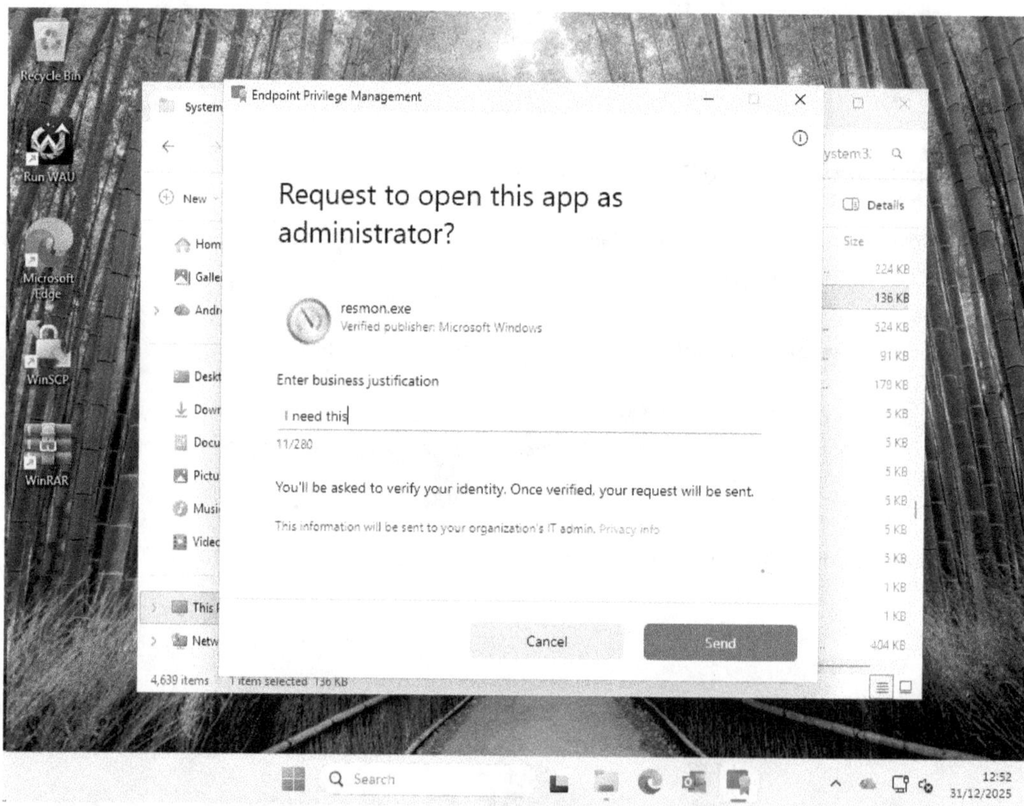

Figure 14.3 – Request elevation

We can then see the request within EPM:

Figure 14.4 – Elevation requests

Clicking on it shows the details, so you do not have to grab them yourself, and it reduces the risk of user error.

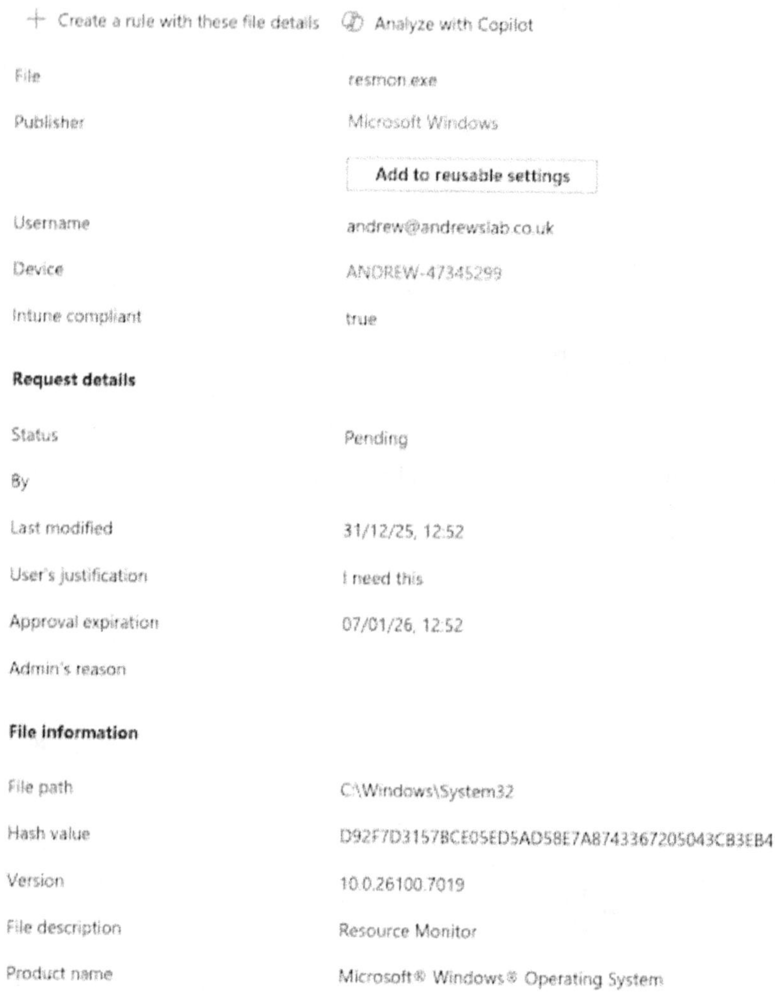

Figure 14.5 – Adding request to rule

You have now configured your first EPM rules policy using PowerShell and Graph.

Deploying certificates with Cloud PKI

Certificate management is often required in larger organizations for authentication, which currently requires on-premises infrastructure, a certificate authority, **Simple Certificate Enrollment Protocol** (**SCEP**), and **Network Device Enrollment Service** (**NDES**), which have to be accessible by the devices.

These can be tricky to configure, as you can see in the official guidance here:

`https://learn.microsoft.com/en-us/mem/intune/protect/certificates-scep-configure`.

The idea behind Cloud PKI is that your **certificate authority** (**CA**) will live within Intune, and you can use that to deploy your certificates. This would eradicate the need for the current on-premises infrastructure and massively reduce the complexity of certificate authentication.

How to do it...

There are numerous use cases for Cloud PKI, such as Wi-Fi authentication, accessing servers, and many others. In this example, we will just configure a root and issuing certificate for you to then work with as per your own internal organizational requirements.

Root CA

To create the root CA, follow these steps:

1. First, in the Intune portal, navigate to **Tenant administration** and click **Cloud PKI**.
2. Click the **Create** button.
3. Enter a name and description.
4. On the next screen, select **Root CA** (we will cover issuing next).
5. Complete other details as required for your organization. When selecting the **Extended Key Usages** option, it will restrict what your issuing certificate can be used for, so select carefully.

> **Note**
>
> A root CA cannot be removed once created!

6. Once you have entered the correct details, click **Next**.
7. We do not require scope tags at this point, so click **Next**.
8. Obviously, you cannot assign a certificate, so double- and triple-check that everything is correct and click **Create**.

Issuing CA

Now that we have the root CA, we need the issuing CA that uses it:

1. Staying in the **Cloud PKI** menu, click **Create**.
2. Select the CA type as **Issuing CA**.
3. Select the root CA source as **Intune**, and then select the certificate created before.

4. Enter any other details as required (you will note that **Extended Key Usage** is restricted to the setting configured in the root CA) and then click **Next**.
5. Again, we do not need scope tags, so click **Next**.
6. Finally, review and click **Create**.

Automating it

Now that we have covered how to create our certificates in the portal, we can look at how to automate it using Graph. Fortunately, these are both very simple to create, as they are all just text fields and do not use Settings Catalog.

Root CA

1. As usual, we start with the URL:

```
$url = "https://graph.microsoft.com/beta/deviceManagement/
cloudCertificationAuthority"
```

2. We then add the JSON, which includes everything included in the UI:

```
$json = @"
{
"certificateKeySize": "rsa2048",
"certificationAuthorityIssuerId": null,
"cloudCertificationAuthorityHashingAlgorithm": "sha256",
"cloudCertificationAuthorityType": "rootCertificationAuthority",
"commonName": "MYCOMMONNAME",
"displayName": "My Root CA",
"extendedKeyUsages": [
{
"name": "Server auth",
"objectIdentifier": "1.3.6.1.5.5.7.3.1"
}
],
"organizationName": "",
"roleScopeTagIds": [
"0"
],
"validityPeriodInYears": 20
```

```
}
"@
```

3. Then, finally, send the request:

```
$rootca = Invoke-MgGraphRequest -Method POST -Uri $url -Body $json -
ContentType "application/json"
```

Issuing CA

Creating the issuing CA is a very similar process; we are only referencing the ID of the root CA created previously. Therefore, we are assuming that both are being created at once and passing the ID from the `$rootca` variable earlier in the script. If you are using two different scripts, you will need to manually set this variable for the issuing CA:

1. Clearly, we need the ID first; if you are not running in one session, replace this with the hardcoded ID within speechmarks as mentioned previously:

```
$rootid = $rootca.ID
```

2. Set the URL:

```
$url = "https://graph.microsoft.com/beta/deviceManagement/
cloudCertificationAuthority"
```

3. Create the JSON:

```
$json = @"
{
"certificateKeySize": "rsa2048",
"certificationAuthorityIssuerId": "$rootid",
"cloudCertificationAuthorityHashingAlgorithm": "sha256",
"cloudCertificationAuthorityType": "issuingCertificationAuthority",
"commonName": "MYCOMMONNAME",
"displayName": "My intermediate CA",
"extendedKeyUsages": [
{
"name": "Server auth",
"objectIdentifier": "1.3.6.1.5.5.7.3.1"
}
],
"roleScopeTagIds": [
```

```
"0"
],
"validityPeriodInYears": 2
}
"@
```

4. Finally, submit the request:

```
Invoke-MgGraphRequest -Method POST -Uri $url -Body $json -ContentType
"application/json"
```

That completes the recipe for using Cloud PKI. Now, we will have a look at how to use EAM to handle your app deployments and updates.

Making app packaging easier with Enterprise App Management

In any organization, keeping your applications updated is a constant battle. First, you have to know whether there is a new version available(the Defender portal will show outstanding CVEs, but apps update for other reasons). You then have to find the new version and package and deploy it. With hundreds of apps, this rapidly becomes a full-time job.

This is where application management tools such as Robopack, Patch My PC, Pckgr, and **Enterprise App Management** (**EAM**) are incredibly useful. They monitor, grab, package, and deploy for you, so you just have to monitor them.

I have reviewed them all here, but this chapter is on Intune Suite, so we are only looking at EAM: `https://andrewstaylor.com/2024/06/03/comparing-package-managers/`.

How to do it...

Deploying Enterprise apps is very similar to standard Win32 apps, as covered in *Chapter 11*, only in this case, you do not have to do the packaging, and most of the information is pre-filled for you:

1. Within the Intune portal, navigate to **App** | **Windows** and click **Create**.
2. In the dropdown, select **Enterprise App Catalog app** and click **Select**.

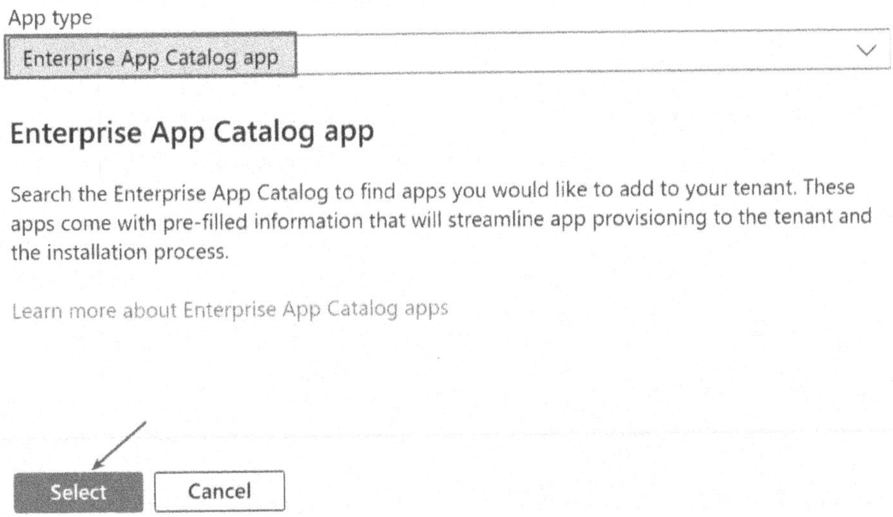

Figure 14.6 – Adding Enterprise App Catalog app

3. Now, click the blue **Search the Enterprise App Catalog** text.

Figure 14.7 – Searching for an app

4. Find your application in the list of apps, select it, and press **Next**. In this case, we will use **WinRAR**:

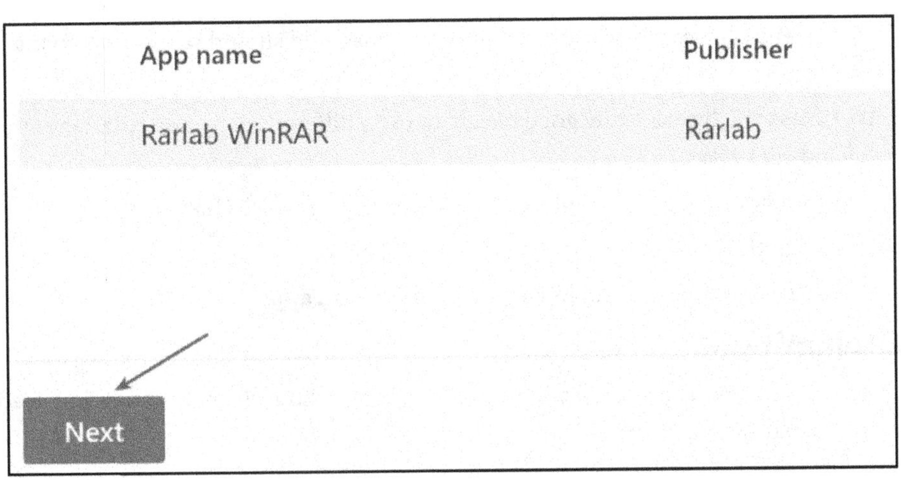

Figure 14.8 – Select your application

5. On the next screen, select the version and language and click **Select**.
6. You will now see the familiar Win32 app screen, only with the data configured for you (except the logo). Confirm everything is as expected and add a logo, then click **Next**.
7. Again, the program details have been preconfigured. In this case, we do not need any changes, but if your application needs a license key or any other install parameter, now is your time to add it.

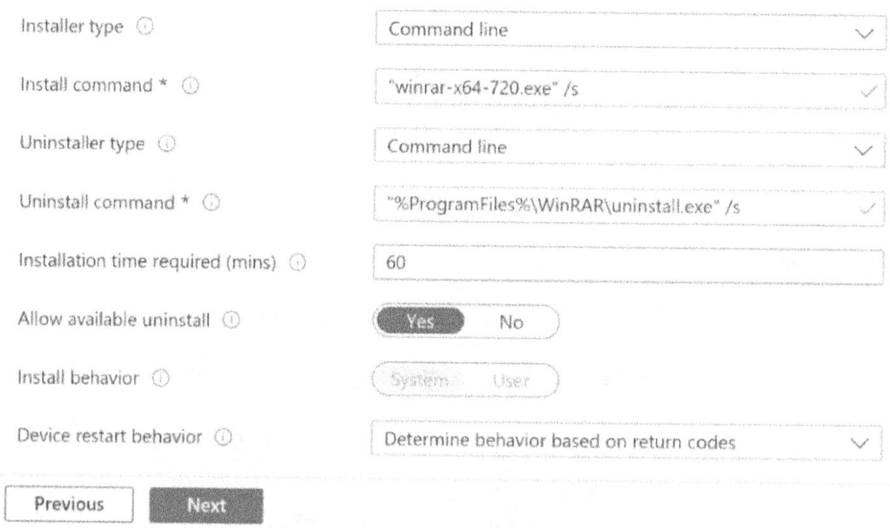

Figure 14.9 – Install commands

8. Once all is correct, click **Next**.
9. The **Requirements** tab has also been pre-filled and should rarely need changing. Click **Next**.
10. Unless you have a really good reason to use a different detection rule, leave these as is and click **Next**.
11. Familiar territory now: unless you need scope tags, click **Next**.
12. Assign the application as required and click **Next**.
13. Finally, check that all looks correct and click **Add app**.

Automating it

Some good news: we can automate app creation, but without the many steps involved when manually creating Win32 apps:

Note

Due to the number of potential apps, we will be using the `getallpagination` function covered in previous chapters, which is included in the full script on GitHub.

1. We start with the standard variables, group ID for assignment, and the name of the application itself. Due to the different locales available, we are setting that as well to ensure that we grab the correct version:

```
$groupid = "xxxxx-xxxxx-xxxxx"
$appname = "Rarlab WinRAR"
$locale = {en-US}
```

2. Now, we grab all of the apps that match the name:

```
$uri = "https://graph.microsoft.com/beta/deviceAppManagement/
mobileAppCatalogPackages?filter=productDisplayName eq '$appname'"
$apps = getallpagination -url $uri
```

3. There will obviously be multiple results here, so we are first sorting on the version number and then only looking for our locale. Finally, grab the top result, which is the latest version. This could be done over multiple commands, but why not use pipes to do it in one?

```
$app = $apps | Sort-Object versionDisplayName -Descending | where-object
locales -EQ $locale | Select-Object * -First 1
```

4. Now, grab the application ID (not the product ID) and drop that into our URL to grab the Win32 app details. You will see the URL is technically a conversion:

```
$appid = $app.id
$converturi = "https://graph.microsoft.com/beta/deviceAppManagement/
mobileApps/
convertFromMobileAppCatalogPackage(mobileAppCatalogPackageId='$appid')"
```

5. Run a request to grab the details:

```
$converted = (Invoke-MgGraphRequest -uri $converturi -Method GET -
OutputType PSObject) | Select-Object * -ExcludeProperty "@odata.context",
id, largeIcon, createdDateTime, lastModifiedDateTime, owner, notes, size
```

6. Now, populate into a Win32 mobile apps `POST` request (we need to convert our output to JSON for the `POST` body):

```
$posturi = "https://graph.microsoft.com/beta/deviceAppManagement/
mobileApps"
$convertedjson = $converted | ConvertTo-Json
$deployedapp = Invoke-MgGraphRequest -Method POST -Uri $posturi -Body
$convertedjson -ContentType "application/json"
```

That is the app deployed; now to assign it.

7. Grab the app ID and populate the URL:

```
$deployedid = $deployedapp.id
$assignurl = "https://graph.microsoft.com/beta/deviceAppManagement/
mobileApps/$deployedid/assign"
```

8. Finally, send a `POST` request with the assignment JSON:

```
$json = @"
{
"mobileAppAssignments": [
{
"@odata.type": "#microsoft.graph.mobileAppAssignment",
"intent": "Required",
"settings": {
"@odata.type": "#microsoft.graph.win32CatalogAppAssignmentSettings",
"deliveryOptimizationPriority": "notConfigured",
"installTimeSettings": null,
"notifications": "showAll",
"restartSettings": null
},
"target": {
"@odata.type": "#microsoft.graph.groupAssignmentTarget",
"groupId": "$groupid"
```

```
}
}
]
}
"@
Invoke-MgGraphRequest -Method POST -Uri $assignurl -Body $json -ContentType
"application/json"
```

You have now successfully deployed a Win32 app using EAM.

There's more...

We also need to look at how to update these applications, which, fortunately, is just a few clicks.

First, we need to check which apps need updating. For this, navigate to **Apps and Monitor**, then click on **Enterprise App Catalog apps with updates**:

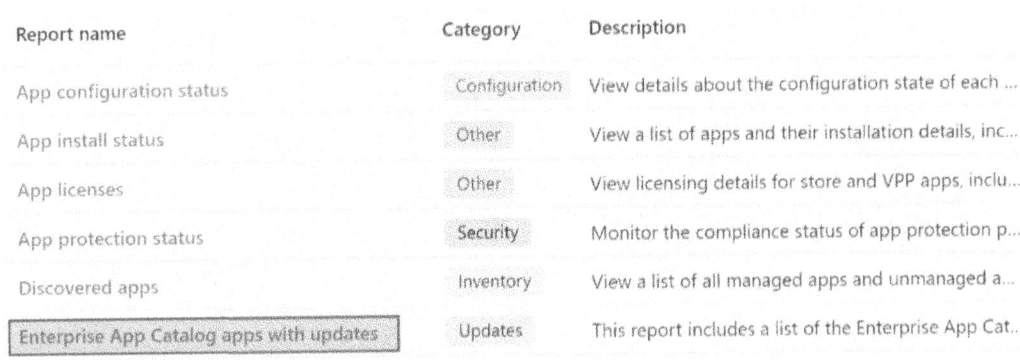

Figure 14.10 – Monitoring apps with updates

Any apps requiring an update will be listed here with the current version and the latest available version.

Simply click on the application and then click the **Update** button at the top, which will take you back to the app creation screens, but this time, creating an app to supersede the previous one (as we covered in *Chapter 11*).

That is the end of this recipe and the chapter on Intune Suite. Next, we will look at what Security Copilot and AI bring to Intune management.

Join us on Discord

For discussions around the book and to connect with your peers, join us on Discord at `packt.link/discordcloud` or scan the QR code below:

15

Using AI with Security Copilot

I am sure that by now you will have heard a lot about AI and how it is going to change the way we perform our daily tasks. So, it seems sensible to have a chapter looking at how the Microsoft-native AI options available within Intune (and **Entra** and **Defender**) can work for you and how to use them.

As AI is, at its heart, just sending Graph commands, you cannot interact with it within Graph, so this will be a less code-heavy chapter without the automation sections; although technically, AI is automation, especially when we look at agents.

Before we look at what is available to use, I will first run through some of the high-level components within **Security Copilot** (and associated agents).

Most AI services you will have heard of use **Large Language Models** (**LLMs**), which have a huge range of parameters available, and that is the reason why they can respond to almost any request.

When looking at Security Copilot, it uses **Small Language Models** (**SLMs**). These are trained on a smaller subset of parameters, in this case, Intune, Defender, and Entra-related, which means they are quicker, more precise, and less demanding on computing requirements.

You can learn more about SLMs here: `https://azure.microsoft.com/en-us/resources/cloud-computing-dictionary/what-are-small-language-models`.

As we are dealing with security information, we also need to cover how the AI is trained and what it does with the data.

Security Copilot (and everything that goes with it) is trained using **grounding data**. This means that the responses are based on the data you have given it (or given it access to). It layers your information on top of the original training data to respond precisely to your request.

You can find more information on grounding data here: `https://learn.microsoft.com/en-us/azure/well-architected/ai/grounding-data-design`.

One final thing to cover before we get into the recipes themselves is pricing. Security Copilot uses consumption-based pricing using **Secure Compute Units** (**SCUs**) with a price per unit, per hour.

If you have Microsoft 365 E5 licensing, you get 400 SCUs per month per 1,000 users included in your subscription, up to a maximum of 10,000. For those on other licenses, at the time of writing, it is $4 per SCU per hour: `https://www.microsoft.com/en-gb/security/security-copilot-in-microsoft-365-e5`.

The number of SCUs you need depends on how heavily you will be using it, but there is a handy price calculator available here: `https://securitycopilot.microsoft.com/calculator`.

You can find more information about current pricing here: `https://www.microsoft.com/en-gb/security/pricing/microsoft-security-copilot`.

This chapter includes the following recipes:

- Enabling Security Copilot in and removing it from your tenant
- Using Explorer to interrogate your devices
- Using Security Copilot within Intune
- Letting agents help you in Intune, Entra, and Defender
- Building your own agents

> **Note**
>
> If you are following these recipes in your own environment and not using E5 licensing, there will be consumption costs. Please be careful and monitor costs closely.

Technical requirements

For this chapter, you will need a modern web browser. You will also need an Azure subscription in which you have permission to add a resource group and resources.

I would suggest using a new resource group to make removal easier if required.

Enabling Security Copilot in and removing it from your tenant

Unlike many aspects of Intune, where everything either just appears or needs a checkbox to enable, Security Copilot has a few more steps involved, primarily because it spans across the entire Microsoft 365 Security suite rather than purely Intune.

In this recipe, you will learn how to deploy it into your tenant, as well as how to remove it, which is especially important for those of you without free SCUs with your licensing.

How to do it...

Here are the steps:

1. Navigate to `https://securitycopilot.microsoft.com`. Assuming you have not yet configured any SCUs, you will be presented with a form to set this up:

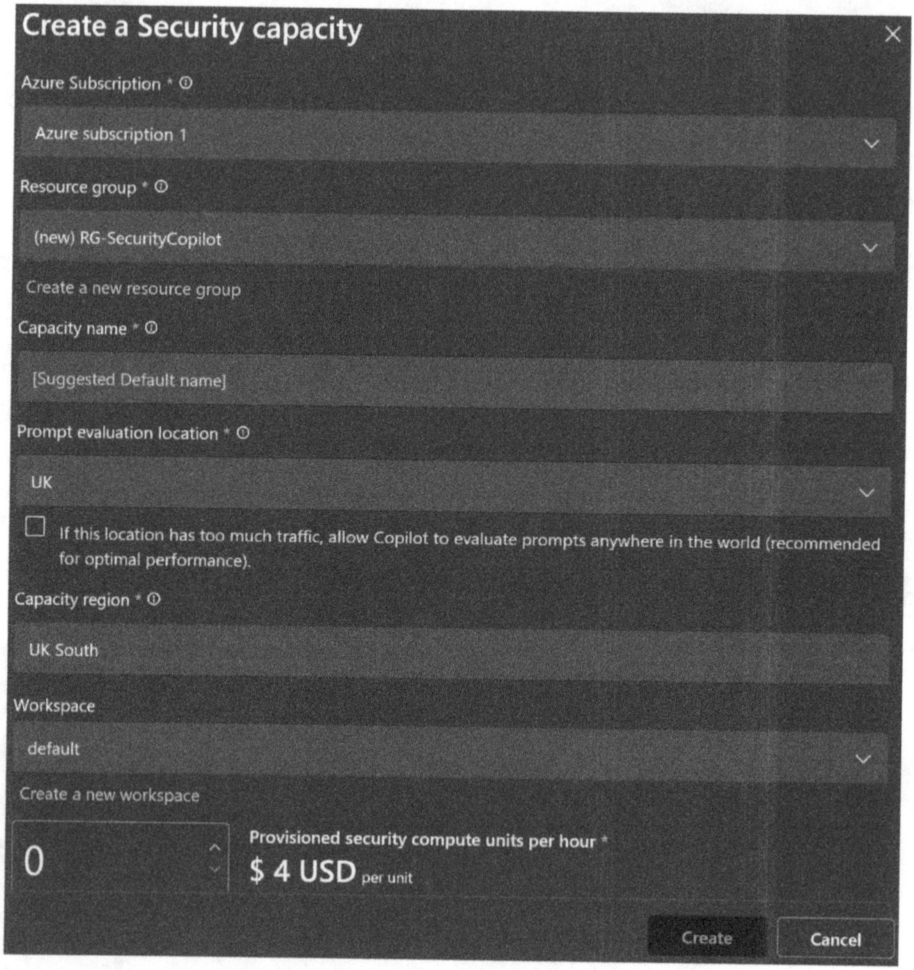

Figure 15.1 – Creating a SCU

2. Complete the details as required. You will see that I have used a new resource group, as mentioned earlier; this is simply to make it easier to remove it at the end to save costs.
3. You can select the location to be global, but consider the data requirements for your company, industry, and country when selecting this option as it will have access to security details.

> **Note**
>
> In this case, we are just going to use one SCU as it is only for testing, but if you plan on using it heavily across multiple users, you may quickly hit limits and want to add more.

4. Once completed, click **Create** and wait for the setup to be completed.
5. You now need to select the capacity you wish to use in Security Copilot, which in this case is the one we have just configured. Then, click **Apply**:

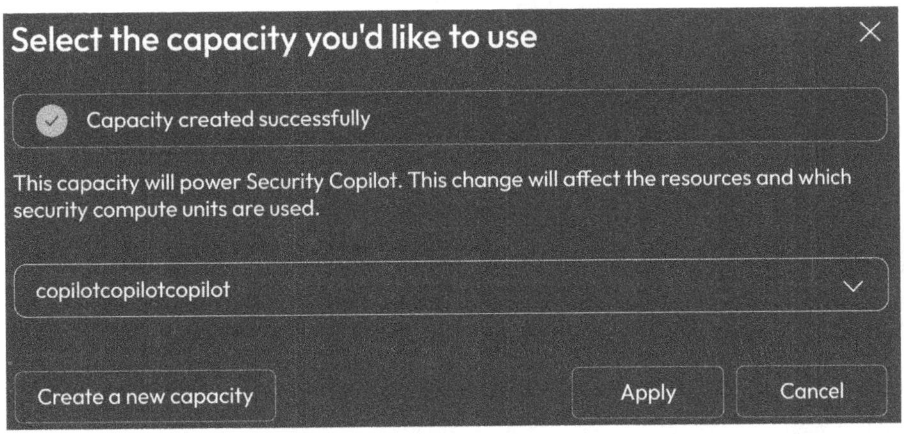

Figure 15.2 – Apply new capacity

6. Click **Done** on the confirmation window.
7. Now click the **Sources** icon next to the search box:

Figure 15.3 – Select the Sources icon

8. Enable any sources as required; for this recipe, we primarily need **Microsoft Entra** and **Microsoft Intune**.

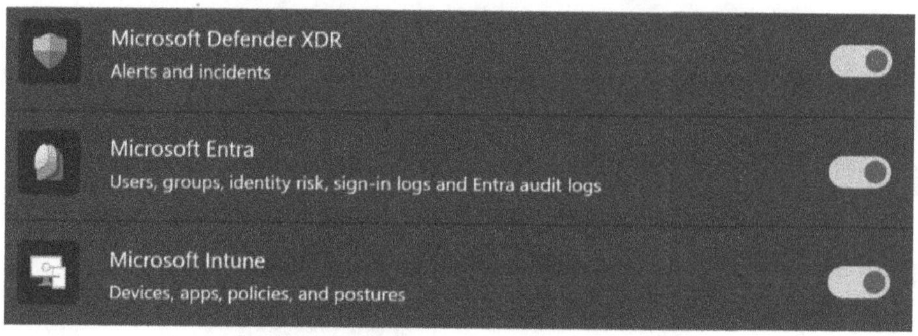

Figure 15.4 – Sources selected

9. To confirm that everything has completed as expected, navigate to the Intune portal.
10. Click on **Tenant administration** and then **Copilot (preview)**, then check that it is showing as enabled:

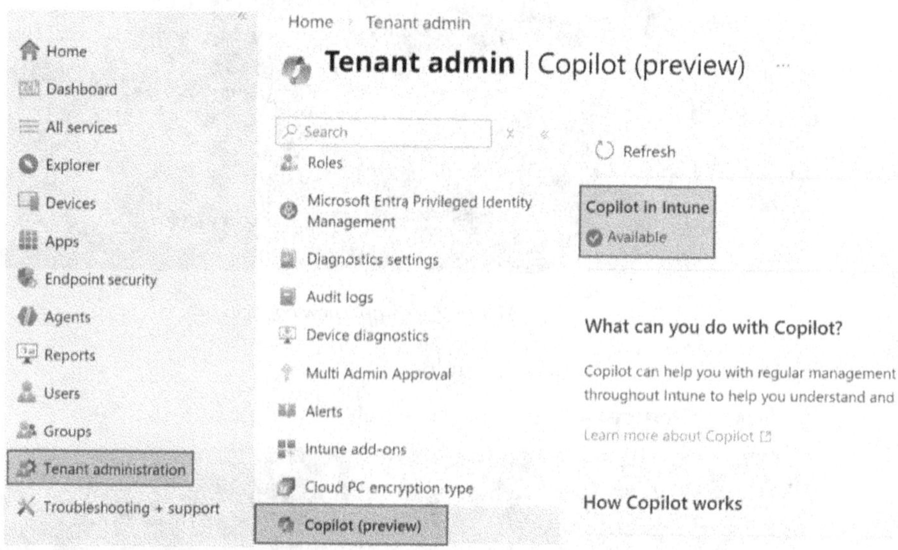

Figure 15.5 – Copilot enabled in Intune

11. If you want to remove Security Copilot in the future, navigate to the Azure portal (`https://portal.azure.com`). Click **Resource Groups** and then on the resource group created earlier, then click **Delete resource group**.

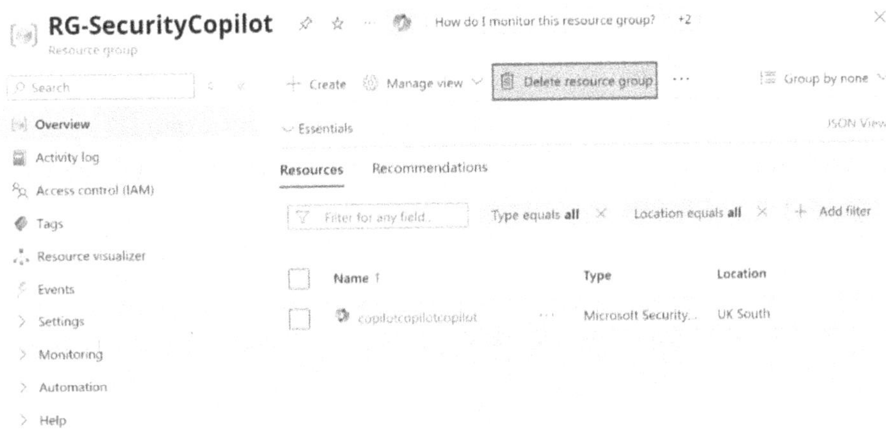

Figure 15.6 – Delete resource group

Confirm by typing the group name at the bottom and clicking **Delete**.

On the home page, you can see some of the many things available to you, which we will cover in the next recipes.

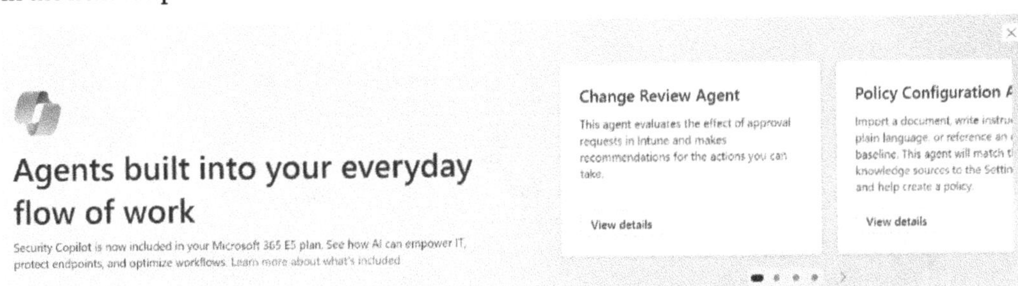

Figure 15.7 – Home page options

Now that we have configured Security Copilot in our tenant, let us see what it can do.

Using Explorer to interrogate your devices

Explorer is a new addition to Intune and, therefore, what is covered here is the functionality available at the time of writing. This recipe will run through how to use it, but the full functionality will likely change, so I would suggest monitoring what is available via this link: `https://learn.microsoft.com/en-gb/intune/intune-service/copilot/copilot-intune-explorer`.

How to do it…

Follow these instructions:

1. Within the Intune portal, click **Explorer** in the left-hand menu.
2. You will be taken to a simple screen with a text box where you can query Security Copilot with natural language.

   > **Note**
   >
   > While Explorer supports natural language, the prompts have to be within the list of the pre-configured options currently supported (it is an SLM, remember).

   There are examples at the bottom of the page with a dropdown to filter different categories, such as devices or compliance.

   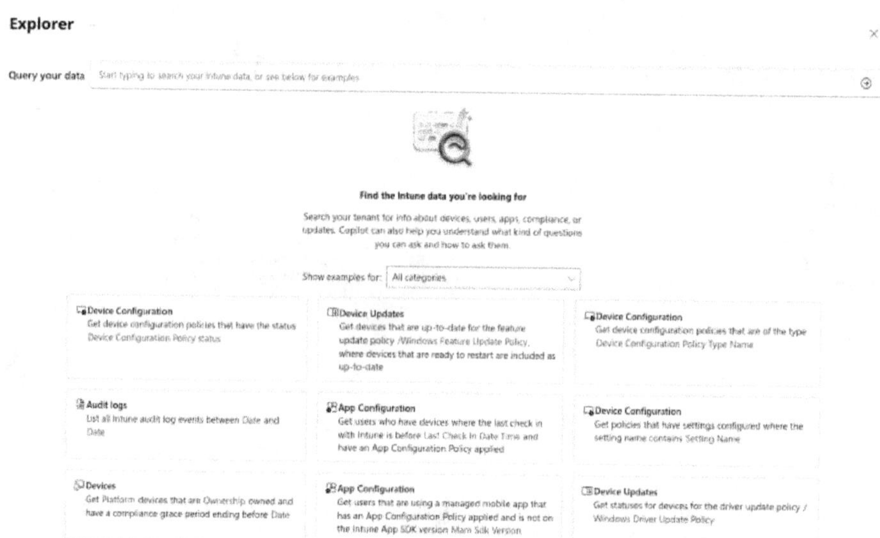

   Figure 15.8 – Device query

   Explorer is a multi-device query, so it is great for aggregating your reporting.

3. In this case, we are going to look for outdated devices. If you start typing into the **Query your data** search box, it will start to display queries that contain or are similar to the text you are entering from the available queries. You can either select the most appropriate one or use the examples to find something better.

   The query I am using here is as follows:

Figure 15.9 – Populated query

As you can see, **Update Version** is in blue text. This signifies that it is a variable you need to set in your query. Click on the blue text and it will provide you with all of the available options for this variable (you can also start typing to filter it).

4. Once you have selected the version, click the arrow to run the request. Copilot will summarize the results, as well as suggesting other queries or next steps.

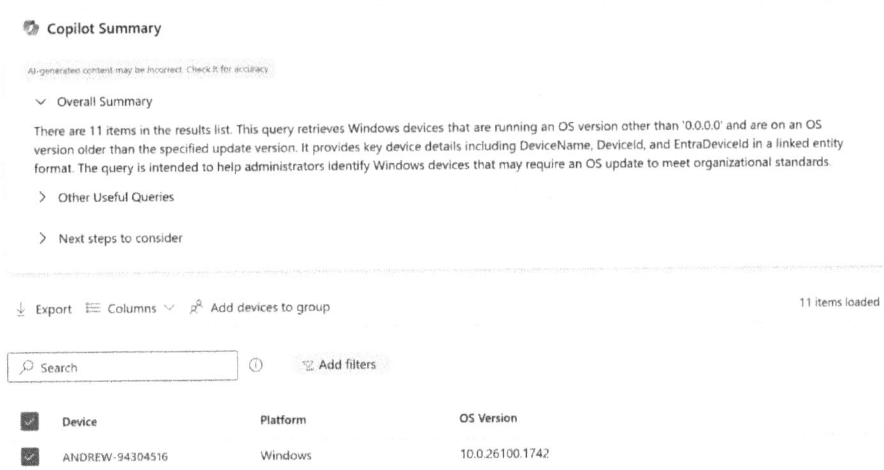

Figure 15.10 – Device query output

5. Underneath that is the raw output of your query, where you can export everything. Alternatively, click on any device to go to the details. Better still, you can add the results into a group that you could then target within Intune with a policy, script, or application to resolve the issue.

Explorer continues to grow in functionality; another recent addition worth highlighting is for **Endpoint Privilege Management** (**EPM**), which we covered in the previous chapter. If you have deployed that to your organization, Explorer will give you a treasure trove of information about not only approved apps but also those that have not been approved but have still been elevated:

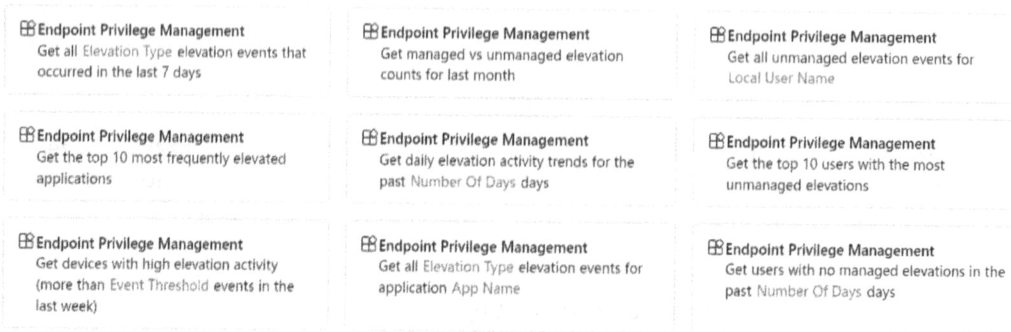

Figure 15.11 – EPM queries

Continuing with Intune Suite additions, Endpoint Analytics has always been my favorite part of Intune Suite. What it offers is just incredible, even more so now that it is in E3 and E5. But throw Security Copilot in and it gets even better. Rather than you having to dig through pages and screens of reports, simply query Explorer and it will correlate all of the data for you. A few clicks and you have full insight into the performance of your devices, and then you can contact users, spot issues before they have even noticed them, and be the most popular person at work!

Here are some of the examples currently available for **Advanced Analytics**.

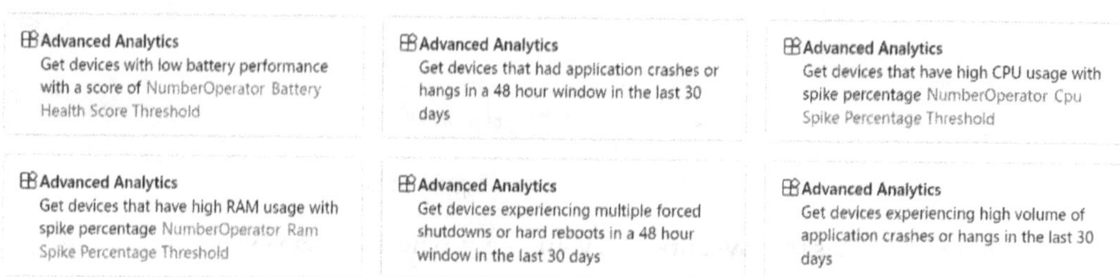

Figure 15.12 – Advanced Analytics queries

Explorer is a useful tool to have within Intune as long as the information you need is in the list of queries. Fortunately, this is not all of the AI functionality available to you; now we can look at what is available within the Intune and Security Copilot portals directly.

Using Security Copilot within Intune

Along with the Explorer functionality, you can also use Copilot directly within the Intune portal.

How to do it...

All Copilot functionality is at the device or policy level, so start by clicking on **Devices** within the Intune portal.

Device prompts

We will start with a look at what can be done within the devices themselves:

1. Within **Devices**, click on **All devices** and then select one of your devices.
2. On the bar across the top, you will find a **Summarize with Copilot** button. Click on that.
3. In the flyout, it will summarize the key details about the device with a text box beneath to query further:

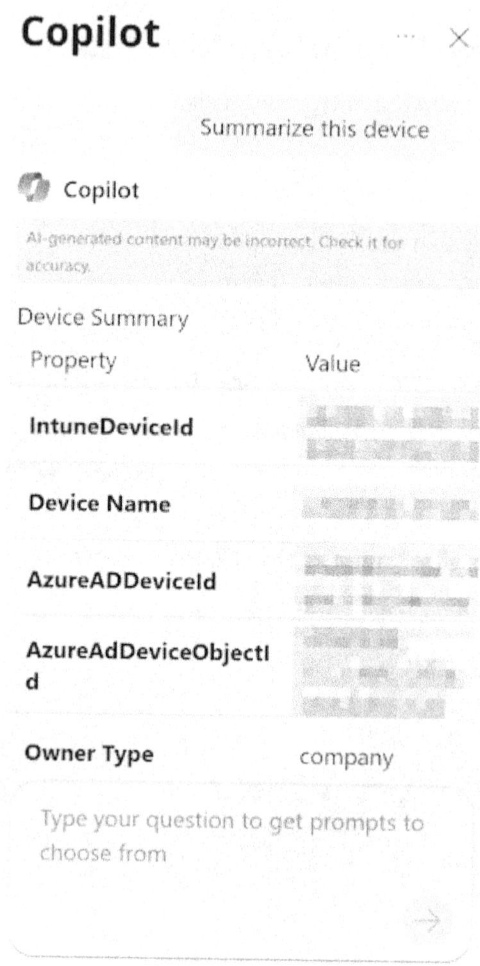

Figure 15.13 – Device Summary

The **Device Summary** section in Copilot is also presented in natural text, where it suggests supported queries to try to match what you are asking. If that fails, it can search the Intune documentation. Some more information can be found here: `https://learn.microsoft.com/en-us/intune/intune-service/copilot/copilot-devices`.

The most useful query, in my opinion, is the ability to compare two devices, which is very useful when troubleshooting.

There is one minor annoyance with most of these options: rather than supplying a dropdown, you have to enter the information manually. For example, when comparing two devices, you have to enter both device names (or device IDs) in the boxes.

Policy prompts

Now we will look at policies:

1. Click on **Devices** | **Configuration** and pick any policy.
2. The **Summarize with Copilot** button will tell you what the policy does and the assignments used in it.

   If we then edit a policy, each setting has a Copilot button that will describe the setting for us:

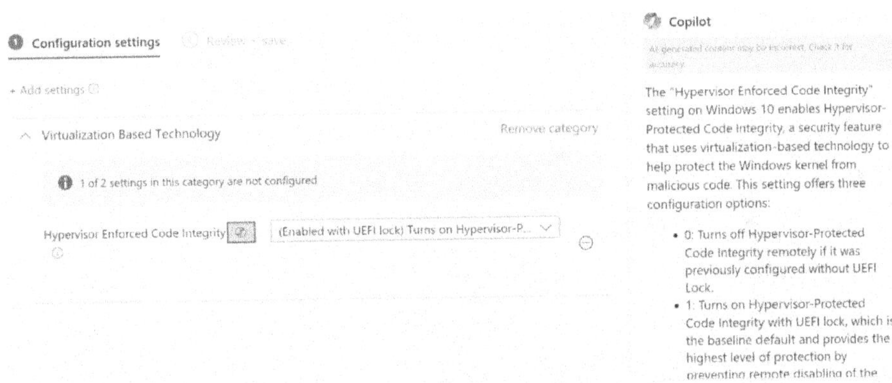

Figure 15.14 – Summarizing a policy setting

This is especially useful with some of the double negatives you can often find within Intune policies (disable a disable to enable a setting, for example).

3. Within the next box, you can also ask Copilot to check whether that setting has already been applied within another policy before hitting any conflicts.
   Another good query is to ask about the impact of that policy, and in this case, it pre-fills the policy ID for you. It will look at risks, assignments, and conflicts and give you an idea of how safe the policy will be to deploy.

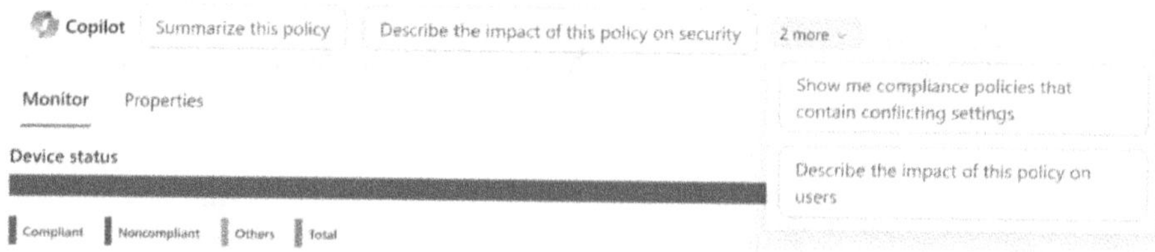

Figure 15.15 – Summarize compliance policy

4. Next, click on **Devices** | **Compliance** and then click on any of your compliance policies.

These are among the most useful settings within Security Copilot that you can pick from:

- **Summarize this policy**: This runs through what the policy contains.
- **Describe the impact of this policy on security**: This looks at the policy from a tenant level; how does it protect you as the administrator?
- **Show me compliance policies that contain conflicting settings**: This does what you would expect; it flags any conflicts (of course, the assignments could differ).
- **Describe the impact of this policy on users**: This looks at the user experience rather than the tenant level. The balance is getting this and the security ones tight enough.

In this example, we will look at the impact of the policy on users. Copilot will outline the policy, look at assignments, and then describe the impact based on what it knows:

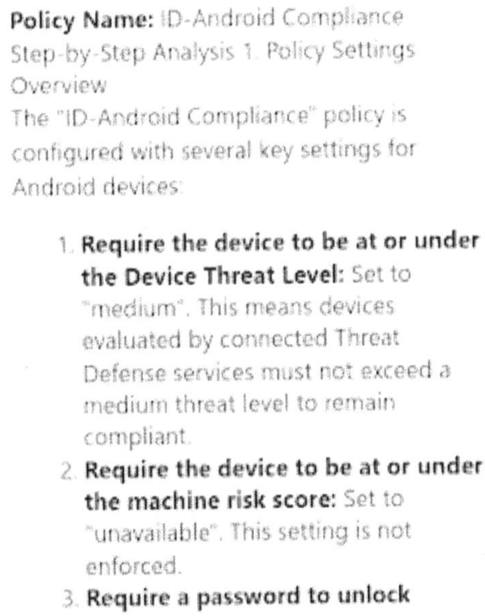

Figure 15.16 – Compliance policy impact

KQL assistance

We have covered **Device Query** already, but knowledge of KQL is required to create your queries.

Fortunately, Copilot can also help here:

1. Navigate to **Devices** and click **Device Query**.
2. The Copilot box at the top accepts all natural language prompts; type your query in here and click the arrow button to create the KQL query:

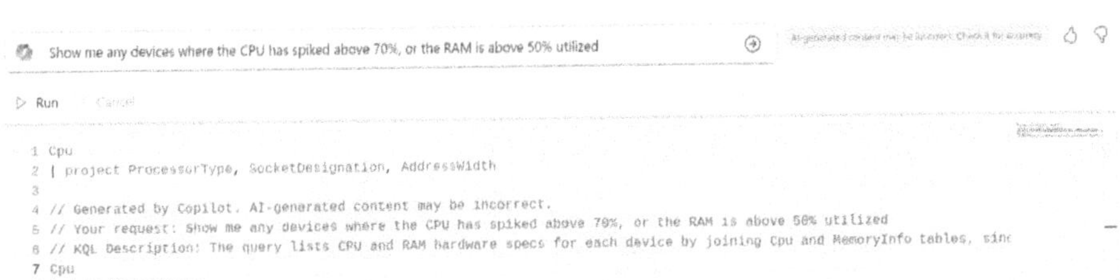

Figure 15.17 – KQL query

3. If the query looks correct, click **Run**.

That completes this recipe covering the native Intune features, but Security Copilot can now take things further with the introduction of agents. We will learn about those next.

Letting agents help you in Intune, Entra, and Defender

Everything we have seen so far has been very reactive and admin-led. **Agents** take a different approach and sit in the background, monitoring your environment for you. At the time of writing, there are four agents available, which will be covered in this recipe, but there will be more added. You can also build your own, which we will cover in the next recipe.

For an in-depth review of the agents, Gerry Hampson has an excellent blog series here: `https://gerryhampsoncm.blogspot.com/2025/12/my-first-look-at-intune-agents.html`.

How to do it...

Agents are available across Microsoft 365, and in this book, we are going to concentrate primarily on Intune and Entra agents as they are most useful for working with Intune. We will also look at the Defender agents and their functionality.

Intune agents

Agents are available in all portals, but as this is an Intune book, we will start there:

1. Navigate to the Intune portal. Click **Agents** in the menu and you will be taken to a screen with the four available options.
   The onboarding process is the same for all agents, so we will run through that here (using the **Change Review Agent** for this example) and then look at the agent-specific information after that.

2. Click the agent required (in this case, **Change Review Agent**), and on the next screen, click **Set up agent**:

Figure 15.18 – Set up agent

3. In the fly-out, it will run through the permissions and plugins required. If you are happy with those, click **Start agent**:

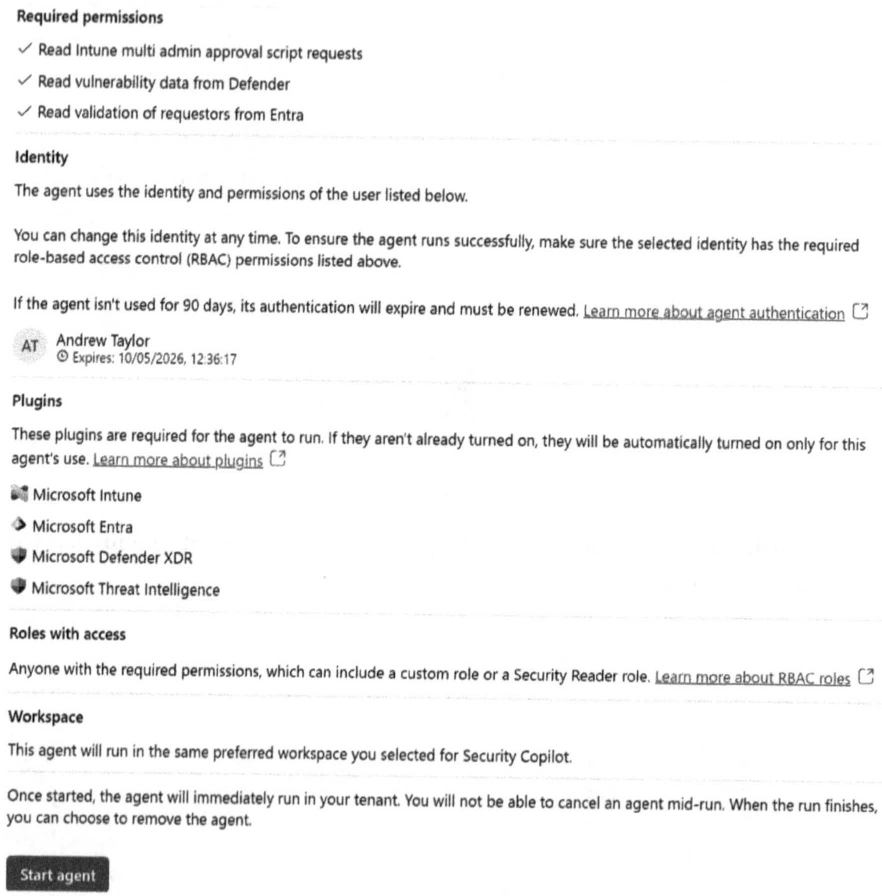

Figure 15.19 – Agent settings

4. Once completed, the agent will display a status of **Running**. We need to wait for it to be completed before we can take any actions:

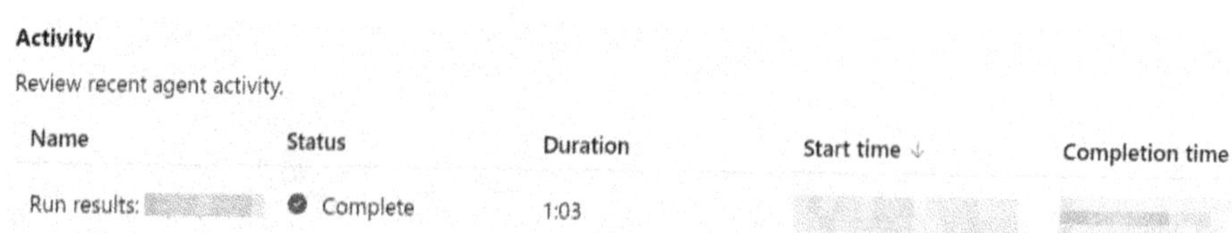

Figure 15.20 – Run complete

Change Review Agent

This agent looks at your outstanding **multi-admin approval** requests; obviously, you need to have multi-admin approval enabled in your tenant for this to work, which we covered in *Chapter 13*.

After this agent runs, it will monitor your environment for any requests and then make suggestions based on what it finds.

1. In this example, I deployed a PowerShell script, which really should not be a platform script (it creates Conditional Access policies in Graph):

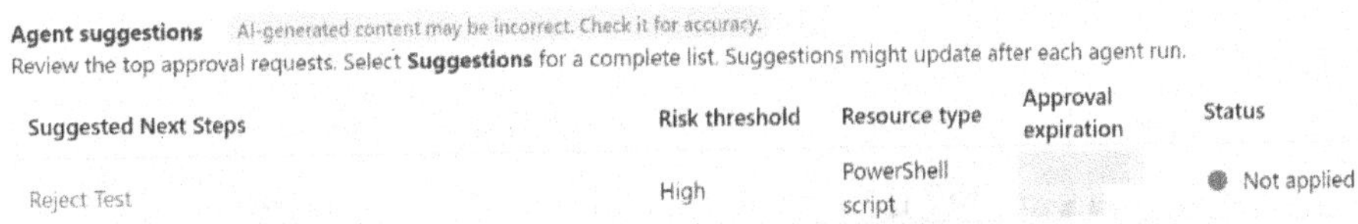

Figure 15.21 – PowerShell script approval

2. Clicking the blue text gives full details and reviews the request to confirm why it is making these suggestions.
3. Clicking **View request** shows the script content for you to make a more informed decision, and you can cancel or complete the request (provided you are logged in as an admin other than the one making the request).

Device Offboarding Agent

This one fixes a long-running issue where Entra lacks the clean-up rules available in Intune, so you find devices still lingering in Entra that have long been removed from Intune.

1. It works in the same way as the Change Review Agent, but it has an additional feature. To see this, click **Settings**.

   Here you will see a Copilot box where, in natural language, you can tell it what to emphasize, include, or ignore.
2. Type your query into the box and click **Generate** (or **Generate again** if you have already sent one).

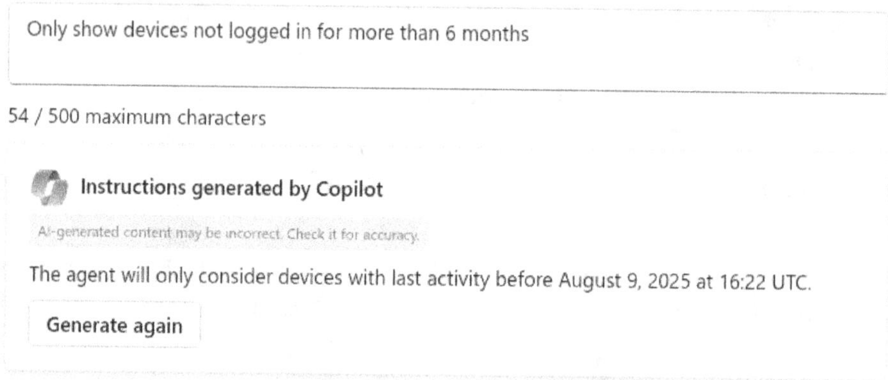

Figure 15.22 – Device offboarding query

In large environments, this will help cut down to just the most important devices.

It will also make some very useful recommendations before removing devices, such as backing up BitLocker keys and LAPS passwords. While it cannot yet complete these tasks and back up the data for you, it is a welcome reminder.

Policy Configuration Agent

This one works slightly differently; rather than monitoring your environment, you can use it to create policies for you (Settings Catalog, Windows only at present).

1. Click **View details** on the agent and you will be taken to the initial screen:

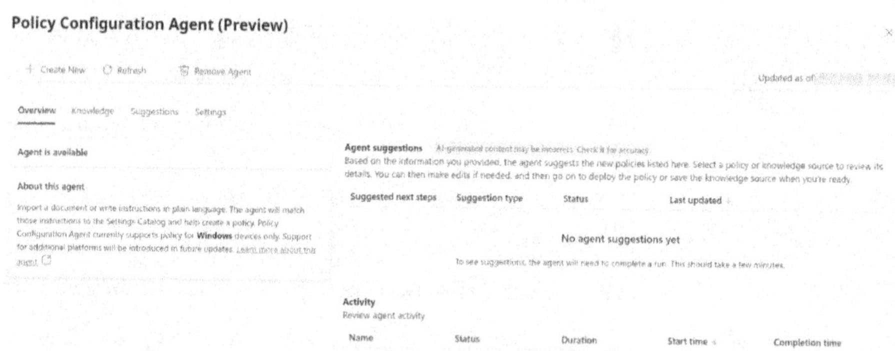

Figure 15.23– Policy Configuration Agent

2. We have two options here: we can either start making a policy or upload a document (**Knowledge**), which the agent can refer to when looking at our request. This could be a baseline such as CIS, or just an internal requirement.
3. To add a knowledge document, click **+ Create New** and select **Knowledge source**.
4. Give the item a name and description and then upload your document. Look out for the file requirements, which, at present, are a `.txt` file that is a maximum of 100 KB. Then, click **Review**.

   The agent will now read the information provided and use that as a reference when responding.

   > **Note**
   >
   > Uploading a knowledge document is optional. The policy creation will work without supplying any knowledge to reference; it will simply use the pre-trained data.

Now that it has a source, we can create our policy:

1. Click **+ Create New** and select **Policy draft**.
2. Enter a policy name and description.

   Optionally, select a knowledge source that has been previously uploaded.
3. Now enter your policy query in the box; in this case, we are going to set the device timezone:

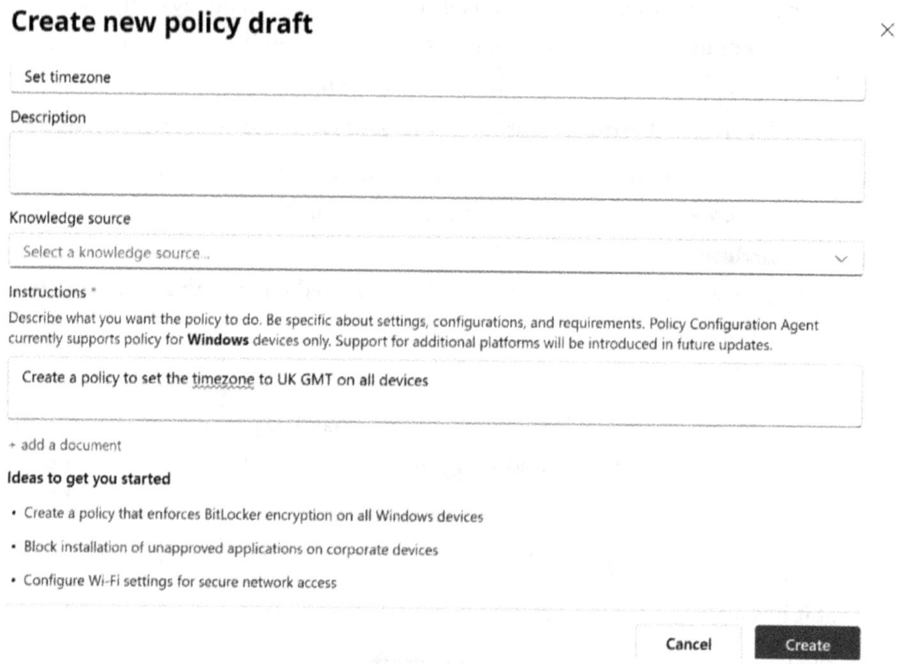

Figure 15.24 – Policy draft

4. Once done, click **Create**.

   The agent will now process your request, and after a few minutes, it will display on the home page:

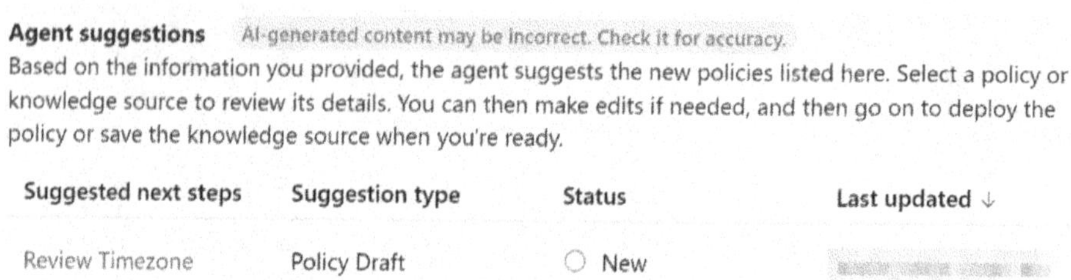

Figure 15.25 – Agent suggestions

5. Click on the blue text (or click **Suggestions** and access it from there).
6. It will outline what has been requested and, at the bottom, the settings found and configured. If all looks OK, click **Create configuration policy**:

Figure 15.26 – Create configuration policy

7. You will now be taken to the familiar policy creation screen, only with the details pre-populated for you. Simply continue as usual from here.

Vulnerability Remediation Agent

This is a Defender agent, but it crosses over with Intune and is also available in the Intune portal. It looks at vulnerabilities across your device fleet and makes suggestions on how to remediate them. It is probably the most important of the agents.

Before we dig into the vulnerabilities, there is one important setting to configure:

1. Click **Settings**, and under **Trigger**, set **Status** to **On** and configure **Frequency (days)** as required, then click **Save**.

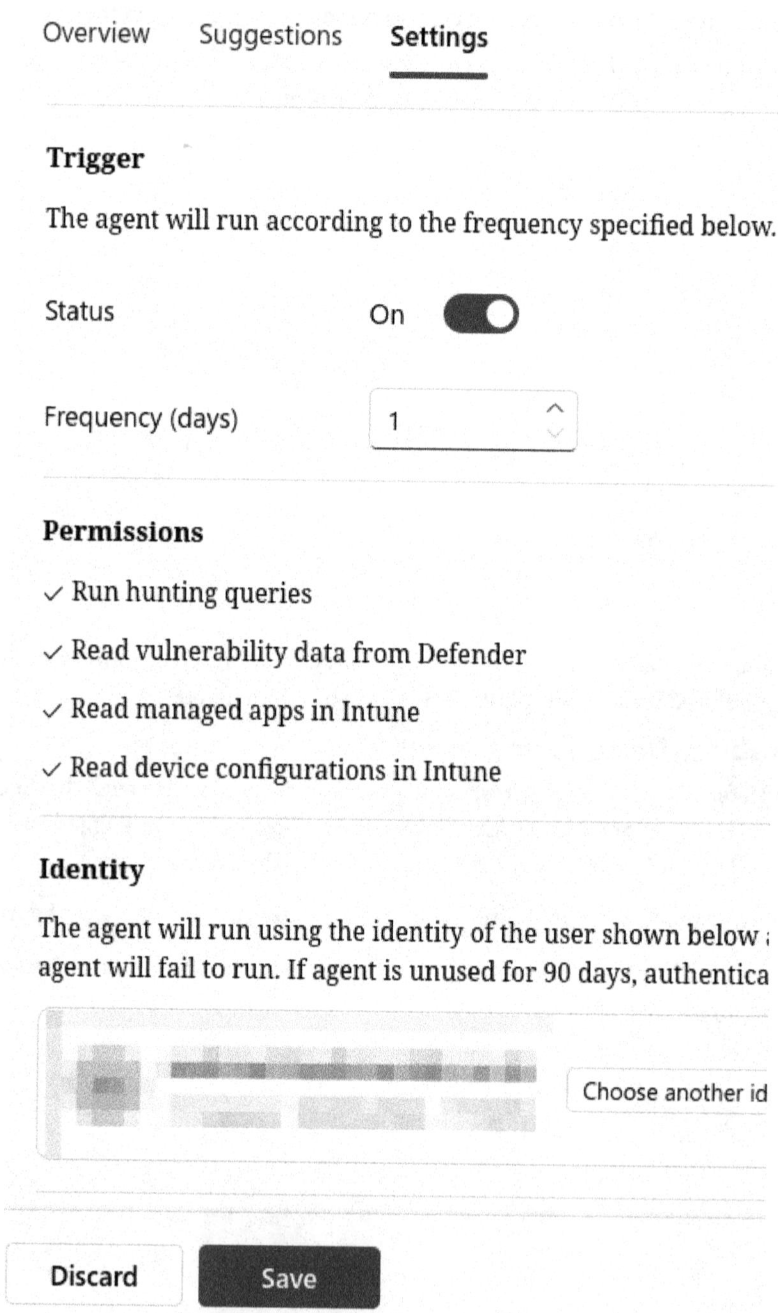

Figure 15.27 – Trigger settings

Configuring this trigger means it will automatically scan your environment, rather than you having to do so manually.

2. Now, click **Suggestions**, and we can see what is outstanding in our tenant:

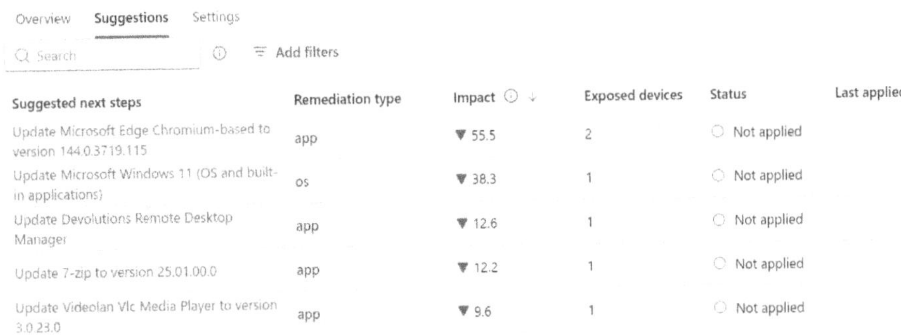

Figure 15.28 – Vulnerability suggestions

It is automatically ordered by impact, which makes things easier in a large environment.

Clicking on a suggestion will give an AI-generated overview of the vulnerability (including the source documentation) and the ability to export a list of exposed devices.

3. It will only give a fix if it can be resolved by a settings catalog policy. If that does not apply, once you have manually remediated the issue, click the **Mark as applied** button.

We can now move on to look at the agents available within Entra ID.

Entra agents

Navigate to the Entra portal (`https://entra.microsoft.com`) and click **Entra agents**:

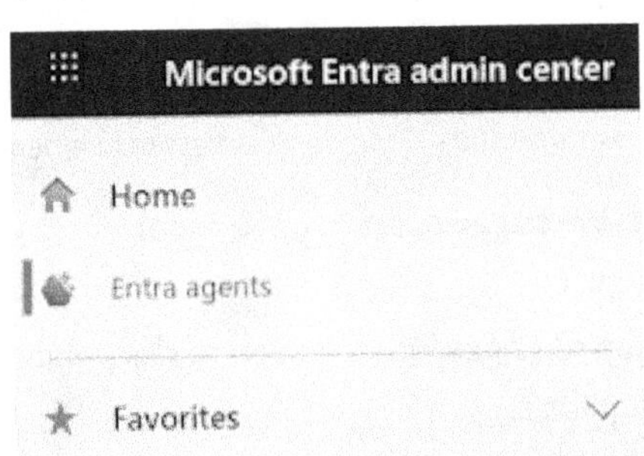

Figure 15.29 – Entra agents

Here, we have another three Entra agents available to us: **Conditional Access Optimization Agent**, **Identity Risk Management Agent**, and **Access Review Agent**.

Enabling these is the same process, so I will enable one here and then run through the use of each individually:

1. Click on **View details** for the agent (in this case, **Conditional Access Optimization Agent**).
2. In the fly-out window, click **Start agent**.

> **Note**
>
> Unlike the Intune agents, the Entra ones have the ability to make changes in your tenant.

Conditional Access Optimization Agent

This agent looks at your users, applications (Enterprise apps, not Win32 apps), and Conditional Access policies. It then looks for any gaps in the protection, whether that is unprotected users, unprotected apps, or unprotected sign-ins.

1. After clicking **Run**, we need to click on **Suggestions**, where it will cover what it has done. In this case, it has created four new Conditional Access policies (fortunately in report-only mode).

Suggested next steps	Actions taken by agent	Last updated ↓	Status	
Turn on policy: **new policy to block high-risk agents (Preview)**	Created new report-only policy	13/02/2026, 12:39:29	Not applied	Review suggestion
Turn on policy: **new policy to enforce device compliance for iOS, macOS, and Windows for 1 group**	Created new report-only policy	13/02/2026, 12:39:27	Not applied	Review suggestion
Turn on policy: **new policy to require app protection for Android users for 1 group**	Created new report-only policy	13/02/2026, 12:39:25	Not applied	Review suggestion
Turn on policy: **new policy to require app protection for Windows users for 1 group**	Created new report-only policy	13/02/2026, 12:39:23	Not applied	Review suggestion

Figure 15.30 – Conditional Access recommendations

2. You can also click **Review suggestion** to have a look at why you need it, what impact it has, and what is configured.
3. Clicking **Review policy changes** will take you to the policy itself, or if you are happy with it, click **Turn on policy**.
   You can also click **Chat with agent** at the top to discuss it further.

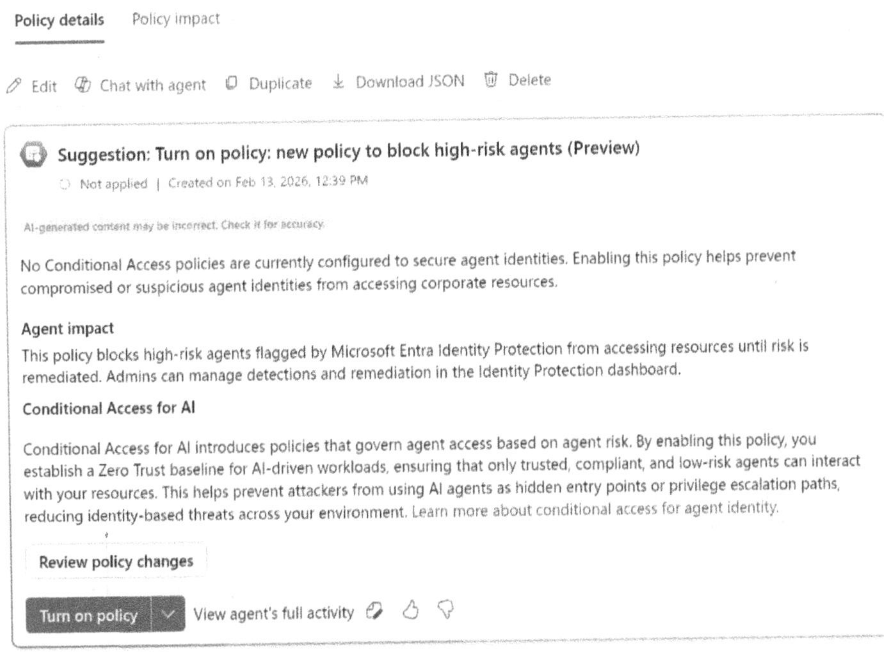

Figure 15.31 – Policy details

4. Within **Settings**, you can also enable/disable the schedule, configure what the agent should monitor, and also disable the ability to create policies if you would rather have greater control:

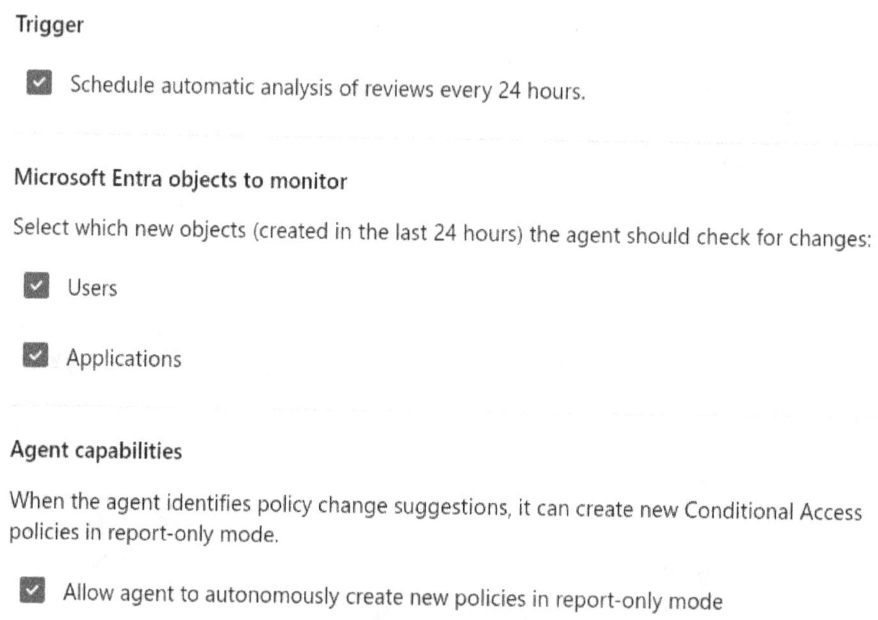

Figure 15.32 – Agent settings

Identity Risk Management Agent

This agent looks at the risky users within your tenant through sign-in logs and other risk data.

1. After running, click **View agent findings**:

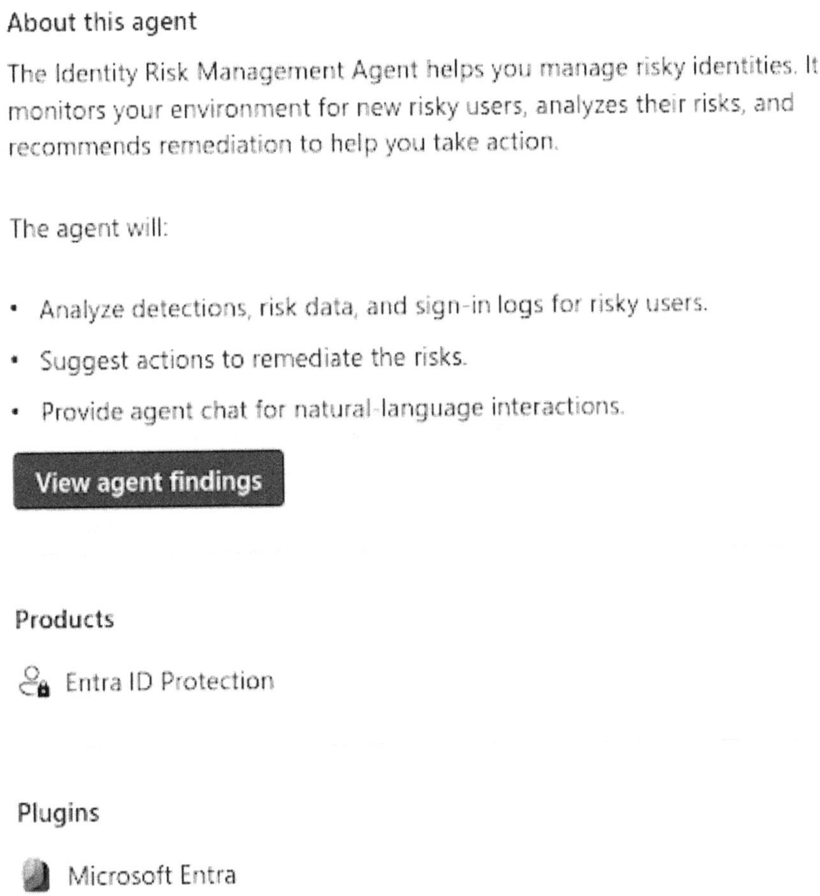

Figure 15.33 – Identity Risk Management Agent

2. Here, you can see a list of your risky users and the risk associated with them. You can see here that my user has been flagged, and I can also click **Chat with agent** to discuss it.

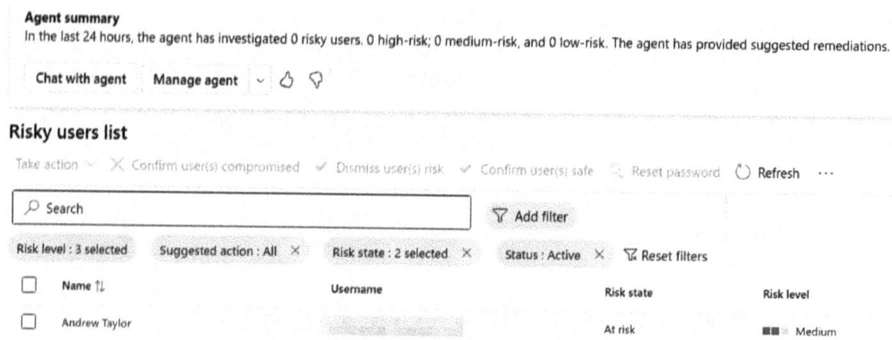

Figure 15.34 – Risky users

3. Clicking on the name loads up details about the risk, with an action bar across the top to quickly remediate it or discuss it further with the agent:

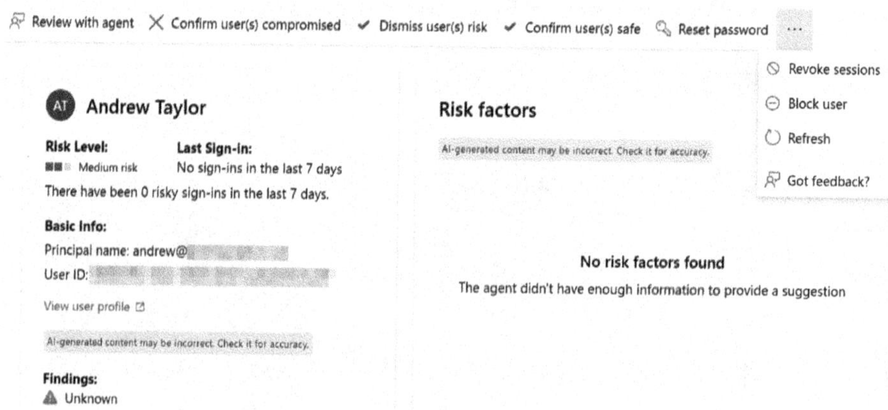

Figure 15.35 – User risk

Access Review Agent

This agent sits mostly in Microsoft Teams. Once enabled in Entra, it reviews access requests and suggests whether they should be approved or denied within a Teams chat. In a large environment, this is invaluable!

Figure 15.36 – Access Review Agent

As access requests are more of a feature of Entra than Intune, we will not dig any deeper into this particular agent, but now you know what it can do and how it can help you.

Finally, we will look at the Defender agents.

Defender agents

Most of these have very little to do with Intune, but as many of you are probably not just Intune admins, we can have a quick look at them here anyway. In Defender, we have **NL2KQL Interactive Agent for Intune Explorer**, **Phishing Triage Agent**, **SIEM Migration Agent**, **Threat Intelligence Briefing Agent**, and **Vibe Hunting Interactive Agent**.

This will not be as in-depth a review of the agents as the others; these agents have very specific purposes and would probably require a book in themselves to cover! You can find out more details here: `https://learn.microsoft.com/en-us/defender-xdr/security-copilot-agents-defender?bc=%2Fsecurity-copilot%2Fbreadcrumb%2Ftoc.json&toc=%2Fsecurity-copilot%2Ftoc.json`.

1. To set them up, click **Set up** under the agent name:

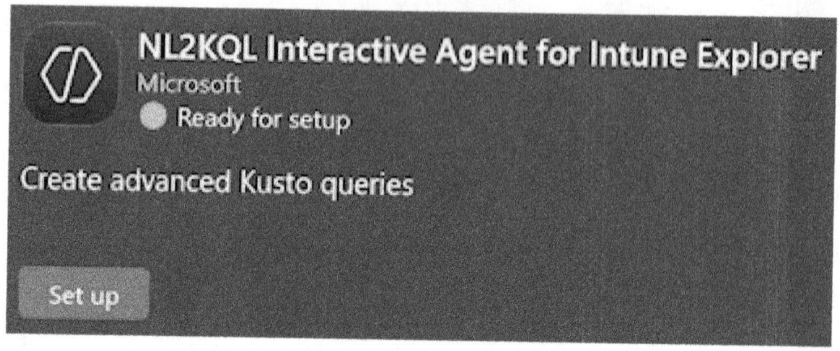

Figure 15.37 – Set up agent

2. Then, click **Set up** in the pop-up window:

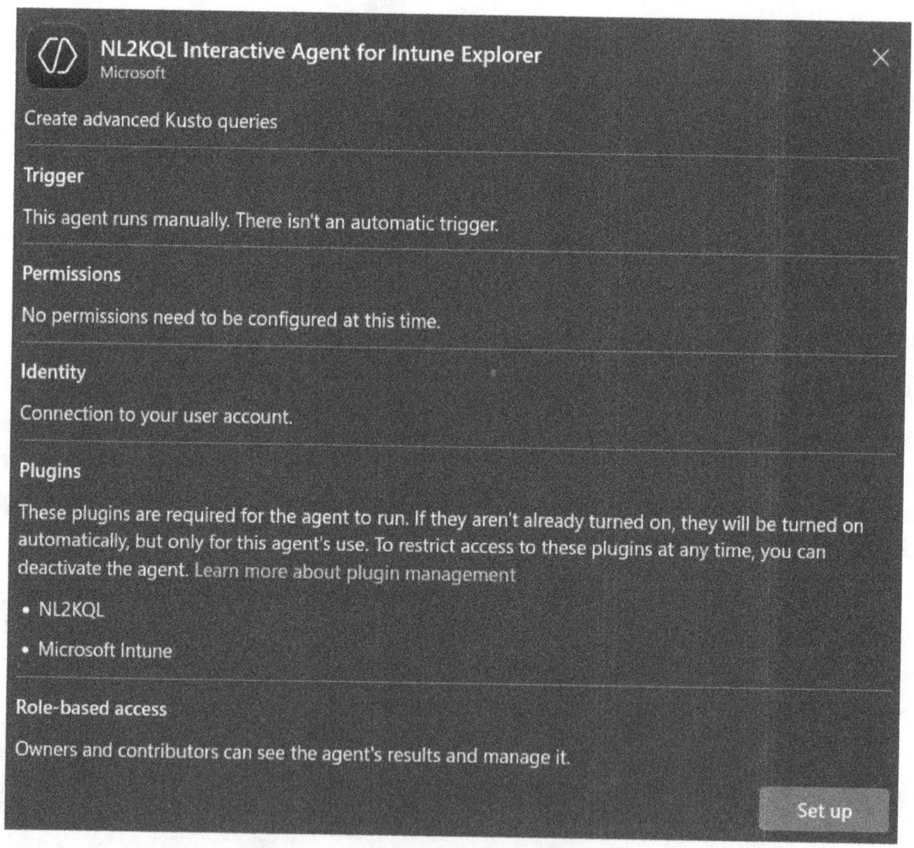

Figure 15.38 – Complete setup

3. You will be prompted to sign in with an account that the agent will use.

L2KQL Interactive Agent for Intune Explorer

This agent can create **Kusto** queries to use within Explorer in Intune.

You can run on a trigger, but in this case, just click **Run** and select **One time**:

Figure 15.39 – Run agent on demand

Phishing Triage Agent

This agent reviews phishing reports from users and reviews them, classifies them, and suggests whether the reported incident is a false alarm or a malicious threat that you need to investigate further.

To enable it, you will need appropriate licensing and to enable **Defender for Office 365** in the Defender XDR settings.

SIEM Migration Agent

This agent is used to migrate any detection rules from any existing **Security Information and Event Management** (**SIEM**) platforms into Sentinel.

Threat Intelligence Briefing Agent

Keeping on top of threats is a full-time job in itself. This agent uses information from your tenant and the wider industry to give you a tailored threat report via email of the things you should be most concerned about.

Vibe Hunting Interactive Agent

This looks at your active hunting investigations and lets you interrogate them using natural language. The agent will generate the KQL queries, interpret the results, and guide you throughout.

That brings us to the end of this recipe. Now that we have seen what the built-in agents can do, imagine what we can do with our own...

Building your own agents

What if we could build our own security agents to build upon the magnificent things we have seen Microsoft manage? That can be achieved in the Security Copilot portal. Read on to find out more...

How to do it...

Follow these steps:

1. Navigate to the Security Copilot portal (`https://securitycopilot.microsoft.com`).
2. On the home screen, click **Build** (in the following screenshot, it says **Preview**, but that will change).

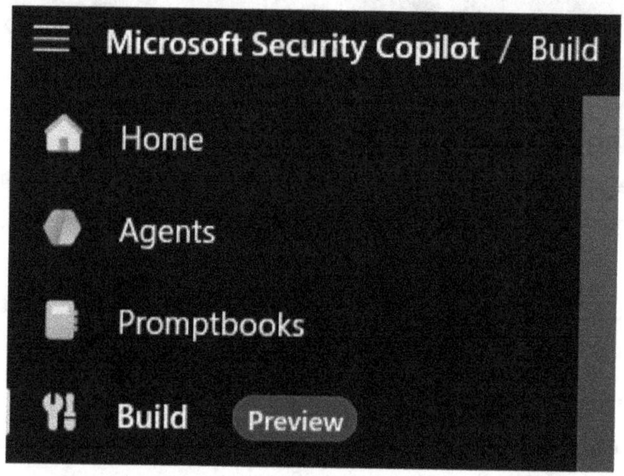

Figure 15.40 – Build agents

3. Here, you can either build from scratch, import YAML, or use natural language to create your agent. As we are using AI here, we will use natural language to build an agent. In this case, we want an agent to email when a device becomes non-compliant:

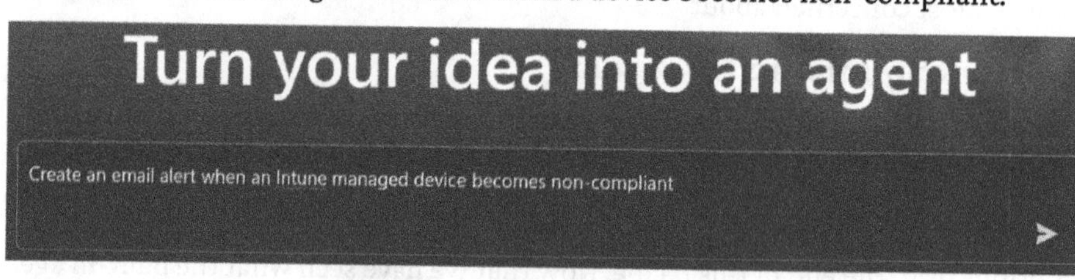

Figure 15.41 – Build agent prompt

4. Copilot will look at the query and ask for clarification (if needed). Respond and click the arrow button.

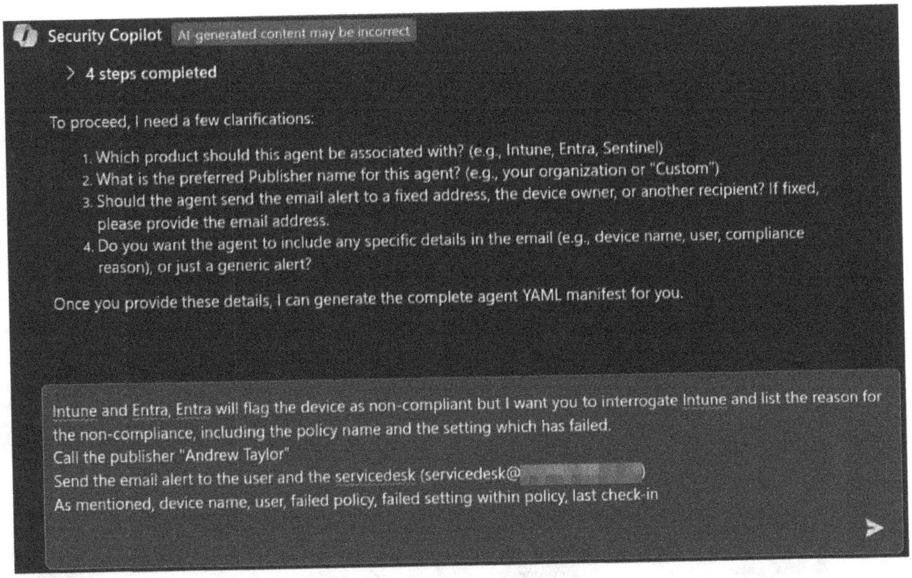

Figure 15.42 – Further prompts

5. Then, it will inform you when the steps have been created. Click **View agent configuration** to build it fully:

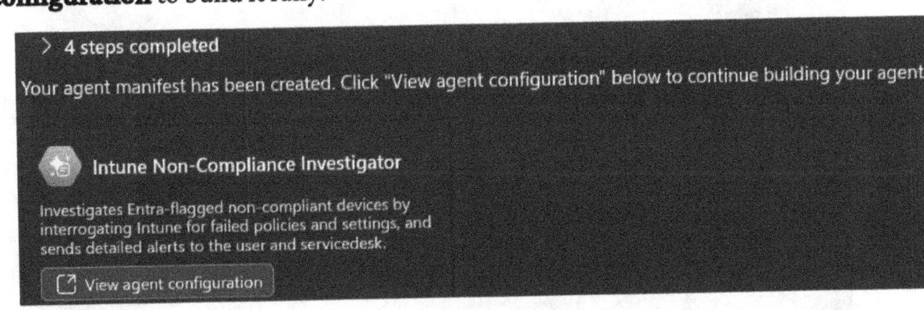

Figure 15.43 – View configuration

You can see the inputs it is using and the tools to provide the output. All of this can be edited as required.

6. Click on **Automation** and set a trigger. You can also optionally constrain it so it can only run one at a time (this will save email clutter and SCUs).

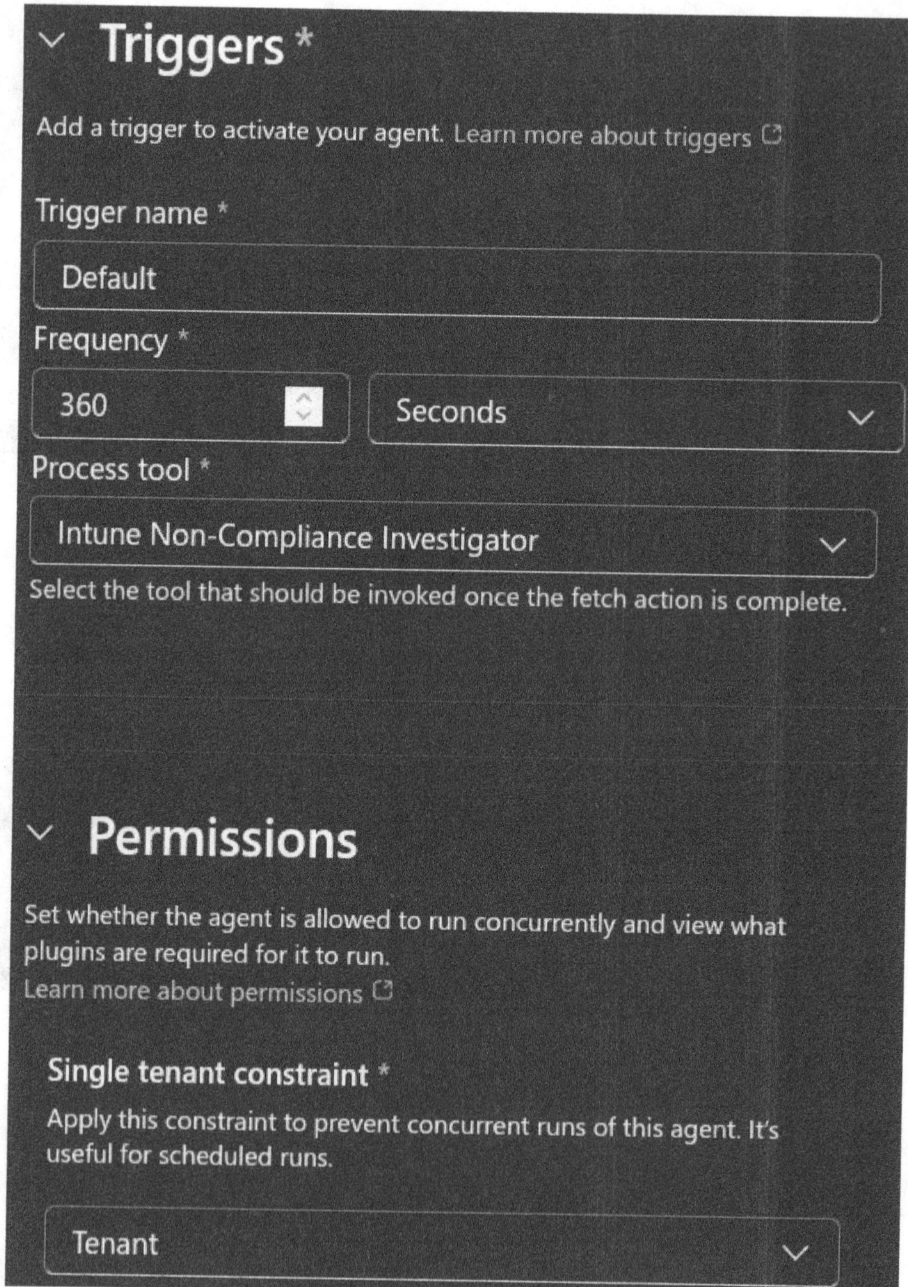

Figure 15.44 – Triggers and permissions

7. Once you are happy with it, click **Test**.

Figure 15.45 – Test trigger

8. Scroll down and enter **Device** and **User** details to test against, and click **Run test**:

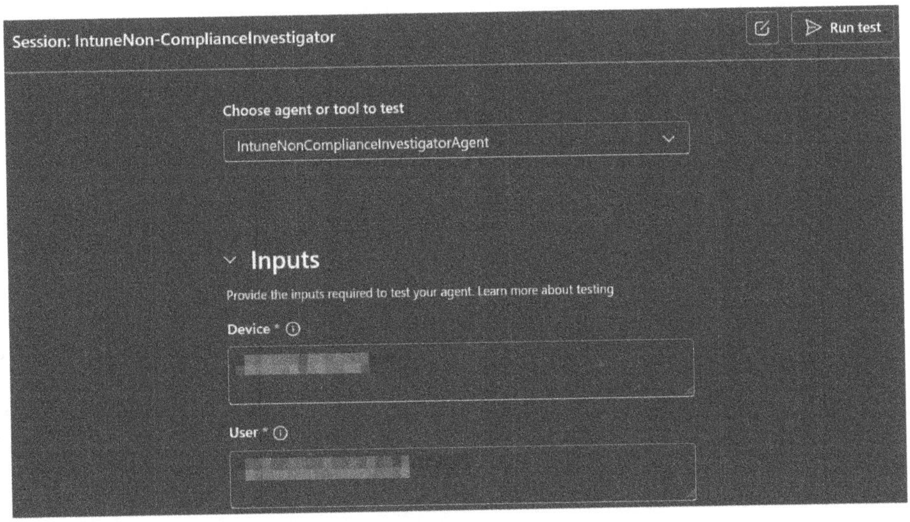

Figure 15.46 – Run test

9. If you are happy with the results, click **Publish**. If not, edit and amend it as required.

That completes this recipe, chapter, and book. I hope you have enjoyed reading it!

Get This Book's PDF Version and Exclusive Extras

Scan the QR code (or go to `packtpub.com/unlock`). Search for this book by name, confirm the edition, and then follow the steps on the page.

UNLOCK NOW

Note: Keep your invoice handy. Purchases made directly from Packt don't require one.

16

Unlock Your Exclusive Benefits

Your copy of this book includes the following exclusive benefits:

DRM-Free PDF Version

Download DRM-free PDF and ePub copies of this book.

7-Day Packt Library Access

Get 7-day unlimited access to 8,000+ books and videos. No credit card required.

Available for first-time Packt+ trial users only.

Next-Gen Reader Access

Read this book on Packt Reader with progress sync, dark mode and note-taking.

Follow the guide below to unlock them. The process takes only a few minutes and needs to be completed once.

Unlock this Book's Free Benefits in three Easy Steps

Step 1

Keep your purchase invoice ready for *Step 3*. If you have a physical copy, scan it using your phone and save it as a PDF, JPG, or PNG.

For more help on finding your invoice, visit `packtpub.com/en-us/unlock?step=1`.

> Note
>
> **Note**: If you bought this book directly from Packt, no invoice is required. After *Step 2*, you can access your exclusive content right away.

Step 2

Scan the QR code or go to `packtpub.com/unlock`.

On the page that opens (similar to *Figure 16.1* on desktop), search for this book by name and select the correct edition.

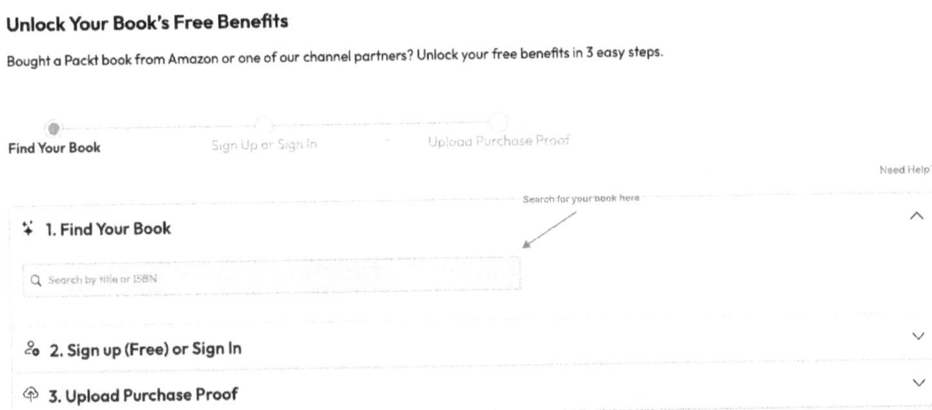

Figure 16.1: Packt unlock landing page on desktop

Step 3

After selecting your book, sign in to your Packt account or create one for free. Then upload your invoice (PDF, PNG, or JPG, up to 10 MB). Follow the on-screen instructions to finish the process.

Need Help

If you get stuck and need help, visit `packtpub.com/unlock-benefits/help` for a detailed FAQ on how to find your invoices and more. This QR code will take you to the help page.

Note

Note: If you are still facing issues, reach out to `customercare@packt.com`.

Other Books You May Enjoy

If you enjoyed this book, you may be interested in these other books by Packt:

Mastering Microsoft Intune – Second Edition

Christiaan Brinkhoff, Per Larsen

ISBN: 978-1-83546-851-7

- Simplify the deployment of Windows in the cloud with Windows 365 Cloud PCs
- Deliver next-generation security features with Intune Suite
- Simplify Windows Updates with Windows Autopatch
- Configure advanced policy management within Intune
- Discover modern profile management and migration options for physical and Cloud PCs
- Harden security with baseline settings and other security best practices
- Find troubleshooting tips and tricks for Intune, Windows 365 Cloud PCs, and more
- Discover deployment best practices for physical and cloud-managed endpoints

Mastering Endpoint Management using Microsoft Intune Suite

Saurabh Sarkar, Rahul Singh

ISBN: 978-1-80602-195-6

- Master endpoint management by effectively managing and securing endpoints with Intune Suite
- Align with Microsoft's Zero Trust principle and least-privilege model by using EPM
- Discover how to troubleshoot effectively by understanding underlying processes and the logs/registry
- Understand real-world setups with detailed screenshots at each deployment step
- Find out how to gain insights and make data-driven decisions by leveraging Advanced Analytics
- Understand how to streamline/automate third-party app deployment with EAM, saving time and effort

Packt is searching for authors like you

If you're interested in becoming an author for Packt, please visit `authors.packt.com` and apply today. We have worked with thousands of developers and tech professionals, just like you, to help them share their insight with the global tech community. You can make a general application, apply for a specific hot topic that we are recruiting an author for, or submit your own idea.

Share your thoughts

Now you've finished *Microsoft Intune Cookbook, Second Edition*, we'd love to hear your thoughts! Scan the QR code below to go straight to the Amazon review page for this book and share your feedback or leave a review on the site that you purchased it from.

https://packt.link/r/1-805-80723-4

Your review is important to us and the tech community and will help us make sure we're delivering excellent quality content.

Index

B

C

D

E

www.ingramcontent.com/pod-product-compliance
Lightning Source LLC
Chambersburg PA
CBHW081302290326
41974CB00012B/59
* 9 7 8 1 8 0 5 8 0 7 2 3 0 *